Handbook of
State Government
Administration

PUBLIC ADMINISTRATION AND PUBLIC POLICY

A Comprehensive Publication Program

Executive Editor

JACK RABIN
Professor of Public Administration and Public Policy
School of Public Affairs
The Capital College
The Pennsylvania State University—Harrisburg
Middletown, Pennsylvania

Additional Volumes in Preparation

Handbook of Public Information Systems, edited by G. David Garson

Handbook of Global Legal Policy, edited by Stuart S. Nagel

Handbook of Global Economic Policy, edited by Stuart S. Nagel

Handbook of Organizational Consultation: Second Edition, Revised and Expanded, edited by Robert T. Golembiewski

Handbook of Global International Policy, edited by Stuart S. Nagel

Handbook of Global Technology Policy, edited by Stuart S. Nagel

Handbook of Global Political Policy, edited by Stuart S. Nagel

Handbook of Global Social Policy, edited by Stuart S. Nagel and Amy Robb

Handbook of Strategic Management: Second Edition, Revised and Expanded, edited by Jack Rabin, Gerald J. Miller, and W. Bartley Hildreth

ANNALS OF PUBLIC ADMINISTRATION

- Public Administration: History and Theory in Contemporary Perspective, edited by Joseph A. Uveges, Jr.
- Public Administration Education in Transition, edited by Thomas Vocino and Richard Heimovics
- Centenary Issues of the Pendleton Act of 1883, edited by David H. Rosenbloom with the assistance of Mark A. Emmert
- Intergovernmental Relations in the 1980s, edited by Richard H. Leach
- Criminal Justice Administration: Linking Practice and Research, edited by William A. Jones, Jr.

Handbook of
State Government
Administration

edited by

John J. Gargan
Kent State University
Kent, Ohio

MARCEL DEKKER, INC.   NEW YORK · BASEL

ISBN: 0-8247-7660-7

This book is printed on acid-free paper.

Headquarters
Marcel Dekker, Inc.
270 Madison Avenue, New York, NY 10016
tel: 212-696-9000; fax: 212-685-4540

Eastern Hemisphere Distribution
Marcel Dekker AG
Hutgasse 4, Postfach 812, CH-4001 Basel, Switzerland
tel: 41-61-261-8482; fax: 41-61-261-8896

World Wide Web
http://www.dekker.com

The publisher offers discounts on this book when ordered in bulk quantities. For more information, write to Special Sales/Professional Marketing at the headquarters address above.

Current printing (last digit):
10 9 8 7 6 5 4 3 2 1

PRINTED IN THE UNITED STATES OF AMERICA

To:

John and Marley

Bridget, Paul, and Hallie

Jim

Pass it on.

Preface

The *Handbook of State Government Administration* considers the range of administrative and management practices employed by state governments in the United States. These practices are discussed and analyzed from both conceptual and applied perspectives. Chapters have been written by individuals with outstanding academic backgrounds and substantial experience dealing with administrative and management issues in substantive policy areas.

For students, scholars, and practitioners of politics and public administration, the topics covered in this handbook are important matters. Media attention to comings and goings in Washington, D.C., notwithstanding, the federal arrangement is one of separate and independent governments sharing authority. Within the federal arrangement, states continue to command, as always, vital legal, political, and policy powers. As demonstrated repeatedly over the past half century, these powers have enabled elected officials to use their states as laboratories. State officials and professionals in government have engaged in policy experimentation, reconsidered functional assignment of program responsibilities between state and local governments, and diffused successful policy innovations to their counterparts in other states.

In very elemental ways, the performance of state governments defines societal capacity to deal with future problems. Growth in the importance of federal law and federal court decisions and expanded federal government involvement in more domestic functions (or at least the funding of functions) is of obvious significance. Yet it is state law, state court systems, and the provision of an array of public services by state and local governments that in most cases determine the contribution of the public sector to the quality of life that individuals and families enjoy.

How well state governments perform is determined by their governing capacity. As a concept, governing capacity involves two dimensions—the ability to do what is required and the ability to do what is expected. High-capacity systems achieve optimal performance levels in meeting requirements and expectations. Capacity is relational and dynamic in that it can be assessed only with regard to the complexity of requirements and expectations confronting a system at a given time. Strains on governing capacity result from increases in the number, differentiation, and interdependence of requirements and expectations. Such has been the case for state governments when, for example, they have confronted the results of global economic change, or when they have been expected to cope with problems with no known solutions, such as drug addiction, or when they have had to plan strategically for major reassignments of responsibilities in the federal system.

Public administration theoreticians and practitioners must address the challenge of specifying the kinds of administrative knowledge and management and technical skills necessary for the ''to meet requirements'' dimension of governing capacity. Although basic management functions continue to be relevant, definitions of state of the art and exemplary management practices have changed as problem and functional contexts change. As ''POSDCORB'' and public sector growth guided public administration thinking of the 1930s, strategic management, postmodernism, and privatization shape public administration thinking at the outset of a new century.

The *Handbook of State Government Administration* is designed to meet the ongoing challenge of specifying the knowledge and skills necessary for building the governing capacity of state (and other) governments. It is also intended to meet particular needs of the public administration community by, first and foremost, serving as a basic text for graduate courses in public administration and management generally, and courses in state government administration specifically. Participants in in-service training programs will find this handbook useful for a review of state administration and management developments and for coverage of topics with which they lack recent experience. Librarians should consider the volume a potentially valuable addition to their reference collections.

Editing the *Handbook of State Government Administration* was eased by the professionalism of many individuals. Chapter authors were uniformly cooperative and understanding of deadlines. Jack Rabin, executive editor of Marcel Dekker, Inc.'s Public Administration and Public Policy series, provided sound advice throughout the project. Production Editors Jeanne McFadden and Paige Force were patient and especially helpful in bringing the project to completion.

John J. Gargan

Contents

Contents

Contributors

Robert Agranoff Professor, School of Public and Environmental Affairs, Indiana University, Bloomington, Indiana

Maria P. Aristigueta Assistant Professor, School of Urban Affairs and Public Policy, University of Delaware, Newark, Delaware

Robert W. Backoff Professor, School of Public Policy and Management, The Ohio State University, Columbus, Ohio

A. Hunter Bacot Assistant Professor, Department of Political Science, University of North Carolina, Charlotte, North Carolina

Evan M. Berman Associate Professor, Department of Public Administration, University of Central Florida, Orlando, Florida

Curtis R. Berry Associate Professor, Department of Political Science, Shippensburg University, Shippensburg, Pennsylvania

Keith Boeckelman Assistant Professor, Department of Political Science, Western Illinois University, Macomb, Illinois

Paul J. Castellani Ph.D. Director, Program Research, New York State Office of Mental Retardation and Developmental Disabilities, and Public Service Professor, The University of New York at Albany, Albany, New York

Keon S. Chi   Professor of Political Science, Georgetown College, Georgetown, Kentucky, and Senior Fellow, Council of State Governments, Lexington, Kentucky

Chung-Lae Cho   Department of Political Science, University of North Carolina, Chapel Hill, North Carolina

James K. Conant   Chair, Department of Public and International Affairs, George Mason University, Fairfax, Virginia

Roy A. Dawes   Assistant Professor, Department of Political Science, Gettysburg College, Gettysburg, Pennsylvania

Joseph Drew   Associate Professor, Department of Political Science, Kent State University, Kent, Ohio

Claire L. Felbinger   Chair, Department of Public Administration, American University, Washington, D.C.

H. Edward Flentje   Professor, Hugo Wall School of Urban and Public Affairs, Wichita State University, Wichita, Kansas

Betsy Fulton   Assistant Professor, Department of Correctional and Juvenile Justice Studies, Eastern Kentucky University, Richmond, Kentucky

John J. Gargan   Professor, Department of Political Science, Kent State University, Kent, Ohio

Peter J. Haas   Professor, Department of Political Science, San José State University, San José, California

F. Ted Hebert   Professor, Department of Political Science, University of Utah, Salt Lake City, Utah

Edward T. Jennings, Jr.   Professor, Martin School of Public Policy and Administration, Department of Political Science, University of Kentucky, Lexington, Kentucky

Thomas P. Lauth   Professor, Department of Political Science, University of Georgia, Athens, Georgia

Lawrence L. Martin Associate Professor, School of Social Work, Columbia University, New York, New York

Michael McGuire Assistant Professor, Department of Public Administration, University of North Texas, Denton, Texas

Karen Mossberger Assistant Professor, Department of Political Science, Kent State University, Kent, Ohio

Paul C. Nutt Professor, Department of Management Sciences, Fisher College of Business, The Ohio State University, Columbus, Ohio

Willard T. Price Professor, Eberhardt School of Business, University of the Pacific, Stockton, California

Julia E. Robinson Assistant Professor, Graduate School of Public Affairs, University of Colorado at Colorado Springs, Colorado Springs, Colorado

Paula E. Steinbauer Political Science Department, University of Georgia, Athens, Georgia

Deil S. Wright Alumni Distinguished Professor of Political Science and Public Administration, Department of Political Science, University of North Carolina, Chapel Hill, North Carolina

Thomas E. Yatsco Health Care Program Evaluator, Health, Education, and Human Services Division, U.S. General Accounting Office, Washington, D.C.

1
Introduction and Overview of State Government Administration

John J. Gargan
Kent State University, Kent, Ohio

State governments fill dynamic roles in the governing of American society, roles as autonomous political systems rather than administrative units of the national government. The performance of the states as political systems over the past four decades is evidence of the vitality of the Constitution's 10th Amendment. On the cusp of the 21st century, as in the past, state governments function as laboratories of democracy, centers of policy experimentation and innovation.

Emphasizing the states' role does not diminish that of the national government but it does address an attention imbalance. Most observers of government and politics are aware of a flow of news about sensational national and global events, and their perspectives have been shaped and reinforced by the proliferation of electronic and print media outlets. The flow of news about state government and policies is significantly more limited.

The national government is, of course, a major stakeholder in domestic policy. In the aggregate, better than 20% of total state revenues are from intergovernmental sources; for particular states and for specific programs that percentage is considerably higher. Beginning with the New Deal, accelerating during the Great Society, and peaking in the late 1970s, federal government involvement by way of financing and regulations has been a central feature of political development in the United States. And the involvement is unlikely to abate. Scholars have pointed out that to maximize efficiency and effectiveness there needs to be a sorting out of domestic functions, with some best handled by the national government and others handled at the state and local levels (Peterson, 1995; Rivlin, 1992).

Allowing for the importance of national government involvement, it is still the case that the set of public services that affect citizens most directly and most fundamentally is a set administered by state and local governments. For example, for all the rhetoric in recent presidential and congressional campaigns about making education a priority item on the national agenda, education—primary, secondary, and higher—continues overwhelmingly to be the responsibility of the states and their local jurisdictions. Similarly for other functions, state and local public employment, in terms of sheer numbers, surpasses federal non-defense-related federal employment by multiples of better than 4 to 1. For the public functions relevant to the citizenry and the greater number of public employees it is the law of state statutes, state constitutions, and state court decisions that is controlling under most circumstances.

Fundamental to state government's ability to cope with existing and emerging problems are well-developed administrative-management practices. The *Handbook of State Government Administration* is designed to provide academics, students, and practitioners with overviews of these practices. The overviews are grouped in three sections addressing the contexts of state government administration and management, essential and emergent management practices, and the administration of specific programs and policies.

I. CONTEXTS OF STATE GOVERNMENT ADMINISTRATION AND MANAGEMENT

The chapters of the first section relate to contextual influences on state government administration and management. One of the most basic is the ideational—how state government should be organized to operate most effectively. As demonstrated by James Conant (Chapter 2), there was derived from the broader field of public administration a set of ideas about reforming state constitutions, executive authority, span of control, staff assistance, and the importance of structural arrangements to effective governance.

Reform efforts were rewarded with successful modernization initiatives, especially during the period 1960 to 1990. The number and character of reforms have varied from state to state but their essential thrust has been to rearrange structural arrangements to promote economy and efficiency. Though modernization did not guarantee effectiveness, it did remove barriers—outmoded constitutional provisions, redundant boards and commissions, multiple elected executive offices—and undoubtedly contributed to the organizational capacity of many state governments.

Long recognized as elemental to state government administration are the legal aspects of federalism and its policy-administrative applications in intergovernmental relations. Relating to these matters, Deil Wright and Chung-Lae Cho (Chapter 3) address federalism, intergovernmental relations, and intergovernmental management as organizing concepts. For each, they assess the roles played by popularly elected generalists, appointed administrative generalists, and policy professionals. Their study traces data collected over nearly two decades on the effects on state governance and state policy of national programs, aid, and regulatory actions. Wright and Cho conclude, albeit provisionally, that evidence is limited for impacts of federal aid and federal regulations on state policy change; that state agencies are in fact more the units of relatively autonomous state governments and forces than simply administrators of federal programs; and future researchers may need to study the possibility that, contrary to the first two conclusions, the reason for the lack of evidence in the longitudinal surveys of federal impacts on the states is that there has been a cumulative effect of aid requirements and regulations which has made state agencies more alike and eliminated interstate variations.

A third contextual factor is political culture, dominant patterns of attitudes and values held by the public and political elite about government and politics (Elazar, 1994; Erickson et al. 1993). H. Edward Flentje (Chapter 4) treats culture as a variable determining the acceptability of approaches to administration and management. Drawing on the work of Aaron Widavsky and his associates, Flentje discusses the relation of cultural types—hierarchy, individualism, and egalitarianism—to the elements of organizations, including their core values, authority structures, and leadership approaches.

With this foundation and an array of examples, Flentje demonstrates the utility of the cultural approach for understanding state government administration. Posited are three ideal types—State Administration as Hierarchy, State Administration as Individualism, and State Administration as Egalitarianism—each of which emphasizes different combinations of core values, authority structures, decision-making approaches, leadership styles, and other variables. Within a state government or state agency, different administrators may hold to one or another of the cultural types. Flentje concludes that, by drawing upon the strengths of each type, alliances of cultures might redirect and energize state government administration.

II. ESSENTIAL AND EMERGENT MANAGEMENT PRACTICES

Chapters in this second section highlight aspects of administrative and management practices in state government. Coverage begins with consideration of the structure of the governorship, proceeds to established management practices, and finishes with an introduction to new management techniques.

Any treatment of state government administration must begin with an acknowledgment that in virtually all states the governor is the focal point for administrative leadership and support for career managers. A recurring theme in this volume is the importance of executive leadership by governors and their offices and staffs.

In his examination of the maturation of governors as administrators, F. Ted Hebert (Chapter 5) indicates the importance governors themselves attribute to management skills. To a considerable degree, this is due to the redefinition in recent decades of the governor's role from that of custodian to policy manager in a complex intergovernmental system. A successful administration is contingent upon the governor's ability to appoint skilled (and loyal) managers to lead state agencies. Hebert assesses changes in the span of gubernatorial responsibilities and formal powers available to governors to influence administrative agencies. Clearly a primary theme of reform has been the concentration of formal budgetry, appointment, and staff power in the governor's office and reduction in the number of state officials with whom the governor must share executive authority. The record of any governor, notes Hebert, will be determined by the interplay of formal and informal influences; those with strong personalities, good communication skills, and formal powers are likely to be more effective than those without.

An important counter to the familiar argument for fortifying the governor's office and reducing fragmentation of the executive branch is offered by Julia Robinson (Chapter 6). She makes the case for independent political executives, those elected to office or appointed to boards and authorities independent of the governor. According to Robinson, independent executives at the state level, unlike those in the national government, tend to have relatively long tenures during which they develop networks based in personal, political, and policy contacts. Since they build upon interpersonal trust and shared policy experiences, the networks facilitate problem solving, particularly for problems requiring cooperation of multiple agencies.

Regardless of the precise administrative structure or the extent of the governor's formal powers, there are basic management tasks which must be dealt with simply to maintain and continue the operations of large scale organizations like state governments. Among the most essential of these tasks are those associated with budgeting and financial management and personnel–human resources management.

Thomas P. Lauth and Paula E. Steinbauer (Chapter 7) assess the relationship between budgeting and management in state government. They characterize the state budget as an instrument of accountability—governmental accountability to the public, executive branch accountability to the legislature, and executive agency accountability to the governor. In addition to being an instrument for accountability and financial control, Lauth and Steinbauer assert, state budgets also are instruments of management—for achieving efficiency and productivity improvements and for determining the degree to which program goals have been accomplished. They note that during the past quarter-century state governments have incorporated program and performance information into their budget systems with the aim of better informing state government resource allocation decisions. Based upon recent information obtained from state budget offices, Lauth and Steinbauer identify the kinds of control and management activities currently used by state budget offices and report on state budget office perceptions of the effectiveness of those activities.

For the second essential task cited, Curtis Berry (Chapter 8) provides a comprehensive overview of personnel-human resources management in state government. Writing from the perspective of the personnel administrator, Berry points up the array of issues with which state personnel offices must deal. Some are of long standing—advantages and disadvantages of alternative personnel structures and procedures; such matters of concern to employees as recruitment and testing, promotion, and compensation. Others issues, according to Berry, have become increasingly complex and paradoxical in that they lead personnel administrators to choices between competing values. Among these are the promotion of merit-based systems while at the same time assuring elected officials of personnel who are repsonsive to their policy agendas; handling professionally, yet realistically, the patronage requests of powerful office holders; recognizing public employee unions and implementing affirmative action policies while balancing the rights of senior employees with those of junior employees from traditionally excluded groups. Neither the longstanding nor the paradoxical issues can be handled by formula or mechanistic regulations. Indeed, it is in the day-to-day operations of human resources agencies that strategic and tactical decisions are made affecting the practical talents brought to jobs and determining which competing values in public administration are to prevail (Kaufman, 1956)—neutral competence, representation, executive leadership.

Strategic management is a more recent addition to the array of critical management tasks. In their chapter, Paul Nutt and Robert Backoff (Chapter 9) are concerned with constraints, such as informal "rules of the game" (media, fiscal, bureaucratic), operating to inhibit initiatives for revitalizing and strategically changing public organizations. Overcoming the constraints is an elementary challenge to those leaders who will be increasingly evaluated on the ability to manage radical change.

Strategic planning experiences with a number of state agencies supply Nutt and Backoff with case examples of the logic of the process of strategic change, what they refer to as "managing the dance of the what and how." They further show how technical developments in group process techniques and decision aids are applicable to public sector contexts. The techniques and aids alleviate the inherent complications of working in groups and help to move agency stakeholders toward support for strategic change and win-win problem solutions.

Financial, personnel, and strategic management are among the critical tasks which most observers would agree strengthen the "technical core of analytic and management skill" (Lynn, 1987, p. 183). Capable handling of these tasks is a prerequisite for competent modern governance. Additionally, new practices have been promulgated which likely enhance the art of public management. To a degree, the innovations have been replies to growing demands for greater effectiveness, responsiveness, and accountability at all levels of government. The innovations have also emphasized the achievement of demonstrable results, an emphasis based on the belief that good management is a means of efficiently allocating scarce resources for increased demands.

Chapters in the second section feature the innovations. Dealing with the most basic, Keon Chi (Chapter 10) covers the management of innovations in state government, distinguishing between political-policy, large-scale "macro," innovations and program management, and smaller-scale "micro" innovations or tools to implement political or policy goals. Chi points out that successful innovations typically are supported by innovation "champions" and frequently result from a "groping along" by individuals or small groups using trial-and-error approaches to new techniques for policies or programs needing help.

Productivity management, "the effective and efficient use of resources to achieve outcomes," is covered by Evan Berman (Chapter 11). For much of the past century, improving productivity has been a concern of theorists and practitioners of public and private administration. As discussed by Berman, current attention to productivity follows on the concerns of the 1980s and 1990s for total quality management to assuage citizen frustration over poor services and undue red tape. Administrators working to make state agencies more effective have used such approaches as public-private partnerships, reengineering of organizations, stakeholder empowerment, and information technologies.

The new management emphases on productivity, client satisfaction, and information are heavily dependent on research, data, and performance indicators. With competing demands and scarce resources, gaining organizational competence to deal with such matters is a challenge. In successive chapters, Peter Haas (Chapter 12) and Maria Aristigueta (Chapter 13) discuss progress in state government.

Peter Haas is concerned with the use of research, particularly policy analysis (more prospective) and program evaluation (more retrospective), to meet the information needs of policy and administrative decision makers in state government. Haas finds that state policy research takes diverse forms, from informal "back of envelope" analysis in smaller agencies to sophisticated performance audits in more institutionalized settings. Though less institutionalized than at the national level, state policy research is conducted within state government units (gubernatorial staff, legislative committees, legislative research sections) and nongovernmental agencies (consulting firms, universities, think tanks, interest groups).

Supportive of efforts to increase productivity and improve administrative performance are quantitative and qualitative indicators of results. Maria Aristigueta gives an overview of developments in benchmarking, measurement performance, and "outcome monitoring" in state government. As she points out, work is under way to establish measures for program productivity, quality, cost-effectiveness, and timeliness. Information gained contributes to management for results systems and such system modules as strategic planning and performance-based budgeting. In turn, the indicators, systems, and modules help to improve organizational performance, accountability to stakeholders, employee motivation, and communications.

III. ADMINISTRATION OF SPECIFIC PROGRAMS AND POLICIES

An axiom of public administration holds that administrative theories are tested in the implementation of public policies and programs by some executive agency. It is further held that the multiple dimensions of public problems dictate that the legislation be formulated in general terms and that administrators use their management expertise to fit programs to particular implementation settings.

Chapters in the third section illustrate the point. Administrative developments and management practices are appraised for a number of policies. Taken in their entirety, the chapters show the importance of effective management to successful policy implementation.

Where possible, chapters have been grouped according to common substantive topics and/or recent political experiences. Because economic growth is of such fundamental importance to so many aspects of public and private life, the section opens with three chapters dealing with state economic development policy. The evolution of that policy is traced by Keith Boeckelman (Chapter 14). Boeckelman identifies three periods or "waves" of economic development policies. In the first period, from the 1920s until the 1980s, states attempted to attract new industries by way of tax concessions and other incentives to reduce the cost of doing business. The second period emerged in the 1980s and emphasized policies to improve productivity and to support within state entrepreneurs. The third period, from the early 1990s to the present, stresses state actions to build support for development—infrastructure, education, and job training—and looks to the operations of the market to determine which businesses will succeed. Development policy in most states is a mix of elements from each of the waves. Boeckelman reviews evaluations of policy effects and concludes that combinations of tax policy, infrastructure investment, and carefully targeted programs can be used in a supportive political context to affect corporate location decisions.

Given the competition for growth industries and firms, economic development policy is difficult under the best of circumstances. Under conditions less supportive of growth, as in rural areas, challenges to public managers are especially great. Robert Agranoff and Michael McGuire (Chapter 15) detail the distinct characteristics of rural development policy—a geographic rather than socioeconomic base, varied administrative locations in state or quasi-governmental agencies, an information–technical assistance focus, and multiorganizational networks for policy formation, implementation, and administration. To a considerable degree, demonstrate Agranoff and McGuire, the success of rural development policy is dependent on administrative capacity to marshall resources, to assist rural communities themselves build capacity, and to sustain networks of public and private organizations.

Regardless of actual circumstances, economic development policy by its very nature is fraught with uncertainty. Karen Mossberger (Chapter 16) explores economic development decision making in five states. With little direct policy experience and a lack of firm knowledge as to factors influencing the locational decisions of firms, administrators had considerable uncertainty in the formation of enterprise zones and in balancing the attraction of businesses into the zones with the protection of public funds. Faced with difficult choices, administrators relied on simplifying strategies for reducing or coping with uncertainty. Analogies were drawn from experience in other policy domains. Symbolism was used to indicate a concern for depressed areas. An emphasis was placed on proceduralism and process. For example, state economic development departments established advisory committees and held public hearings. Uncertainty was also reduced through the use of multiple information sources—intergovernmental networks, networks of practitioners, and professional associations—for the diffusion of ideas and published information about program experiences. Mossberger suggests that the enterprise zone research may have a broader relevance to other programs where state administrators have limited control over policy stakeholders or broader policy influences.

Among the most fundamental challenges for state administrators are those resulting from court decisions and/or fundamental policy shifts in intergovernmental programs. A sampling of results is reported in three chapters reviewing recent changes in social policy. In reviewing developments in developmental disabilities policy, Paul Castellani (Chapter 17) illustrates the variety of state policy approaches resulting from legislative, judicial, and administrative actions. These actions have altered the overall framework of disabilities policy and the number and characteristics of a clientele that often has a life long relation with the services in that framework. Mental retardation and developmental disabilities programs in many states have been transformed from large institutional settings to community-based public and private facilities. Accompanying the transformations have been varying patterns of state-local fiscal responsibilities, new types of services, and innovative modes of service delivery, in some cases involving sophisticated contractual arrangements. Castellani advises of the importance of experienced middle managers and state management capacity to the successful handling of developmental services. Where the experience and capacity are absent or deficient, centrifugal policy forces may lead to the disintegration of the developmental disabilities framework for administering services.

Even when affected by the same court decisions and intergovernmental policy shifts, states vary in their responses. Contributing to the variation, and complicating generalizations about state government, are differences in institutional arrangements established for state human service agencies. As described by Lawrence Martin (Chapter 18), arrangements differ on mundane matters of agency name, and also on more substantial matters including the number of functions dealt with and the division of responsibility for human service programs between state and local governments.

Intergovernmental policy reforms induce state government administrative and management consequences. This has been conspicuous in the case of welfare policy in general, as reviewed by Edward Jennings (Chapter 19), and in detail for the ET Choices program in Massachusetts during the 1980s and changes in the State of Washington following adoption of the federal Personal Responsibility Act of 1996. The 1996 act involved the devolution of greater program control to the state government level and the redefinition of welfare policy from entitlement to a block grant and job-related. Jennings concludes that management challenges derive from changing policy goals and policy designs; the greater the changes proposed, the greater the management challenges. Among the challenges he cites are the design and management of advanced information systems, collection of details on client characteristics and benefit eligibility, and appraisal of performance data. As reforms become more intricate there is a heightened need for coordination of networks of relatively autonomous public, private, and nonprofit service providers.

Of domestic policies of the past half-century few have occupied the attention of state policy makers and attentive publics as Medicaid, the federal entitlement program adopted to provide health care to the poor. As analyzed by Joseph Drew and Thomas Yatsco (Chapter 20), the rate of growth in Medicaid spending has crowded out spending increases for other functions. Medicaid issues mirror health care policy concerns in the United States—how to increase access to health care while maintaining costs and not reducing service quality. In the chapter Drew and Yatsco address major reforms adopted by the states in the 1990s, including shifts in the mix of covered populations, reorganization of providers into managed care, reductions in payments to providers, and increased state regulation of services provided.

State level administrators may enjoy discretion in the implementation of programs and policies. That discretion is bounded, however, by assumptions advancing policy and program choices. Betsy Fulton (Chapter 21) explains how the "get-tough-on-crime" assumptions guiding corrections policy in the United States have had profound implications for state government managers. Operationalized in "three-strikes laws" (conviction of three felonies automatically resulting in life imprisonment), mandatory sentences, reinstatement of the death penalty, and community-based punishment, get-tough assumptions have produced an incarceration rate five times that of other industrialized nations and state spending on corrections for adults and juveniles increasing at dramatic rates.

If punishment satisfies cultural and political preferences, research reviews of get-tough assumptions are mixed. Some researchers credit the policies for declining crime rates. Other researchers conclude that more cost-effective strategies for reducing crime could be based in early intervention programs and rehabilitation programs for adults. Fulton notes that among promising management practices for longer-term solutions are more rigorous case classification to determine the probability of recidivism, better measures of organizational performance, and tests of the effectiveness of privatization of entire corrections facilities or specific elements of the corrections function.

The importance of constructive intergovernmental cooperation is illustrated by Roy Dawes and A. Hunter Bacot in their appraisal (Chapter 22) of environmental program management. For environmental policy, and for other policy domains, the achievement of national goals has been contingent upon successful implementation of federal programs by state governments and other service providers. Management of program implementation has been complicated by the interaction of several factors: differing standards for air, water, and waste pollutants; changing knowledge bases regarding contaminants and technologies for pollution abatement; regional variations in the severity and character of pollution problems; and differences in the ideological and partisan support for management options such as standard regulations and market-based incentives.

Dawes and Bacot conclude that the devolution movement is congruent with state government preferences for decentralized federal rather than centralized national methods. Management of successful implementation requires a cooperative work relationship between national and state officials, agreement on primary roles and responsibilities, and sustained commitment to program objectives.

Essential to economic growth strategies, and more fundamentally to the quality of life enjoyed by the citizenry, is the adequacy of a jurisdiction's physical infrastructure. Involved are the basic facilities of modern life—water resources systems, waste management plants, highways, bridges, flood control, public power networks, etc.—and the public works agencies responsible for their administration. As covered by Claire Felbinger and Willard Price (Chapter 23), infrastructure policy, funding, construction, and management have involved all levels of government and the private sector. Administration and oversight are vested in structural arrangements from the multistate authority, to the within state multicounty district, to the single-purpose special district. Drawing on the intricate

California experience, Felbinger and Price discuss the likely benefits of the integration of public works administration at all levels of government. They suggest that more integrated programs would result from making the consideration of infrastructure and natural resources policy proposals the responsibility of a very limited number of legislative committees, by creating single funding pools based on specified and earmarked revenue sources, and placing a resource administrator as agency head or as a member of the governor's staff to coordinate infrastructure policy and related decision making.

In the final chapter consideration is given to the administrative and management practices related to the governing capacity of state governments. Governing capacity is defined as the ability of state governments to meet the requirements of effective functioning in a federal system and to satisfy expectations of key stakeholders both within and outside the state. High-capacity systems achieve optimal performance levels in meeting requirements and expectations; low capacity systems fail to achieve minimal requirements and expectations. Use of the administrative and management practices discussed in this volume is a necessary but not sufficient condition for high governing capacity. Satisfying stakeholder expectations in an era of public cynicism and distrust of government compound the difficulty of achieving high governing capacity status. Confronting elected, appointed, and career state managers are administrative and management challenges of a high order. Those officials who best meet the challenges will furnish effective, efficient, and beneficial government to their fellow state citizens.

REFERENCES

Elazar, D. J. (1984). *American Federalism: A View from the States*, 3rd ed., Harper & Row, New York.

Erikson, R. S., Wright, G. C., and McIver, J. P. (1993). *Statehouse Democracy: Public Opinion and Public Policy in the American States*, Cambridge University Press, Cambridge.

Kaufman, H. (1956). Emerging conflicts in the doctrines of public administration, *American Political Science Review, 50*: 1057–1073.

Lynn, L. E. Jr. (1987). Public management: What do we know? What should we know? And how will we know it? *J Policy Analysis and Management, 7*: 178–187.

Peterson, P. E. (1995). *The Price of Federalism*, Brookings Institution, Washington.

Rivlin, A. (1992). *Reviving the American Dream: The Economy, the States, and the Federal Government*, Brookings Institution, Washington.

2

Management Consequences of the 1960–1990 "Modernization" of State Government

James K. Conant
George Mason University, Fairfax, Virginia

"[T]he democratic state has yet to be equipped for carrying out those enormous burdens of administration which the needs of this industrial and trading age are so fast accumulating."

—Woodrow Wilson, "The Study of Administration," 1887

"What we need is not a new principle, but a modernizing of our managerial equipment."

—President's Committee on Administrative Management, 1937

During the 1960s and early 1970s, it was not uncommon for scholars and journalists to refer to the states as the "fallen arches" in the federal system. Today, it seems as though the states are everywhere being celebrated as "laboratories of democracy." While the former generalization probably exaggerated the weaknesses of the states, the latter generalization may be an overly optimistic appraisal. Yet, there is very little question that state governments today are larger, stronger, and more visible entities in the American federal system than they were 30 or 35 years ago (Conant, 1989). What accounts for this dramatic change in observers' perceptions of the states? The most important factor may be the remarkable modernization of state legislative, executive, and judicial branches that occurred between 1960 and 1990. While the pace of modernization and the degree of change achieved varied considerably from state to state, no state was left untouched by the powerful forces that propelled the drive to modernize.

The purpose of this chapter is to examine the modernization of one of the three branches of state government: the executive branch. Specifically, we will look at some of the factors that contributed to the modernization initiatives in the states between 1960 and 1990, the principal means by which modernization was pursued, and some of the management consequences of the modernization initiatives. Perhaps the most important consequence was the expansion of the chief executives' authority and capacity to manage the executive branch. Comprehensive reform initiatives aimed at streamlining the structure of the executive branch and expanding gubernatorial power were the principal means through which this result was achieved. The single most important causal factor in the results achieved may have been the set of ideas reformers in the states had about how to modernize state government. These reform ideas emerged from the field of public administration, and they were developed over a period of more than 50 years. Ironically, at the very time this intellectual heritage might be celebrated for the remarkable contribution it made to the modernization of the states, it is being challenged from a variety of directions and by a variety of sources. Consequently, whether the ''classical'' conception of modernization will continue to serve as the intellectual foundation for executive branch reform in the 21st century now seems to be an open question.

I. MODERNIZATION AND A SCIENCE OF ADMINISTRATION

Since the word modernization is used frequently in this chapter, it seems appropriate to begin with a definition of this key term. In Webster's dictionary, the word ''modernize'' means ''to adopt modern ways.'' The word ''modern,'' according to Webster's, has two principal meanings: (1) ''of, relating to, or characteristic of a period extending from a relevant, remote past,'' and (2) ''involving recent techniques, methods or ideas.'' Both of these definitions are important for the discussion in this chapter. The drive to modernize the executive branch of state government between 1960 and 1989 was an attempt to employ ''recent techniques, methods or ideas.'' The drive to modernize was also an attempt to bring to fruition a particular conception or model of government. The intellectual roots of this model can be traced back to 1887, when Woodrow Wilson's article ''The Study of Administration'' was published in *Political Science Quarterly*.

At the time Wilson's article was published, more than 80% of the U.S. population was employed in agriculture. Yet, Wilson recognized that the change from an agrarian society to an industrial and commercial society was well under way. Furthermore, he realized that an industrial society would be much more complex than an agrarian society, which, in turn, would require a much greater degree of governmental activity than had previously been the case. More active governmental engagement in societal affairs would not only require more legislative activity, Wilson believed, but also greater administrative capacity.

Yet, the governmental conditions of the time did not inspire confidence. As Wilson put it:

> [T]he poisonous atmosphere of city government, the crooked secrets of state administration, the confusion, sinecurism, and corruption . . . in the bureaus at Washington forbid us to believe that any clear conceptions of what constitutes good administration are as yet widely current in the US.[1]

The antidote Wilson offered to these problems had three central components: (1) the expansion of civil service throughout government; (2) the development of a science of administration by which the structure and processes of government agencies could be improved; and (3) a "drill" (training) for prospective members of the public service in the science of administration. Indeed, Wilson maintained that the development of a science of administration was so important that the best minds in the field of political science needed to turn their attention to this task.

During the 50 years that followed Wilson's challenge, concerted efforts were made to extend the reach of civil service within national, state, and local governments. Additionally, a concerted effort was made by management practitioners and scholars to define a science of administration. These intellectual efforts culminated in an edited volume published in 1937, *Papers on a Science of Administration*. The book featured the most up-to-date thinking of people who were writing about administration in both the public and private sectors. In their chapter, the editors of the volume, Luther Gulick and Lyndal Urwick, articulated what they understood to be the key principles of the "science of administration." The four principles were supposed to apply to both public and private sectors: (1) unity of command; (2) a limited span of control (for supervisors); (3) specialization of labor; and (4) organization (work division and coordination) on the basis of purpose, process, place, or people.

II. MODERNIZATION AND ADMINISTRATIVE MANAGEMENT

In 1937, President Franklin D. Roosevelt's Committee on Administrative Management (Brownlow committee) attempted to apply the principles of the "science of administration" to the national government. Indeed, the committee noted early in its report that the principles of the science of administration were well known. The problem, the committee maintained, was that the principles were not being followed. In fact, the committee compared the executive branch to an old farm,

---

[1] Woodrow Wilson, p. 201.

where the "barns, shacks, silos, tool sheds and garages" had "grown up without plan or design."[2] Whenever Congress created a new program, the committee complained, legislators frequently created a new agency to administer that program. The result, the committee argued, was a haphazard structure and a span of control far greater than any President could successfully handle.

The committee recommended that the 100 executive branch agencies and departments be consolidated by function into 12 large departments, with the head of each department appointed by the President. Additionally, the committee recommended that the President's personal staff be increased, the managerial agencies be expanded, and the financial and accounting processes of government be brought up-to-date. Last, but not least, the committee recommended that civil service be expanded throughout government. The purpose of the changes, the committee argued, was to "make democracy work" by making the national government an "up-to-date, efficient, and effective instrument for carrying out the will of the nation."[3]

In putting forward its recommendations, the committee was not only applying the "science of administration" but also presenting a normative argument about what the framers of the Constitution intended. At the time the committee was writing, the legislative branch (Congress) was the dominant institution in both policy making and administration. However, the committee had serious reservations about the ability of legislatively controlled governments to get things done. In order to have effective and efficient implementation of the laws that the American people want, the committee argued, the chief executive had to be "the center of energy, direction, and administrative management."[4] Administrative management, the committee said, "concerns itself in a democracy with the executive and his duties, with managerial and staff aids, with organization, with personnel and with the fiscal systems because these are the indispensable means of making good the popular will in a people's government."[5]

In this respect, the President's committee not only employed the principles of administration developed during the 50 years after Woodrow Wilson's article appeared but also made a critical contribution to the development of the science. In his 1887 article, Wilson noted that the science of administration would have to deal with an important constitutional issue: the distribution of authority within government. Yet most scholars and practitioners who had attempted to articulate the elements of a science of administration between 1887 and 1937 shied away from this potentially explosive issue. In contrast, the President's committee made the constitutional issue its principal focus.

---

[2] President's Committee on Administrative Management, p. 29.

[3] *Ibid.*, p. 3.

[4] *Ibid.*, p. 2.

[5] *Ibid.*, p. 3.

III. ADMINISTRATIVE MANAGEMENT IN THE STATES

The desire to improve administrative effectiveness and efficiency by making the chief executive the center of energy, direction, and administrative management was the central thrust of the major reform efforts in the states during the 1940s and '50s, as well as the '60s, '70s, and '80s. At the state level, however, advocates of modernizing the administrative machinery of government and expanding executive control over that machinery faced a major hurdle that President Roosevelt and the Brownlow committee did not have to confront. At the national level, the limitations on the chief executive's formal power were primarily established through statutory provisions and custom. At the state level, the limitations on the chief executive's power were established by explicit constitutional provisions, as well as statutory provisions and custom.

The constitutional limits on the formal powers of states' chief executives were the result of the colonial heritage, the Progressive movement, and legislative action. The constitutional framers in the original 13 states, as well as many who joined the Union in later years, were suspicious of executive power. Their experience with the British monarchy was the principal reason for this suspicion. The result was that early state executives were provided very few powers (Beyle, 1983). For example, gubernatorial terms were often limited to one or two years, and in some states, governors were limited to a single term.

In addition to these early constitutional limitations, the 19th century reform movement brought with it an increase in the number of separately elected executive branch officials such as the attorney general, secretary of state, state treasurer, and superintendent of education. Furthermore, as state legislatures responded to constituent demands and public problems, they created a host of new programs—and with them a host of new agencies and departments.

In many states, the number of executive branch agencies grew to 100 or 200 before a reorganization occurred. State legislatures generally established boards and commissions as the governing bodies to oversee the programs and agencies they created. In addition, state legislatures generally reserved for themselves the power to appoint board and commission members. In short, the premodernization position of most governors was that they had very little power to influence the executive branch agencies.[6] Nevertheless, governors were generally assumed by state voters to be responsible and accountable for the activities and performance of these agencies.

Given this situation, the "cabinet" model of government became the re-

---

[6] In addition to the formal limitations described here, most of the states' chief executives had little power in the budgetary process. Consequently, budget reform proposals aimed at giving the chief executive a key role in the process were sometimes a part of the reorganization proposal.

form ideal for the states (Bell, 1974). Advanced by reform advocates like A. E. Buck (1938), the reform ideal consisted of six principles:

1. Concentration of authority and responsibility in the hands of the chief executive
2. Departmentalization or functional integration of independent agencies
3. Elimination of boards or commissions for purely administrative work
4. Coordination of staff services
5. Independent audits
6. Recognition of the governor's cabinet

Not all state reformers used the reform ideal (cabinet model) for framing their reorganization plan, however. Some used the "traditional" model, and some used the "secretary/coordinator" model. Indeed, in historical terms, the traditional model has been used more frequently than the cabinet model; the secretrary/coordinator model has been used relatively infrequently (Garnett, 1980; Conant, 1986b).

As the information in Table 1 shows, the traditional model called for less dramatic structural and legal modifications than those prescribed in the cabinet model. In the traditional model, some functional consolidation (reduction in the number of agencies) and some expansion of gubernatorial appointment power are considered desirable. However, elimination of all elected constitutional officers, boards, and commissions is not considered to be necessary—or even desirable.

There are two principal reasons why the traditional model has been employed more frequently than the cabinet model as the structural objective of state executive branch reorganization initiatives. The first is tactical. The reorganization initiators hoped or assumed that state legislators would find a change from a pretraditional (or prereorganized) stage to the traditional model more palatable than a more comprehensive change (Elling, 1983; Conant, 1986b). The second

Table 1 Models and the Reform Ideal

	Cabinet	Secretary coordinator	Traditional
Number of agencies	Low	Very low	Moderate
Degree of functional consolidation	High	Low/moderate	
Gubernatorial appointment of department heads	High	Moderate	Low
Number of departmetns with single executive	High	High	Low/moderate
Department executive's control over consolidated department	High	Low	Low

reason is that some—perhaps even many—of the reorganization commission members themselves were not prepared to endorse the substantial expansion of executive power called for in the reform ideal (cabinet model). In short, the degree of change called for in the reorganization seems to have been a key sticking point.

There may be a historical lesson here that is worth highlighting. There seems to be a logical progression or sequence with respect to executive branch reorganization in the states: from the pretraditional to traditional model, and then from traditional model to the cabinet or secretary/coordinator model. This progression was clearly visible in the 1960s, '70s, and '80s. While a few states moved from a pretraditional structure (and constitution) to a cabinet structure or secretary/coordinator structure, most moved from a pretraditional to traditional or from traditional to the cabinet or secretary/coordinator form.

IV. STATE EXECUTIVE BRANCH REORGANIZATION: 1965–1979

A wave of comprehensive reorganization initiatives in the states followed the publication of the Brownlow report. Another wave of reorganization initiatives followed the publication of the report by the successor at the national level to the Brownlow commission, the Hoover commission (Garnett, 1980). During these two waves, reorganization initiatives were likely to be ignored by state legislatures or defeated by voters at the polls (Bosworth, 1954; Garnett, 1980). In contrast, the 15-year period between 1965 and 1979 could be called the golden era of state reorganization (Conant, 1987). During those years, the executive branch was reorganized in 21 states. In chronological order, the states were: Michigan, Wisconsin, California, Colorado, Florida, Massachusetts, Delaware, Maryland, Montana, Maine, North Carolina, Arkansas, Virginia, Georgia, South Dakota, Kentucky, Missouri, Idaho, Louisiana, New Mexico, and Connecticut.

In most of these 21 comprehensive reorganization initiatives, the passage of the reorganization bill and approval of the constitutional changes required to implement the reform could be described as a "bittersweet victory" for reform advocates. Many of these reformers had experienced "decades of frustration" during which reorganization proposals were launched with some fanfare, and then defeated or ignored by the legislature.[7] Indeed, the average germination or

---

[7] This phrase, which seemed so appropriate to the subject matter, was actually the title of a Wisconsin publication. The publication was cited by Governor Warren Knowles in his "Special Message to the Legislature on Reorganization" (April 5, 1967).

development time for these 21 executive branch reorganizations was 45 years (Conant, 1987).[8]

As shown by the rhetoric of the reorganization initiatives, unplanned growth, waste, duplication, overlap, and inefficiency were the problems the reformers wanted to overcome. Since the fragmentation and diffusion of both agencies and executive authority were generally regarded as the cause of these problems, the cure was to streamline the structure (consolidate agencies into departments) and expand executive power. In many of these states, the efforts to expand the chief executive's formal power included an expanded (four-year) term, a larger staff, new staff agencies, and the authority to develop executive budget recommendations.

The ability to appoint (and dismiss) the heads of the executive branch agencies has often been considered the most important of the expanded executive powers, but the extent to which this power was pursued in the 21 states varied. This fact is demonstrated by the structural objectives articulated by the reformers in each state. The reform ideal or cabinet model was the objective in seven of the 21 states, while the traditional model was the objective in eight. The secretary/coordinator was the model in four states; in two states the objective was a hybrid of other models.

One of the most interesting findings from the 21 states relates to the level of executive/legislative conflict over the reorganization proposal. In 16 of the 21 states, conflict was either low or moderate. This may seem to run contrary to expectations, since legislative opposition to reorganization has previously been identified as the key factor in the high failure rate of this type of reform initiative. It is important to note, however, that these 21 executive branch reorganization initiatives were "successful" because they gained legislative approval.

Support from legislative leaders and a majority of legislators is required to gain passage of the statutory changes needed to proceed with the reorganization. Thus, a low to moderate level of conflict seems, almost by definition, to be an important factor in the "success" scenario. Indeed, in many of these successful executive branch reorganizations, legislators—and particularly legislative leaders—played a role in the reorganization study commission or study and in the development of the reorganization plan.

Data on the results of the reorganization initiatives show that a substantial degree of consolidation took place in all states. Indeed, in some states the numbers of departments and agencies before reorganization exceeded 150, while the number of departments (and agencies) after reorganization was generally 30 or fewer. In the seven states where the cabinet model was the structural objective, the

---

[8] Data presented on these 21 reorganization initiatives in the following two pages are taken from this source. Specifically, the data are displayed in the Appendix of the 1987 publication.

governor gained the authority to appoint most cabinet heads or secretaries. In the states where the traditional model was the structural objective, the number of department heads the governor could appoint after the reorganization ranged from approximately 25% to 60%.

In addition to the structural consolidation and the expansion of gubernatorial appointment powers, most of the reorganization initiatives yielded important results in other areas, too. For example, in some states, gubernatorial terms were expanded from two to four years, the size of the governor's personal staff was expanded, and governors were given authority and responsibility for producing a state budget. New staff agencies, such as budget, personnel, and finance, were created and new auditing procedures were established.

Having discussed the remarkable results achieved during the 21 comprehensive reorganizations that took place between 1965 and 1979, it is now necessary to discuss the factors that propelled these modernization initiatives. As already noted, a conception or model of what a modernized executive branch should look like was an important starting point for reform initiatives in the states. Yet, even though this model may have been a necessary condition for modernization, it was certainly not a sufficient condition. A host of other powerful factors came into play during the 1960s and early '70s that provided the impetus for this fourth wave of reorganization initiatives. Among these factors were: rapid growth in state expenditures, from $27.6 billion in 1964 to $81 billion in 1974; reapportionment of state legislative districts; the expansion of state service and regulatory activities; citizen demands for better governmental performance; the new breed of legislators who recognized that effective administration was the key to making policy mandates work; the carryover into government of sophisticated management and budget techniques; federal officials who recognized that strong state administration was required for the implementation of federal programs; changes in party control of the statehouse and the executive office; the desire to emulate or keep up with other states; and governors who recognized that they could not effectively govern under the old organizational mode. These factors, as well as other factors and conditions specific to each state, contributed to the initiation and to the success of the reorganization efforts.

V. EXECUTIVE BRANCH MODERNIZATION IN THE 1980s

During the 1980s, the focus of efforts to modernize the executive branch of state government shifted away from comprehensive reorganization initiatives to smaller-scale efforts. Indeed, only one comprehensive reorganization initiative came to fruition during the decade, and this initiative (Iowa, 1985) differed from the reorganization initiatives of the 1960s and '70s in several important respects. The most important of these differences was principal objective of the initiative.

The Iowa reorganization was aimed at reducing fiscal stress, rather than modernizing the administrative machinery of government (Conant, 1992).

What factors account for the move away from comprehensive reorganization? Four factors have been cited in the scholarly literature:

1. The success of the extensive modernization and reform efforts initiated during the 1960s and '70s
2. The shift in gubernatorial, legislative, and administrative interest from structure and power to budget and management processes, additional revenue requirements, and critical policy issues (Beyle, 1982; Garnett, 1983; Sabato, 1983)
3. Legislative resistance to expanded executive power (Conant, 1988)
4. Resistance of executive branch officials and agency clientele to comprehensive reorganization initiatives (Conant, 1986b).

The fifth factor that may have come into play here could be described as the "climate of the times." For example, in his 1981 inaugural address, President Reagan said: "Government is not the solution to our problems. Government is the problem." Reflecting this view, Reagan's key commission on governmental management, the Grace commission, put heavy emphasis on cutting costs by eliminating government programs and agencies. A similar drive, the drive to "downsize," was going on in the private sector during the 1980s. The key objective in this drive was the elimination of middle managers and others who performed "overhead" or "nonproductive" functions. Such functions included staff support, budgeting, personnel, and auditing. In short, there was no equivalent of the President's Committee on Administrative Management at the national level to inspire or encourage comprehensive modernization efforts at the state level. Additionally, the most visible private sector management initiatives seemed to involve mindless chopping of personnel rather than modernization.

Despite these factors, however, one large-scale modernization initiative did take place in the states that is worth noting. This initiative took place in the state of New Jersey, between 1982 and 1984 (Conant, 1986a). Among the most important features of the New Jersey initiative was that it applied the "principles" of administration in a new and interesting way.

VI. GOVERNOR'S MANAGEMENT IMPROVEMENT PROGRAM IN NEW JERSEY

Initiated in June 1982 by Governor Thomas Kean, the Governor's Management Improvement Plan, as it was called, differed from the comprehensive reorganization initiatives that took place from 1965 to 1979 in four areas: structural objectives, evaluation process, adoption strategy, and implementation strategy (Conant, 1986b).[9] The New Jersey effort involved all 20 executive branch departments, but its focus was on modifying the structure of existing departments (intradepartmental reorganization) rather than on consolidating agencies with related functions into a few large departments (interdepartmental reorganization).

The unusual design of the New Jersey reorganization effort was based in large part on the strategy and tactics chosen by the governor and his key advisers. Undoubtedly, the fact that the opposition party controlled both houses of the legislature played an important role in the development of this strategy. But a historical factor, a cabinet model reorganization in 1947, made this design feasible. As part of the 1947 cabinet model reorganization, the formal powers of the governor were expanded, the state agencies were consolidated into large departments, gubernatorial appointment of department commissioners was established, and an executive budget process was set up. As a result, the pursuit of administrative economy, efficiency, and effectiveness with limited structural (and procedural) objectives was possible in 1982.

Like the structural objectives, the evaluation process used in the New Jersey reorganization was unusual. Generally speaking, the study of state agency structures and administrative procedures is conducted by private sector executives (volunteer) and by consulting firms hired for the study. The recommendations for change are usually developed by these same parties. In the New Jersey study, however, approximately 1200 public sector managers from all 20 state departments were teamed as "co-consultants" with the 250 private sector executives. Furthermore, the public managers had the primary responsibility for developing the recommendations for change.

The "technology" used to do the organizational assessment was also unusual. Indeed, the consulting firm employed for the reorganization was selected precisely because it had a "unique" methodology for doing the analysis. Described as a "bottom-up" rather than a "top-down" approach to reorganization, the consulting firm used a "data-based" methodology rather than formal organizational charts and personal interviews to identify and analyze the existing structure of the state departments. Part of this data base was established through the firm's work with private sector organizations and part through its survey of the departments.

The study of each state department began with the development of a "dictionary" or catalog of all work activities performed in the department. Then all managers and supervisors within the department were asked to fill out survey forms. They were asked to identify: (1) how they allocated their time among the work functions described in the dictionaries, and (2) how their employees spent

---

[9] All of the remaining text in Section IV is taken from this source. Permission to reprint the text from this article was granted by *State Government*.

their time. Using this survey information, "house plots" were generated and then analyzed by the coconsultants on the basis of several key indicators: (1) total overhead costs, (2) the number of management levels, (3) the ratio of managers to workers, and (4) the functional distribution of salary dollars and employees. Target figures for each of these measures were established during the organizational analysis. In the areas where the department numbers exceeded or fell below the desired levels, or where functional tasks were "fragmented," reductions or changes were recommended.

Among the target figures used in the organizational analysis, the "span norms" were the most important of the evaluation tools. Developed during the data-gathering stage through a process of negotiation between the public managers, private sector executives, and representatives of the consulting firm, the span norms were the number of employees each manager or supervisor was supposed to be able to oversee. For example, a span norm for a clerical supervisor might be 10 to 15; a span norm for an engineering supervisor 5 to 10. Whenever the number of workers fell below the span norm, "targets of opportunity" were available. These "targets" were particularly visible where managers had only one or two employees (or other managers) reporting to them.

As it turned out, the data showed that in every department the number and levels of middle managers could be reduced. The consulting firm argued that streamlining the structure of the organization offered not only the opportunity for immediate savings but also the potential for more efficient performance. It is important to note, however, that the co-consultants were not required to accept the computer-generated recommendation for changes in the organizational structure. In most cases, the public managers spent days or even weeks analyzing the recommendations. Then they were reexamined in meetings with the private sector executives. Once the co-consultants made their final recommendations, they were submitted to the department commissioners, who had final decision making authority.

A. Adoption and Implementation

Like the structural objectives and evaluation process, the adoption and implementation strategies of the New Jersey reorganization effort were different from those of most previous state reorganizations. Generally speaking, after the organizational analysis is completed, a reorganization plan is submitted to the legislature. In the 1982 New Jersey reorganization, however, most of the departmental reorganization plans could be adopted without legislative approval. Because most of the plans involved the reassignment or reduction of personnel within the individual departments, the only approval required was civil service approval. Furthermore, even in cases where functions were being transferred from one division to another within a department, new statutory language was generally not required. Under the Executive Reorganization Act of 1969, the governor was required to submit reorganization plans for the transfer, abolition, or consolidation of agency functions to both houses of the legislature, but the plans went into effect within 60 days unless the legislature passed a concurrent resolution opposing the proposal.

The adoption strategy, like the implementation strategy, was unusual in its design. The architects of the reorganization clearly understood the fact that successful implementation of a reorganization plan required cooperation from public administrators. One vehicle used to develop this cooperation was to employ the public sector managers as "co-consultants"; another method was to give the department commissioners final decision-making authority over reorganization plans for their departments. As a result of these tactics, in most departments there was a commitment to the reorganization plans that does not usually exist in these efforts. Furthermore, this "ownership" of the planned changes was enhanced through public commitments made in press conferences. More than half the commissioners announced the changes they intended to make and the savings they intended to achieve during these sessions.

In addition, two other tactics were used in New Jersey to encourage implementation. Each commissioner was asked to submit a copy of the department's reorganization plan to the governor. In effect, this step could be viewed as the establishment of an agreement between the governor and the commissioner. Also, the implementation process was monitored by the Office of Management and Budget. The monitoring at least raised the possibility of budgetary penalties if department executives failed to implement their reorganization plans and realize their promised savings.

B. Findings and Recommendations

The quantitative findings and recommendations of the New Jersey organizational analysis were published in book form. The findings show that all 20 New Jersey departments shared some similar characteristics. In almost every department, the cost to manage was too high, the percentage of middle managers too high, the ratio of workers to managers too low, the maximum management levels too high, and the average management levels too high. For example, in the Department of Environmental Protection the cost to manage was almost 30% higher than the recommended level, the percentage of middle managers approximately 25% higher than the target level, the ratio of workers to managers 18% lower than the recommended level, and the average management level about 8% greater than the target level (Conant, 1986b).

When the proposed levels for each of the measures or indicators are compared with actual levels, it is clear that significant changes in the structure of the individual departments were envisioned. Furthermore, there was an expectation that these changes would result in substantial savings. The data from the organization analysis seemed to support the consulting firm's operating assumption that significant savings could be achieved by streamlining the structure of the individual departments. The primary target for the savings was the number of middle-level managers. The data showed that many managers had only one or two employees reporting to them, even though the span norms showed that they could supervise 5 to 15 employees.

C. Results

The results achieved through the structural changes implemented in New Jersey were sometimes impressive. Savings (economies) were achieved, efficiency improved, and in some cases effectiveness in service delivery or regulation was enhanced. Yet even the most carefully constructed reorganization design is not likely to have a uniform impact on all departments, and that was the case in New Jersey. The effect the reorganization had on the structure of the state departments was not uniform across departments, nor was it uniform across divisions within departments. The degree of structural change was higher in some departments than in others, and it was higher in some divisions than in others. Likewise the savings realized varied from department to department and division to division.

Although the estimated savings achieved through the structural changes were only a small percentage of the total base budget for four of the five departments listed in Table 2, the importance of realizing incremental savings should not be overlooked. Administrators, legislatures, and scholars all regard incremental increases as a critical element of the political process, so there is no reason

Table 2   Structural Change and Estimated Savings

	Number of management positions redesignated to worker status[a]	Personnel reductions	Estimated savings[b] (in millions)
Education	59	159	$3.6
Environmental protection	—	46	$1.1
Human services	205	—	$1.5
Labor	160	126	$2.7
Transportation	356	140	$2.8

[a] Redesignation did not necessarily mean reduction in pay.
[b] Estimated savings from Aug. 1, 1983, through Dec. 31, 1984.

to dismiss or ignore incremental savings. Furthermore, in addition to the savings, gains in efficiency and effectiveness were realized in some New Jersey departments. Indeed, most of the 130 public managers interviewed for this study said that the reorganization had a positive effect on the performance of their divisions and departments.

D. Evaluating the New Model

Unlike the cabinet, secretary/coordinator, or traditional models, the New Jersey reorganization was not designed to overhaul the entire structure of the executive branch. While all 20 state departments were affected to some degree by the reorganization, the structural objectives were limited rather than comprehensive, and the focus was intradepartmental rather than interdepartmental. Like other reorganization initiatives, it was an effort to expand gubernatorial power by increasing control over administration, but no attempt was made to change the governor's formal powers, nor was it required. As a result, the balance of power issue was not sharply focused, and direct conflict between Governor Kean and the legislature over proposed structural changes emerged only in a few areas.

Like the structural-legal objectives of the New Jersey reorganization, the process used to evaluate the departmental structures was limited and carefully focused. The technology employed was innovative: coded survey forms replaced formal organization charts and personal interviews as the means used to gather existing data on existing structures, and the computer was used as a key tool in the assessment of those structures. Likewise, the theory underlying the assessment technology (specialization, functional integration, and limited span of control) was applied in an innovative manner. The operating assumption was that costs could be reduced and performance improved by cutting unnecessary levels of management and by more clearly defining authority, communication channels, and decision-making responsibility. As it turned out, the data showed that for most managers the span of control could be expanded (rather than reduced), which meant that the number of both managers and management levels could be reduced. In short, the data seemed to show that these public bureaucracies were heavy at the middle levels, as some critics have maintained.

There are, however, two potential problems with this new application of the old principles of administration. First, trimming middle-management levels may reduce costs, but changes in structure alone do not guarantee improved performance. Other areas, like strategy, systems, staff, style, skills, and values, may also need overhauling. Governor Kean and the architects of the New Jersey reorganization seemed to be well aware of this fact. For example, an assessment of the state's data processing system was an important part of the New Jersey initiative, and a $20 million investment in new data-processing equipment was one of its principal outcomes.

The second potential problem is that while cuts in personnel can mean more clearly defined reporting relationships and better accountability, they can also have a negative effect on morale and thus hurt, rather than improve, performance. This phenomenon was particularly visible in the Department of Labor, where reduction in force procedures were used during the reorganization to reduce and reclassify positions. Approximately 285 positions were affected by these actions, but more than double that number of personnel changed chairs as employees exercised their civil service "bumping" rights. In other departments, however, where the bumping affected only small numbers of people or where attrition was the primary vehicle used to streamline the structure or cut staff, negative consequences were less pronounced. Furthermore, among the managers who seemed most sensitive to the short-term negative effect these personnel actions had on morale, many said that the long-term effects would be positive. They anticipated clearer lines of communication and responsibility and more efficient decision making as a result of the streamlined structure.

The design of the adoption and implementation strategies, like the structural objectives and evaluation process, seem to show a good understanding of the critical political and administrative factors that can block or inhibit change. As previously noted, most of the proposed changes in departmental structure and procedure could be adopted without new statutory language—a pivotal factor in New Jersey since the opposition party controlled both houses of the legislature. Likewise, bureaucratic resistance to the changes was minimized, at least at the top levels, because the public managers played a key role in developing the recommendations for change.

The "Achilles heel" of the reorganization initiative, however, was civil service rules. Not only did those rules limit and slow down the process of change, but the rules and regulations were actually direct causal factors in the excessive numbers and levels of middle-level managers discovered in the organizational analysis. The source of the problem was the link between pay and management responsibility. The base pay for professionals, like scientists, engineers, and accountants, was fixed for the group, and the only way to significantly improve an individual's pay was to award that person a management title. In order to retain professionals whose expertise and experience were needed to make government work, management titles were often given to people who did little or no managing. The result, as one division manager described it, was "an organizational structure that looked like a nuclear reactor rather than a pyramid." Horizontal and vertical relationships were ill defined, and communication and decision making were slow and cumbersome.

As part of the solution to this problem, several departments asked civil service to provide a "high-tech" title series that would compensate top-flight professionals at competitive salaries without the assignment of a management title. However, civil service's initial response to the request for the new personnel series was not particularly encouraging. Consequently, most department commissioners were reluctant to fully implement the reorganization plans because they did not want to lose key personnel. Thus, both the scope and depth of the potential structural changes were limited in important ways by this single factor.

E. Application in Other States

Since most states have experienced some form of comprehensive reorganization in which the executive branch agencies have been consolidated and gubernatorial authority has been expanded, the new model could be used in almost all states. However, the New Jersey model is likely to be most effective in the states where a cabinet reorganization has taken place or where the governor's powers of organization are strong: Alaska, Michigan, Maine, Massachusetts, Maryland, South Dakota, Hawaii, Missouri, Montana, Virginia, New York, Pennsylvania, Utah, Connecticut, and New Hampshire.

Like all management tools, the new model of reorganization has some shortcomings that need to be kept in mind, yet it appears to provide a means to systematically assess and modify the structure of government departments while minimizing legislative involvement. Thus the administrative issues, like the cost and performance of the government, can be addressed without directly raising the more difficult and divisive political issue of the balance of power between the executive and the legislature that so often becomes the focal point in a reorganization initiative. Given the enormous size of most state bureaucracies, the vast scope of their responsibilities, and the importance of their performance, the New Jersey experience seems to provide a workable reorganization model for modern times.

VII. CONCLUSION

During the three decades between 1960 and 1990, the executive branch of government was modernized in the states. While the degree of modernization varied from state to state, no state was left untouched by the powerful forces that propelled the drive to modernize. These forces included citizen demands for better governmental performance, the new breed of legislators who recognized that effective administration was the key to making policy mandates work, the desire to emulate or keep up with other states, governors who recognized that they could not effectively govern under the old organizational mode, the expansion of state service and regulatory activities, and other conditions specific to each state.

In this chapter, the discussion of modernization initiatives and the results of those initiatives have focused on large-scale or comprehensive initiatives. During the 1960s and '70s, this type of initiative was undertaken in many states.

Important outcomes of those initiatives included the restructuring of the executive branch, the expansion of gubernatorial authority, and the expansion of gubernatorial capacity to manage the executive branch agencies. During the 1980s, the focus of elected and administrative officials in the states shifted away from large-scale modernization efforts. Only the Governor's Management Improvement Program in New Jersey (1982–1984) fits the definition employed here of a large-scale modernization initiative. While this initiative differed from previous large-scale initiatives in a variety of ways, it does seem to be an appropriate model for future modernization initiatives in states that have a "cabinet" structure.

In states that have a pretraditional or traditional structure, a large-scale modernization initiative aimed at establishing the cabinet structure may be a precondition for more effective administrative management. Whether the cabinet model and the concept of administrative management will serve as normative ideals for modernization initiatives in the 21st century is, however, an open question. Downsizing, contracting out, reengineering, and reinvention have been the principal management "drives" in both the national government and the private sector during the 1990s. As of this writing, there is no particular reason to think that the appeal of these approaches will soon fade. In fact, the reduction of operating costs (economy), which downsizing, contracting out, reengineering, and reinvention seem to have as their primary objective, may be positioned at the top of governatorial and legislative agendas. If this does happen, the assembly of information about these approaches will be an important task for public administration scholars who want to contribute to the debate about modernization initiatives in the states.

REFERENCES

Bell, G. (1974). State administrative activities, 1972–73, *Book of the States, 1974–75*, Council of State Governments, Lexington, KY.

Beyle, T. (1982). The governors and the executive branch, *Book of the States, 1982–83*, Council of State Governments, Lexington, KY.

Bosworth, K. (1953). Management improvement in the states, *American Political Science Review*, 47:84–89.

Buck, A. E. (1938). *Reorganization of State Government in the United States*, New York Municipal League, Columbia University Press, New York.

Conant, J. K. (1986a). Reorganization and the bottom line, *Public Administration Review*, 46(1):48–56.

Conant, J. K. (1986b). State reorganization: a new model? *State Government*, 58(6):130–138.

Conant, J. K. (1988). In the shadow of Wilson and Brownlow: executive branch reorganization in the states, 1965–79, *Public Administration Review*, 48(5):59–69.

Conant, J. K. (1989). The growing importance of state government. *Handbook of Public Administration* (J. E. Perry, ed.), Jossey Bass, San Francisco.

Conant, J. K. (1992). Executive branch reorganization in the states, 1965–1991, *Book of the States, 1992–93*, Council of State Governments, Lexington, KY.

Elling, R. (1983). State bureaucracies, *Politics in the American States* (V. Gray, H. Jacob, and K. Vines, eds.; 4th ed.), Little, Brown, Boston.

Garnett, J. L. (1980). *Reorganizing State Government: The Executive Branch*, Westview Press, Boulder, CO.

Garnett, J. L. (1983). Management structures, *State and Local Government Administration* (J. Rabin and D. Dodd, eds.), Marcel Dekker, New York.

Sabato, L. (1983). *Good-bye to Good-time Charlie*, Congressional Quarterly Press, Washington, D.C.

President's Committee on Administrative Management (1937). *Report of the President's Committee*, Government Printing Office, Washington, D.C.

Wilson, W. The study of administration, *Political Science Quarterly*, II(2):192–222.

3
State Administration and Intergovernmental Interdependency: Do National Impacts on State Agencies Contribute to Organizational Turbulence?

Deil S. Wright and Chung-Lae Cho
University of North Carolina, Chapel Hill, North Carolina

Any attempt to understand the functioning of state government and administration in the American political system must take account of the concepts of federalism (FED), intergovernmental relations (IGR), and intergovernmental management (IGM). The distinctive features of these three concepts and the contrasts among them are summarized in Figure 1. That figure also displays along a time line the approximate evolution in the development of the three terms in the U.S. historical experience (Wright, 1990, 1997, 1998). Of special relevance to this essay on state administration is the distinctive and prominent roles played by ''leading actors'' under each concept. Those featured actors are:

    FED: Popularly elected generalists (PEGs)
    IGR: Appointed administrative generalists (AAGs)
    IGM: Program policy professionals (PPPs).

These three sets of actors, as discussed below, interact within and between each level or *plane* of governance.

To understand the idea of a governmental *plane* as well as the involvement of the three types of officials, a visual image is useful. Figure 2 represents the

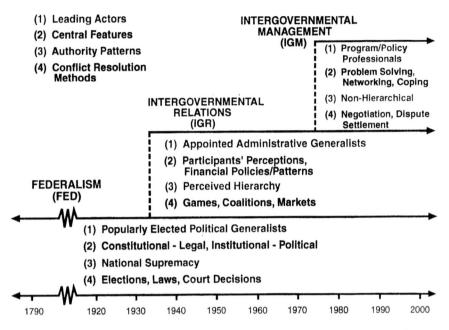

Figure 1   Historical evolution of interjurisdictional concepts: federalism (FED), intergovernmental relations (IGR), and intergovernmental management (IGM).

three levels of government(s) in the United States when viewed as planes of
governance. The three-dimensional rectangular cube depicts each jurisdictional
level (national, state, local) as a vertical plane standing on edge (upright), parallel
to the other planes.

   This conceptualization does not deny the presence of some (or several)
patterns of hierarchy in various interjurisdictional relationships. One that first
comes to mind is Dillon's Rule, which defines (for most American states) the
fundamental legal subordination of local governments to state governmental pow-
er(s). Local legal subservience, however, is only one aspect of a wide range of
state-local relations (Zimmerman, 1995). A broader understanding of state-local
dynamics lends credence to the idea that state-local as well as state-national and
national-local relations can be properly viewed as interjurisdictional interactions
that occur between and among *planes of governance.*

   The arrays of reciprocal arrows that connect the three planes convey the
multiple and varied interactions. Absent from Figure 2 are the intraplane interactions, of which two are most obvious. First, within the state plane are the 50
American states, so there are 50 sets of state-local and state-national relations as
well as all the permutations of interstate relations within the state plane. Second,

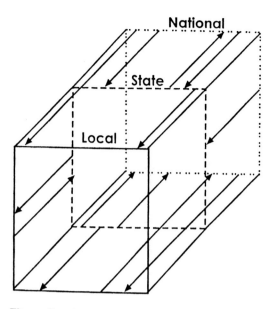

Figure 2   Planes of governance in the United States: national, state, and local planes and intergovernmental interactions. Arrows indicate intergovernmental interactions and influence, not necessarily in proportion to the number and direction of the arrows.

within the local plane are over 86,000 local governments (counties, cities, school districts, etc.). There are therefore innumerable inter-local interactions, all of which take place within the confines of a particularized set (one of 50) of state-local relations. In short, Figure 2 is grossly oversimplified. The figure helps, however, to establish the essential idea of *planes* of governance.

With this simplified visual framework as a starting point let us return to the three types of leading actors identified earlier: PEGs, AAGs, and PPPs. Our aim is to locate each set of actors within the respective three planes.

Figure 3 helps illustrate the positions of these actors. Two new features appear in Figure 3. First, a cylindrical core is inserted within the rectangular cube. This core traverses and connects the three planes of governance, from national to local. The second new feature is the display of short-hand terms for the three sets of actors on the edges, inside the margins, and in the central core.

The focus of this essay can be specified visually within the framework of Figure 3. It is within the state governance plane and on the types of state administrative agencies located in that plane, especially the administrators who head those agencies. The agencies, and their respective agency heads, cluster predominantly into two categories: (1) program policy professionals (PPPs) located

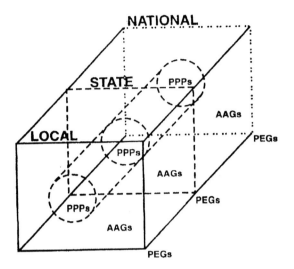

Figure 3 Planes of governance in the United States: distinctive positions and roles of three types of intragovernmental and intergovernmental actors. PEGS, popularly elected generalists; AAGs, appointed administrative generalists; PPPs, program policy professionals.

chiefly in the central cylindrical core of the cube, and (2) appointed administrative generalists (AAGs), who occupy spaces within the state plane between the interior edges of the plane and the cylindrical core. The third set of actors, the PEGs, are ones for whom we have only a limited set of representatives. These are the elected heads of several types of state agencies of which the four most common are attorneys general, auditors, secretaries of states, and treasurers. These popularly elected officials are not representative of the most powerful PEGs occupying the edges of the state plane—namely, governors and legislators. Nevertheless, these popularly elected administrators are directly accountable to the voting public. In this respect their roles, actions, and attitudes offer a relevant, albeit imperfect, set of clues as to how other PEGs may participate in the state governance plane.

I. FLUIDITY AND INTERDEPENDENCY: THE POLICY CONTEXT OF STATE ADMINISTRATION

We have asserted that the states are embedded in dynamic sets of intergovernmental networks of interdependency. We document and describe selected aspects of those interdependencies below. Prior to that exposition, however, it is important to demonstrate the fluid, or dynamic, dimensions of state level administrative operations. This can be achieved by first assessing the extent of change in agency program priorities. Secondly, the role of various actors in initiating the changes can be compared.

A. Agency Program Fluidity

To what extent do state agency programs change? How stable or how fluid are the priorities and policies set by state agencies? To answer these questions we rely on data collected from periodic mail questionnaire surveys of state agency heads across the 50 states. This ongoing research effort is called the American State Administrators Project (ASAP) (see Bowling and Wright, 1998). Table 1 displays responses on the extent of program changes from ASAP surveys in the years 1978, 1984, 1988, and 1994. In each instance the questions probed the degree of change over the preceding four-year span. The percentages arrayed in Table 1 reveal that program priorities in state agencies are quite fluid.

Table 1 Changes in State Administrative Agencies' Program Priorities, 1978–1994

	1978	1984	1988	1994
Extent of change[a]				
None	2%	2%	2%	2%
Minor	18	21	21	20
Moderate	40	42	42	42
Major	40	35	34	37
(N=)	(1371)	(1110)	(1429)	(1211)
Initiators of change[b]				
Governor	41%	47%	53%	55%
Legislators	57	58	59	65
Agency staff	71	64	67	61
Clientele groups	29	27	30	34
National officials	38	31	32	28
Local officials	13	8	11	10
(N =)	(1341)	(1105)	(1370)	(1226)

[a] *Question*: Within the past four years what changes or shifts have taken place in the ordering of priorities among programs within your agency?
[b] *Question*: Were any shifts in program priorities the result of policy initiatives or actions originated by any of the following? (Check wherever applicable.)
Note: Because of rounding the percentages may not add to 100.
Source: D. S. Wright, American State Administrators Project (ASAP) Surveys, Institute of Research in Social Science, University of North Carolina, Chapel Hill, NC.

The percentage of agency heads reporting the absence of program changes was so small, 2%, as to be inconsequential. At the other end of the change continuum, 30–40% of the agency heads indicated "major" shifts in programs during the preceding four years. When those proportions are added to those in the "moderate" category (40–42%), the exceptionally fluid character of state agency program operations is confirmed. Between 75% and 80% of all state agencies were reported to have experienced moderate or major shifts among and between programs during the preceding four years.

This picture of fluid and flexible state agencies, from a program priorities standpoint, contradicts conventional wisdom. It runs counter to the stereotype of staid, stable, and stodgy bureaucratic operations, whether in state government or elsewhere.

We may assign a variety of terms to this program fluidity—responsiveness, adaptability, or merely change-capacity. Whatever the term, it strips away some stereotypes of organizational rigidity and inflexibility in state government. Furthermore, the consistency of the findings on fluidity across the four ASAP surveys lends added credence to the substantive results and interpretations.

B. Initiators of Change

Let us assume that the program changes discussed above can be construed as agency responsiveness, at least in the aggregate. A question which logically follows from such an interpretation is: To whom or what are state agencies responding when engaged in these reported program shifts? We address the "to whom" question based on ASAP survey data from 1978 to 1994. Table 1 also shows the percentage of respondents indicating that the program shifts were "the results of policy initiatives or actions" originated by one or more of the indicated actors.

Both governors and legislators were prominent participants in the program change processes of state agencies. This is no surprise. On the other hand, it is noteworthy that legislators are more active initiators than governors. While administrative agencies are formally a part of the "executive" branch, they are clearly and understandably responsive to legislator initiatives.

Note that the percentages for both the governor and legislators consistently increase, albeit modestly, across the four surveys. This may be a reflection of increased institutional assertiveness in the competition for power and influence over administration in the states (Abney and Lauth, 1986; Rosenthal, 1989). Whatever the case, it should also be noted that by 1994, governor- and legislator-initiated changes approached or exceeded the role of agency staff in inducing program changes.

This latter finding stands out prominently in Table 1, namely, the high percentages indicated for agency staff involvement in initiating program changes.

With the exception of 1994, staff-initiated program changes exceeded all other sources of program change. Those proportions, however, declined somewhat from 1978 to 1994, and in the latter year were exceeded by legislator-initiated program changes. Not only state agency programs are in a constant state of flux; so also is the pattern of pressures from various actors to whom the agencies are responsive.

We have identified three central participants in the program change process: agency staff, governor, and legislators. Three other, less central participants, depending on the situation, are identified in Table 1. These "external" actors are clientele groups, national officials, and local officials. The role of these actors in prompting agency change is considerably less than the roles of the three central actors discussed above. With the possible exception of local officials, however, these external actors are far from bit players on the stage of state agency actions. For clientele groups and national officials, from one-fourth to one-third of the agency heads indicate agency responsiveness to initiatives from these sets of actors. For clientele groups there is no apparent trend across the years from 1978 to 1994.

In the case of national officials it is possible to argue that there has been a decline in their role as initiators of state agency change. This point reflects a trend in the proportions across the four sequential ASAP surveys: 38%, 31%, 32%, and 28%. A separate, earlier analysis on state administrators perceptions of national influence documented a distinct shift toward reduced national influence between 1978 and 1988 (Yoo and Wright, 1993). The decline (to 28%) in 1994 suggests that there may be some further attenuation in national impact(s) at the state level. Any stronger or firmer statement concerning this apparent trend is contingent of further analysis of the ASAP as well as other data.

Quite apart from the modest and perhaps significant trend toward declining national influence and impacts in the state plane, one clear parameter is present. Over the past two decades from 28% to 38% of state administrators report that national officials have affected agency program priorities. This is a substantial and consequential national presence, one that cannot and should not be ignored. The remainder of this essay is devoted to describing, understanding, and explaining the character of that presence.

II. FEDERAL AID

The state governance plane has been established in the American intergovernmental system. The location and roles of three types of policy actors have been identified (PEGs, AAGs, and PPPs). Additionally, the dynamic nature of state programs and policies has been described, accompanied by an exploration of actors who have contributed to the program/policy shifts.

In the latter analysis we devoted special attention to the role of national officials in initiating program shifts within state agencies. The next step in this exposition looks at the most prominent and historic instrument by which the national government has attempted to influence state agency/administrator behavior, namely, through the use of grants-in-aid (or federal aid).

A. Studying Grants-in-Aid

It is useful to be reminded at the outset of the historic, distinctive, and significant character of federal aid (MacDonald, 1928; Wright, 1968; Derthick, 1970; ACIR, 1977, 1978). There is a tendency to view federal (i.e., national) aid as uniquely American in origin. The extensive use of this intergovernmental fiscal transfer device does have long-standing roots in American history (ACIR, 1978). The instrument, however, took its modern form in early 19th century England (Webb, 1911). Indeed, the first formal analysis of the device was authored by Sidney Webb of Fabian Society fame, under the title *Grants-in-Aid: A Criticism and Proposal* (1911).

Despite numerous prior analyses of federal aid, there is much that remains to be understood about its *administrative* impact(s). Political analyses abound (see Peterson, 1995, and references therein). Economic, econometric, and geographic assessments are nearly numberless (Chubb, 1985a,c). But systematic, empirically based analyses of the administrative impacts of federal aid are scarce and often sketchy (ACIR, 1977; Haas, 1985; Yoo and Wright, 1993, 1994). The existence of data sets from replicated ASAP surveys offers the opportunity for an analysis that focuses on these administrative impacts.

B. Three Decades of Federal Aid

Federal aid as a conditional grant of funds to the states has existed for more than a century (ACIR, 1978). Its growth and consequences over the past four decades, however, have transformed it into a political-administrative issue of major importance. In 1978, for example, federal aid constituted 26% of state-local general revenue and about one-sixth of the national budget. These proportions prompted many voices calling for restoring a "balance" in national-state/local relations. A state-focused, agency-based review of federal aid since the 1960s is therefore warranted. Table 2 provides the basis for pursuing a temporal overview.

The receipt of federal aid by state agencies in the early 1960s was modest, at best. About one-third of the ASAP respondents in 1964 reported that their agency received federal aid. By 1968 the proportion exceeded 50% and it approached two-thirds by 1974. The reach of federal aid peaked in 1978 with slightly more than three-fourths of all responding administrators heading agencies

Table 2 Federal Aid Patterns Among State Administrative Agencies, 1964–1994

		1964	1968	1974	1978	1984	1988	1994
Receipt of aid		34%	54%	63%	76%	70%	69%	73%
	(N=)	(910)	(987)	(1587)	(1363)	(1078)	(1439)	(1205)
Dependency	under 25%	47%	49%	48%	44%	45%	45%	45%
	25–49%	23	23	20	21	22	22	20
	50–74%	17	20	19	19	20	19	21
	75% or more	13	8	13	15	14	14	14
	(N=)	(309)	(522)	(983)	(1014)	(746)	(981)	(863)
Diversity	1	NA	NA	37%	34%	36%	38%	31%
	2	NA	NA	27	28	26	25	27
	3	NA	NA	17	19	18	17	21
	4	NA	NA	8	9	11	11	12
	5 or more	NA	NA	11	10	9	9	10
	(N=)			(975)	(996)	(741)	(974)	(845)
Complexity	Project	NA	NA	71%	72%	67%	63%	70%
	Formula	NA	NA	55	60	58	59	63
	Block	NA	NA	30	25	34	31	32
	Nonmatching	NA	NA	20	21	16	16	19
	Loans	NA	NA	4	3	3	4	5
	(N=)			(989)	(1037)	(750)	(987)	(867)

Note: Because of rounding the percentages may not add to 100.
Source: D. S. Wright, American State Administrators Project (ASAP) Surveys, Institute of Research in Social Science, University of North Carolina, Chapel Hill, NC.

receiving aid. Since that apogee the penetration of federal aid among state agencies has stabilized at about 70%.

Of what significance are these trends and fluctuations? Beyond the simple quantitative statement that the administrative reach of federal aid doubled between 1964 and 1978, what broader conclusions or interpretations can we attach to the patterns? At a somewhat higher descriptive level the escalation of aid among state agencies documents and even dramatizes the heavily interdependent character of national-state relations. In addition, and in the face of episodic devolution initiatives from both presidential and congressional sources, the level of interdependency has remained high since 1978.

It may be true, as Chubb (1985a) argued over a decade ago, that the "bias toward centralization" has ceased. But these ASAP survey results show that any marked movement toward decentralization has yet to reveal itself using federal aid as an indicator. As one observer (Walker, 1997:38) recently noted, "Devolution has not entered a new and accelerated phase...[but] instead it has proven to be just one dynamic among the many that drive the system, and its success to date clearly indicates that it is no *Big Deal* and in no sense a *Revolution*." Obviously, the 1996 welfare "reform" legislation (P.L. 104–193) is not reflected in the ASAP federal aid impacts. But even that devolutionary legislation contained prescriptive nationalizing elements. In short, the fabric of national-state administrative interdependency appears to remain as broadly and perhaps as tightly woven as at any time in the past two decades.

Indeed, 40 years ago President Dwight D. Eisenhower made a modest proposal to "unwind" federal aid interdependency (Grodzins, 1960a,b). Two small grant-in-aid programs and some tax revenues were offered as "turn-backs" to the states. The Gordian Knot of federal aid interdependency could not be cut then, nor has it been dramatically reconfigured in more contemporary times. To understand why federal aid is so durable and pervasive, we need a better grasp of its configurations. The following sections present analyses of federal aid dependency, diversity, and complexity—all viewed from the standpoint of state administration.

1. Dependency

A prominent if not dominant interpretation of the power relations involved in federal aid is one of *dependency* or, as Pressman describes it, the donor-recipient relationship (Pressman, 1975). This asymmetric power pattern is far from an exclusive view, however (Ingram, 1977). Our approach to understanding federal aid influence is to argue that the fiscal transfers create the preconditions but not the certainty of a subordinate relationship. Dependency is, then, a continuous variable (or interval) whose measurement is fiscal. The power relationship created by dependency remains problematic.

The degree of dependency on federal aid by state agencies is reported in Table 2 for the years 1964–1994. The figures reveal the extent to which state agencies receiving federal aid rely on that revenue source for varying proportions of their budgets. The number of cases on which the percentages are based vary for two reasons. First, increasing proportions of state agencies received federal aid (from 1964 to 1978). Second, the response rates to the different ASAP surveys varied from about 70% in 1964 and 1968, to slightly under 40% in 1984 and 1994.

A review of the dependency percentages across the seven ASAP surveys discloses a singular and striking feature. There are insignificant and inconsequential variations from 1964 across the intervening years to 1994. Despite dramatic agency program and policy fluctuations in the decades of the 1960s through the 1990s, federal aid dependency among state agencies has remained remarkably stable. How can we account for this unexpected fact?

There is no simple, sure, straightforward explanation that comes to mind. We might posit two sharply contrasting sets of conditions and then hypothesize that a combination of factors falling between the extremes offers avenues for testing alternative explanations.

One approach is to hypothesize a sharp or even complete discontinuity between the high politics of federal aid in Washington and the operational reality of state agency acquisition of federal funds for program implementation. In visual terms this would emphasize the insulation or isolation of the PEGs (located on the outer surfaces of the cube in Figure 3) from the PPPs, positioned in the cylindrical core of the cube.

This separation between broad ideological cleavages over "federalism issues," for which federal aid is a convenient surrogate, and the prosaic processes of aid administration has been uncovered earlier. Peterson and associates (1986) used a volcanic eruption metaphor to describe the unanticipated findings of their research on the workings of federalism in the early 1980s. Their research on the implementation of distributive and redistributive aid programs through the contentious years of the first Reagan Administration prepared them "to record the dying moments of Pompeii shortly before Mount Vesuvius erupted" (1986: xii). To their surprise, "Vesuvius erupted, all right, but the lava it spewed forth reached only to the edges of Pompeii, or, more exactly, the town fought back, dousing the fires that a new political leadership in Washington had been igniting" (1986:xii).

We doubt that the stable patterns of federal aid dependency are produced by the fire brigade capacity of state administrative agencies. We might suppose, however, that the state agencies have some built-in fire retardant features that might buffer, smooth, or protect them from the vicissitudes of national political conflagrations over federal aid. Clearly, the issue is ripe for further creative and systematic research.

A second approach to understanding the unexpected stability of federal aid dependency is to question what seems obvious. The apparent stability is just that—apparent, superficial, and false. The aggregate proportions for the varying degrees of dependency may actually mask wide variations depending on different agency, administrator, and contextual characteristics. Here, too, for illustrative purposes we may take a page from Peterson (1981, 1986, 1995) and his research on federalism and intergovernmental relations.

Peterson has consistently advanced the proposition across two decades that functional efficiency in performing certain activities is fundamentally linked to the capacity (or incapacity) of particular jurisdictions within the American political system. This functional linkage, in the case of ASAP findings on federal aid dependency, suggests the need for disaggregation by type(s) of agency programs, activities, or functions. To understand the dynamics of intergovernmental interdependency we need to understand the differences among aid programs and policies. Or, as Peterson (1979:157) expressed it, "Public policy structures political relationships." It is necessary to know the type or arena of policy to understand the politics associated with it (Lowl, 1970, 1972). This issue is addressed later.

2. Diversity

Escalation in the number of grant-in-aid programs in the 1960s and its continuation through the 1970s raised many issues among the actual and potential recipients of federal aid. One significant one was: How many different aid programs should we (our agency) pursue? Another was: What types or forms of aid shall we secure? The first question involves the issue of diversity—the multiple or varied sources from which monies are obtained. The second poses the problem of complexity—how many different forms of aid can our agency manage?

This juncture is not the place for a wide-ranging review of types of federal aid programs. Some brief historical data, however, on the numbers and types of programs are useful for placing the subsequent analysis in context. The total numbers of programs in operation from 1960 to 1995 are shown below for selected years (ACIR, 1995).

1960: 132	1984: 392
1967: 379	1989: 478
1975: 443	1993: 578
1981: 534	1995: 618

Apart from a significant drop during the first Reagan Administration (1981–1985), the clear trend regarding the number of grant programs has been upward. This presents state agencies (and other recipients) with a cafeteria of opportunities. These grant programs, of course, tend to be concentrated in or among a few major national agencies. For example, nearly 300 grant programs are administered by the Department of Health and Human Services and over 100 by the Department of Education. One part of the ASAP survey was aimed at ascertaining how many different national agencies funded the state agency's programs.

The diversity percentages in Table 2 show that, quite consistently since the 1970s, roughly one-third of the state agencies secure federal aid from a single federal department or agency. This substantial proportion suggests the prominence of what might be termed a "single-shot" strategy; one national agency is the exclusive source of federal aid. At the second level of diversity—receipt of aid from two national agencies—about one-fifth of all aid-dependent state agencies rely on a two-track strategy in securing federal aid funds. At the third tier of aid acquisition, another one-fifth of the state agencies obtain funds from three major national sources. At the top two levels of aid diversity, four and five (or more) sources, about 10% of the state agencies operate in each of these two multisource environments. Here, as in the case of dependency, the distributions across the five ASAP surveys are strikingly similar.

The diversity dimension can be positioned within the visual framework of Figure 3. Imagine that state agencies receiving federal aid exist in the state-level plane and are in the center of the plane where the core cylinder passes through the state plane. That cylindrical core, of course, represents the conduit through which federal aid funds pass. Imagine further that the several hundred grant-in-aid programs are grouped within 10 large conduits which represent the main national agencies that channel aid to the states (and localities). The configuration of aid diversity discussed above represents the manner or pattern by which different state agencies intersect with the various national agency aid conduits.

Two concluding points can be made concerning the diversity dimension. First, the row percentages across the five ASAP surveys reveal again how stable the aid distribution patterns are. The proportions for 1994 are not much different from those in 1974. This consistency exists despite major shifts in national politics and significant pressures to alter intergovernmental policies, including federal aid programs. In short, state agencies still appear to connect or intersect with national aid agencies in ways that have been quite stable over the past two decades. Is this some immunity from the "Vesuvius effect" noted earlier? Or has the political shock from the 1994 national elections produced effects that will not surface until 1998 or later? Only more recent data and further careful analysis will shed light on the question.

The second point involves link(s) between diversity and dependency. Are the state agencies most dependent on federal aid also more reliant on a single national source for funds? In short, are diversity and dependency inversely related? The availability of five ASAP data sets permitted multiple testing of this hypothesis for the years 1978 through 1994. None of the five bivariate analyses revealed any relationship, positive or negative, between diversity and dependency. In other words, the most aid-dependent state agencies are not more likely to pursue single-shot aid acquisition strategies than the least dependent. Diversity and dependency appear to be uncorrelated federal aid variables.

3. Complexity

It is common knowledge that a variety of federal aid instruments are used as intergovernmental transfers. The existence of different ways of classifying federal aid lends confusion to the analysis because the types of aid are not mutually exclusive. For ASAP survey purposes we relied on a simplified scheme shown in the lower segment of Table 2.

Some background on aid patterns by types of grant is useful in understanding and interpreting the percentages in Table 2. The numbers below serve this purpose (ACIR, 1995).

Number of Grant Programs by Type of Federal Aid

Year	Project grants	Project-formula grants	Formula grants	Block grants
1975	296	35	96	4
1984	267	27	80	12
1989	323	21	117	14
1995	446	30	125	15

Two features are prominent in the figures listed above. The first is the predominance of project grants from a purely numerical standpoint. This is *not* the case with regard to dollar amounts, however, since nearly 80% of all federal aid funds ($230 billion in 1995) are disbursed through only 25 formula-based aid programs.

A second comment on the above numbers involves the small number of block grants, virtually all of which are formula based. These few broad-based grants, however, still channel about 10% of all federal aid to the states (ACIR, 1995). Of course, the most featured of all recent block grants is the TANF grant (Temporary Assistance to Needy Families) enacted under the Personal Responsibility and Work Opportunity Act of 1996 (P.L. 104–193). This block grant program allocated over $16 billion among the 50 states in the fiscal year 1997.

The percentages in Table 2 for complexity show some initially unsurprising results. First, project grants, the most numerous type of grant, lead in the proportion of state agencies receiving them. Second, formula grants, the next most extensive type of aid instrument, follow closely behind project grants in terms of recipient frequencies.

Somewhat unexpected are the figures for block grants. While far less numerous in the scheme of grant types, these flexible funds make an impact across a substantial proportion of state agencies. Block grants number less than 5% of all grant programs and allocate about 10% of all federal aid. Yet those funds reach the coffers of about one-third of all aid-receiving state agencies. This somewhat surprising finding may be a factor contributing to the reduced level of perceived national influence on the part of state administrators (Yoo and Wright, 1994).

Reinforcing the idea of reduced national influence are the proportions of agencies receiving nonmatching grants. From one in five to one in six of the administrators report that their agency receives some nonmatching grant money. While some (or several) conditions may be attached to nonmatching grant funds, the lack of fiscal effort on the part of the recipient makes this type of funding particularly attractive.

A final point brings this discussion of federal aid complexity to a close. It constitutes the reiteration of a theme mentioned earlier. A scan of the row percentages for each type of funding instrument from 1974 to 1994 shows a striking consistency in the proportions. The figures seldom vary more than three to five percentage points from one ASAP survey to the next. The complexity associated with managing multiple types of aid instruments does not appear to have changed greatly across three decades of monitoring aid arrangements by ASAP survey methods. This leads us to conclude that the cylindrical core populated by program policy professionals is relatively insulated from the political shocks impacting on the surface(s) of the rectangular cube (see Figure 3). It may in fact be very difficult for PEGs to reshape and redirect intergovernmental relationships among the PPPs.

These findings and their implications can be framed in broader and less technical terms. They support the view that federal aid penetrates state agencies extensively and significantly. Furthermore, the patterns of federal aid receipt suggest that aid processes are quite stable and institutionalized. The apparent distance of elected officials from influence and impact on aid receipt and effects raises questions of democratic control and administrative accountability. Are federal aid impacts, trends, and shifts largely immune from the efforts of electoral coalitions to redirect or reset policy priorities? Our analyses and findings are better at helping us pose the question than answering it.

III. FUNCTIONALISM, FEDERAL AID, AND FLUIDITY

In discussing federal aid dependency we noted that the type of agency contributes to an understanding (or explanation) of the politics and administration associated with the policy arena (Lowi, 1970, 1972; Peterson, 1979, 1986). Measuring policy "types" according to Lowi's categories of distributive, regulatory, and redistributive has been both difficult and controversial. For the descriptive and explanatory purposes of this essay we do not use Lowi's macrocategories. Instead, we employ a less aggregated and more nominal classification scheme. We use clusters of the types(s) of state agencies, a scheme that we call "functionalism."

The row headings in Table 3 reveal one grouping of the many different types of state agencies whose administrative heads have responded to ASAP questionnaires from the 1970s to the 1990s. We classified the diverse agencies into the 13 categories shown in Table 3. From this set of functional categories we look for patterns present between the variable of functionalism and two measures of federal aid—receipt and dependency. We carry the functionalism approach one step further in Table 4. There we assess the relationship between functionalism and fluidity—the extent of agency policy change.

A. Functionalism and Federal Aid

Different types of state agencies have distinctively different degrees of involvement with federal aid. Very high proportions of social service, education, and health agencies have been federal aid recipients since the 1970s (and before). Environmental and energy-related agencies were somewhat less involved in the 1970s but now approach near-universal participation in the aid process.

A second cluster of agencies—natural resources, transportation, criminal justice, and economic development—was somewhat less participative in federal aid in the 1970s but recorded increased involvement by the 1990s. On the simple criterion of receipt or nonreceipt of federal aid, it appears that there has been a consistent and broad-based rise in state agency involvement with federal aid between the 1970s and the 1990s. This has occurred despite the efforts and impacts of the Reagan "Restoration New Federalism" of the 1980s (Yoo and Wright, 1993).

There is a substantial cluster of state agencies that are marginal to (or are reluctant participants in) the federal aid process. This group includes two types of staff agencies (fiscal and nonfiscal) as well as regulatory agencies. Also on the periphery are agencies headed by popularly elected officials, for example, attorneys general, auditors, secretaries of state, and treasurers. In most instances only about one-third or fewer of these types of agencies have received federal aid during the 1970s, '80s, and '90s.

When the question moves beyond the receipt of aid to the degree of aid dependency, some additional variations and nuances appear. The right section of Table 3 shows the percentages of agencies depending on federal aid for 50% or more of their budget. Clearly, the social service (income security) agencies

Table 3 Functionalism and Federal Aid (Receipt and Dependency)

Functionalism (type of agency)	Receipt of aid (% yes)					Aid dependency (50% or more)				
	1974	1978	1984	1988	1994	1974	1978	1984	1988	1994
Income security & social service	94%	97%	97%	99%	95%	85%	85%	80%	81%	73%
Education	85	96	92	94	96	28	30	26	24	42
Health	85	99	100	99	96	30	45	25	28	46
Environment & energy	73	87	80	86	93	26	41	43	24	34
Natural resource	84	93	91	83	96	5	4	7	4	6
Transportation	84	80	83	93	93	41	30	20	27	25
Criminal justice	77	93	65	78	85	26	14	3	8	10
Economic development	55	79	68	72	77	27	20	30	34	34
Regulatory	23	37	36	38	37	2	9	8	8	4
Fiscal staff	18	32	24	23	32	5	4	4	1	1
Nonfiscal staff	51	71	22	20	28	35	23	9	11	5
Elected officials	17	27	15	30	30	0	0	3	1	2
Other	73	72	75	73	63	60	31	37	37	29
Total sample	63	74	65	68	71	28	26	23	22	24

Source: D.S. Wright, American State Administrators Project (ASAP) Surveys, Institute of Research in Social Science, University of North Carolina, Chapel Hill, NC.

Table 4 Functionalism and Fluidity

Functionalism (type of agency)	Fluidity (% major change)				(Illustrative N's)	
	1978	1984	1988	1994	1978	1994
Income security & social service	46%	36%	39%	51%	(115)	(134)
Education	40	38	45	55	(70)	(71)
Health	54	33	41	48	(85)	(67)
Environment & energy	47	40	40	29	(142)	(143)
Natural resource	32	31	24	22	(146)	(114)
Transportation	33	38	27	38	(82)	(58)
Criminal justice	50	34	30	39	(134)	(96)
Economic development	45	57	45	37	(96)	(100)
Regulatory	37	29	32	36	(148)	(148)
Fiscal staff	29	21	27	29	(94)	(87)
Nonfiscal staff	40	39	36	33	(82)	(58)
Elected officials	35	27	31	25	(51)	(49)
Other	31	37	37	41	(98)	(86)
Total sample	40	35	35	37	(1343)	(1211)

Source: D.S. Wright, American State Administrators Project (ASAP) Surveys, Institute of Research in Social Science, University of North Carolina, Chapel Hill, NC.

outdistance all others in aid dependency. Three-fourths or more of these agencies were thus heavily dependent on federal aid from the 1970s into the 1990s.

The other agencies in the top cluster—education, health, and environment—had much smaller percentages of aid-dependent agencies. High dependency applies to only 25–40% of these agencies. Perhaps the main point among these agency types was the noteworthy fluctuations across the ASAP survey years.

The second tier of agency types in Table 3 shows notable interagency differences in dependency. Very small proportions of natural resource and criminal justice agencies are heavily dependent on federal aid. Transportation and economic development, however, stand out as having one-fourth to one-third of these agencies relying on aid for half or more of their budgets. While these proportions have varied across the ASAP surveys, they have done so within a fairly well defined range. In this respect these state agencies may have secured a well-established if not stable pattern of aid-based relationships with national government agencies. Of course, highway aid, as part of the transportation package of agencies, is traceable back to 1914.

The third and final cluster of state agencies in Table 3 demonstrates the smallest reliance on aid. This result is not surprising given the initial low rates of aid receipt. While nonfiscal staff agencies were exceptions in the 1970s (35% and 23%), they dropped sharply in the 1980s and recently fit well within the group with the lowest dependence on federal aid.

The character and configuration of federal aid impacts on state administrative agencies have been topics of long-standing speculation and research (MacDonald, 1928; Wright, 1968; ACIR, 1978; Yoo and Wright, 1993). Table 3, with its two different indicators of aid-based linkages, reveals the variations in national-state connections. In some respects federal aid might be said to partition state administration into three compartments, or arenas of interdependency.

In one compartment are the extensive and heavily dependent aid recipients. These are largely the welfare, health, and education sectors. The second segment or arena is composed midlevel players in the federal aid "game." While they may "play" in a widespread way, they have not become highly dependent on aid for the bulk of their budgets. These second-order participants consist largely of natural resource, transportation, criminal justice, and economic development agencies.

The third-order set of agencies is a relatively peripheral set of participants in the federal aid arena. This outer segment or cluster consists of agency types in which a third or less receive any aid and under 10% secure half of their budget from federal aid. These are agencies headed by elected officials, are executive staff units, or have primarily regulatory functions. Most of these agencies are clearly on the outer orbit of the federal aid "solar" (monetary) system.

B. Functionalism and Fluidity

Functionalism is important in understanding the general character of state administration, and is especially significant with respect to federal aid. We now return to the concept of fluidity and program change to further elucidate how functionalism shapes state government and administration. Table 4 serves this purpose by tabulating across four ASAP surveys the relationship between functionalism and fluidity.

At the outset we note that the contrasts across the three types of agency clusters are far less clear for fluidity than they are for federal aid. There is some tendency for a greater degree of program change to occur among agencies in the health-education-welfare cluster. Most percentages fall in the range of one-third to one-half. The average of the percentages is 40. While there are a few high figures in the second cluster, especially for economic development, the remaining figures are nearly all in the 20–40% range. If economic development is excluded, the average is 34%. The third cluster consists, with one exception, of percentages in the 20s or 30s. The average percentage is 32. There is, then, a tendency for functionalism and fluidity to be slightly related. A more extensive and rigorous analysis is needed, however, to confirm the clarity and strength of such an association.

C. Federal Aid and Fluidity

Both federal aid and policy fluidity demonstrate distinctive patterns in relation to functional categories of state agencies. The next query turns attention to the subtitle of this essay: Are federal aid patterns correlated with policy fluidity? Does aid dependency, for example, contribute to turbulence (policy change) in state agencies?

We test the dependency-turbulence hypothesis with four ASAP data sets— 1978, 1984, 1988, and 1994. Table 5 displays the product of the separate analyses. The percentage distributions warrant two brief observations.

First, as in several prior cross-section analyses across ASAP data sets, the percentages are quite close and consistent. For example, among agencies with minor policy shifts, the proportions not receiving federal aid ranged from only 33% to 38% across the survey years. Among the same set of policy-stable agencies the proportions heavily dependent on federal aid were 19% and 21%. Among agencies reporting major policy shifts the proportions across the four surveys were not as close or consistent, but the contrasts were hardly extreme or dramatic.

Table 5 Policy Fluidity and Aid Dependency

| Policy shift | Year | Aid dependency | | | (N=) |
		None	Under 50%	50% and more	
None and minor	1978	34%	47%	19%	(275)
	1984	38	43	19	(240)
	1988	37	42	21	(337)
	1994	33	46	21	(253)
Moderate	1978	25	51	23	(516)
	1984	28	49	23	(441)
	1988	30	47	23	(592)
	1994	28	48	24	(492)
Major	1978	18	49	33	(532)
	1984	28	46	26	(380)
	1988	29	48	23	(484)
	1994	23	48	29	(432)

Note: Because of rounding the percentages may not add to 100.
Source: D.S. Wright, American State Administrators Project (ASAP) Surveys, Institute of Research in Social Science, University of North Carolina, Chapel Hill, NC.

The second observation bears directly on the hypothesis linking policy turbulence to aid dependency. It can be assessed best by examining the three sets of percentages in the final (right-hand) column of Table 5. These are the proportions of agencies most dependent on federal aid grouped by the three graduations of policy shifts—minor, moderate, and major. For the top cluster (minor) the percentages average 20 while for the bottom cluster (major change) the percentages vary from 23 to 32 but average 27. There is, then, only a slight or weak relationship between federal aid and policy turbulence.

This finding is consistent with earlier results and fits the general framework of public administration within the plane of state governance. First, recall that one-third or less of the respondents attributed the initiatives for policy changes to national officials. This was substantially below the proportions tracing policy change initiatives to governors, legislators, and agency staff. In short, national officials, through aid-based interactions, do not appear to be the creators of substantial policy turbulence in state administration.

Second, when state agency heads do attribute policy change to the actions of national official(s), those who acknowledge this source of initiative are far more likely to be state administrators whose agencies are heavily dependent on federal aid. For example, among agencies not receiving federal aid, only 10–15% of the agency heads across the four ASAP surveys mention national officials as a source of policy change. By way of contrast, 50–60% of the agency heads with high aid dependency (50% or more) indicated national officials as a source initiative for policy change. This finding was consistent across the four ASAP surveys from 1978 to 1994. Federal aid is an avenue along which national influence(s) may travel. Despite the width and direction of the avenue, however, there is no assurance that a specified amount of national influence will automatically accompany this distinctive fiscal vehicle.

Third, to the extent that *some* policy shifts are induced by federal aid, these appear to filter through or across basic tensions or fault lines within the plane of state governance. One fault line is the cleavage between the PPPs (program policy professionals) and the AAGs (appointed administrative generalists). This division can be observed visually in Figure 3. There is a distinct separation between the administrative generalists and the program specialists (Yoo and Wright, 1994). Fiscal and nonfiscal staff, elected officials, and regulatory agency administrators are clearly a breed apart from the dominant core of state administrative agency heads (the heads of major functional or line agencies). The noncore component of state administrative establishments is challenged not only to "make its mark" within the plane of state governance, but also to define and assert its status in relation to officials in the national and local planes.

A fourth interpretation of the findings is possible. This attributes the preponderance of policy turbulence to state-level forces modestly augmented or accentuated by intergovernmental factors, especially federal aid. This interpretation emphasizes the primacy of political and institutional dynamics pressing on the edges of the state governance plane and into its internal surfaces. This view is more promising and optimistic with regard to democratic accountability. It suggests that despite the regularities and continuities in aid policies, in legislative oversight/control, and in executive support, there are realistic prospects for agency policy shifts caused by several political actors in the state governance plane (Bowling and Wright, 1998a).

The preceding point prompts us to revise and extend V. O. Key's (1956) provocative question posed over four decades ago: "Is there an autonomous state politics?" Our version of this query is, "Are there autonomous state administrative systems?" Just as there has been no definitive answer to Key's long-standing question, so too have we not established a definitive answer to its administrative counterpart.

What does emerge from our analyses and results, however, is a provisional assessment. First, there are multiple and diverse administrative systems within each state government (Elling, 1992). The nature of a particular state's administrative establishment has been variously described as a holding company (Kunde, 1987), a kaleidoscope of fluid and conflicting forces (Thompson, 1993), and a web of interconnected relationships involving sharply demarcated institutional boundaries. (Robinson, 1998).

Our research, here and elsewhere, confirms the sprawling character of state administrative systems (Jenks and Wright, 1993). There is no single or unified "executive branch" of state government. Rather, there are numerous semiautonomous constellations of administrative authority and influence *within* state governments. Any one or several of these constellations may be subject to national-level influences, whether by the "carrots" (incentives) of federal aid, or through the "sticks" of national mandates or sanctions. Furthermore, the nature and extent of national influences clearly vary in significant ways across the irregular landscape that constitutes state administration.

National legislation and various administrative actions may contribute to selected turbulence in the state plane(s) of governance. A national presence is evident among several state administrative constellations through federal aid conduits. We do not find, however, a compelling or uniform reach of national influence that seems destined to overpower the political and administrative foundations of state agencies. Consistent with a recent Supreme Court decision, we conclude that, "States are not mere political subdivisions of the United States; State governments are neither regional offices nor administrative agencies of the Federal Government" (New York v. United States 505 U.S. 186, 1992). The fluidity or turbulence associated with program changes in state agencies is generated as much or more by within-agency and within-state variables than by federal aid features.

IV. NATIONAL REGULATORY IMPACTS

Elazar (1984:252) argued over a decade ago that "the American federal system may be passing into a new phase, one in which grants, while remaining important, will no longer set the tone of intergovernmental relations. . . . Now the move seems to be in the direction of new relationships in the field of governmental regulations." Elazar's statement captured a prominent and widely discussed shift in the character of national-state relations in the 1980s. "Regulatory federalism" was only one manner of describing the shift (ACIR, 1984; Hanus, 1981). A more pointed and pejorative way of describing the new regulatory era was "from cooperative to coercive federalism" (Kincaid, 1990).

Federal aid is often cited as the defining instrument of cooperative federalism. To the extent that there is a singular or distinctive feature of regulatory (or coercive) federalism, it derives from legally based national actions. The varied scope and content of regulatory federalism have been amply explored (ACIR, 1984, 1993; Chubb, 1985b; Conlan, 1986, 1995; Kettl, 1983; Kincaid, 1990, 1993, 1996). Several of its general and specific features are examined below since the 1994 ASAP survey was aimed in part at assessing national regulatory impacts on state administration.

A. Generic and State-Level Impacts

Our empirical exploration of regulatory federalism focused at three levels. One was at the generic nature of national regulatory impacts on state government power(s) generally. This was measured by asking state administrators, "Have national legal/regulatory actions (court decisions, statutes, regulations) infringed on the reserved powers of the States?" The phrase "reserved powers" referenced broad claims under the 10th Amendment constitutional authority retained by the states.

The second level of national regulatory impact was targeted at state-specific effects. The question asked was, "Have National legal/regulatory actions altered your State's program and policy priorities?" The aim here was to measure administrators' assessments of national actions on program and policy priorities within their respective states. This could be viewed as interagency or statewide impacts.

The third level of national impacts was agency-specific. Administrators were asked, "In your opinion, how would you rate, negatively or positively, each of the following types of National actions *on your agency*?" There followed a list of four types of national actions, e.g., mandates, court decisions. For each type of action the response alternatives ranged from "no impact" and "very negative" impact to "very positive" impact. We cannot be assured that these levels of measurement and the several types of impacts cover the full scope and content of regulatory federalism. We are confident, however, that the queries address directly an important dimension of the "new phase" of federalism highlighted by Elazar, Kincaid, and others.

State administrators' responses on the first two levels of regulatory impacts are reported in Table 6. Both the reserved-powers issue and policy change questions prompted high levels of impact responses. Nearly three-fourths of the respondents agreed that national actions had infringed on the reserved powers of the states and 80% indicated that national actions had program/policy impacts within their state.

These levels of agreement on national impacts are not surprising. The

Table 6 National Regulatory Impacts: Reserved Powers and Program/Policy Changes

	Reserved powers[a]	Program/policy changes[b]
Some impact		
Yes	72%	80%
No	10	11
Don't know	18	9
	(N = 1180)	(N = 1171)
Degree of impact		
Low	13%	11%
Moderate	29	31
High	38	41
Very high	20	18
	(N = 849)	(N = 920)
Direction of impact		
Positive	15%	23%
Neutral	19	23
Negative	66	54
	(N = 731)	(N = 822)

[a] *Question asked*: Have national legal/regulatory actions (court decision, statutes, regulations) infringed on the reserved powers of the states? ____ Yes; ____ No; ____ Don't know
    If YES: On a scale of 1 (low) to 5 (high) indicate the degree of infringement or intrusion.
              (low) 1   2   3   4   5 (high)
         On balance, has the infringement been ____ positive; ____ neutral; ____ negative?
[b] *Question asked*: Have national legal/regulatory actions altered your state's program and policy priorities? ____ Yes; ____ No; ____ Don't know
    If YES: On a scale of 1 (low) to 5 (high) indicate the extent of impact of national legal/regulatory actions on your state's program/policy priorities.
              (low) 1   2   3   4   5 (high)
         On balance, has the impact been ____ positive; ____ neutral; ____ negative?
Note: Because of rounding the percentages may not add to 100.

anger, anguish, and angst surrounding only *one* type of national regulatory action, unfunded mandates, for example, have been clearly documented (Conlan, 1995). A counterpoint might also be noted. About 10% of the respondents indicated no impact in either arena, and 10–20% offered Don't Know replies. For a modest proportion (20–30%) of state agency heads, regulatory federalism is a nonissue.

The preponderance of agreement regarding national impacts on the generic and statewide levels does not tell us much, apart from the fact that these may be highly visible, lightening rod issues. The extent and the character of the impacts need to be pursued. For that purpose follow-up questions were asked regarding the extent and direction (positive/negative) of the impacts. The tabulations for these queries are provided in the lower segments of Table 6. The degree of impact was rated on a five-point scale, from 1 (low) to 5 (high). The follow-up on the direction of impact was a three-category response option: positive, neutral, or negative.

On both the reserved-powers and policy change items nearly 60% of the respondents rated national regulatory impacts as high or very high. Clearly, national presence and impacts through regulatory routes have achieved considerable significance among state agency heads in the 1990s. Unfortunately, no earlier comparable data are available on which to base a judgment about regulatory trends. On purely qualitative grounds—such as articles, lobbying efforts, and public statements by state officials—we might expect the 1990s to reflect an increased attentiveness and reaction to regulatory federalism.

Regulatory federalism has entered the intergovernmental scene on a distinctively negative note. The term "coercive federalism" is only one illustration of this bias. We should entertain the possibility, however, that national regulatory actions, regardless of their coercive character, might be viewed as having positive consequences at the state level. An example might be court decisions or administrative regulations that prohibit discrimination in the delivery of state services because of race or gender in violation of the equal protection provisions in the 14th Amendment.

The possibility of positive as well as negative reactions to national impacts is reflected in Table 6 as "direction of impact." In the case of reserved powers, there is a small positive component of 15%, and a slightly larger segment (19%) judging national infringement on reserved powers as neutral. On the other hand, two-thirds of the state administrators found national impacts on the reserved powers of the states as negative. The weight of opinion on this generic issue is clearly negative.

When the focus of national impacts shifts to statewide or interagency policy effects, the views of state agency heads are slightly more balanced. Nearly one-fourth (23%) see positive effects and the same proportion sees essentially neutral impacts. Nevertheless, over half report negative effects. The nature of the question and the responses about statewide impacts offer a limited base for interpretations. While negative assessments are in a bare majority, the positive and neutral judgments together produce a more tempered distribution. The negative consequences of regulatory federalism for statewide programs and policies appear less severe in the eyes of state agency heads than we might expect.

B. Agency-Specific Impacts

The third level of regulatory federalism impacts was agency-specific. State administrators were asked to assess the impacts of four types of national actions as they directly affected their own agency. Table 7 provides tabulations of responses to four regulatory items: administrative regulations; national mandates (either statutory or administrative); statutory preemptions; and federal court decisions.

The distributions reveal general consistencies across the different national actions, but also show some distinctive differences. First, less than 10% of all respondents indicate the absence of any impacts for each of the four types of national actions. At the unfavorable end of the evaluative spectrum national preemptions prompt nearly 20% of the administrators to report "very negative" impacts. Mandates, court decisions, and administrative regulations follow in descending order.

If the "negative" responses are added to the "very negative," a pattern emerges. Over half (55%) of the agency heads indicate negative effects from mandates and preemptions. Barely half report negative impacts from administrative regulations and about 40% view federal court decisions negatively. Mandates and preemptions clearly stand out as focal points of administrators' ire with regulatory federalism. The neutral category again contains some substantial proportions. The lowest level of neutrality (24%) involves mandates whereas court decisions are viewed as neutral by nearly 40% of the state agency heads.

Positive and very positive responses are grouped because of the low proportions in each category. They vary modestly, from 6% to 15%, with mandates the

Table 7 Impacts of National Regulatory Actions on Own Agency

Type of national action		Character of Impact				
	None	Very negative	Negative	Neutral	Positive	(N=)
Administrative regulation	8%	9%	41%	30%	12%	(1141)
Mandates	6	14	41	24	15	(1142)
Preemption	8	19	36	30	6	(1122)
Federal court decision	8	12	29	38	13	(1139)

Note: Because of rounding the percentages may not add to 100.

highest and preemption the lowest. These small positive percentages for own-agency impacts can be compared to those for statewide policies and reserved powers (Table 6). They are generally lower, and suggest that administrators' opinions shift away from a positive valence as regulatory federalism becomes more agency-specific. Further analysis of these data and the gathering of comparative trend data are needed to develop firmer and broader interpretations.

C. Regulatory Impacts and Program Fluidity

Earlier we examined the relationship between federal aid and program/policy changes in state agencies. We found only a modest positive association between aid dependency and shifts in agency program priorities. We found no relationships between policy fluidity and federal aid complexity or diversity. The above exploration of regulatory federalism makes it logical to pursue a similar analysis. Are national regulatory impacts related to policy change/fluidity in state agencies?

Analyses at the generic impact level reveal no clear or strong association between national regulatory actions and state agency policy fluidity. That is, administrators' views about national infringement on the states' reserved powers was uncorrelated with reported shifts in agency programs and policy priorities. This applied to the presence/absence of national impacts, the degree of impacts (low-high), and the direction of impacts (positive or negative). Second-level (statewide) impacts showed a modest positive association between reportedly high impacts and changes in agency program priorities. For example, among state agencies with only minor policy shifts, less than half (48%) reported high legal/regulatory impacts. This contrasted with state agencies indicating major policy shifts, where nearly two-thirds (65%) of the administrators reported high national regulatory impacts.

The next step was to examine agency-specific national regulatory impacts. For this purpose interval rankings were used (from very negative to very positive) for the four types of national actions reported in Table 7. The numerical averages below indicate the impact scores for the four items, where 3.0 is neutral, 1.0 very negative, and 5.0 very positive.

Type of National Actions	Average Impact Scores
Preemptions	2.26
Mandates	2.43
Administrative regulations	2.50
Federal court decisions	2.59

Table 8 Agency Shifts in Program Priorities by Impacts on State Agency of National Regulatory Actions (Average Scores)

Agency program shifts	Types of national action							
	Administrative regulations		Mandates		Preemptions		Court decisions	
None/minor	2.49	(216)[a]	2.37	(225)	2.25	(213)	2.57	(218)
Moderate	2.54	(446)	2.42	(452)	2.26	(436)	2.54	(451)
Major	2.47	(379)	2.48	(389)	2.28	(377)	2.66	(371)
Total	2.50	(1041)	2.42	(1066)	2.26	(1026)	2.59	(1040)

[a] Numbers in parentheses.

The above listing, of course, simply condenses the percentage distributions in Table 7 into a single number. It also orders the national actions in accord with their impact valences on the state agency—from preemptions and mandates to administrative regulations and court decisions. The impact scores are used to assess the question of whether agency-specific national legal/regulatory actions are correlated with policy fluidity. Table 8 reports the scores for the four types of national actions according to the extent of agency program shifts.

To confirm the hypothesis of an association between regulatory impacts and policy fluidity there should be a consistent and substantial rise (or fall) in the impact scores depending on the extent of policy fluidity. An inspection of the column scores reveals no consistent pattern up or down the program shift categories. Furthermore, the differences among the impact scores within the national action columns are inconsequential. We therefore reject the stated hypothesis and accept the null hypothesis. There appears to be no association between the impacts of regulatory federalism and policy fluidity within state agencies.

V. SUMMARY OBSERVATIONS

We initiated this exploration with a simple question: Do national actions impacting on state administrative agencies contribute to policy fluidity or turbulence within the agencies? We pursued the query both conceptually and empirically.

From a conceptual standpoint, state agencies (and their administrative heads) were positioned in both their intergovernmental and intragovernmental contexts. Intergovernmentally, state government was posited as a vertical plane with extensive state-national, state-local, and interstate relations. In presenting a verbal (and visual) model of interjurisdictional interactions we relied on the concepts of federalism (FED), intergovernmental relations (IGR), and intergovernmental management (IGM). These concepts underlay distinctions among three types of public officials operating intragovernmentally within the plane of state governance—PEGs (elected generalists), AAGs (appointed generalists), and PPPs (policy professionals). The three types of officials were also acknowledged as active in the intergovernmental arena.

This conceptual approach guided the empirical analysis, which relied on seven ASAP data sets covering 30 years of mail questionnaire surveys of state agency heads. The four most recent surveys (1978–1994) provided the data bases to identify consistent patterns and trends and to look for confirmation (or rejection) of the hypothesis that national actions are linked to state agency policy change.

State agency policy change, referenced as fluidity or turbulence, was measured by asking the agency heads the extent of change in program and policy priorities over the prior four-year period. Two major types of instruments of national impacts on the states were measured: federal aid, and national legal/regulatory actions.

Federal aid is a historic, significant, and extensively employed method of intergovernmental collaboration. It is the hallmark instrument of "cooperative federalism." National legal/regulatory methods impacting the states have generated considerable attention and debate over the past two decades. Extensive use of these instruments of intergovernmental relations has earned the dubious appellation, "coercive federalism."

We charted several trends from the 1960s to the 1990s in three main features of federal aid—dependency, diversity, and complexity. National presence and impacts through federal aid escalated rapidly from the 1960s to the 1970s. Since the 1970s, however, the general features and several specific characteristics of federal aid to state agencies have remained remarkably stable. One interpretation of this stability is that federal aid programs, policies, and patterns are largely insulated from the prominent political rhetoric and blunt political efforts aimed at macro- as well as microsystem changes in intergovernmental fiscal relations.

Our test of the hypothesis linking federal aid to state agency policy fluidity broadly paralleled the insulation interpretation. We found only modest or fragmentary evidence of correlations between federal aid features and agency policy fluidity. Only among the relatively few state agencies with the highest levels of federal aid dependency did we find higher levels of policy fluidity. Even here, however, the association was not strong and definitive.

An auxiliary but noteworthy finding accompanied the results of the aid-fluidity analysis. Our hypothesis testing uncovered the strong functional fragmentation forces that characterize the nature of state-level public administration. We observed that for all practical purposes, *the* executive branch (singular) is a nonexistent entity in state government. Rather, state administration is composed of agencies analogous to corporate holding companies. These findings and interpretations are hardly new or original (Allen, 1949; Fesier, 1955, 1967; Ransone, 1956; Weinberg, 1977). Furthermore, there are recent offsetting developments and trends that lend greater coherence to state administration than has long been imagined (ACIR, 1985; Bowman and Kearney, 1986; Bowling and Wright, 1998a,b; Brough, 1992; Brudney et al., 1999; Garnett, 1980; Van Horn, 1993).

One interpretation relevant to the fragmentation issue comes from the general acceptance of the null hypothesis regarding the aid-fluidity association. The functionalism and fragmentation present in state administration are not precipitated by federal aid features. Intragovernmental forces within the state plane of governance seem to be stronger forces contributing to the unwieldy character of state administration.

Our analyses of regulatory federalism and its link to state agency policy fluidity parallel the findings of federal aid impacts. Despite the attention garnered and appellations assigned to regulatory federalism, our findings involving national regulatory impacts on the states push us toward acceptance of the null hypothesis. We searched hard-to-find fragmentary hints that the degree and/or direction of national regulatory impacts might be linked to state agency policy/program shifts. We examined regulatory impacts at three levels, or layers. The dominant results were in favor of accepting the conclusion of no association.

Where do these analyses and findings leave us? What larger or broader interpretations are suggested? Three provisional conclusions can be offered, each of which deserves, in our estimation, further thoughtful exploration.

First, our findings, if valid and reliable, call into question the state-level consequences of national policy instruments, i.e., federal aid and regulatory actions. Is it possible that the significance and efficacy of national policies and programs have been overrated? Is there more smoke than fire, more rhetoric than reality in the complaints of state officials over national intergovernmental policy intrusiveness? These questions cast doubt on much of the received wisdom involving state-national relations, but to paraphrase Justice Holmes, we need to question the obvious more than we need to investigate the obscure.

A second conclusion, also provisional, is the obverse of the first. Questioning the scope and significance of national impacts on the states returns us to V. O. Key's query about state autonomy. We rephrased it to ask: Are there autonomous state administrative establishments? The degree(s) of structural and policy fragmentation in state administrative arrangements and the apparent absence of consequential national impacts incline us toward an affirmative response. State agencies, under this interpretation, are not extensions or subordinates of either national patrons or national policy prescriptions. Instead, the varied state agencies constitute administrative streams of identity, integrity, reliability, and resiliency that are appropriately (or inappropriately) channeled by potent state-level forces.

Prominent among the state power vectors are the agencies themselves and their administrative leaders. Key's notion of autonomous state politics is supplemented and perhaps strengthened by this conclusion about autonomous state administration. As Friedrich (1940:50) noted over a half-century ago, "bureaucracy [administration] is the core of modern government." In comparison to many political systems of the world, the 50 American states reasonably qualify as "modern" governments.

There is a third and rather radical conclusion we might draw from the findings reported in the body of this essay. We have relied heavily on analyzing, reporting, and interpreting results that tend to confirm the null hypothesis. We cannot explain variations in state program/policy fluidity with variations in national impacts via federal aid or regulatory actions. Suppose, however, that the cumulative character of national impacts on state agencies over the past one, two, or five decades has been so substantial that national actions have greatly reduced the variations within and among state administrative operations (Rose, 1973). In other words, interstate, intrastate, and intra-agency variations may be so modest or minor that there is little variance to be explained! This could lead to the same empirical findings we found so prevalent, namely, the absence of correlations between national impacts and state policy fluidity. (The same conclusion could also result, of course, from an invalid or unreliable measure of policy fluidity.)

Whatever interpretations or conclusions are favored from among those stated above, one matter is clear. There are important and significant research questions that remain to be pursued in attempting to explain state administrative differences using national policy instruments.

ACKNOWLEDGMENTS

We wish to acknowledge assistance and support of this research provided by the Earhart Foundation of Ann Arbor Michigan and the Institute for Research in Social Science at the University of North Carolina.

REFERENCES

Abney, G., and Lauth, T. P. (1986). *The Politics of State and City Administration*, State University of New York Press, Albany.

ACIR (Advisory Commission on Intergovernmental Relations) (1977). *Improving Federal Grants Management*, Government Printing Office, Washington, DC.

ACIR (1978). *Categorical Grants: Their Role and Design*, Government Printing Office, Washington, DC.

ACIR (1984). *Regulatory Federalism: Policy, Process, Impact, and Reform*, Government Printing Office, Washington, DC.

ACIR (1985). *The Question of State Government Capability*, Government Printing Office, Washington, DC.

ACIR (1993). *Federal Regulation of State and Local Governments: The Mixed Record of the 1980s*, Government Printing Office, Washington, DC.

ACIR (1995). *Characteristics of Federal Grant-in-Aid Programs to State and Local Governments: Grants Funded in 1995*, Government Printing Office, Washington, DC.

Allen, R. S., ed. (1949). *Our Sovereign State*, Vanguard Press, New York.

Bowling, C. J., Wright, D. S. (1998a). Public administration in the fifty states: a half-century revolution, *State and Local Government Review*, 30(Winter):50–62.

Bowling, C. J., Wright, D. S. (1998b). Change and continuity in state administration: administrative leadership across four decades, *Public Administration Review*, 58(Sept/Oct):429–444.

Bowman, A. O., and Kearney, R. C. (1986). *The Resurgence of the States*, Prentice Hall, Englewood Cliffs, NJ.

Brough, R. K. (1992). Total quality management in state government, *Journal of State Government*, 65(Jan–March):4–8.

Brudney, J. L., Herbert, F. T., and Wright, D. S. (1999). Reinventing government in the American states: measuring and explaining administrative reform, *Public Administration Review*, 59(Jan/Feb):19–30.

Chubb, J. E. (1985a). Federalism and the bias for centralization, *The New Direction in American Politics* (J. E. Chubb and P. E. Peterson, eds.), Brookings Institution, Washington, DC, pp. 273–306.

Chubb, J. E. (1985b). Excessive regulation: the case of federal aid to education, *Political Science Quarterly*, 100(Summer):287–311.

Chubb, J. E. (1985c). The political economy of federalism, *American Political Science Review*, 79(Sept):994–1015.

Conlan, T. J. (1986). Federalism and competing values in the Reagan Administration, *Publius: The Journal of Federalism*, 16(Winter):29–48.

Conlan, T. J., Riggle, J. D., and Schwartz, D. E. (1995). Deregulating federalism? The politics of mandate reform in the 104th Congress, *Publius: The Journal of Federalism*, 25(Summer):23–40.

Derthick, M. (1970). *The Influence of Federal Grants: Public Assistance in Massachusetts*, Harvard University Press, Cambridge, MA.

Elazar, D. J. (1984). *American Federalism: A View from the States*, 3rd ed., Harper and Row, New York.

Elling, R. C. (1992). *Public Management in the States: A Comparative Study of Administrative Performance and Politics*, Praeger, Westport, CT.

Fesler, J. W., ed. (1955). *The Forty-Eight States: Their Tasks as Policy Makers and Administrators*, American Assembly, Columbia University, New York.

Fesler, J. W., ed. (1967). *The 50 States and Their Local Governments*, Alfred A. Knopf, New York.

Friedrich, C. J. (1941). *Constitutional Government and Democracy*, Ginn and Company, revised ed., New York.

Garnett, J. L. (1980). *Reorganizing State Government: The Executive Branch*, Westview Press, Boulder, CO.

Grodzins, M. (1960a). American political parties and the American system, *Western Political Quarterly* 13(Fall):974–998.

Grodzins, M. (1960b). The federal system, *Goals for Americans: The Report of the President's Commission on National Goals*, Prentice-Hall, Englewood Cliffs, NJ. pp. 265–282.

Haas, P. J. (1984). *The Causes and Effects of Administrative Expansionism: State Bureaucratic Attitudes Toward Budgetary Growth*, Ph.D. dissertation, Department of Political Science, University of North Carolina, Chapel Hill, NC.

Hanus, J. J., ed. (1981). *The Nationalization of State Government*, D. C. Heath, Lexington, MA.

Ingram, H. (1977). Policy implementation through bargaining: the case of federal grants-in-aid *Public Policy*, 25(Fall):499–526.

Jenks, S. S., and Wright, D. S. (1993). An agency-level approach to change(s) in the administrative functions of American state governments, *State and Local Government Review* 25(Spring):78–86.

Kettl, D. R. (1983). *The Regulation of Federalism*, Louisiana State University Press, Baton Rouge, LA.

Key, V. O. (1956). *American State Politics: An Introduction*, Alfred A. Knopf, New York.

Kincaid, J. (1990). From Cooperative to Coercive Federalism, *Annals* 509(May):6–152.

Kincaid, J. (1993). From cooperation to coercion in American federalism: housing, fragmentation, and preemption, 1980–1992, *Journal Law Politics* 9:333–430.

Kincaid, J. (1996). From dual to coercive federalism in American intergovernmental relations, *Globalization and Decentralization: Institutional Contexts, Policy Issues, and Intergovernmental Relations in Japan and the United States* (J. S. Jun and D. S. Wright, eds.). Georgetown University Press, Washington, DC, pp. 21–47.

Kunde, J. (1987). The politics of excellence: managing more with less in the Western states. Paper presented at the Western Governors' Association.

Lowi, T. J. (1970). Decision making vs. policy making: toward an antidote for technocracy, *Public Administration Review* 30(May/June):314–325.

Lowi, T. J. (1972). Four systems of policy, politics, and choice, *Public Administration Review* 32(May/June):298–310.

MacDonald, A. F. (1928). *Federal Aid: A Study of the American Subsidy System*, Crowell, New York.

Peterson, P. E. (1979). Redistributive policies and patterns of citizen participation in local politics in the USA, *Decentralist Trends in Western Democracies*, (L. J. Sharpe, ed.). Sage Publications, Beverly Hills, CA.

Peterson, P. E. (1981). *City Limits*, University of Chicago Press, Chicago.

Peterson, P. E., Rabe, B. G., and Wong, K. K. (1986). *When Federalism Works*, Brookings Institution, Washington, DC.

Peterson, P. E. (1995). *The Price of Federalism*, Brookings Institution, Washington, DC.

Pressman, J. L. (1975). *Federal Programs and City Politics*, University of California Press, Berkeley, CA.

Ransone, C. B. Jr. (1956). *The Office of Governor in the United States*, University of Alabama Press, University AL.

Robinson, J. E. (1998). The role of the independent political executive in state governance: stability in the face of change, *Public Administration Review* 58(March/April):119–128.

Rose, D. D. (1973). National and local forces in state politics: the implications of multilevel policy analysis, *American Political Science Review* 67(Dec):1162–1173.

Rosenthal, A. (1989). *Governors and Legislators: Contending Powers*, CQ Press, Washington, DC.

Thompson, F. (1993). Introduction: critical challenges to state and local public service,'' *Revitalizing State and Local Public Service* (F. Thompson, ed.), Jossey-Bass, San Francisco, CA, pp. 1–40.

Van Horn, C. E., ed. (1993). *The State of the States*, CQ Press, Washington, DC.

Walker, D. B. (1997). Devolution: a big deal or only one dynamic in the system? Paper presented at the annual meeting of the New England Political Science Association, New London, CT, May 3, 1997.

Webb, S. (1911). *Grants-In-Aid: A Criticism and a Proposal*, Longmans Green, London.

Weinberg, M. W. (1977). *Managing the State*, MIT Press, Cambridge, MA.

Wright, D. S. (1968). *Federal Grants-in-Aid: Perspectives and Alternatives*. American Enterprise Institute, Washington, DC.

Wright, D. S. (1990). Federalism, intergovernmental relations, and intergovernmental management: historical reflections and conceptual comparisons, *Public Administration Review* 50(March/April):168–178.

Wright, D. S. (1997). Understanding intergovernmental relations, *Classics of Public Administration* (J. M. Shafritz and A. C. Hyde, eds.), Harcourt Brace, Fort Worth, TX. pp. 578–594.

Wright, D. S. (1998). Federalism, intergovernmental relations, and intergovernmental management: the origins, emergence, and maturation of three concepts, *Handbook of Public Administration* (J. Rabin and others, eds.), Marcel Dekker, New York, pp. 381–447.

Yoo, J. W., and Wright, D. S. (1993). Public policy and intergovernmental relations: measuring perceived change(s) in national influence—the effects of the federalism decade, *Policy Studies Journal* 21:(Winter):687–699.

Yoo, J. W., and Wright, D. S. (1994). Public administration education and formal administrative position: do they make a difference?, *Public Administration Review* 54(July/Aug):357–363.

Zimmerman, J. F. (1995). *State-Local Relations: A Partnership Approach*, Praeger, New York, 2d ed.

4
State Administration in Cultural Context

H. Edward Flentje
Wichita State University, Wichita, Kansas

Daniel Elazar introduced the idea of political culture to students of U.S. federalism in 1966. In his initial review he asserted that political culture shaped political structures of individual states and specifically "the administration of state government." He described how the development and operation of state and local bureaucracies were influenced by political cultures citing variances in the impact of federal assistance on the administration of state government as leading evidence of the impact of political culture on state government. Political culture, he observed, helped explain differences in the way that Hatch Act requirements of federal assistance were carried out in Minnesota as compared to Kentucky, as well as substantive variations in state administration of federal assistance (Elazar, 1966:81–82). While these sketches were largely anecdotal, Elazar opened a new chapter for understanding federalism and sparked interest in the relationship of political culture to state administration.

Elazar defined political culture as "the particular pattern of orientation to political action in which each political system is imbedded" and saw its importance as "the historical source of such differences in habits, concerns, and attitudes that exist to influence political life in the various states" (1966:79–80). Political culture could be observed in "(1) the set of perceptions of what politics is and what can be expected from government, held by both the general public and the politicians; (2) the kinds of people who become active in government and politics, as holders of elective offices, members of the bureaucracy, and active political workers; and (3) the actual way in which the art of government is practiced by citizens, politicians, and public officials in light of their perceptions"

(Elazar, 1966:84–85). Finally, the influence of political culture could be observed "in the kind of civic behavior dictated by conscience and internalized ethical standards; in the character of law-abidingness displayed by citizens and officials; and in the positive actions of government" (1966:85).

Based on his observation of state politics, Elazar identified three primary political cultures in the U.S.—an individualistic political culture, a moralistic political culture, and a traditionalistic political culture. An individualistic political culture "emphasizes the centrality of private concerns," encourages individual initiative and access to markets, and discourages governmental intervention in the market. In such a culture, politics is conceived as bargaining among individuals and groups acting out of self-interest. Political parties form, according to Elazar, to coordinate the interests of individuals and groups. Government is constituted on a utilitarian basis, that is, to respond to the demands of individuals and groups and not for any sense of the collective good (1966:85–94).

In a moralistic political culture, according to Elazar, politics "is considered one of the great activities of man in his search for the good society." Self-interest is tempered by the intervention of government "when it is considered necessary to do so for the public good or the well-being of the community. . . . Government is considered a positive instrument with a responsibility to promote the general welfare. . . ." This culture places a moral obligation on citizens and officeholders to engage in issues that define a good society and similarly devalues the pursuit of self-interest by individuals, private groups, or political parties (1966:90).

A traditional political culture, in Elazar's view, "accepts a substantially hierarchial society as part of the ordered nature of things, authorizing and expecting those at the top of the social structure to take a special and dominant role in government." Government takes on a paternalistic role in the community, seeks to maintain the existing social order, and adjusts to change "with the least possible upset." Political power is confined to "a relatively small and self-perpetuating group drawn from an established elite who often inherit their 'right' to govern through family ties or social position" (1966:93).

This chapter examines the administration of state government in a cultural context, drawing upon relevant literature to review the relationship of political cultures to state administration. The evolving concept of political cultures—introduced by Daniel Elazar just over 30 years ago—is explored with particular attention to the scholarly work contributed by Aaron Wildavsky and associates. Within the Wildavsky framework of political cultures, social organization and state administration are then examined in terms of underlying values and concepts of authority, decision making, and leadership. The main body of the chapter assembles available state experience suggesting that state administration mirrors ideal types of political cultures. Finally, the relevance of viewing state administration through cultural lenses to the practice of administration is discussed.

I. POLITICAL CULTURES

In Elazar's view, the taproots of political cultures may be traced to differences among ethnic and religious groups beginning with their arrival in America or even earlier times and continuing with their westward movement across the continent. Basic patterns "were set during the period of the rural-land frontier by three great currents of American migration that began on the east coast and moved westward after the colonial period." The first wave were "the Puritans of New England and their Yankee descendants . . . [who] came to these shores intending to establish the best possible earthly version of the holy commonwealth . . . a moralistic political culture." After establishing cultural roots in New England the Puritans moved westward, leaving the imprint of a moralistic political culture in New York, northern Pennsylvania and Ohio, Michigan, Wisconsin, Minnesota, and Iowa, later branching farther west into other states (1966:99–100).

A second wave composed primarily of ethnic and religious groups from England and Germanic states settled initially in the Middle Atlantic states. According to Elazar, these highly diverse groups "established the basic patterns of American pluralism . . . [and] were united by one common bond in particular— the search for individual opportunity in the New World." In contrast to a moralistic political culture, these settlers fashioned an individualistic political culture "dedicated to individual freedom to pursue private goals, to the point of making religion a private matter. . . ." From the mid-Atlantic states these groups spread an individualistic political culture through their westward movement into Pennsylvania, central Ohio, Indiana, and Illinois, Missouri, and ultimately across a belt reaching west into California (1966:101–102).

A third wave originating in the South shaped a traditionalistic political culture. Economics reminiscent of the Old World, "a plantation-centered agricultural system based on slavery and essentially anticommercial in orientation," cast the ordered, elitist political structure of this culture, according to Elazar. Settlers carried this culture into the border states of Kentucky and Tennessee, the southern parts of Ohio, Indiana, and Illinois, and Alabama, Mississippi, Louisiana, Texas, and Oklahoma (1966:102–103).

Elazar concludes that these three waves of political culture have spread across the United States, blended to some degree, and left unique amalgams of political culture in each of the 50 states. He then boldly places each state into one of eight classes of political culture:

1. Moralistic dominant
2. Moralistic dominant, strong individualistic strain
3. Individualistic dominant, strong moralistic strain
4. Individualistic dominant

5. Individualistic dominant, strong traditionalistic strain
6. Traditionalistic dominant, strong individualistic strain
7. Traditionalistic dominant
8. Traditionalistic dominant, strong moralistic strain (1966:107–111).

Over the past 30 years, Elazar's classifications of state political cultures have been reprinted repeatedly in articles and textbooks often as an indelible definition of political cultures in the 50 states and used as independent variables in explaining various political and governmental phenomena in a multitude of cross-state research endeavors.[1] At minimum, Elazar's work represents a starting point for any serious study of the subject.

II. POLITICAL CULTURES À LA WILDAVSKY AND ASSOCIATES

A second stream of scholarly work on political culture has been led by Aaron Wildavsky and his associates (Wildavsky, 1987; Thompson et al., 1990; Ellis, 1993; Coyle and Ellis, 1994; Ellis and Thompson, 1997; Chai and Swedlow, 1998). These scholars commend the pioneering work of Elazar but suggest improvement may be made in his categorization of political cultures. They have advanced the concept of political cultures by drawing upon theoretical work of anthropologist Mary Douglas—defining political culture as a set of values and beliefs upheld by social relations (Douglas, 1978). These cultural theorists assert that social organization may best be understood by examining an organization's underlying cultural biases which are justified and sustained by patterns of interpersonal relations (Thompson et al., 1990:1–24).

In contrast to Elazar's categories derived inductively from observation of state politics, Wildavsky and associates deduce inferences on political cultures from Douglas' assertion that essential cultural biases in social relations may be analyzed through cultural polarities, specifically a two-dimensional, grid-group typology (see Figure 1).[2] The group dimension, according to Douglas, measures the degree to which "the individual's life is absorbed in and sustained by group membership." Strong group suggests a high level of group involvement, strong boundaries separating group members from nonmembers, group restrictions on

---

[1] Illustrative of this research is "State Political Subcultures: Further Research," an issue of *Publius: The Journal of Federalism* 21 (Spring 1991):2.

[2] A six-state study of the impact of political cultures on state policy in education suggests "the importance of understanding culture as sets of polarities. At the core of the cultural paradigm are polarities of preference and social relations that give meaning to the whole. Intuitively, as well as analytically, such a view of culture seems to fit—to describe, explain, and predict—the political activity in the American states" (Marshall et al., 1989:162).

Strong Grid

Fatalism

- seeing the world as random and capricious--immune to rational action or management;

- believing that community action is hopeless; and

- hoping for luck or divine intervention.

Hierarchy

- promoting individual sacrifice in behalf of collective good;

- establishing order through rule of law, hierarchial structures, division of labor, and standards generated by experts;

- redeeming individual deviation through good institutions; and

- utilizing the power of conscience and reason to regulate and restrain baser passions and impulses.

Weak Group ─────────────── │ ─────────────── **Strong Group**

Individualism

- enhancing individual liberty through political competition and limits on political authority;

- enhancing liberty through free markets, bidding and bargaining, barter and exchange;

- maximizing self regulation and minimizing the scope of governmental regulation;

- encouraging innovation, trial and error, experimentation; and

- promoting equality of opportunity.

Egalitarianism

- promoting equality of conditions through measures such as redistribution of wealth, progressive taxation, and quotas based on sex or race;

- rectifying social inequity and injustice by reducing differences; and

- equalizing power relations by diminishing established authority.

Weak Grid

Figure 1   Political cultures.

individual autonomy, and individual reliance on the group for residence, work, recreation, or other life-sustaining resources. Weak group suggests greater individual autonomy in social relations either through a low level of group involvement or multiple group involvements of a nominal kind. The grid dimension, according to Douglas, involves external prescription or regulation "leaving minimum scope for personal choice." Strong grid suggests strict regulation of individual behavior through environmental forces; weak grid suggests "a good degree of independence" in negotiating social relations (1978:16).

From the grid-group typology, Douglas defines four essential cultures underpinning social relations: individualism (weak grid–weak group), hierarchy (strong grid–strong group), egalitarianism (weak grid–strong group), and fatalism (strong grid–weak group). Wildavsky and associates draw upon and extend these constructs to develop a theoretical basis for political cultures. Culture, they argue, aids understanding of a wide range of political phenomena, most importantly, political preferences which take form in social relations:

> People . . . get their preferences from their involvement with others. Social relations are the great teachers of human life. They provide us with our conception of what is desirable, beautiful, horrible, normal, outlandish. . . . Preferences are formed from the most basic desire of human beings—how we wish to live with other people and others wish to live with us (Thompson et al., 1990:56–57).

Such relationships, mostly without conscious design, create cultural biases, that is, the "shared meanings, the common convictions, the moral markers, the subtle rewards, penalties, and expectations common" to a particular political culture (Thompson et al., 1990:59).

At the same time political culture is not deterministic: "Our theory of cultural biases attempts to leave room for individual discretion by viewing individuals as actively pursuing their preferred way of life, as well as by testing rival ways to determine which is preferable." Further, cultural theory envisages "a permanent dynamic imbalance in which adherents are constantly changing positions and, in so doing, transforming the relative strength of the rival ways." From this framework, politics may be seen as a contest among rival political cultures: "Political culture is transmitted from generation to generation, but it is not transmitted unchanged, nor is it transmitted without question or by chance. . . . It is a lively and responsive thing that is continually being negotiated by individuals" (Thompson et al., 1990:177–177, 186, 218).

Wildavsky and associates then explain the political cultures of individualism, hierarchy, egalitarianism, and fatalism in terms of core values, world view of man and nature, assessment of blame when things go wrong, and principal prescriptions for society underlying these cultures (see Thompson et al., 1990).

A. Hierarchy

Hierarchs value order and seek collective order through social relations character-ized by the rule of law, hierarchial structures, division of labor and specialization, and standards based on scientific methods and expertise. Individual sacrifice is believed to be essential for collective order, and therefore duty, obligation, defer-ence, and service for the benefit of the whole are emphasized. If cooperation among individuals is needed, those in authority ordain it by defining the collective good or enacting laws. When things go wrong, blame is likely placed on social deviants who do not know their place.

Hierarchial views of human nature and the natural world often call for collective action to assure order. For example, hierarchs believe that human be-ings "are born sinful but can be redeemed by good institutions. This conception of human nature helps sustain a way of life rich in institutional constraints" (Thompson et al., 1990:35). Such collectivists rely on the power of conscience and reason to restrain baser passions and impulses of human beings. Hierarchy views nature as tolerant and forgiving but vulnerable to unusual occurrences and therefore in need of regulation.

The organization of the military, the Roman Catholic church, and other bureaucratic structures exemplify hierarchy.

B. Individualism

Individualists seek individual liberty and believe that social relations character-ized by free markets, bidding and bargaining, barter, and exchange provide the best assurance of liberty. Innovation, trial and error, and experimentation are encouraged by competitive individualists. They view nature as wonderfully for-giving and natural resources as unlimited and therefore embrace a laissez-faire approach to this natural world. In politics, individualists prefer self-regulation and therefore want to minimize the scope of governmental regulation. They seek to enhance liberty through political competition and limits on political authority.

Individualists view human nature as extraordinarily stable. Human beings "remain essentially the same: self-seeking. By making man self-seeking and un-malleable, individualists can justify a way of life that attempts to channel existing human nature rather than change it" (Thompson et al., 1990:34). Cooperation is secured through one-on-one negotiations. Individualists promote equality of opportunity, but when things go wrong, poor judgment, personal incompetence, or just bad luck is to blame.

Free markets exemplify individualism.

C. Egalitarianism

Egalitarians value equality and seek to equalize conditions in human affairs. They concern themselves with inequities and injustice in society and therefore promote measures that produce equality of results, such as redistribution of wealth, progressive taxation, and quotas based on sex, race, or other divisions.

Egalitarians prefer social relations based on equal status and are therefore suspicious of any structure that gives one person more authority than another. They look for ways to diminish differences in established authority and equalize power relations. As a result, they promote cooperation through direct participation and consensus among participants with equal status—which often makes the resolution of conflict difficult.

To egalitarians, the natural world "is a terrifying, unforgiving place and the least jolt may trigger its complete collapse." For this reason, the environment must therefore be managed with "great care" and timidity. Further, egalitarians "believe that human beings are born good but are corrupted by evil institutions." Therefore, while human nature may be good, it is also "highly malleable" and "susceptible to institutional influences." Evil institutions, external forces, "the system," the establishment, or some alliance of government and business is most likely to blame when things go wrong (Thompson et al., 1990:25–38).

Certain religious sects and animal rights organizations exemplify egalitarianism.

D. Fatalism

Fatalists are excluded from groups yet shackled by external prescription. They exercise little control over their lives, enduring "the social isolation of individualism without the autonomy; the constraint of hierarchy without the support of a loyal group" (Coyle and Ellis, 1994:4).

Fatalists view the world as random and capricious—immune to individual or community influence. Human nature "is unpredictable. Some people may be benevolent . . . but more are hostile. . . . Never knowing what to expect from others, fatalists react by distrusting their fellow human beings" (Thompson et al., 1990:35). Whom do fatalists blame when things go wrong? Fate, of course.

Examples of fatalists might be individuals living in servitude or welfare recipients caught in a cycle of dependency.

E. Cultural Alliances

While these cultural theorists argue the viability of the four political cultures, they also assert that no single culture can effectively govern alone:

> The incapacities of the three active ways of life (hierarchy, egalitarianism, and individualism) prompt them to reach out for cultural allies who can compensate for their weaknesses. Thus, adherents of each way of life try to undermine the other ways and simultaneously rely on these competitors. . . .

As a result, alliances are formed in order to govern: "An alliance can help make up for the defects of a single way of life, but it can never provide a lasting solution. Allies remain competitors; antagonism is always there beneath the surface" (Thompson et al., 1990:88–89). Governing regimes within individual states of the U.S. may be viewed as alliances comprised of distinct, yet fundamentally incompatible and competing political cultures.

The dominant U.S. political parties may be viewed as cultural alliances (see Wildavsky, 1991). The modern Democratic party, for example, took original shape during the Jacksonian era as an alliance of individualism and egalitarianism. These two cultural types—one promoting economic opportunity through the least government, the other equality of results—could agree on reducing national authority by abolishing the national bank, cutting congressional funding of internal improvements, and decrying governmental interference in the economy. Jackson justified such actions by arguing that a disempowered national government could not favor the rich and powerful. A national political party evolved committed to the idea that "equality of opportunity, meticulously followed, would lead to an approximation of equality of result" (Wildavsky, 1991:38).

The origins of the present-day Republican party may be traced back at least to the Whigs also of the Jacksonian era (see Ellis and Wildavsky, 1989:177–204). As a party oriented to hierarchial views, the Whigs embraced a positive, even paternal, vision of government that showed concern for the needy and stimulated the economy through a strong national bank and congressional appropriations for internal improvements. As a former Whig, Lincoln "was instrumental in creating a new Republican party in which individualism was tempered but not led by hierarchy" (Ellis and Wildavsky, 1989:177). Lincoln embraced the program of the defeated Whigs, but through his actions raised the themes of competition and self-regulation to a preeminent position. The Republication party evolved as a cultural alliance of individualism and hierarchy.

In sum, Wildavsky and associates argue that their approach to political cultures inferred deductively from Douglas' typology offers "measures of culture that allow for comparisons across time and space and relate values and beliefs to social relations and institutions" (Coyle and Ellis, 1994:2). This focus on mutually reinforcing values and social relations may be applied any social organization—to state administration as well as to political parties, tribes, or individuals. The test of any theory, however, is its explanatory power. Does cultural theory aid in understanding and explaining political phenomena? How does the approach of Wildavsky and associates compare to Elazar?

F. Wildavsky and Associates Compared to Elazar

The work of Wildavsky and associates and that of Elazar have much in common (see Thompson et al., 1990:233–245). Elazar classifies political cultures of states and even regions within states by variations in the strength of core cultures (for example, moralistic dominant, strong individualistic strain, etc., noted above)—a concept which corresponds to the idea of governing regimes as cultural alliances, promoted by Wildavsky et al. The concept of individualist political culture also aligns closely between the two.

Wildavsky and associates take issue with the label but not the substance of Elazar's concept of traditionalistic political culture. They believe Elazar's traditionalistic political culture compares well substantively with the political culture they term to be hierarchy, both emphasizing—in contrast to individualism—ambivalence toward free markets and self-regulation. However, they observe that the traditionalistic label "suggests that at its core is a commitment to doing things the way they have been done in the past, regardless of the substance of those past behaviors and beliefs" (Thompson et al., 1990:234). Wildavsky and associates believe "hierarchy" more accurately characterizes the substantive beliefs of this culture, including those of the culture described by Elazar as traditionalistic.

Wildavsky and associates find serious substantive confusion between Elazar's concepts of traditionalistic and moralistic political cultures.[3] First, they point to Massachusetts in the late 1700s and early 1800s, described by Elazar as the seedbed of a moralistic political culture in which each citizen has a duty to participate in community affairs for the good of the whole (Elazar, 1966:89–92, 99–100). Citing historical research, they find Massachusetts political culture of the period to be hierarchial (or traditionalistic, using Elazar's term) dominated by the Federalists, the party of hierarchy; its politics, they argue, were largely deferential not participatory. Participation was "limited to the few who were virtuous, wealthy, and wise." Second, Wildavsky et al. find fault with Elazar's moralistic category that lumps together groups as divergent as radical abolitionists and conservative Whigs. Conservative Whigs, they maintain, were hierarchs who upheld "a politics of deference and noblesse oblige" (Thompson et al., 1990:236). Radical abolitionists were egalitarians suspicious of authority in all forms and committed to universal emancipation including women—a far cry from the Whigs. Third, they question Elazar's traditionalistic category for being "virtually synonymous" with southern states and for making no cultural distinction between Virginia and Alabama—citing V.O. Key's observation that lightyears in political distance exist between the two states.

In sum, Wildavsky and associates believe their political cultures of hierarchy and egalitarianism offer enhanced explanatory power over Elazar's concepts of traditionalistic and moralistic political cultures. Their concepts clarify the dis-

---

[3] Wildavsky and associates also take issue with the "moralistic" label, arguing that each political culture has a distinct basis in moral beliefs.

tinctive substantive beliefs and social relationships of these political cultures and provide a theoretical basis for analyzing political cultures and cultural alliances of state governments.

III. POLITICAL CULTURES AND ORGANIZATION

Cultural theory suggests that key cultural values are integral to social organization—to organizational structure, decision making, and leadership, among other practices—and that organization may best be understood through a cultural framework. The Wildavsky framework of political cultures suggests a typology for understanding organizations which Dennis Coyle has recently applied to social organization in general—conceptualizing organizations in terms of their underlying values and the social relationships which uphold those values. Coyle's work and related literature help construct ideal cultural types of social organization (Coyle, 1997; deLeon, 1993; Wildavsky, 1989; Fiske, 1991). Figure 2 summarizes three active cultural types—hierarchy, individualism, and egalitarianism—in terms of essential elements of organization, specifically, underlying values, structure of authority, decision making, and modes of leadership, which are discussed as follows.[4]

A. Organization in Hierarchy

A preference for collective order represents the principal value underlying organization in hierarchy. All elements of the organization—people, positions, superiors and subordinates, offices—have their place and status. Rational behavior supports the collective order. The ethics of discipline, obedience, and duty instruct individual behavior. Loyal members of the organization who willingly make sacrifices for the benefit of the organization as a whole are rewarded. When things go wrong in hierarchical organization, deviant behavior is usually to blame. Such behavior—disobedience, lack of discipline, or disregard for duty—threatens hierarchy, undermines collective order, and is punished.

Organizational structure in hierarchy is hierarchic, fixed, and prominent. Authority is hierarchically arranged position by position in a chain of command with control centralized in the hands of a few. Structure provides for a clear division of labor, requiring specialized competence in the performance of organizational tasks. Superiors and subordinates know their prerogatives, as well as

---

[4] The three active cultural types—hierarchy, individualism, and egalitarianism—are emphasized because of their relevance to state administration in the U.S. While administration in fatalistic culture may also have relevance here, available literature on its application is sparse.

Organization in Fatalism

- unknown.

Organization in Hierarchy

- *underlying value*: collective order

- *authority*: centralized, hierarchic

- *decision making*: ordained by hierarchy

- *leadership*: limited, positional

- *vulnerability*: individual alienation, totalitarianism

- *form of organization*: bureaucracy

Organization in Individualism

- *underlying value*: individual liberty

- *authority*: competitive, polyarchic

- *decision making*: through negotiation, accomodation, bidding and bargaining

- *leadership*: entrepreneurial, meteoric

- *vulnerability*: creation of inequities

- *form of organization*: markets

Organization in Egalitarianism

- *underlying value*: equality, equal results

- *authority*: participative, group based

- *decision making*: group consensus and norms

- *leadership*: illegitimate or charismatic

- *vulnerability*: disorganization, conformity

- *form of organization*: collegial

Figure 2   Organization within political cultures.

the limits of those prerogatives. Organizational boundaries are defined clearly distinguishing the organization from its environment.

Organizational decisions are ordained from above in hierarchy. Cooperation among the elements of the organization is secured through the rule of law, written rules and regulations that prescribe behavior and routinize decision making throughout the structure of the organization. Standard operating procedures control decision making in the organization.

Hierarchial culture is supportive of organizational leadership and assures continuity in leadership, but the scope of leadership is constrained by the rule of law and position. Officials in hierarchial organization are expected to lead but may become autocratic within their sphere of authority.

Police organization often typifies hierarchy.

B. Organization in Individualism

A preference for individual liberty underpins organization in individualism. Self-regulation, the freedom to make individual choices, represents the ultimate value. Rational behavior is self-seeking. When mistakes are made, individual judgment, personal competence, or just bad luck is to blame.

Power in this cultural form is competitive and polyarchic; self-regulation is the ideal. Individual and minority rights are emphasized. Public authority is diffuse and limited. Separate and competing power centers are encouraged in order to limit central authority. Organization boundaries are fluid and subject to continuous fluctuation.

Decision making in this organizational form resembles a free market. Conflicting preferences are mediated through marketlike processes—bidding, bargaining, and one-on-one negotiation. Contracts secure cooperation among individuals. Individuals may choose to align temporarily in coalitions with those of similar interests in order to accomplish immediate objectives. Resulting compromises make public purposes ambiguous.

Pure markets function through individual bidding and bargaining and do not require leadership. Competitive individualists are therefore not generally supportive of leadership but may be drawn to leaders who produce results in a free market. For example, an entrepreneur achieving meteoric success in the market may attract a following among individualists—as long as the success continues— but such leadership is likely short-lived. On occasion, individualists may contract for leadership but such contracts will be of limited scope and duration.

C. Organization in Egalitarianism

A desire for equality motivates members of egalitarian organizations. They seek to rectify inequities and achieve equal results. Egalitarians concern themselves with conspiring outsiders who foster inequality as well as impure insiders not fully committed to values shared among members of the organization.[5]

---

[5] In the field of public administration the movement known as the "new public administration" embraces egalitarian values, advocating that administrators have an ethical obligation to promote social equity and defend against external forces that would sustain or cause inequities. According to proponents of this view, public administrators should concern themselves with equity in the external distribution of goods and services and integrative structures that equalize power relations (see Marini, 1971; Frederickson, 1980).

Power among members of egalitarian organization is equalized, and structure is at best collegial but often ambiguous. Office may rotate perpetually among members. Clarity as to who does what is normally absent, for authority in the sense of superior-subordinate relations is alien to egalitarians. In contrast to the high and tight structure of hierarchy, egalitarian structure is flat and loose. Rigid organizational boundaries protect members from a forbidding environment, but dissension may easily splinter the organization into factions.

Decision making among equals requires group consensus—on procedures as well as the substance of issues under consideration. Building consensus involves full participation by all group members and calls for careful deliberation which may become interminable. Further, dissident members may disrupt decision making and even threaten the existence of the group. Decisions arrived at through consensus among equals may also be fragile and tentative. In the absence of formal decision making, informal group norms guide behavior.

Formal leadership is foreign to egalitarian organization, for it upsets a structure of equalized power. Members of egalitarian organization view inequities in power as illegitimate and therefore seek to eradicate distinctions in individual power. A member may convene or facilitate but not lead. While egalitarians are inherently suspicious of leadership, charismatic leadership is possible and, according to Wildavsky, possible *only* in egalitarian culture. A charismatic leader who embodies egalitarian spirit and virtues may emerge as a total but temporary substitute for authority when equalitarian organization is subject to external threat (Wildavsky, 1989:100–110).

Purer forms of egalitarian organization might be a faculty senate, a professional association, or a voluntary association committed to eradicating social injustice.

IV. POLITICAL CULTURE AND STATE ADMINISTRATION

The application of cultural theory to social organization suggests its potential use for understanding administration in state government. In other words, cultural theory may give insights into state administration, that is, the key cultural values underlying state administration and related structures of authority, decision making, and leadership. However, the state of empirical knowledge relevant to political cultures and state administration is primitive. Cultural theory is a new and evolving field of study, and the application of cultural theory to public organization is virgin territory. To complicate the task further, as one student of political cultures has concluded, isolating, specifying, and measuring ''the characteristics, intensities, manifestations, and effects '' of political cultures is no simple matter (Kincaid, 1982:7). Research on political cultures and state government is at best rudimentary, and hardly any research specifically applying a cultural framework to state administration has been conducted.[6]

Ideally, research on political cultures and state administration would start with ethnography, applying methods of cultural study to state administration. An ethnography of state administration would focus on the underlying value biases of a particular state agency and the relationships that uphold those biases. Thick description of values and related structures, decision making, and leadership in segments of state administration could provide building blocks for a base of knowledge on political cultures and state administration. Ethnographic study, really in-depth case study with a cultural focus, would be quite familiar to the field of public administration.

Given the primitive state of knowledge on political culture and state administration and the absence of an ethnography of state administration, empirical knowledge on the subject must be extracted from available research relevant to state administration that may also be applicable to a cultural framework. Using the parameters indicated by the application of cultural theory to social organization, available state experience suggesting that state administration mirrors ideal cultural types is assembled. From this compilation a cultural view of state administration is constructed—isolating ideal cultural types in state administration, working hypotheses if you will, of key cultural values and related practices of state administration.

A. State Administration in Hierarchy

Hierarchy comprises the historic home of the field of public administration, and therefore the character of administration in hierarchy, if not its underlying cultural biases, should be immediately familiar. Max Weber's classic concept of bureaucratic organization—based on rule of law, written rules and regulations, hierarchial structure, division of labor, and specialized competence—mirrors organization in hierarchial culture. Woodrow Wilson's prescription that public administration be separate from politics and policy, and Frederick Taylor's embrace of scientific method in organizing work and search for the "one best way" further supplement the model. The essential characteristics of administration in hierarchy often constitute the starting point for empirical research in public administration—as well as state administration.

Most empirical research on state administration documents some aspect of the cultural type, state administration in hierarchy. One recent case study vividly details this ideal cultural type and its continuing hold on the practice of state

---

[6] Frederick Wirt identifies state implementation as a fruitful topic for research on political cultures but concludes, "no research in this phase is known"(Wirt, 1991:9).

administration (Barzelay, 1992). While analyzing administrative reforms undertaken in the 1983–90 period in Minnesota state government and specifically in the Minnesota Department of Administration, Michael Barzelay identifies "the reigning bureaucratic paradigm" which resulted from Progressive-era ideals, "a compelling system of beliefs in the early twentieth century." This belief system of public administration "promised order and rationality in that new domain of public affairs denominated as administration. . . . The theory also provided a reason to believe that the work of public servants served the public interest." Serving the public interest meant a government "cleansed of particularism," requiring that all segments of state administration be subordinate to the collective good of state government. (Barzelay, 1992:4, 22–27, 117, 122).

The preference for order, rationality, and service in the public interest, according to Barzelay, led to a number of related administrative beliefs and practices, as follows:

> *On authority and structure*: Specific delegations of authority define each role in the executive branch. Officials carrying out any given role should act only when expressly permitted to do so either by rule or by instructions given by superior authorities in the chain of command. . . . Authority was the right to make decisions and demand obedience from subordinates on matters related to the grant of authority. Formal structure referred to the system of superior-subordinate relationships, which matched delegated authority with subdivided functions ultimately to the level of individual positions (Barzelay, 1992:5, 126).

> *On rules*: The bureaucratic paradigm encouraged control activities to develop ever-denser networks of rules in response to changing circumstances or new problems. When rule systems became extremely complex, staff operations of substantial size—located in both staff and line agencies—were needed to understand, administer, and update them (Barzelay, 1992:124; see also Bardach and Kagan, 1982:34–39).

> *On uniform rules and procedures*: In exercising authority, officials should apply rules and procedures in a uniform manner. The failure to obey rules should be met with an appropriate penalty (Barzelay, 1992:124).

> *On control*: Within the bureaucratic reformer's vision of government, control was the lifeblood of efficient administration . . . [carried out through] accounting systems, budgetary freezes, reorganizations, reporting requirements, and countless measures to reduce the exercise of discretion by most public employees. . . . Control was essential to realize the aim of a unified executive branch . . . to purge administrative decisions of particularistic influences (Barzelay, 1992:123–124).

> *On professionalism and expertise*: The purpose of the bureaucratic reforms was to enable government to serve the public interest. . . . A central element of that strategy was to recruit, develop, and retain experts in such fields as accounting, engineering, and social work. This strategy was designed not only to achieve results, but also to use expertise as a way to legiti-

mate the actions of unelected officials in an administrative state. . . . [T]hese officials came to presume that the public interest was served whenever they applied their various bodies of knowledge and professional standards to questions within their respective domains of authority. . . . [D]ecisions made in accord with professional standards were congruent with citizens collective needs . . . (Barzelay, 1992:117–119).

The executive reorganization movement which has swept through state governments in waves throughout most of this century reinforces beliefs and practices associated with state administration in hierarchy. The most important benefits of state reorganization

> are the rationalizing of the executive branch machinery and the expansion of the chief executive's formal powers over the consolidated executive branch departments. These changes seem to be necessary conditions for enabling a state's chief executive to be the "center of energy, direction, and administrative management" (Conant, 1992:71).

In a 50-year review of administration in state governments, Bowling and Wright conclude that compared to the late 1940s, administrative structures are reorganized and central control is strong:

> The void in central controls which existed in the 1940s has been filled. Most state administrations have experienced a major turnabout, with the governor exerting a centralizing force. . . . Centripetal forces in state administration in the 1990s are in sharp contrast to the centrifugal factors dominant in the 1940s (Bowling and Wright, 1998:57).

This enthusiasm for hierarchial administration is also promoted through materials of the governors' vehicle for collective action, the National Governors' Association (*Governing the American States . . .*, 1978).

Another state study documents the enduring viability of Wilson's politics-administration dichotomy in state administration. Based on a survey of 847 state administrators in 10 states, Richard Elling concludes that "these state administrators continue to believe that maintaining some sort of politics-administration separation is a good way to assure efficient and effective administration of the public's business." Similarly, these state managers "tend to believe that good management is enhanced to the extent that the influence of external political actors is reduced." Nearly two-thirds of these managers viewed legislative review of proposed administrative rules and regulations as not positive in terms of the effect on the implementation of agency programs. They also expressed a similar negative assessment of whistle-blowing, which was likely viewed as an act of disobedience and a threat to agency administration (Elling, 1992:90–92, 97, 196).

In a study of state educational structure, Frederick Wirt found that states with hierarchial cultures had more centralized control and less local autonomy in education (1977:177–79). Further, an in-depth, six-state study of state policy in education found that political cultures "roughly distinguish which state policy mechanisms and program approaches are selected"(Marshall et al., 1989:159). For example, the study documented that elites in states having political cultures with hierarchial tendencies opposed local control by school administrators and favored state mandates with respect to student discipline. Specifically, elites in Arizona and West Virginia "opposed the strengthening of local administrators' control by giving them more discretion, by reorganizing their districts, and by mandating their evaluation and employee discipline programs," and "favored more control of students by mandating their discipline and modifying their suspension or expulsion regulations . . ." (Marshall et al., 126).

The values and administrative practices associated with state administration in hierarchy likely permeate, or at least in the past have permeated, a number of substantive fields that fall within the jurisdiction of state government. In environmental regulation, for example, a dominant view of ideal state administration has been termed command-and-control enforcement, which includes "the reliance on formal, precise, and specific rules; the literal interpretation of rules; the reliance on the advice of legal technicians (attorneys); the quest for uniformity; and the distrust of and an adversarial orientation toward the regulated" (Shover et al., 1986:11). According to this model of state regulation, vigorous enforcement coupled with sanctions and penalties effectively corrects violations of environmental laws and deters potential violators. While strict adherence to the law would limit administrative discretion, Hunter and Waterman found that state environmental regulators "respond to political clues from their hierarchial superordinates" (1996:195).

Brendon Swedlow discerns a hierarchial world view in the first two reform movements in the field of mental health—the first, "collecting all undesirables in asylum warehouses," and the second, "psychiatric treatment in state hospitals." Both reforms, according to Swedlow, exhibited a paternalistic belief that "some of us can decide that some others are different and therefore deserve to be treated differently. Psychiatrists replaced wardens as the new custodians of these others' welfare. The hierarchical doctor-patient relationship was substituted for the hierarchical keeper-kept relationship . . ."(1994:73).

Swedlow then reviews civil commitment procedures for the mentally ill to illustrate how professionals "make decisions for the rest of us" based on state authority exercised through the courts and professional standards interpreted by psychiatrists. The suggested legal standard for civil commitment, with the hierarchical meaning inserted in parentheses by Swedlow, is as follows:

> Would a reasonable man (as determined by the court), given the patient's serious illness and suffering (as determined by the court's confidence in the testifying psychiatrist), be willing to give up a certain amount of freedom in

that particular institution in exchange for a treatment that (according to the psychiatrist) in similar cases produces a specific range of results? (1994:74).[7]

This procedure helped to preserve proper roles in the administration of mental health and assure the maintenance of social order in the community—underlying values of state administration in hierarchy. According to Swedlow, "Judges and psychiatrists retain their unique, well-delineated place in the society . . . in part by being able to make certain sorts of decisions for other people which of course also 'helps' those people retain their 'mentally ill' roles or positions" (1994:74–75).

Lawrence Mead (1997) and associated researchers document a recent wave of state paternalism that has permeated the administration of numerous social services including those dealing with welfare, teenage pregnancy, child support, homelessness, drug addiction, and public education. In this "new paternalism" the collective interests of the state override individual choice: "Society claims the right to tell its dependents how to live . . ."(1997:4). In welfare, for example, Mead finds that

administrators prescribe certain responses such as work and require the clients to conform. . . . [P]enalties are imposed if people fail to comply. . . . The goal is to supervise behavior, largely outside institutional walls, something that can be done by routines where staff members check up on clients. . . . The idea is that the poor need support, but they also require structure. And behavioral rules are to be enforced through government (Mead, 1997: 21–22).

James Q. Wilson summarizes the prescription underlying the research of Mead and his associates as follows:

[P]aternalism needs to be revived and strengthened where it is already accepted (the schooling of children) and enlarged and extended for people—the homeless, criminals, drug addicts, deadbeat dads, unmarried teenage mothers, and single mothers claiming welfare benefits—who have by their behavior indicated that they do not display the minimal level of self-control expected of decent citizens (Wilson, 1997:340–341).

When carried to the extreme, state administration in hierarchial culture reveals totalitarian impulses and loss of individual liberty. Early in the 20th century certain states enacted laws that gave state officials and medical professionals authority to sterilize inmates of state institutions. In Kansas during the height of

---

[7] The suggested legal standard is taken from Stone (1975:69). The parenthetical phrases are Swedlow's.

the Progressive era, for example, state lawmakers authorized superintendents and wardens of state hospitals and prisons to initiate sterilization if he or she:

> believes that the mental or physical condition of any inmate would be improved thereby or that procreation by such inmate would be likely to result in defective or feeble-minded children with criminal tendencies, and that the condition of such inmate is not likely to improve so as to make procreation by such persons *desirable or beneficial to the state* (my emphasis) (Kansas, 1913, 1917).

Once the administrator's recommendation was reviewed and sanctioned by superior state officials and medical officers, the treatment could be executed. Presumably, the state would then benefit.

B. State Administration in Individualism

Another model of state administration began gaining new life in the 1970s and 1980s. David Osborne chronicled an emerging paradigm based on the policies and administrations of a new class of state governors (Osborne, 1988: particularly 326–332). This paradigm rejected bureaucratic solutions and looked to decentralization, competition, and market-based solutions for managing state issues. Private sector and third sector organizations, rather than agencies of government, emerged as an alternative for state administration. While not entirely new, this model helps illustrate another distinct cultural type, that is, state administration in individualism.

Osborne, teamed first with Ted Gaebler in *Reinventing Government* (1992) and more recently with Peter Plastrik in *Banishing Bureaucracy* (1997), developed this paradigm more fully in two best-selling books, which prescribed a broad range of approaches for administration of government at all levels—state, national, and local. These prescriptions included empowering citizens, injecting competition into service delivery, focusing on customer needs, leveraging change through markets, enterprising, and decentralizing, among others. For purposes here, this discussion will focus on key elements of this paradigm—customer choice as the underlying value, diffusion of authority through competition and empowerment, decision making through negotiation, and entrepreneurial leadership—with applications drawn from state administration.

The free market ideal of customer choice permeates the practice of administration in individualism. Public services are viewed as contracts in which customers receive specified benefits at a certain cost, and quality of service is measured by customer satisfaction with benefits and costs. Public dollars follow customer choice, making administration accountable to customers. Osborne and Plastrik report, for example, that Minnesota has given parents the power of school choice with public funds shifted to the school of choice. School choice in Minnesota is based on the belief that:

> the key to transforming schools was changing the system of incentives, accountabilities, and control within which they operated. By giving customers choices, making districts compete for their students and dollars, and encouraging teachers, parents, and others to create new schools free of the red tape that constrained most principals and teachers, they believed they could create a system that would produce not just a few excellent schools, but thousands of excellent schools (Osborne and Plastrik, 1997:160).

One early study of open enrollment under school choice in Minnesota concluded:

> Open enrollment has stimulated an increase in parent decision-making power, which is characterized initially by administrators involving parents more in school planning efforts and day-to-day operations. School administrators were seen to become more responsive to parent wishes and demands in an effort to keep them satisfied (quoted in Osborne and Plastrik, 1997: 166).

A more recent study similarly found:

> Open enrollment impacts the parent-educator dynamic by subtly changing the degree of power held by each player in the system. . . . Parents are flexing their political muscles by demanding desired programs and services. If the requests are not honored, many threaten to leave the district. Findings suggest it doesn't take a large number of families threatening transfer for administrators to take seriously the requests (quoted in Osborne and Plastrik, 1997: 172).

School choice had an immediate impact as schools made adjustments to compete for students. These changes included ''lengthening their hours, adding more counseling, and developing new educational programs, new after-school programs, new career programs, and new programs for gifted and talented students'' (Osborne and Plastrik, 1997:172). Smaller schools expanded offerings, cutting administrative costs rather than programs, in order to stay competitive.

The value of customer choice was also used to transform the Minnesota Department of Administration, a traditional control-oriented state agency into a customer-oriented service provider. In this case, the preference for customer choice was defined as follows:

> A customer relationship is a mutually adjustive working relationship in which a provider's main purpose is to meet user's needs. In a typical customer relationship, users believe that providers should be accountable to them . . . for fulfilling this purpose, and providers recognize that they ought to be accountable. Built into the definition of a customer relationship is an additional

key presumption: as a rule, customers' informed and reflective judgements about how well a service meets their needs are accurate. Therefore the most relevant information and evidence for judging how well a provider fulfills the main purpose of providing a service are users' evaluation of service quality and value, however expressed (Barzelay, 1992:110).

This customer focus resulted in enhanced information sharing with customers, more face-to-face contacts, and more two-way communication with customers, empowering customers in decision making, assessing customer satisfaction, and market research on customer needs. Further, Minnesota adopted the basic market philosophy that customers should pay for service. In other words, centralized service agencies should be financed through revenues earned by selling services to line agency customers, which further heightened customer service and accountability (Barzelay, 1992:58–78, 102–114).

Diffusion of authority in the delivery of public service—which takes many forms—represents another key element of state administration in individualism. Customer choice obviously individualizes authority. Other means of diffusing authority include the familiar, for example, local control and home rule, and more novel strategies, such as competition, privatization, and empowerment.

A deep-seated belief in local self-government has shaped institution building and state administration throughout U.S. history. Tocqueville observed that self-government was a widely held principle for organizing U.S. governments in the early part of the 19th century. Americans believe, he observed, that each individual:

> is the best and sole judge of his own private interest and that society has no right to control a man's actions unless they are prejudicial to the commonweal or unless the commonweal demands his help. . . . Municipal independence, in the United States, is therefore a natural consequence of this very principle of the sovereignty of the people (De Tocqueville, 1945:64–65).

In Kansas, for example, the ideal of local self-government spawned over 11,000 counties, cities, schools, and townships from statehood in 1861 to the mid-1890s. Nationally, over 80,000 locally governed instrumentalities of the state deliver a broad array of public services (see Krane et al., forthcoming).

In his study of political culture with respect to public schools, Frederick Wirt states that local control:

> is one expression of the fundamental value of individualism, which is characterized by a belief that the individual can best be protected if one can see what government is doing to one's interests. . . . [T]he individualistic culture might fear the use of centralized power, and hence its institutions would be more localist in school power; centralism is always a threat to the expression of individual preferences . . . (Wirt, 1982:82, 95).

One study of state and local expenditures found, for example, that in "individualistic states, expenditures are higher for local governments and lower for state government" (Miller, 1991:100).

Research on state educational elites and statutory provisions suggests that the extent of local autonomy varies from state to state in response to political cultures. For example, in Illinois, a state with an individualistic political culture, researchers found "considerable localism, a preference for local control paired with a suspicion of state control" and "pervasive distrust of political authority." Education elites "seem to adopt consistently one view . . . let locals handle it." Specifically, elites opposed long-range capital planning by the state and favored incremental approaches in building maintenance. Statutory provisions were designed to protect against the abuse of authority and left issues of curriculum up to local authorities mandating few requirements (Marshall et al., 1989:127, 141, 144–145).

Osborne and his associates take this long-standing ideal of local control at least one step further to "community empowerment," suggesting that local authorities diffuse authority further by empowering neighborhoods and others within local jurisdictions. According to the authors, compared to bureaucratic service delivery, empowered communities have more commitment to their members, understand problems better, solve problems rather than deliver services, are more flexible and creative, and are cheaper (see Osborne and Gaebler, 1992:25–48; Osborne and Plastrik, 1997:203–240). Citizen empowerment in which citizens deliver services through volunteerism and coprovision would take diffusion of authority a step further (Percy and Baker, 1980; Powers and Thompson, 1994). Most states, for example, make provision for fire protection in rural or sparsely populated areas through volunteer fire departments.

Another means of diffusing authority in the delivery of service is competition through privatization of services. Privatization takes many forms, some of which are readily familiar in the administration of state government. Almost all major state agencies procure services through competitive bidding among private vendors, both profit and not-for-profit organizations (Kettl, 1993:155–177). Most state transportation agencies, for example, have for years contracted for road construction and maintenance, as well as professional services for design and engineering of roads. Many state social service agencies have procured a broad array of social services through contracts with a multitude of private providers.

Since the early 1980s, a new level of competition has been injected into service delivery, extending and deepening privatization in the administration of most state governments. In a recent 50-state survey of state agency heads in 15 substantive areas, 60% of the state officials reported an expansion of privatization in their jurisdiction over the past five years, and 55% indicated that the level of privatization would increase over the next five years. Fewer than one in eight officials responded that no privatization was taking place (Chi and Jasper, 1998:

7). Officials indicated that over 3000 specific programs had been privatized reaching into every area of state activity surveyed with privatization reported most frequently in transportation, administration and general services, corrections, higher education, social services, natural resources and environment, mental health and retardation, juvenile rehabilitation, and health.

According to the Council of State Governments survey:

> Many states are turning to privatization to achieve cost control, efficiency and administrative expediency . . . [T]here are few comprehensive privatization initiatives. Instead, individual agencies privatize their activities as necessary and manage the projects on a case-by-case basis (Chi and Jasper, 1998:4).

Over 80% of the privatization is executed through contracts with private providers. Less widely used forms of privatization, no one of which was used in more that 5% of the cases according to the survey, include public-private partnerships, service shedding, franchises, vouchers, deregulation, and asset sale.

Michigan has used privatization as strategic tool through a review process labeled PERM for privatize, eliminate, retain in current form, or modify. Privatization was defined as "the act of reducing the role of government, or increasing the role of the private sector, in an activity or in the ownership of assets" (Kost, 1996:17). John Kost concludes from his experience with privatization in Michigan that the process requires "a sound analytical process" and assurance of "quality and value rather than . . . simply the lowest price." Assuring performance from private vendors requires "precise specification of outcomes in advance," "complete and binding contractual language" including accountability, and "comprehensive after-the-fact evaluation" (Kost, 1996:18, 21).

State administration in individualism—whether through customer choice, diffusion of authority, or competition—suggests decision making through negotiation, bargaining, and incremental adaption, rather than top-down orders. For example, in the case of the Minnesota Department of Administration, in which a control-oriented department was transformed into a customer-oriented service agency, mutual adjustment, not unilateral direction, characterized decision making. According to Barzelay:

> . . . mutual adjustment becomes valued. . . . Once employees are conscious that they and the users are engaged in coproduction, attention can focus on optimizing their interactive working relationship. . . . As a further consequence, improving working relationships and optimizing mutual adjustment processes can come to be valued by staff agency employees, substituting for the value conventionally placed on delineating roles and responsibilities and on the unilateral adjustment of line agencies to staff agencies (Barzelay, 1992:106–107).

State regulatory agencies may opt for negotiation between regulator and regulated over command and control enforcement due to the nature of regulation, as indicated by one study of water pollution control:

> Negotiation is carried on in various ways reflecting the officer's own style and his personal judgement as to the most fruitful approach to employ with a particular discharger. . . . Enforcement activity in pollution control is centered upon the handling of individual cases . . . [which] has the potential for fragmented and particularistic enforcement work since each case tends to be treated on its merits, according to its own special problems. Practical policy is expressed in the accumulation of individualized decisions (Hawkins, 1984: 141, 153).

According to Joel Handler, the decision-making process is characterized by informality, consultation, and persuasion, a style of regulation "rooted in *reciprocity*—the agency bargains on the less serious offenses, treats the regulated with respect, exchanges information, is responsive to the problems of compliance, and is considerate of good faith. Forbearance is exchanged for access, information, and compliance" (1996:60). In a comprehensive 50-state study of water quality regulation Hunter and Waterman similarly find that bargaining is "rampant" and conclude that state officials will "continue to rely quite heavily on bargaining, compromise, and negotiation with permittees . . . for pragmatic reasons" (1996: 226).

A recent four-state study of child care regulation identified different roles chosen by state inspectors of child care facilities, including the roles of persuader, bargainer, and enforcer. Inspectors in Pennsylvania, a state with an individualistic political culture, more often selected the roles of persuader and bargainer, compared to inspectors in North Carolina, a state with a hierarchial culture, who were more likely to choose the enforcer role indicating vigorous and punitive enforcement (Gormley, 1997:290–293).

States also opt for regulatory strategies other than strict law enforcement to secure compliance. Regulatory administration is being accomplished through self-regulation, voluntary compliance, private regulation, public disclosure, and liability requirements, among other mechanisms (see Bardach and Kagan, 1982: 217–299; Handler, 1996:133–168). Enforcement officials in motor carrier safety for the California State Highway Patrol, for example, are encouraged to achieve "voluntary compliance" and regard formal prosecution under the law as a failure. Some state environmental protection agencies prefer "telephone calls, site visits, warning letters, and conferences" over court action (Bardach and Kagan, 1982: 38–39). Keith Hawkins concludes:

> The voluntary compliance of the regulated is regarded by the agencies as the most desirable means of meeting water quality standards . . . [and] a

> relatively cheap method of achieving conformity. . . . Compliance takes on
> the appearance of voluntariness by the use of *bargaining*. . . . Bargaining
> implies the acquiescence of the regulated . . . [and] suggests some compro-
> mise from the rigours of penal enforcement (1984:122).

Terms such as entrepreneurial and innovative are often used to describe
leadership in state administration committed to customer choice, diffusion of authority, and competition in service delivery. Risk and failure are also associated
with such leadership. Research on innovation relevant to state and local governments suggests, according to Laurence Lynn, that such leadership is individual-
ized:

> Innovation is fueled by creativity. . . . Creativity is individual, a product of
> passion and intellect, and the natural inclination of iconoclasts who thrive
> on taking risks and challenging the status quo. Committees organized to rep-
> resent affected interests and to produce innovations through teamwork are
> extremely unlikely to be creative or the wellsprings of innovation, though
> they will congratulate themselves on having been just that. . . . An innovative
> organization is flexible to the point of being a bit chaotic. Turf is up for
> grabs. The ambitious, clever entrepreneur thrives. The intellectual tone is
> active, contentious, and exciting. Young turks challenge "the bureaucrats."
> Contempt is evident for seniority, expertise, and hierarchy. It is not who is
> right, but what is right, that counts (Lynn, 1997:97).

Lynn also observes that political skills—bargaining, negotiating, and collaborat-
ing—will likely be required to carry innovation into full implementation (1997:
91).

"Entrepreneurial" is often used to describe recent state leadership in economic development. Activist governors and economic officials have crafted initiatives to enter into partnership with private companies, underwrite product development, stimulate technology-based industry, target industries with venture
capital, reinvent production processes, subsidize business incubators, and seed
the development of value-added companies, among many other interventions in
the state economy. These state leaders believe they can influence "which businesses start, grow, innovate, develop and market new products, improve their
productivity, develop export markets, contract, decline, relocate, and fold"
(Fosler, 1988:319). In such cases the state becomes, according to Peter Eisinger,
"a risk-taker, a path-finder to new markets" (1988:9). State officials become
entrepreneurs, often investing public funds in high-risk projects in order to generate long-term results. This focus on "discovering, developing, expanding, and
creating new markets for indigenous industries" distinguishes this new brand of
state leadership from earlier experience, according to Paul Brace (1993:29).

Such high-risk ventures are obviously subject to failure. In some cases governors who have led entrepreneurial ventures to stimulate the economy have been

replaced with governors much less inclined to such endeavors, which, according to Brace, "underscores the fragility of state economic development efforts. Like a house of cards, they may be assembled with great care, yet, with a single jolt, come tumbling down" (1993:121). In Kansas, during an economic downturn in the mid-1980s, the chair of the state public employees retirement fund convinced the governor and other state officials to divert a significant portion of state retirement funds from secure low-interest securities into higher-risk investments with potential for big payoffs. Initial results were exceedingly favorable, but then a number of investments failed. The chair resigned amid allegations of conflicts of interest. Suits were filed challenging poor investment practices. High-risk ventures were sharply curtailed. Leadership here could be described as meteoric—rising in spectacular brilliance then plummeting into the depths of darkness.

C.   State Administration in Egalitarianism

Egalitarian administration may be an oxymoron. Egalitarians are suspicious of formal authority, particularly that based in hierarchial structures, division of labor and specialization, professional status and expertise—pillars upon which the field of public administration is founded. Administration requires structure which egalitarians naturally suspect because of likely inequities. So, how could egalitarians administer? Or, of relevance here, does any experience with state administration in egalitarianism even exist?[8]

Coyle suggests that egalitarian organizations tend to be "small or short-lived" (1997:74). Consequently, egalitarian principles may not be applicable for administering major functions of state government—many of which are sizable and require continuity. At the same time, egalitarian units may exist within large state bureaucracies, for example, as a research center or academic department within a large, complex state university; and a number of state agencies may exhibit egalitarian behavior on occasion. Two experiences with egalitarian organization within state government—state administration during the populist movement of the late 1800s, and state management of indigent defense—give some insight into state administration in egalitarianism. These experiences and others will be examined from the perspective of underlying values and concepts of authority, decision making, and leadership.

Research into the populist movement of the 1890s leaves little doubt that the populists were egalitarians of the purest sort (see Malecha, 1997; Ellis, 1993: 48–56). This time period also gives a rare snapshot in American history when egalitarians took control of government—at least a few state governments. Kan-

---

[8] Coyle observes that egalitarianism is "the lost culture of organization" and that a dearth of research is available on egalitarian organization (1997:73–77).

sas was a hotbed of the populist movement nationally and for two years populists took control of state government in Kansas.[9] Populist leadership in Kansas makes clear that equality was the underlying value of the movement—not simply equality under law, a hierarchial view, or even equality of opportunity, a view of individualism. Populists wanted equality of results; they saw government as the means for rectifying inequities (Ellis, 1993:49–53).

In his inaugural address of 1893, the newly elected populist Governor Lorenzo Lewelling declared: "The survival of the fittest is the government of brutes and reptiles, and such philosophy must give place to a government which recognizes human brotherhood. It is the province of government to protect the weak." (quoted in Ellis, 1993:200). Populist activist Frank Doster, who would two years later be elected chief justice of the Kansas Supreme Court, stated at the time: "All government and all necessity for government grows out of the fact of inequalities and that government which does not provide for the leveling and equalizing of the conditions which grow out of the unrestricted exercise of the natural powers of its citizens has failed in the purpose of its creation" (quoted in Ellis, 1993:54). Both Kansans were reflecting the aspirations written into the 1892 platform of the People's Party that "oppression, injustice, and poverty shall eventually cease in the land."

In Kansas, populist legislators sought to rectify inequities resulting from raw individualism through a broad range of egalitarian measures. Populists introduced and advocated legislation providing for regulation of railroad rates, telephone rates, and interest rates, liberal credit through coinage of silver, protection of the working man, public ownership of utilities, public employment of jobless, initiative and referendum, women's suffrage, assistance to those in economic distress, and the creation of an office of public defender, among others. The populists, however, were not successful in enacting a significant body of legislation. Apparently, as could be surmised from cultural theory, these egalitarians were poorly organized, lacked unity and discipline, and discovered traitors within their ranks (Argersinger, 1995:176–212). Populist rule in Kansas, often characterized by factional disputes, was short-lived. By the end of the 1890s Republicans had regained control of most state offices.

---

[9] In 1890, a year in which 125 seats in the Kansas House of Representative were up for election, Kansas populists running under the banner of the Kansas Alliance took control of 91 seats. No other state offices were up in 1890. Two years later, in the elections of 1892, Kansas populists, running this time under the imprimatur of the People's Party, elected a governor, a lieutenant governor, an attorney general, a secretary of state, a state treasurer, a state auditor, 25 of 40 state senate seats, and somewhere between 58 and 68 of 125 state house seats, depending on whose vote count was certified. From 1893 through 1894, these populists controlled the governorship, all state executive offices elected statewide, the state senate, and possibly the state house. For at least two years they ruled almost by themselves.

While little research has been published on populists as administrators, a profound commitment to social equality and justice would seemingly pervade their administration of state government.[10] Modern-day egalitarians—proponents of a new public administration—have similarly called for administration imbued with an ethical commitment to social justice and equality (see Marina, 1971; Frederickson, 1980). According to George Frederickson: "Administrators are not neutral. They should be committed to both good management and social equity as values, things to be achieved. . . . Simply put, new Public Administration seeks to change those policies and structures that systematically inhibit social equity," (1980:312). Further, representative democracy has allowed the "continuation of widespread unemployment, poverty, disease, ignorance, and hopelessness," conditions which are "morally reprehensible," and new public administrators as change agents should commit to rectifying such inequities (1980:310–321). Disciples of this new public administration are proselytizing an old populist faith.

One obligation of state government imbued with a commitment to social justice and equity is indigent defense, provision of which was advocated by the populists 70 years in advance of its becoming a Constitutional obligation of state governments. Speaking for the U.S. Supreme Court in *Gideon v. Wainwright*, Justice Hugo Black maintained that every defendant should stand equal under the law and have access to fair and impartial justice: "This noble ideal cannot be realized if the poor man charged with crime has to face his accusers without a lawyer to assist him." With this decision, the court mandated that state governments make legal defense available to any indigent accused of a felony at every stage of the legal proceedings against the accused. As a result, in every state in the Union, indigent defenders—sometimes called public defenders—are daily engaged in carrying out this Constitutional commitment to equal justice under the law.

Law professor and former public defender Charles Ogletree writes that young, idealistic public defenders embark on a legal career to fight injustice, represent the underdog, and aid the underprivileged who have been charged with a crime. Public defenders find motivation, according to Ogletree, in an heroic view of their work: "I saw myself as a kind of 'hero' of the oppressed, the one who fights against all odds, a sort of Robin Hood figure who can conquer what others cannot . . ." (Ogletree, 1993:1275). Another law professor and former defender agrees: "A lawyer performs good work when he helps to prevent the imprisonment of the poor, the outcast, and minorities in shameful conditions" (Babcock, 1983–84:178). Defenders develop empathy for the accused, see the

---

[10] Homer E. Socolofsky reports that Governor Lewelling stayed in a cheap, "dollar-a-day" room, sent state troops to protect miners from strikebreakers, and issued a "tramp circular" condemning local enforcement of vagrancy laws against the unemployed (1990:116–122).

defendant as a victim facing "a hostile world . . . the police, the prosecutor, the judge, and the jury. Within this hostile world the defender was the client's best ally" (Ogletree, 1993:1,286). With the scales of justice tilted toward law enforcers, defenders stand alone in assuring that the guarantee of equal justice afforded by the Bill of Rights is met.

Egalitarian values help indigent defenders cope with what they perceive as a hostile environment for their organization as well as for the accused but also call defenders to a higher purpose—championing social justice in society as a whole. The public demands stricter law enforcement, stiffer sentencing, and harsher punishments. Courts and jails are overburdened with defendants. Police and prosecutors have all the resources. Compassion for the accused and devotion to equal justice provide essential motivation for daily engagement in indigent defense. However, defenders' deep sense of injustice against a hostile public and politicians grandstanding on crime moves them to become political advocates for social justice. In Kansas, state agency staff committed themselves to educating the public "in order to create fair and just legislation" which meant organizing the agency in coalition with external allies to oppose reinstatement of the death penalty by the legislature (Flentje and Newton, 1995:41–52).

Authority in egalitarian organization is amorphous. Egalitarian disciples of the new public administration call for "integrative" solutions to the issue of authority and "search for less structured, less formal, less authoritative integrative techniques in publicly administered organizations" but come up short on answers (Frederickson, 1980:321–323). Trainers of public officials at the University of Virginia advocate a "communitarian strategy" based on democratic values in which

> [the] whole organization is based on team-ness . . . shared leadership and management as everyone's business. . . . A strategy is to urge everyone to take a mental promotion, to act as though they were personally responsible for the whole organization and community. . . . Teamness is an attitude . . . [t]he belief that each member is a teammate, not a customer or competitor (Roberts, 1995:5–10).

Egalitarians in mental health experiment with eliminating distinctions between patients and doctors (Swedlow, 1994).

Kansas populists had an idealized view of public authority which included aversion to the use of force or the intervention of government—except for the cause of equalizing conditions. Populist Governor Lewelling saw the issue of government authority as "how to make the State subservient to the individual, rather than to become his master. Government is a voluntary union for the common good" (quoted in Malecha, 1994:109). He preferred to avoid coercion in resolving conflict. Doster sought to "discover and enforce those laws of harmony which raise men above the barbarous antagonisms of the natural state into relations of unity and fraternity.'' Another populist advocated that government should be an ''agency through which the associated people of the nation would carry on universal co-operation. It would not be paternalism; that would be dead; but fraternalism—an association of brothers for the common good'' (Ellis, 1993: 54, 110).

In the Kansas state agency charged with administering indigent defense, the exercise of formal authority was avoided like the plague. Actual defense work was lodged in the hands of hundreds of public and private defenders who operated largely as sole practitioners—essentially subject to no supervision in their defense of the accused. The state board authorized by statute to supervise indigent defense exercised little or no direction, owing primarily to cooptation by staff and the criminal defense bar. Ironically, in an agency dominated by attorneys, the board had no written policies on the authority, appointment, or removal of the agency's director and subordinate officers, no bylaws for the conduct of board business, no official minutes of board meetings, and no written procedures for preparation of budgets, recruitment of personnel, or the conduct of external relations (Flentje and Newton, 1995).

Informal authority was exercised through a network of defenders, primarily chief public defenders operating in the field. They effectively neutralized any oversight by the board or the central staff of the agency. Over the agency's 13-year history, numerous management initiatives to account for costs, manage caseload, track cases, assess efficiencies, or negotiate contracts for defense were successfully thwarted. The constitutional mandate for equal justice, interpreted when necessary by state and federal courts, further immunized the agency from any serious incursion by legislative or executive officials. Professional norms of indigent defenders and the criminal defense bar, rather than any exercise of state authority, guided the internal operation of the agency.

One clear aspect of authority in egalitarian organization is the delineation of boundaries insulating the organization from its external environment. Kansas populists developed internal cohesion through rituals and sponsorship of various social, political, and cooperative service activities. Kansas populists and indigent defenders both solidified their followers and internal organization through their assault on external injustice. Committed to high purpose on the inside, egalitarian organizations challenge evil on the outside (Malecha, 1994:105). Indigent defenders in particular saw their agency as separate from a public hostile to the cause of equal justice. A survey of agency employees showed that while over 90% of the staff believed the agency was delivering a valuable service, a similar percentage believed the public did not value what the agency did. Defenders' perception of a public ill informed on criminal justice and elected officials ill advised on indigent defense served to unify staff in their struggle to assure equal justice for the accused.

The nature of decision making, like authority, in egalitarian organization is not completely clear. Little research has been conducted on the topic, particularly with respect to state administration. Egalitarian decision making likely approximates what Joel Handler describes as "unitary democracy" which "assumes a high degree of common interests and an equality of respect—more like friendship among its members. Thus, unitary democracy is characterized by face-to-face assembly and consensus" (1996:232). Organizations in which members have common identity, equal status, and shared interests, and are

> able to make decisions unanimously. . . . [I]n a great many decisions votes aren't taken. Rather, a consensus is reached. . . . [T]he desire for harmony creates informal pressure to reach unanimity. The norm of consensus drives the group to consider the common good, to draw the dissidents into the group, to encourage listening and empathy, and the development of moral bonds" (Handler, 1996:232–234).

In cases of disagreement, however, a second-order decision rule on consensus evolves, one which asks objecting members if they can "live with" a decision, in order to keep dissenters from leaving the group.

A requirement or norm of consensus in decision making challenges any organization's stability. Kansas populists assured consensus by specifically excluding merchants, lawyers, and bank owners from membership, and by purging traitors. Members who dissented from the faith or provoked dissension, discouraged participation, or disparaged other members were expelled and shunned, but Populists continued to suffer from factions and disorganization (Malecha, 1994: 98). Kansas indigent defenders used the absence of consensus to defer decisions on the internal management of the agency which eventually subjected the organization to external scrutiny and criticism.

Leadership in egalitarian organization is similarly murky. Trainers at the University of Virginia profess:

> Instead of solitary heroes or authoritative directors, we focus on helping people to exercise servant leadership as stewards, coaches, facilitators, and enablers. . . . Power dynamics shift from control to commitment and empowerment. . . . All employees, even first line workers, can contribute to the work of leadership, and share more self-management responsibility" (Roberts, 1995:7–8).

This assertion coincides with Kansas populists who declared: "We have no leaders. We formulate our demands in our own way. . . . We never have and never will permit dictation inside, nor will we from outside the order" (Malecha, 1994: 99–100). At the same time a number of charismatic leaders emerged in the populist movement and gained national attention, for example, "Sockless" Jerry Simpson and the popular Mary Elizabeth Lease, who urged farmers to "raise more hell and less corn." Employees of the state agency for indigent defense were mostly critical of agency leaders, though supportive of their immediate supervisors. Informal leadership dominated the agency.

V. GOOD STATE ADMINISTRATION AS CULTURAL ALLIANCE

Viewing state administration in a cultural context reveals distinguishing value biases and social relations of pure cultural types (see Figure 3). The underlying beliefs and connected social practices of state administration point to what energizes and what constrains different forms of administration. With this framework the strengths and vulnerabilities of distinct cultures also become more discernible. A culturally based assessment may be useful to state administrators in self-evaluation, that is, in examining the values and practices underpinning individual management styles or administration within their own agencies or administration of state government in general. At minimum such evaluation provides an alternative to assessment using ambiguous concepts such as effectiveness and efficiency. Understanding the culture of state administration may provide an alternative framework for improving administration—in redirecting state administration through insights into the cultural basis of administrative history, patterns of current management, and even predictions concerning future direction.

Cultural theory provides insight into sources of energy and inertia in state administration. For example, service in the public interest energizes administration in hierarchy; individual discretion and competition motivates administration in individualism; and pursuit of equality inspires administration in egalitarianism. Centralized authority constrains administration by both individualists and egalitarians. Individual deviation, for example, whistle blowing or disloyalty, wreaks havoc on hierarchic administration.

The strengths and vulnerabilities of different cultural forms of administration are also more visible. For example, according to Coyle:

> When value agreement and factual certainty are high, the corresponding organizational form (and culture) is hierarchy. In these cases, group identity and role differentiation are strong. . . . It is knowledge that provides order; when knowledge is complete, the organization is like a fully analyzable machine, held together by standard operating procedure. . . . [H]ierarchies excel at replicating routine tasks, but are ill-suited to environmental turbulence (Coyle, 1997:63, 66).

Hierarchial administration tends toward state paternalism and dampens individual initiative.

Administration in individualism offers responsiveness and adaptability but is subject to higher risk of failure or even complete collapse; it stimulates experi-

State Administration in Fatalism

• unknown.

State Administration in Hierarchy

• serving the public interest through: 1) rule of law;
2) hierarchial structures; 3) division of labor and
specialization; 4) merit selection of personnel; and
5) standards generated through scientific method
and technical expertise;

• unifying administration through centralized
executive control;

• decision making by those in positions of authority
with decisions executed through written rules and
regulations;

• insulating administration from politics; and

• expanding the professionalization of work and
professionalizing workforce through full-time
occupations and professional career paths.

State Administration in Individualism

• enhancing individual liberty and restraining
government through customer choice, diffusion of
authority, and reciprocity in decision making;

• promoting customer choice as the underlying
value: 1) state services are viewed as contracts in
which customers receive specified benefits at a
certain cost; 2) quality of service is measured in
terms of customer satisfaction with benefits and
costs; and 3) service providers are accountable to
customers;

• diffusing authority in service delivery through: 1)
local autonomy, home rule, charter schools, and
other forms of local control; 2) competition and
privatization through contracts, franchises,
vouchers, and sale of assets; and 3) empowerment
of citizens through neighborhood associations,
voluntarism, and coprovision;

• decision making through reciprocity, negotiation,
mutual adjustment, and bargaining; and

• exercising innovative and entrepreneurial
leadership, with high risk of failure, in stimulating
the economy and promoting customer choice.

State Administration in Egalitarianism

• imbuing organization and employees with ideals of
socal justice and equality;

• promoting equality of conditions;

• avoiding the exercise of formal authority by
cooperating through informal means such as
teamwork, harmony, fraternity, brotherhood and
sisterhood, and professional networks;

• insulating organization and employees from
external environment through internal activities
solidifying organizational cohesion and critique of
external social inequities and injustice;

• deciding the quality and quantity of work through
norms of employee groups and associated
professions;

• decision making through direct participation and
consensus among employees with equal status; and

• leading through stewardship, coaching, facilitation,
and enabling.

Figure 3   State administration within political cultures.

mentation and innovation but shows little concern for resulting inequities. Such administration can function in an environment of rapid change, conflicting demands, and turmoil. Its preference for restrictions on public authority limits public accountability and makes administration susceptible to conflicts of interest resulting from negotiated deals.

Egalitarian organization, as Coyle has indicated, is likely small and short-lived and therefore may not be capable of administering large, complex state functions which require continuity. Egalitarianism aspires to decision making through direct participation and consensus among equals and challenges managers to work with idealistic forms—organization without formal authority and leadership without formal leaders—which may spawn stalemate and disorganization. The norm of consensus in decision making likely precludes quick action, defers action on matters of internal conflict, and may produce conformity in outlook. Egalitarian administration also acts as a constant thorn in the side of society as a whole by pointing out existing social inequities and injustice.

The inherent vulnerabilities of each cultural type suggests that public institutions would not mirror any one culture but are more likely organizational compounds in which different cultures are stronger or weaker (Wildavsky, 1989:107). According to Coyle:

> The fundamental types may best be thought of as tendencies or pressures rather than organizational forms. Other organizational structures may develop as hybrids, and gradual movement from one pole to another through trial-and-error experience more plausibly describes organizational change. . . . Even supposedly unfettered markets move far enough on the grid and group axes to enforce basic rules against force and fraud, for example. And as long as human perception is flawed and individualized and cooperation and understanding depend in part on the imperfections of language, hierarchy can never be pure. In the case of hybrids, the basic types indicate the kinds of tensions they internalize or the dissonance they will experience (1997:64–65).

Good state administration, then, would likely be comprised of alliances among these political cultures.[11]

By way of illustration, state administration as an alliance of the cultures of hierarchy and individualism would be an organizational compound valuing both liberty and order, which could take numerous forms depending on the strength of the cultural elements. For example, such organization could strive to derive the benefits of a market orientation by expanding customer choice while

---

[11] Marshall et al. explore this concept of cultural alliances with respect to state school statutes and more generally as an ongoing tension among cultural values (1989:146–150, 162–174).

retaining the accountability of public organization. Or, using the counsel of Osborne and Gaebler, state administration could delineate between the functions of steering and rowing, retaining the steering duties within government and assigning rowing—that is, the delivery of services—to private providers. Current state developments in competition and privatization of service delivery, indeed, seek to foster both liberty and order.

State administration as an alliance of hierarchy and egalitarianism would be an organizational compound valuing both order and equality. Such organization might have "loose-tight" qualities, for example, tight in serving the public interest under the rule of law and loose in allowing public employees to determine through agreement how best to serve those ends. Many state agencies have advanced both order and equality by professionalizing work and the work force and then relying on the authority and decisions of professionals to carry out public purpose.

An alliance of individualism and egalitarianism—of liberty and equality—may be an unlikely compact for state administration. Proponents of such a compound would have to be convinced that enhancing liberty—for example, by expanding customer choice—could achieve equality of conditions. Further, an organizational compound disconnected from the rule of law is not readily apparent in state administration.

In sum, viewing state administration in cultural context illuminates cultural biases and related practices and offers a cultural perspective in gaining self-knowledge and undertaking self-assessment. Such knowledge could presumably be applied to improving state administration. No cultural type of state administration is best in any universal sense; each has strengths and vulnerabilities. One may be more applicable than another under certain environmental conditions. Historically, society has been shifting away from beliefs and social relations based in hierarchial culture toward individualism and egalitarianism. Good state administration is moving in these directions as well but will likely continue as organizational compounds relying upon an alliance of cultures.

REFERENCES

Argersinger, P. H. (1995). *The Limits of Agrarian Radicalism: Western Populism and American Politics*, University Press of Kansas, Lawrence.

Babcock, B. A. (1983–84). Defending the guilty, *Cleveland State Law Review* 32(1):175–187.

Bardach, E., and Kagan, R. A. (1982). *Going by the Book*, Temple University Press, Philadelphia.

Barzelay, M. (1992). *Breaking Through Bureaucracy: A New Vision for Managing in Government*, University of California Press, Berkeley.

Bowling, C. J., and Wright, D. S. (1998). Public administration in the fifty states: a half-century administrative revolution, *State and Local Government Review* 30(1):52–64.

Brace, P. (1993). *State Government and Economic Performance*, Johns Hopkins University Press, Baltimore.

Chai, S., and Swedlow, B. (1998). *Culture and Social Theory: Aaron Wildavsky*, Transaction Publishers, New Brunswick, NJ.

Chi, K. S., and Jasper, C. (1998). *Private Practices: A Review of Privatization in State Government*, Council of State Governments, Lexington, KY.

Conant, J. (1992). Executive branch reorganization in the states, 1965–1991, *Book of the States. 1992–93*, Council of State Governments, Lexington, KY, pp. 64–73.

Coyle, D. J. (1997). A cultural theory of organizations, *Culture Matters: Essays in Honor of Aaron Wildavsky* (R. J. Ellis and M. Thompson, eds.), Westview Press, Boulder, CO, pp. 59–78.

Coyle, D. J., and Ellis, R. J., eds. (1994). *Politics, Policy, and Culture*, Westview Press, Boulder, CO.

de Leon, L. (1993). As plain as 1, 2, 3 . . . and 4 ethics and organizational structure, *Administration and Society* 25(3):293–316.

de Tocqueville, A. (1945). *Democracy in America*, (P. Bradley, ed.), Alfred A. Knopf, New York.

Douglas, M. (1978). *Cultural Bias* (Occasional Paper 35), Royal Anthropological Institute of Great Britain and Ireland, London.

Elazar, D. J. (1966). *American Federalism: A View from the States*, Thomas Y. Crowell, New York.

Eisinger, P. (1988). *The Rise of the Entrepreneurial State*, University of Wisconsin Press, Madison.

Elling, R. C. (1992). *Public Management in the States: A Comparative Study of Administrative Performance and Politics*, Praeger, Westport, CT.

Ellis, R. J., and Thompson, M., eds. (1997). *Culture Matters: Essays in Honor of Aaron Wildavsky*, Westview Press, Boulder, CO.

Ellis, R., and Wildavsky, A. (1989). *Dilemmas of Presidential Leadership from Washington Through Lincoln*, Transaction Publishers, New Brunswick, NJ.

Ellis, R. J. (1993). *American Political Cultures*, Oxford University Press, New York.

Fiske, A. P. (1991). *Structures of Social Life: The Four Elementary Forms of Human Relations*, Free Press, New York.

Flentje, H. E., and Newton, J. P. III (1995). *Indigent Defense in Kansas: A Report on State Policy and Management*, Hugo Wall School of Urban and Public Affairs, Wichita State University, Wichita.

Fosler, R. S., ed. (1988). *The New Economic Role of American States*, Oxford University Press, New York.

Frederickson, H. G. (1980). *New Public Administration*, University of Alabama Press, Birmingham.

Gormley, W. T. Jr. (1997). Regulatory enforcement: accommodation and conflict in four states, *Public Administration Review*, 57(4):285–293.

Governing the American States: A Handbook for New Governors (1978). National Governors' Association, Washington, DC.   .

Handler, J. F. (1996). *Down from Bureaucracy: The Ambiguity of Privatization and Empowerment*, Princeton University Press, Princeton, NJ.

Hawkins, K. (1984). *Environment and Enforcement*, Clarendon Press, Oxford.

Hunter, S. and Waterman, R. W. (1996). *Enforcing the Law: The Case of the Clean Water Acts*, M. E. Sharp, Armonk, NY.

Kansas (1913). *Session Laws of Kansas* (chapter 305), State Printer, Topeka.

Kansas (1917). *Session Laws of Kansas* (chapter 299), State Printer, Topeka.

Kettl, D. F. (1993). *Sharing Power: Public Governance and Private Markets*, Brookings, Washington, DC.

Kincaid, J. (1982). Introduction, *Political Culture, Public Policy, and the American States* (J. Kincaid, ed.), Institute for the Study of Human Issues, Philadelphia, pp. 1–23.

Kost, J. M. (1996). *New Approaches to Public Management: The Case of Michigan*, Brookings, Washington, DC.

Krane, D., Rigos, P. N., and Hill, M., eds. (forthcoming). *Home Rule in America: A Fifty-State Handbook*, Congressional Quarterly, Washington, DC.

Lynn, L. E. Jr. (1997). Innovation and the public interest: Insights from the private sector, *Innovation in American Government: Challenges, Opportunities, and Dilemmas* (A. A. Altshuler and R. D. Behn, eds.), Brookings, Washington, DC, pp. 83–103.

Malecha, G. L. (1994). A cultural analysis of populism in late-nineteenth century America, *Politics, Policy, and Culture* (D. J. Coyle and R. J. Ellis, eds.), Westview Press, Boulder, CO, pp. 93–116.

Marini, F., ed. (1971). *Toward a New Public Administration*, Chandler, Scranton, PA.

Marshall, C., Mitchell, D., and Wirt, F. (1989). *Culture and Education Policy in the American States*, Falmer, New York.

Mead, L. M., ed. (1997). *The New Paternalism*, Bookings Institution Press, Washington, DC.

Mead, L. M. (1997). The rise of paternalism, *The New Paternalism* (L. M. Mead, ed.), Brookings Institution Press, Washington, DC, pp. 1–38.

Miller, D. Y. (1991). The impact of political culture on patterns of state and local government expenditures, *Publius: The Journal of Federalism* 21(2):83–100.

Ogletree, C. J. Jr. (1993). Beyond justifications: seeking motivations to sustain public defenders, *Harvard Law Review* 106: 1239–1294.

Osborne, D. (1988). *Laboratories of Democracy*. Harvard Business School Press, Boston.

Osborne, D., and Gaebler, T. (1992). *Reinventing Government: How the Entrepreneurial Spirit Is Transforming the Public Sector*, Addison-Wesley, Reading, MA.

Osborne, D., and Plastrik, P. (1997). *Banishing Bureaucracy: The Five Strategies for Reinventing Government*, Addison-Wesley, Reading, MA.

Percy, S. L., and Baker, P. C. (1980). *Citizen Coproduction of Public Services: An Annotated Bibliography*, Council of Planning Librarians Bibliographies, Chicago.

Powers, K. J., and Thompson, F. (1994). Managing coprovision: using expectancy theory to overcome the free-rider problem, *Journal of Public Administration Research and Theory* 4(2):179–196.

Roberts, D. D. (1995). Delivering on democracy: high performance government for Virginia, *University of Virginia Newsletter* 71:1–11.

Shover, N., Clelland, D. A., and Lynxwiler, J. (1986). *Enforcement or Negotiation: Constructing a Regulatory Bureaucracy*, State University of New York Press, Albany.

Socolofsky, H. E. (1990). *Kansas Governors*, University Press of Kansas, Lawrence.

Stone, A. A. (1975). *Mental Health and Law: A System in Transition*, U.S. Government Printing Office, Washington, DC.

Swedlow, B. (1994). Cultural influences on policies concerning mental health, *Politics, Policy, and Culture* (D. J. Coyle and R. J. Ellis, eds.), Westview, Boulder, CO, pp. 71–89.

Thompson, M., Ellis, R., and Wildavsky, A. (1990). *Cultural Theory*, Westview Press, Boulder, CO.

Thompson, M., and Wildavsky, A. (1986). A cultural theory of information bias in organizations, *Journal of Management Studies* 23(3):273–286.

Wildavsky, A. (1987). Choosing preferences by constructing institutions: a cultural theory of preference formation, *American Political Science Review* 81(1):3–21.

Wildavsky, A. (1990). Introduction: Administration without hierarchy? Bureaucracy without authority?, *Public Administration: The State of the Discipline* (N. B. Lynn and A. Wildavsky, eds.), Chatham House, Chatham, NJ, pp. xiii–xix.

Wildavsky, A. (1991). A cultural theory of leadership, *Leadership and Politics* (B. D. Jones, ed.), University Press of Kansas, Lawrence, pp. 87–113.

Wildavsky, A. (1991). *The Rise of Radical Egalitarianism*, American University Press, Washington, DC.

Wilson, J. Q. (1997). Paternalism, democracy, and bureaucracy, *The New Paternalism* (L. M. Mead, ed.), Brookings Institution Press, Washington, DC, pp. 330–343.

Wirt, F. M. (1977). School policy culture and state decentralization, *The Politics of Education* (J. D. Scribner, ed.), National Society for the Study of Education, Chicago, pp. 164–187.

Wirt, F. (1982). Does control follow the dollar? School policy, state-local linkages, and political culture, *Political Culture, Public Policy, and the American States*, (J. Kincaid, ed.), Institute for the Study of Human Issues, Philadelphia, pp. 81–100.

Wirt, F. M. (1991). 'Soft' concepts and 'hard' data: a research review of Elazar's political culture, *Publius: The Journal of Federalism* 21(2):1–13.

5
Governors as Chief Administrators and Managers

F. Ted Hebert
University of Utah, Salt Lake City, Utah

Governors have been near the center of the recent reinvigoration of American state governments and the general enhancement of their governing capacities. In this era of greater state responsibility, the governor's role has expanded, making it easier for governors to influence both public policy and administration. Many states have enlarged their governors' staffs and strengthened governors' positions so that they can better cope with the demands of the office.

Individually and working together through their regional and national associations, today's governors have assumed important roles in national policy debates. They have spoken out forcefully on welfare reform, education policy, health policy, and many other fields. They seek to influence policies of the federal government that directly and indirectly affect state administration. Governors have led efforts to reform the federal system, sought the devolution of federal programs to the states, and encouraged expansion of state responsibilities.

The governor has emerged as a prominent policy leader on the American scene in the late 20th century (Herzik, 1991). This marks the latest phase in development of an office that has evolved slowly over the course of American history. Understanding the present relationship between governors and state administrative agencies requires both a historical perspective and knowledge of the position of governors in the states today, including the wide variation among the states. In all of the states, the governor's position as "chief executive" leads people to hold the chief executive to some degree accountable for actions of administrative agencies. Therefore, it is in the governor's interest to attend to agency management (Beyle, 1996; Muchmore, 1983; Ransone, 1982). Numerous studies have shown, however, that governors do not necessarily dominate state administrative agencies (Abney and Lauth, 1986; Brudney and Hebert, 1987). They compete for influence with the legislature, with interest groups, and even with federal agencies.

Terry Sanford, former governor of North Carolina, was an early observer who noted the important role that governors could play. Thirty years ago he catalogued state weaknesses, observing that the states at the time could be called indecisive, antiquated, timid, unresponsive, and unwilling to face their problems, especially those of the cities (Sanford, 1967). However, regarding governors, Sanford saw great potential in gubernatorial leadership, pointing out that every governor had leadership potential and an important role in both molding public opinion and managing state government. "[The governor] must prod the institutions of state government to the service of the people" (Sanford, 1967:185).

Governors of the late 20th century are no longer the " 'flowery old courthouse politicians,' 'machine dupes,' 'political pipsqueaks,' and 'good-time Charlies' " that Larry Sabato (1983:1) describes from the earlier part of the century.

> Governors today are more concerned about the substantive work of the office than about its ceremonial aspects. Once parochial officers whose concerns rarely extended beyond boundaries of their home states and whose responsibilities frequently were slight, governors have gained major new powers that have increased their influence in national as well as state councils (Sabato, 1983:2).

In taking the position of policy managers today, governors are assuming a broader set of responsibilities than they held during most of American history.

I. THE DEVELOPING GOVERNORSHIP

As states created their governmental systems during and just after the Revolutionary War, they provided for legislative assemblies and governors, but the governors' positions they created varied widely in type and function. Several states established plural executives, while others established a post filled by a single person. Several created popularly elected governors' posts, but others set up governorships chosen by the legislature. All but three states specified a one-year term, and many limited reeligibility (Kallenbach, 1966:15–18). Generally, the states severely limited their governors' powers. A common feature was an executive council to advise, assist, and even restrict the governor. Few governors had veto authority, and few had an unlimited ability to grant pardons.

Beginning weak, the governors were in some respects weakened further in the early 19th century. Jeffersonian and Jacksonian democracy introduced widespread popular election and established the long-ballot tradition of separate elections to fill various state administrative posts. To the benefit of the chief executives, however, more of the governors themselves came to be chosen by popular election rather than by legislative appointment. This helped to establish a foundation of gubernatorial authority separate from the legislature and to strengthen separation of powers at the state level.

As the 19th century progressed, the governors recorded other gains and losses. The veto power became more common, and governors' terms were lengthened. With the progressive movement at century's end, though, the number of administrative agencies in state government multiplied, and many states placed some of these new agencies under boards or commissions over which governors had only limited authority or no authority at all.

During the Progressive era, prominent governors emerged as policy leaders. Several not only affected their own states but became nationally prominent as well. This group included Theodore Roosevelt in New York, Woodrow Wilson in New Jersey, and Robert La Follette in Wisconsin.

A. Development of Governors as Administrative Managers

Administrative management, characterized by strong executive leadership and efforts to centralize control, characterizes the development of the modern presidency in the 20th century. The federal government led the way in recognizing the need for both strong executive leadership and emergence of a separate administrative "branch." For the most part, states and their chief executives lagged significantly behind. Although some states undertook important administrative reforms, these often followed in the wake of such notable federal reform efforts as the Taft Commission in 1912, the Brownlow Committee in the 1930s, and the two Hoover commissions following World War II.

Central to all of these major reform ventures at the federal level were attempts to strengthen the chief executive, to emphasize the president's managerial role (Arnold, 1986). Especially with expanding federal activities in the 1930s, the Brownlow Committee sought to enhance the chief executive's ability to set managerial direction and to effectively control administrative agencies. "To administrative theorists and reformers, it was self-evident that the presidency must perform as the manager of the bureaucratic state. The managerial presidency is the product of that understanding" (Arnold, 1986:362).

Reformers urged that states adopt this administrative management paradigm, too. Its proponents (notably Luther Gulick and A. E. Buck in the 1930s) argued for structural reforms that would help the states enhance executive management and thereby strengthen governors. They argued for a reduction in the number of state agencies, for concentration of executive authority, for formal recognition of the governor's cabinet, and for clear lines of agency accountability to the governor (Garnett, 1980). Accomplishing these goals in the states was a difficult task, made more difficult by the need to pass constitutional amendments (sometimes significant ones) and to eliminate the separate election of persons to fill executive offices. Additionally, strong interest groups protested abolishing independent boards and commissions (e.g., higher education boards, insurance commissions), and even some governors were less than fully enthusiastic about the reforms—perhaps unsure that the gains were worth the political cost of achieving them.

Many of the state executive branch reforms that have succeeded over the decades have effectively consolidated separate state agencies into larger departments, some of them collapsing over 200 separate agencies into 30 or fewer departments. Potentially, at least, this sort of state government modernization has strengthened governors, especially where full cabinet systems have been created and governors have been given power to name agency directors and department heads. To make this type of reform complete, most independent boards and commissions must be eliminated (and their jobs assigned to appointed cabinet members). Similarly, many formerly elected offices might be made appointive.

Some states have settled for a reduction in the total number of agencies through more modest restructuring, leaving in place various independent boards and commissions and numerous elected officials. This type of less extensive reform has been labeled a ''traditional''reorganization (Bell, 1974), but even it realizes some of the goals reformers set out. However, it fails to create a strong gubernatorial cabinet system, one with a limited number of appointed executives reporting to the governor. Over the decades, though, the traditional approach to reform has been the most commonly employed (Conant, 1992).

There is a third type of reform, one that attempts to hold a middle ground. It is the least commonly adopted. The ''secretary/coordinator'' reform consolidates agencies into superdepartments headed by gubernatorial designees, but the agencies themselves retain considerable operating independence. Thus, while it has some of the form of a cabinet system, the individual agencies (within the larger departments) more easily escape central direction and control (Conant, 1992).

B. The Governor's Cabinet

Whether or not a state has formally adopted a ''cabinet system'' as an organizational arrangement, the governor may assemble key department heads and agency managers to form a cabinet. Scholars examining the evolution of the President's cabinet at the federal level have noted that many of its members today are not appointed solely for the advice and counsel they can give the President, nor just for their abilities to manage the agencies they will head, but rather they are chosen for a combination of reasons that may include those two as well as close connections the persons chosen have to particular interest groups or the ties they have to political party factions (Heclo, 1977). Appointments made in this way serve some the chief executive's purposes and may even help cement relations to some administrative departments, but they probably diminish the cabinet's value as a collective source of advice for the President.

Governors assembling a cabinet must address similar challenges on the state level. Persons named to cabinet positions are chosen for a variety of reasons. Collectively, though, the governor hopes to have a cabinet that can further the administration's policies.

States vary in their use of organized cabinet structures. In some states where governors hold regularly scheduled cabinet meetings, these are open to the public and to media representatives, and consequently they are formal sessions where little of substance is accomplished. In others they are closed to the public. Twelve states have no formal cabinet system at all, but 24 have a cabinet system that is required either by the state constitution or by statute. The remaining 14 have cabinet systems founded on state tradition or that operate because particular governors have chosen to establish them (Council of State Governments, 1996).

State executive branch reforms and the expanded use of cabinets (and even subcabinets with a functional focus) provide part of the context in which today's governors serve as "chief administrators." To understand how governors carry out their management tasks in these systems, it is critical to recognize that oversight of administration is only one part of the governor's job—and for some, it is not even the most important part. As Conant noted, "while structural consolidation and enhancement of the governor's formal powers may be necessary conditions for improving executive branch performance, they are by no means sufficient. Some governors will have very little interest in administrative management. . . . [Others] will have little aptitude for it" (Conant, 1992:72). Further, the press of other state affairs and limitations on the governor's time reduce the attention that the governor can give to supervising administration, regardless of the formal structure in place for doing so. The balance of this chapter explores the job of the governor as it relates to administration and the mechanisms and tools that are available to a governor who seeks to influence administrative agencies.

II. GOVERNORS AS POLICY ADMINISTRATORS

The state executive establishments over which governors assume oversight responsibilities have exploded in recent decades. In 1970, there were 2,755,000 state employees, but by 1995 that number had grown to 4,719,000. During that same 25-year period, states added many new agencies to their administrative structures, and others became more common across the states. Among the newer but nevertheless important departments, divisions, and bureaus are those concerned with each of the following topics: energy; arts; environmental affairs;

mass transit; Medicaid; ethics; community affairs; drug abuse; and consumer protection. Even with the organizational simplification that may have eased governors' administrative chores, in important respects their responsibilities have grown significantly more complex. They must confront a multitude of major new policy issues.

A. The Governor's Roles and Responsibilities

Thad Beyle (1996), drawing on the handbook for new governors prepared by the National Governors' Association and other sources, identified a long list of duties governors must assume: head of the executive branch; legislative leader; head of party; national figure; family member; ceremonial chief; intergovernmental actor; policy leader; and chief crisis manager. Add to these the possibility of seeking reelection or election to another office (U.S. Senate or even President or Vice President) and hoping to leave a legacy of his or her incumbency, the governor's role becomes even more complex. Further, unpredictable events often expand or restrict a governor's freedom of action, complicating the choices the governor must make.

Because the public expects governors to assume responsibility for managing executive agencies in their "chief executive" capacities, it is difficult for them to avoid this responsibility. Some governors have noted the prominent importance they attach to management. Lynn Muchmore quotes Governor Calvin Rampton of Utah (1965–77) as saying, "If a Governor is going to do his job, he has got to be the manager," and Governor Dan Walker of Illinois (1973–77) as declaring even more strongly, "What counts is management, and there isn't enough emphasis on management in government. . . . [W]e have to get the Governors to concentrate on management" (Muchmore, 1981:184, 243–244). Governor John Ashcroft of Missouri (1985–92) wrote, "If government does its job well . . . the governor receives the credit; if government seems to be operating for its own benefit without regard for the people it's designed to serve, the governor gets the blame" (Ashcroft, 1991:75).

Several scholars have sought to identify principal elements in the governor's management task and to better understand relationships to administrative agencies. Muchmore (1983) describes gubernatorial management as consisting of four components: basic stewardship (concern to avoid ethical breakdown, even in a minor agency); response to crisis (natural or human-caused, again in any agency); administrative routine (imposed by state or federal law); and active manager (setting a policy agenda). She dubs the first three of these components "custodial relationships," but notes that they are the relationships that account for most of the contact governors have with agencies. This is so despite the extensive efforts of recent reforms to strengthen governors' abilities to engage in policy management.

In a particularly careful study of one governor's involvement with administrative agencies, Martha Weinberg (1977) described Gov. Francis Sargent's relationships with agencies in Massachusetts. She noted that the governor had only limited control over development of relations with agencies. Rather, governors monitor some agencies carefully because they are large or because any crisis that might occur in them would be spectacular in nature, and the potential fallout for the governor would be disastrous. A few smaller agencies may be monitored because of prior crises, events that the governor feels must be managed to either gain or retain public support. Some others are managed closely because they represent particular policy interests of the governors. Most agencies, though—by far the largest number—are simply left alone; the governor pays them little attention and makes little or no effort to actively manage them.

Raymond Cox III (1991:55) notes that "the shift from a custodial, administrative style to a proactive, policy focused style is key to understanding the modern role of the governor." Today's governors seem to recognize that they will be judged by their success in policymaking and implementation. The reduction of federal funds available to the states has compelled governors to assume a larger policy leadership role, and they are expected to overcome limitations that may be imposed by institutional arrangements, finances, and even state personnel restrictions. Cox (1991:66) suggests that the governor can carry out this policy responsibility by taking "an expanded view of management as a tool of policymaking."

Today's governors are younger, better educated, more thoroughly trained, and a more heterogeneous group than they were in the past (Beyle, 1996). They are better prepared to use the organizational and institutional tools that are available to them for policy making and management, and in recent years the quality of these tools has been improving significantly. The governor's appointive power has been expanded; governors' office staffs are larger and more complex; and planning and budget offices are better prepared to provide the policy analysis capability required by a governor engaged in policy leadership.

B. The Governor's Policy Management Tools

Reformers hoped that creating a cleaner hierarchical structure, with the governor at the top, would make it possible for the chief executive to control agencies and more easily influence both policy and administration. Eliminating the election of agency heads and abolishing independent boards and commissions were steps to give the governors direct access to a wider range of agencies. Most important, reformers believed that governors would be better able to influence and control agencies if they were given appointment and removal power over agency directors (Conant, 1992). Beyle and Dalton (1981) confirmed through interviews of former governors that the chief executives themselves believed that these changes were important ones.

1. Appointment and Removal Power of the Governor

Governors may have responsibility for making hundreds of appointments, naming persons to top departmental positions, to many second-level posts, and to slots on numerous boards and other bodies. Often, important appointments are subject to state senate confirmation (and sometimes confirmation by both legislative chambers). In some states, the total number of appointments the governor makes has been reduced by placing many smaller administrative units under larger "umbrella" departments, giving the department heads authority to name smaller units' directors or providing that they be named according to merit system procedures.

The 1994 American State Administrators Project survey of directors of state agencies asked respondents to report the mechanism of their appointment.[1] In that study an "agency" might have been at any of several hierarchical levels, depending on how a particular state was organized. The results revealed that 25.2% of respondents indicated their positions were covered by their state's civil service or merit system and 3.5% reported that they were popularly elected to their positions. Others were politically appointed, with 19.5% named by a department head; 17.4% named by a board, commission, or some other means (such as by a legislative committee); and 34.3% appointed by the governor. The governor's appointees were almost evenly split between those who required legislative confirmation (18.7%) and those who did not (15.6%).

In making appointments, governors seek persons who have the ability to manage the agencies they will head. For this they need individuals with both appropriate administrative skills and professional competence in the particular substantive area of the agency's activities. In some cases, that means an incoming governor will retain some agency heads from a previous administration, even if the previous governor was from the opposite political party (Beyle and Dalton, 1981). Weighing against doing so, however, is a third criterion governors use to choose appointees. They want administrators who will demonstrate loyalty to policy directions the governor chooses. By selecting fellow party members, governors may help ensure loyalty.

Considering that elections continue to be used to fill directorship positions in some administrative areas (most prominently in education and agriculture

---

[1] These data are from the American State Administrators Project (ASAP) survey, a mailed survey of heads of 93 types of agencies in all 50 states. Because some agencies are not represented in all states, the total population of agency heads surveyed was 3365. There were 1229 respondents, for a response rate of 37%. I appreciate Prof. Deil S. Wright's making these data available, and acknowledge support of the ASAP survey provided by the Earhart Foundation of Ann Arbor, MI.

agencies in some states, but occasionally in others as well) and that alternative mechanisms are used to fill a variety of agency head positions in many states, governors generally have only limited appointment authority. Beyle and Dalton (1981) tracked changes in governors' appointment powers that have resulted from reorganization efforts and found that the number of elected positions has declined only slowly. That continues to be the case. Examining 11 specific positions across the 50 states, in 1965 there were 298 posts filled by election; by 1980 the number dropped to 286; by 1996, the number had dropped further to 280 (Beyle and Dalton, 1981; Council of State Governments, 1996). Thus governors cannot rely on the appointment power to influence or control agencies in all circumstances. At best, they must couple it with other mechanisms of influence.

The "flip side" of appointments is the power to remove. Newly elected governors, or even governors who want to make administrative reassignments, might find it important to be able to remove appointees from administrative positions. To the extent that a governor sees the chief executive's office as analogous to a private sector CEO's position, having and potentially using the removal authority may be especially important. Former Gov. James Edwards of South Carolina (1975–79) reflected that position: "I firmly believe that if I'm the boss, I should be able to give you walking papers if I don't like the way you part your hair" (Muchmore, 1981:92). However, governors do not have unlimited removal authority. Although there is great variation from state to state, constitutional and statutory provisions in many states restrict the scope of each governor's removal powers (limiting it to certain positions or excluding others), provide that removals be accomplished only for cause (for certain enumerated reasons), or provide specific procedures that must be followed to remove even persons the governor has appointed (Beyle and Mouw, 1989). Beyond these legal limitations, governors may find themselves politically restrained in exercising removal authority. Since they often consider the wishes of various interest groups and party factions as they fill positions, they may have to consider those same interests before an appointee is removed. Further, the vacant position must be filled. Cox (1991:66) quotes Gov. Norman Bangerter of Utah (1985–93) as saying, "You never replace someone until you know you have found a replacement who can improve the situation."

2. The Executive Budget

Beginning with adoption of the executive budget process early in the 20th century (in Ohio in 1910 and Maryland in 1916), governors have gradually been extended the power of executive budgeting. Today it is the process followed in almost every state. Governors are responsible for preparing a budget and submitting it to the legislature for consideration and adoption. In doing so, they have an important opportunity to influence the financial well-being of individual agencies and to affect the future of particular programs. Lee Bernick (1979) surveyed state senators in 11 states and found that they identified the budget authority as the most important power available to governors—even exceeding the informal power governors could command to muster popular support.

Budget office staffs, some located directly in governor's office and some housed in other agencies, vary considerably in size, with the number of personnel directly engaged in the budget function ranging from fewer than 10 in several states (Maine, Mississippi, North Dakota, South Dakota) to more than 100 in others (California, New York). While some offices concentrate on preparation of the budget, others assume strategic planning, management analysis, and program evaluation chores on behalf of the governor as well (National Association of State Budget Officers, 1997).

Recent research by Thurmaier and Gosling (1997) examined the approach that budget analysts in three midwestern states take to their jobs. They compared their findings with evidence from the same states in 1985 and found a considerable shift toward a policy orientation. In the earlier year, only analysts in the Wisconsin office had a clear policy focus, while today those in Iowa and, to a lesser degree, Minnesota do so as well. In both Wisconsin and Iowa, the analysts report close contact with their governors, participating in briefing the governor and becoming familiar with the governor's views about the programs for which they are responsible. Assistance of budget office staff is thus potentially very important to the governor in analyzing policy options.

3. Gubernatorial Staff

One of the first tasks for a new governor is to assemble a competent staff. Although the size of governors' staffs vary a great deal (from fewer than 10 to more than 200), and the responsibilities assigned to the governors' offices also vary from state to state, governors depend on the staff both for specific advice and to maintain critical relationships on behalf of the governor (Sprengel, 1988). Additionally, members of the staff function as "gatekeepers" for the governor, determining which individuals and what particular issues reach the governor's attention.

Noting the dramatic changes in state programs and the sharp increase in responsibilities that states have assumed, Beyle (1996:239) points out specific important changes that have helped governors provide policy leadership:

> The first level of change has taken place in the governor's office itself. In recent years the office has increased greatly in size, ability, functions, and structure. What used to amount to a few close associates working together with the governor has now been transformed into a much larger and more sophisticated bureaucratic organization in many of the states.

The professional staff of governors' offices are generally well educated, with many of the staff holding graduate degrees (Sprengel, 1988). Among the critical positions and functions on the staff are chief of staff, media relations, legal counsel, appointments secretary, intergovernmental relations, legislative relations, and policy advisers. Because governors find it critical that these staff members consider the chief executive's program and provide sound advice, key staff positions are likely to be filled by persons the governor knows well—perhaps from the campaign organization or from prior political or business connections.

To assess the role of the governor's staff, state agency heads responding to the 1994 ASAP survey reported the frequency of their contact with members of the governor's staff, as well as with other key political actors. They were asked to indicate whether such contact was "daily," "weekly," "monthly," "less than monthly," or "never." Of these agency heads, 49.5% had weekly or daily contact with the governor's staff; only 19.8% had weekly or daily contact with the governor. Contact with legislative staff was quite similar to contact with governor's staff, with 43.7% reporting such contact occurring weekly or daily. A similar level of contact was reported with legislators, 44.5%. The important role for the governor's staff is evident, especially in comparison to contact with the governor personally.

III. ADMINISTRATORS' REACTIONS TO THE GOVERNOR'S INFLUENCE

To what extent do governors influence administrative agencies? Clearly, the public expects that in their positions as chief executives they will exercise influence. Some tools of the office are designed to give them influence. However, in the context of separation of powers, they compete with legislatures to control administration. Both governors and legislatures attempt to provide close administrative oversight, sometimes even to provide detailed instructions or guidance that thwarts the desires of the other. Rosenthal (1990:173–174) describes this competition as follows:

> Although the governor is chief administrator, it is not unusual for the head of a department to spend as much time relating to the legislature as to the governor and the governor's staff. Nor is it unusual for those at the top of the ladder in the career service to spend more time trying to pacify the legislature than trying to figure out what the governor might want to do. The governor's concern is episodic, the legislature's . . . is continuous.

Several investigations of the governor's influence over administrative agencies have been explicitly comparative, examining the influence of both the governor and the legislature (Abney and Lauth, 1986; Brudney and Hebert, 1987; Elling, 1992). From the perspective of agency directors, these two major formal institutions, or "external actors," are especially salient features of their environments. Public agencies, however, are relatively open to external influences, and consequently are affected by other important external actors as well. Among the more prominent ones that compete with the governor and legislature are interest groups, federal agencies, Congress and the President, local officials, and professional associations (Abney and Lauth, 1986; Brudney and Hebert, 1987).

Abney and Lauth (1986) asked department heads in all 50 states to rank the impact of various external political actors on agency programs and objectives. The governor and legislature dominated the first-place rankings, with 43% of respondents placing the legislature first and 38% placing the governor first. While this difference is not great, it indicates both the slight advantage the legislature might have in total "impact" on agencies and the degree to which these two actors contend with each other for influence over state administration.

Elling (1992) reported findings from a study of 10 states and similarly found that the legislature has somewhat greater influence over administrative agencies than does the governor, especially in matters concerning agency budget levels.

The 1994 ASAP survey, as well as similar surveys dating back to 1964, asked state agency heads to compare the amount of control and oversight that the governor and legislature exercise over their agencies. Administrators' responses to this question are displayed in Table 1. Throughout this 30-year period, somewhat over one-fifth of respondents have indicated that the two actors are roughly equal in influence. Notably, though, in three of the four survey years, more than two-fifths of the administrators indicate that the governor has the most control and oversight—and this figure approaches 50% in 1994.

It appears, then, that in terms of broadly described "control and oversight," the governor has the upper hand relative to the legislature, and this may have grown in recent decades. Perhaps, however, more is concealed than revealed by this general comparative question. Table 2 reports administrators' responses to two questions concerning the legislature's and the governor's influence over

Table 1 Agency Heads' Assessments of Governor's and Legislature's Control and Oversight

	1964	1974	1984	1994
Exercises more control & oversight				
Governor	33.2	47.4	42.1	48.3
Each the same	22.6	26.3	23.3	21.4
Legislature	44.2	26.3	34.6	30.3
Total	100.0	100.0	100.0	100.0

Source: American State Administrators Project surveys, years indicated.

Table 2 Agency Heads' Assessments of Governor's and Legislature's Budget Control

	1974	1984	1994
Exercises more detailed review			
Governor	35.5	30.4	32.6
Each the same	32.4	35.3	37.0
Legislature	32.1	34.3	30.4
Total	100.0	100.0	100.0
Greater tendency to reduce requests			
Governor	31.9	36.2	39.2
Each the same	24.3	20.0	24.2
Legislature	43.8	43.8	36.7
Total	100.0	100.0	100.1

Source: American State Administrators Project surveys, years indicated.

agency budgets. Specifically, agency heads were asked whether the governor or the legislature exercises the more detailed review of the agency's budget, and whether it is the governor or the legislature that has the greater tendency to reduce the agency's budget request.

Comparing the governor's and the legislature's influence over budget matters, and examining changes in responses since 1974 (the first year these questions were asked), we see that the two institutions exhibit more nearly equal influence. Regarding who exercised more detailed review of agency budget requests, 32.6% of respondents in 1994 indicated the governor did, compared to 30.4% who said the legislature did. A plurality of 37.0% indicated the two had equivalent influence.

Clearly, in the 1994 survey as well as in the surveys from the two earlier decades, the governor and the legislature are shown to be closely competitive in their abilities to review agency budgets—but did this similarity extend to action they took on those budgets? Agency heads were also asked whether the governor or legislature had the greater tendency to *reduce* budget requests. Since administrators often support the programs their agencies provide, and this requires seeking increases in annual appropriations, it is interesting to inquire about the reactions to their requests. These requests afford the governor (and the legislature) a unique opportunity to review an agency's activities and to either reward it or, potentially, impose sanctions. A clear tendency to reduce requests may indicate that the governor is using the budget as a tool of influence.

The lower section of Table 2 shows that in 1994, administrators were divided on who was more likely to impose reductions. The governor held a slight edge. Across the 20-year span a trend seems to emerge, with governors becoming more likely to reduce budget requests.

A.   A Complex Environment: The Governor Is Only One Player

From the perspective of a state agency, the governor is only one in a group of environmental actors, although the chief executive is often a particularly important one. Wamsley and Zald (1973:21) note that "one of the relatively distinctive features of public organizations is the greater degree to which external actors are directly involved in setting goals, allocating resources, and granting or withholding legitimacy from them." Like other organizations, public agencies engage in exchanges with important environmental actors in order to obtain support for agency survival and growth.

To explore the character of the agency environment more fully than is possible with questions that ask simply for direct comparisons of the influence of the governor and the legislature (as critical as those two actors are), some investigations of state administration (Hebert et al., 1983; Elling, 1992) have used measures of actors' influence that are independent of each other. Such a measure was incorporated into the 1994 ASAP survey. It included a set of items that asked responding agency heads to assess the degree of influence (from "none" to "high") exercised by five actors: governor; legislators; clientele groups; professional associations; and state courts. The influence of each actor was assessed across four influence domains: total agency budget level; budgets for specific programs; major policy changes; and agency rules/regulations.

One advantage of this approach over the direct comparison or even a ranking of external actors is that it does not require zero-sum gains and losses of influence across actors, but permits changes of influence to be positive-sum. It recognizes, for example, that even though the governor and legislature may compete for influence, both may exercise high (or low) influence and over time increase their ability to influence administrative agencies.

Cheryl Miller (1987) examined whether influence levels of various actors on agency policy are likely to be zero-sum in nature. Her conclusion was that they do not seem to be so. When asked to indicate present levels of influence that various actors have over their agencies and to further indicate what the levels *should be*, state administrators recognized that influence of a number of actors (five out of seven—in addition to themselves) could and should increase (Miller, 1987). Correlation analysis of administrators' responses revealed mostly weak positive relationships, suggesting that there was no clear zero-sum pattern. Only in the case of agency personnel versus the legislators was there a significant (but weak) negative relationship, suggesting a zero-sum relationship might be present. Miller found no such relationship regarding the governor. Administrators indicated they would prefer greater gubernatorial influence than existed at present, and this was not inconsistent with preferring greater influence for themselves.

Table 3 shows state agency heads' assessments of external actors' influ-

Table 3 Mean Influence of Critical External Actors, by Influence Domains

	Influence domains[a]				
External actors	Total agency budget	Specific program budgets	Major policy changes	Rules and regulations	Total influence
Governor	2.56	2.49	2.48	1.91	9.47
Legislators	2.59	2.56	2.35	1.89	9.40
Clientele groups	1.13	1.25	1.39	1.47	5.23
Professional assns	0.75	0.81	0.97	1.07	3.59
State courts	0.42	0.39	0.84	0.92	2.55

[a] Means of responses to items measuring individual influence domains are calculated on 0–3 scale, "none" to "high" influence; total influence is an additive scale, across the four domains, resulting in a range of 0 to 12. Number of valid responses for total influence varied from 1097 (court influence) to 1172 (legislators' influence).

Source: American State Administrators Project survey, 1994.

ence, as revealed by the 1994 ASAP survey. The scale used here ranged from 0 (low) to 3 (high), so it is clear that both governors and legislatures exercise considerable influence over agency budget matters—with both achieving scores on these two items in the range of 2.5 and above. Clientele groups fall in a middle position, influencing budgets to some degree, but not to the extent that the two formal institutions do.

Regarding whatever rivalry there may be for influence between the governor and the legislature, these data seem to indicate the contest is a draw. Administrators report that the legislature's influence only slightly exceeds the governor's on both total budget and program budget matters.

As might have been expected, the governor plays a larger influence role in nonfiscal agency matters. Table 3 shows that with regard to "major policy changes" and "agency rules and regulations," the governor's influence surpasses the legislature's—but only slightly. Regarding rules and regulations, clientele groups rival the two formal institutions for influence. No doubt, this reflects the important role that administrative agencies have in the promulgation of rules and regulations and the importance of this process to interest groups.

Agency heads report that neither professional associations nor state courts exercise extensive influence over their budgets, policies, or rules. The score of 1 is designated "slight," and it appears that this may appropriately characterize the level of influence these two external actors demonstrate. As might be expected, the influence of the courts is greatest over rules and regulations, but substantially less in the two budget areas. Professional associations similarly show highest influence on rules and regulations.

The final column of Table 3 presents a total score for each external actor, constructed across the four policy domains. The governor's influence slightly exceeds the legislature's, and these two actors clearly surpass the influence of all others. Scores of four of these actors can be compared to similar scores reported by Brudney and Hebert (1987), based on data from the 1984 ASAP survey (courts were not included in the previous survey). Ten years earlier, the scores for both the governor and the legislature were very slightly lower (at 9.2 and 9.3, respectively); those for clientele groups and professional associations stood at 4.9 and 3.0, respectively. It thus appears that influence of all these external actors over state administrative agencies may have increased slightly over the decade, especially that of the less formal actors.

B. Explaining the Governor's Influence

While administrators report that governors have substantial influence over some features of agency operations (most particularly matters related to their budgets), there is ample evidence that governors cannot attend regularly to all agency affairs. Hence, it is not surprising that the amount of gubernatorial influence reported by individual agency directors varies from agency to agency and across the states.

Weinberg (1977) and Ransone (1982) have noted the importance of distinguishing among agencies, and the likelihood that governors will exercise more influence over some agencies than others. Variations may result from differences in perceived "importance," from contrasts in structural character (e.g., whether the governor appoints the director), from how the agency is funded, or from particular emergent situations.

1. Formal Gubernatorial Powers

Elling (1992), in his study of administrators in 10 states, considered five specific elements of gubernatorial power that might relate to administrative influence: appointment authority; budget authority; organizational authority; veto authority; and tenure potential. He also constructed a combined index from these five indicators. With the exception of tenure potential, he found that these elements of formal gubernatorial power positively related to variation in gubernatorial influence.

Hebert et al. (1983) also measured the effect of variations in the governor's formal powers. Specifically, they examined the relationship between an index of formal gubernatorial power developed by Dometrius (1979) and administrators' reports of gubernatorial influence, and found that the governor's formal powers are positively associated with gubernatorial influence.

In addition to examining the broad array of formal powers, which includes a measure of appointive authority, Abney and Lauth (1986) suggested that whether or not the governor appoints a particular agency head will affect the amount of influence the chief executive has over that agency. They confirmed this effect, finding that administrators who had been appointed by the governor are far more likely than other administrators to report that the governor's influence exceeds the legislature's influence.

Beyond the appointment process, an agency's position in the state's organization structure may affect the degree of gubernatorial influence over it, as may the agency's size (Weinberg, 1977; Brudney and Hebert, 1987). Agency directors reporting to the governor (even if not appointed by the governor) are more responsive to gubernatorial influence than are those several layers removed in the state hierarchy. Weinberg has suggested that major agencies are more likely to be worth the governor's limited time and attention, and the potential difficulties that may arise from them are sufficiently great to deserve the chief executive's attention. Consequently, these nearby, larger agencies are especially subject to the governor's influence.

In a multivariate analysis reported in 1987, Brudney and Hebert examined some of these variables together. While the level of total explained variation was not dramatically large (22%), the investigation revealed a number of variables that accounted for significant amounts of variation across agencies. The governor's formal powers, the process by which the agency director was named, and organizational structure were particularly important. Staff agencies (those most closely linked to the governor) reported higher levels of influence. "Independent" agencies (those that are often established under independent commissions or regulatory bodies) reported particularly low levels of gubernatorial influence.

2. Informal Gubernatorial Powers

Both research scholarship and efforts to reform state government have emphasized the governor's formal powers, the institutional authority that the office receives from the state's constitution and statutes. In addition to these formal powers, though, there is a set of informal or personal powers that governors may wield (Beyle, 1996). Some of these the individual may bring to the office (such as personal ambition, management skill, and leadership style) and others the governor may have less ability to control (public performance rating, electoral mandate).

When state agency heads were asked to indicate the degree of "help" a set of formal and informal powers provided the governor in exercising control over their agencies, the result showed that both formal and informal ones made important contributions (Hebert and Brudney, 1988). While respondents ranked two formal powers first and third (governor's budget authority and appointment power), other powers that they placed near the top were informal powers: governor's interest in agency programs (2nd); governor's staff's skill (4th); governor's management skill (5th); and governor's legislative skill (6th). Completing the 11 items in order were the removal power, the general veto authority, the governor's reelection prospects, the governor's electoral mandate, and the item veto authority.

Beyle (1996) examined relative formal and informal powers of governors in all 50 states. Because of the nature of the informal powers, these may change with individuals who hold the governor's chair. From the perspective of the governor who seeks to influence administrative agencies, it is important that a number of the critical informal powers lie well within the governor's control. It may not be necessary for the chief executive to wait until statutes are changed or constitutions are amended to further extend influence over agencies.

IV. CONCLUSION

In fulfilling their present roles, today's governors have emerged as policy leaders. It is not possible for them to attend constantly to the management details of all state agencies, even with the added capacity that recent reforms have provided them. They compete with legislatures, interest groups, and important other actors seeking to influence state agencies as they make policy choices and implement programs.

Although it is probably accurate to say that governors today are in a stronger position to influence state administration than they ever were before, they still must use their authority selectively. Flentje (1981) suggested that an activist governor interested in exercising managerial influence across a broad front will run a risk of incurring substantial liability. Chief executives will find that, although they have important formal powers (appointive authority, removal power, cabinet structures, and budget power) and many informal ones as well, applying these in all situations may not prove equally productive, and they may sometimes be forcefully opposed.

By having clearly defined policy agendas and specific policy interests, governors may select particular agencies on which to focus their attention. While others cannot be totally ignored—and events will place some in the spotlight—the governors as policy leaders are in positions to select certain agencies to accomplish policy initiatives. Using the combination of their formal and informal powers selectively, governors have the potential to influence those agencies to direct their efforts toward their administrations' policy objectives.

REFERENCES

Abney, G., and Lauth, T. P. (1986). *The Politics of State and City Administration*, State University of New York Press, Albany.

Arnold, P. E. (1986). *Making the Managerial Presidency*, Princeton University Press, Princeton, NJ.

Ashcroft, J. (1991). Leadership: the art of redefining the possible, *Governors on Governing* (Robert D. Behn, ed), National Governors' Association, Washington, DC.

Bell, G. A. (1974). State administrative activities, 1972–73, *The Book of the States, 1974–75*, Council of State Governments, Lexington, KY, pp. 137–146.

Bernick, E. L. (1979). Gubernatorial tools: formal vs. informal, *Journal of Politics* 41: 656–664.

Beyle, T. (1996). Governors: the middlemen and women in our political system, *Politics in the American States: A Comparative Analysis*, 6th ed. (V. Gray and H. Jacob, eds.), CQ Press, Washington, DC.

Beyle, T. L., and Dalton R. (1981). Appointment power: does it belong to the governor? *State Government* 54:2–12.

Beyle, T. L., and Mouw, S. (1989). Governors: the power of removal, *Policy Studies Journal* 17:804–827.

Brudney, J. L., and Hebert, F. T. (1987). State agencies and their environments: examining the influence of important external actors, *Journal of Politics* 49:186–206.

Conant, J. K. (1992). Executive branch reorganization in the states, 1965–1991, *The Book of the States, 1992–93*, Council of State Governments, Lexington, KY, pp. 64–73.

Council of State Governments (1996). State cabinet systems, *Book of the States 1996-97*, Council of State Governments, Lexington, KY, pp. 27–28.

Cox, R. III (1991). The management role of the governor, *Gubernatorial Leadership and State Policy* (E. B. Herzik and B. W. Brown, eds.), Greenwood Press, Westport, CT.

Dometrius, N. C. (1979). Measuring gubernatorial power, *Journal of Politics* 41:589–610.

Elling, R. C. (1992). *Public Management in the States: A Comparative Study of Administrative Performance and Politics*, Praeger, Westport, CT.

Flentje, H. E. (1981). Governor as manager: a political assessment, *State Government* 54: 76–81.

Garnett, J. L. (1980). *Reorganizing State Government: The Executive Branch*, Westview Press, Boulder, CO.

Hebert, F. T., and Brudney, J. L. (1988). Controlling administrative agencies in a changing federal system: avenues of gubernatorial influence, *American Review of Public Administration* 18:136–147.

Hebert, F. T., Brudney, J. L., and Wright, D. S. (1983). Gubernatorial influence and state bureaucracy, *American Politics Quarterly* 11:243–264.

Heclo, H. (1977). *A Government of Strangers: Executive Politics in Washington*, Brookings Institution, Washington, DC.

Herzik, E. B. (1991). Policy agendas and gubernatorial leadership, *Gubernatorial Leadership and State Policy* (E. B. Herzik and B. W. Brown, eds.), Greenwood Press, Westport, CT.

Kallenbach, J. (1966). *The American Chief Executive: The Presidency and the Governorship*, Harper and Row, New York.

Miller, C. M. (1987). State administrator perceptions of the policy influence of other actors: is less better? *Public Administration Review* 47:239–245.

Muchmore, L. (1981). *Reflections on Being Governor*, National Governors' Association, Washington, DC.

Muchmore, L. R. (1983). The governor as manager, *Being Governor: The View from the Office* (T. L. Beyle and L. R. Muchmore, eds.), Duke University Press, Durham, NC.

National Association of State Budget Officers (1997). *Budget Processes in the States*, National Association of State Budget Officers, Washington, DC. (Available from www.nasbo.org/pubs/budpro/frame.htm; accessed Aug 3, 1998.)

Ransone, C. B. Jr. (1982). *The American Governorship*, Greenwood Press, Westport, CT.

Rosenthal, A. (1990). *Governors and Legislatures: Contending Powers*, CQ Press, Washington, DC.

Sabato, L. (1983). *Goodbye to Good-time Charlie: The American Governorship Transformed*, 2d ed., CQ Press, Washington, DC.

Sanford, T. (1967). *Storm over the States*, McGraw Hill Book Co., New York.

Sprengel, D. P. (1988). Trends in staffing the governors' offices, *Comparative State Politics Newsletter* 9:9–20.

Thurmaier, K., and Gosling, J. J. (1997). The shifting roles of state budget offices in the midwest: Gosling revisited, *Public Budgeting and Finance* 17(4):48–70.

Wamsley, G. L., and Zald, M. N. (1973). *The Political Economy of Public Organizations*, Lexington Books, Lexington, MA.

Weinberg, M. W. (1977). *Managing the State*, MIT Press, Cambridge, MA.

6
The Independent Political Executive in State Governance

Julia E. Robinson
University of Colorado at Colorado Springs, Colorado Springs, Colorado

I. DISPERSED AUTHORITY IN THE STATES

After the Civil War and into the 20th century, the state's role in governance was extremely limited. The Depression and World War II focused public attention on achieving national solutions. The postwar development of the welfare state and burgeoning federal bureaucracy continued this trend.

In the 1980s, however, emphasis shifted away from continuation of federal policy initiatives to state innovation. Authors such as Van Horn and Bowman and Kearney argued that by the middle 1980s that a quiet revolution in governance was occurring across the nation. They documented the resurgence of state government as the most responsive, innovative, and effective level of government in the American federal system (Bowman and Kearney, 1986; Van Horn, 1989). The 1990s brought increasing power and prominence of states in shaping the national agenda (O'Neill, 1990). The zenith of this state governance movement may well prove in hindsight to have been the 1995 Republican Congress' "Contract for America," seeking to turn the federal social programs back to the states. Dag Ryen (1992:53), executive director of the Council of State Governments, captures the dramatic realignment in the relationship between federal and state governments when he writes:

> A great deal of fermentation is going on in state cauldrons. Having achieved a level of influence and activity unprecedented since the 18th century, state governments face extremely challenging problems and decisions in the coming years.

The resurgence of state governments has paralleled an increasing emphasis on gubernatorial power. For example, between 1955 and 1982, 11 states ratified new Constitutions strengthening executive powers of the governor and eliminating some elected officials. Numerous reorganizations took place across the country consolidating agencies and developing cabinets with the intention of giving governors more control over state bureaucracies (Reeves, 1989:21–24).

The goal of strengthening gubernatorial powers has been to reduce fragmentation and thus improve accountability and responsiveness (Thompson, 1993a). In this model of public administration, a centralized governmental structure presided over by the governor as chief executive is seen as desirable. Dispersed authority with a number of independently elected officials or appointed officials is viewed as an obstacle to good governance. In Thompson's (1993b) conclusion on how to revitalize state government, Thompson characterizes the current dispersion of authority at the state level as a "sloppy governmental system" and a "barroom brawl" (p. 310).

This belief in the effectiveness of the powerful chief executive is so fundamental to theory in public administration that the Winter commission (1993) recommendations on state and local reform advocate "strengthening executive authority to act by reducing the number of independently elected cabinet-level officials" (p. 10). Chester Newland, long-term editor of the *Public Administration Review*, describes this orientation as "the orthodoxy of public administration since the short-ballot movement—glorifying the chief executive at the expense of dispersed authority systems and legislatures" (personal communication, Feb. 3, 1995).

The fact remains that in the face of continuing theoretical emphasis and ongoing reform efforts to centralize gubernatorial power, a large number of independently elected and appointed officials maintain extensive authority in state governments throughout the country. For example, most governors share their elected powers with other elected state officials. Massachusetts and New Jersey are the only two states where the governor is the sole elected state official.

American public administration theory and research have traditionally failed to deal much with the normative political dimensions of appointed and elected executive governmental positions below the chief executive (Fisher, 1980).[1] Public administration, with the exception of presidents and local government managers, tends to deemphasize the role of individuals (Doig and Hargrove, 1987). The omission of political actors apparently stems from a continuing theoretical emphasis on technical rationality, persistent positivist research approaches, and the widely shared belief that leaders in government make little difference (Doig and Hargrove, 1987; Fischer, 1980, 1986; Moe, 1990).

While there have been some studies of the roles, actions, and impacts of federal executives, mayors, governors and gubernatorial appointees, there has been very little research on state political executives who are elected in their own right or who are gubernatorial appointees but serve on boards and commissions independent from the governor and his/her cabinet.[1] This omission occurs even though the orientation of appointees and elected officials is different from other public managers. Thus, the presence of political officials in the governmental process alters the dynamics of the process (Lorentzen, 1985).

In 1993, the Winter commission report *Hard Truths/Tough Choices: An Agenda for State and Local Reform* recommended that efforts be made to streamline state government by eliminating these independently elected officials and political executives appointed to oversee boards and authorities independent of the governor. Until such action occurs in states across the country, however, the public authority of independent political executives makes them distinct players in developing state policy and brokering public values on a tier which is quasi-independent of the state bureaucracy (Moe, 1990). Their actions contribute toward establishing what Kirlin (1994) has termed "place value," or the effectiveness of political structures, civic institutions, and individual property rights that influence the quality of life in the state.

This chapter addresses the question, "What is the role of the independent state executive in the state governance process?" Five themes emerge from examining this question.

The first theme is that the existence of and persistence of these positions in state government is a reflection of embedded public values woven into state constitutions and statues (Beyle, 1993). Independent state government executives originated to capture the deeply held public values of democratic responsiveness and bureaucratic neutrality in governmental design. In the public administration literature, these values are presented as being inherently at odds. The creation of independent state political executive positions, however, is a direct result of efforts to achieve both of these ends at differing points in American history.

The second theme that emerges is that the dispersion of authority at the state level means that state government processes must be understood as a web of interconnecting relationships (Kettl, 1994; Robinson, 1998). In a political system in which power is shared, a hierarchical model of government does not capture much of the political action and efforts to define the public good.

The third theme is that political executives in state government are different than political executives in the federal bureaucracy and serve a different function in the governance process than executives at the national level (Heclo, 1977; Wilson, 1989; Thompson, 1993a,b; Roberts, 1993). The difference between federal political executives and state executives results from two structural factors

---

[1] Examples of this research include Ammons and Newell, 1989; Banfield and Wilson, 1963; Doig and Hargrove, 1987; Garvey, 1993; Golembiewski and Gabris, 1995; Ingraham, 1987; Kravchuk, 1993; Montjoy and Watson, 1995; Rosenbloom, 1995; Svara, 1985, 1988, 1989; Wilson, 1989.

in states: the dispersion of authority at the state level among a number of political executives who are independent of the governor and the relative longevity of these executives in their positions (Roberts, 1993; Robinson, 1998; Thompson, 1993a; Winter, 1993).

The fourth theme of this chapter assumes that independent political executives play a key role in the development of a state's unique political and social institutions. This role means that these executives help establish the distinctive character of each state and are prominent actors in brokering and determining a state's unique "place value" (Kirlin, 1994; Robinson, 1998).

The fifth and final theme is that dispersion of authority at the state level among a number of long-term independent political executives has positive consequences for states (Robinson, 1998). This theme is in contrast to arguments by the centrist school that gubernatorial power should be strengthened through reducing the number of or eliminating state political executives who function independently of the governor (Thompson, 1993a,b; Winter, 1993).

II. WHO ARE THE INDEPENDENT POLITICAL EXECUTIVES IN STATE GOVERNANCE?

In identifying the independent political executive, the three key terms are *independent, political,* and *executive.* "Independent" is understood as relational vis-á-vis the governor. Individuals meeting this definition are able to operate relatively independently of the governor if they choose (Elling, 1994; Winter, 1993).

"Political executive" is understood to mean that these executive positions operate at the extreme end of the public continuum characterized as the state. These positions have been granted public authority emanating from constitutional or legislative mandates to oversee governmental operations. Backoff et al. (1976) refer to these agencies as the "hard core" of public agencies, which undertake typical government activities and are easily identified by the public.

Delineating this political context is important when examining the role of the political manager. Graham Allison (1992) found that managers who have served in both industry and federal appointed positions "all judged public management as different from private management and harder" (p. 16).

This chapter is premised on the assumption that political management in public organizations is fundamentally different than management in the private sector (Bozeman and Coursey, 1990; Dahl, 1947; Denhardt, 1993; Lindblom, 1979, 1992; Marini, 1971; Milakovich, 1991; Swiss, 1992; Waldo, 1988). Independent political executives in state government operate in a distinct sphere emanating from public authority and involving the concept of "publicness" (Bozeman and Coursey, 1990; Moe, 1990). Because the context is disparate, political managers confront different management demands from those facing high-ranking private-sector managers, or even public-sector civil service managers. Consequently, understanding the uniqueness of the political context is essential to analyzing the role of the state political executive.

The concept of public sphere is a value-laden, linguistic category implying shared societal understandings of both moral and political good (Ryan, 1990). This shared understanding is found in such concepts as the "public interest" or "search for the common good." Because of the values implicit in the concept of "public," political managers, especially elected political managers, symbolically speak for the community and articulate commonly shared understandings of public policy. The power of the public is best understood by the fact that, once agreed to, public policy can overrule private interests, and the public domain is the only sector authorized to use sovereign force in the public interest.

The above definition of independent political executive excludes individuals who are elected to Congress, the state legislature, or to the state court system. These individuals are politically independent of the governor but do not qualify because they are not executives of state agencies. Also excluded are cabinet appointees who serve at the pleasure of the governor and therefore are not independent of the governor's authority.

Applying this definition to state executives, the most obvious independent political executives are those who run for office and are elected in their own right and administer a state agency. Examples of this group include lieutenant governor, secretary of state, treasurer, attorney·general, superintendent of public instruction, and auditor. However, not every state has each of these positions and not every one of these positions is independent of the governor. On average there are six statewide elected officials per state (Beyle, 1993). This represents about 14.5% of the executive positions in state government.

There are three other categories of state executives who meet the definition of independent political executives:

1. Individuals who are appointed by and serve at the pleasure of some other officer such as a statewide board or commission which may be appointed by the governor but which may act without the consent of the governor.
2. Individuals elected or appointed by the legislature with only advice of the governor.
3. Individuals who are appointed by the governor for a set term and may not be removed at the governor's pleasure.

Thus, executives in the above three categories may choose to act independently of the governor without fear of being removed.

When independent political executives are identified as distinct actors in state government, it becomes clear that governance responsibilities are scattered among a number of officers commonly independent of the governor. These positions may control a great deal of the personnel and financial responsibilities in state government. For example, in Utah only 33% of 90 agencies report to the governor and only 40% of the state funds and employees are under the control of the governor (Kunde, 1987).

The orthodoxy of public administration portrays the governor as the chief executive with centralized authority over a large governmental bureaucracy. In reality, state government is better understood as a complex arrangement of actors and institutions in which dispersed authority means that many actors are involved in most decisions (Kunde, 1987:21). Because of this array of actors in state government, the Western Governor's Association in a manual on governing describes state government as a holding company (Kunde, 1987:3). The characteristics shared by state government and a holding company are lack of clear executive control, varying goals based on position, shifting external forces, and ambiguous measures of overall success.

III. THE NUMBER OF INDEPENDENT POLITICAL EXECUTIVES

The exact number of these independent appointees is difficult to identify. The Council of State Governments notes that state governments are organized in diverse ways; thus, various approaches to identifying state officials do not necessarily apply to all states.

The Winter commission (1993:16–17) notes that:

> Yet, of the nearly 2,000 major administrative officers serving American state government, almost 300 were elected directly by the public while another 750 were appointed by somebody other than the governor. Over half the officers of state government are independent in one way or another from the chief executive. Consider the following figures:
>
>   36 states elect a separate secretary of state
>   38 elect a treasurer
>   25 elect an auditor
>   16 elect a comptroller
>   12 elect an agriculture commissioner
>   11 elect public utility boards or commissioners
>   10 elect an insurance commissioner
>   5 elect a land commissioner
>   15 elect a superintendent of education

Governors who appoint and remove without any other body involved are considered most powerful (Beyle, 1991:121–129). There are, however, very few of these governors. Beyle (1991) in his study of the powers of governors identified only one state, New Mexico, where a governor has strong removal powers. The number of independent executives vastly increases beyond the Winter commission estimates when the definition of independent political state executives is expanded to include executives appointed by the governor, but independent because they are appointed for set terms and not removable by the governor except in the cases of malfeasance. For all intents and purposes, once these individuals are in office they are no longer directly responsible to the governor. Using this definition, independent appointed state political executives are relatively autonomous because they may or may not choose to follow their governor's wishes. The choice, however, does not impact these executives' expectations of fulfilling the appointed terms.

The Council of State Governments has identified 163 separate functions of state government sometimes filled by either elected officials or appointees. The functions range from adjutant general to fish and wildlife, to gambling, to oil and gas regulation, to secretary of state (Jones and Minton, 1993.). Once appointed, many of the individuals filling the multiple functions of state government become for all intents and purposes independent of the governor because of removal limitations. When this group is considered with the independently appointed and elected officials, the number of independent state executives is substantial.

Thad Beyle (1993), who has done extensive research on gubernatorial powers, estimates the average number of independent executives in states as follows: There are about six statewide elected officials per state, North Dakota having the largest number with 11 separately elected officials. There are on average 17 appointees per state who are appointed by some other officer or the legislature. Oregon has the most independent appointees with 28 positions outside the Governor's direct purview. Overall, Beyle estimates that governors appoint on average 18 or 19 state administrative officials, or about 45% of the total offices involved.

IV. THE NORMATIVE DIMENSIONS OF THE INDEPENDENT POLITICAL EXECUTIVES

The philosophical roots of elected independent political state executives can be traced to back to the Articles of Conferdation's emphasis on republicanism protected through limited governmental jurisdictions (Beyle, 1993; Lockard, 1969). This political model stressed popular sovereignty. Elections afforded the opportunity for the people to translate their will into public action. Direct election of a number of major officials to govern a state not only ensured that state government remained responsive to its citizens but also prevented the development of a more formalized central authority in the form of the governor. In other words, while this construction may seem contrary to traditional theories of direct line control of large bureaucracies, a number of separately elected cabinet positions in state government were expressly intended to dilute gubernatorial direction and control and provide for a pluralist response from the state executive branch.

T. Mitau (1996:2) summarizes the structure of state constitutions with numerous elected officials when he writes: "The political ethos of American State constitutions is frankly antagonistic to social engineering. State constitutions emphasize minimal government . . . highly decentralized executive . . . diffusion of political power."

While numerous elected state officials reflect America's early constitutional debates, appointed independent positions were frequently created in a different era and reflect a different set of American values. These new values emerged after the Civil War in response to growing negative public sentiment toward the spoils system of appointment. Early public administration theorists such as Woodrow Wilson (1887) emphasized neutral competency and separation of politics and administration in the design of governmental agencies. These theories were further institutionalized into governmental design with the publication of Goodnow's *Politics and Administration* (1900). National efforts at designing governmental systems which separated politics from administration can be seen in the Pendleton Act of 1883 and the recommendations of the Bronlow commission (1937).

Appointed boards acting as regulatory bodies with quasi-judicial responsibilities and independent commissions to administer a variety of programs were created by the thousands during this period (Lockard, 1969). These boards and commissions were given statutory appointment authority to select career professionals who would be neutrally competent in managing large bureaucracies. The establishment of various commissions throughout state government essentially diluted gubernatorial authority in general in order to block patronage and favoritism.

As noted in the introduction between 1955 and the 1990s, there have been a number of reform efforts in state government to strengthen the role of the governor. Over this time period, however, the number of separately elected executive officials has changed very little. Beyle notes that in 1955 there were 514 officials, and in both 1981 and 1994 there were 511 separately elected officials (Beyle, 1995). The tenacity of these positions leads Beyle to conclude that there is an irreducible minimum of state elected officials (p. 21). The retention of these positions in the face of reform demonstrates that:

> The ultimate aim of our political structure (referring to state government) is not orderliness and efficiency, and it is not simply to break bottlenecks or avoid blockage by state action. . . . Instead the citizens of the United States need diversified political strengthens. . . . Diverse political strength develops varied answers to assorted problems (Stanford, 1967:7).

V. HOW THE INDEPENDENT POLITICAL EXECUTIVE IMPACTS THE STRUCTURE OF THE STATE GOVERNMENT POLITICAL PROCESS

The second theme in this chapter is that state government is better understood as a "web" than as a single hierarchical structure. Thompson describes state governance like "a kaleidoscope—very complex and shifting" (1993:1). The dispersion of authority at the state level suggests that " our thinking about executive leadership in state government also needs to deepen. . . . No governor can single-handedly 'lead' his or her state" (Roberts, 1993:63). In fact, Beyle's research has indicated that governors often face some of their greatest conflicts within the executive branch (Beyle, 1993).

Governor Booth Gardner, former Governor of Washington (as quoted by Governor Norman Bangerter, former Governor of Utah), captured the reality versus the public impression when he said: "Governing a state is simply different from running a company . . . The public is genuinely confused about how state government functions and who is accountable for its operations" (Kunde, 1987: vii).

Using Thompson's (1993) metaphor of state government as a kaleidoscope, governmental processes can best be understood as a myriad of fluid, conflicting forces buffeting each other (p. 1). Carolyn Lukensmeyer (1990), chief of staff to former Ohio Governor Richard F. Celeste, notes that the dispersion of authority in state government means that many of the most important issues a state faces extend beyond the jurisdiction of a single agency or even the authority of the governor (p. 82). Thus, state government is better understood as a web of interconnecting public authority, institutions, and formal and informal relationships (Robinson, 1998). As a web, focusing on the pieces does not necessarily lead to an understanding of the whole. As one independent executive wrote for a speech on economic development, economic development policy in government does not exist in neat packages:

> We do ourselves a disservice if we focus just on the Department of Commerce "programs." We have layer upon layer of tax credits, tax exemptions, spending programs (water, highways), and miscellaneous government activities which have been historically justified on economic development arguments. It is difficult to get these bundles back up on the table for policy analysis (N. Freudenthal, personal communication, June 24, 1994).

When state government is understood as a web, points on the web are demarcated by institutional boundaries and public authority. Public authority attached to political roles gives occupants of the roles (political executives) unique and enormously valuable property rights by virtue of holding a public office (Moe, 1990). Moe argues that state government can best be understood as a two-tier system in which politicians and interest groups interact, on one tier deciding the manner in which political authority will be exercised. Governmental managers operate in another tier carrying out the everyday activities of the bureaucracy. In this two-tier model, understanding the role of the state political executives in the governance process is essential to understanding political struggles. Deborah Roberts (1993) captures this dispersion of authority when she writes: ''The executive leadership system (of states) sits atop the operating levels of state government and cuts across the institutional boundaries of agencies that focus more narrowly on their function and policy areas'' (p. 63).

Once state governance is understood as a complex web in which public authority is shared, analysis of political executives shifts from focusing on internal management of organizations to junctures where the public authority of various players meets or overlaps. These junctures occur at the boundaries of agencies, the areas where public authority leads to complex interrelationships and shared responsibility (Kettl, 1994).

Kettl argues that the boundaries between government organizations are where the balance of power is set and mutual influence is exerted. He sees that a key role of a political executive is maintaining and reaching across boundaries. He contends that ''coping at the boundaries of government thus imposes substantial and novel burdens on top officials'' (Kettl, 1994:194). Kettl writes that political executives act as ''gatekeepers'' stationed at organizational boundaries. The skill of the political executive influences the balance of power between organizations. As Kirlin (1994) notes:

> Governments with all their attendant constitutions, institutions, policies, programs, regulations and more are social constructions. They were created by human action and can be recreated in endless variety by human action. Governments are not static, nor immutable, but rather changing and changeable. As a consequence, ''design'' of government and all their parts is a critical, on-going activity (pp. 5–6).

Through participation in the ongoing political dynamics of the state, each independent political executive plays a unique role in the design of their state governmental process.

VI. INDEPENDENT STATE POLITICAL EXECUTIVES ARE DIFFERENT FROM POLITICAL EXECUTIVES IN THE FEDERAL GOVERNMENT

A third theme that emerges from studying independent state political executives is that these individuals are different from political executives at the federal level and play a somewhat different role in governance than federal executives.

When analyzing the federal bureaucracy, James Wilson argues that federal political executives have weakly defined roles: "They are less bound by daily routines and peer expectations and are less dominated by situational and technological imperatives" (Wilson, 1989:209). Independent political state executives also have weakly defined roles. State executives, however, vary from federal executives in their expectation for longevity in their positions. Federal political executives anticipate staying two years or less while state political executives can expect to be in positions in state government an average of 13 years. The longevity of independent political state executives allows these executives to operate in a context very different from their federal counterparts. A comparison of the different characteristics between federal and independent political state executives is presented in Table 1.

In 1977, Hugh Heclo published his now classic study about characteristics, roles, and relationships of federal political executives in Washington, DC. The title of his work, *A Government of Strangers*, captures a major characteristic of federal political executives. These executives arrive in Washington, DC, with little knowledge of governmental processes or the necessary political networks to help them learn how to make government work for them. Heclo (1977) describes the relations between executives and bureaucrats as "an accidental collection of individuals with little past commitment to political leadership and few enduring stakes in government's own capabilities and performance" (p. 154). Thus, the short-term nature of federal political appointees, from diverse backgrounds and geographic locations, makes them virtual strangers attempting to provide national political leadership through the federal government. Appointees come and go in such rapid succession that Heclo termed them "birds of passage."

Heclo argues that good management requires open communication, trust, and confidence in order for organizations to achieve long-term goals. The short-term tenure of the federal political executives, however, limits even the most skilled executive's efforts to make a significant difference and alter core government functions.

> [Federal] political executives have to learn, however, that it is not enough to help themselves. Those few important characteristics that appointees share—impatience, short-term tenures, and inexperience as a group—are at war with what they most need—a patient fashioning of relationships of trust and confidence. The latter require time and experience, both of which are in short supply in the political layers (Heclo, 1977:170–171).

Heclo (1977) portrays federal political executives who are unable to master the short learning curves necessary just to survive in their positions as unable to "find their way around" (p. 156).

This phenomenon of short tenure in top political positions in the federal government has not changed substantially since the 1970s. Michaels (1995) notes

Table 1 Comparison of Characteristics of Federal and Independent Political State Executives

Characteristics of political executives	Federal political executives[a]	Independent political state executives[b]
Longevity in position	Short tenure—average 2 years	Average years in state government—13
Experience with government	Extremely limited—short, fast learning curve needed to succeed	Highly developed expertise about state government technical processes and state politics
Policy objectives	Few or none—emphasis on self-promotion "maintenance of the executive" and controlling agency autonomy	Clear goals to be achieved Agency autonomy taken as a given Successful movement towards goals results in increased personal power and public authority
Knowledge of internal operations and agency staff	Limited—(1) Immediate staff may be hired for political or stakeholder payoffs. (2) Bureaucrats are long-term career employees with limited reason to trust or assist.	Extensive—(1) Deputy is likely to have extensive experience in state government and long work history with executive. (2) Because of longevity, executive may eventually be able to hire a majority of career positions. (3) Potential long tenure of executive affords protection of career employees and the development of lasting loyalty.
External networks and contacts	Few in Washington; need to be developed quickly to succeed	Already in place through years of careful management
Authority structure	The executive is easily expendable; must constantly tend connections with those with more power and authority, i.e., cabinet secretary, White House	Independent—may choose to cultivate relationship with governor, but not required to because of independent status; in fact, may choose to actively oppose the governor
Descriptive terms	"Birds of passage", "Government of strangers"	"In and arounders", "Government of acquaintances"

[a] Composite developed from Heclo, 1977; Wilson, 1989.
[b] Composite developed from Wright et al., 1991:31–37; Thompson 1993a; Roberts, 1993.
Source: Robinson (1998).

that presidential appointments (PAs) in the Reagan years were understood to be 18–24 months, but those who stayed longer than 8 months were considered "old-timers" (p. 279). A Government Accounting Office study of tenure during the Reagan/Bush years found that cabinet, department, and agency heads served 2.1 years (Michaels, 1995:282). Michaels argues that the advent of President Clinton's Democratic Administration, after 12 years of Republican rule, brought back a government of strangers. The figures presented above suggest at least at the top of the federal government Heclo's findings of short tenure of political appointees has applied into the late 20th century.

State political executives do not, however, reflect this short-term phenomena. Research shows a great deal of stability in the people involved in leadership positions in state government (Wright et al., 1991:31–37). State executives have spent an average of 13 years in state government, a figure virtually unchanged over two decades (Thompson, 1993a:21). This longevity of people (the positions that an individual holds may change) has led Roberts (1993) to describe government executives as "in and arounders" (p. 61). Governance at the state level moves from policy development by strangers to a "stable government of acquaintances" (Roberts, 1993:61).

The prospects for longevity of these executives and their staffs at the state level changes the dynamics of the potential role these executives may play in the state governance process. Wilson argues that federal political executives' short tenure and constant federal turf wars necessitate that the federal political executives work on issue of agency maintenance using strategies that enhance the executives' personal, external reputations. Wilson describes federal political executives as in an ongoing state of siege, both internally and externally.

Thirteen years in a position is a long time in the rapidly changing world of politics. State political executives, unlike their federal counterparts, have the luxury of time on their side and are not in constant battles over the very existence of the agencies which they head. Independent political state executives have a detailed knowledge of internal agency operations as well as extensive understandings of technical processes that make state government work. They have over time surrounded themselves with staff who are loyal to them. Most of these individuals have a deputy who has worked with them for years and can handle the internal operations of their agency with little oversight from the executive.

The internal loyalty and trust of their staff combined with their expertise in government and state politics allows the executive to stay externally focused, developing long-term goals and mapping out successful strategies for achieving desired outcomes. Freed from internal threats to his/her administration, the political executive can focus on issues of public authority, negotiate boundaries between other agencies and other governmental sectors and become a prime actor in debates on normative issues of state governance.

Over time, independent political state executives can develop extensive networks of colleagues, loyal supporters, and friends throughout government and throughout the state. The longevity and thus the success of the independent political state executive builds on itself. The longer the executive stays in his/her position, the more goals he/she achieves, and the more influence and power within the state the executive acquires (Pfeffer, 1992).

Independent political state executives' public authority initially emanates from state constitutions and statues. This formal authority provides political executives with a base from which to acquire power (Pfeffer, 1992). As Pfeffer (1994) notes, a good position for acquiring power provides an executive with control over budgets and positions, control over and access to information and formal authority (p. 69). This power affords the independent political executive a prominent role in the state governance process. Powerful independent political executives are in the position to influence, shape and reshape public authority and policy to be consistent with their values and visions. These executives have years to carefully expand their sphere of influence.

For political executives who choose to broaden their scope of influence, their initial public authority emanating from their political position provides some protection for their activities. Since the executive is elected in their own right or appointed for a set term, the executive can determine in advance how much controversy they are personally willing to sustain. Their staff may have more protection than staff in a typical bureaucracy if their activities generate what the politician feels is defensible controversy (K. Karpan, personal communication, April 15, 1994).

The weakly defined roles of the state political executives combined with their prospects of longevity for themselves and their immediate staff, allows the executives to create distinct spheres of influence by building on their particular areas of expertise and personal talents. These individuals are able carve out niches which become their personal spheres of influence in the state governance process.

For independent state political executives, public authority and institutional boundaries are not rigid but fluid. Both evolve based on the individuals involved in the political struggles. Some independent political executives are willing to seize opportunities as they become available. These individuals are willing to exert their political power and expertise "to influence behavior, to change the course of events, to overcome resistance, and to get people to do things that they would not otherwise do" (Pfeffer, 1994:30). When they successfully exert their power, independent political executives also augment their authority. This is especially the case in political arenas in which legal authority among various actors is ambiguous.

This shaping process is possible because all public authority is not absolute but, rather, is a social construction. As such, it is a value-laden linguistic category implying shared societal understandings of both moral and political good that evolve over time (Ryan, 1990). Understanding the value-laden nature of the public is fundamental to analyzing the impact of independent political executives on the state governance process. Since this process is fluid, the authority, power, and boundaries established by one person filling a particular position do not necessarily transfer to the next person who inhabits that position.

Independent political state executives have broad latitude in developing their concepts of public authority and in delineating their personal spheres of influence within a state's governmental process. The techniques by which the executives build their sphere of influence varies by personal style and skill. This process can be understood as an artisan carving a niche in the political terrain. The successful state executive meets Goodsell's definition (1992:247) of an artisan who performs each individual task well with a sure sense of execution and mastery. The state political executive masters the political terrain by learning to harness personal creativity and distinctive style. The independent political state executive daily engages in an artistic performance responding to complexity and proceeding with only partial information (Etzioni, 1989). Like any true artisan, the independent political state executive takes pride in what he/she does. Schon (1983) captures the artistry of the state political executive when he writes:

> His artistry is evident in his selective management of large amounts of information, his ability to spin out long lines of invention and inference, and his capacity to hold several ways of looking at things at once without disrupting the flow of inquiry (p. 130).

The choice and skill to pursue power from these positions is, of course, an individual one. Obviously, not every executive is interested in expanding their sphere of influence, authority, and political power. Some political executives are satisfied with the status quo and narrowly define their public authority. These individuals take little action outside prescribed boundaries. But the potential for these individuals to move into their state's larger political terrain outside of the executive clearly defined jurisdictional boundaries remains.

VII. THE INDEPENDENT POLITICAL STATE EXECUTIVE'S ROLE IN CREATING A STATE'S "PLACE VALUE"

The fourth theme of this chapter is that as independent political executives engage in state political struggles they are also contributing to a state's unique political and social institutions. A deeper analysis of executive leadership in states beyond the role of governor acknowledges that independent political executives are key actors in developing the distinctive political terrain of the state. These executives are central in developing "place value" in each state.

Place value can best be understood as a shared understanding of why people choose to live in a state. Place value is the sum total of a location's characteristics including governmental, economic, sociocultural and natural factors that lead to shared understandings by inhabitants of the assets and worth of the locale. The shared understandings of a locale's value may be taken for granted by its inhabitants. As Pulitzer Prize–winning poet Gary Snyder writes, "of all the memberships we identify ourselves by (racial, ethnic, sexual, national, class, age, religious, occupational), the one that is most forgotten . . . is place" (Snyder, 1995: 44). Place value implies that where an individual lives defines and shapes his experiences and perceptions in a variety of ways. Thus, place value has important ramifications in terms of economics, politics, and quality-of-life issues.

This understanding develops from the ongoing interaction of government, the economy, and both the sociocultural and natural environment. Kirlin (1994) notes that place values are important:

> Place values include effectiveness of political structures, civic institutions, individual, property and other rights . . . that influence the quality of life in an area, such as personal safety, environmental quality and opportunities for individual to shape their destinies (p. 1).

Independent political executives help to shape a state's place value by acting as political brokers who mediate competing demands. These executives also regularly articulate their personal understandings of shared public values in a state. The combination of these activities helps create a state's place value.

Kirlin argues that every geographic location has a place value. Place value, however, is not a static concept but is constantly evolving through a complex interaction of inhabitants, political structures, civic institutions, rights, quality-of-life issues, environmental factors, and individual opportunities. Paul Gruchow (1995) captures the evolution of place value when he writes:

> The word "wilderness" acquired positive connotations only quite recently. Before the mid-19th century, in the European-American tradition, wilderness—especially those features of wilderness that we now think particularly lovely: seacoasts, islands, mountains, forests—was regarded as frightful, ugly, even evil. The idea of wilderness as a good thing took root and prospered as our culture became more urban and industrial. What unfulfilled need in contemporary life does wilderness satisfy? (p. 51)

Each state has chosen to design its institutional structures in a distinct manner as a result of differing values, cultural and economic differences, and geography. The end product of this design process is a state's place value.

Independent political state executives can be key actors in developing a state's distinctive place value. The manner in which these executives choose to exercise their public authority can over time change the structure of a state's civic institutions, individual and property rights, and, ultimately, the state's place value.

This role of the independent political executive is a different concept than the more traditional view of government executives being responsible for delivering services, arbitrating interest group conflicts, or developing structures that remedy market failures (Kirlin, 1994:3). This view focuses on the executive as a key player in the ongoing evolution of state governmental structures. This perspective changes the emphasis of analysis from management styles to meanings, processes, and outcomes.

Independent political executives, however, do not have free reign in developing place value since they operate within the constraints of existing laws and institutional structures. In fact, as Kirlin notes, the greatest opportunities to impact place value are in the beginning, the moment of creation of a policy. Once institutionalized, as Selznick (1957) notes, the institution can have remarkable staying power. A role of the political executive is to recognize when existing governmental structures have outlasted their usefulness and are negatively impacting the place value of their state and then actively attempt to change these structures.

Political executives cannot assume that their chosen values will become the preferred "public value" for their state. Political executives operate in "a politically negotiated order held together by political bargains and agreements" (Fischer, 1986:11). The executives are engaged in power struggles characterized by uncertainty and risk. In this ever-changing terrain, the political executive's conception of the public good is just one of many possible constructions which are vying for acceptance.

Every state has ongoing public policy debates designed to strengthen the worth and assets of the state for its citizenry. Those individuals with the power to help enforce their definitions of what should be valued can position themselves to play a major role in this definitional process. Thus, independent political state executives who effectively use their formal authority have the potential of brokering values, developing policy and ultimately creating place value in every state.

VIII. THE POSITIVE FUNCTIONS OF DISPERSED AUTHORITY IN STATE GOVERNANCE

The final theme of this chapter is that centrist positions recommending elimination of the independent political executive position have been developed without research into the role of these executives in state government. This chapter has suggested that independent political executives make a positive contribution to the governance process and that the elimination of these positions might dramatically alter state governments, not necessarily in a favorable manner. Table 2 presents a comparison of the centrist position versus the beneficial role of the independent political executive.

Proponents of strengthening the state leadership role of governors by eliminating other independent political state executives suggest that restructuring would revitalize state government by providing a structure which is more efficient, effective, and democratically responsive (Thompson, 1993a). For example, the first report of the National Commission on the State and Local Public Service argued that fragmentation of authority among a number of political actors denies governors the opportunity to effectively lead.

> Chief executives need the authority to forge their own leadership teams. Too many governments, especially state governments, have scattered that authority among too many elected cabinet-level officials, boards, and authorities (Winter, 1993:10).

Public administration theorists who advocate for centralizing state authority in the hands of the governor note that electorial choices for the populace would be easier with the only choice for state elected position being that of governor. With a shortened state ballot, it can be assumed that the voting public would have better information about a limited number of candidates to make reasonable choices.

Even if the candidate elected proved unworthy of the voter confidence, the responsibility for leadership would be clearly delineated. Bad leaders would be held accountable and removed in the next election. Research has shown that in cases where authority is not clear, the public sometimes has a difficult time identifying exactly who is responsible for programs (Thompson, 1993a). Thus, dispersed authority raises a variety of issues about public accountability.

Finally, centrists argue that dispersed authority in state government results in excessive friction among the various actors. This fragmentation of authority leads at best to inconsistent policy and at worst to total policy stalemate.

On the surface, the rationale outlined above provides a convincing argument for centralizing authority in state government in the hands of the governor. These centrist arguments, however, do not look at the the role of independent political state executives in the state government process. In fact, contributions by independent political state executives to the governance process are usually omitted in centrists' discussions.

This chapter has suggested that given the ongoing efforts to streamline government and the tenacity of these positions in absolute numbers, these positions must make some positive contributions to a state or efforts to eliminate them would be more effective. Reformists have had trouble eliminating these executive positions because the public perceives that the positions protect strongly held values of republicanism and bureaucratic neutrality. The longevity

Table 2 Arguments For and Against Centralizing of Authority with the Governor

The positives of centralization	Arguments against centralization
1. State election ballot shortened to one choice. Possible for voters to know more about candidates and make better decisions.	1. Other state political executives provide continuity across gubernatorial terms providing stability on some ongoing initiatives.
2. Strong leader as governor can provide clear direction for the state and achievable goals and objectives.	2. Strong governor and cabinet system could politicize state governance structure leading to similar short tenure, lack of trust, and communication at apex of federal political structure.
3. Provides for a governmental structure with clear lines of authority and responsibility. Possible to hold governor accountable for outcomes.	3. Elimination of other independent political state executives makes state government dependent on the outstanding leadership qualities of one person. Dispersion of authority allows the state to utilize leadership skills of a variety of men and women.
4. Reduces friction among a variety of actors which could potentially lead to fragmentation and stalemate on state policy issues.	4. Electing a number of state executives provides a variety of avenues for citizens to access state government and have responsive representation.
	5. Independent political state executives' active participation in political struggles helps create a state's shared understanding of place value.
	6. Diversity in political struggles can moderate extremist positions and provide for broader definitions of the "public good."

Source: Robinson (1998).

of independent political executives provides continuity in the state governance process. Dispersion of authority at the state level means independent state political executives are key actors in demarcating the boundaries of governance. Individuals in these roles come to play important parts in a state's political struggles to develop a unique sense of "place."

Changing the state governance structure to a strong governor and appointed cabinet, at the expense of independent political state executives, could potentially affect the stability of state government. At the present time, state executives have a tenure in state government on the average of 13 years. As noted previously, the longevity of independent state executives changes the dynamics of state government interactions from those at the federal level.

State executives in cabinet positions, however, have a much shorter tenure. For example, in the 1970s and early 1980s, turnover for agency heads was about 50% every two years (Haas and Wright, 1989a,b). Controversial positions such as corrections commissioners, welfare commissioners, or mental health commissioners may stay three years or less (Hargrove and Glidewell, 1990). These executives, however usually do have state government experience. Thompson (1993a) argues that this turnover does not result in a government of strangers similar to the federal level because, "first, exempt positions in state government do not as readily turn over when a newly elected governor takes office. . . . Second, top administrators in state agencies usually have considerable experience in the public sector" (p. 21).

The risk, however, of moving to a single elected official with total appointment power is that the tenure and role of state government executives will be politicized to the extent that characteristics of state executives will come to mirror those of federal political executives. Admittedly, movement toward politicizing the apex of state government might vary across individual states and even between governors in the same state. Without independent political state executives, however, the potential for a governor to extremely politicize a state governmental terrain exits. By asking for and accepting the resignations of all political executives, a newly elected governor could transform overnight state government management structures previously based on long-term relationships of trust and loyalty.

Centrists assume that governors will appoint qualified executives to provide leadership to their proposed streamlined state government structure. The centrist proposal, however, places tremendous power in the hands of one individual and his/her appointees. Centralized authority requires that leadership at the top be outstanding. As Richard Neustadt (1990) notes, when describing presidential power, "the responses of our system remain markedly dependent on the person of the President. . . . A dangerous dependence on the expertise of the top man—dependence on his 'feel' for power in the ongoing system" (p. 162). As Neustadt's work also chronicles, different men have brought different approaches and skills to the presidency with varying results.

Dispersed authority gives the public a number of avenues to responsive governance. As former Wyoming secretary of state Kathy Karpan (personal communication, June 15, 1995) notes:

> Independently elected officials have the power of people's consent. They are picked by the people and this makes them powerful. They must remain in direct communication with the people; in order to be re-elected, they have to keep the electorate happy.

In the dispersed approach, emphasis is not on finding the one great leader but on developing systems that produce a number of good political leaders. In a dispersed authority model, "what is needed is not just able and strong leaders, but leadership systems rooted in institutional reform" (Nathan, 1994:156–174). Under such a system, states should encourage able men and women to run for or apply for a variety of independent political executive positions.

Independent political executives also allow for a diversity of opinions as part of the governance process. In a complex society with settled institutions and difficult problems, a variety of viewpoints may result in more positive outcomes than a single-minded response to an issue. Wyoming state auditor Dave Ferrari, a proponent of centralizing gubernatorial powers and the architect of the Wyoming cabinet system, notes:

> I believe in a strong governor but it is important not to go overboard. A number of elected officials from different parties is valuable to a state. It allows for differing positions to be debated and issues other than those focused on by the governor to be raised (Personal communication, April 27, 1994).

Finally, independent political state executives help define and create a state's distinctive place value. The existence of independent political state executives insures greater diversity in the ongoing social construction of a state's place value. The elimination of these positions from a state's governmental process will reduce the viewpoints presented in policy debates and the potential for these officials to moderate and/or change strongly held or extreme positions of the governor or one or two powerful interest groups in a state. Part of the variety of states' political structures and cultures can be attributed to the existence and diversity of independent political state executives serving in various positions across the United States.

Thus, while centrists argue for centralizing power in the hands of the governor to create clear lines of authority, this chapter has argued that dispersed authority structures account, in part, for the responsiveness, innovation, and other distinctive governmental features which have made states the focal points for governmental changes in the 1990s. The longevity of independent political state executives in these positions provides a stabilizing force in states during times of great political volatility. This continuity has allowed states to engage in a clear pursuit of policy outcomes not possible in the more transient structure of political actors at the federal level.

IX. CONCLUSIONS AND FUTURE IMPLICATIONS

Hal Rainey (1990) has argued that more research is needed on the commonalties and variations of officials at different levels of government and between different organizations. He has noted that it is also important to research differences between political and career officials at all levels. He writes, "Politically appointed officials have been relegated to the twilight zone in political analysis" (p. 159).

The discussion presented in this chapter supports Rainey's contention that additional research at different levels of government between political and career professionals will generate valuable data for better understanding the complex dynamics of governmental processes. This chapter has reviewed the existing literature and research on independent state political executives and found that while there is only limited research available, that which exists raises questions about traditional public administration theory. These questions include the applicability of findings concerning federal executives to state government executives' roles and behaviors, and the assumptions of centrists on the best method to further streamline state governance processes.

This chapter has suggested that political actors must deal with a stream of variables that change throughout time (Kotter and Lawrence, 1974). A justifiable action from the actor's perspective at one point may prove to be a detriment at another point in time. In addition, context is important to understanding actions and outcomes. The process approach to analysis emphasizing history and context challenges technical-rational assumptions in public administration and other social sciences. "Borrowing its approach from turn-of-the-century physical science, social science remains dominantly committed to the notion of developing knowledge or certainty through a-temporal causality" (Adams, 1992:366).

The U.S. cultural emphasis on technical rationality is also found in the centrist's arguments for strengthening gubernatorial authority. Centrists' arguments are grounded in themes that careful structuring of legitimate authority serves as a positive force in the operation of large governmental bureaucracies (Adams, 1992:368). The centrists' arguments for centralizing power and authority are not based on research about the negative and/or positive aspects of dispersed power in state governmental processes, since only limited research has been undertaken about political actors in this setting.

Implicit in the discussions of independent political executives building a base of support over time and developing independent networks is the notion that in government, as in most other endeavors in life, knowing colleagues and coworkers makes a difference in interaction patterns and outcomes. Longevity at the state level builds improved communication and trust between political actors and their employees and allows these individuals to direct their efforts to external problem solving. These discussions raise significant questions about the ultimate advisability of term limits. Enforced shortened stays in government may not lead to more responsiveness and accountability. Term limits in fact may create even more government instability and distrust than now exists.

This chapter has also raised the possibly that governors may never achieve the role of sole executive in a state. Given that states may continue to have dispersed authority structures, governors and other state leaders need to develop alternative approaches to governance than traditional leadership approaches based on control structures. The information in this chapter suggests that recent public administration theorists who have suggested that "process must triumph over structure" may be providing new directions for executive leadership in contemporary society (Kettl, 1994:176). Using these theoretical models, the potential for reform in government lies in finding incentives for political actors to develop interdependent networks committed to identifying and achieving new definitions of the public interest rather than creating new governmental structures.

Ultimately, the literature presented in this chapter is consistent with Robert Putnam's (1993) research on democracy in Italy. Democracy seems to work best in settings where citizens know each other and know their elected officials. Efforts at long-lasting governmental reform might be better focused on creating horizontal linkages of reciprocity and cooperation between citizens than on structural changes. Building trust and communication among citizens, government workers, and political executives has the potential of strengthening the very fiber of governmental processes.

REFERENCES

Adams, G. (1992). Enthralled with modernity: the historical context of knowledge and theory development in public administration, *Public Administration Review 52(4)*: 363–373.

Allison, G., Jr. (1992). Public and private management: Are they fundamentally alike in all unimportant respects? *Current Issues in Public Administration* (Lane F. S., ed.), St. Martin's Press, New York.

Ammons, D., and Newell, C. (1989). *City Executives*, State University of New York Press, Albany.

Backoff, R., Levin, C., and Rainey, H. (1976). Comparing public and private organizations, *Public Administration Review* March/April: 233–244.

Banfield, E., and Wilson, J. (1963). *City Politics*, Harvard University Press, Cambridge, MA.

Beyle, T. (1993). Being governor, *The State of the States*, 2nd ed. (C. Van Horn, ed.), *Congressional Quarterly*, Washington, DC.

Beyle, T. (1995). Enhancing executive leadership in the states, *State and Local Government Review 27(1)*: 18–35.

Beyle, T. (1991). The powers of the governors, *State Government Congressional Quarterly's Guide to Current Issues and Activities*, 1990–91 (T. Beyle, ed.), *Congressional Quarterly*, Washington, DC.

Bowman, A., and Kearney, R. (1986). *Resurgence of the States*, Prentice-Hall, Englewood Cliffs, NJ.

Bozeman, B., and Coursey, D. (1990). Decision making in public and private organizations. A test of alternative concepts of publicness, *Public Administration Review* Sept./Oct.: 525–535.

Brownlow, L., Gulick, L., and Merriam, C. (1937). *Report of the President's Committee on Administrative Management: Administrative Management in the Government of the United States*, United States Government Printing Office, Washington, DC.

Dahl, R. (1947). The science of public administration, *Public Administration Review 7*: 1–11.

Denhardt, R. (1993). *Theories of Public Organization*, 2nd ed., Wadsworth Publishing, Belmont, California.

Doig, J., and Hargrove, E. (eds.). (1987). *Leadership and Innovation: A Biographical Perspective on Entrepreneurs in Government*. Johns Hopkins University Press, Baltimore.

Elling, R. (1994). The line in winter: an academic assessment of the first report of the National Commission on the State and Local Public Service, *Public Administration Review 54(2)*: 197–198.

Etzioni, A. (1989). Humble decision making. *Harvard Business Review* July/Aug.: 122–126.

Fischer, F. (1980). *Politics, Values, and Public Policy: The Problem of Methodology*, Westview Press, Boulder, CO.

Fischer, F. (1986). Reforming bureaucratic theory: toward a political model, *Bureaucratic and Governmental Reform* (D. J. Calista, ed.), JAI Press, Greenwich, CT.

Garvey, G. (1993). *Facing the Bureaucracy: Living and Dying in a Public Agency*, Jossey-Bass, San Francisco.

Golembiewski, R., and Gabris, G. (1995). Tomorrow's city management: guides for avoiding success-becoming failure, *Public Administration Review 55(3)*: 240–246.

Goodnow, F. (1900). *Politics and Administration: A Study in Government*, Russell & Russell, New York.

Goodsell, C. (1992). The public administrator as artisan, *Public Administration Review 52(3)*: 246–253.

Gruchow, P. (1995). Where does the landscape end? And where do we begin? *Utne Reader 69*: 50–51.

Haas, P. J., and Wright, D. S. (1989a). Administrative turnover in state government: a research note. *Administration and Society 21*: 265–277.

Haas, P. J., and Wright, D. S. (1989b). Public policy and administrative turnover in state government: the role of the governor. *Policy Studies Journal 17*: 788–803.

Hargrove, E. C., and Glidewell, J. C. (eds.). (1990). *Impossible Jobs in Public Management*, University Press of Kansas, Lawrence.

Heclo, H. (1977). *A Government of Strangers: Executive Politics in Washington*, Brookings Institution, Washington.

Ingraham, P. (1987). Building bridges or burning them? The president, the appointees and the bureaucracy, *Public Administration Review* Sept./Oct.: 425–135.

Jones, D., and Minton, J. (1993). *State Administrative Officials Classified by Function 1993–94*, Council of State Governments, Lexington, KY.

Kanter, R. M. (1977). *Men and Women of the Corporation*, Basic Books, New York.

Kettl, D. (1994). Deregulating at the boundaries of government: Would it help? *Deregulating the Public Service* (J. J. DiIulio, ed.), Brookings Institution, Washington, 175–197.

Kirlin, J. J. (1994). *Where is the value in public entrepreneurship?* Working draft presented at Entrepreneurship and Development Conference, University of Texas at Arlington, Dec. 6.

Kotter, J. P., and Lawrence, P. (1974). *Mayors in Action*, John Wiley and Sons, New York.

Kravchuk, R. (1993). The "new Connecticut": Lowell Weicker and the process of administrative reform, *Public Administration Review 53(4)*: 329–339.

Kunde, J. (1987). The politics of excellence—managing more with less in the Western states, Paper presented at the meeting of the Western Governors' Association, July 6, Salt Lake City, Utah.

Lindblom, C. (1992). The science of muddling through, *Classics of Public Administration* (J. M. Shafritz and A. C. Hyde, eds.), Brooks/Cole, Pacific Grove, CA.

Lockard, D. (1969). *The Politics of State and Local Government* (2nd ed.), Collier, Macmillan Limited, London.

Lorentzen, P. (1985). Stress in political-career executive relations, *Public Administration Review* May/June: 411–414.

Lukensmeyer, C. (1990). Six not-so-easy lessons for new governors (and others), *Governing 4(2)*: 82.

Marini, F., ed. (1971). *Toward a New Public Administration: The Minnowbrook Perspective*, Chandler, San Francisco.

Michaels, J. (1995). A view from the top: reflections of Bush presidential appointees, *Public Administration Review 55(3)*: 273–283.

Milakovich, M. (1991). Total quality management in the public sector, *National Productivity Review*, Spring: 195–213.

Mitau, T. (1966). *State and Local government,Politics and Process*, Charles Scribner & Sons, New York.

Moe, T. (1990). The politics of structural choice: toward a theory of public bureaucracy, *Organization Theory* (Williamson O., ed.), Oxford University Press, New York, pp. 116–153.

Montjoy, R., and Watson, D. (1995). A case for reinterpreted dichotomy of politics and administration as a professional standard in council-manager government, *Public Administration Review 55(3)*: 231–239.

Nathan, R. (1994). Deregulating state and local government: What can leaders do? *Deregulating the Public Service: Can Government Be Improved* (J. J. DiIulio Jr., ed.), Brookings Institution, Washington, pp. 156–174.

Neustadt, R. (1990). *Presidential Power and the Modern Presidents: The Politics of Leadership from Roosevelt to Reagan*, Free Press, New York.

O'Neill, W. (1990). Meeting the challenge of leadership, *Journal of State Government 63(1)*: 3–5.

Pfeffer, J. (1994). *Managing with Power: Politics and Influence in Organizations*. Harvard Business School, Boston.

Putnam, R. (1993). *Making Democracy Work: Civic Traditions in Modern Italy*, Princeton University Press, Princeton, NJ.

Rainey, H. (1990). Public management: recent developments and current prospects, *Public Administration: The State of the Discipline* (N. Lynn and A. Wildavsky, eds.), Chatham House, Chatham, New Jersey.

Reeves, M. M. (1989). State activism as a balance in preserving federalism, *Journal of State Government* Jan./Feb.: 21–24.

Roberts, D. (1993). The governor as leader: strengthening public service through executive leadership, *Revitalizing State and Local Public Service* (F. J. Thompson, ed.), Jossey-Bass, San Francisco.

Robinson (1998) The role of the independent political executive in state governance: stability in the face of change, *Public Administration Review 58(2)*: 119–128.

Rosenbloom, D. (1995). Politics and administration in the late 20th century, *Public Administration Review 55(3)*.

Ryan, M. (1990). *Women in Public*, Johns Hopkins University Press, Baltimore.

Ryen, D. (1992). The challenge ahead: the state agenda for the coming years, *Journal of State Governments* April/June: 53–57.

Schein, E. (1992). *Organizational Culture and Leadership*, Jossey-Bass, San Francisco.

Schon, D. (1983). *The Reflective Practitioner*, Basic Books, New York.

Selznick, P. (1957). *Leadership in Administration: A Sociological Interpretation*, University of California, Berkeley.

Snyder, G. (1995). Current, *Utne Reader 69*: 44.

Stanford, T. (1967). *Storm over the States*, McGraw Hill, New York.

Svara, J. (1985). Dichotomy and duality: reconceptualizing the relationship between policy and administration in council-manager cities, *Public Administration Review 45*: 221–232.

Svara, J. (1988). The complementary roles of officials in council-manager government. *The Municipal Year Book* (M. A. Shellinger, ed.), International City/Country Management Association, Washington, DC.

Svara, J. (1989). Policy and administration: city managers as comprehensive professional leaders. *Ideal and Practice in Council-Manager Government* (H. G. Frederickson, ed.), ICMA, Washington, DC, pp. 70–93.

Swiss, J. (1992). Adapting total quality management to government, *Public Administration Review 10(4)*: 356–362.

Thompson, F. (1993a). Introduction: critical challenges to state and local public service, *Revitalizing State and Local Public Service*, Jossey-Bass, San Francisco, pp. 1–40.

Thompson, F. (1993b). The challenges revisited. *Revitalizing State and Local Public Service*, Jossey-Bass, San Francisco, pp. 309–328.

Van Horn, C. E. (ed.) (1989). The quiet revolution, *The State of the States, Congressional Quarterly*, Washington.

Waldo, D. (1980). *The Enterprise of Public Administration*, Chandler and Sharp Publishers, San Francisco, California.

Wilson, J. (1989). *Bureaucracy: What Government Agencies Do and Why They Do It*, Basic Books, New York.

Wilson, W. (1987). The study of administration, *Political Science Quarterly 2*: 197–222.

Winter, W. F. (1993). The first report of the National Commission on the State and Local Public Service, *Hard Truths/Tough Choices; An Agenda for State and Local Reform*, Nelson A. Rockefeller Institute of Government, New York.

Wright, D., Yoo, J., and Cohen, J. (1991). The evolving profile of state administrators, *Journal of State Governments 64(1)* 30–38.

7

Budgeting in State Government: Control and Management

Thomas P. Lauth and Paula E. Steinbauer
University of Georgia, Athens, Georgia

Public budgets are instruments of accountability—governmental accountability to the public, executive branch accountability to the legislature, and executive agency accountability to the chief executive. In addition to being instruments for accountability and financial control, public budgets are also instruments of management—for achieving efficiency and productivity improvements, and for determining the degree to which program goals have been accomplished. This chapter first identifies several functions of public budgets and describes the development of the *executive budget* in state governments. Next, it discusses trends of the past half-century toward the incorporation of program and performance information into state budget systems. Finally, based on recent information obtained from state budget offices, it identifies the kinds of control and management activities currently used by state budget offices and reports state budget office perceptions of the effectiveness of those activities.

I. PUBLIC BUDGET

A public budget is a document that states the relationship between proposed expenditures and anticipated receipts. It is also a record of past spending and a plan for future spending. More precisely, it may be any one of three documents: the governor's budget recommendation to the legislature, the legislature's appropriation act or acts, and an agency's annual operating budget. These documents are closely related, but because they emerge at different stages in the budget process they may present slightly different pictures of state spending. If they are based on different budget formats, such as a program budget in the executive branch and a line-item budget in the legislature, they also will have quite different appearances.

In addition to being a document, a public budget is a technique for allocating scarce resources among competing agencies, activities, or programs. Line-item or traditional budgets typically allocate resources to agencies; performance budgets allocate resources to agencies based on agency activities or tasks, and program budgets allocate resources to programs which represent the purposes for which governments exist.

A public budget is also an instrument for legislative control of the executive branch, as well as a device through which the chief executive attempts to direct and control agencies within the executive branch. In this century, state legislatures have chosen to exercise fiscal control over the executive branch of government by concentrating responsibility for budget preparation and execution in the office of the governor. This places the governor in the position of actively presenting the agenda of state spending for the next fiscal period (Gosling, 1991), while the legislature is for the most part reacting to the governor's policy initiatives. Legislative reliance on the governor to formulate and present the budgetary agenda has had the effect of strengthening the office of governor in state government, but at the same time it has enabled legislatures to focus and assign responsibility for the resource and expenditure decisions made in the executive branch (Schick, 1971).

Most states have some form of executive budget operating within a separation-of-powers system, but the strength of the executive and relative influence of the governor and legislature vary from state to state (Abney and Lauth, 1987; Clynch and Lauth, 1991). The executive budget is based on the premise that an executive-centered budget process reduces waste and inefficiency because agency requests are submitted to the legislature only after being coordinated and reviewed by the governor. The governor's budget recommendation to the legislature is a comprehensive document which not only has verified the accuracy of agency estimates and the soundness of agency requests, but also has weighed their importance in relationship to each other, and assessed their compatibility with the policy goals and program objectives of the governor (see Appendix A).

Most states have developed an executive budget office to assist the governor in budget preparation and program planning, and to review agency budget requests (see Appendix B). Some central budget offices are an agency within a department of administration, finance, or management and budget ($n = 30$), some are organized within the executive office of the governor ($n = 11$), and some are freestanding agencies within the executive branch ($n = 9$) (NASBO, 1997). Executive budget offices also differ from each other in their orientation toward the budget tasks of expenditure control, and policy planning and evaluation (Gosling, 1987; Duncombe and Kinney, 1987; Willoughby, 1992).

II. PROGRAM AND PERFORMANCE BUDGETING IN THE 20TH CENTURY

The double entendre in the title of S. Kenneth Howard's *Changing State Budgeting* (1973) suggested that although state budgeting had undergone significant changes during the middle decades of this century, further changes in state budgeting practices and procedures were desirable. Howard identified the rational budgeting techniques associated with program budgeting as particularly well suited for improving the quality of budgetary decision making. During the past 50 years, budget reforms have attempted to integrate program and performance information into budget deliberations. The goals of reform have been to focus greater attention on planning, policy analysis, and program evaluation, without diminishing the importance of financial control.

At the end of the century, states continue to struggle with their efforts to use budgeting as a tool for management improvement. Increasingly, states have attempted to shift the focus of their budget process from inputs to outcomes, from items purchased to program results. Fiscal constraints and the desire for greater public accountability have been motivating factors for the trend toward results-based budgeting.

Yet, public budgets, initially intended for spending control, are only partially suited for the task of management improvement. Budgets are important policy instruments because they allocate resources annually or biennially for the entire government. As such, they may be used to encourage agencies to comply with the policy goals and objectives of the governor and legislature, or to improve the quality of agency service delivery. When agencies submit their spending requests, they may also be required to submit performance data on their programs. In principle at least, governors and legislatures may choose to allocate resources based on program performance. However, the decision rules for allocating resources based on program performance are not entirely clear. Should poorly performing agencies or programs be punished in resource allocation for poor performance, or should they be given additional resources in the hope that added resources will improve performance? Similarly, should high-performing agencies or programs be rewarded in resource allocation for their successful programs and activities predicated upon the expectation that they might perform even better with additional resources? Or should new resources be placed elsewhere based on the presumption that a high-performing agency/program does not need additional funding to continue a high level of performance? In budgeting as in other aspects of administration, it sometimes appears that no good administrative deed goes unpunished.

A further complicating factor in using the budget for management improvement is that budget cycles and program evaluation time frames may be mismatched. An annual or biennial budget cycle may be an insufficient time period to accurately measure the effectiveness of many government programs. And, the outcomes of some government programs truly are difficult to measure. Also, loading program and performance data into the budget process where they are linked with fiscal data may overburden the budget process and produce neither good budgeting nor good management. Despite these caveats, it is easy to understand why advocates of management improvement would choose the budget process as the optimal venue for inducing agencies to take seriously the assessment of program outcomes. The budget is where the policy action is and agencies seeking resources will assess program outcomes if required to do so as a condition of acquiring resources. In this connection Donald Axelrod has noted, ''The power of the purse, if exercised, can be a formidable weapon to alter organizational structures, operating systems, programs and policies (Axelrod, 1989:85).

III. CONTROL, MANAGEMENT, AND PLANNING

Allen Schick (1971) identified three operationally indivisible but analytically separable orientations in public budgeting: control, management, and planning. To that trio, accountability might be added as a fourth orientation. Each of these orientations roughly corresponds to the budget formats: line-item, performance, program, and what John Mikesell (1999) calls the new performance budgeting.

The line-item budget focuses on goods and services to be purchased by government agencies, e.g., salaries, equipment, or commodities. In systems terms, it focuses on inputs. Typically, line-item budgets have an object-of-expenditure classification which is uniform across all government agencies. Appropriations are made to departments as organizational units and within departments to specific object classifications, or line items. Funds must be spent according to the conditions of the line item. The objective of the line-item budget is to control expenditures. Control is a fiduciary responsibility to ensure that public funds are not stolen or otherwise mishandled. Control also aims to ensure that funds are spent for the purposes for which they were designated in the governor's budget recommendation or the legislative appropriation. Further, control may entail efforts to limit the size and scope of government. Line-item budgets sometimes are referred to as traditional budgets. This is especially the case when the attendant budget process is characterized by incremental approaches to decision making.

The performance budget focuses on agency activities and tasks, e.g., repairing roads, performing audits, or patrolling highways. The objective of the performance budget is to encourage the efficiency of activities and tasks. Workload information and cost information for each unit of work are necessary ingredients of performance budgeting. Comparisons may be made between actual and projected workload and cost information. Performance budgeting seeks to improve internal management and to achieve more favorable relationships between activities and the cost of performing those activities. Improved internal management might result in a higher level of activities at a constant cost level, or a constant level of activities at a lower cost level.

Program budgeting focuses on programs which represent the purposes for which governments exist, e.g., educational development, human services, or public safety. Programs may be grouped across departmental boundaries. Educational development as a program category might include activities within departments of elementary and secondary education, higher education, and adult and technical education. Human services as a program category might include activities within departments of physical health, mental health, and vocational rehabilitation. Program budgets, sometimes with the aid of a formal planning process, define goals and identify activities that contribute to achieving a particular goal. Funds are then allocated in an effort to reach those goals. Planning horizons, when planning is part of the budgeting process, often extend beyond one year. Program budgets, to a far greater degree than performance or line-item budgets, enable decision makers to consider spending decisions as levels of support for public policy alternatives. Budget debates about alternative policy goals and means for achieving those goals might be informed by quantitative analysis comparing the costs and benefits of alternative uses of available funds.

The Planning, Programming, Budgeting System (PPBS), which was initiated in the U.S. Department of Defense in 1961 and extended to all federal agencies from 1965 to 1971, represents the prototype of program budgeting. PPBS was implemented in a number of states, including California, Michigan, New York, Vermont, and Wisconsin, as part of a common implementation project, and in Pennsylvania, which has generally been regarded as one of the more successful PPPS experiences. PPBS was a rational-decision system requiring specification of program goals and objectives, specification of alternative means for achieving objectives, systematic analysis of the costs and benefits of alternatives means, and budget allocations based on systematic analysis. It was an attempt to introduce planning into the spending process, and impose cost considerations on the planning process. Reasons for the demise of PPBS have been thoroughly discussed elsewhere (Schick, 1973) and will not be recounted here.

Zero-base budgeting (ZBB) is another kind of program budgeting. ZBB links various service levels and levels of program activity with their costs. Service levels and levels of program activity are presented as *decision packages* which then are *ranked* according to their priority for agencies from the most essential (i.e., from zero base) to the desirable but less essential. In principle, at least, ranked decision packages representing agency priorities would be funded in their order of priority according to the level of resources available to the government for the fiscal period. Georgia adopted zero-base budgeting beginning with the 1973 fiscal year. It had a much publicized beginning, but on balance was only moderately successful. The formal documents and procedures including decision packages, multiple funding levels, and ranking processes were in place during the 1970s. However, the Georgia budgetary process was not able to assimilate the program focus or decision making techniques of ZBB into existing budget practices and procedures. Rational comprehensive techniques failed to penetrate incremental decision strategies at the micro level and never were perceived as useful at the macro resource allocation level (Lauth, 1978, 1997; Lauth and Rieck, 1979). In contrast, a modified ZZB system had some success in Idaho, where both the executive and legislative branches found it useful (Duncombe, 1981).

Recent efforts to achieve greater accountability in service delivery and overall government performance have spawned new dimensions in program budgeting, which variously are called performance-based budgeting, results-based budgeting, and *new* performance budgeting (focusing on outcomes rather than activities and tasks). The essential features of these new dimensions in program budgeting are agency identification of outcomes to be produced by programs, and the development of performance measures to gauge progress toward achieving those outcomes. Results-based budgeting for the State of Georgia is described in the following way:

> For each program, a program purpose, goal, and desired result that can be accomplished during the fiscal year will be developed. This desired result will be measured at the completion of the funding period and progress toward achieving the result will be measured. . . . This initiative is designed to relate program results with program expenditures. The Governor and the General Assembly can then decide through public debate whether or not the State is making the proper investment.

Similar results-based innovations can be found in other states, e.g., Virginia's Goal Setting and Performance Budgeting Process, and Florida's Government Performance and Accountability Act.

The structure of each budget format encourages different kinds of budgetary conversations. The line-item format permits comparisons of spending levels across fiscal years and permits the monitoring of spending within a fiscal year. It does not support conversations about operational efficiency or the appropriateness of public policy alternatives. The performance budget format invites conversations regarding operational efficiency, but not about policy alternatives. The program budget format is intended to shift the focus of budgetary conversations away from items purchased, beyond operational efficiency, and toward considerations of public policy priorities and alternatives.

Because these different budget formats have different advantages and disadvantages, many governments have hybrid budget formats consisting of elements from all three types. Because concern for control is critical to budgeting, the line-item format usually is the basic component of organization budgets. Program budgets sometimes are used in conjunction with the line-item format, with cost information in line-item format and program information presented in narrative form. Far less frequently are standalone performance budgets used, although elements of performance budgeting are found in a number of state budgets.

The National Association of State Budget Officers (NASBO) periodic survey of *Budget Processes in the States* (1997) contains information regarding "budget approach" used by the states. States self-report their "budget approach" as incremental, program, zero-based, or performance budgeting. While line-item budgets and incremental decision making are not the same thing, they often are linked as elements of traditional budgeting. The "incremental" category in the NASBO survey may be considered a proxy for the line-item budget format. In the NASBO survey, five states identified their approach as incremental, eight identified their approach as program, one identified its approach as zero-based, and none identified the approach as performance budgeting. Most of the other 36 states identified their "approach" as various combinations of incremental, program, zero-based, and performance budgeting. Three identified their budget procedures as using all four approaches, 12 identified their procedures as using three approaches, and 21 identified their procedures as using two approaches. The modal category was program/incremental ($n = 16$). Clearly, "budget approaches" in the states are hybrids, not pure types.

IV. STATE EXPERIENCES WITH PROGRAM AND PERFORMANCE BUDGETING

Researchers have been examining state budgeting practices and management techniques for decades. Important and ongoing studies by Robert D. Lee, a periodic survey by the National Association of State Budget Officers, and one-time studies by other researchers have provided a rich description of current and future trends in state budgeting. These studies also provide a context for the survey results presented later in the chapter.

Efforts to link program and performance analysis with budgeting have been attempted for decades by states and by the federal government. One of the earliest reforms dates back to 1949. Executive Order 10072 established an Advisory Committee on Management Improvement and required heads of all federal agencies to make periodic and systematic appraisals of their operations (Yamada, 1972). The latest movement follows the tenets of total quality management (TQM) and strategic planning. At the federal level, Vice President Gore continues to implement the National Performance Review program. Congress has supported these efforts and passed the Government Performance and Results Act of 1993 (P.L. 103–62), which requires state agencies to develop annual performance plans. In the same year, President Clinton issued Executive Order 12862 which requires federal agencies to develop and to measure customer service standards (Lee, 1997a).

Several projects are under way to develop performance standards for managing government entities. The National Advisory Council on State and Local Budgeting (NACSLB) was formed by several budget and governmental associations to determine what constitutes "best practices" in state and local budgeting. "The council has agreed on 59 practice statements on what it considers to be components of a commendable budget process" (NACSBL, 1997). The recommendations incorporate many of the goals of strategic planning such as using a long-term perspective, establishing linkages to broad organizational goals, focusing budget decisions on outcomes and results, involving and promoting communication with stakeholders, and providing incentives to government management and employees.

The Government Performance Project, coordinated by the Alan K. Campbell Public Affairs Institute at Syracuse University, designed a method for assessing and rating management. Performance measures have been specified in six management areas: financial management, managing for results, capital management, human resource management, information technology and executive capacity.

A recent project report, "Grading the States: A Management Report Card" (*Governing*, 1999), notes that "more and more states are deciding to hold themselves accountable for the results produced by the dollars they spend every year. Strategic planning, performance measurement, bench-marking, and performance-based budgeting are all in use in a growing number of places, though the way the terms are defined varies widely." State grades range from A− in two states where "managing for results" is an integral part of government, to F in one state which seems to have ignored performance-based management completely. Most states are graded somewhere in between, with a 50-state average of C+ in the managing for results category.

Looking primarily for achievements in performance-based budgeting, a perusal of the study's report on each state leads to three generalizations. First, the quality of the performance data varies from a few states where "excellent examples of outcome measures are easy to find," to several states where "outcome measures are still being used in budgeting decisions in only a limited way," to many states where "the quality of the data and many of the measurements could use improvement." Output measures apparently are much more prevalent than outcome measures. Second, many states have initiated performance-based budgeting by using a small number of pilot agencies before expanding to a larger number of agencies, and pockets of success with measuring outcomes is more common than state-wide success. Third, legislatures tend to be disinterested in performance-based budgeting. Some appear to be wary of performance-based budgeting because they fear such data might be used to strengthen agency claims for increases in spending, or to shift the balance of power between the executive and legislative branches to the disadvantage of the executive. However, some legislatures have realized that good performance data is information to help them carry out their legislative functions more effectively.

Robert D. Lee over the past 25 years has surveyed state budget offices at 5-year intervals regarding their budget preparation procedures, use of program analysis, accounting procedures, and personnel qualifications. Lee's surveys demonstrate that these offices are dynamic, continuing to search for methods of improving budgeting practices and fiscal control. Higher levels of education among analysts and computerization have permitted states to thoroughly analyze and develop data on agencies and funding requests.

Jon Yunker identified several issues as important for managing a state budget office. Yunker (1990) believes four matters must be addressed: defining the role of the budget office in relation to the governor's office and the legislature; defining the organizational structure that best supports that role; finding and developing the right personnel; and adopting a management style and strategy to maximize the effectiveness of personnel. According to Yunker, an effectively managed office is a necessary precondition for a successful budget process because management and staff energy can only then be devoted to resource allocation and policy guidance.

The primary focus of the central budget office is budget preparation and fiscal guidance for agencies. According to Al Kilman (1990), a successful budget process is defined by five criteria: the budget is produced; it is "on time"; it reflects the priorities of the top decision maker; the document is accurate; and it has sufficient backup detail for defense. Furthermore, Kilman contends these elements are fundamental, extending beyond where the budget is produced or the process used for budget development (e.g., PPBS or MBO). These elements are necessary whether the process is defined through policy or political outcomes.

Lee describes six forms of budget guidance (1992). These include imposing budget ceilings for agency requests, maintaining minimum or current levels of service, mandating which types of policies will receive favorable reaction by the governor, inclusion of necessary or mandatory program improvements or expansions (e.g., court orders or federal requirements), and requiring agencies to rank requests. These kinds of ceilings or guidance on agency requests have grown in popularity over the past 20 years and reflect the need to "weed out" lower priority spending in order to accommodate critical programs such as Medicaid and public safety. For example, in 1970, 59% of the states reported not using any form of budget ceilings to constrain agency requests. By 1990 only 11% reported not using any form of budget ceiling. However, in 1995 the trend was reversed, with 28% of state budget offices reporting that they did not impose budget ceilings for agency requests (Lee, 1997a). This may a sign that states have rebounded from the recessionary pressures of the early 1990s and are permitting agencies to expand programs after several years of constrained spending.

In 1995, nearly half the states reported using specific dollar-level ceiling techniques for agency budget preparation compared to no states imposing specific dollar-level ceilings in 1970. The use of written policy guidance has increased over the past 25 years from 2% to 39% in 1995. Interestingly, the practice of ranking priorities among programs decreased from 1990 to 1995 but it is still utilized by more than three-fourths of the states (Lee, 1997a).

In 1995, Francis Stokes Berry and Barton Wechsler surveyed state agencies on several aspects of strategic planning including, the kinds of processes employed, and the objectives and outcomes of the process (Berry and Wechsler, 1995). The authors defined strategic planning as ''a systematic process for managing the organization and its future direction in relation to its environment and the demands of external stakeholders, including strategy formulation, analysis of agency strengths and weaknesses, identification of agency stakeholders, implementation of strategic actions, and issue management.'' The study found approximately 60% of agencies responding used some type of strategic planning. Although this is a significant portion, the results should be viewed with caution because states have only recently begun implementing the process.

Reasons considered important for using strategic planning from highest to lowest response (96% to 60%) included setting program and policy direction, a desire to emulate good business practices, government budget and fiscal pressures, and a need to resolve competing agency resource allocation priorities. Agencies have begun connecting strategic planning to the budget process. In fact, three-quarters of the respondents link the strategic planning process and the agency's budget process. One important way to tie the two processes together is through workload measures that quantitatively reflect the achievement of objectives. Of course, one problem with the linkage is the inherent conflict between the long-term plan and the single year budget cycle of most governments. The authors are optimistic about the future of strategic planning by state agencies, expecting its importance to expand in the future.

Lee outlines the changes in the usage of program analysis and effectiveness and productivity measures over time. States report significant declines in conducting program analysis by central budget offices. There were 18 and 16 percentage-point decreases in effectiveness and productivity analyses from 1990 to 1995, respectively (Lee, 1997b). Other central offices appear to be doing this work instead (Lee, 1997a). However, states that conduct productivity analysis do use the information for decision making (Lee, 1997b). How this will effect budget practices and decisions is unknown at this point.

Detailed performance measures have also appeared to reach their maximum use in 1990, when 95% of all states included program effectiveness measures in budget requests for new or revised programs (Lee, 1997a). In 1995, states were not using this kind information as much (72%), but it is still much higher than 1970 levels (24%). These measures are substantially employed for revising funding levels though. Effectiveness and productivity measures were used by 57% and 60% of the states respectively in 1995, up from 49% and 51% in 1990. One reason for the overall decline may be the difficulty in establishing useful measures and in gathering the data, particularly for effectiveness measures. Of course, as state executive and legislative budget offices become more sophisticated in using indicators, these difficulties will wane, enabling the most efficient use of the information. Lee concludes that the executive branch has probably ''balanced out'' in using these forms of analysis (Lee, 1997a).

In another survey of state budget offices, Julia Melkers and Katherine Willoughby found that 47 of the states have some form of performance-based budgeting requirements (Melkers and Willoughby, 1998). The authors define performance-based budgeting as requiring strategic planning regarding agency mission, goals and objectives, and a process that requests quantifiable data about program outcomes. The requirements are statutory for 31 states or administrative in 16 states. Only Arkansas, Massachusetts, and New York do not have either type of mandate.

Confirming other research, the study found that the budgeting requirements were recent, with the exception of Hawaii and Illinois. Sixteen of the states with statutory requirements tie performance measures to strategic planning in the law. In most cases, responsibility for developing measures lies with the line agencies, which is sensible since these are the agencies with programmatic knowledge. Melkers and Willoughby (1998) include a cautionary note in reporting their findings, stating that ''the effectiveness and contribution of performance measures to the budgeting process in the states remains unclear.'' Constraints on time, resources, and data limit the full utilization of measurements.

NASBO's 1997 survey results confirm much of the information of the previously cited surveys and offer interesting additional information. In 32 states, budget offices monitor performance measures, and in 29 states the results are published. States use these measures for a variety of reasons including public accountability (24 states), goal or priority building (21 states) and budgeting decisions (24 states).

Based on his research on state budgetary reforms, Lauth (1992) concludes that several conditions must exist for the efforts to be successful. The existing system must be perceived as unsatisfactory. The governor's commitment is necessary. The program should not be oversold with grand promises. Managers and budgeters implementing the effort must be thoroughly trained and their support obtained. The program should be selectively installed, i.e., pilot agencies. Requisite data bases and accounting processes must be compatible and support the new information requirements. The reformers must consider the political ramifications. The effort ought to have a good implementation strategy consisting of a clear statement of goals and an understanding of how existing organizational units and procedures contribute to those goals. The reform is an ongoing effort, probably requiring adjustments. Finally, it its important not to overemphasize the rational/technical features of budget innovation at the expense of political/democratic values.

The federal government has been following the states' lead on budget reform, as can be seen from the previously mentioned National Performance Review (NPR) and the mandatory development of performance standards. Philip G. Joyce cautions the leaders and the public about being overly optimistic for the future of these reforms in his essay, "The Reiterative Nature of Budget Reform: Is There Anything New in Federal Budgeting?" (Joyce, 1993a). Joyce links the current reform efforts to past ones such as PPBS and ZBB to demonstrate how the federal government has tried to implement performance budgeting several times previously. He asserts that the system failed for two reasons: first, the reforms were not consistent with the political process and second, the paperwork requirements were too burdensome. These problems are also possible for the latest reform efforts so those implementing the NPR need to (1) appreciate that the reforms may be resisted by those who have a stake in the traditional incremental budgeting process, (2) ensure the information provided is necessary and used, and (3) analyze how the reforms will be implemented and the information used before instituting universal requirements (Joyce, 1993b). Furthermore, the stakeholders must realize that reform will occur at the margin rather than through a wholesale effort (Joyce, 1993a).

For the new generation of reforms to take root, policy makers must expect a relationship between money spent and performance. Before this can happen, though, the Executive, Congress, and stakeholders must first agree on the agencies' most important goals. In other words, agencies have competing functions, and for there to be an accurate assessment of success, everyone must agree on what success means; only then can objectives be quantified (Joyce, 1993b). Developing outcome measures for some departments and functions may be very difficult where outcomes are vague or implementation is dependent on outside actors such as the Defense Department and intergovernmental programs. Over time, performance measures may be able to provide information that legislators and the President can use making fiscal decisions, but as mentioned previously, this will be in context to other political and policy decisions. In the end, the greatest use of performance indicators may be as a management tool to track spending and efficiency.

Beyond budget processes and performance, central budget offices use several techniques to control agency spending and ensure expenditures do not exceed revenues. One is reviewing interim expenditures through reports. Thirty-nine states use this method, and most do so on a monthly basis. Budget offices can also limit the amount of revenue allotments to agencies; however, most choose not to do so. In fact, the states vary widely in allotment request using quarterly, annual, or "as requested" time frames. Only Utah has allotment requests on a monthly basis (NASBO, 1997). The ability to transfer funds between programs or departments is another widely used form of control over agencies. In performing this function, budget offices must achieve a balance between adhering to legislative intent as expressed in the appropriations act, and permitting agencies to accommodate changed circumstances or respond to unforeseen events. Only 11 states permit the agency to transfer appropriations between programs or units in a department, and no agency is allowed to transfer funds between departments without approval of some other entity such as the legislature, budget office, or controlling board. In nearly half the states (21), these kinds of transfers are not even permitted (NASBO, 1997).

V. SURVEY OF STATE BUDGET OFFICES

To better understand the activities state budget offices currently use to manage state government and control government spending, a survey was sent in the spring of 1998 to all state budget offices (State Budgeting Survey, 1998). The survey asked respondents to identify from a list provided those activities used in their state to maintain control over state spending and to enhance the management of state government. Respondents were invited to identify any other activities they use for these purposes. Respondents also were asked to rate the level of effectiveness for each activity on a 4-point scale (very effective, effective, somewhat effective, and not effective). Forty-six states returned the survey, for a response rate of 92%.

Spending control activities include the following:

Stipulating limits on agency budget requests
Providing budget preparation instructions for agencies
Providing policy guidelines for agencies
Review and analysis of agency operating budget requests
Review and analysis of agency capital equipment requests
Recommendations to the governor on agency funding levels
Review and analysis of agency revenue increases (e.g., fees)
Quarterly allotments to agencies
Review and analysis of budget amendments for agencies
Review and analysis of supplemental appropriations for agencies
End-of-year revenue reconciliation for agency budgets
End-of-year spending reconciliation for agency budgets
Quarterly or periodic reviews of expenditure reports
Monitor expenditures regularly through a centralized accounting system

Most of these spending-control activities are performed by budget offices in three-fourths or more of the states. Stipulation of spending limits is performed by budget offices in two-thirds of the states, end-of-year reconciliation is performed in fewer than one-half of the states, and quarterly allotments are performed in fewer than one-third of the states. A large majority of respondents from states performing each activity reported that the activity is *effective* or *very effective* in maintaining control of spending.

Management enhancement activities include the following:

Perform program evaluations for efficiency
Perform program evaluations for effectiveness
Perform management studies as directed by the governor
Review implementation of new programs
Coordinate development of statewide strategic plan
Establish statewide standards and procedures for agency plans
Facilitate development of strategic plans of state agencies
Review or approve final strategic plans for state agencies
Facilitate development of agency performance indicators
Oversee agency achievement of performance indicators
Oversee agency adherence to legislative directives or management recommendations
Oversee agency compliance with legislative audit recommendations or findings

Most of the management enhancement activities are performed by budget offices in approximately one-half of the states. Three activities are performed by budget offices in approximately two-thirds of the states: management studies as directed by the governor, review of the implementation of new programs, and oversight of agency adherence to legislative directives. The point to be emphasized is that activities generally associated with results-based budgeting, such as strategic planning, performance measurement, and program evaluations, are being carried out by budget offices in approximately one-half of the states. Respondent perceptions of the degree of effectiveness of management enhancement activities differs somewhat from their perceptions of the effectiveness of spending control activities. Respondents from states performing each activity reported that the activity is *effective* or *somewhat effective* in improving the management of state agencies.

Spending and management control activities also include the following:

Maintenance of personnel position counts
Review and approve new positions
Review and approve position classifications
Review and approve agency contracts
Review and approve equipment purchases
Pre-audit other categories of agency expenditures

The budget offices in three-fourths of the states review and approve the creation of new personnel positions, and budget offices in approximately one-half of the states maintain personnel position counts. However, budget offices in fewer than one-third of the states perform the other functions. Review and approval of position classifications, preaudits, and approval of contracts and purchases tend to be performed by other state government agencies, not the budget office.

Several respondents listed one or more additional activities they use to control spending and enhance management in their states. However, with one exception, most activities appeared to be state-specific. The activity listed by four respondents is a form of impoundment—the withholding of funds appropriated by the legislature. One budget office described the activity: "With the governor's approval, authority to restrict appropriated funds during the fiscal year." A second budget office called it "withholding." A third wrote, "We can reduce appropriations if we believe revenues will be short." The fourth budget office described it in the following way: "As needed institute contingency plans whereby a percentage of operating funds are held in reserve and released upon compelling justification." Each state characterized such activity as "very effective." Impoundment sometimes signals policy or partisan disagreement between the governor and the state legislature. At other times, as when faced with revenue shortfall, it is prudent fiscal management.

Based on the literature summarized in the previous section, one might conclude that state governments are actively engaged in results-based or new performance budgeting. However, our survey results suggest caution in embracing this conclusion. Many state budget offices report engaging in activities usually associated with results-based or the new performance budgeting. Yet, those activities are judged by respondents to be only moderately effective.

Approximately one-half of the state budget offices ($n = 23$) report using program evaluations to enhance the efficiency and effectiveness of their governments. However, only one respondent judged program evaluations to be "very effective" and none reported that program evaluations were "not effective." Ten respondents judged program evaluations to be "effective," and 12 judged them to be only "somewhat effective."

Approximately one-half of the budget offices are involved in the strategic planning process, either generally, by coordinating development of a statewide plan or establishing statewide standards and procedures for agency plans, or specifically, by facilitating the development of agency plans or by reviewing and approving final drafts of agency plans. The majority of state budget offices found these activities either "effective" or "very effective" with percentages ranging from 62% for review and approval of agency strategic plans to 87% for establishing statewide standards. Interestingly, budget officers found the more general coordinating function rather than the more specific review and approval function to be where they achieved the greatest degree of effectiveness. This may be because state budget offices possess the expertise to develop a statewide strategic plan but lack the programmatic expertise to evaluate individual agency strategic plans.

Budget offices are involved in the development of agency performance indicators (83%), but only 52% of the offices oversee agency achievement of performance indicators. Of those budget offices facilitating the development of agency performance indicators, 53% consider this activity "very effective" or "effective" for managing state government. Similarly, of those budget offices overseeing agency achievement of performance indicators, 58% consider that activity "very effective" or "effective" for managing state government.

There are several activities that budget offices consistently undertake and find useful. For example, 45 of 46 budget offices responding to the survey recommend funding levels to the governor for individual agencies, and 42 of those offices (93%) find this activity either "effective" or "very effective" maintaining control over state spending. Thirty-nine budget offices review and analyze the effect of agency fee increases on the public, and 73% of them find this activity "effective" or "very effective." Budget offices also are concerned with budget amendments and supplemental appropriations. Seventy-one percent of budget offices find the examination of budget amendments "effective" or "very effective," and 87% of budget offices find analysis of supplemental appropriation requests "effective" or "very effective" for controlling state spending.

These response patterns suggest that not only do state budget offices continue to perform traditional budgeting activities, they also perceive those activities to be effective in their efforts to control state spending and manage state government. Despite the efforts in the past quarter-century to move state government budgeting from traditional approaches to a greater utilization of program and performance information, from an emphasis on items purchased to an emphasis on program results, the traditional budget has had strong staying power (Wildavsky, 1978).

VI. CONCLUSION

Throughout the 1900s reform movements have sought to increase state government accountability to the public. The budget movement was an attempt to reduce waste and inefficiency in the use of public funds. The executive budget advocated an integrated administrative system with the governor as chief administrator. It aimed at strengthening the governor's capacity to control and direct agencies within the executive branch so as to increase responsiveness and responsibility to the legislature and to the public. The line-item budget sought to control expenditures as a fiduciary responsibility, to ensure that funds are spent for the purposes for which they were designated, and to limit the overall size of government. The performance budget was advocated as a technique for increasing efficiency in the internal management of government. The program budget sought to make planning and analytical decision making part of the budget process, thereby improving the quality of public programs. The most recent reform, performance-based, or results-based, budgeting aims at explicit identification of outcomes to be produced by government programs, the development of performance measures to gauge progress toward achieving those outcomes, and use of such information by governors and legislatures to determine the worth of government programs. The common element in each of these reform movements is government accountability. Efforts to achieve accountability by linking program and performance data with fiscal data in the budget have had mixed success. The quality of management activities and the quality of public services no doubt have improved as a result of efforts to rationalize the budget process, but those efforts have only partially succeeded.

Throughout this century budgets have been important instruments for public management and accountability. As we look to the next century, we can expect budgets and budgeting to occupy a central place in the never-ending quest for government accountability to the public.

Appendix A: Budget Management as a Fiscal Necessity in Georgia

Henry M. Huckaby, Former Director, Office of Planning and Budget

At the outset of the second term of [Georgia] Governor Zell Miller, the staff of the Office of Planning and Budget (OPB) was forced to devise a new approach to constructing the Governor's annual budget proposal to the Georgia General Assembly. Miller had set specific policy objectives for his second term whose costs exceeded the projected yearly revenue growth for the succeeding four years. Consequently, a means of managing the state's revenues to match the Governor's strongly held policy and program objectives was conceived and labeled "Budget Redirection." Under the rubric of "Redirection," powerful tools were put in place which allowed the OPB to address agency budget behaviors many of which have been the bane of all executive budget directors for a long time.

1. *Limit Agency Budget Acquisitiveness.* Faced with the necessity to redirect current funds to support the Governor's highest priorities, the allocation decisions to be made by the Governor would only be made more difficult were agencies allowed to continue their traditional pattern of unrestrained requests for increasing funding for existing programs or establishing new ones. Consequently, the percentage of new funds requested was to be limited to the value of the projected growth level for the forthcoming fiscal year. In addition to making the universe of new agency requests more manageable, there are at least two other positive attributes to this approach: (a) limiting the amount an agency may request reinforced the Governor's commitment to making "Redirection" work; (b) secondly, it forced agency heads to establish priorities for new funding rather than merely shifting those decisions forward to the OPB and the Governor.

2. *Negotiated Budget Base.* Many budget scholars as well as budget practitioners have long known that the budget base is the best predictor of future appropriation levels. Therefore, it was important that the budget base for each agency be established as early in the budget cycle as possible. To that end redirection required that the value of the

budget base be negotiated prior to the agency's formal budget submission to the OPB on September 1. This approach sought to limit the amount of game-playing as to what is to be included and what is to be excluded. By requiring that this amount be negotiated early in the process, all of the Governor's review period could focus on the agency redirection proposals and new funding requests.

3. *Linkage of Requests to Agency Strategic Objectives.* In 1993 Governor Miller had introduced and successfully passed major budget reform legislation. One of the new components of this legislation was the requirement for state agencies to prepare a strategic plan which was consistent with and reflective of the larger goals and objectives of the State's Strategic Plan. However, until the introduction of redirection, the fiscal imperative for the implementation of agency plans in the context of resource allocation decisions was missing. Now, the strategic objectives of an agency provide a program framework for budget analysis rather than the traditional line-item focus.

4. *Agency Program Performance Versus Expenditure Accounting.* Companion to the requirement for strategic planning is the move toward performance budgeting or in Georgia known as "results-based budgeting." Budget redirection provided a formal budget structure to change the focus and content of fiscal analysis both within the agency and the Office of Planning and Budget. Linking resource allocation to agreed-upon policy and program outcomes provides a powerful tool to both agency heads and the Governor in achieving the State's policy objectives.

The introduction of "Budget Redirection" has potentially changed state budgeting in Georgia for decades to come. Critics of this new approach argue that in the next fiscal crisis (recession) the Governor and legislature are likely to revert to the old ways. I would argue the contrary. In fact, Redirection was introduced in a period of self-induced fiscal crisis caused by the Governor's unyielding commitment to specific costly policy initiatives. These policy initiatives could be funded only by the reduction of the budget base of some agencies. Consequently, both agency personnel and OPB analysts are now accustomed to collecting data and conducting fiscal analysis for competing priorities. Also, agency heads have experience in making difficult resource allocation decisions—experience that will be invaluable during periods of modest or little net revenue growth. Consequently, budget redirection provides strong and effective budget management tools that are likely to be strengthened during periods of fiscal crisis.

Appendix B: Budget Management Practices in Nevada

Don W. Hataway, Deputy Director, Budget Division, Department of Administration

The Nevada Revised Statutes (NRS) requires all departments, institutions and other agencies of the executive department of state government and all agencies of the executive department receiving state money, fees or other funds under the authority of the state to submit agency budget requests to the Budget Division (Budget) for each biennium on or before August 15th preceding the next legislative session. The use of the agency budget request to construct the Governor's *Executive Budget* for presentation to the legislature is the point where the state budget management cycle is initiated.

Budget issues instructions that contain detailed guidelines for completing the payroll and line-item agency budget requests. Although the budgets are developed on the basis of the state strategic plan and agency measurements of performance, as well as the fact that the Executive Budget is presented in a summary format to the legislature, we have yet to move totally away from the line-item budget method of evaluation.

The budget is in three parts—an adjusted base budget, the program maintenance budget(s), and the enhancement budget(s). Maintenance budgets are the cost to continue existing programs, but at levels affected by external factors. Those factors include such issues as costs associated with inflation, demographic/caseload changes, fringe benefit rate adjustments, federal mandates, court orders, and consent decrees. Enhancement budgets are the cost of funding agency proposals to address the state's functional goals identified through the strategic planning process and program improvements and changes in service levels not related specifically to a functional goal. Maintenance and enhancements are displayed in separate numbered and titled sections reflecting the incremental costs for and supporting revenue associated with the specific decision.

The three-part budget process is designed to allow the legislature to concentrate on policy issues and the enhancements contained in the Executive Budget. Every effort is made by the executive and legislative fiscal staffs to come to closure on adjusted base budget issues and for the most part on fiscal issues required to maintain current services. Although this portion of the budget process is still evolving, experience to date indicates it has minimized the amount of time the legislature spends on routine issues.

Of special interest is the fact that a ballot initiative will be considered by the electorate in November 1998 to limit the biennial legislative session to 120 days. On the basis of the fact that the 1997 session lasted 169 days, it will be imperative that the budget process become even more streamlined in the event this measure is approved. In addition to the basic budget directives, there are a number of additional requirements that could require considerable investment of agency personnel time. These features include: the review and updating of the agency strategic plan; the review and updating of agency measurements of performance; the development of Business Plans for all projects that have an ultimate cost in excess of $1,000,000 or an increase in a current service program by 50%, whichever is less; the development of Technology Improvement Project and Investment Justification Documents for all information technology projects over $25,000; the projection for the operation and maintenance costs associated with new building construction; and the development of reports to address legislative Letters of Intent issued by previous legislatures.

The legislative approved budget allocates funds by expenditure category with a majority of the allocations to the categories of salaries, out-of-state travel, in-state travel, operating, equipment, information technology and training. The NRS states that it is a misdemeanor for an agency head to commit the state to expenditures in excess of category authority. An agency may submit budget amendments to Budget. Within certain financial thresholds, Budget is authorized to approve the amendments. However, major revenue and expenditure adjustments must be approved by the legislative Interim Finance Committee. Unless there is statutory authority or authority provided in the appropriation and authorization budget bills for transfers between budgets and/or fiscal years, the agency must "live within" the parameters of the original legislatively approved budget for both years of the biennium.

Many other aspects of the use of agency funds are controlled, reviewed, and approved by Budget. This activity includes review and approval of all contracts with independent contractors, lease agreements for non-state building rent, purchase requisitions and journal vouchers for transfers between budget accounts and account categories. In order to minimize the "micro-management" of state agencies beyond the otherwise tight restrictions, Budget staff is directed to limit decisions to whether the request is legal, within the agency mission and state goals, within state statutory and regulatory requirements, within federal regulatory requirements, and whether the proposal is cost-effective, technically correct, and good public policy.

Throughout this entire cycle, close communication and coordination are maintained with the Governor's Office. Every effort is made to present a "united front" to the legislature, with Budget concentrating on fiscal issues and the Governor's staff concentrating on the policy issues.

REFERENCES

Abney, G., and Lauth, T. P. (1987). Perceptions of the impact of governors and legislatures in the state appropriations process, *Western Political Quarterly*, 40: 335–342.

Abney, G. and Lauth, T. P. (1989). The executive budget in the states: Normative idea and empirical observation, *Policy Studies Journal, 17 (summer)*: 829–840.

Axelrod, D. (1989). *A Budget Quartet: Critical Policy and Management Issues*, St. Martins Press, New York.

Berry, F. S., and Wechsler, B. (1995). State agencies' experience with strategic planning: Findings from a national survey, *Public Administration Review, 55 (March/April)*: 159.

Clynch, E. J., and Lauth, T. P., eds. (1991). *Governors, Legislatures, and Budgets: Diversity Across the American States*, Greenwood Press, Westport, CT.

Duncombe, S., Andreason, J., and Seale, L. (1981). Zero-base budgeting in Idaho: An evaluation after five years, *Government Accountants Journal, 30 (summer)*: 24–35.

Duncombe, S., and Kinney, R. (1987). Agency budget success: How it is defined by budget officials in five western states, *Public Budgeting and Finance, 7 (spring)*: 24–37.

Gosling, J. J. (1991). Patterns of stability and change in gubernatorial policy agendas, *State and Local Government Review, 23 (winter)*: 3–12.

Gosling, J. J. (1987). The state budget office and policy making, *Public Budgeting and Finance, 7 (spring)*: 51–65.

Grading the States: A Management Report Card. (1999). *Governing*, February: 17–90.

Howard, S. K. (1973). *Changing State Budgeting*, Council of State Governments, Lexington, KY.

Joyce, P. G. (1993a). The reiterative nature of budget reform: Is there anything new in federal budgeting? *Public Budgeting and Finance, 13 (fall)*: 36–48.

Joyce, P. G. (1993b). Using performance measures for federal budgeting: Proposals and prospects, *Public Budgeting and Finance, 13: (winter)*: 3–17.

Kilman, A. (1990). A successful budget process, *Public Budgeting and Finance, 10 (summer)*: 110–114.

Lauth, T. P. (1992). State budgeting: Current conditions and future trends, *International Journal of Public Administration, 15*: 1067–1096.

Lauth, T. P. (1987). Budgeting productivity in state government: Not integrated but friendly, *Public Productivity Review, 10 (spring)*: 21–32.

Lauth, T. P. (1997). Zero-base budget, *International Encyclopedia of Public Policy and Administration* (J. Shafritz, ed.) Westview Press, Boulder CO.

Lauth, T. P. (1978). Zero base budgeting in Georgia state government: Myth and reality, *Public Administration Review, 38 (September/October)*: 420–430.

Lauth, T. P., and Reick, S. C. (1979). Modifications in Georgia zero-base budgeting procedures: 1973–1980, *Midwest Review of Public Administration, 13 (December)*: 225–238.

Lauth, T. P., and Steinbauer, P. E. (1998). *State Budgeting Survey.* University of Georgia, Athens, GA.

Lee, R. D. (1997a). A quarter century of state budgeting practices, *Public Administration Review, 57 (March/April)*: 133–140.

Lee, R. D. (1997b). The use of program analysis in state budgeting: Changes between 1990 and 1995, *Public Budgeting and Finance, 17 (summer)*: 18–36.

Lee, R. D. (1992). The use of executive guidance in state budget preparation, *Public Budgeting and Finance, 12 (fall)*: 19–32.

Melkers, J., and Willoughby, K. G. (1998). The state of the states: Performance-based budgeting requirements in 47 out of 50, *Public Administration Review, 58 (January/February)*: 66–73.

Mikesell, J. L. (1999). *Fiscal Administration: Analysis and Applications for the Public Sector,* Harcourt, Brace and Co., Orlando, FL.

National Association of State Budget Offices. (1997). *Budget Processes in the States,* National Assoc. of State Budget Offices, Washington, D.C.

National Advisory Council on State and Local Budgeting. (1997). *A Framework for Improved State and Local Government Budgeting and Recommended Budget Practices-Draft.* Http://www.gfoa.org/nacslb/framework.htm

Schick, A. (1971). *Budget Innovations in the States,* Brookings Institution, Washington, DC.

Schick, A. (1973). A death in the bureaucracy: The demise of federal PPB, *Public Administration Review, 33 (March/April)*: 146–156.

Wildavsky, A. (1978). A budget for all seasons? Why the traditional budget lasts, *Public Administration Review, 38 (November/December)*: 501–509.

Willoughby, K. G. (1993). Decision making orientations of state government budget analysts: Rationalists or incrementalists?, *Public Budgeting and Financial Management, 5 (winter)*: 67–114.

Yamada, G. T. (1972). Improving management effectiveness in the federal government, *Public Administration Review, 32 (November/December*: 764–770.

Yunker, J. (1990). Managing a budget office, *Public Budgeting and Finance, 10 (summer)*: 96–101.

8
Developments in Personnel/Human Resources Management in State Government

Curtis R. Berry
Shippensburg University, Shippensburg, Pennsylvania

At the close of the 20th century a wide array of challenges and expectations confront personnel/human resource management officials in state government. The so-called "devolution" of governmental responsibilities appears to be shifting increased responsibility back to the states. Governors frustrated with Washington have been demanding a greater role in the formulation and delivery of domestic policies, and it appears that their concerns have been heard. States now face the prospect of having to "put up or shut up." For the personnel staff at various levels within the states, this challenge means increased pressure to provide effective, meaningful, and timely assistance to agencies (and their employees) as they strive to meet the expectations of elected officials and the public. Simultaneously, efforts continue to reduce or at least rein in the size and rate of growth of bureaucracies in many locales.

The discussion which follows provides an overview of the current status and recent developments in the field of personnel/human resources management in state government. An effort was made to examine as wide array of personnel issues as possible. Topics are addressed from the perspective of the practitioner striving to cope with the myriad personnel issues that arise in contemporary state government. Chapter length restrictions limit the amount of attention given to any one area.

I. STRUCTURAL ARRANGEMENTS IN STATE PERSONNEL ADMINISTRATION

A. Organization of the State Personnel Office

As with most governmental activities, tremendous variation exists when one examines and compares the personnel operations of state governments. While all states except Texas have a centralized personnel function, there are major differences in the organizations that have responsibility for the function. For example, the number of employees the office is responsible for ranges from about 10,000 in New Hampshire to 188,000 in New York (Sheibley, 1997: App. B).

Some state personnel offices have responsibility for serving only state agencies or departments; others have additional responsibilities for educational institutions and/or local government administrative units. The legal basis for the state personnel department varies as well. It may be rooted in state constitutional language, statutes enacted by the legislature, gubernatorial executive order, or some combination of these (NASPE 1996:1–5).

In about half the states the personnel function is handled by a stand-alone administrative entity, while in the remaining states the function is in a division of a larger administrative structure such as an Office of Administration, Management Services, or the like. The chief personnel official in most states (26) is selected by the governor; officials in 15 states are appointed by the department head of the agency in which the personnel office is located; and in the remaining states a personnel board makes the appointment (*Book of the States*, 1996:295–296).

In 47 states a single personnel office has primary responsibility for most if not all activities associated with the personnel function. In some of these states, however, one or more functions (e.g., labor relations or appeals of adverse actions) may be assigned to a separate organization. Two states, Pennsylvania and California, divide responsibilities associated with directing the state merit system between two separate agencies (Sheibley, 1997, p. 2).

In California, the constitutionally established state personnel board (SPB) is responsible for ensuring that employment decisions are based on merit and that the state's civil service system is free of improper patronage influences. Additionally, the board has responsibility for recruitment, selection, position classification, appellate review of adverse actions, goal setting, training, and consultation services to other state departments. Also responsible for personnel matters is the statutorily created department of personnel administration (DPA) which represents the governor on all matters concerning employee relations, including labor-management relations, classification and compensation, employee benefits, health and safety matters, training and continuous improvement efforts, and litigation of personnel matters (SPB & DPA Web Sites Oct. 1998).

Responsibility for persons in the classified service in Pennsylvania rests with the state civil service commission (CSC) and the office of employee relations in the governor's office of administration. The CSC recruits applicants, develops and administers employment and promotion tests, conducts investigations of possible Civil Service Act violations, and supervises various other aspects of Pennsylvania's civil service system. The office of employee relations and three of its four bureaus are responsible for position classification, maintaining the compensation plan, labor relations and collective bargaining, equal employment opportunity, and oversight of operating agency personnel offices. A fourth bureau, state employment, has responsibility for developing and maintaining procedures related to recruitment, selection, promotion, and termination of personnel in nonclassified positions in agencies under the governor's jurisdiction (PA Legislative Budget & Finance Committee, April 1998:8–11).

B. Functions of the Central Personnel Agency

The state government central personnel agency typically has responsibility or shares responsibility with operating agencies for a number of personnel functions. The more significant of these include recruitment, test development and administration, issuing hiring rules, classification and compensation administration, labor-management relations, and appeals of personnel actions. The range of functions and roles handled by the central personnel agency in the states is shown in Table 1.

Table 1 Functions and Responsibilities of Central Personnel Agencies in the States

Establishes minimum qualifications	HR development	Productivity systems
Merit system testing	Training	Employee attitude surveys
Human resources planning	Employee health and wellness programs	Dependent care
Classification	Affirmative action	Workers' compensation
Position allocation	Labor and employee relations	Group health insurance
Compensation	Collective bargaining/ labor negotiations	Deferred compensation
Recruitment	Grievance and appeals	Drug and alcohol testing
Selection	Alternative dispute resolution	Retirement
Performance evaluation	Employee incentive programs	Employee promotions
Position audits		Budget recommendations to the legislature
Personnel function audit of agencies		
Employee assistance and counseling		

Source: National Association of State Personnel Executives, 1996.

1. Recruitment

Because the public sector is largely "labor-intensive," recruitment of personnel is a vital function. Recruitment involves identifying and developing favorable contacts with qualified and motivated persons and securing applications from them. In this process, the central personnel agency normally develops and disseminates recruitment literature and maintains a pool of applicants certified for appointment for the various state agencies, educational institutions, and local governments served by the office.

2. Test Development and Administration

A second major area of responsibility typically under the jurisdiction of the central personnel office is test development and administration. While a considerable discussion has centered on decentralization of testing in recent years, the reality is that testing essentially remains the responsibility of the central personnel office. For example, while Wisconsin has been recognized for decentralizing testing, the actual extent of that decentralization is somewhat limited. Additionally, states having strong merit traditions are more apt to rely on centralized test development and administration (Sheibley, 1997:4–5).

   The development and validation of tests is a highly technical, time-consuming, and expensive endeavor. These efforts must be undertaken in a manner consistent with the requirements of Title VII of the Civil Rights Act of 1964, as amended; the Uniform Guidelines on Employee Selection Procedures; as well as specific and perhaps unique requirements of specialized agencies being served. For example, tests developed for Wildlife Conservation Officers in the Commonwealth of Pennsylvania combine questions addressing law enforcement issues and wildlife management. Examinations developed for law enforcement positions are not sufficient for assessing the qualifications of applicants for these more specialized positions.

   In addition to developing paper-and-pencil examinations, the central personnel agency may be called on to assist in developing procedures or standards utilized by panels of administrators conducting oral interviews of applicants. Additionally, the central personnel agency frequently has responsibility for certifying test results and for applying the veteran's bonus points to passing test scores. Civil service lists of "Eligibles for Appointment" must be continually updated. Names of newly tested applicants are added to the list; some persons previously certified and listed as available are selected; and names are purged from the list due to the failure of applicants to respond positively to inquiries as to their availability for appointment.

3. Hiring Process Constraints

Closely related to the previous two functions is the matter of rules agencies must adhere to in extending job offers to applicants of agencies under the jurisdiction of the central personnel agency. Several factors affect this aspect of the process. One is the desire to achieve a socially representative bureaucracy as expressed in concept of workforce diversity. Agencies must be cognizant of requirements set forth in Title VII of the Civil Rights Act of 1964 as amended, the Uniform Guidelines on Employee Selection Procedures, court orders and consent decrees, state statutes, and executive orders addressing EEO and affirmative action. In recent years the backlash associated with affirmative action has caused states to rethink policies designed to achieve a socially representative work force and in some cases to adopt policies that are less aggressive and less threatening to majority group males (Ridge, Executive Order 1996–9, 1996).

The hiring process is also influenced by statutory rules mandating the so-called rule of 3 which requires the hiring agency to contact and interview the persons with the highest three qualifying civil service test scores. Operation of the rule of 3 may not be as restrictive as popularly perceived.[1] Nevertheless, a number of jurisdictions have expanded the pool of persons eligible for consideration through interviews by adopting a "rule of 5" (e.g., Alaska, Kentucky, Maryland, Nevada, South Carolina); a "rule of 6" (Maine); a "rule of 7" (Washington), a "rule of 10" (Alabama, Arkansas, Idaho, Ohio, Oklahoma, West Virginia); or a "rule of 15" (e.g., Delaware, Missouri). In Connecticut and Kansas anyone who passes the examination may be interviewed. In some states agencies base hiring decisions on the specific requirements of the position. (Sheibley, 1997:App. B).

"Veterans' preference bonus points"[2] represent yet another major constraint on

---

[1] The "rule of 3" essentially restricts the hiring agencies' ability to interview and consider applicants certified by the central personnel agency as possessing the minimum qualifications for appointment. Beginning at the top of the "registry," agencies must contact and interview the persons with the highest three civil service test scores. Where individuals have the same test score, the agency may end up interviewing significantly more than three persons. For example, based on the distribution of test scores, it may end up interviewing one person who scores a 95%; the four persons who have next highest score at 94%; and the two persons next on the list who scored 93%.

[2] "Bonus points" are typically added to the test scores of qualifying veterans who attain a passing score on civil service examinations. A qualifying veteran normally would include persons who serve or served in U.S. active duty or reserve Armed Forces units, National Guard units, or the Coast Guard and were honorably discharged. At least 42 states award bonus points of 2, 5, or 10 points to qualifying veterans. Ohio provides a 20% bonus of the test score to qualifying veterans. Disabled veterans or veterans with service/combat-connected disabilities may receive bonus points 10, 15, or 20 points depending upon the state they are seeking employment in. New Jersey appears to have the most extreme form of absolute preference, whereby all veterans go to the top of the eligibility list. In Pennsylvania, where veterans are entitled to 10 bonus points, they enjoy an absolute preference in hiring if they are among the top three candidates for a vacant position. It is reported that Pennsylvania's requirement for absolute preference has contributed to the expansion of the number of job classifications in place in the state. The state's 3120 separate classes are narrowly tailored in part to mitigate the effect of absolute veterans' preference on selection practices in the Commonwealth. Legislative Budget and Finance Committee.

the hiring process. The preference may entail one or two elements. The first constitutes awarding of bonus points to the test scores of qualifying veterans who attain a passing score of the civil service examination. At least 42 states award 2, 5, or 10 bonus points to qualifying veterans. Disabled veterans or veterans with service/combat-connected disabilities may receive 10, 15, or 20 bonus points, depending upon the state. The second form veterans' preference takes is an absolute preference in appointments. At least seven states have some form of absolute preference (PA Legislative Budget & Finance Committee, 1998:19–20; Sheibley, 1997:App. B).

4.   Position Classification and Compensation

Position classification and compensation administration represents another functional area for which the central personnel agency has major responsibility. Position classification usually has entailed analyzing the content of jobs and preparing position descriptions for specific positions; organizing positions having similar duties, level of authority, and minimum qualifications into classes; and developing a comprehensive pay plan linked to the classifications established. Classification is a function that the central personnel agency often shares with operating agencies under its jurisdiction or those who contract with it for services.[3]

The number of separate classifications tends to vary considerably. The Council of State Governments in the 1996–97 edition of the *Book of the States* reports that the number of classifications ranged from 551 in South Dakota to 6169 in New Jersey. Major industrial states with work forces responsible for a wide array of activities have larger numbers of classes. Growth in the number of classes is also linked to ''grade creep'' and efforts to circumvent the restrictive nature of the compensation plan linked to the classification system. The frequency with which the system undergoes a comprehensive updating significantly affects the number of classifications. Lastly, the number of classifications can be linked to a system of absolute veterans preference which causes agencies to prepare very narrow position description and classification specification to mitigate against the negative impact such systems have on sound personnel selection procedures (States Update Personnel Systems, 1995; PA Legislative Budget & Finance Committee, 1998:19–20).

The central personnel agency also possesses authority and responsibility for developing the overall compensation plan and assigning classes to particular pay schedules within the plan. Control over the compensation plan is influenced by several external considerations. Political decisions made by the elected officials responsible for providing funding for cost of living increases represent one such consideration. These same persons may have authority to determine the

---

[3] The operating agency may have responsibility for classifying individual positions but must do so consistent with the classification standards formulated by the central personnel agency.

number of classification schedules, pay grades within each, number of steps in the class, and magnitude of increase between increments on the pay schedule. Another major consideration impacting the pay schedule is that of collective-bargaining agreements which dictate the level of periodic increases for persons in bargaining units. These agreements tend to influence the compensation plans for managers and others outside the unit(s).

Though discussions of compensation typically focus on wages or salaries, benefits administration represents a major responsibility of the central personnel agency. Employee benefits ranging from leave with pay, to health and medical insurance, to disability pay, to retirement pensions, constitute a major expense for public employers. Costs can range from 30% to 40% of employee base pay. The central personnel agency has responsibility for fixing standards of eligibility and participation as well as negotiating with vendors that provide benefit services. Such benefits include vision care, dental coverage, prescription drugs, life insurance, employee assistance, and counseling services, among others.

5. Labor Relations and Collective Bargaining

Collective-bargaining rights for state employees exists in some 28 states and the District of Columbia. Statutory coverage of collective bargaining rights for public employees is found in over 100 separate state statutes, civil service regulations, local ordinances, court decisions, attorneys-general opinions, and executive orders. State legislation ranges from a single state statute which covers all public employees in the state in the case of Iowa, to the state of Wyoming, whose legislation applies only to firefighters; to North Carolina, which has a statutory ban on all public-sector collective bargaining. In two states, Kansas and Washington, employees may not bargain over wages and fringe benefits (Kearney, 1992: 67; Public Employee Department, 1997:1, 3–5).

Bargaining in the public sector is modeled after the system that has been in place for the private sector for much of this century. However, some differences exist which significantly affect the operations of the central personnel agency. A very detailed timetable for conducting negotiations linked to the jurisdiction's "budget submission date" is typically present since personnel costs represent such a large portion of agency operating expenses. Specific and detailed bargaining impasse procedures (e.g., mediation, fact finding, and interest arbitration) are also built into the enabling legislation to serve as a substitute for the right to strike or to minimize its use where the strike right exists. Finally, in most states strikes by public employees are strictly prohibited with severe penalties imposed in the event of an illegal strike or job action. Nevertheless, a "limited right to strike" is currently recognized for a portion of the state workforce in 10 states (Ban and Riccucci, 1993:79).[4]

---

[4] Note the states which allow their employees the right to strike include: Alaska: all public employees

While attention is often directed at the strike right in the public sector, from the standpoint of the state's central personnel agency a number of other issues are equally important. As such, several states have established separate administrative entities whose sole function is labor-management relations. These offices are typically responsible for contract negotiations with a number of separate bargaining units (and unions), representing a wide array of employees, negotiating in succession, with each attempting to gain a better deal than the one arrived at previously by other units. Once contracts are negotiated, the labor relations office has responsibility for advising line agencies on the implementation and enforcement of the "master" collective bargaining agreement in a wide array of units which may have local agreements or "side letters" which impact on the bargaining relationship (Kenyon, 1998; Office of Administration, 1996:1–161).

During the life of the collective-bargaining agreement a wide array of grievances, real and fancied, are likely to arise. These involve matters such as assignment of bargaining unit work, denial of promotions, disciplinary actions, and overtime. Processing grievances, investigating claims filed, advising line agencies on settlement possibilities, and preparing for arbitration cases are normal office responsibilities. Arguing cases before the state labor relations board regarding the certification of bargaining units, as well as investigating and responding to unfair practice complaints filed with the board, take up a considerable amount of time and resources (Kenyon, 1998; Kearney, 1992:373).

6. Appeals of Adverse Actions

Employees in the states enjoy a number of due process protections from adverse actions by management. Appeals may arise due to employment discrimination, position reclassification, imposition of disciplinary sanctions, and numerous other actions violating merit system standards or other employee rights.

Adverse action appeals are handled through administrative reviews in the operating agency and/or the central personnel agency. When facts are in dispute, hearings before hearing examiners or administrative law judges, acting as impartial decision makers, lead to factual determinations and recommendations for resolution. These "preliminary" determinations are subject to final review by the agency head and/or merit protection panel. In some states a separate agency

---

except for police and firefighters; Hawaii: all public employees; Illinois: all public employees except police, firefighters, and paramedics; Minnesota: all public employees except police and firefighters; Montana: all public employees; Ohio: all public employees except police and firefighters; Oregon: all public employees except police, firefighters, and correctional officers; Pennsylvania: all public employees except police, firefighters, guards at prisons and mental hospitals, and employees necessary to operation and functioning of the courts; Rhode Island: all public employees; California: a state supreme court decision granted all public employees, except police and firefighters, *providing* a court or California PERB does not rule that striking is illegal.

similar to the federal merit system protection board adjudicates appeals (Sheibley, 1997:6).

Critics of the merit system frequently cite the amount of time and documentation necessary to terminate public employees. The time and documentary requirements may contribute to the generally low number of disciplinary terminations. In Pennsylvania, for example, involuntary terminations other than furloughs have averaged less than 1% of the workforce during much of the 1990's. Interestingly, termination rates were similar for merit system employees and exempt, non-classified personnel. Another concern is the amount of time necessary to adjudicate appeals and arrive at a final decision. Again to cite the experience in Pennsylvania, it took an average of 16.6 months from filing date to final adjudication to resolve merit system appeals in 1997. Delays are often a function of a backlog of cases and the inability to schedule hearing until months after petitions are filed. Requests for continuances by one or both of the parties and the need for multiple hearing dates also push back the final decision date (*Governor's Workforce Report*, 1998, pp.27–29; PA Legislative Budget & Finance Committee, April 1998, pp. 45–46).

C. Growth in State Bureaucracies in the 1990s

The U.S. Bureau of Labor Statistics Data indicates that in January 1998 the seasonally adjusted number of persons employed by the 50 states totaled some 4,613,000. According to the bureau, the number of state employees increased in 8 of the past 10 years, with an overall increase of 14.8% since January 1988. This increase might come as a surprise if one listened to the political rhetoric of governors who campaigned on pledges to reduce the size of bureaucracy in the 1990s. A closer look indicates that while substantial growth did take place, it was not evenly distributed across the 50 states or among agencies or programs within the states (U.S. Bureau of Labor Statistics, 1998).

Census bureau data indicate that between October 1990 and October 1995 36 states experienced a net increase in state employment, with eight states experienced growth of 10% or more. States with the highest level of growth were in the South (Kentucky at 18.4%) and Far West (Arizona at 18.2%). During the same period 14 states experienced net declines in state government employees. Declines were heaviest in the Northeast and upper Midwest, with Wisconsin witnessing a net decline of 16.2%. Table 2 provides a state-by-state comparison of state government employment levels from 1990 to 1995.

Growth in state employment during.the 1990s has been driven by several factors. Significant staffing increases in law enforcement and corrections resulted from efforts to address the crime problem and the imposition of more severe sanctions on those convicted of crime. Exploding prison populations brought on by "get-tough" policies of the 1980s and the 1990s set the stage for a prison

Table 2 State Government Employment Growth (Decline), 1990–1995

State	No. state employees			No. per 10,000 population		
	1990	1995	Percentage change	1990	1995	Percentage change
Kentucky	84,177	99,660	18.39	228	258	13.16
Arizona	60,674	71,713	18.19	165	170	3.03
Idaho	22,818	26,700	17.01	227	230	1.32
Texas	258,905	302,074	16.67	152	161	5.92
Utah	43,012	49,890	15.99	250	256	2.40
Missouri	86,507	97,918	13.19	169	184	8.88
Hawaii	57,595	65,009	12.87	520	548	5.38
Washington	112,110	125,402	11.86	230	231	0.43
Colorado	68,854	75,287	9.34	209	201	-3.83
Louisiana	99,572	108,570	9.04	236	250	5.93
Connecticut	66,939	72,853	8.83	204	222	8.82
Arkansas	49,245	53,162	7.95	209	214	2.39
Mississippi	52,854	56,673	7.23	205	210	2.44
North Dakota	20,081	21,452	6.83	314	334	6.37
Delaware	24,878	26,504	6.54	374	370	-1.07
North Carolina	122,535	130,198	6.25	185	181	-2.16
Florida	180,597	191,368	5.96	140	135	-3.57
Pennsylvania	150,008	157,920	5.27	126	131	3.97
New Hampshire	21,011	22,084	5.11	189	192	1.59
California	389,805	409,021	4.93	131	129	-1.53
Georgia	123,249	128,857	4.55	190	179	-5.79
Ohio	171,742	179,298	4.40	158	161	1.90
South Carolina	87,724	91,413	4.21	252	249	-1.19

Tennessee	91,811	95,578	4.10	188	182	−3.19
Alabama	92,124	95,759	3.95	228	225	−1.32
Oregon	62,221	64,644	3.89	219	206	−5.94
Indiana	106,536	110,597	3.81	192	191	−0.52
West Virginia	39,407	40,819	3.58	220	223	1.36
Oklahoma	78,006	80,758	3.53	248	246	−0.81
Montana	22,807	23,410	2.64	285	269	−5.61
Virginia	141,309	144,771	2.45	228	219	−3.95
New Mexico	51,535	52,670	2.20	340	313	−7.94
South Dakota	17,300	17,662	2.09	314	242	−22.93
Rhode Island	24,274	24,525	1.03	242	248	2.48
Iowa	62,445	62,906	0.74	225	221	−1.78
Minnesota	84,898	85,394	0.58	194	185	−4.64
Wyoming	12,679	12,676	−0.02	279	264	−5.38
Nevada	21,705	21,675	−0.14	181	142	−21.55
Kansas	57,824	57,423	−0.69	233	224	−3.86
Nebraska	35,751	35,471	−0.78	227	217	−4.41
New Jersey	125,430	123,822	−1.28	162	156	−3.70
Alaska	25,021	24,640	−1.52	455	408	−10.33
Vermont	14,743	14,465	−1.89	261	247	−5.36
Illinois	170,438	167,134	−1.94	149	141	−5.37
Maine	26,659	26,105	−2.08	217	210	−3.23
Michigan	177,721	173,575	−2.33	191	182	−4.71
New York	305,475	282,190	−7.62	170	156	−8.24
Maryland	101,522	93,773	−7.63	212	186	−12.26
Massachusetts	107,901	97,984	−9.19	179	161	−10.06
Wisconsin	90,367	75,747	−16.18	185	148	−20.00

Source: Developed from PA Legislative Budget and Finance Committee, 1992, 1998a.

building and staffing binge. Another cause of this growth in the size of state bureaucracies was the significant population growth, primarily in the Sunbelt and Far West which forced many governments to increase employment levels to keep pace with public demand for expanded services (Walter, 1998:17–19).

D. Tools for Controlling Growth in the Size of Bureaucracy

Governors and political executives who establish overall policy direction for the central personnel agencies have at their disposal a variety of tools to control personnel costs. Societal, economic, and political considerations determine which combinations of these will be pursued. Gubernatorial candidates in the early 1990s pledged to reduce the excess of public employees performing outdated or undesirable functions and free up resources for tax cuts or new policy initiatives. The economic recession of the early 1990s gave way to substantial and sustained economic growth by the mid-1990s and tax revenues expanded greatly in most states. While the improving economy reduced the immediate pressure to cut costs, political executives committed to rolling back the size and scope of government held constant or scaled back budgets and continued to restructure, reorganize, or downsize agencies and programs.

Use of attrition to reduce personnel complements creates a number of potential problems for agencies. Decisions to leave an organization are not evenly spread across the bureaucracy. Departments having large numbers of older employees may be hit hard by normal retirements. This problem is often exacerbated by incentives offered to encourage more senior staff to take early retirement. Critical functions must continue to be performed regardless of whether authorization is granted to permanently replace separated employees. Despite claims to the contrary, there is typically sufficient leeway for the politically connected manager to secure a ''special exemption'' and thus fill a ''critical need.'' The inability to permanently fill positions during such times may also produce an increased reliance on temporaries and part timers. In some cases organizations have even brought back former employees who ''retired'' on so-called personal services contracts to perform critical needs (often the same or similar to what they did as a career civil servant). However, as a ''contract'' employee they do not appear on the official complement lists.

In some cases bureaucratic reorganizations resulted in the consolidation of multiple agencies into single administrative structures. Politically weak programs experienced cuts and downsizing. Elected officials asserted such moves enabled government to deliver vital services at lower costs and with fewer people, that government could do more with less. On the other hand, costs can be shifted to the public in the form of increased time delays in processing applications and the like or the possibility that more and more will simply fall through the administrative cracks and only become apparent when some significant disaster befalls the community.

1. Outsourcing and Privatization

In the 1990s a renewed interest in shifting certain government functions and responsibilities to the private sector has emerged based on the perception that it can deliver many public services more efficiently and effectively than existing bureaucratic structures. Privatization efforts can range from the modest, such as employing a clerical employee from a temporary service while a permanent employee is on maternity or military leave, to private-sector construction and lease back of facilities, to construction, staffing, and operation of correctional facilities (U.S. General Accounting Office, 1997:1).

While proponents of privatization are quite enthusiastic in advocating wider usage in state government, attaining the advertised benefits is substantially more complex. Since the potential for substantial disruptions exist for long-term public employees and their families, every effort should be made to enable in-house operations to compete on a level playing field with private firms which promise much and may deliver less. Public organizations may find that the spirit of competition will inspire unions and managers to develop cooperative strategies for both preserving jobs and achieving significant improvements in service delivery (U.S. General Accounting Office, 1997:14–15).

Personnel departments need to carefully develop appropriate administrative controls prior to implementation of privatization initiatives. Promised savings should be closely scrutinized to ensure that they are real and that private delivery of such services is not more expensive than those by public systems replaced. Additional staff may have to be hired and trained to draft complex contracts that cover the specific services for which government is seeking private-sector bids. Poorly crafted bids and contract language can result in vendors delivering far less than expected. Contract compliance officers must be employed to monitor and oversee the implementation of contracts with vendors to ensure that government is getting what it has paid for. Agencies need to develop tools to effectively and accurately measure performance and account for all relevant costs so as to realistically determine if tax dollars are being saved and the public is being served better (U.S. General Accounting Office, 1997:10–14, 16–19).

2. Complement Control

A number of governors concerned about paring down the size of government or creating opportunities for tax cuts or both, pledged publicly in the early 1990s to reduce the size of their bureaucracies by instituting hiring freezes, placing caps on employment of new staff, or relying on attrition. Examination of the data for the period 1990–1995 suggests that in most states governors and/or other elected officials were successful (see Table 2). During this period, the ratio of state employees to population in the state declined in 32 states, including a number in which there were increases in the number of state employees (e.g., Colorado with a 9.3% increase) (PA Legislative Budget & Finance Committee, 1992, 1998).

Political decisions made in the governor's mansion or in the state house to slow bureaucratic growth to reduce the absolute number of employees created pressures for state personnel departments to tightly control the personnel complement of agencies under the governor's jurisdiction. Growth in state bureaucracies in the 1990s occurred rather grudgingly (averaging less than 1% per year in 30 states between 1990 and 1995) due to the existence of strict complement control mechanisms.

Controlling the personnel complement, the total number of persons an administrative entity is officially permitted to have on the payroll, became a vital tool for controlling the size of bureaucracy, the scope of its responsibilities, and the activities of affected agencies. In most agencies there are in reality two complement levels. The first is the official complement level, controlled by the jurisdiction's central personnel office or directly by the governor's office, serves as the basis for an agency's budgetary allotment. The second represents an unofficial, yet constraining real complement level, generally somewhat lower than the official complement level. This unofficial complement level may represent the effects of a hiring freeze ordered by the governor; it may represent an effort by the agency to temporarily free up agency resources for acquisition of new technologies or equipment or other contingencies; or such a strategy may be adopted to attain a modification in the organizational culture by forcing it to adapt or accept changing conditions; or force improvements in levels of productivity and efficiency. Surpluses created by leaving positions vacant for significant periods of time may enhance the stature of agency officials or perhaps allow them to avoid the wrath of budget chiefs or governors committed to doing "more with less."

There is a risk that the official complement level will be revised downward permanently if the lower unofficial complement level is allowed to remain for lengthy periods of time. Absent some significant demonstration of the adverse affects on the public health, safety, or welfare, official complement level reductions are likely to be made permanent. Of course the official complement can be increased in the future. Emphasis in the current era on capping, shrinking, cutting, downsizing, right-sizing, and outsourcing makes the likelihood of complement levels being enhanced or restored to prior levels somewhat remote unless there is fundamental political change (Kaufman, 1998; PA Legislative Budget & Finance Committee, 1997:70; Office of Administration, Commonwealth of Pennsylvania, 1982, 1995).

A primary tool of the personnel agency to control agency complement is the "job requisition" or "personnel action request" form. The completed form serves as the formal request from an operating unit for authorization to fill a vacant position, create a position, reclassify a position, promote an employee, or take some other personnel action involving a specific position and/or its incumbent. In the present political environment, such authorization may require the approval of the bureau director, the agency's personnel director, agency head, and officials outside the agency, such as that from the office of administration in the Governor's office.

In recent years a number of factors have contributed to the use of "Requisition Forms" as a tool in classifying positions. Among these are the federal government's Equal Employment Opportunity specifications as found in Title VII of the Civil Rights Act of 1964, as amended, the 1978 Uniform Guidelines on Employee Selection Procedures, and provisions of the 1990 Americans with Disabilities Act requiring that "essential job functions" be identified, have forced public employers to carefully consider the contents of a position description. Court cases dealing with the exemption of policy-making positions from First Amendment restrictions on patronage hiring and dismissals have also forced personnel agencies to review the nature of a position when it becomes vacant. Lastly, tighter agency budgets have also contributed to the trend, insuring that recruitment is not none for nonexistent positions.

A job requisition form will generally require the following information:

1. Title of the position
2. Organizational unit, division or department in which the position is located
3. Salary range for the position
4. Minimum academic qualifications
5. Previous work experience requirements
6. Duties of the position
7. Employment status of the position incumbent—permanent/temporary; full/part-time
8. Any other pertinent information (e.g., type of action involved such as dismissal, suspension, demotion, etc.)

An important step in the process of preparing the job requisition/personnel action request form is to review and update the existing position description to reflect changes in the duties and responsibilities, work processes, and technologies which have occurred since the position was last filled. Once approved, the job requisition serves as the agency recruitment staff's authorization to fill a vacant or newly created position (Sylvia, 1994:182–183; Klingner & Nalbandian, 1998:197; Office of Administration, Commonwealth of Pennsylvania, 1982).

II. PERSONNEL REFORM IN THE STATES

A. Evolution of the Merit System

Historically, two mechanisms for filling public service positions have been utilized in the states: appointment via a "spoils" patronage system, or a "merit"-based personnel selection system. The political patronage or "political sponsorship" system, which exited prior to the founding of the Republic, bases appointment upon membership and support of a particular political party or candidate. Scarce government jobs are given out as rewards for hard work during the campaign on behalf of the party's candidates. When there is a change in party control, or even a faction within a party, the public employee may be fired or is expected to resign and is replaced by a partisan supporter of the party or faction coming to power (Freedman, 1994:9).

In merit-based public personnel systems, decisions on employee selection, retention, and promotion are based on ability, knowledge, and skills of applicants after fair and open competition. Hiring and promotion examinations are formal, standardized, and typically are written. In a merit system individuals are actively and publicly recruited and screened via open competitive examinations, which evaluate candidates' abilities to perform position specific functions. Further, in a merit-based system, no personnel actions are based on or influenced by an individual's political affiliation and participation or lack thereof.

The historic challenges to instituting a merit-based personnel system in state government can be seen in often quoted comments of Stanley (1974). Stanley opened a symposium on "The Merit Principle Today" with the following:

> The late Henry Aronson, who spent some 30 years developing and enforcing merit system standards for state agencies, used to tell this story: In the late '30's a certain Southern state paid little attention to the federal merit requirements newly established for grant-in-aid programs. Persuasion and threats accomplished nothing and finally Uncle Sam began action to "cut off the water"—as politically unthinkable an action then as now. The governor of the state sent an assistant to see Aronson, who gave him the full sales business on merit system principles. When Henry paused, the emissary said, 'Well, Mr. Aronson, the guv'nor—he b'lieves in the merit system—he just b'lieves that his friends have more merit than his enemies.

And there we are today. One person's merit is another's favoritism. One person's excellence is another person's unreasonable requirement" (Stanley, 1974:425).

1. Historical Overview of Civil Service Reform in the States

Civil Service reform has focused on efforts to minimize political patronage and to bring about a politically neutral and professionally competent workforce. Following the Civil War, a significant political backlash emerged and was directed toward the bosses and their machines. Reformers dedicated to the destruction of the machines and machine control over the process of staffing bureaucracy became quite active. By the late 1870s numerous civil service reform associations sprang up across the country, in states as well as cities (Aronson, 1991:133–134).

Adoption of the Pendleton Act at the national level in January 1883 set the stage for similar efforts in the states. In 1883 New York became the first state to adopt a civil service law under the sponsorship of then Assemblyman Theodore Roosevelt. The New York legislation signed into law by Governor Grover Cleveland was very similar to the Pendleton Act, providing for a three-member board responsible for implementing the law; a system of open competitive examinations for appointments; a provision forbidding the levying of assessments on any state or local officer and granting authorization for mayors of cities with more than 50,000 residents to apply civil service regulations to their cities. On June 3, 1884, the state of Massachusetts adopted its own version of civil service reform based on both the Pendleton and New York acts (Aronson, 1991:134; Hoogenboom, 1961:256–257).

The actions of New York and Massachusetts in 1883 and 1884 represent a "high water" mark in the reform effort in the late 19th century. Political opponents to reform were able to regroup and launch a "counteroffensive." In 1877 the Massachusetts stature was amended to allow the appointment of veterans without any testing requirement, and in December, 1896 the New York commission's rules were revised, substantially corrupting the reformers' ideal of civil service reform. More significantly, the drive for civil service reform in other states bogged down as well. Bills focused on reform were introduced in Pennsylvania, Maryland, New Jersey, Ohio, Virginia, Rhode Island, Indiana, Illinois, Wisconsin, Missouri, and California but failed to be enacted into law. In fact, it would be another 20 years before another state would adopt civil service reform legislation (Hoogenboom, 1961:260).

Support for reform after the turn of the century received a major boost as a result of the crusading efforts of so-called muckrakers who exposed corruption, abuse of public office, and spoils patronage in the cities and state legislatures. Their work generated renewed interest in civil service reform. Ida Tarbell's *History of Standard Oil Company* in 1903, Lincoln Stevens' *The Shame of the Cities* in 1904, *The Treason of the Senate* by David Graham Phillips, Upton Sinclair's novel *The Jungle* and others served as the catalyst for renewed interest in reform. Consequently, civil service systems were advocated by reformers and adopted in a number of states from 1905 to 1920 (Aronson, 1991:134).[5]

---

[5] Between 1905 and 1920 the following states adopted civil service reform legislation: Wisconsin and Illinois in 1905; Colorado in 1907; New Jersey in 1908. In 1912 Ohio adopted a general provision for civil service in its state constitution and in the following year enacted a statutory basis for civil

Renewed interest in civil service reform in the states was manifest in the mid-1930s. The Commission of Inquiry on Public Service Personnel in 1935 issued its final report, entitled *Better Government Personnel*. The report stressed the need for a career service that would attract the best minds in the nation. In the commission's view a merit system focused on selection was not enough. "True careers" for those who entered the public service, including recruitment of graduate and undergraduate degree recipients, and real opportunities for satisfying career advancement to retain them in the public service, needed to be established. The report helped to renew and promote interest in both extending and improving merit systems in state government. New state civil service laws were enacted in Maine, Michigan, Connecticut, Arkansas, and New Mexico in 1937, and in 1939 new laws were enacted in Alabama, Rhode Island, Minnesota, and Pennsylvania (Hoogenboom, 1961:333; Aronson, 1991:139–140).

2. Pressure from the Federal Government for Merit-Based Reform

The traditional view of federalism and the proper relationship between the national government and states, coupled with the Tenth Amendment to the Constitution, served to limit opportunities for the national government to dictate standards for personnel administration to the states. This all changed drastically during the New Deal era of the 1930s as the national government began to attach strings to various funding mechanics.

The Social Security Act amendments of 1939 compelled states desiring to receive federal funds for welfare programs to develop state merit systems for employees paid in whole or in part by those funds. Approved overwhelmingly by Congress, these amendments went into effect on January 1, 1940. In the same year the original Political Activities Act of 1939, the Hatch Act, was extended to cover state and local government positions receiving funding from the national government. The statute imposed on the states the obligation to adopt merit principles designed to ensure "neutral competency" by limiting the partisan political activities of employees in state civil service systems. The act applied to all federally aided agencies except educational institutions. Additionally, the law applied to nonelected heads of departments and other employees exempted from the merit system (Aronson, 1991:137).[6]

---

service. In 1913 California and Connecticut adopted civil service laws, although Connecticut's law fell out of favor, became moribund, and was repealed in 1921. In 1915 Kansas enacted a civil service law but it became inoperative in 1919 because the legislature failed to provide funding. Maryland in 1920 enacted a personnel law, which was noteworthy in that it provided for the first time a single administrator rather than a bipartisan commission some 59 years before the federal government would create the Office of Personnel Management.

[6] The Hatch Act of 1940, which was repealed in 1974, imposed the following types of restrictions

In the late 1990s the federal government's principal influence in mandating a merit-based personnel system in state government rests with requirements imposed on recipients of grants-in-aid. The federal Office of Personnel Management has identified the standards for a merit system of personnel administration. These standards are part of the basic personnel management requirements for administering all federal intergovernmental assistance programs, and require that state and local government assistance recipients maintain a merit-based personnel system. Among the merit requirements are standards related to recruitment and selection of personnel; promotions; equitable compensation; access to training opportunities; continued employment based on adequate performance; identifies prohibited partisan abuses; and fair treatment in all aspects of personnel administration (PA Legislative Budget and Finance Committee, 1998a:6).[7]

The federal government in recent years has taken a rather relaxed approach to the requirements. Specific compliance audits to verify adherence to the requirements are not conducted; rather, recipients are allowed to submit letters of certification stating compliance with the law. For example, the Office of Personnel Management under provisions of the law accepted as sufficient documentation a letter from the Commonwealth of Pennsylvania indicating that merit system welfare fraud investigators employed by the state's Department of Public Welfare who had been administratively transferred into "exempt" positions in the newly

---

on the activities of covered employees: serving as a delegate or alternate to a political convention; soliciting or handling political campaign contributions; being an officer or organizer of a political club; engaging in "electioneering" activities; being a candidate for partisan elected office; and leading or speaking to a partisan political meeting or rally.

[7] 5 C.F.R. Section 900.603 states in part:

The quality of the public service can be improved by the development of systems of personnel administration consistent with such merit principles as—

a. Recruiting, selecting and advancing employees on the basis of their relative ability, knowledge, and skills, including open consideration of qualified applicants for initial appointment.

b. Providing equitable and adequate compensation.

c. Training employees, as needed, to assure high quality performance.

d. Retaining employees on the basis of the adequacy of their performance, correcting inadequate performance, and separating employees whose inadequate performance cannot be corrected.

e. Assuring fair treatment of applicants and employees in all aspects of personnel administration without regard to political affiliation, race, color, national origin, sex, religious creed, age or handicap and with proper regard for their privacy and constitutional rights as citizens. This "fair treatment" principle includes compliance with the Federal equal employment opportunity and nondiscrimination laws.

f. Assuring that employees are protected against coercion for partisan political purposes and are prohibited from using their official authority for the purpose of interfering with or affecting the result of an election or a nomination for office.

created Office of Inspector General which reported to the governor were still part
of a merit system (PA Legislative Budget and Finance Committee, 1998a:6).

B. Demise and (Near?) Disappearance of Political Patronage

1. First Amendment Freedom of Association Protections

Beginning in 1976, a trilogy of U.S. Supreme Court cases addressing First
Amendment freedom of association protections began to have a profound impact
on the manner in which governors, state legislators, and other elected officials
carried out or influenced the process of staffing and maintaining public bureaucracies. The U.S. Supreme Court in that year handed down a landmark decision in
the case of *Richard Elrod v. John Burns*, wherein the Court found that patronage
dismissals violate a person's constitutional right of freedom of association. In
this case, Republican John Burns, a non–civil service employee of the Cook
County, Illinois, Sheriff's office, brought suit in federal district court against the
newly elected sheriff, Richard Elrod, a Democrat, and the Cook County democratic organization (i.e., the Daley political machine). Burns alleged that Elrod
violated the First and Fourteenth Amendments of the U.S. Constitution and various federal statutes, including the Civil Rights Act of 1871, for discharging department employees or threatening to discharge for the sole reason that they were
not affiliated with or sponsored by the Democratic party.

A divided Court found that patronage dismissal severely restricts an individual's First Amendment rights of political belief and freedom of association.
To paraphrase Justice Brennan, government may not force a public employee to
relinquish the right to political association as the price of holding a public job
without severely inhibiting First Amendment rights. While First Amendment
rights are not absolute, they may be curtailed only for very limited reasons, with
the burden of proving the reason resting with the employer. If patronage practices
are to survive constitutional challenge, they must serve a vital government end
by means of a "least restrictive" "freedom of belief" and "association," and
the benefit gained must outweigh the loss of the constitutionally protected rights
(*Richard Elrod v. John Burns*, 1976).[8]

---

[8] In the "judgment of the Court" announced by Justice William J. Brennan, several important principles regarding harm done to the 1st and 14th Amendments by patronage dismissals were articulated,
including the following: (1) Patronage dismissals severely restrict political belief and association,
which constitute the core of these activities protected by the 1st Amendment, and government may
not, without severely inhibiting 1st Amendment rights force a public employee to relinquish his
right to political association as the price of holding a public job. (2) 1st Amendment rights are not
absolute; they may be curtailed only by interests of vital importance, the burden of proving the
existence of which rests with the employer. If conditioning the retention of employment on the

Because the U.S. Supreme Court was philosophically divided on the proper application of First Amendment protections to patronage dismissals, there was no "opinion of the court" in *Elrod v. Burns*. Such was not the case in 1980, when the High Court handed down its decision in *Branti v. Finkel*. The Court in a 6-3 decision affirmed the position outlined in *Elrod v. Burns* four years earlier. Justice John Paul Stevens, in writing the "Opinion of the Court," found that the First and Fourteenth Amendments protected the respondents in the case from discharge solely because of political beliefs. Stevens' opinion had the effect of providing clarity to the process of identifying the narrow group of appointees, which might properly suffer dismissal without constituting a violation of the First and Fourteenth Amendments. Stevens stated in part:

> The ultimate inquiry is not whether the label "policy maker" or "confidential" fits the particular position, rather the question is whether the hiring authority can demonstrate that party affiliation is an appropriate requirement for effective performance of the public office involved (*Branti v. Finkel*, 1980, p. 519).

The final decision in the Supreme Court's trilogy was *Cynthia Rutan et al., v. Republican Party of Illinois, et al.* (1990). The Rutan decision was significant due to the fact that the court both affirmed and expanded its earlier decisions on patronage dismissals. In a 5-4 decision the court ruled that "promotions, transfers, and recalls after layoffs based on political affiliation or support are an impermissible infringement on the First Amendment rights of public employees. . . ." (p. 63). Additionally, the Court held that patronage hiring places burdens on free speech and association similar to those imposed by patronage promotions, transfers, and recalls, and that "conditioning hiring decisions on political belief and association plainly constitutes an unconstitutional condition, unless the government has a vital interest in doing so," (p. 64). Justice Brennan, in his Opinion of the Court, effectively summarized the Court's current position:

> To the victor belong only those spoils that may be constitutionally obtained,
> . . . we are asked to decide the constitutionality of several related political

---

employee's support of the party in power is to survive Constitutional challenge, it must further some vital government end by a means *least restrictive* of "freedom of belief" and "association" in achieving that end, and the benefit gained must outweigh the loss of the constitutionally protected rights. (3) The inefficiency resulting from wholesale replacement of public employees on change of administrations belies the argument that employees not the same political persuasion as the controlling party will not be motivated to work effectively; nor is it clear that patronage appointees are more qualified than those they replace. Since unproductive employees may always be discharged and merit systems are available, it is clear that less drastic means than patronage dismissals are available to insure the vital need for government efficiency and effectiveness. (4) The need to insure that policies that the electorate has sanctioned are effectively implemented can be fully satisfied by *limiting patronage dismissals to policymaking positions*.

patronage practices—whether promotion, transfer, recall, and hiring decisions involving low-level public employees may be constitutionally based on party affiliation and support. We hold that they may not. (p. 65)

These Supreme Court decisions have vital implications for personnel managers and agencies. It is essential that personnel departments clearly identify those positions which are legitimately policy making in character and therefore may be properly filled on the basis of political sponsorship.[9] This information is crucial when the personnel department is instructed to locate a position for the person who is highly recommended by the governor, legislative leaders, or other politically influential and connected person seeks a government job for a friend, relative, or constituent. This information may be even more important when a position has already been identified for the politically connected applicant and the personnel department is directed to hire the individual into that specific slot (Heidorn and Moran, 1997).

Further, prior determination of the policy making status of a job is especially significant if a personnel action involving the position is challenged administratively or judicially on the grounds that an unsuccessful applicant or an adversely affected incumbent's First Amendment freedom of association rights were violated. Given the litigious nature of American society, it may be impossible to prevent determined individuals who believe they are victims of improper partisan political influence in personnel decisions from taking legal action. However, clear evidence that the positions involved are policy making may make such challenges more difficult and less likely to be successful (Berger, 1998; PA Legislative Budget & Finance Committee, 1997:84).

2. Collective Bargaining Impacts on Patronage

The advent of public-sector collective bargaining in the states had a greater impact on hastening the demise of patronage than civil service reform or the recognition of First Amendment freedom of association rights limiting patronage practices. The vast majority of persons occupying nonmanagerial positions that were once prizes to be claimed after an election, are today covered by collective bargaining agreements. These agreements typically contain very specific language related to dismissals of bargaining unit employees. Relevant sections of agreements limit dismissals to ''for-cause'' reasons, subject to appeal through the grievance procedure to binding grievance arbitration. These provisions, coupled with the union's ''duty of fair representation,'' create a powerful incentive to

---

[9] The position description developed for the job should clearly and concisely demonstrate the policy making nature of the position so that there can be no doubt as to the ''political/policy making'' nature of the position.

challenge the legitimacy of terminations which smack of patronage dismissals (Act 1970-195; Elling, 1996:304).

3. Litigation Costs Associated with Patronage Dismissals

The litigation of cases alleging improper political influence in personnel decisions is time-consuming and quite expensive in terms of staff and legal resources (often external law firms retained at a premium rate) even if the agency prevails or is able to reach an amicable out-of-court settlement. Substantial legal expenses are likely to be incurred defending the organization against charges alleging patronage employment practices. Attorney fees for outside legal counsel or the staff time of in-house legal counsel can be quite substantial. Expenses associated with deposing of witnesses, discovery, legal research, filing of briefs and motions, settlement negotiations, going to trial, or out-of-court settlements are burdensome for fiscally strapped public sector organizations.[10]

If the legal challenge is sustained, the agency faces a number of complex issues. Liability may involve actual damages, including awarding of the position or promotion to the litigant with back pay and benefits. Among possible additional issues confronting the agency are punitive damages, attorney fees and court costs, adverse employee morale and publicity, and the dilemma of what to do with the person who was improperly hired into the position in question (Rosenbloom and Carroll, 1990:30–31; *Smith v. Wade*, 1983).

Administrative steps can be taken to minimize organizational exposure to judicial challenges of alleged patronage practices. Organizations need to develop and disseminate clear statements concerning patronage and nepotism in the workplace. Partisan interference in internal personnel decisions should be clearly prohibited and organizational commitment to "neutral competency" articulated through the use of open and competitive recruitment, screening, and selection procedures to gain qualified personnel (PA Legislative Budget & Finance Committee, 1997:84, 89–91).

III. FINANCIAL ISSUES IN PERSONNEL SYSTEMS: COMPENSATION AND BENEFITS ADMINISTRATION

A. Filling Positions High in Demand

Ongoing challenges confront state central personnel offices dealing with compensation packages, recruiting candidates for entry level positions, and competing

---

[10] An illustration of this can be seen in the experiences of the Pennsylvania Turnpike Commission during the mid to late 1990s. The commission incurred legal expenses from outside legal counsel of over $2.9 million in five cases litigated between December 1993 and April 1997. In addition

for those specialists in high demand. Illustrative of the complexity of these challenges is the year 2000 computer problem. The serious problems resulting from the inability of computer systems to recognize the year 2000 have caused many organizations to seek talented persons capable of upgrading the systems. Given the demand for individuals with the necessary programming skills, shortages exist and salaries are being forced upward.

Personnel issues are highlighted by this specific problem and similar ones. First, there is the matter of maintaining the integrity of a compensation plan. Increases in salaries for these positions may have a ripple effect of profound proportions and impact on organizations for many years to come. Second, there is a risk that once the year 2000 problem is resolved, a surplus in computer programmers may arise necessitating furloughs and organizational disruptions associated with such actions.

B. Step and Increment Increases in the Compensation Plan

Critics of bureaucracy often argue that public employees enjoy a compensation system that rewards longevity rather than superior performance. State compensation plans frequently have annual longevity and/or step increases for 20 or more years (Office of Administration, 1996). If an employee remains with a state agency and performs satisfactorily, he or she can expect a ''step increase'' and perhaps a contractually or administratively mandated cost-of-living adjustment. An implication of these pay plans is that even when a ''0%'' increase in salaries is contemplated, actual wages for many employees will rise since they are entitled to a step or longevity increase.

When the central personnel agency administratively revises the compensation plan or undertakes contract negotiations which drive the compensation plan, several important concerns need to be addressed. The organization should reconsider how many longevity steps or levels there should be in the compensation plan. The manner in which this is addressed has a substantial impact on employee morale and relationships among newer and better-educated or credentialed employees and more senior, often less-educated, personnel. An appropriate balance has to be struck between longevity and qualifications. Further, if employees are guaranteed step increases and cost-of-living adjustments for most of their careers,

---

to these costs you can add $125,000 paid to a plaintiff in an out-of-court settlement, plus the in-house legal and staff resources expended to respond to these suits. The turnpike during this time frequently asserted its need to vigorously defend itself against charges that it acted improperly. Additionally the turnpike frequently cited its view that since it had not lost a single case in the courts its employment practices were appropriate. Media reports contradicted these assertions and served to support the view patronage employment practices were still the norm on the ''Pike.''

there is a risk they will become complacent. The organization therefore needs to consider the size of the percentage change between increments in the salary plan. Generally, the larger the increments, the more time an employee should remain within a pay grade (Sylvia, 1994:155–159; Klingner and Nalbandian, 1998:128–138).

1. Bonuses vs. Changes in the Base/COLAs

Establishing future pay increases is often one of the most contentious areas at the bargaining table of contract negotiations. To minimize the implications of a compensation article, the central personnel agency may seek an agreement providing for the payment of a one-time bonus to employees in lieu of an increase in the base pay structure. Such a strategy has advantages for management. The strategy allows managers to claim that they have addressed the needs of employees to keep pace with inflation in a particular year without making the long-term commitment resulting from modifications in the base. By limiting growth in the base, the employer's related expenses for Social Security, Medicare, pensions, and the like are held constant. Unions will likely resist bonuses in lieu of cost-of-living adjustments to the base since, with bonuses, future compensation levels and other benefits are not positively enhanced or adjusted to keep pace with inflation (Mayer, 1998).

2. Overtime Usage

While there is a prevailing view that overtime is cheaper than taking on additional staff, there are negative implications of excessive reliance on overtime. One implication is the long-term impact on the retirement benefits of employees with sizable overtime earnings. Retirement payouts are increased and these higher costs continue for an long as the retirees or their heirs are collecting payments from the state retirement system. In some state agencies an organizational climate may exist in which employees enjoy a tacit "entitlement" to maximize overtime opportunities in the final years of employment to expand their monthly retirement benefits (Hildreth, 1995:403; PA Legislative Budget & Finance Committee, 1997:110).

A second implication of excessive usage of overtime is employee fatigue. Evidence exists which clearly demonstrates that at a certain point employee productivity, workplace safety, and quality decline as a result of employee fatigue. For example, for overworked emergency response workers dispatched to the site of a serious accident, the implications of fatigue could be quite substantial.

3. Indirect Compensation

Historically, public employee wage and salary levels were less attractive than those for comparable positions in the private sector. To attract and retain qualified employees the public sector has relied on indirect compensation. Referred to as "fringe benefits," the costs of the indirect compensation are anything but "fringe" or marginal. Public employees in the typical state enjoy a variety of benefits including medical and health care, life insurance, disability insurance, retirement pensions, etc. Collectively these benefits represent a third or more of employee compensation and constitute a sizable expenditure for the employer (Hildreth, 1995:405–408; Ridge, 1998:39).

These benefits have been extended to employees and their spouses and dependent children. With the growing number of dual-career families, nontraditional households, and "alternative lifestyles," the public employer is being challenged on the type of benefits provided and manner in which benefits are made available. Single employees and employees without dependent children express concern that the current structure short changes them since they generally receive no additional compensation comparable to the added expenses associated with benefits provided to employees with traditional families.

Among the most important and sought of employee benefits are medical and health care coverage for individuals and their dependents. In the past coverage was provided through a traditional/indemnity commercial insurance or hospital service plan such as Blue Cross/Blue Shield with premiums primarily paid by the employer. More recently, with health care costs running well ahead of the inflation rate and many employees desiring programs to assist them to stay well rather than treat them when they are sick, HMOs/managed care providers have received increased attention. These alternatives to the traditional medical and hospitalization coverage have to some extent shifted a portion of the health care burden back to employees.

4. Controlling Benefit Costs

Concern has been expressed about the cost associated with public-sector compensation packages and the fringe benefits which more than offset any inequity between public and private salary levels. Tight agency budgets and the desire to "bring under control" compensation costs have caused central personnel agencies to take a close look at benefits. Today organizations may well take the approach that benefits have as much value to employees as salary or wages, and perhaps more, since the value of benefits is typically exempt from taxation as income (Elliot and Vocino, 1995:371–372; Rosenbloom and Hallman, 1986: 204–205).

Employers are telling employees and/or their unions that they may have to choose between improving wage levels and preserving existing benefits, and minimizing the shift to employee contributions or reducing levels of coverage. Many organizations originally installed pensions, health care insurance, and life insurance plans on a shared basis, but gradually employee contributions were phased out. However, changing demographics, special-purpose benefits, and cafeteria plans have all influenced the renewed acceptability of contributory plans, at least from the employer's perspective (McCaffery, 1988:203; Hildreth, 1995: 412; Klingner and Nalbandian, 1998:373).

Higher deductibles are a significant cost containment strategy. The employee pays out of pocket the first $100 or higher amount, and the benefit plan covers the remaining costs. The deductible must be satisfied annually. Generally, the greater the deductible the lower the premium the employer and/or employee pays. A second strategy is use of an offset, which represents a benefit paying something less than 100% of the lost income or expense replacement. Coordination of benefits has become commonplace and entails ascertaining if a scheduled payment can be reduced or rejected since it is covered by a spouse's plan. Finally, coinsurance/copay is a benefits provision in which the employee generally must pay a fixed percentage of the cost each time a service is used (McCaffery, 1988: 78–84; Rosenbloom and Hallman, 1986:204–205).

5. Cafeteria Benefits Plans

The increased prevalence of dual-career couples and singles in the workplace is causing many organizations to rethink the manner in which employee benefit programs are defined. So-called cafeteria benefits programs allow employees to personalize, to some extent, the range of benefits and levels of coverage contained in their compensation packages. The central personnel office has several choices in terms of the specific type of cafeteria plan it implements. For example:

1. Core-type plans. "Core" coverage for such benefits as retirement, medical, disability, life insurance, and vacations remain in place but at reduced levels of required coverage. The employee has the option of using the difference between the value of the required benefit in a "preflexible" system and the value of benefits that are required in a flexible system to increase their levels of coverage of desired benefits.

2. Participant option ("opt up/opt down") plans. Participants may elect an "average level" of benefit coverage and are not required to contribute to the cost of the plan; a "liberal level" of coverage whereby the employee increases the level of coverage in certain areas, but must pay the added cost of coverage through additional payroll deductions; or a "conservative level" the employee receives less than the average level of coverage on certain benefits, but receives a cash payment for the difference between the average level of coverage and the conservative level.

3. Additional allowance type (add-on). Flexible credits are calculated each year on the basis of an employee's salary and years of service. Using flexible credits, salary deductions, or both, employees may select additional benefits in a variety of areas such as life insurance, dental coverage, paid leave, educational

subsidies, cash, etc. (McCaffery, 1988:169–185; Elliot and Vocino, 1995:372; Henderson, 1985:470–480; Rosenbloom and Hallman, 1986:473–479).

Flexible spending accounts represent yet another option to assist employees in tailoring a benefits program to meet their unique needs. This form of cafeteria benefits allows an employee to set aside pretax dollars for recurring or routine medical, dental, and dependent-care expenses. The employer creates a special account in which the employee can annually specify the amount to be set aside for these expenses. Funds are then deducted from the account to pay the incurred expenses. The principal advantage of these accounts is that the employer and the employee are not obligated to pay income or Social Security taxes on the funds set aside. The risk to the employee, under some systems, is that if he or she fails to spend all of the funds set aside for a given year, the remaining funds are forfeited and retained by the employer. However, employers may choose to create a system whereby unused dollars are returned to the employee as income subject to normal taxation (Henderson, 1985:478–479; McCaffery, 1988:174–175).

C. Early Retirement Incentives and Cost Savings

Because senior employees are compensated at higher levels, have greater entitlement to paid leave, and utilize some medical benefits relatively frequently, they are more expensive to retain than newer personnel. A number of jurisdictions concerned about personnel costs and seeking creative approaches in the 1990s have developed and offered lucrative early retirement incentives to employees. The incentives frequently take the form of "bonus" credits added to an employee's retirement computations, providing a higher monthly pension, or a pension equal to full year's of service for those lacking sufficient years of service to qualify for full benefits. "Window" periods are established which allow employees to exit the personnel system prior to the normal retirement age and/or with fewer years of service than normally required (Hildreth, 1995:412–413; Klingner and Nalbandian, 1998:12; Public Employee Retirement Commission, 1995:3–6).

A number of issues must be considered in determining the appropriateness of early retirement incentive programs. The first is determining which employees are to be targeted and how the incentive will impact their decision and the decision of other employees to leave the system. Secondly, clarity as to the "intent" of the incentive plan to alter the workforce is important. The system must decide whether its objective is to permanently eliminate positions or merely replace older, more expensive personnel with younger, less expensive employees. Actual savings are a function of the number of employees replaced, the amount of time positions remain vacant, and the salary differential between retirees and their replacements (Public Employee Retirement Commission, 1996:iii).

Administrative expenses associated with carrying out the early-retirement effort must also be anticipated and accounted for. Employer and/or retirement systems must provide a sufficient number of retirement counselors at appropriate times to respond to the questions and concerns regarding the myriad options and choices that potential retirees have and must make before signing up for retirement. Staff resources must also be devoted to preparing the mountains of paperwork and reviewing documentation necessary to place persons in a retired status and remove them from active employee status (Public Employee Retirement Commission, 1995:13).

Early retirement incentives or windows may not yield the cost savings expected when initially announced. Careful analysis must be undertaken to avoid a situation in which, rather than producing substantial financial savings, the effort ends up costing the jurisdiction substantial amounts for years to come and thereby creates major barriers to future early-retirement efforts. An example of this can be seen in the "Mellow early retirement" legislation adopted in Pennsylvania in the mid-1990s. Total amortization costs for the 15,000 eligible state employees were estimated between $274 million and $369 million (depending on the level of utilization) over 20 years (PA Public Employee Retirement Commission, 1995).[11]

IV. EMPLOYEE RELATIONS AND RIGHTS OF STATE EMPLOYEES

A. Performance Appraisal

Performance appraisal entails a systemmatic review of an individual employee's job performance to evaluate his or her effectiveness or the adequacy of the work. Ideally, the appraisal involves formulation of a plan for improved performance. In the organizational context, performance appraisal data may be utilized in a wide variety of personnel actions, including:

Compensation decisions such as "merit" increases
Staffing decisions such as promotions, demotions, layoffs, or disciplinary dismissals
Succession planning (whereby the organization determines if it can fill future vacancies with internal applicants)

---

[11] If bonuses are used to encourage an early exit or if the number of years of service is reduced from, say, 35 or 30 years, some computation of additional costs over the next 10, 15, or 20 years may well be necessary to get relevant data on the actual costs of the incentive program. It should also be kept in mind that future cost-of-living adjustments provided to all system retirees may be another cost to be added to the overall price of the effort. Other related costs are often associated with the implementation of such programs. For example, employers can incur additional costs in the form of payouts for unused vacations/annual leave or unused sick leave, which can be partially redeemed as cash by the retiring employee.

Assessing the validity and reliability of recruitment, selection, and placement decisions
Providing timely and accurate feedback to employees
Identifying employee training needs (Klingner and Nalbandian, 1998:275–
278).

B. Workforce Diversity

The Equal Employment Opportunity Act of 1972 extended protections of Title
VII of the Civil Rights Act of 1964 to employees of state government, thereby
providing a legal basis for equal employment opportunity and for prohibiting
illegal discrimination in personnel actions. Equal employment opportunity (EEO)
refers to policy and practices designed to guarantee individuals fair access to all
available jobs and training programs, under equal terms and conditions, with
equal benefits and services, and without consideration of the applicant's race,
religion, sex, national origin, or age. EEO is essentially a passive concept designed to remove overt employment barriers rooted in illegal discrimination. EEO
policy does not rectify the effects of past discrimination; rather, it is forward-
looking in its perspective and strives to create a "level playing field" for all
employees (Shafritz et al., 1992:226, 229–232; Ledvinka, 1982:24–45).

In contrast to EEO, affirmative action involves positive, "active," and, if
necessary, aggressive steps to correct or overcome the continuing effects of past
discrimination. Affirmative action seeks to create opportunities which presumably would have existed for protected groups had they not been adversely affected
by the effects of past racism or illegal discrimination (Shafritz et al., 1992:224,
232–235; Ledvinka, 1982:118–124). In terms of employment law, the term "affirmative action" has its origin in a provision of Section 706(g) of Title VII of
the Civil Rights Act of 1964:

> If the court finds that the respondent (i.e., employer generally) has **intention-
> ally engaged in or is intentionally engaging in an unlawful employment
> practice** charged in the complaint, the court may **enjoin** the respondent from
> engaging in such unlawful employment practices and **order such affirmative
> action as may be appropriate**, which may include but is not limited to:
>
> 1. reinstatement or hiring employees with or without backpay;
> 2. **any other equitable relief as the court deems appropriate** (42 U.S.C.
>   Section 2000e-5(g)(1)) (emphasis added).

Of late, a backlash has developed against affirmative action. In some instances popular initiatives, legislation, or gubernatorial executive orders have restricted or banned its use. The jargon of the personnelist has even changed to
reflect a softer, more politically correct concept—work force diversity. Work
force diversity is in keeping with the concept of a socially representative bureau-

cracy and equal employment opportunity, without generating the emotional hostility associated with affirmative action, a term which to some implies "reverse discrimination" against majority-group males. This change is more than mere semantics. Efforts at achieving, through aggressive means if necessary, a socially representative bureaucracy throughout the administrative hierarchy have been stunted (Sylvia, 1994:82–91;Riccucci, 1997:57–69; Ridge, 1996).

C. Nepotism and Workplace Romances

With more dual-career marriages and concerns regarding sexual harassment in the workplace, renewed interest has been shown in developing and promulgating nepotism and nonfraternization policies. Nepotism policies prohibit relatives and spouses from being employed in the same organization, the same office, or in a supervisor-subordinate relationship. Such policies have traditionally existed in public-sector settings to protect the "merit principle" by preventing the appointment of employees on the basis of family connection rather than competence. Additionally, such policies are intended to prevent the potentially disruptive consequences that may arise when married couples work together (Tompkins, 1995: 319).

Organizations that enforce restrictive nepotism policies are under attack because such policies adversely affect the employment opportunities of dual-career couples. If an employer is prohibited from hiring both spouses, then one spouse (more often than not the woman) may have to choose between marriage and career. Those who favor abolishing nepotism rules argue that in white-collar occupations it is possible for married couples to work in close quarters and even supervise one another without problems of favoritism or marital discord (Tompkins, 1995:319).

Organizations may minimize inequities created by antinepotism policies by clearly defining the family relationships covered by the policy—spouses (including "significant others"), children, parents, brothers, sisters, blood relatives. The policy should stipulate that these persons are not permitted to work in the same department, under the direct line of supervision of each other (first and second line), or be involved in decisions affecting each other in such matters as compensation, benefits, promotion, performance appraisal, etc. (PA Fish and Boat Commission, 1995).

D. Nonfraternization Policies

In addition to nepotism policies, personnel offices increasingly have had to deal with employees who date one another or who may cohabit. Promulgating policies that balance the employer's legitimate interest in maintaining an efficient and effective workplace while respecting employees' right to privacy is problematic.

Office romances may undermine employee morale if coworkers believe a colleague is receiving special treatment as a result of the relationship with a superior. The employer may also have legitimate concerns about the possibility of the romance turning sour and the subordinate employee raising allegations of being sexually harassed or punished for ending the relationship (Levine, 1998).

It cannot realistically be expected that nonfraternization policies will prevent office romances from developing. Such policies, however, can minimize the negative potential of such relationships for the organization. An employer who becomes aware of a relationship may have some obligation to ascertain whether it is consensual. The employer might further seek to ensure that there are not direct reporting lines for persons involved with each other. If possible, one of the persons should be transferred to another department or agency, particularly where the relationship has begun to adversely affect the mission of the office (Winning, 1998; Levine, 1998).

E. Harassment

1. Sexual Harassment

Sexual harassment is egregious, unwelcome behavior of a sexual nature that profoundly affects the work environment and can disrupt workplace productivity if personnel are made to feel uncomfortable, embarrassed, and fearful of coming to work. Harassment impairs employee morale and job performance and can result in serious disciplinary actions up to and including discharge. In a 1995 study the U.S. Merit System Protection Board estimated that sexual harassment cost the federal government $327 million between 1992 and 1994 in increased sick time, employee turnover, and decreased individual and group productivity. Since sexual harassment constitutes a violation of federal and state law, the central personnel agency must develop and promulgate specific policies that assist agencies in identifying and rooting it out of the workplace (U.S. Merit System Protection Board, 1995:viii, 26; Greenbaum, 1992).[12]

---

[12] Sexual harassment represents a form of sex discrimination prohibited by Title VII of the Civil Rights Act of 1964 as Amended and the EEOC's Guidelines on Discrimination because of Sex (29 Code of Federal Regulations Section 1604. Sexual harassment entails ''unwelcome sexual advances, requests for sexual favors, and other verbal or physical conduct of a sexual nature constitute sexual harassment when: a. Submission to such conduct is made either explicitly or implicitly a term or condition of an individual's employment, b. Submission to or rejection of such conduct by an individual is used as the basis for employment decisions affecting such individual, or c. Such conduct has the purpose or effect of substantially interfering with an individual's work performance or creating an intimidating, hostile or offensive working environment.''

2. Types of Harassment

Sexual harassment may take several forms. The first, a "hostile work environment" entails actions directed toward the victim designed to humiliate, embarrass, or intimidate victims to the extent that the workplace is so intolerable that the employee has no choice but to resign. A second form is superior-subordinate or, "quid pro quo," harassment. Here a supervisor or superior with authority to affect the subordinate's working conditions, compensation, and opportunities for continued employment or promotion makes sexual advances or asks for sexual favors. Giving in to these demands is an explicit or implicit condition of continued employment, favorable performance evaluations, or promotions. A refusal to submit to the demands of the harasser results in retaliation and reprisals such as poor assignments, poor performance appraisals, disciplinary action, demotion, or discharge for pretexual reasons (Greenbaum, 1992).

A "paramour claim" is a third form of harassment. It arises when a superior becomes romantically involved with a subordinate. In addition to violating nonfraternization policies, this relationship may result in the subordinate's receiving certain tangible benefits, such as better assignments or schedules, or pay increases or promotions at the expense of others who are more deserving in the work unit. This may result in complaints or lawsuits alleging that the paramour has received special treatment (Greenbaum, 1992).

"Third-party harassment" is a final form that organizations need to be aware of. This type of misconduct can be by employees or against employees by outsiders such as clients, patients, passengers, customers, or outside vendors such as contractors and subcontractors, repair and service personnel, salespersons, and others. The organization's interest in addressing this type of harassment derives from its responsibility for maintaining a workplace free of harassment and its liability in these cases (Greenbaum, 1992).

3. Sexual Harassment Policy

Central personnel offices, in consultation with employee representatives, should develop and disseminate to all agencies, departments, and bureaus under its jurisdiction a clear and unequivocal policy against all forms of sexual harassment. Education and training programs for supervisors and managers are a key component in the success of the policy. All employees need to be informed of what constitutes harassment, their right to raise the issue, and how to file a complaint. An in-house grievance or complaint procedure can be developed, with appropriately trained individuals to hear and investigate fully and fairly all claims of sexual misconduct. In the effective organization, staff responsible for conducting the investigation are sensitized to the special aspects of sexual harassment cases, and investigators listen and take complaints seriously. Immediate steps are taken to stop the harassment and rectify any wrongs that have been documented. When the evidence warrants, transfers, training and education, or disciplinary actions are taken against persons engaging in harassing conduct (Greenbaum, 1992; U.S. Merit Systems Protection Board, 1995:29–39).

F. Workplace Violence

1. Extent of the Problem

The central personnel agency has a major role assisting units under its jurisdiction to prepare policies and strategies for addressing the ever-increasing problem of violence in the workplace. Workplace violence runs the gamut from verbal abuse to homicide. According to AFSCME's *Preventing Workplace Violence*, violence is defined as:

> . . . any act of aggression that causes physical or emotional harm, such as physical assault, rape, verbal abuse, threats (including bomb scares) and even sexual harassment. Types of assaults include pinching, biting, hitting, grabbing, kicking or being stuck by a weapon. Almost any object can be used as a weapon (AFSCME, 1998).

Other disruptions found in the workplace include:

a. Stalking and armed threats by spouses, former lovers, etc.
b. Overreaction/hostility by angry clients or customers turned violent
c. Telephone bomb or suicide threats
d. Obscene, harassing, or threatening phone calls
e. Stressed employees who go"postal"—i.e., bring firearms into the workplace and assault current or former coworkers, supervisors, and whoever else is present

During the 1990s there has been a growing awareness of the problem of violence in the workplace. A few high-profile incidents have captured a great deal of media attention. Examples include shootings of teachers and students at public schools by students in 1997 and 1998, violent outbursts in post offices around the country, and most notably the tragic bombing of the Alfred P. Murrah Federal Office Building in 1995. And the problem of workplace violence is much more pervasive than suggested by these incidents (National Institute of Occupational Safety and Health, 1996; Williams, 1997:2; Bachman, 1994).[13]

---

[13] The following statistics provide an overview of the extent of the problem: every week 18,000 (nearly 1 million per year) persons are victims of violent crime while working; every week on average 20 workers (1071 in 1994) are murdered on the job in the United States; 30% of violence in the workplace is directed at public employees even though government employment equals only 18% of the total U.S. workforce; 260,000 women are annually victims of violent crime in the workplace; 8% of all rapes, 7% of all robberies, and 16% of all assaults occur at work; homicide is the leading cause of death of women on the job; nonfatal assaults result in millions of dollars in lost workdays and employee wages.

2. Employer Responsibility in Addressing Violence in the Workplace

Public employers have a legal obligation to provide a workplace that is reasonably safe. Where a credible threat exists, the employer is required to take appropriate steps to address the threat including seeking restraining order or injunctions prohibiting aggressors from coming in contact with staff or into the workplace. The failure of employers to treat threats prudently exposes them to financial liability (Williams, 1997:6; Defense Personnel Security Research Center, 1995).[14]

The central personnel agency can do a variety of things to minimize threats to employees in the workplace. Initially it can develop and promulgate a comprehensive policy on workplace violence that provides clear direction to agencies. Such a policy contains information that helps employees identify the warning signs that an employee, former employee, client, or vendor who is potentially violent. The policy also provides direction to employees to help them minimize personal threats they may encounter and to deescalate potentially violent situations. Additionally, the comprehensive policy provides a detailed reporting mechanism to document and communicate to superiors threats or incidents that employees observe, receive, or encounter on the job. Finally, like the U.S. Postal Service's "zero tolerance" policy with respect to employees bringing firearms to the workplace can be adopted (Williams, 1997:6; Defense Personnel Security Research Center, 1995).[15]

Potential threats to the workplace may be addressed by pre-employment background checks on prospective employees and inquiries of previous employers about prior incidents of violence. Persons with a history of workplace threats or violence obviously cannot be employed, particularly if a potential for similar behavior is identified. Additionally, the central personnel agency, in consultation with the department of general services or similar entity responsible for facilities should evaluate security measures, and the use of barriers and security devices to minimize threats to employees (Williams, 1997, p. 6; Defense Personnel Security

---

[14] Liability may arise as a result of: the dangerous acts of employees it has hired if harm was foreseeable; its failure to intervene in situations of harassment of employees by its supervisors and managers; actions of employees who are drunk or under the influence of drugs if the employer exercises control over them and is negligent in exercising that control; a failure to warn an employee, spouse, or third party of threat made by another to do physical harm to that person.

[15] In response to the growing threat of workplace violence, the U.S. Postal Service has adopted a "zero tolerance" policy with respect to employees bringing firearms to the workplace. The U.S. Office of Personnel Management has organized an interagency working group on violence in the workplace to address the problem and February 1998 disseminated "Dealing with Violence in the Workplace: A Guide for Agency Planners." The publication provides direction to federal agencies on matters related to preparing policy statements, prevention, case studies, etc. State personnel agencies should proceed in consultation with OPM and other consultants in preparing polices and procedures tailored to their own specific needs and situations.

Research Center for the Private Sector Liaison Committee of the International Association of Chiefs of Police, 1995).

G. Qualified Immunity/Civil Suits for Damages

Central personnel offices are responsible for disseminating clear statements to all personnel that violating the constitutional or statutory rights of public employees, agency clients, or persons incarcerated or on parole unacceptable. Long gone are the days in which public servants enjoyed absolute immunity from civil suits for damages alleging violating of rights during the exercise of their official duties. At present the employee enjoys what might be characterized as "qualified immunity." The public employee who violates an individual's protected rights may be sued personally for actual and punitive damages. Actual damages would include reimbursement to the victim for lost income, medical and rehabilitation expenses, etc. Additionally, so-called punitive damages may be assessed and serve as a deterrent causing others to avoid a similar violation of protected rights. The guilty employee might also incur considerable expenses in the form of attorney's fees, court costs, etc. (Rosenbloom and Carroll, 1990: 29–52; *Bryce Harlow and Alexander Butterfield v. A. Earnest Fitzgerald*, 457 U.S. 800 (1982)).[16]

Public employers may or may not be liable for a violation of rights associated with actions by their employees. Employees should know that a claim of merely following orders (the so-called Nuremberg defense) is insufficient to counter possible liability. In fact, the employer may well place the employee on paid or unpaid administrative leave and tell him or her to resolve legal difficulties before submitting a request for reinstatement and return to work. The organization can undertake an internal investigation to determine if any of its policies or rules were violated that might subject the employee to discipline or discharge before the application for reinstatement is approved (Rosenbloom and Carroll, 1990: 29–52)

V. MANAGEMENT OF STATE HUMAN RESOURCES SYSTEMS IN THE 21st CENTURY

A. Civil Service Reform

First articulated in the early 1980s, the assessment that government was the "problem" rather than the "solution" continued to enjoy popular support in

---

[16] Rosenbloom (1997) states:

> ". . . the main purpose of constitutional tort doctrine is to protect the public. But that goal is balanced against the government's interest in exercising discretion and functioning cost-effectively. Most public employees and officials have qualified immunity in such suits. They are liable for money damages only if they violate clearly

the late 1990s. Bureaucracy was not viewed positively as a tool for formulating strategies and implementing programs to solve problems. Public employees continued to be characterized by some politicians as underworked, overpaid, and too immune from disciplinary mechanisms even if incompetent. After 100 years of viewing the merit system principles as the cornerstone of civil service reform, the system and its protections of employees from partisan abuses and arbitrary actions are the target for a new generation of "reformers" (Thompson and Radin, 1997:1; Perry and Mesch, 1997:21).

The state of Georgia provides a most dramatic illustration of this change in direction. On July 1, 1996, the Georgia's Senate Bill 635 became law creating two classes of public employees. All persons employed prior to July 1, 1996, continued to be covered by merit system protections and retained associated rights. When state positions previously covered by the merit system become vacant and are filled by persons hired on or after July 1, 1996, merit system protections do not apply and the employee is assumed to be an "at-will employee" of the state. Such employees, at least in theory, can be hired, promoted, transferred, demoted, and even dismissed without the constraints normally associated with merit system rules (Walter, 1997:17).

The reforms adopted in Georgia may add up to less than advertised. While newly hired employees are exempt from the state's merit system, the agencies which hire them must adhere to merit principal requirements mandated by the federal government. By the requirements, the new employees are recruited, screened, selected, and promoted based on their skills, knowledge, and abilities. Their compensation is to be equitable and adequate, based on performance and merit, and they are to be protected against partisan coercion. Even in disciplinary cases resulting in termination, due process protections must be afforded to them (Walter, 1997:17; PA Legislative Budget and Finance Committee, 1998:64).

Reforms like those enacted by Georgia are often justified by the rationale that they will enable the public sector to enjoy the type of flexibility found in the private sector. Flexible organizations can presumably adapt and change quickly to meet evolving environmental conditions and thus be more responsive to new policy and political direction by elected officials. Critics of the reforms have reservations about the potential for arbitrary and capricious treatment of employees and the reappearance of widespread partisan abuses. Whether these concerns are valid or merely designed to block real change remains to be seen. It may be that First Amendment freedom of association protections coupled with Constitutional due process requirements, along with "just cause" requirements found in

---

established constitutional rights which a reasonable person would have known. Public employees and officials generally retain absolute immunity when engaging in adjudicatory or legislative functions. Immunity is from suit itself, not simply a defense against being assessed with compensatory or punitive damages. . . ."

the disciplinary clauses of collective bargaining agreements, will provide public employees with adequate protections. Additionally, the possibility of negative press revelations of abuses arising as a result of rolling back merit system protections may also minimize blatant violations of employee rights.

B. Internet Use of Emerging Technology

The late 1990s are a very exciting and challenging time for the central personnel office in most states. The offices are laboring to acquire and master new technologies and information systems. To a large extent, the Internet represents the future of public personnel administration, providing a virtually unlimited opportunity for agencies to share as well as gather information on a wide array of topics of concern to personnelists. Increasingly, state central personnel offices and civil service commissions are establishing sites and expanding the range of information posted or services that employees or the public may access.

The Internet has the promise of making it considerably easier for the personnel office to fulfill its mission. Recruitment efforts, for example, can be and have been enhanced as agencies post information about position vacancies, civil service position announcements, testing requirements, submission of applications, and the like. Test development and validation efforts have the potential for significant improvement given the capacity to have nearly instantaneous access to information from operating agencies, professional associations, personnel agencies in other states, and the federal government.

Today the central personnel office staff has instant access to information from federal data bases, organizations like the National Association of State Personnel Executives, the National Academy of Public Administration, and the Society for Human Resource Management, as well as from counterparts in other states, without ever having to telephone anyone or send a written request for information. As the knowledge explosion continues, the Internet affords personnel agencies a low-cost means of keeping pace with available information. States which devote the time, talent, and resources to develop and exploit the potential of the Internet will be well on the way of meeting challenges of the 21st century. Those who don't will be left behind trying to figure out why others are succeeding while they struggle with outmoded practices and technologies.

VI. CONCLUDING THOUGHTS

The organizing themes of this chapter and the professional literature cited demonstrate that personnel/human resources management in state government is a vital and dynamic endeavor. As suggested by the array of managerial, political, and legal constraints addressed in this chapter, states must continually attract the best and brightest to personnel positions if they are to deliver the services demanded by the public. Since the demands for quality services and the litigious nature of personnel administration are unlikely to subside in the near term, personnelists, line supervisors, and other managers must have a well-honed understanding and appreciation of the personnel matters addressed in this discussion.

Over the next 10 years, a number of significant changes are expected in the environment of state government personnel administration. The shift in domestic policy leadership away from Washington and back toward the states is under way. Work force demographics will be altered as more women and minorities enter the public-sector work force and attain leadership positions. Employees are expected to change careers frequently and the technological revolution will re-shape the nature of work and where and how it is performed. For the most part, however, the public sector will remain "labor-intensive" and personnel costs will claim the central portion of agency budgets.

Into the next century, calls for reforming state personnel systems will be made by elected officials and academics. Civil servants must also be heard given their exceptional insights regarding the environments in which their agencies operate. Personnel departments need to be given resources dedicated to formulating new strategies and approaches to present and future problems. Unfortunately, tight budgets force agencies to focus on putting out fires and reacting to, rather than anticipating, problems. Personnel departments will have to reconsider the protected position of "sacred cows" and the notion that "if it ain't broke, don't fix it," and central personnel office and line agencies must develop mechanisms for genuinely harnessing the creative potential of their employees. Reform is not the end but the means by which agencies more efficiently, effectively, and economically serve the public—a notion that has not changed much in 100 years.

REFERENCES

Aaron, B., Najita, J. M., and Stern, J. L. (1988). *Public Sector Bargaining*, 2d ed., Bureau of National Affairs, Washington, DC.

Act 1970-195, Public Employee Relations Act, 43 PA Statutes Annotated, Section 1101.101 et seq.

Aronson, A. H. (1991). State and local personnel administration, *Classics of Public Personnel Policy*, 2d ed., revised and expanded (F. J. Thompson, ed.), Wadsworth Publishing Company, Belmont, CA, pp. 133–142.

AFSCME. (1998). Workplace violence facts, *Preventing Workplace Violence*, American Federation of State, County and Municipal Employees, AFL-CIO, Washington, DC, pp. 1–4.

Bachman, R. (1994). *Bureau of Justice Statistics Data Brief—Violence and Theft in the Workplace: National Crime Victimization Survey*, U.S. Department of Justice, Office of Justice Programs, Bureau of Justice Statistics, Washington, DC.

Ban, C., and Riccucci, N. M. eds. (1997). *Public Personnel Management: Current Concerns, Future Challenges*, 2d ed., Addison, Wesley Longman, New York.

Ban, C., and Riccucci, N. M. (1993). Personnel systems and labor relations: steps toward a quiet revitalization, *Revitalizing State and Local Public Service* (F. J. Thompson, ed.), Jossey-Bass, San Francisco, pp. 71–103.

Berger, P. A. (1998). Comments provided to Curtis Berry regarding the application of the *Rutan* decision and litigation involving the PA Turnpike Commission.

Branti v. Finkel. (1980). 445 U.S. 507.

Brvce Harlow and Alexander Butterfield v. A. Earnest Fitzgerald. (1982). 457 U.S. 800.

California Department of Personnel Administration. (1998). *The State Personnel Management System*, Author.

California State Personnel Board. (1998). *About the State Personnel Board*, Author.

Cayer, N. J. (1996). *Public Personnel Administration in the United States*, 3d ed., St. Martin's Press, New York.

Civil Rights Act of 1964, As Amended. 42 U.S.C. Section 2000e.

Council of State Governments. (1996). *The Book of the States, 1996–1997 ed., Vol. 31*, Council of State Governments, Lexington, KY.

Cozzetto, D. A., Pedeliski, T. B., and Tipple, T. J. (1996). *Public Personnel Administration: Confronting the Challenges of Change*, Prentice-Hall, Upper Saddle River, NJ.

Cynthia Rutan et al. v. Republican Party of Illinois et al. (1990). 497 U.S. 62., 110 S. Ct. 2729.

Defense Personnel Security Research Center for the Private Sector Liaison Committee of the International Association of Chiefs of Police. (1995). *Combating Workplace Violence—Guidelines for Employers and Law Enforcement*, International Association of Chiefs of Police, Alexandria, VA.

Edwards, H. T., Clark, R. T. Jr., and Craver, C. B. (1991). *Labor Relations Law in the Public Sector: Cases and Materials*, 4th ed., Michie Company, Charlottesville, VA.

Ehrenhalt, S. M. (1997). The new geography of government jobs: hiring in state and local government shifts to South and West, and to medium and small states, *Government Employment Report*, Center for the Study of the States, Nelson A. Rockefeller Institute of Government, SUNY, Albany, NY.

Elling, R. C. (1996). Bureaucracy—maligned yet essential, *Politics in the American States: A Comparative Analysis*, 6th ed. (Virginia Gray and Herbert Jacob, eds.), Congressional Quarterly Press, Washington, DC.

Freedman, A. (1994). *Patronage: An American Tradition*, Nelson-Hall Publishers, Chicago.

Greenbaum, M. L. (1992). Sexual harassment in the workplace, Presentation at the 14th annual summer program of the American Arbitration Association, Ogunquit, ME.

Hays, S. W., and Kearney, R. C. eds. (1995). *Public Personnel Administration: Problems and Prospects*, 3d ed., Prentice-Hall, Englewood Cliffs, NJ.

Heidron, R. Jr., and Moran, R. (1997). The turnpike takes its toll: Family, political ties pave the way to jobs, *Philadelphia Inquirer*, Oct. 27, p. A1.

Heidron, R. Jr., and Moran, R. (1997). The turnpike takes its toll: Why you pay to cross Pa., *Philadelphia Inquirer*, Oct. 26, p. A1.

Heidron, R. Jr., and Moran, R. (1997). The turnpike takes its toll: millions in contracts go to the connected, *Philadelphia Inquirer*, Oct. 28, p. A1.

Henderson, R. I. (1985). *Compensation Management: Rewarding Performance*, 4th ed., Reston Publishing Company, Reston, VA.

Hoogenboom, A. (1961).*Outlawing the Spoils: A History of the Civil Service Reform Movement—1865–1883*, University of Illinois Press, Urbana, IL.

Kaufman, L. (1998). Comments provided to Curtis Berry, during Pennsylvania Legislative Budget & Finance Committee Budget Audit of the Fish and Boat Commission.

Kearney, R. C. (1992). *Labor Relations in the Public Sector*, 2d ed., revised and expanded, Marcel Dekker, New York.

Kenyon, C. F. (1998). Comments related to personnel and collective bargaining issues within the Commonwealth of Pennsylvania, PA Bureau of Labor Relations, Harrisburg.

Klingner, D. E., and Nalbandian, J. (1998). *Public Personnel Management: Contexts and Strategies*, 4th ed., Prentice-Hall, Englewood Cliffs, NJ.

Ledvinka, J. (1982). *Federal Regulation of Personnel and Human Resource Management*, Wadsworth, Belmont, CA.

Lefkowitz, J., ed. (1985). *The Evolving Process: Collective Negotiations in the Public Sector*, Labor Relations Press, Fort Washington, PA.

Levine, D. S. (1995). Dangerous liaisons: why your employer wants to tell you with whom you can sleep and why they probably don't, *Disgruntled Feature* 1,(4).

Mayer, D. F. (1998). Comments of Dr. Donald F. Mayer, chairperson, negotiating team, 1998 Association of Pennsylvania State College and University Faculties.

McCaffery, R. M. (1988). *Employee Benefit Programs: A Total Compensation Perspective*, PWS-Kent Publishing Company, Boston.

National Association of State Personnel Executives. (1996). *State Personnel Office: Roles and Functions*, 3d ed., Council of State Governments, Lexington, KY.

National Institute of Occupational Safety and Health. (1996). *Violence in the Workplace: Risk Factors and Prevention Strategies*, DHHS (NIOSH) Publication No. 96-100, National Institute of Occupational Safety and Health, Washington, DC.

Office of Administration, Bureau of Personnel. (1996). *Pay Plan 1996: M525.2*, Commonwealth of Pennsylvania, Office of Administration, Bureau of Personnel, Harrisburg, PA.

Office of Administration, Commonwealth of Pennsylvania. (1982). *Management Directive 505.4 Amended, Salaried Complement Control*, Commonwealth of Pennsylvania, Office of Administration, Bureau of Personnel, Harrisburg, PA.

Office of Administration, Commonwealth of Pennsylvania. (1995). *Management Directive 505.20, Wage Complement Management and Control*, Commonwealth of Pennsylvania, Office of Administration, Bureau of Personnel, Harrisburg, PA.

PA Fish and Boat Commission. (1995). *Nepotism Policy, Memo to All Managers and Supervisors*, from Executive Director, Pete Colangelo, PA Fish and Boat Commission, Harrisburg, PA.

PA Legislative Budget and Finance Committee. (1992). *1992 Statistical Digest*, PA Legislative Budget and Finance Committee, Harrisburg, PA.

PA Legislative Budget and Finance Committee. (1997). *PA Turnpike Commission Performance Audit: Issues Related to Turnpike Organization, Management and Operations: Report II*, PA Legislative Budget and Finance Committee, Harrisburg, PA.

PA Legislative Budget and Finance Committee. (1998a). *1998 Statistical Digest*, PA Legislative Budget and Finance Committee, Harrisburg, PA.

PA Legislative Budget and Finance Committee. (1998b). *Study on Civil Service Reform: Pursuant to Senate Resolution 1977–44*, Legislative Budget and Finance Committee, Harrisburg, PA.

PA Public Employee Retirement Commission. (1995a). *Advisory Note on Senate Bill 614, Printer's Number 638 and Senate Bill 615, Printer's Number 639*, PA Public Employee Retirement Commission, Commonwealth of Pennsylvania. Harrisburg, PA.

PA Public Employee Retirement Commission. (1995b). *Feasibility of Early Retirement Incentives in the Public Sector*, Public Employee Retirement Commission, Commonwealth of Pennsylvania, Harrisburg, PA.

PA Public Employee Retirement Commission. (1996). *Fiscal Impact of the Early Retirement Incentive for Public School Employees Provided by Act 186 of 1992 and Act 29 of 1994*, Public Employee Retirement Commission, Commonwealth of Pennsylvania, Harrisburg, PA.

Perry, J. L., and Mesch, D. J. (1997). Strategic human resource management, *Public Personnel Management: Current Concerns, Future Challenges*, 2d ed. (C. Ban and N. M. Riccucci, eds.), Addison, Wesley Longman, New York.

Public Employee Department, AFL-CIO. (1997). *Public Employees Bargain for Excellence: A Compendium of State Labor Relations Laws*, Public Employee Department, AFL-CIO, Washington, DC.

Rabin, J., Vocino, T., Hildreth, W. B., and Miller, G. J. eds. (1994). *Handbook on Public Personnel Administration and Labor Relations*, Marcel Dekker, New York.

Rabin, J., Vocino, T., Hildreth, W. B., and Miller, G. J. eds. (1995). *Handbook of Public Personnel Administration*, Marcel Dekker, New York.

Richard Elrod v. John Burns. (1976). 427 U.S. 347.

Ridge, T. (1998). *Governor's Annual Workforce Report 1998*, Governor's Office, Commonwealth of Pennsylvania, Harrisburg, PA.

Ridge, T. (1996). *Executive Order 1996-9, Equal Employment Opportunity*, Office of Administration, Governor's Office, Commonwealth of Pennsylvania, Harrisburg, PA.

Rosenbloom, D. H. (1997). Constitutional problems for the new public management in the United States (K. Thai and R. Y. Carter, eds.), *Current Public Policy Issues: The 1998 Annals*, Academic Press, Boca Raton, FL.

Rosenbloom, D. H., and Carroll, J. D. (1990). *Toward Constitutional Competence: A Casebook for Public Administrators*, Prentice-Hall, Englewood Cliffs, NJ.

Rosenbloom, J. S., and Hallman, G. V. (1986). *Employee Benefit Planning*, 2d ed., Prentice-Hall, Englewood Cliffs, NJ.

Shafritz, J. M., Riccucci N. M., Rosenbloom, D. H., and Hyde, A. C. (1992). *Personnel Management in Government: Politics and Process*, 4th ed., revised and expanded, Marcel Dekker, New York.

Sheibley, L. B. (1997). *Survey of Other States: Decentralization of Personnel Functions*, Pennsylvania Civil Service Commission, Harrisburg, PA.

Smith v. Wade. (1983). 461 U.S. 30.

Stanley, D. T. (1974). A symposium: the merit principle today, *Public Administration Review 34(5)*: 425–452.

State & Local Sourcebook for 1998. (1998). Supplement to *Governing, Congressional Quarterly*, Washington, DC.

Sylvia, R. D. (1994). *Public Personnel Administration*, Wadsworth Publishing Company, Belmont, CA.

Tompkins, J. (1995). *Human Resource Management in Government*, HarperCollins College Publishers, New York.

Thompson, F. J., ed. (1991). *Classics of Public Personnel Policy*, 2d ed., revised and expanded, Wadsworth Publishing Company, Belmont CA.

Thompson, F. J., ed. (1993). *Revitalizing State and Local Public Service*, Jossey-Bass, San Francisco.

Thompson, F. J., and Radin B. A. (1997). *Reinventing Public Personnel Management: The Winter and Gore Initiatives—National Commission on the State and Local Public Service Occasional Paper*, Nelson A. Rockefeller Institute of Government, SUNY, Albany, NY.

Unknown. (April/May 1995). States update personnel systems, *State Trends Bulletin, 1(3)*: 1, 6–7.

Unknown. (Feb./March 1995). Downsizing: the mantra for state personnel directors in the '90's, *State Trends Bulletin 1(2)*: 1.

U.S. Bureau of Labor Statistics. (1998). *Nonfarm Payroll Statistics from the Current Employment Statistics, National Employment, Hours, and Earnings, Seasonally Adjusted: State Government*, BLS, Washington, DC.

U.S. Department of Labor. (1996). *Report of the Secretary of Labor's Task Force on Excellence in State and Local Government Through Labor-Management Cooperation: Working Together for Public Service*, U.S. Department of Labor, Washington, DC.

U.S. Equal Employment Opportunity Commission, *Guidelines on Discrimination Because of Sex, 29 Code of Federal Regulations* Section 1604.

U.S. General Accounting Office. (1997). *Report to the Chairman, House Republican Task Force on Privatization*: Privatization: Lessons Learned by State and Local Government, GAO/GGD-97-48, U.S. General Accounting Office, Washington, DC.

U.S. Merit Systems Protection Board. (1997). *Sexual Harassment in the Federal Workplace: Trends, Progress, Continuing Challenges*, U.S. Merit Systems Protection Board, Washington, DC.

U.S. Office of Personnel Management. (1998). *Dealing with Violence in the Workplace: A Guide for Agency Planners*, United States Office of Personnel Management, Office of Workforce Relations, Washington, DC.

Williams, H. A. H. (1997). Violence in the workplace: a reality for men and women, *California Labor and Employment Law Quarterly*, spring.

Winning, E. A. (1998). *Romance in the Workplace*, E. A. Winning Associates, Walnut Creek, CA.

9
Strategic Management in State Governments

Paul C. Nutt and Robert W. Backoff
The Ohio State University, Columbus, Ohio

The agencies and departments[1] of state government are faced with their greatest challenge in decades (Osborn and Gaebler, 1992). The pressure to change the missions and practices of inertia-ridden and politically protected agencies has been growing for some time (Wechsler and Backoff, 1986). This pressure has prompted shifts in expectations that are becoming ever more frequent in their occurrence and comprehensive in their scope. How does one create new directions for the inertia-ridden organization, make change seem attractive to the politically protected agency, and help the proactive agency leader cope with rapidly changing and often contradictory expectations of a governor and a legislature? This chapter builds on our change ideas (e.g., Nutt and Backoff, 1992, 1995a, 1996a, 1997a) and addresses these concerns by showing how agency leaders can carry out transformational as well as less radical change.

The agencies and programs operated by state government are facing many challenges. We provide a brief summary of these challenges and show how the revitalization desperately needed in state government and its agencies can be, and often is, thwarted by the "rules of the game." The forces that hold back change are being met as other different forces that are demanding it. We show how these "action triggers" are pushing state agencies toward change in the face of others that are holding leaders back.

This "tension" between the status quo and pressures for change creates a paradox that often bewilders agency leaders. The leaders get a message to be

---

[1] Hereafter we use "agency" to describe all types of state government organizations.

proactive and to be careful not to offend anyone or be conspicuous at the same time. We address this dilemma by showing its origins and ways to cope by creating a proactive agency. We also identify constraints that make change very high risk and prone to failure. Principles for change and transformation are offered that help the proactive leaders cope with forces that hold them back and call for change at some time. These principles take shape as managing a dance of the what (strategic action) and how (process of change) for both nonradical and transformational change efforts.

I. PRINCIPLES OF CHANGE

Transformational and nonradical change are both very risky. We seek to lower this risk by laying out what we call "change principles." These principles are derived from our reading of the literature, our experiences in facilitating change and transformation, the special needs of a state agency, and from the special demands posed by a transformation. We believe that transformation will redirect and channel much of the energies of strategic leaders in the future. To transform an agency, leaders must offer a vision that suggests what the agency can become. The change process provides a vehicle for key people to contribute to developing and implementing the vision. To carry out change management, leaders must make a commitment to change, articulate aims and purposes, determine the context that must be managed, make choices about the process intensity and duration, select the type of strategy to be sought, and make decisions about the type of process to be used. The challenge faced by state agency leaders is to carry out a change effort in a systematic manner without losing sight of its purpose. Leaders overly focused on the content of a change may ignore process stages and steps that are central to success. Leaders overly concerned with process can get bogged down in procedure.

To deal with this challenge, we call on leaders to "walk the vision" with stakeholders and tailor the change process accordingly. To do this, leaders engage what we call "the dance of the what and how." The leader communicates a vision (the what) and provides a way to shape and evolve it (the how). This allows stakeholders to embellish the change strategy in a vision and give it detail. Agency leaders who carefully manage the dance of the what and how, or the interplay between content and process, improve their chances of creating and sustaining a transformation.

Change principles guide "the how" of strategic change, suggesting choices that can be made and options that are available. These principles call for the leader to identify whether an agency is susceptible to change, match enacted environment and type of strategy, manage the dance of the what and how, select techniques according to expectations to support the process, create ownership, accept multiple roles, and recognize and reach for a vision, a set of ideals. Change requires an ongoing management effort in which the agency leader takes an active role. To engage the what-and-how dance, a change process is carried out in which directions are determined, vision or ideals articulated, situational assessments carried out, issue tensions uncovered and tested for comprehensiveness, strategies sought to manage priority issue tensions, strategic actors aligned, resources and support needed to implement determined, and implementation plans devised.

II. BARRIERS TO REVITALIZATION

State government agencies are mostly service-providing organizations. These organizations offer or contract for services and provide information about service transactions. For example, bureaus of unemployment service connect job seekers with leads and keep statistics about unemployment. Economic development commissions broker the transactions carried out to entice firms to locate in their area and keep data on the jobs created. These functions are often misunderstood and undervalued (Jones, 1998; Levine, 1984; Kettl, 1993; Dilulio et al., 1993). Because contracting and information roles seem nonessential, there is an eagerness to cut agency budgets or to eliminate them. In addition, there is a widespread perception of waste and goldbricking in state agencies. This perception has prompted a string of initiatives to reform government. In the Johnson years, programming, planning, and budgeting systems, or PPBS, was proposed to cut cost and increase efficiency. Under Nixon, management by objectives was attempted. Carter called for zero-based budgeting. Reagan appointed the Grace Commission to root out inefficiencies and tax dollar waste (Volker et al., 1989). Bush called for "right-sizing," reducing agency size to cut governmental spending. Recently, several U.S. governors have mounted "total quality management" campaigns. Clinton has bought into TQM and the contracting ideas that Osborn and Gaebler (1992) proposed to "reinvent" government (Gore, 1993).

Lack of understanding, perception of low value, and claims of waste have lead to disillusioned public servants and agencies in "free fall," spiraling downward without a safety net. As missions erode and people leave, the reputed ineffectiveness of state government agencies becomes a self-fulfilling prophecy. The value of an exemplary public service is recognized in Europe and elsewhere, but less so in the United States (Salamon and Lund, 1984; Blumenthal and Michael, 1979).

The belt-tightening of the 1990s has added to these problems. Poor economic conditions and the growing resistance to new taxes have caused state agencies to face maintenance and bust cycles. Services are maintained, and then cut when declines in business activity produce state tax revenue shortfalls. Taxing authorities are caught in a dilemma when this occurs. New taxes are vigorously resisted because they are believed to hinder economic recovery. As a result, budget cuts are made which disillusion the state agency service provider. Idealistic providers often leave when the prospect of providing adequate service becomes unlikely, leaving the disgruntled to "do more with less." For instance, social workers in children's services agencies can see their caseload more than doubled in hard economic times, making it impossible to meet the needs of troubled juveniles and their families. This makes oversights in which children are returned to abusive homes more likely.

A. Rules of the Game

Problems experienced by agency leaders are intensified by the "rules of the game" (Nutt and Backoff, 1996a). These informal but very real rules restrict what leaders can do and often hamstring them before they can move into their offices. The rules of the game stem from the fallacies of media oversight, accountability, merit systems, collective bargaining, financing, discretion, proaction, and the voters' willingness to accept the status quo.

1. Media Oversight

Sunshine laws require open meetings, making it difficult for agency leaders to experiment with ideas. It is difficult to innovate without speculating about possibilities, some of them outrageous, as do private organizations. Agency managers are often put into situations that crimp what they can consider to learn about objections and ways to overcome these objections. For the media, considering an idea is tantamount to proposing it. The belief of wide-scale wrongdoing by public officials, whether real or imagined, limits the development of creative and innovative ideas.

Identifying ineffective public organizations has become the special responsibility of the media. Private organizations must satisfy customers in a market, providing something of value for a competitive price. The media see themselves as providing the equivalent of market mechanisms for public organizations. Media scrutiny is thought to expose waste and corruption. The exposé is believed to force the state bureaucrat to reduce the cost of state operations. The media, however, have market responsibilities much like a firm. Advertisers respond to high ratings and high ratings stem from exposés. People have a 3 to 1 preference for negative (Tversky and Kahneman, 1973), so the media sells negativism with a little fluff. Finding something negative is fairly easy because the investigative reporter, using the Freedom of Information Act, can get access to all information, both negative and positive. If nothing is uncovered, the media have been known to invent incidents that confirm their suspicions. Because media awards are based on exposés, there is considerable pressure to seek out the negative and ignore the positive. When errors are made, reporters and media backers hide behind Constitutional guarantees of freedom of the press.

This run of negative information about state agencies is contradicted by actual experiences people have with state government (Rainey, 1991). Surveys find that people using government services, such as employment and economic development, typically have good experiences and believe that they are well served. These same people, however, believe that state government services are generally bad and ineffective. The personal experience contradicts the generalization. People accept the media's interpretations because they seem more representative than a personal experience.

A state official attempting to get out a success story finds little interest in positive accomplishments systematically ignored and their failings systematically magnified. For example, the head of a state corrections agency attempted to bring reforms in the treatment of juvenile offenders carried out by the agency to the media's attention (Card, 1992). The story about past abuses became a front-page feature article in the Sunday paper, without mentioning that all of the abuses had been corrected. The agency director wrote a lengthy rebuttal, but the paper did not print it.

Such experiences suggest that media "oversight" provides little balance in the information that is used by people to evaluate agency performance. The cumulative effect is to gradually characterize every state agency as ineffective, inefficient, and unworthy of the funds it receives. This is reinforced by candidates for public office who run on platforms to "clean up government" and headlines that identify what's wrong and needs fixing. Agency heads with a success story find that no one is listening.

2. Discretion Limits

Rules, regulations, and procedures under which a state agency must operate are made ever more strict with each exposé and failure jolt. Each new set of rules and regulations lowers discretion and limits action by leaders. Job descriptions are tightened to say more about what someone cannot do, again limiting discretion. Alleged scandals often force leaders to let senior people go, whether involved or not, and to take personal charge (Card, 1992). Both actions bleed away valuable time and energy, lowering discretion. Also, civil service and unions take defensive action to protect their people when a scandal is alleged, sapping still more state agency time and energy.

3. Accountability

People expect elected officials to make the bureaucrats who lead state agencies accountable for what they do and spend. Elected officials, however, are pulled in many ways at the same time by interest groups that try to orchestrate what they do. Interest groups are becoming even more vocal, pointing out state agencies and programs that are not doing what they want. The media become a partner in creating this pressure, making it easy for a state agency to be whipsawed by the demands of elected officials and interest groups. State agencies are often required to cope with a new barrage of queries and requests before the last round of demands can be met.

More importantly, targeting a bureaucracy for accountability ignores how tax dollars are spent. Nearly all state and federal agencies are nothing but conduits for entitlements (Milward, 1991). Eighty percent of the funds spent by government goes to fund the entitlement, and 20% to staffing the entitlement's conduit (the actual cost of government operations). And four-fifths of the 20% is contracted out (Kettl, 1988). Accountability in governmental operations involves efficient disbursement of funds and little more. Accountability for the bulk of government spending rests with elected officials who authorize spending, expand programs, and determine who will be served.

4. Merit Systems

The civil service system dates to the Pendelton Act of 1883. Its purpose was to control political appointments and to professionalize the civil service, ensuring that knowledgeable and competent people will keep government going during transitions. Political appointees and the "spoils system" have been under control in most places for over 100 years. Today state civil service rules are thwarting badly needed incentives to promote efficiency and effectiveness in governmental operations. For instance, President Carter's attempt to set in place incentives for senior federal official was removed before it could be given much of a try (Goodsell, 1993). Also, state collective bargaining agreements insist on across-the-board increases and scales by classifications, much like civil service. Without some form of incentive system, the best people will continue to leave government service, making the disaffected and unmotivated an ever-growing segment of its work force (Kouzes and Posner, 1993).

New initiates through the Volker Commission (Ingraham and Rosenbloom, 1990; Volker et al., 1989) are looking for ways to enhance governmental service. Similar commissions have been studying state civil service (Winter et al., 1993). Both initiatives are seeking ways to empower the civil servant working under the constraints posed by instability in mission, programs, and resources that have created rules-following bureaucracies. To move away from this situation, a new vision of governmental management is needed. A new sense of possibilities seems essential to bring new blood and encourage the best to enter public service (Rosen, 1986).

5. Funding Preferences

Most of the funds for state agencies are allocated by a legislative body. Legislatures prefer to provide money for bricks and mortar because the results are visible, drawing attention to job creation and the prospects of better economic conditions. Computer systems and training that can help a state agency improve its level of service are often given a low priority. As a result, approvals for projects such as computer purchases are dragged out, which makes agencies seem even more ineffective. Bewildering complications in redtape and oversight make this situation even worse. For example, the General Services Administration's approval process takes up to three years, rendering equipment such as a computer obsolete before it can arrive (Gore, 1993). Similar delays are typical in state agencies.

6. Proactive Roles

The extent of proactivity desired for a state agency is seldom debated, muddying what is wanted of the agency and its leader. There is no systematic information collection about the state of a state. No one walks through a state service system to see what is and is not happening. Instead, people in power prefer to listen to the single complaining customer. As a result, state legislatures and elected officials have little insight into what is being accomplished in state agencies, state universities, and other organizations that they fund. The level of information is so poor that initiatives from oversight bodies tend to jerk the agency about with little rhyme or reason. Being told to spend as little as possible, do as little as possible, and avoid controversy allows for very little proaction by a leader. The first priority of a state agency leader is not to get into a newspaper.

7. Perceptions About Politics

Voters are oblivious to the rules of the game. Most people are critical of government spending, but oppose changes that would revitalize state agencies (Rosen, 1986). The current "fix" is to privatize services as much as possible by contracting out (Osborn and Gaebler, 1992). The motivation is to reduce state agency involvement in service provision by encouraging entrepreneurship. Privatizing by contracting out makes services seem more "businesslike" and encourages state agencies to be run more like a business (Straussman, 1981). This movement also reduces the size of civil service and public unions, which are thought to be inefficient and hard to motivate.

B. State Agency Leadership

The rules of the game pose many thorny problems for the strategic leader and prompt a formidable set of obstacles. These obstacles arise from the leader being exposed politically, coping with subordinates that have divided loyalties, being accountable to many groups with little authority, and keeping a low profile that is expected by political leaders.

State agency leaders are often exposed politically. The media and others make presumptions of wrongdoing and mount efforts to find a controversy. When wrongdoing or a controversy appears to surface, the feeding frenzy that results can make it impossible for anyone to act. No one wants your message. The problems of leadership are exacerbated by the short tenure of most leaders. Most last less than two years (Card, 1992), and many must live with a tainted selection process (Oroz, 1991), producing threat-driven management. Team building is ignored because top aides have suspect or divided loyalties. Key subordinates are often appointed because of patronage and have little motivation to support a leader. Also, it is pragmatic to give lip service to the leader's agenda when one knows the leader will soon leave. Many take a "let's-wait-them-out" posture and offer token efforts (Kelley, 1992). The need to be responsible to many oversight bodies further complicates things. For instance, the head of a state mental health department takes walking orders from volunteers' associations made up of parents, state legislatures, the governor, service contractors, and many others.

In such milieus, leadership, let alone strategic leadership, can become an oxymoron. The state agency leader can become little more than a figurehead for people to abuse when they are upset, a cutback manager when the agency is to be downsized, or a caretaker. Clearly, a person's leadership can be severely tested under these conditions. Transformational change is a formidable challenge.

III. FORCES FOR CHANGE IN STATE AGENCIES

After an appraisal of the obstacles to be faced, many agency leaders try to slide into a "figurehead" role. However, there are several emerging forces that make such a posture untenable. To bring these forces into focus, we offer some illustrations of state agencies that are being pushed toward change. (We must disguise some agencies and some key players too because we promised them anonymity.) We use these agencies to illustrate some of the forces for change and, later, to illustrate how we carried out the principles and processes of strategic change.

A. Ohio Department of Mental Health

Historically, states provided mental health services through a network of state-operated hospitals. Ohio's Mental Health Act of 1988 called for a change from an inpatient to a community orientation and a transfer of control to community mental health boards that were to operate an integrated system of care. Treatment of patients was to be done in the least restrictive setting, close to family and friends. The reform legislation mandated a phased-in transfer of resources from state hospitals to community-managed mental health service units to support this effort.

To facilitate the mandated change in Ohio, the Ohio Department of Mental Health (ODMH) was to divert funds away from state hospitals for local use in community-based treatment. The amount of funds to be placed under local control was to gradually increase from 1990 to 1996. Each community mental health board was required to reimburse the state for state hospital use. Local community mental health boards were allowed to choose whether to accept increased financial responsibility and, with it, more state funding. A 1994 amendment made local responsibility a requirement. The Ohio legislation was intended to gradually grow local responsibility and reconfigure the state hospitals accordingly.

By 1992, the State of Ohio had a very mixed bag of experiences in attempting to implement the law. Most boards had accepted responsibility, drawing funds away from state hospitals in these areas. State hospitals were changing to accommodate the new payer and payer expectations, but there was conflict and even litigation about the funding distribution. This led to global planning for hospital downsizing and fund transfer, resulting in sweeping plans for hospital consolidation and closure.

The state's hospitals were under considerable stress. The threat of downsizing had put many jobs at risk, including those of hospital CEOs and treatment professionals. Reform had brought massive downsizing with some closures and mergers, making the pain of massive change very real to the survivors. Within the next several years, downsizing from what had been 17 hospitals in 1989 to seven by 1998 had to be completed to significantly reduce state hospital costs. This called for:

1. Reducing the number of hospital beds from 1800 to 1200, placing clients and some staff in community-based treatment organizations. (The hospital bed capacity had been 4000 in 1988 and had been reduced to 1500 by 1995.)
2. Cut FTEs from 3200 to 2500 (there had been 6000 employees in 1988).
3. Ensuring that the remaining 1200 beds are used to treat only the most severely ill individuals and court-ordered hospitalizations.
4. Cutting $70 million annually in hospital operating cost below 1994 levels by 1998 and reinvesting it in community care.
5. Cost containment by consolidations to support service mergers, and affiliations.

These changes had to consider unionized employee groups by dealing with layoffs and outplacement. Mental health care quality was also a concern, as was the state's new role in the provision of mental health services. To downsize successfully, the state's responsibilities in operating hospitals and funding local mental health boards to provide services needed a complete rethinking.

No large state had successfully achieved such a broad-based change designed to deal with the provision of impatient care within a community system. The result calls for unprecedented levels of cooperation between state and local agencies and a sharing of responsibilities and accountabilities for the care of all mental health patients in the state.

The broad strokes for this effort had been set to provide a basis for hospital downsizing, consistent with legislative mandates and departmental values. The department CEO had wanted to build a consensus about the role of the hospital in each region to incorporate local differences and develop agreements with unions to transition staff to outpatient settings. There was considerable disagreement about the most significant issues to be addressed and how best to move forward.

B. Historical Society

The historical society is operated by a large industrial state through a 12 member board appointed to staggered terms by the governor of the state. The board is charged with providing oversight for the executive director and a top management team of seven professional managers. The society manages the state's historical museum, which houses documents and artifacts deemed to have historical significance. It also operates a number of smaller museums and park sites that contain historical landmarks. The society also supports historical societies in local communities, and programs and events important to the state's history. The society operates a pioneer village that has preserved historically important buildings and puts on reenactments of historical events that occurred in the state.

The society has a number of volunteer groups that assist in its programs and give input on issues thought to be important. The volunteers provide much of the labor required to put on special events and programs at historical sites. This free labor is essential to keep these programs and activities going.

The executive director has become frustrated with the difficulties of managing the demands from the volunteers and the board and finding compromises when the volunteers and the board disagree. The turnover of one-third of the positions on the board every year creates additional difficulties. Every year a massive educational effort is needed to get the new members up to speed.

During one of these annual education programs for the historical society's new board members, a new board member, who represented business, asked why the society did not plan "like a business," and volunteered to help. The society was still reeling from its last attempt to plan, which had been a complete failure. This effort had produced considerable conflict over priorities. Staff had engaged in turf battles to promote and protect their interests. Sympathetic board members were approached to gain support for the staff members' programs, areas of responsibility, and budgets. The coalitions that emerged produced a stalemate. This stalemate effectively blocked a plan in which the society had invested considerable time and money.

The executive director of the society sees planning as a good thing. However, he is reluctant to go through it again with all of the hassles and the prospect that the effort will fail. The director is planning a two-day retreat for the annual education program for board members. The new board member who advocated planning wants to initiate strategic management at this meeting, and has hired a facilitator. The executive director is being forced to go along.

C. Ohio Bureau of Worker's Compensation

The Ohio Bureau of Worker's Compensation (BWC) processes claims of workers who have been injured on the job. The bureau applies guidelines drawn from legislation and makes rulings on claims by determining eligibility, after reviewing medical needs statements. As in many other states, the BWC had formed a partnership with employers. An employer could pay into a state fund or be self-insured. The state paid out claims from the funds collected from employers, acting as an underwriter. A few employers were self-insured. Claims from people in these organizations were handled in the same way as other claims.

The BWC operated like a classic input-throughput-output system with its case management. Individuals filed claims and the bureau applied the guidelines to make recommendations. If a claim is approved, a check is written to providers to underwrite the cost of medical treatment and rehabilitation. Claimants can appeal to a commission in another agency if they are dissatisfied with the outcome of a claim. This agency schedules a formal hearing. Lawyers and state examiners assemble to hear appeals and render judgments.

The BWC had been under fire for some time. Critics contended that the long wait for a decision caused serious delays in obtaining payments for providers. It took five months to process a clear-cut claim. Claimants often waited in long lines at the bureau's office without even being able to get the simplest of inquiries answered. This unresponsiveness frustrated claimants and resulted in calls to legislators, who eventually protested to the governor. Bureau procedures were in a shambles. The bureau often lost claims, in part because of its manual claim handling system and the poor management of bureau staff.

Employers were concerned about the mounting cost of their worker's compensation charges and called for reform. Inefficient bureau practices were linked by critics to these increased charges. The governor was being inundated with calls from injured workers, medical providers, and legislators, who cited unresponsiveness of the bureau and indifference to people's needs; and from employers, who called for reduced costs in claim processing.

The governor, frustrated by endless complaints and the BWC's inaction, fired its director and initiated changes that he thought would create private sector management practices. An oversight board was appointed. An executive director was hired who had considerable experience in organizational turnaround. The BWC director's annual salary of $260,000 was set in part to signal the governor's commitment to reforming the bureau. The new executive director has to move quickly to show that reform is under way.

D. Some Key Forces

The concerns and difficulties being faced by these three agencies are typical. Many state agencies recognize the need to modify old practices and traditional ways of doing business. Each faces a number of complex and intertwined change forces, and feels considerable pressure to act and act decisively, prompting the call for strategic change (Nutt and Backoff, 1995b). We offer a brief description of these forces.

1. New and Changing Initiatives

In a state, legislature initiative creates new programs, drops old ones, and modifies still others. New programs can create new energy. For example, the Ohio department of education faced with providing competency-based education put together a measurement scheme, garnered some funding for their initiatives, and experienced some success. This success led to growing legitimacy and questions about the future. There was uncertainty about what to emphasize. Should the agency serve as evaluator/monitor or show how schools with poor records could improve? Explaining a new or an expanded rule is often essential before such an agency can ensure continuity. The program leaders feel considerable pressure to quickly decide what the agency will do before the inevitable criticism of spending without doing anything useful begins. Similar difficulties can be found in ongoing agency programs and activities. For instance, the historical society had to explore its role in preservation before it could plan for the future. Welfare agencies had to consider how their mission had changed when the State of Ohio shifted authority for disbursement of welfare benefits to counties. State departments on aging had to implement programs to keep people out of nursing homes, which forced them to work through the impact of these new programs on their operations.

2. Need to Stabilize Funding

State agencies feel pressure to diversify and stabilize their sources of funding. Selling services in a state agency is often limited or prohibited. ODMH knows that fees would drive away many of the people who most need their help. Also, the prevailing culture of low taxation and mandates from oversight bodies can make fee increases difficult. For instance, increases in license plate fees and toll charges can help to offset shortfalls in revenues for state agencies that operate these activities, but are politically difficult to implement.

The perceived need to privatize is often prompted by funding problems, as noted in the BWC case. Instead of increasing budgets, state legislatures change eligibility rules to have more services paid for by clients. The leaders of the affected organizations see the consequences of these acts as leading to cutbacks in professional staff and to clients who are unable to pay, prompting the need to rethink aims and directions. Savvy leaders in such agencies see the need to think strategically as they financially reposition their agencies. A financial crisis, or an impending one, often raises questions about the needs for change.

3. Desire to Grow Services

State agencies often see the need to expand their services through branches or affiliates and by offering more variety in their services. Universities start branch campuses. The Ohio Department of Natural Resources created a state park system by charging fees to offset the cost of programs, such as natural-area preservation and protection, that the legislature would not fund.

A state agency in this situation needs a strategic plan to justify expansions to people who have oversight authority. Frequently, this requires a process in which the agency hoping to expand gradually brings along a group charged with oversight authority, until its members see the need for expansion and the agency's rationale.

4. Expanded Roles Thrust on an Agency

A state agency can be faced with a demand to enlarge its role. The addition of new services and activities typically brings new clients that have special needs. Alcoholism programs were added to mental health agencies. Water quality was folded into the mandates of state EPA agencies. Tracking abused women was forced on health service agencies. Health care capital expenditure review, a control function, was given to state health agencies with a planning function. State health departments were expected to develop shared commitments to improve health care delivery among health providers as they controlled expenditures by people who were to be collaborators.

Agencies like ODMH often have a board and an executive group which contracts with a provider organization for services. Groups must work together toward a common aim, which tends to shift over time. This opens the agency up to a new interpretation of what needs to be done by each party. The leader of such an agency must move quickly to gain control, or be swamped by special interests. To make things more complex, changes in the board are often mandated by law. Each year a leader loses several board members who had been carefully cultivated and could be counted on for support.

Turnover in oversight groups brings in new members who must be informed about the practices and traditions of the agency. New working arrangements with provider organizations must be forged. The leaders of such agencies realize the need to work together toward a common goal. They seek a way to steer the new board, an executive group, and providers at the same time.

5. Education of Oversight Bodies

Oversight bodies require frequent updating. Board members periodically leave, and new issues that pose threats or offer opportunities arise. Both situations call for programs to educate the board members. The state historical society had one-third of its members replaced every year. Boards that oversee the Public Utilities Commission of Ohio (PUCO), BWC, and higher education (in many states) have their members appointed to fixed terms. The members of such oversight bodies have to be educated before they can be approached to approve new initiatives.

Leaders of such agencies are faced with the challenge of creating insight simultaneously into traditions that must be preserved and needs that call for change. Such leaders struggle to find a way to meet the dual aims of getting board members to see the value in current practices and the need to change practices at the same time. The dilemma of presenting the need for preservation and transition often frustrates and stalls needed action, as noted in the historical society.

6. Leadership Changes

State agency leaders often have short tenures (Card, 1995). Many new leaders bring with them a vision for the agency, and try to get boards and key organization staff members to buy into their ideas. Others seek to create a vision working with these same groups. Savvy leaders realize that they must redirect momentum and establish a shared vision before radical change will be adopted. The vision attempts to clarify what the organization stands for, its values and centers of excellence with distinctive competencies, to ensure that these values and competencies will be preserved. Some leaderless agencies can also make such a move. For instance, a college of business in a state-assisted university mounted a massive strategic development effort to ensure that its values were recognized by the university's top management, and then looked for a new dean who shared the values.

There is often a misconnection between a leadership change and a process of change. State agencies and state-supported programs can be seen shifting between leaders who have ''stander and shaker'' and ''stroker'' styles. The stander and shaker wears out his/her social credit and is replaced by a stroker. The stroker gets nothing done and is replaced by a new stander and shaker. This pattern repeats over and over again, suggesting that the agency oversight has no idea what the agency needs or where it is going.

Being clear about needs indicates whether a leader with idea skills or implementation skills is needed. The style of the leader selected then makes sense, in part because key people have thought through their needs and agreed on them. This calls for determining the magnitude of change and the extent to which rapid action is required as a basis for leader selection. In such situations, an agency oversight body needs to plan before they select a new leader.

7. Legal Mandates for Planning

Many state agencies face new mandates that require some form of planning. Federal programs for health, transportation, mental health, aging, and mental retardation and other developmental disabilities call for states to create plans before monies are released that show how the money is to be used. County mental health boards must have a plan to access state support for mental health services. Hospitals must submit five-year plans before state departments of health will consider a proposal for facility expansion or modernization.

In each case, plans must be skewed to fit the categories demanded by regulators and funding agents. In many instances, the agency must do ongoing agency management as it responds to these demands. Getting the most from such an effort is becoming an important part of good agency leadership.

8. Demands for Integration

Increasingly, states see the need to integrate services across their departments. Integration is needed to keep people from falling into an abyss created by the lines of authority that separate state departments offering related services. Separate offices have been created to do coordinational planning that integrates a cluster of departments to ensure follow-through. These offices have been charged with reducing duplication of effort and finding gaps in services. State departments unaware of their complementary missions are brought together to jointly fashion services and improve the efficiency of service provision.

Many states have initiated such programs. Forming cluster groups around topics such as youth services, economic development, environmental protection, utility regulation, taxation and budget, physical resources, and health services has become a widespread practice of state governments in recent years. The leaders of such groups are faced with the pressing need to develop strategic plans and to get the agencies that are affected to adopt them.

9. Coordination of Action

Changes in elected officials often bring new mandates and programs to state agencies. The leaders of such an agency must create a shared vision of where the agency has been, its current commitments, and where it must go. These steps are needed to give everyone a common direction, creating order and continuity in the change-making process. Leaders want everyone marching to the same tune. The director of the BWC will face such a test as programs are fashioned and new aims created. Strategic change in the historical society also calls for this type of coordination.

10. Caught in a Rut

Many agencies are caught in a rut, producing the same responses over long periods of time. There are lethargy and considerable inertia. Such agencies create motion, but little of value. In some instances, outside pressure can mount that shocks such an agency by replacing its leader, as in the BWC case. The new agency leader knows that the agency needs renewal and must grope for a way to revitalize services and operations and challenge a bored and underused staff.

The historical society had fallen into such a rut and was seeking ways to break out. ODMH found that the phase-out of state hospitals had stalled because the hospital CEOs were reluctant to change old ways of doing business and create a shared commitment to support the radical changes in their service provision role. Similar difficulties arose when the Ohio Bureau of Motor Vehicles sought to improve its service by eliminating the long lines that had prompted so many complaints that the agency's image had been seriously tarnished.

11. Political Threats

Developments can pose threats. Politically motivated oversight bodies have few restraints when doing the work of elected officials. Such a body can take action that seriously harms or eliminates a state agency or program. In Indiana, for example, the Board of Regents, responding to legislators who complained about poor teaching, made substantial increases in the funding of state universities with a teaching mission with funds taken from all other state-assisted universities. The legislature and employers demanded that the BWC improve its practices without granting the time and resources to make the needed changes.

When political pressure becomes intense, state agencies are forced to respond. A proactive strategy that heads off political action can be a good defense in such a situation. A massive change was needed in BWC to keep the governor from feeling heat in the worker's compensation situation. The Bureau of Motor Vehicles handled such pressure with new systems.

12. Visions of What Might Be

Some agency leaders see a way to meet previously unmet needs by clever orchestration of an agency and its oversight body (Nutt and Backoff, 1997a). For example, the executive director for a board of regents recognized that if he could get people ready for school and ready for jobs he could make the regents a broker for education. He could mediate between employers and universities by recognizing and dealing with the needs of each. Universities in this state had a mandate to admit any of the state's high school graduates who apply, on a first-come basis. Universities were being burdened by compensatory education and employers by on-the-job training. Each saw its own needs but not the needs of the other. This created a new possibility. The director challenged his staff and board to creatively rethink the commitment to education in these terms and offer suggestions.

The director wanted to initiate a strategic management process that could give detail to his vision and help key people contribute to it. The link among education, economic development, technological development, and business was to be created through a collaborative process that embellished the vision. The process was to empower others by having them fill in the details. Communicating the vision (the what) and giving it detail (the how) is essential when strategic leaders act in this way.

Other public leaders see a new world and want to help in fashioning implementation plans, much like John F. Kennedy and his "New Frontier." They want everyone to "walk the vision" with them. Connection with and then transfer of the vision is sought much like Gorbachev's *Glasnost* and *Perestroika*. Such leaders also want key people to walk the vision with them and help them create specific plans that will lead to connection and transfer, as in the ODMH case.

IV. FACILITATING A CHANGE PROCESS

Savvy leaders in state agencies have an acute appreciation of constraints that limit what they can do (Bozeman, 1987). However, as the cases illustrate, state agencies are facing turbulent times in which developments can alter the nature of an agency overnight (Ansoff, 1988; Shortell et al., 1988). A new administrator enters or a board member unexpectedly leaves, and old commitments are "out the window," as in the cases of the historical society and the BWC. These developments can alter markets, goals, accountability, and performance expectations in unexpected ways. Such agency leaders face a tension between forces that limit change and those that are demanding it. The savvy leader is wary of this tension and seeks a way to manage it. To rethink an agency's strategy can flush out critics who seek to abolish the agency or reduce its budget. Proactive agency leaders need a change process that helps them steer around such obstacles as they consider and test ways to change.

Agency leaders mount a change effort by addressing aims, identifying key players, recognizing the setting in which development is to take place, specifying timing, and carrying out steps in a change process. The key players are stakehold-

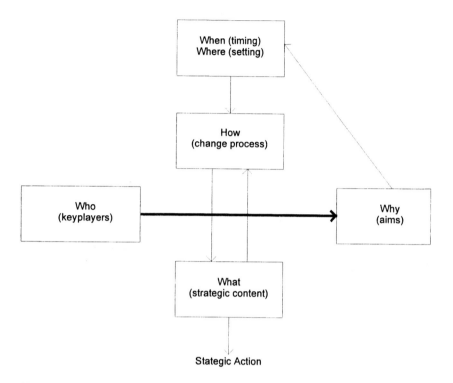

Figure 1 Key features of a change process.

ers, who must play a role in the formation and implementation of a change strategy. Some of the stakeholders become members of the change management group (CMG) that will undertake change development and implementation. CMG members often enter and exit as the change strategy takes shape. Influential stakeholders should also be consulted during feasibility assessments. The process, or the how of change management, is used by the CMG to create content, or what makes up a change strategy. The change strategy is devised to meet aims (the why) and is carried out in a particular setting (where) and with certain timing (when). The elements of the change process have the relationship shown in Figure 1.

A. Process as a Dance

The arrows between the how (process) and the what (content) in Figure 1 attempt to capture the interplay between process and content. One merges into the other as a change strategy is fashioned. This "dance of the what and how" is central to our approach of doing change management. The agency leader energizes a process with ideas, and uses process to fashion ideas. Learning occurs during energizing and developmental efforts. Strategic leaders use the process to position their agency so that change is both desirable and possible. To dance and manage the process, the agency leader alters agency practices, activities, and services. This poses several key questions. We consider leadership, aims, timing, and the steps to be followed to provide guidance now and carry out a change effort.

B. Leadership

The dominant force in fashioning a strategy is the agency leader who takes action to initiate a change process (Nutt and Backoff, 1996a). Recall the cases. The leader of ODMH wanted to push the deinstitutionalization effort forward; the director of the historical society sought new directions and funding continuity. Leaders prompt action by recognizing the need for change, which provides impetus and purpose. To do this leaders must determine who is to be involved and their role in the process. Decisions about who is to be involved answer questions about "where" that help to determine the context to be managed. The context becomes more inclusive as more outside influences are accepted into the change effort.

C. Forming a Change Management Group (CMG)

A CMG is formed to guide the change effort. It is made up of people who represent key power centers inside and/or outside the organizations that are asked to formulate and implement change. Participation promotes ownership. The social world of a CMG arises out of its members' interaction as they explore and interpret their views (Selznick, 1979; Berger and Tuckman, 1966). What counts are the constructions of reality that the CMG makes (Boulding, 1956). This social construction of reality guides what is seen or believed. Participation is crucial in helping the CMG make constructions that square with reality. It also creates an opportunity to create shared meanings that can be sustained to provide a basis for action. The dance of the what and how is designed to build the knowledge and insight in a CMG that is needed to formulate and implement a strategic change. Participation helps the CMG members appreciate what can be done and their role in carrying out the change. When a CMG develops ideas, an appreciation of the needs and stakeholder interests that created the basis to act, also emerges.

1. Insiders and Outsiders as CMG Members

The CMGs can be made up of key insiders or both insiders and outsiders, answering in part the "where" question. When outsiders make up the CMG, a consortium arrangement is used (Nutt, 1992). In a consortium, members represent the interests and point of view of agencies that must act together to fashion a change. Consortia are becoming more important as demands for integration in service delivery increase. For instance, the State of Illinois has mandated "councils" and the State of Ohio has initiated "cluster groups" made up of state agencies that deal with aspects of a particular topic, such as economic development, to coordinate action. Such a group is needed to deal with the equitable delivery of services and to appreciate important values such as seeing that needs are met, eliminating duplication, and ensuring continuity.

2. Team Formation

Even when insiders make up a CMG, communication and promoting ownership can be formidable tasks. To cope with this, we use a Kiva approach (Nutt and Backoff, 1992) with a two-tiered group of stakeholders. The CMG has an "inner circle" with about 10 key stakeholders and an "11th" chair. In the ODMH project, the inner-circle members were selected by its executive committee in consultation with others in the department. The inner circle included five members representing the top management of hospitals (CEOs and nursing directors) and five central office staff members with important hospital liaison and coordinating roles. Invitations were sent to other stakeholders (e.g., other hospital CEOs, medical directors, and people in key hospital central office liaison roles, such as district managers) to join the outer circle. Inner-circle membership was fixed; outer-circle members varied depending on topic and interest. The agenda was faxed or e-mailed to all interested parties. The outer-circle members could elect someone to fill the 11th inner-circle chair for any meeting. Each inner- and some outer-circle members also had liaison responsibilities to key interest groups. As concerns developed, these people were encouraged to become part of the outer circle to express them at the next meeting. These steps were taken to facilitate implementation via participation (e.g., Likert, 1967; Nutt, 1987).

In summary, the inner circle was to:

Lead off with ideas
Help to sort ideas
Present outer-circle ideas
Do preliminary rating
Provide reflective dialogues on their ideas and votes
Call for process "time-outs" to resolve disputes and differences of opinion
Provide liaison to groups and points of view that they represented

The outer circle was asked to:

Listen to the discussion
Do silent reflection listing in parallel with the inner circle
Huddle with inner-circle members during "time-outs"

Hand suggestions to an inner-circle member
Identify who is to occupy the "11th" chair
Do between-meeting liaison and analytical work as skills dictate
Serve as inner-circle number if needed
Provide liaison to groups and points of view they represent

The Kiva process allowed reflections of the outer-circle members to be expressed to the inner circle. The outer-circle members were not allowed to talk during the process. To express their ideas, an outer-circle member could pass a note to an inner-circle member at key process points, such as idea generation. The inner-circle member receiving a note was obligated to interpret the idea and include it with his/her own. Also, both the inner- and outer-circle members were asked to vote on priorities. The inner and outer priorities were compared. Presenting differences in priorities when they appeared created pressure to resolve differences before moving forward.

3. Leader Roles

Agency leaders must take on various roles in a change effort, moving from observer or participant to process manager, facilitating the work of a CMG and changing its members as required. Leaders need to develop skills in being a process manager, including facilitator, teacher, technician (or technical supervisor), and politician (Quinn et al., 1990).

Facilitators should develop a broad knowledge of techniques that can support the strategic management process (Howe and Kaufman, 1979; Nutt, 1992). Such a repertoire allows the strategic leader to fashion hybrid techniques that combine useful features of several techniques according to the demands for quality, acceptance, innovation, or preservation. Techniques that support the strategic management process are selected according to these needs (Nutt and Backoff, 1992). Facilitators and strategic leaders with these insights can become very good technician supervisors.

D. Aims

Aims (why) indicate the type of change that is sought. The strategic leader determines whether transformational, large-scale radical change or traditional change is called for. Traditional change, which alters current arrangements, calls for leaders to determine whether quality, innovation, acceptance, and/or preservation (e.g., identifying centers of excellence that will not be changed) outcomes will be sought. These choices help to identify the best way to collect and organize information needed by the process to increase the prospect that the desired outcome can be realized (Nutt and Backoff, 1992). Often a "qualified comprehensive change strategy," which calls for quality, acceptance, and innovation while preserving important programs, is sought for nonradical change efforts. We provide a target to shoot for that guides each type of change. Transformational change demands a vision, and traditional change calls for ideals as targets. We will say more about the distinctions between radical-transformational change and traditional change and how to fashion visions and ideals later in the chapter.

E. Timing

Timing demands (when) also shape the process. Scaled-down one-day experiences will differ from those that call for one-process cycle. A one-time cycle differs from the commitments and resources required to do continuous change strategic management, shown in Figure 2. Change efforts can be undertaken in a variety of settings. We recommend locations that take people away from their daily interruptions to encourage reflection and to prompt creativity.

F. Special Needs of State Agencies

The agencies of state government have several unique needs (Levine et al., 1976; Allison, 1984; Neustadt, 1989; Rainey, 1989). These needs call for new ways to think about how to go about strategy development that differs from private sector approaches (Nutt and Backoff, 1993a,b). The markets, constraints, goals, author-

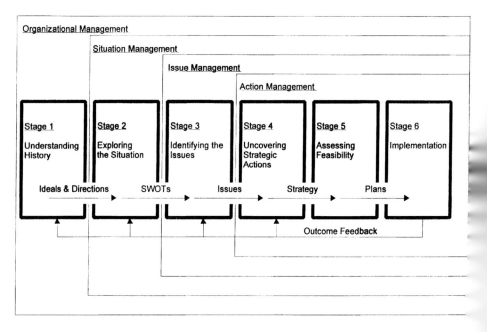

Figure 2 Continuous change in a strategic management.

ity, authorization to act, accountability, and performance expectations of a state agency differ from those faced by commercial firms, which create strategy to produce profit (Perry and Rainey, 1988). The market in a state-operated organization is made up of rule-making bodies, such as boards of trustees or legislatures. Service recipients often must work through such a body to make their wishes known. Other features include constraints that limit flexibility and autonomy, goals that are often vague and in dispute, limited leader authority, political interference and scrutiny by outsiders, broad accountability, and shifting performance expectations. For example, ODMH, BWC, and the historical society have their services dictated by their oversight bodies. The oversight body stipulates the scope of services to be offered and philosophy for charges. An oversight body can call for free services, target indigent clients for fee waivers, or mandate treatment, as in mental health treatment for people who plead not guilty by reason of insanity (NGRI). State structures govern what the historical society can do to get block grants, which made up a significant part of the society's budget. Goals were articulated in terms of the scope of services and clients to be served by ODMH. A politically appointed board was calling for the BWC to increase the speed of claim resolution and increase the speed of provider payments, with reduced funding. These features create a volatile environment in which change must take place. The process that is used to fashion change must be able to deal with each of these considerations.

Savvy leaders of state agencies have an acute appreciation of the constraints and possibilities that characterize their situation (Bozeman, 1987). However, as the cases illustrate, these organizations are facing turbulent times in which new developments can alter the nature of an organization overnight (Ansoff, 1988; Shortell et al., 1988). A new administrator enters or board members unexpectedly leave and old commitments are "out the window," as in the case of the historical society. These developments can alter markets, goals, accountability, performance expectations, and the other features in unexpected ways. The proactive leader must study how his/her organization can change and the impact of these changes. These developments also bring with them the need to rethink the old strategy and consider the value of change.

G. Change Process: The What and How

To be successful leaders must deal with the developments that are prompting action. Each poses questions that we use to engage the "what" and the "how" of a strategic process of change. Our approach deals with what we call the "dance of the what and the how" by moving between content and process in several waves or stages of activity. Each move creates content and provides a way to take the next step. Strategic principles flow from the guidelines we provide to cope with the who, why, when, where, how, and what of a change process, as noted in Figure 1. These principles are summarized in Table 1. In the discussion

Table 1 Principles of Strategic Change

Strategic action elements	What is required
Who (Strategic leader makes a commitment)	Recognize that a change in agency capacity and responsiveness is needed to become *proactive*
Why (articulate aims)	Provide target that articulates a *vision* or an *ideal*
Where (determine context to be managed)	Identify *context* from which CMG membership is to be drawn (agency, mixed board and agency, or consortium)
When (choices about scope)	Select *type of process* to be established (trial-experiment, one cycle, or continuous change)
What (select content of strategy)	Note special needs of the agency and how the agency is apt to change, producing new constraints and possibilities.
	Match environments to *types of strategy*
	1. Bureaucracy strategy to placid environments
	2. Accommodator strategy to placid clusters
	3. Director strategy to disturbed environments
	4. Mutualist strategy for turbulent environments
	5. Use strategies to focus effort by providing plans, ploys, patterns, positions, and perspectives

How (decisions about process)

Craft *strategic change:*

1. Recognize *issues* as tensions, made up of competing concerns. Test the concerns in terms of their tractability and public support to suggest ways to package them to win support. Test the tensions made up of these concerns to uncover hidden issues

2. Uncover *win-win* strategic action for each core issue tension and *align* these actions

3. Manage the dance of the what and how.

   Engage the dance by:

   a. Determining and evaluating directions, establishing vision or ideals, uncovering SWOTS, forming an agenda of issue tensions, find "win-win" strategic actions, align action, assess feasibility, form implementation plans.

   b. Recycle as needed to create action management, issue management, situational management, and agency management

   Organize the dance by:

   a. Forming a CMG

   b. Leader choosing among roles of process manager, process participant, or observer

   c. Decide on process timing

4. Promoting ownership by having CMG interpret needs and create repsonses based on shared meanings

5. Select information generating techniques to support the process according to expected results

6. To make *transformational* change, follow the principles for radical change by:

   a. The development of a vision

   b. Using continuous change strategic management

   c. Coaxing leaders to become a process facilitator, teacher, technician manager, and politician

   d. Emphasizing a mutualist strategy and consortiums

that follows, we outline a change process and show how it can cope with the concerns and difficulties facing the leaders of state agencies. To engage the dance of the what and how, we call for the staging of activity shown in Figure 2.

1. Understanding History

State agency leaders, seeking to mount a change effort, must inform staff and board members of the agency's origins and founding ideas, as well as current events that call for a response. These educational efforts create a shared interpretation of where the organization has been and the forces for change. Knowing where the agency has been is essential before people can decide where the organization should go in the future.

To create a shared understanding of the agency's history and forces for change, we have the CMG uncover trends, events, and directions. Directions indicate where the organization has been and where it will go without change. Trends and events capture key developments that have forged this direction and will influence it in the future. For example, a Department of Natural Resources (DNR) had to immerse its new board into the trends and events that shaped its effort to create a state park system. At the same time, new trends and events (e.g., wetland and scenic area preservation) were considered that suggested new directions. As these developments were discussed, the DNR determined what it wanted to preserve and what it could change. Going back into history is an essential step in making a conceptual forecast of future directions (El Sawy, 1985). Precise and vivid descriptions of past trend events provide a vehicle with clear and compelling imagery on which to build (Weick, 1979). These reference projections (Ackoff, 1981) suggest directions that may not be desirable and that merit redirection.

We use this discussion to set the stage for the development of a target. The target represents the best-case situation for an agency. For instance, a target for the DNR could call for programs in the several areas that balance the interests of its many factions (e.g., hunters, fishermen, environmentalists, naturalists). The target provides an image of what an organization can become, stated in concrete terms, such as clients and programs, that are preferred by agency leaders. Two types of targets can be devised, depending on whether the agency seeks transformational or nonradical change.

Visions propose a radical change in the agency's services, clients to be served, approach to service provision, competence and skill, basis and means used for collaboration, current sources of funding, and persona that the agency seeks. A vision must be fleshed out to determine how a radical change in some of these aspects of a strategy influence the others. The integration of old with the new offers a target that can prompt transformational change.

Agencies seeking or limited to nonradical change can use *ideals*. Ideals uncover answers to these same questions, concentrating on modifying what is currently in place. Ideals suggest targets that indicate who should be served and what the agency should be doing to serve these clients and how the agency can promote a desired persona, suggesting how the agency is regarded by its key oversight bodies. The current strategy is fine-tuned by ensuring that the agency's current clients and customers are being served, that services meet best-practice standards and are delivered efficiently and effectively, that available revenue sources are being tapped, that competency is sufficient, that strategic alliances are being fine-tuned, and that steps are being taken to improve agency image. Ideals sum up needed moves in several of these areas.

Vision or ideals replace goals. There is no generic goal for a state agency comparable to profit in private firms. In state agencies, goals are often vague and in dispute (Nutt and Backoff, 1993b). To avoid goal mania in which the goal-setting process becomes an end in itself, we use a target articulated as a vision or an ideal.

2. Exploring the Situation

Exploring history gives the CMG an understanding of the agency's past and, from its vision or ideals, an appreciation of an idealized future. The next step is to explore factors that obstruct or enhance the prospect of reaching this desired future state. The organization's strengths, weaknesses, opportunities, and threats, or SWOTs, are uncovered and explored to identify things that enable or limit strategic change. Agencies such as the BWC identified competencies (strengths) and possibilities (opportunities) which were mobilized to deal with weaknesses (staff and systems) and blunt threats (political pressure to ignore inadequate reserves).

3. Identifying Issues

Historical and situational assessments help an organization develop a shared view of core concerns that must be managed. Priority concerns produce an issue agenda. Issues capture tensions in the agency that are pulling or pushing it away from its vision or its ideals. In the Board of Regents example, a key issue tension was "job readiness and college preparation," calling for educational change. We call this a "productivity-productivity" tension, moderated by a transition (educational change). We help organizations search for other values such as human relationships and preservation. In the example, the learner's needs (human relations) may be in tension with educational change and preservation (profit for firms; research productivity for universities), which may be in tension with the learner's needs and college preparation and job readiness. When agencies uncover an agenda of issues in this way, we find that they are more apt to identify and deal with chronic concerns and difficulties. Support for framing issues as tensions can be found in Janusian thinking (Rothenberg, 1979) and in the literature on dialectics (Mason and Mitroff, 1981). Considering values that organizations often overlook helps to uncover hidden concerns that have been ignored in the past and merit attention (Quinn, 1988). The steps we take to uncover an issue agenda are detailed in the next section.

4. Uncovering Strategic Actions

The issue agenda directs the search for strategic actions, beginning with the most important issue tension to be managed. A search is carried out to find ways to manage this issue tension by uncovering a "win-win" action for each of the core issue tensions that can hold back strategic change. For instance, the regent's executive director could use such an approach to find ways to deal with the "job readiness and college preparation tension," seeking a win-win in which both values are accepted and affirmed. To align strategic action, the win-wins uncovered for each core tension are linked. To align action leaders ensure that actions to manage a given issue tension complement the others. When oppositions are noted, the CMG alters the action until it supports and integrates with others. The steps we recommend to uncover and align strategic action are discussed in detail in the next section.

5. Assess Feasibility

The feasibility of a strategic move can be determined by whether needed resources are obtainable and whether key stakeholders, not a part of the inner or outer circle, are apt to support proposed changes. To make these determinations, we identify needed resources to carry out the change and individuals and organizations with interests in proposed changes. These resources and individuals/organizations are evaluated by locating them on the grids shown in Figure 3 and 4. This evaluation (detailed in Nutt and Backoff, 1992), reveals crucial concerns that must be attended to during an implementation effort. The strategic leader inventories both available funds and potential sources of support. The prospect of using these sources of support to underwrite implementation costs provides one test of feasibility.

Stakeholders are inventoried and assessed much like resources. Stakeholders are identified, their positions determined, and plans forged to capitalize on supporters and to manage antagonists. The nature and number of stakeholders in each category of Figure 3 suggests whether implementation is apt to be successful.

6. Implementation

During implementation plans are devised to deal with the concerns posed by the resources and stakeholder assessments. These plans are devised to garner the

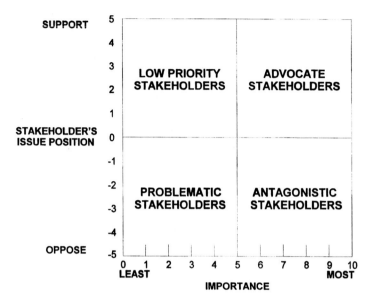

Figure 3 Stakeholder assessments.

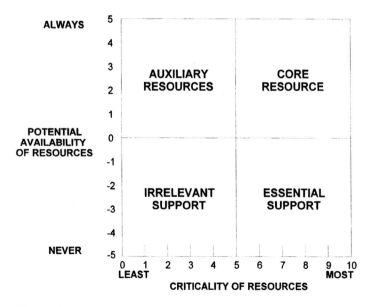

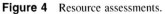

Figure 4 Resource assessments.

required resources and build stakeholder support to take the actions called for in a strategic change. Tactics for dealing with each type of stakeholder and resource should be considered (see Nutt and Backoff, 1992).

State agencies can get resources from internal reallocations and from new sources. For instance, diverting funds from employer collections to underwrite change in the Bureau of Workman's Compensation, although seemingly desirable and supported by key stakeholders, may be prohibited by law. Implementation in this case would identify people who must authorize such action to work for a change in agency rules. New sources of funding may be required. To carry out new strategic actions, state-assisted universities may be able to increase tuition or increase their grant and contract activity. Historical societies may have to increase their efforts to secure federal grants. With this in mind, Ohio's Department of Natural Resources began to charge user fees and now supports two-thirds of their budget in this way. To coax stakeholders into authorizing such resource moves or to overcome their resistance to proposed changes may involve lobbying, negotiation, bargaining, education, coalition building, cooptation, selling, and promotion. Stakeholders thought to be amenable to one or more of these tactics are approached by the agency leader to win them over.

H. Continuous Change

Process recycles are shown in Figure 2. The first recycle is to pick up additional issue tensions from the issue agenda and repeat stages 4, 5, and 6. This is called *action management*. Second, leaders should periodically revise the issue agenda, repeating stage 3, as well as stages 4, 5, and 6. This is called *issue management*. Third, leaders reassess the situation repeating stage 2, and then carry out stages 3 to 6. This is called *situation management*. Finally, leaders repeat stage 1 to look at directions and new targets as visions and ideals that call for agency renewal, and then carry out stages 2 to 6. This is called *agency management*. Together, these recycles provide a way to carry out the continuous strategic management of a state agency (see Figure 2).

V. FASHIONING STRATEGIC CHANGE

To manage a process of change requires agency leaders to make several crucial moves. The first calls for a matching of their strategic action with their environment and determining whether change is possible for their agency. The type of change that seems feasible helps a leader uncover the type of ''strategic action'' that fits the situation, and the extent to which it can be changed. When change seems feasible three additional moves are made: treat issues as tensions; uncover win-win actions; and align these actions. This gives the leader a map to follow that shows how useful strategic changes can be fashioned.

A. Agency Positioning and the Prospects of Change

Some state bureaus and agencies find themselves in situations of limited capacity and/or low responsiveness to expectations (Nutt and Backoff, 1993b). Capacity gets eroded by years of budget cutting, limitations on prerogatives from court rulings, rule making by legislatures, assignment of duties to other agencies during reorganization, and chronic staff turnover. As capacity reaches a low ebb complacency sets in, making change difficult. Also, change can be difficult when a state agency is buffeted by events it is unable to manage. Demands are experienced at a rate that exceeds the agency's ability to understand the proposed actions or requests. Such an agency may react by adopting a "learned helplessness posture," in which elaborate rationales for avoiding action supplant building capacities.

Strategic change attempts to move such agencies toward increased capacity and increased control over their environment. In this section, we discuss how state agencies get in such situations and when it is possible to move an agency toward change. This is shown by moving up the diagonal, running from lower left to upper right, as indicated by the arrows in Figure 5. The path along the diagonal toward a more proactive posture identifies conditions that make change feasible. An agency with an imbalance between external control over its actions and internal capacity seldom engages in strategic change. A balance in control and responsiveness is required to make strategic change seem desirable and pragmatic.

B. Agencies That Resist Change

Figure 5 shows how agencies can be classified by their capacity and the extent to which prerogatives are dictated by outsiders, such as legislatures. Stable types with little motivation to change arise when internal competence and external control have become seriously imbalanced. Because either competence or control dominates, attention is focused on the maintenance of the competence or control and not on using competence to exercise useful control. Such agencies are found far off the diagonal describing the path of change in Figure 5.

1. Professional Agencies

Agencies with high internal capacity, real or perceived by outsiders, and little external control are called professional. Activity is directed internally by professional values. Control is low because the political, legal, and economic structures

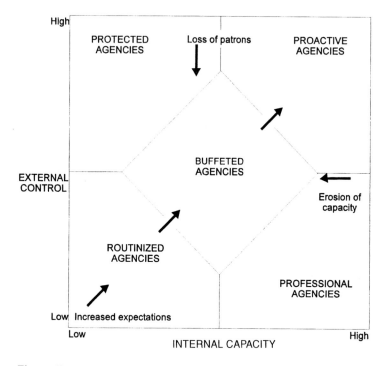

Figure 5   Forces prompting change in state agencies.

that ordinarily direct and channel energies and ensure accountability are not in place. Typically, such an agency has protected its budget or resource base and has considerable prerogative to act in a prescribed arena. Departments of taxation and the attorney general's office provide examples.

Agencies that rely on highly skilled and self-regulated staff members to provide key services can also become professional-type organizations. Examples include state-run mental health and acute care hospitals, university facilities, social work agencies, and others dominated by a professional elite who control the terms of services that are provided. Strategic change with professionals who seek to maintain this kind of control is not apt to be successful.

The professional bureau or agency can ignore client or stakeholder preferences, the political agenda of reformers, and public support and may even be insulated from budget cutting. In some instances, the professional agency can even turn aside legal mandates and judicial orders. Such agencies have little motivation to change and often adopt a drifter strategy, shown in Figure 6.

Environmental Types

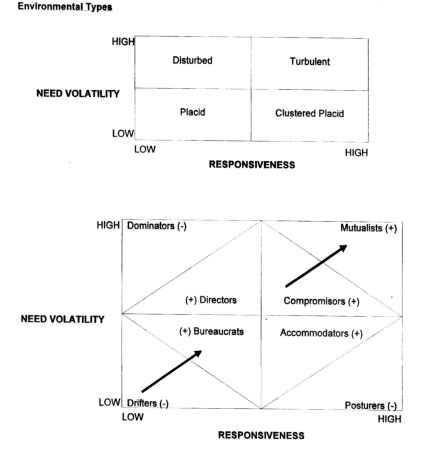

Figure 6 Matching strategy and agency environments.

2. Protected Agencies

Agencies that allow high control over their actions and lack internal capacity are termed "protected." Such an agency exploits its leverage by carving out a domain in which it has an exclusive right to act. Legislation can be written to give exclusive rights or responsibilities. For example, the Iowa legislature gave the University of Iowa Medical School exclusive rights to provide all tertiary care in the state. In a protected agency, old-boy networks are carefully maintained to deflect criticism and routine accountability and to harness the forces that would normally be used to monitor actions. Control of turf in this way by agencies creates little incentive to improve capacity, and makes the agency quite political. Many protected agencies take control of the domain in which they have been given an exclusive right to act. For example, departments of development (DOD) are often viewed as essential by Republican legislatures and governors. Such an agency can be expected to carefully maintain such a network to harness forces that would normally call for accountability. For example, when a critic asks how many new jobs have been created by DODs and how much tax base has been given away, the network is mobilized to deflect the critic's questions or make them seem unwarranted or politically motivated.

3.   Routinized Agencies

Agencies low in competence or capacity with few expectations become routinized. To justify their existence, highly codified routines are developed and rigidly followed. Because no one questions what such an agency produces, it can go about its processing with very little accountability. Examples include state highway patrols, contract activities in departments of transportation, claim processing in bureaus of worker's compensation, and service departments such as travel, records and transcripts, and stores in universities. Former students who complain about poor service, such as delays in getting a transcript, are ignored by university leaders and oversight bodies that have more important things to do. Delays in receiving compensation benefits fall on deaf ears, charges of unfair or unethical contracting for highways are ignored, and questions about how the highway patrol spends the bulk of its budget go unanswered. In each case, oversight bodies have little motivation to question long-standing practices.

C.   The Forces for Change

The protected, professional, or routinized agency can be pushed toward change by loss of control and/or a loss in capacity. When this occurs these agencies become buffeted and begin to field pressure to change. This movement can occur in three ways, as shown by the arrows in Figure 5.

1.   Change for a Professional Agency

Strategic change in a professional agency is difficult even when forces calling for more control over the agency's actions are clear and compelling unless the agency's capacity is thought to be declining. The agency is moved toward the diagonal in Figure 5 as perceived competence falls, making strategic change both possible and desirable.

The strategy of a professional agency rests on maintaining its internal capacity. The FBI's reputation after the death of J. Edgar Hoover went into eclipse, forcing the FBI to become more concerned about public relations and to reexamine its role. A similar impact was felt by Ohio's Department of Corrections after the Lucasville riots. A decline in competence (real or perceived) is a necessary precursor for change to occur in professional agencies. This prompts the agency to try to maintain an image of competence as new practices are being forged and adopted. As real or perceived competence declines, such an agency requires new positioning. Defending past practices coupled with small adaptations is carried out. For example, the IRS, stung by reports that they unmercifully harassed tax payers, confiscated the bank accounts of children, and gave inaccurate tax advice mounted strategy to do damage control and to reform its procedures. In the aftermath of Lucasville riots in Ohio, a task force was set up to study the needs for change bringing a number of reforms in the use of computer technology, training, and accreditation.

2. Change for a Protected Agency

Agencies that cultivate patrons and ignore building capacity end up in the upper left corner of Figure 5. The strategy in such an agency is to maintain the old-boy network and other arrangements that protect turf. Real change is not apt to occur unless these arrangements erode. Erosion of turf or prerogatives can occur when agency patrons lose elections or leave office or when an old-boy network ceases to function. This tosses the protected agency into the mainstream. The political agenda of newcomers or a shift in power among stakeholders signals the need for action. The clear and compelling call for better services and the like can no longer be ignored. The agency must increase its internal capacity, shifting it toward the diagonal in Figure 5.

Ohio's Department of Public Welfare experienced such a shift, moving from a protected position to one of increased expectation after a new governor took office. The status quo was no longer acceptable and a posture of change was adopted. The welfare department had to abandon a dominator strategy, in which clients were expected to respond as directed, and move toward a posture that emphasized helping clients, which provided the impetus for strategic change (Figure 6).

Increased awareness of low internal capacity often accompanies shifts in environmental control. Exposing this low capacity invariably forces rapid action to improve matters, increasing the need for and desirability of strategic change. Leadership transitions and increased consensus to adopt a new practice often result.

3. Change for a Routinized Agency

State agencies with modest to low competence can be ignored for decades. Such agencies go about their activities with little accountability until there is a shift in expectations for both competency and control. For instance, complaints about long waits and inept staff prompted change in a state bureau of motor vehicles. New funds were provided and new systems were designed to allow mail-in license plate renewals that separated taxpayers and staff, thereby reducing both dysfunctional contacts with the public and the time involved. Note how complaints had to become intense before action was taken that recognized the need to increase competence (new systems).

Such attention is necessary, but sometimes not sufficient to move an agency out of its routine posture. For instance, when an Ohio highway patrolman killed his wife, the resulting media scrutiny spilled over into agency practices. This attention, however, proved to be short-lived and the agency soon returned to its bureaucratic ways.

D. Promoting Change

Agencies on the diagonal fall into less stable states in which change will be considered. This occurs when internal capacity and external control are balanced. The match of capacity and control calls into question whether the organization's directions have or can produce hoped-for outcomes. This questioning can arise externally through the preferences of stakeholders, shifts in political agendas, erosion of public support, budget shortfalls or windfalls, and legal rulings. It can also arise internally as the result of shifts in consensus or changes in leadership. Internal and external pressures to change make strategic change seem pragmatic, and lower the barriers to change erected by political or professional postures. This create two new agency types: the buffeted, and the proactive.

1. The Buffeted Agency

When the professional, protected, or routinized agency experiences an erosion of competence and/or increased control it becomes buffeted. The buffeted agency gets pulled about by fickle public support, changing legal mandates, shifting political agendas, and shifting preferences of clients or key benefactors. As mandates shift, budget support may shrink and constraints about the use of resources often emerge. As a result, priorities provide moving targets that can lead to frustrated staff and turnover of key personnel. Turnover forces large investments in training that further bleed away resources. Agencies experiencing such buffeting become susceptible to change.

Strategic change can help the buffeted agency come to grips with the forces at work in its environment. Capacity to act is built by finding ways to increase control over the environment. This control can lead to happier and more challenged staff and reduce turnover. As capacity is built and environmental control established, the agency develops an increased interest in strategic change. To accommodate shifts in competence, the agency is encouraged to move toward the mutualist strategy in Figure 5, assuming that a measure of environmental control is possible.

2. The Proactive Agency

High internal capacity balanced with high external control and the obligations of this control leads to an ideal type called proactive. Such an agency is prompted to develop a shared understanding of needs and potentials to act.

Consider the Ohio Department of Natural Resources (DNR), which moved toward a proactive organization with high environmental responsiveness by strategic change management. Key stakeholders who had expressed criticisms were folded into task forces to deal with important issues such as wildlife protection, natural areas, hunting and fishing rights, waterways, and recreation. Programs were identified and funds sought to operate them through licensing the use of wild areas, through park programs, and through new types of fishing and hunting licenses. The fees collected were turned back to fund program development, which produced more fee-generating activities until tow-thirds of the DNR's funding was outside the state's budget process. By responding to stakeholders in this way, the DNR became a self-sustaining proactive state agency that is highly responsive to stakeholders as well as high in action.

E. Ideal Types of Strategy

Needs and responsiveness to these needs describe the environment in which state agencies must operate. These environments are often "socially constructed": created by beliefs held by agency leaders and oversight bodies about what people need and the extent to which the agency should respond. The agency leader or its oversight body may see these needs and their ability to respond to them realistically, or they may misrepresent them (Daft and Weick, 1984). Change is difficult when a leader wants to be more proactive than an oversight body sees as being appropriate or necessary, or when an oversight body calls for acting on low-priority or nonexistent needs. Both create unstable states that cause an agency difficulty, and will ultimately derail a change effort.

We consider the aftermath of this in which leaders and oversight bodies have come to an agreement. When this occurs the agency has several choices for strategy. Within each enacted environment there are two strategic moves possible, with one superior to the other (Emery and Trist, 1965; Miles and Snow, 1978; Agor, 1986).

As shown in Figure 6, an agency's responsiveness to perceived pressures for action creates the environment in which they operate (Nutt and Backoff, 1995a). Figure 6 also shows how state agencies can shape a strategy to fit this environment, indicating effective and ineffective strategies. The lower left corner of Figure 6 depicts an agency that is functioning without producing much useful action. The aim is to move such an organization as far as possible up the diagonal from lower left to upper right, gradually making it more proactive in need recognition and fashioning arrangements to meet these needs. Instead of merely responding, a state agency can alter its relationship with other agencies and stakeholders that make up their environment. The expected level of responsiveness is modified as the organization makes these commitments. This can prompt a move to a director, accommodator, compromiser, or collaborator strategy and attempt to sustain this strategy, showing how environments can be constructed agency actions.

Agencies that respond as if needs are at a low ebb create a placid environment, as in the bureau of worker's compensation before its leadership change. A *drifter* strategy can result in which gold bricking is widespread. A *bureaucratic* strategy moves such an agency to a minimally acceptable posture. The *bureaucratic* strategy carries out programmed action by standardized procedure. An agency with this strategy takes a defensive posture to protect seemingly important practices through budget maximization and the creation of slack for the inevitable budget cutbacks. The equivalent of protectionism in firms is sought. The strategist becomes a custodian and uses sagas in which heroic exploits are used to reaffirm values and protect important competencies (Rubin, 1987). For example, sagas were used by professionals in mental health hospitals facing elimination under deinstitutionalization to fashion war stories that protected their treatment prerogatives (Nutt and Backoff, 1997b).

Agencies with high responsiveness to low demands for action prompt a clustered placid environment. Such agencies often adopt a *posturer* strategy. Issues are brought to others for action, which can make the organization seem irresponsible to an outsider. Illustrations include Common Cause, the American Association of Retired Persons, and the NAACP.

State agencies that frequently bring problems to the state legislature for action display some of these attributes. For instance, the new head of BWC posed questions about the adequacy of agency reserves and called for increased funding. Legislators saw the request for higher fees and/or more tax support as irresponsible. In fact, they had commitments to firms to keep fees low and to the electorate to keep a lid on taxes, so this was the legislature's priority. The BWC leader was told to bring solutions, not problems, in the future. Agencies, such as aging, that lobby for assisted living for the elderly are expected to bring solutions, not just problems, to the table.

A more effective approach applies an *accommodator* strategy to deal with each cluster by recognizing and dealing with the unique needs in each cluster, as in the aging example. Priorities must be set to allocate available funds among clusters, based on the compelling nature of the needs in each cluster. Such a strategy was used by many publicly assisted universities in the early 1990s to deal with the Draconian cuts in instructional subsidies imposed by state legislatures. Allocation is carried out by parlays, in which a move is made to create an opportunity to make a subsequent move (Rubin, 1987). This tactic is used in budget hearings, media reports, and the like to gradually reveal allocations and read reactions.

Disturbed environments arise when responsiveness has been low and the need for action abruptly increases. Agencies that deal with these emerging needs with little or no new types of responsiveness create a *dominator* strategy. The motivation is to maintain discretion in the choice of action and divorce it from accountability. State departments of taxation use such a strategy. A better approach calls for a *director* strategy, in which new demands are dealt with by taking measured action. Before the deinstitutionalization legislation of 1988, hospitals in state departments of mental health used a dominator strategy to provide mental health services. When their service area and patient population were eroded, the better-led hospitals could be seen moving toward a director strategy. New ways to meet the mental health needs of people were tried out as ventures, in which speculations about emergent needs and ways to respond were considered (Rubin, 1987).

Turbulent environments arise when responsiveness and the need for action both increase dramatically. This often prompts a *compromiser* strategy. The agency plays one constituency off against another, meeting the needs of important constituents, needy constituents, or both when resources permit. Such a strategy was adopted by the BWC to prompt internal process changes that increased the speed of claim processing and reduced costs to allow employer fees to fall. A *mutualist* strategy is a better approach because it attempts to create collaborative arrangements to meet all important needs that arise with umbrella organizations, such as the National Kidney Foundation and the highway safety consortia. Attempts by the Ohio Department of Mental Health to fold county mental health boards into a partnership to pursue quality care and better insurance coverage describe a contemporary effort to follow a mutualist strategy.

A mutualist strategy calls for novel arrangements to be created to meet emergent needs. A mutualist strategy calls for (1) key people to set the tone by subordinating personal and organizational interests, (2) issue-centered effort, (3) a consortium that draws together key stakeholders into an umbrella organization to address priority issues, (4) creating or shaping a vision to meet emergent needs, (5) seeking win-win arrangements for all affected parties, and (6) promoting trust so stakeholders will cooperate toward resolving the issue, guiding stakeholders away from competition toward cooperation (Nutt and Backoff, 1995a). A mutualist strategy takes shape as a quest, which mounts new initiatives to create a grand vision. Agency leaders who create the sense of adventure and tests of courage of a quest produce such a vision. A mutualist strategy gets stakeholders to search for new ways to meet emergent needs and entices key people to collaborate in meeting needs that prove to be crucial.

Strategy is used by an agency to focus effort in reaching for its visions or ideals by providing plans, ploys, positions, and perspectives (Mintzberg, 1987). As a plan, a strategy offers a way to take action, such as finding new clients and services. Ploys are strategies invented to deceive an opponent. Note how ploys are not useful in a mutualist strategy, but are essential to a compromiser strategy. Strategy as position seeks services that seem needed by reading environmental signals. Positioning, such as protecting budgets or becoming territorial by staking out a service area, often accompanies director and accommodator strategies. As a perspective, strategy captures an organization's traditions and commitments, becoming a touchstone for future action.

F. Formulating Strategic Action

We identify and illustrate a way for strategic leaders to fashion strategic change. The key steps in the process involve uncovering diagnostic issues, finding issue relationships, identifying innovative responses to crucial issues that have connections, and synthesizing strategic responses to connected issues. We suggest ways to deal with important aspects of issue diagnostics, issue relationships, identification of strategic actions, and tying together these actions into a circle of strategic change.

1. Building an Issue Agenda

Issues are crucial to strategic management because they direct the search for strategy, as problems do in problem solving (Nutt and Backoff, 1992, 1993a). Trends or events produce developments that capture attention and often become issues. Trends and events arise from the threat of budget cuts, limits on responsibilities or prerogatives, changes in those eligible for services, increases or decreases in service intensity, limits placed on charges or fees, hiring freezes, union activism, erosion of image, reorganization plans, shifts in the views of oversight bodies, judicial rulings, technological advances, pollution and environmental awareness, equal opportunity, law suits, user-need shifts, leadership changes, and other developments. A development that appears to be holding an agency back, or one that offers a significant advantage, becomes a ''concern'' and people call for action.

Most concerns are linked to other concerns. Taking action to deal with one of these concerns can be viewed as dismissing the other. This may prompt stakeholders with strong interests to take a position. For example, a state department of instruction may have to reduce spending because of a budget cutback and, at the same time, be forced to deal with edicts from a state legislature that call on them to mount new programs to improve the graduation rate of disadvantaged groups. Responding to one of these concerns without considering the other creates a potentially explosive situation in which the department can be battered by the media and various interest groups. Such a situation can arise in any state agency when the connection between concerns arising from programs, budgets, personnel, goals, and the like are overlooked or treated as a dilemma that calls for a choice between two ways to interpret needs.

To capture this, we treat issues as *tensions* between competing concerns. The tension points out conflicting interests and values within the agency or between the agency and its environment. The notion of a tension highlights these conflicts. This helps to capture the tangled web of political and social forces that push and pull a state agency in several ways at the same time. Agency leaders who deal with one of the forces in a issue tension and neglect the other are less apt to be successful (Cameron, 1986). For example, ODMH has to deal with court orders to treat clients and with federal funding agents that call for budget reductions at the same time. If these concerns are not managed as a tension, the department can be whipsawed by powerful people in its authority network. Tensions also arise from arguments offered by media, professional interest groups, and branches of government that support or oppose an action. For example, calls to privatize the Ohio Bureau of Workers Compensation were made by some groups and opposed by others. Agency leaders who deal with but one of the two opposing concerns, and ignore the other, create potentially dangerous situations.

2. Uncovering Strategic Issues

Most issue tensions are organization-specific. The shared experiences of key people create beliefs about agency values that must be understood before strategic change can be initiated. As a result, we begin issue identification by uncovering these concerns. This helps participants appreciate now key people view the local situation. We construct an issue agenda by following steps 1 and 2 listed in Table 2.

In the ODMH project, the inner circle was asked to uncover issues and then form them as tensions. Using an SRGP (Table 2), the inner circle was asked to identify anticipated or actual conditions that, if continued, would influence ODMH's ability to reach the desired future of budget reallocations. Issue tensions were formed by asking inner-circle members to examine each concern and then find the most significant concern that was pulling in the opposite direction. Examples were used to describe what was wanted, such as a medical school department's loss of a subsidy from a state legislature that was paired with increased demands to serve low-income patients in a state subsidized clinic (Nutt and Backoff, 1992).

Table 2 Key Steps in Fashioning a Strategic Change

Steps	Actions	Supporting techniques
Assessment	1. Issue agenda building	
	a. Elicit concerns	SRGP[a]
	b. Test concerns	Concern framework
	c. Find opposing concerns to form and issue tension	Dialectics
	d. Test issue agenda for missing values	Tension framework
	e. Add to issue agenda	Mapping
	2. Identify priority issue tension and related tensions.	
Strategic actions	4. Map the win-win space	Hampden-Turner maps
	a. Find lose-lose outcomes	Creativity
	b. Find best win-lose outcomes	Stakeholder teams
	c. Find compromise strategy	Negotiation
	5. Find win-win strategy	SRGP
	a. Move up the diagonal	
	b. Create bigger space	Laddering
	c. Modify context	Reverse figure and ground
	d. Search for win-win	Creativity, dialectics
	6. Create change circle	Spoke and wheel
Integrating strategic changes	a. Offer win-win strategy (intervention)	
	b. Tensions arrayed as spokes in the wheel	
	c. Identify actions that amplify the win-win and deal with concerns	Cybernetics 2
	in the adjacent issue tension (amplification)	Find and root out perverse incentives
	7. Fine-tune cycle	
	8. Co-align with other change circles	Coalignment

[a] SRGP: Salient reflective group process using a Kiva approach (see Nutt and Backoff, 1992).

3. Testing the Emerging Agenda of Issues

Two steps are taken to test the suggestions of an CMG (the inner circle in the ODMH project). First, concerns that make up an issue tension are classified by their stakeholder support and tractability to identify the portfolio of issues facing an agency (Figure 7). Sitting Ducks are concerns that are resolvable and have stakeholder support. Angry Tigers have stakeholder support but pose concerns that are difficult to successfully resolve. Dark Horses can be resolved but stakeholder support is lacking. Sleeping Dogs are concerns that lack both stakeholder support and tractability. The proportion of types found in the agency's issue portfolio gives a picture of environmental conditions.

We classify the portfolio of concerns in this way to suggest how people will react to strategic efforts and the manageability of the issue agenda. For example, ODMH had considered Sitting Ducks (downsizing, RIF, cost cutting), suggesting that some manageable issues were being considered. This would allow players to experience some success and provide impetus to change. ODMH also faced up to Angry Tigers (union agreements, winners and losers in the hospitals and, to some extent, in central office). However, ODMH had misjudged the intensity of the decentralization-centralization (central office–hospital) issue, until it was treated as a tension. Classifying concerns in this way would have given "heads up" on this early on. There were also Sleeping Dogs (integrated system,

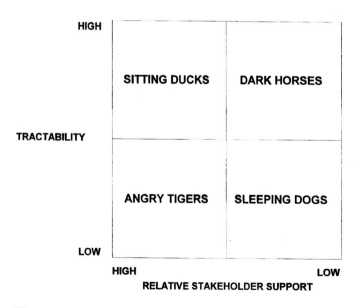

Figure 7 Agency portfolios of concerns.

safety net, client quality perceptions, and ODMH doing quality monitoring). It may have been too early to confront these concerns, except as contingency plans. There was no current support for ODMH to become a system guarantor, as these concerns imply. Also, no Dark Horses emerged, suggesting that ODMH may have overlooked some concerns for their contingency planning. Classifying issues in this way reveals what can become sensitive issues for damage control. Also, it points to the importance of seeking out concerns that could become threats (Dark Horses and Sleeping Dogs) to make contingency plans. This example illustrates how state agencies can gain such insights by classifying the initial concerns as they are uncovered.

The second test is more comprehensive. The concerns, formed as issue tensions, are examined to find tensions that have been overlooked. To look for these hidden tensions, we test the initial list against a framework of generic tensions that can arise in an organization (Nutt and Backoff, 1993a). Tensions that fall to surface suggest suppressed difficulties. Organizations have failed to deal with these issues over long periods of time. Testing a list of issue tensions helps to reveal these overlooked tensions, providing new insights into barriers to action.

A generic issue tension can be formed from four types of concerns that often arise in organizations—equity, preservation, transition, and productivity. The network of relationships that run a public organization and make interpretations of what needs attention prompts *equity* concerns. Equity concerns can arise for both clients and people who run the organization. For insiders, equity concerns may call for an investment in their growth, or their support of one another. Equity concerns also arise as the demands of service providers and clients and the merits of these claims. Concerns often also take shape as a call to meet needs with increased staffing or more training. The need to maintain tradition underlies *preservation* concerns. This concern will take shape as the preservation of cultures, practices, or treaties forged and validated over the life of the agency. *Transition* concerns suggest how the organization is being asked to change, such as new programs that can provide the agency with larger budgets or greater influence. Concerns that arise from *productivity* stem from calls to make modifications that can improve performance or increase efficiency, such as the "do more with less" call made by many state governors.

Each potential concern is paired with each other concern to define 10 types of issue tensions, as shown in Table 3. Four tensions arise from similar concerns. For example, a tension between employers stressing job readiness and universities calling for adequate college preparation was observed by the leadership of a state board of regents for higher education (Nutt and Backoff, 1993b). This produced a "productivity-productivity" tension because each party was calling for a productivity-based action. Other issue tensions arise from combinations of the four different concerns. In the board of regents example, the learner's needs (equity)

Table 3 The 10 Issue Tension Types

Type	Often signaled by	Illustration[a]
1. Equity-equity	Whose interests will be served	Clashes between clients and/or key providers that have different interest
2. Transition-transition	Several plans for change	Each plan calls for a different set of actions that appear to benefit a different set of stakeholders
3. Productivity-productivity	Disputes over diagnostics	Several different measures of performance are being use by stakeholders that suggest different actions
4. Preservation-transition	Groping for core values	Allocating resources among agencies that have different sources of funding some that support traditional services, others with innovative services
5. Preservation-preservation	Dealing with inertia during change	Inertia causes organizations to get sucked into a degrading cycle with no apparent way to break out
6. Productivity-equity	Reconciling cost cutting with human commitments	Agencies forces to cut costs but must so so in accordance with union contracts and commitments to key people
7. Equity-transition	Who get what during change	Disputes over anticipated utility surpluses in which new services or internal operations are being claimed by political appointees
8. Transition-productivity	Meeting demand during change	Agencies facing a budget cutbacks that are attempting to mount new programs
9. Preservation-productivity	Squeezing a stressed system wedded to tradition	Agencies with a critical need to increase output purposes change that is resisted by people who argue that the new norms violate important agency traditions
10. Preservation-equity	When fairness clashes with tradition	When Congress instituted performance-based compensation for civil servants implementation was stalled by rules that called for compensation based an seniority

[a] Examples of a single tension are difficult to provide. This stems from our basic premise: an issue agenda is connected or implicated in all of the other tensions. Each of the examples that we use to illustrate the tensions can be reframed to make it fit any of the other tensions. We believe that all issue tensions have this characteristic.

can be in tension with college preparation (productivity), and educational system change (transition) can be in tension with inertia in higher education (preservation). Also, educational needs (equity) and inertia (preservation) can be hidden in claims by students and faculty that slide past the other party. The learner's needs (equity) can also be in conflict with the need for new taxes (transitions) which will be resisted by people who represent firms in the behind-the-scenes maneuvering with the board.

An issue agenda is tested by classifying an initial list of issue tensions as one of the 10 types on Table 3. This makes missing tensions easier to spot. An additional search is carried out to uncover concerns that can be fashioned into the missing issue tensions. At least one in each category should be uncovered. A fully diagnostic issue agenda considers each of the 10 types of issue tensions.

To illustrate, ODMH identified concerns about centralization, local control of hospitals, care system integration, system cost cutting, safety nets for low-income patients, the magnitude of cuts, assuring treatment quality, constraints posed by union agreements, and how to carry out a huge reduction in force. To create issue tensions, the CMG linked these concerns with others that were most apt to pull in the opposite direction. This suggested tensions between decentralization-centralization, integrated system–safety net, client perceptions of quality-productivity, downsizing-maintaining care quality, union agreements–reductions-in-force. These issue tensions fell into the following categories:

> Equity-equity: Centralization-decentralization (who gets what)
> Productivity-productivity: Cost cutting–perceived quality (what is to be emphasized)
> Transition-productivity: System integration–safety net (comprehensive care and coverage)
> Downsize–maintain quality (who is responsible for quality)
> Preservation-productivity: Union agreement–RIF (outplacements acceptable to the union)

Six issue types were not uncovered: preservation-preservation, transition-transition, transition-preservation, productivity-equity, equity-transition, preservation-equity. ODMH had worked through preservation. Key people knew that old ways of providing care were untenable and that change was essential in which some people would be hurt. This suggests that equity-preservation had been managed. Several other issue tensions had been ignored. Transition-transition clashes could arise in the future as options for change surface. Beliefs about who gets what during change (equity-transition) could prompt winners and losers to square off. The performance expectations of different groups (e.g., hospitals and central office) were not clear, signaling a productivity-equity issue. These three tensions should be considered when the issue agenda is revised for future issue management efforts. This will help ODMH deal with hidden concerns that can block full implementation of their ideals.

4. Selecting Issue Tensions for Management

Issue tensions often deal with core values and practices that are interrelated. These relationships are captured to find the best place to start as well as crucial interdependencies among issue tensions that must be considered in any change attempt. We do this by mapping the tensions using paired comparisons (Nutt and Backoff, 1992).

We have the CMG consider all of the tension pairs and give their view of precedence (which issue tension must be managed first) and producer-product (which issue tension is more likely to produce or result from another). We capture these relationships by arrows that connect all pairs tensions according to the CMG's views, as shown in Figure 8.

The precedence relationship indicates priority, which issue tension comes first. The issue tension with the most arrows pointing outward is a candidate for the priority issue tension. The precedence relationship in Figure 8 suggests that tension A is the priority issue tension. Most of the arrows point outward, suggesting that tension A precedes the others. The precedence diagram also uncovers reciprocal relationships. Note that tensions B, C, and D are interdependent (Figure 8). To deal with these interdependencies, these tensions must be considered together as strategy is crafted.

The producer-product relationship is described by two arrows between each pair of issue tensions shown in Figure 8. The thickness of the arrow is used to indicate the strength of the relationship. Solid lines depict producer relationship and dotted lines depict a product relationship. The priority tension will be a producer and have more dark lines coming from it. For example, in Figure 8, tension A is the producer of tensions B, E, and F. Because these relationships are strong (as signified by the dark line) and because tension A is not the product of other tensions, the producer-product relationship in Figure 8 identifies tension A as the priority tension. Also note that tension B is the producer of tension C and the product (or result) of dealing with tensions A and F. This shows that tensions F, B, and C must be considered together so that these interdependencies can be managed in a strategic change process as strategy is crafted.

Interdependent precedence (e.g., tensions B, C, and D) and producer product relationships (e.g., tensions F, B, and C) identify issue tensions that cannot be considered separately during strategy development. Such tensions are synergistic and call for a change strategy that coordinates the actions taken to deal with them (Senge, 1990). Issue tensions with interdependent relationships become "*related tensions*" that make up a strategic change cycle.

The inner circle in the "inpatient futures" project identified the issue ten-

Precedence Relationships

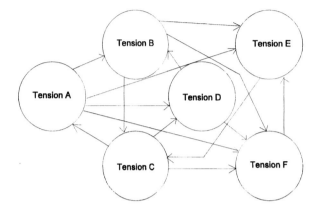

Producer-Product Relationship

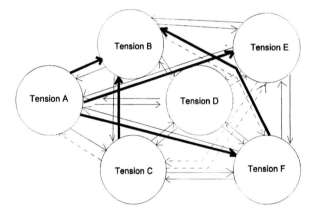

Figure 8   Finding priority tensions.

sion relationships shown in Figure 9. The figure shows that the centralization-
decentralization tension preceded the others and was a producer, not a product,
of the other tensions, making it the core tension. The centralization vs. decentralization of hospital functions after downsizing and mergers posed questions about
what was to be done centrally and what regionally, by the hospitals. The critical
functions, from the mental health accreditation standards, included appointment

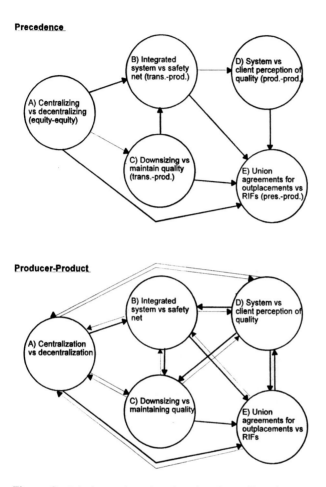

Precedence

A) Centralizing vs decentralizing (equity-equity)

B) Integrated system vs safety net (trans.-prod.)

D) System vs client perception of quality (prod.-prod.)

C) Downsizing vs maintain quality (trans.-prod.)

E) Union agreements for outplacements vs RIFs (pres.-prod.)

Producer-Product

A) Centralization vs decentralization

B) Integrated system vs safety net

D) System vs client perception of quality

C) Downsizing vs maintaining quality

E) Union agreements for outplacements vs RIFs

Figure 9 Priority tensions for "inpatient futures" project.

authority, control of budgets, ability to contract for services, environmental control, human resource function, management information systems, clinical education and reeducation, patient-driven services and treatments, staff competency determinations, and program improvements. We selected "integrated system vs. safety net" and "downsizing vs. maintaining quality" as related tensions because both of these tensions were seen as intermediate steps, with important interrelationships with the downsizing effort. The remaining tensions were deferred because both were consequences of dealing with the others (Figure 9).

G. Identifying Strategic Action

Next we fashion strategic win-wins for important issue tensions. The notion of a "strategic win-win" draws on ideas found in the conflict management (Thomas, 1976; Fisher and Vry, 1984), integrated negotiation (Lewicki and Litterer, 1985), leadership (Covey, 1989), and systems thinking. In our treatment, a strategic win-win must satisfy both concerns that make up an issue tension. Such a strategy creates commitment and support for actions to be taken (Pettigrew, 1987). This occurs because a cooperative culture has been created, disposing of the destructive competitive urges that lie behind most organizational tensions (Pascale, 1990). Win-win strategy assumes that actions provide something of value for all parties with interests.

1. The Win-Win Map

The core issue tension is put on a map as shown on Figure 10, (Hampden-Turner, 1981, 1990). Each axis of the map represents one of the concerns that make up the core issue tension. The strategic solution space is filled with lose-lose (down the diagonal), win-lose (at each axis), compromise (at the midpoint), and win-win (up the diagonal, upper right). Using the map, a leader-facilitator makes a series of moves that work toward a strategic win-win.

We begin by calling attention to lose-lose, or what can happen if the core tension is ignored or left unmanaged. This step motivates action. The next move is to create a win-lose strategy for each concern that makes up the tension. This step helps group members to work out the interests of the key stakeholders in concrete terms. Next, we look for a compromise. This step promotes the notion of working together. To sanction searching for a strategic win-win, we ask the group if they are willing to invest some additional time looking for a better strategic solution—one that increases the net payoff to all of the stakeholders. The prospect of increasing net payoff is usually sufficiently seductive to get the group to authorize further effort.

The outcome created for ODMH is shown in Figure 10. The lose-lose outcome of inaction leads to a diminished organizational credibility because legislative mandates to trim money from hospital operations would not be met. The prospect of sanctions, such as severe budget cuts, were very real to the CMG should community funding not be available. The prospect of local rebellion, focused through legislators representing these areas, could have devastating consequences for the ODMH.

The win-lose solutions for centralization called for improved central office capacity to provide technical assistance that could benchmark how hospitals best do things. Such an approach was thought to suggest a central office reorganization around hospital functions called for by the Joint Commission on Accreditation

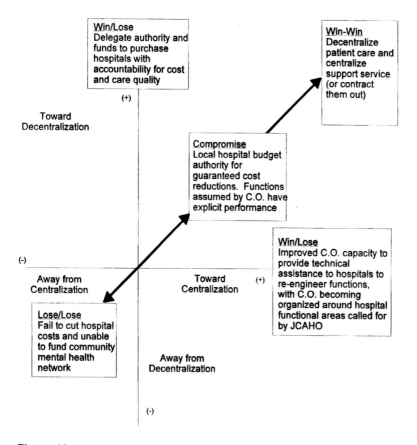

Figure 10 Solutions for the centralization-decentralization tension.

of Healthcare Organizations (JCAOH) accreditation standards. The other win-lose solutions called for a delegation of authority to purchase needed services to the local level, with clear performance expectations (e.g., cost, quality of care). Central office would allocate funds currently being used for support to viable local hospitals. The local hospitals would buy services from the ODMH central office or from others, as needed.

The compromise solution had local hospitals getting increased budget responsibility by guaranteeing a 2% reduction in cost per day per bed. For each function assumed by central office (e.g., medical records), an agreed-upon turn-around time and performance expectations were to be set. Hospitals also asked for more clinical education in exchange for some loss in local autonomy. This third compromise was rejected because it was thought to increase costs in the short run, and possibly in the long run as well.

A strategic win-win was created that called for a "redesign" in which both parties were asked to do what they could do best. Hospitals were to be delegated patient care authority and accountability. Central office agreed to provide all support services or contract them out, whichever proved to be the most cost-effective. Note how the net payoff to ODMH was increased by assuming an abundance mentality and avoiding compromise solutions.

The procedure to create strategy has four steps (Table 2). The steps call for a leader-facilitator to move up the diagonal in Figure 10, create a bigger space that allows for more possibilities, carry out context reversal, and explore the space with a key group, such as an inner circle.

2. Move Up the Diagonal

Moves too far from the diagonal in Figure 10 often cause an organization to "get stuck." One power center gets favored and interest groups square off—one to protect further erosion, the other to get more consideration. To counter this, leader-facilitators move away from a lose-lose and toward a win-win strategy in small steps. In the ODMH project, focusing on problems in hospitals enticed stakeholders to fixate on the "injustices" visited on the hospitals by cutbacks and call for a spreading of the misery. An emphasis on central office ignored the very real problems of hospitals and their distinctive competencies.

The inner circle was divided into two subgroups to create win-lose (or win) options. People with sympathies or commitments to hospitals (e.g., the hospital CEOs) were placed on the subgroup to deal with the decentralized pull of the core tension; people with central-office sympathies or commitments dealt with centralized pull. The subgroups were asked to identify the best solutions for the centralized and decentralized pulls of the core tension. The outer circle was also divided along their apparent loyalties and asked to join one of the two groups, participating as described previously. The Kiva group process was used to generate and prioritize suggested actions for each subgroup.

During the generation of each proposed action, subgroup members also listed facts, assumptions, and valued outcomes associated with each action. The fact set was summarized in the presentation to the other group to demonstrate the basis each subgroup used to form its recommendations. For example, facts behind centralization proposed actions included: central office budget control; hospitals must cut 500 people; hospitals $10 million underfunded with current client load; and friction between central office and hospitals and the local communities. Facts behind the decentralized proposed actions included hospital uniqueness (size, scope of service), local autonomy required by some hospital boards, competence in clinical practice, and responsiveness to local systems of care and needs.

The assumptions behind each action were listed to identify beliefs held by each subgroup. The assumptions were open to challenge by members of the other subgroup during presentations. The assumptions cited by the centralization subgroup included: inconsistent central office decisions; hospitals lack timely information from central office; central office must balance hospital and community needs; and some hospitals unaware of their need to radically change. The decentralization subgroup assumed that hospitals must respond to local community needs, political realities call for local decision making, and few interactions among hospitals were needed. The facts and assumptions were pooled to indicate areas of agreement and contention to set the stage for the development of a compromise strategy. (In some cases it is desirable to test the assumptions to find which are both important and certain [Mason and Mitroff, 1981]. Actions linked to assumptions that fail to meet these requirements would have questionable value. Subgroups could explore an action set in this way before presenting it to the other group.)

The two subgroups reported out their suggestions to the other, with the outer circle listening. To promote compromise, each subgroup met again after the presentations to consider how they could realize their priority actions. Each subgroup member made a list of what they would have to give up to realize each of their recommended priority actions. The list of "give up" to "get" actions were then prioritized to identify compromises that each subgroup was willing to make. The two subgroups then reported out their proposed compromises. The top priority proposed actions from each group became the compromise strategy (see Figure 5).

3. Enlarge the Arena

Constraints often emerge during problem solving that narrow the scope of search (Guilford, 1967). To broaden solution search, Warfield (1990) calls for "outscoping" and Delbecq (1977) calls for "problem-centering" activity. Both approaches enlarge the arena in which search will be conducted by removing implicit constraints. Opening up the solution search to new possibilities follows widely accepted maxims derived from studies of problem solving and expert practitioners. A broad-based search produces the best results (e.g., Maier, 1970). Delaying action until the nature of key issues becomes clearer is an essential step in successful strategic management efforts (e.g., Lyles and Mitroff, 1981; Lyles, 1981). Studies of expert practitioners find that the best results occur when both means and ends are kept fluid (Schon, 1983). This helps to keep people "issue-centered," forcing them to linger in formulative activities until a more complete understanding of needs can emerge (Nutt, 1993).

A laddering technique was used to enlarge the arena in which the search for strategy was to be conducted (Nadler, 1981; Nutt, 1992). The valued outcomes identified by the subgroups were used to form the ladder. The centralized group identified the following valued outcomes; improved central office (CO) performance; clear CO responsibilities; reduced CO administrative overhead; increased hospital responsiveness to client needs; and support hospital functions, as given by JCAOH accreditation requirements. The decentralized group identified reduce CO costs, strengthen community system of care, enhance hospital's ability to collaboratively compete, clarify CO responsiveness to hospitals, and increase (hospital) income for hospital budgets. To begin a ladder construction, the most basic valued outcome was identified. The ladder was then built by adding unique valued outcomes in small increments.

A review of the valued outcomes suggests that the most basic was to "support hospital functions." To construct the ladder, a facilitator asks the purpose of the lowest scope-valued outcome: Why support hospital functions? An answer is to clarify CO responsibility to hospitals. The same type of question is posed again: Why clarify responsibilities? An answer was to improve CO performance. By continuing in this way a hierarchy for the ladder was created that moves from the least to most inclusive valued outcome, as shown in Figure 11. Valued outcomes dealing with the same type of expectations were combined at an appropriate ladder rung. For example, cost and overhead called for similar outcomes, so they were combined.

The ladder poses why and how questions. Moving up the hierarchy answers the *why* question (increases in hospital budget enhance service provision). Moving down the hierarchy poses the *how* question (improved performance reduces overhead). ODMH could increase hospital responsiveness by strengthening the system of care (why) and strengthen the system of care through hospital responsiveness (how), and so on. By moving up the hierarchy in this way, stakeholders can be shown progressively larger spaces in which strategic solutions can be sought. The bigger space is better because it has fewer constraints (Rothenburg, 1979). Laddering broadens the scope of a search, opening up the search process to more possibilities (Nadler and Hibino, 1990).

The inner and outer circle members explored the scopes of action open to them and voted to select the valued outcome that would guide their efforts to select a win-win strategy. After differences were reconciled through discussion, enhancing hospitals ability to provide services was selected (Figure 11).

4. Context Reversal

To guide the search for a win-win strategy, concerns that make up the core tension were reversed by subordinating each pull in the tension to the other (Table 2). If the priority tension concerns equity-transition, search is directed to find transition possibilities in the equity concerns of key people and equity concerns in the transition possibilities being considered. In the "inpatient futures" project, search

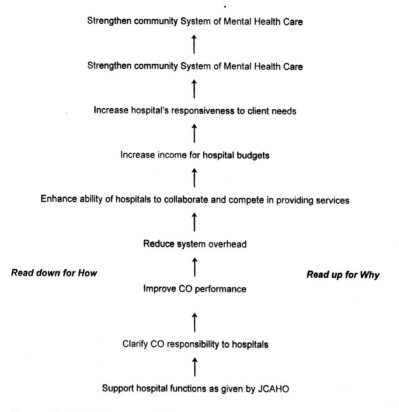

Strengthen community System of Mental Health Care

↑

Strengthen community System of Mental Health Care

↑

Increase hospital's responsiveness to client needs

↑

Increase income for hospital budgets

↑

Enhance ability of hospitals to collaborate and compete in providing services

↑

Reduce system overhead

Read down for How   ↑   **Read up for Why**

Improve CO performance

↑

Clarify CO responsibility to hospitals

↑

Support hospital functions as given by JCAHO

Figure 11   Valued outcomes ladder.

was initiated to find ways to increase decentralization as centralization was carried out and ways to centralize as decentralization was realized. A win-win strategy embraces both pulls in this tension. This approach reverses figure and ground, following problem-solving tactics found in gestalt psychology (Maier, 1970; Guilford, 1967). A context reversal is insightful because it helps people see new possibilities. Such an approach is also supported by the basic dictum of creativity: make the familiar strange and the strange familiar (de Bono, 1970).

The inner circle was asked to ''hold the tension'' as they searched for win-win ideas. Search was guided by looking for centralized actions that affirmed decentralized values (e.g., autonomy, practice skills) and decentralized actions that affirmed centralized values (e.g., legislative mandates to cut costs and become community-based). Listing by the inner-circle members was assisted by beginning with a centralized action and then adding decentralized values, moving then to a decentralized action and adding centralized values. Switching back and forth in this way both maintained values as priorities during search and helped group members hold the tension. The silent reflective phase of the Kiva group process was enhanced by this structure to make the strange familiar, a key tenet of creativity (Stein, 1975). These steps were taken to help people gain more access to the right hemisphere of their brain (Rothenburg, 1979; Goldberg, 1983; Agor, 1986; Anthony et al., 1993), which improves the prospect of finding creative ideas.

H. Aligning Strategic Action

The ''spoke and wheel'' configuration shown in Figure 12 offers a way to picture the logic of alignment (Nutt and Backoff, 1997c). Leaders take the win-win strategy for the priority issue tension and, using other important tensions as a guide, mount a search for additional actions that amplify the strategic win-win. The win-win strategy is to be enhanced by all subsequent actions. These actions must

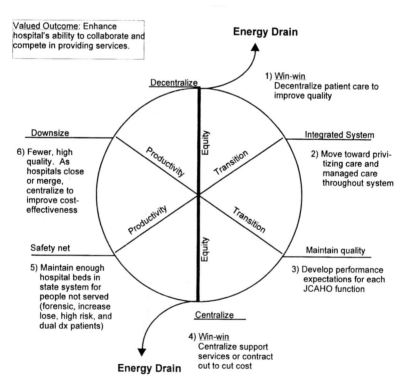

Figure 12   The change circle.

also fit together to create a succession of action steps that, when carried out, cope with key issue tensions. This makes actions connect to and deal with issue tensions that have interdependent relationships. First, the priority issue tension or core tension is located on the wheel as a spoke. Other issue tensions that have interdependent relationships (the related tensions) are also arranged as spokes. The win-win strategy is located next to one of the two concerns that make up the priority issue tension. One then circles the wheel and searches for actions that close the circle.

1. The Change Circle

Figure 12 summarizes the results obtained for the ODMH effort. The core tension was equity-equity. How would ODMH share the burden of cost cutting? The related issue tensions both involved transition-productivity: integrated system vs. safety net, and downsizing vs. maintaining quality. The point of intervention is given by the win-win strategy. The components of the win-win strategy were put on the wheel next to the appropriate pull of the core tension. To amplify, the inner-circle members looked for actions that build on the win-win strategy and respond to the pull in the adjacent issue tension. For example, action 1 calls for a decentralization of patient care to improve quality, holding the hospitals accountable for quality care. This action deals with ODMH's needs to decentralize while maintaining centralized values. Action 2 moves toward privatizing care while maintaining quality. The hospitals would be integrated with a specific set of community mental health centers to provide care, preserving the skills and competencies in each hospital that were needed. This action maintains safety net values to ensure that people needs will be meet. Action 3 calls for the development of performance expectations for each accreditation function. Performance assessed in this way could serve as a basis to close and merge hospitals during downsizing. Action 4 provides a safety net by identifying number of beds required to meet the needs of underserved or unserved clients (clients that are forensic or court-ordered, long length of stay, high risk, or dual diagnosis). The limits to integration crop up because these patients often lack health care coverage, which keeps them out of private hospitals. Action 5 commits to fewer, higher-quality hospitals, centralizing funds and activities as closures and mergers take place.

The actions supporting the win-win strategy that deal with related tensions were devised by a group made up of inner- and outer-circle volunteers. The group was asked to list actions that could realize the valued outcome, enhance the win-win strategy, and deal with each pull in the related tensions. To help in the listing, each person was asked to work around the wheel, starting with action 2 (integrate) then affirm the other pull (safety net) in action 4, move to action 3 (maintain quality), and affirm the other pull (downsize) in action 5. The actions were then tested to be sure that they would complement the others, fine-tuning them as needed. To generate the next set of actions, group members emphasized the tension pulls subordinated in the last set, moving back and forth in this way and testing each set of proposed actions for integration before moving on.

In a strategic circle of change, a win-win strategy is amplified by each trip around the wheel in Figure 12. After several trips, actions begin to transcend the issue tensions that make up the spokes of the wheel. For example, in the ODMH effort patient care decentralization, privatization, performance expectations, centralizing support services, safety net bed selection, and the close-and-merge-hospitals circle of action realize the ODMH's valued outcome of enhancing hospitals' ability to provide services. Several cycles must be completed in which these actions are carried out before the issue tensions will be managed.

2. Change Cycle Maintenance

A number of trips around the wheel in Figure 12 will be made before energy losses begin to occur (Maruyama, 1983). A change circle can lose momentum through ill-advised actions by higher-ups, the lack of feedback, and unfocused activity. Momentum losses occur when an issue tension recurs, as shown by arrows that draw energy outward from the core tension in Figure 12. *Blocking* arises when someone, wittingly or unwittingly, takes action that has a dampening effect on the strategic change cycle, producing an energy drain. For instance, ever-increasing demands by ODMH management for hospitals to account for their actions could create an undercurrent of distrust that unravels synergistic relationships. *Feedback failures* can also cause an energy drain. For instance, failing to recognize the accomplishments of hospitals or undervaluing their distinctive skills in treatment would suggest that hospital competency was not valued (Kouze and Posner, 1987). Many *unfocused projects* will fritter away the time of a team with too much unfocused activity. Start-up time becomes excessive, making specific accomplishments more difficult to realize.

Even the best-oiled change cycle will gradually run down. Entropy arises when people gradually lose their zeal, potentials for strategic change are depleted, and new strategic issues draw away attention. For example, in the ODMH effort, should the target reduction of $70 million not be reached after several cycles around the strategy wheel, new issues may emerge. These issues could involve preserving hospitals with distinctive competencies facing the budget axe or finding ways to provide a safety net for types of clients found to be outside the care system.

To maintain the strategic cycle of action in a cybernetic loop, one looks for negative synergy that slows the energy flow or seeks ways to restore or enhance amplifying actions (Quinn and Cameron, 1988; Smith, 1989). For example, in the ODMH effort, renewed efforts to cut the cost of support services or to get reimbursement for services rendered may be able to infuse needed resources. Periodically fine-tuning the strategic change cycle in this way can keep the change cycle operating smoothly for a period of time.

In most organizations, more than one strategic change circle will be required to deal with the strategic issues on an issue agenda. This calls for several strategic change circles to be built to deal with bundles of issue tensions that seem important. Leaders must then align the actions called for in each strategic change cycle (Thompson, 1967). Strategic actions are integrated across several strategic change cycles to create amplification among the cycles. For example, actions that limit privatization of mental health care in another change circle would be investigated to eliminate this intercircle energy drain. Also, ways to promote intercircle change amplification can be sought. The coalignment of an amplifying set of strategic actions provides a powerful engine of strategic change.

VI. TRANSFORMATIONAL CHANGE

State agencies are apt to face a future of increased turbulence. This calls for a process of continuous change in which leaders take an active role in fashioning and shaping a vision for an agency. This seldom occurs today, but will be essential to meet the turbulent times ahead (Ansoff, 1985; Shortell et al., 1988). Agency leaders will be expected to find a way to create and manage transformations. This will continuously alter both internal structure and external commitments in response to dynamically changing needs that will characterize the future of most state agencies. Turbulent environments call for collaborative responses in which state agencies form alliances and garner and allocate resources in response to the emergent needs. This will require the development of a vision, continuous strategic management that is carried out by the organization leader, and the use of mutualist strategy.

A. What Is Transformation?

Turbulent environments prompt the need for radical change. A radical change transforms an agency by providing greater variety, more skill, and increased ability to serve its customers/clients in new and different ways, which allows the agency to cope more effectively with its changed world (Senge, 1990; Pauchant and Mitroff, 1992). To transform a state agency, its leaders must to go beyond making efficiency and effectiveness improvements, using maintenance and control activities. Fundamental changes in traditional practices and ways of doing business are required. A transformation calls for new ways of thinking that alter taken-for-granted and often hidden organizational rules, which limit how people think about change (Wilber, 1983; Pribram, 1983; Torbert, 1987; Fisher and Torbert, 1995).

A transformation calls for a vision. A vision provides energy (Block, 1991), has inspirational qualities (Nanus, 1989), and brings organizational distinction (Covey, 1990). Transformations result when leaders see and act on visionary possibilities, drawing on their knowledge of their agency—its sources of funds, services, customers, and human resources, to mobilize action with ideas (Galbreath et al., 1993). The vision suggests ways to make radical changes in an organization's strategy. To find radical changes, agency leaders must abandon an orientation rooted in the present and adopt one focused on the future (Hamel and Prahalad, 1994). Many state agency leaders can think strategically by asking hard questions about their ideals: their current services, customers served today, current service provision channels and skills, the basis for today's current collaborative advantage, current sources of funding, and persona (Porter, 1985; Nutt and Backoff, 1997a). These same leaders find it difficult to find answers to these same questions, put in a future context. To transform a state agency, its leaders must find a vision that suggests future services, customers, channels, skills, bases for collaborative advantage, sources of funding, and persona that can offer the agency distinction (Wheatley, 1992). Transformations go beyond tinkering with today's strategy, projecting today's thinking into the future to imagining what a desired future would look like. A transformation takes place when a vision that makes radical, creative, and coherent changes in several aspects of an agency's current strategy has been integrated with its core capabilities.

For instance, the Ohio Department of Natural Resources (ODNR) was transformed with a vision to incorporate critics into its programs to build joint interests. Conflicts between sportsmen and environmentalists were managed by opening up new hunting and fishing areas and using fees for hunting and fishing licenses and park use to support wildlife, environmentally threatened areas, and state parks. Cooperation between historically antagonistic groups, representing sportsmen and environmentalists, was created and resulted in broad support for tax-based funding to protect endangered areas and wildlife and support recreation programs. Recreational areas were expanded, increasing revenue from user fees and providing revenues to fund other initiatives. The synergy of protection and use programs led to a ODNR budget that relied on the state funding for less than one-third of its programs, making a state agency take on the characteristics of a private, nonprofit organization. Note how ODNR moved to a higher order of complexity in which change, such as new services, was not just added on but emerged from the integration of old and new services. As a result, the transformed organization is able to respond in new and different ways to the emergent demands and opportunities found in turbulent environments. State agencies with a vision, that anticipate client needs can use these anticipated needs to make changes in their core services and procedures, can produce a similar result. Synergy between the agency's new and old services and other aspects of its strategy increase flexibility and adaptability (Linden, 1994).

A transformation goes beyond fostering growth, which adds to existing capability by serving existing clients more efficiently or effectively. A transformation engages in a *continuous* appraisal of visionary possibilities and systematically *integrates* viable ideas into the repertoire of capabilities and other aspects of the organization's strategy (Weisbord, 1988). For example, novel ways to meet the needs of a different set of clients would be integrated with current services, channels, etc., that make up an agency's strategy. Each successful integration provides a quantum jump in the *capacity* of the agency and its ability to cope with abrupt environmental shifts. The transformed state agency brings these new capacities to bear as services for clients that can be internal or external to the agency, turning upside down traditional notions, such as who is a customer or client.

Many strategic management efforts in state agencies are unable to mobilize and sustain a radical change. By their actions, if not their public pronouncements, governors support only efficiency improvements, such as TQM, and fear transformations. Agency leaders in such a situation can rethink current strategy and by doing so set the stage for more radical change when forced by outside events or allowed by a more tolerant climate. For example, since 1988, ODMH has been guided by a vision of treating people in the least restrictive setting, close to family and friends, which we have called "deinstitutionalization." A new vision of integrated care that merges acute and mental health care and their insurance coverage frightens state politicians, who have blocked such initiatives. Until a new vision emerges, ODMH can only make nonradical changes in its current strategy. This suggests that the window of opportunities for transformation opens and closes quickly. To be ready, leaders must be prepared to initiate change efforts that can shape the leader's vision or create a vision in response to emergent demands.

B. Make Continuous Change

Organizational leaders often treat development as a one-day affair or as a single concerted effort, facilitated by outsiders. In the future, this should change. Transformation calls for a continuous process of change management, in which cycles of action, issue, situation, and agency management are carried out repeatedly (see Figure 2). The state agency should periodically test its vision, shaping it as new ideas and understandings emerge.

C. Use Mutualist Strategies

A mutualist strategy deals with turbulent environments in which compelling needs explosively emerge with little warning by substituting collaboration for competition. The best outcome from a competitive posture would have competing state agencies serving people thought to fall under their jurisdictions. Such an approach leaves important needs unmet or undeserved and encourages duplication. A collaborative posture calls for negotiation with taxing and budgeting authorities and sister agencies to parcel out service areas so that all service responsibilities can be met. The mutualist strategy calls for consortia and other kinds of umbrella organizations to be created to serve emergent needs. Although relevant examples such as the Highway Safety Program and the National Kidney Foundation can be identified, they have occurred far too infrequently in the past and will become more essential in the future.

A collaborative approach is needed to ensure that emergent needs in a dynamically changing environment will be met. The mutualist strategy is managed by resources and programs drawn from many sources. The self-interests of these sources are subordinated to the greater interest of serving people's needs. The mutualist strategy recognizes the need to develop model structural arrangements and to create new ways to meet emergent needs.

To initiate a mutualist strategy, tomorrow's strategic leader must have vision, commitment, and leadership qualities. Vision is needed to recognize compelling ideas that anticipate needs with an innovative strategy (Vaill, 1989). Commitment is required to set an example for others (Bennis, 1989). One must sacrifice personal aims and parochial interests to set the tone called for by a mutualist strategy. Leadership skill is needed to strike a posture that avoids being pretentious but takes a moral position, which calls for collective action. Many are apt to interpret such a posture as a clever way to promote the agency leader's interests. Successful and unsuccessful agency leaders engage in many of the same behaviors. Success depends on putting things into a frame in which mutualist values are believable, so others will adopt and emulate these values.

VII. SUMMARY

Strategic leaders face several notable challenges. To improve the prospects of success, we believe that leaders must recognize and deal with both the content and the process of a change process. We call this managing the dance of the what and how. To manage the dance, agency leaders must see content and process as complementary. To help leaders successfully manage the dance of the what and how, we offered several strategic principles. The principles were derived from the unique needs of state departments and agencies and their ''public'' nature, our experience in making such changes, and recent theoretical developments in change and transformation. The principles of strategic change include identifying departments and agencies susceptible to change, matching strategy to environments, recognizing issue tensions, finding win-win actions, aligning these actions, managing the dance of the what and the how, promoting ownership that encourages implementation, selecting leaders who accept the roles of facilitator, coach, technician, and politician. The ability to manage a process of radical change appears to be an essential attribute of tomorrow's leaders. The need for transformation prompted by environmental turbulence, seems essential for agencies and departments to be successful in the 21st century. Radical change that can prompt a transformation calls for vision, the management of continuous change, innovation and creativity, and using mutualist strategies.

REFERENCES

Ackoff, R. (1981). *Creating the Corporate Future*, Wiley, New York.

Agor, W. H. (1986). *The Logic of Intuitive Decision Making*, Quorum, New York.

Allison, G. T. Jr. (1984). Public private management: Are they fundamentally alike in all unimportant aspects, *New Directions in Public Administration*, B. Bozman and J. Straussmon, (eds). Brooks/Cole, Belmont, CA.

Ansoff, In. (1988). *The New Corporate Strategy*, Wiley, New York.

Anthony, W. P., Bennett, R. H. III, Maddox, E. N., and Wheatley, W. J. (1993). Picturing the future: using mental imagery to enrich strategic environmental assessment, *Academy of Management Executive* 7(2):43–56.

Argyris, C., (1982). *Reasoning, Learning, and Action: Individual and Organizational*, Jossey-Bass, San Francisco.

Axelrod, R. (1978). *Structure of Decision: The Cognitive Maps of Political Elites*, Princeton University Press, Princeton, NJ.

Bennis, W. (1989). *Why Leaders Can't Lead*, Jossey Bass, San Franciso.

Bennis, W., and Nanus, B. (1985). *Leaders*. Harper and Row, New York.

Berger, P, and Luckman, T. (1966). *The Social Construction of Reality*, Doubleday, New York.

Block, P. (1991). *The Empowered Manager*, Jossey Bass, San Fransisco.

Blumenthal, M., Michael D. (1979), Candid reflections of a businessman in Washington, *Fortune* Jan 29.

Bolding, K. (1956). *The Image*, University of Michigan Press, Ann Arbor.

Bozman, B. (1987). *All Organizations Are Public*, Jossey-Bass, San Francisco.

Burns, J. M., (1978). *Leadership*, Harper & Row, New York.

Cameron, K. S. (1986). Effectiveness Paradoxes: consensus and conflict in perceptions of organizational performance, *Management Science*, 32(5):539–553.

Card, M. (1992). Creating you job. Unpublished PhD dissertation, Ohio State University.

Collins, J. C. and Porras, J. I. (1994). *Built to Last: Successful Habits of Visionary Companies*, Harper, New York.

Covey, S. R. (1990). *Principled Central Leadership*, Summit, New York.

Covey, S. (1989). *The Seven Habits of Highly Effective Leaders*, Simon and Schuster, New York.

de Bono, E. (1970). *Lateral Thinking: Creativity Step by Step*, Harper and Row, New York.

Daft, R., and Weick, K. (1984). Toward a model of organizations as interpretive systems, *Academy of Management Review* 9(2):284–295.

Delbecq, A., Van de Ven, A., and Gustafson, D. (1986). *Group Techniques for Program Planning*, Greenbrier, Middletown, WI.

Delbecq, A. (1977). The management of decision making within the firm: three strategies for three types of decision making, *Academy of Management Journal* 10(4):329–339.

Delbecq. A. L. (1989). *Sustaining Innovation as an American Competitive Advantage*. Institute for Urban Studies, University of Maryland, College Park.

Dilulio, J. J., Garvey, G., and Kettl, D. (1993). *Improving Governmental Performance: An Owners Manual*. Brookings, Washington, DC.

Eden, C. and Radford, J. (1990). *Tackling Strategic Problems: The Role of Group Decision Support* Sage, Beverly Hills, CA.

El Sawy, O. A. (1985). Exploring temporal perspectives as a bias to managerial attention, Center for Futures Research, Graduate School of Business Administration, University of Southern California, May.

Emery, F. E., and Trist, E. L. (1965). Causal texture of organizational environments, *Human Relations* 18(1):21–32.

Fisher, D., Torbert. W. R. (1991). Transforming managerial practice: beyond the achiever stage, *Research In Organizational Change and Development* 5:143–173.

Fisher, R. Brown, S., (1988). *Getting Together. Building a Relationship That Gets to Yes*, Houghton Mifflin, Boston.

Fisher, R., and Ury, W., (1981). *Getting to Yes*, Houghton Mifflin, New York.

Freeman, R. E. (1984). *Strategic Management: A Stakeholder Approach*. Pittman Press, Boston.

Galbraeth, J. R., Lawler, E. E. III. (1993). *Organizing for the Future*, Jossey Bass, San Fransisco.

Goldberg, P. (1983). *The Intuitive Edge*. Tarcher, Los Angeles.

Goodsell, C. T., (1993). Reinvent government or rediscover it?, *Par* 53(1):85–87.

Gore, A. (1993). From red tape to results: creating a government that works better and costs less, Report of the National Performance Review, Washington, DC.

Gullford, J. P. (1967). *The Nature of Human Intelligence*, McGraw-Hill, New York.

Hamel. G., and Prahalad, C. K., (1994). Competing for the future, *Harvard Business Review*. July-Aug, 122–128.

Hampden-Turner, C. M. (1990). *Charting the Corporate Mind*. Free Press, New York.

Hampden-Turner, C. M., (1981). *Maps of the Mind*. Macmillan, New York.

Howe, E., Kaufman, J. (1979). The ethics of contemporary American planning, *Journal of the American Planning Association*, 45(3):242–255.

Ingraham, P. W., and Rosenbloom, D. H. (1990). The state of merit in the federal government, National Commission on the Public Service, Washington, D.C.

Jantsch, E. (1975). *Decision for Evolution: Self Organization and Planning in the Life of Systems*, Brazilla, New York.

Johnson, B. (1992). *Polarity Management*, HRD Press, New York.

Jones, C. O. 1988. *The Reagan Legacy*, Chatham House, Chatham, NJ.

Kelley, R. (1992). *The Power of Followership*. Doubleday, New York.

Kettl, D. F. (1988). *Government by Proxy: (Mis?)Managed Federal Programs*. CQ Press, Washington DC.

Kettl, D. F. (1993). *Sharing Power: Public Governance and Private Markets*, Brookings, Washington, DC.

Kingdom, J. W. (1984). *Agendas Alternatives and Public Policies*, Little, Brown, Boston.

Kouzes, J. M., and Posner, B. Z. (1993). *Credibility*, Jossey Bass, San Fransisco.

Kouzes, J. M., and Posner, B. Z. (1987). *The Leadership Challenge*, Jossey-Bass, San Francisco.

Levine, C. H., Backoff, R. W., Cahon, A. R., and Siffin, W. J. (1976). Organizational design: a post Minnowbrook perspective for the "new" public administration, *Public Administration Review* July/Aug: 425–435.

Lewicki, R., and Littener, J. (1985). *Negotiation*, Irwin, Homewood, IL.

Likert, R. (1967). *The Human Organization*, McGraw-Hill, New York.

Linden, R. (1994). *The Seamless Government: Re-engineering in the Public Sector*, Jossey Bass, San Fransisco.

Lyles, M., and Mitroff, I. (1980). Organizational problem formulation: an empirical stud, *Administrative Science Quarterly* 25:102–119.

Lyles, M. (1981). Formulative strategic problems: empirical analysis & model development, *Strategic Management Journal* 2:61–73.

Maier, N. R. F. (1970). *Problem Solving and Creativity: In Individuals and Groups*, Brooks-Cole, New York.

Maruyama, M. (1983). Second order cybernetics: deviation amplificating mutual causal processes, *American Scientist* 51.

Mason, R. O., and Mitroff, I. I. (1981). *Challenging Strategic Planning Assumptions*, Wiley-Interscience, New York.

Miles, R. E., and Snow, C. C. (1978). *Organizational Strategy, Structure and Process*, McGraw Hill, New York.

Mintzberg, H. (1987). Crafting strategy, *Harvard Business Review* July-Aug:65–75.

Mitroff, I., and Pauchant, T. (1990). *We're So Big and Powerful Nothing Bad Can Happen*, Buchtone, New York.

Morgan, G. (1988). *Riding the Waves of Change*, Jossey Bass, San Francisco.

Nadler, G. (1981). *The Planning and Design Approach*, Wiley, New York.

Nadler, G., and Hibino, S. (1990). *Breakthrough Thinking*, Prima, Rocklin, CA.

Nanus, B. (1989). *The Leader's Edge*, Contemporary Books, Chicago.

Neustadt, R. E. (1989). American residents and corporate executives, National Academy of Public Administration, Oct 7–8.

Nutt, P. C., and Backoff, R. W. (1997a). Crafting vision, *Journal of Management Inquiry* 6(4):308–328.

Nutt, P. C., and Backoff, R. W. (1997b). Organizational transformations, *Journal of Management Inquiry* 6(3):235–254.

Nutt, P. C., and Backoff, R. W. (1997c). Transforming organizations with second order change, *Research in Organizational Development and Change* 10:229–274.

Nutt, P. C., and Backoff, R. W. (1996a). Walking the visions and walking the talk: transforming organizations with strategic leadership, *Public Productivity and Management Review* 19(4):455–486.

Nutt, P. C., and Backoff, R. W. (1996b). Fashioning and sustaining strategic change, *Public Productivity and Management Review* 19(3):313–337.

Nutt, P. C., and Backoff, R. W. (1995a). Strategy for public and third sector organizations, *JPART* 5(2):189–211.

Nutt, P. C., and Backoff, R. W. (1995b). The dance of the what and how: creating and sustaining organizational transformation, in A. Halachmi and G. Bouchaert (eds.), *The Enduring Challenges in Public Management: Surviving and Excelling in a Changing World*, Jossey-Bass, San Fransisco.

Nutt, P. C., and Backoff, R. W. (1994). Transforming public and third sector organizations facing difficult times, *Technological Forecasting and Social Change* 45(2):131–150.

Nutt, P. C. (1993). The formulation processes and tactics used in organizational decision making, *Organization Science* 4(2):226–251.

Nutt, P. C., and Backoff, R. W. (1993a). Organizational publicness and its impact on strategic management, *JPART* 3(3):209–231.

Nutt, P. C., and Backoff, R. W. (1993b). Strategic issues as tensions, *Journal of Management Inquiry* 2(1):28–43.

Nutt, P. C. (1992). *Managing Planned Change*, Macmillan, New York.

Nutt, P. C. (1987). Identifying and appraising how managers install strategy, *Strategic Management Journal* 8:1–14.

Nutt, P. C., and Backoff, R. W. (1993c). Strategic issues as tensions, *Journal of Management Inquiry* 2(1):28–43.

Nutt, P. C., and Backoff, R. W. (1992). *The Strategic Management of Public and Third Sector Organizations*, Jossey Bass, San Francisco.

Oroz, J. (1991). Leadership transitions of state government executives. Unpublished Ph D dissertation, Ohio State University.

Osborn, D., and Gaebler, T. (1992). *Reinventing Government*, Addison-Wesley, Reading, MA.

Pascale, R. T. (1990). *Managing on the Edge*, Simon and Schuster, New York.

Pananowsky, M. (1994). Teamwork for wicked problems, *Organizational Dynamics* Spring:36–56.

Perry, J. L., and Rainey, H. G. (1988). The public private distinction in organization theory: a critique and research strategy, *Academy of Management Review* 13(2):182–201.

Pettigrew, A. M. (1987). Context and action in the transformation of the firm, *Journal of Management Studies*, 11(2):31–48.

Pettigrew, A. M. (1985). Context and action in the transformation of the firm, *Journal of Management Studies* 11(2):31–48.

Porter, M. E. (1985). *Competitive Advantage*, Free Press, New York.

Porter, M. E. (1980). *Competitive Strategy: Techniques for Analyzing Industries and Competitors*, Free Press, New York.

Pribam, K. J. (1983). The brain, cognitive commodities, and the enfolded order, in K. Boulding and L. Senesch, eds., *The Optimum Utilization of Knowledge*, Westview Press, Boulder, CO.

Quinn, J. B., Mintzberg, H., and James, R. M. (1988). *The Strategy Process*, Prentice-Hall, Englewood Cliffs, NJ.

Quinn, R. A., Faerman, S., Thompson, M. P., and McGrath, M. R. (1990). *Becoming a Master Manager* Wiley, New York.

Quinn, R. E. (1988). *Beyond Rational Management: Mastering the Paradoxes and Competing Demands of High Performance*, Jossey-Bass, San Francisco.

Quinn, R. E., and Cameron, K. (1988). *Paradox and Transformation*, Ballinger, Cambridge, MA.

Quinn, R. E., and Rohrbaugh, J. (1983). A spatial model of effectiveness criteria: towards a competing values approach to organizational analysis, *Management Science* 29(3):363–377.

Rainey, H. E. (1989). Public management: recent research on the political context and the managerial roles structures, and behaviors, *Journal of Management* 15(2):229–250.

Rainey, H. E. (1991). *Understanding and Managing Public Organizations*, Jossey Bass, San Fransisco.

Rosen, B. (1986). Crisis in U.S. Civil Service, *PAR* 46(3):487–501.

Ring, P. (1987). Strategy issues: what are they and where do they come from?, *Strategic Planning* (J. Bryson and R. Einsweller, eds.), Planners Press, Chicago.

Rothenburg, A. (1979). *The Emerging Goddess*, University of Chicago Press, Chicago.

Rubin, M. S., (1988). Sagas ventures, quests and parlays: a typology of strategies in the public sector. In J. Brysen and Einsweller, R. (eds.), *Strategic Planning* APA, Chicago, 84–105.

Salamon, L. M., and Lund, M. S. (1984). *The Raegan Presidency and Governing America*, Urban Institute Press, Washington, DC.

Sashkin, M., and Kiser, K. J. (1993). *Putting Total Quality Management to Work*, Berrett-Koehler, San Francisco.

Schon, D. A. (1983). *The Reflective Practitioner: How Professionals Think in Action*, Basic Books, New York.

Seiznick, P. 1949. *TVA and the Grass Roots*, University of California Press, Berkeley.

Senge P., (1990). *The Fifth Discipline: The Art and Management of the Learning Organization*, Doubleday, New York.

Shortell, S., Morrison, E. M., and Friedman, B. (1988). *Strategic Choice for Americas Hospitals: Managing Change in Turbulent Times*, Jossey-Bass, San Francisco.

Smith, K. K. (1989). The movement of conflict in organizations: the joint dynamics of splitting and triangulation, *Administrative Science Quarterly* 34:1–20.

Stein, S. (1992). The relationship between human resource development and corporate creativity, *Human Resource Development Quarterly* 3(3).

Straussman, J. D. (1981). More ban for the buck or how local governments can rediscover the potentials (and pitfalls) of the market, *PAR* 41:150–157.

Thomas, K. (1976). Conflict and conflict management, in M. Dunnette (ed.), *Handbook of Industrial Organizational Psychology*, Wiley, New York.

Thompson, J. D. (1967). *Organizations in Action*, McGraw Hill, New York.

Torbert, W. R. (1989). Leading organizational transformation, *Research in Organizational Change and Development* 3:83–116.

Tversky, A., and Kahneman, D. (1973). Availability: a heuristic for judging frequency and probability, *Cognitive Psychology* 5:207–232.

Vaill, P. B. (1989). *Managing as a Performing Art*, Jossey Bass San Francisco.

Van Grundy, A. B. (1981). *Techniques of Structured Problem Solving*, Van Nostrand Reinhold, New York.

Volker, P. A., et al. (1989). *Leadership for America: Rebuilding the Public Service*, Report of the National Commission on the Public Service, Washington, DC.

Warfield, J. N. (1990). *A Science of Generic Design*, Interscience, Salinas, CA.

Warwick, D. (1975). *A Theory of Public Bureaucracy*, Harvard University Press, Cambridge, MA.

Wechsler, B., and Backoff, R. W. (1986). Policy making and administration in state agencies: strategic management approaches, *Public Administration Review* July/Aug: 321–327.

Weick, K. (1979). *The Social Psychology of Organizing*, Addison-Wesley, Reading, MA.

Weisbord, M. R. (1988). Towards a new practice theory of OD: notes on snapshooting and movie making, *Research in Organizational Change and Development* 2:59–96.

Wheatley, M. J. (1992). *Leadership and the New Science*, Berett-Kohler, New York.

Wilber, K. (1982). *The Holographic Paradigm and Other Paradoxes*, Shombala, Boulder, CO.

Winter, W. F. (1993). *Hard Truths/Through Choices: An Agenda for State and Local Reform*, Rockefeller Institute of Government, Albany, NY.

Woodman, R. W., Sawyer, J. E., and Griffin, R. W. (1993). Toward a theory organizational creativity, *Academy of Management Review* 18(2):293–321.

Yeung, A. K., and Ulrick, D. (1994). How organizations learn: an experimental study of the antecedents and organizational learning styles, *Academy of Management Conference*, Dallas, TX, August, 14–17.

10

Administration of Innovations in State Government

Keon S. Chi
Georgetown College, Georgetown, Kentucky and Council of State Governments, Lexington, Kentucky

As reflected in the voluminous literature, the subject of policy and program innovations in state government has attracted a great deal of attention from both academic researchers and practitioners in the past three decades. It seems, however, that we still have a long way to go to claim mastery of the subject matter. More than 10 years ago, one scholar reported to the National Science Foundation that the study on innovations might be linked to the "six-blind-men-and-the-elephant approach to knowing" (Cox, 1985). This description of innovations seems appropriate even today. Indeed, it is confusing, difficult, and even frustrating to offer a set of guidelines and strategies to foster innovations in state government.

There are several issues and questions to address when initiating, administering, and transferring innovations in state government. Among major issues and concerns are: How should we define an innovation? Are there certain types and models of innovations? Why innovate? Who should innovate? How are innovations diffused? How can we create an innovative organization? What are barriers to innovation diffusion? How can state officials overcome such obstacles? And, How can they sustain innovations? This chapter addresses these and other relevant questions about innovations in state government based on findings of academic research and practical experiences.

I. DEFINITIONS, TYPES, AND MODELS

For various reasons, scholars tend to think about innovations differently from practitioners. This is true particularly when defining an innovation in state government. Broadly stated, academic researchers tend to define an innovation as a discovery or the adoption of a policy or program which is new to an adopting agency or a state. In fact, nearly all political scientists and public management specialists who have done extensive research on state innovations have defined an innovation in very much the same way. To put it differently, they defined innovations from the adopter's perspective, not from the inventor's perspective. For example, in his pioneering study on innovation diffusion in state government, Walker defined an innovation as ''a program or policy which is new to the states adopting it, no matter how old the program may be or how many other states may have adopted it.'' According to him, innovation is not an invention or creation (Walker, 1969). For Savage, ''an innovation is a policy adopted by a state for the first time'' (Savage, 1978). Downs and Mohr defined innovation as ''the earliness or extent of use by a given organization of a given new idea, where 'new' means only new to the adopting agent, and not necessarily to the world in general'' (Downs and Mohr, 1979). Similarly, Nice regards innovations as policies or programs new to the state adopting them, even if the policy was first adopted in other states years earlier (Nice, 1994).

On the other hand, practitioners and others tend to define an innovation as an invention or a brand new policy or program that has not been adopted previously by other jurisdictions. They tend to define an innovation as creation or novelty, not a mere replication of a policy or program initiated by others. The Council of State Governments' (CSG) innovations awards program, for example, has used this definition since the program's inception in 1975. The national innovations awards program recognizes creative and novel initiatives in place that have proven to be effective in addressing significant policy, program, and management issues but that have not been adopted by other states. According to this definition, therefore, replicating a program originated in other states would not be considered truly innovative.

Although innovations in state government take many forms, these forms may be grouped under the two broad types: political or policy innovations, and program or management innovations. The first type includes large scale or ''macro'' innovations, while the second type includes smaller-scale or ''micro'' innovations. In his study of innovations in the federal government, Polsby defined a political innovation as ''a policy or a set of policies that seem to have altered (or promise to alter) the lives of persons affected by them in substantial and fairly permanent ways'' (Polsby, 1984). And Bingham, in his study of innovation in local government, defined a political innovation as a public policy (Bingham, 1976). Thus, political or policy innovations in state government, as in the federal and local governments, may include those initiated often, but not exclusively, by enabling legislation. Policy innovations include statewide education reform laws, restructuring court systems, and ongoing welfare-to-work reforms.

On the other hand, program or management innovations are initiated as creative tools or means to implement political or policy goals more effectively and efficiently with or without legislation measures. Examples of program and management innovations include productivity and management improvement measures as well as technology application. Experiences with the CSG and Ford Foundation–Harvard University innovations awards programs indicate that nearly 90% of innovations selected as semifinalists or finalists are program and management innovations, not policy innovations. Therefore, public administration and management specialists tend to regard innovations in terms of program and management innovations.

The process of originating innovations in state government has been analyzed in two models: policy planning and "groping along." Under the policy-planning model, innovations are initiated, for example, with prior planning and well-designed, comprehensive implementation plans. This model is usually found in political or policy innovations. Under the groping-along model, innovations are taking place without much systematic planing. This model deemphasizes the initial policy-planning idea or legislative requirements in favor of discretionary or more flexible ways of accomplishing policy objectives through trial and error, often modified by experience. As one researcher observed,

> The policy-planning model encourages managers to pay careful attention to identifying the right innovative idea, drafting a statute or execute policy that fully reflects it, and planning in advance for problems that might arise in implementation. The groping-along model, by contrast, involves much less attention to the original idea or policy—quite a number of different policies might be effective at starting an organization down a useful path—and much more attention to the organization's ability to gather and respond to operational experience along the way (Golden, 1990).

The policy-planning model may be more appropriate when explaining political-policy innovation processes, and the groping-along model can better explain program or management innovation processes.

A review of innovations in state government by the CSG innovations awards program suggests that most program and management innovations fall under the groping-along model. The same is true with the Ford Foundation and Harvard University innovations awards program. According to researchers for the Ford-Harvard innovation award program,

> Rather than emerging from systematic research projects or policy analysis, they [innovations] have involved one person or a small group drawing upon past experience and/or informal communications with colleagues in other

settings. Following initial conception the ideas have generally been quickly tried out in practice and have subsequently evolved via trial and error rather than formal experimentation or analysis. Given that the state and local governments almost never invest in research and development, this pattern was perhaps to be expected (Altshuler and Zegans, 1990).

II. WHY INNOVATE?

The question "Why innovate?" has been discussed in terms of purposes, causes, and motivations of innovations. This question has also been answered by examining political culture, organizational environment and personal qualities that attribute to initiating or adopting innovations by a state government. Below we offer several direct and indirect reasons for policy and program innovations in state government (Altshuler, 1997; Behn, 1997; Chi, 1990; Schall, 1991).

Alternatives.   New ways of managing government agencies and delivering public services are needed because many traditional and ongoing programs are not working as well as they should. State policy makers and agency managers need to come up with alternative policies and programs.

Public Confidence.   State policy makers and administrators innovate policies and programs because they want to meet the public's expectations and ultimately gain voter confidence.

Doing More with Less.   Increasingly, American taxpayers have tended to refuse to pay more taxes for government services. As a result, state policy makers and administrators are expected to "do more with less," especially during periods of fiscal austerity and retrenchment.

Managers.   Unlike in the past, state managers and workers today tend to regard innovations as part of their responsibilities. They also innovate because they attempt to apply rational approaches to problem solving. State workers in many jurisdictions are also concerned about self-efficacy, self-esteem, and legacy.

Businesses.   State officials innovate because private businesses do. The influence of the private sector in state policy making and administration has been tremendous, particularly when embarking upon strategic planning and benchmarking, quality management, productivity improvement, and privatization activities.

Competition.   The states are competing with each other in nearly every policy and program area, and the level of competition has heightened in recent years. To compete with other states, they need to create new programs or replicate policies and programs implemented by other states.

Technology.   The availability of technology makes it possible to innovate from old ways of conducting business in state government, especially in telecommunications and management information systems. In fact, many program and management innovations are linked to new technology application in state agencies.

Funding. For practical purposes, innovations are needed to obtain outside funding. State policy makers and administrators have to be more innovative to experiment with pilot projects or to acquire waivers from federal agencies, for example. They also need to develop new ideas for implementation to raise money from private sources.

III. WHO INNOVATES?

In the past three decades, there has been a gradual shift in research focuses from the state level to the individual and agency levels. For example, scholarly research between the late 1960s and mid-1980s centered around "innovative states" issues, and in the 1990s, a series of conferences and research projects have focused on innovators and creating innovative organizations. Some of the most often asked questions to address when discussing individual innovators in state agencies include: Who are innovators in state government? How can we characterize their personal and professional profiles? In what kind of work environment do they work? How do they get new ideas for policy and management improvement?

Initiators of new ideas in state government include elected officers, appointed managers and ordinary workers. Innovators tend to possess certain qualities, however. Based on a review of background information on selected innovations and interview data on innovators, for example, a Ford Foundation innovations specialist characterized the distinguished qualities of state and local innovators as "product champions," who can communicate their visions and mobilize support for new ideas. The major attributes of typical innovators include energy, persistence, knowledge of the problem, political astuteness, the ability to inspire people, and the capacity to work effectively with diverse groups (Arnold, 1990).

One national survey of innovators in state government conducted by the Council of State Governments revealed that innovators are very well educated, with virtually one-half of the innovators possessing an advanced degree from a four-year institution. Innovators tend to have a diverse array of academic majors with concentrations in social sciences, business, education, and public administration as the dominant educational backgrounds. Many innovators appear to be midcareer employees who returned to school to advance to managerial opportunities and have prior experience in the private sector, mostly in nonprofit organizations or in private consulting firms dealing with government programs. The innovators in the survey sample were very active professionally. The majority belonged to at least one state and one national professional association. Close to a majority belong to two or more associations at some level. Interestingly, national associations appeared to be more important to innovators than regional associations. (Chi and Grady, 1990).

The most common singular role pattern is for innovators to generate innovations themselves as part of their day-to-day professional responsibilities. The primary groups involved in helping the innovator develop the innovation are those individuals working with the innovator on a day-to-day basis, such as his or her coworkers and supervisors. Innovators usually find their strongest support from those they worked with and from the groups most dependent upon their agencies' services. In more than 80% of the cases, according to the CSG survey, the innovation had a potential effect on the organization.

The innovators identified by CSG relied primarily on their immediate coworkers for professional information and secondarily on the professional associations to which they belonged. The innovators appeared to be aware of what other states were doing within their respective policy areas. One-half of the respondents said that they used innovations originated in other states as a source of information. More than 60% of the states mentioned as innovative were outside the innovators' region. These results depart from the notion that innovators look primarily to regional neighbors when contemplating a new venture for their agencies.

IV. INNOVATIVE STATES

One popular question on state-level innovation studies has been, "How should we measure the innovativeness of states?" This question has been analyzed by many political scientists since the mid-1960s. These studies have certain characteristics. First, the political scientists defined an innovation as a state law, not anything else. Second, they used laws in selected policy areas during certain periods to measure the innovativeness of states. And third, researchers measured and ranked states according to date or speed of adopting innovations. Thus, states that adopted laws earlier than others were deemed to be more innovative. For example, Walker ranked states according to composite scores of innovations based on 88 state laws in 11 policy areas enacted by at least 20 states between 1870 and 1966 (Walker, 1969). Gary's innovativeness rankings are based on only 12 laws in three areas: education, welfare, and civil rights (Gray, 1973). Savage used 181 laws from 15 policy areas to measure innovativeness of the states: 58 laws in the 19th century, 54 laws in the early 20th century, and 69 laws in the late 20th century (Savage, 1978).

As for future research, at least three points may be made regarding methodologies to measure the innovativeness of the states. First, as mentioned earlier in this chapter, most scholars define innovations as adoptions of innovations implemented elsewhere. If this definition is used, however, as a former NSF intergovernmental program coordinator once pointed out, "every state is an innovator" because all states borrow ideas from each other. Some would argue that truly innovative states are "pioneering" or "bellwether" states. Therefore, not every state adopting another state's programs should be considered a pioneer or a bellwether state. The question is, should we continue to define innovations from an adopter's perspective?

A second point has to do with the use of state laws to determine the innovativeness of states. The question is, can we measure the innovativeness of the states based solely on their adoption of laws? Laws are certainly a major source of information on how states are doing. Using laws might be a convenient, but not necessarily the most comprehensive, way of measuring a state's innovativeness. There appear to be several inherent problems when relying solely on laws in the study of innovation diffusion in state government. First of all, the date of adoption of a law does not necessarily correspond with the timing of implementation of policy. In many states, significant policy or program initiatives are implemented even before relevant laws are enacted. The delay in policy implementation may be attributable to several factors such as the state's budgetary constrains and administrative rules and regulations. The issue is the elapsed time between the date of adoption of legislation and the time when the policy or program is actually implemented. The gap might prove to be significant in the study of innovation diffusion. In addition, some laws are subsequently changed or repealed. One might ask, therefore, can we consider a state innovative even if it failed to implement a new law adopted earlier?

In addition, when measuring innovativeness based on laws, the content of the legislative measure might need careful examination. The early innovation studies virtually disregarded the nature and extent of an innovation. Perhaps the researchers assumed the same or similar types of titles of laws would contain the same or similar provisions. What they needed was, it seems, a list of laws with years of adoption by the states. Although states tend to replicate laws adopted by others, more often they also tend to revise or sometimes improve such laws to fit their own situations. While the intent of laws might be the same, the implementation process can be substantially different. Should we pay attention only to the intent of laws and not to the methods of implementation? It is possible to think about a situation where a laggard state can come up with more effective legislation that is more beneficial to the people. Finally, perhaps most importantly, the previous studies on innovations virtually disregarded program and management innovations which account for most innovations occurring in state agencies. It should also be pointed out that most innovations fall under the groping-along model, not the policy-planning model.

A. Creating Innovative Organizations

How can state leaders and managers create innovative agencies? An innovative agency may be defined as "one in which everyone—from those on the leadership team, to middle managers, to front-line supervisors, to front-line workers—acts on a sense of responsibility for inventing, developing and implementing new ways of achieving the organization's mission" (Behn, 1995). To make a state agency innovative, leaders, managers, and front-line workers all must have clearly defined goals and proper roles to play.

First, goals are important when creating innovative organizations because goals can set directions organizations want to go, set specific targets to reach, and be measured by both quality and quantity. Goals can help define outcomes in meeting the public's expectations and demands. Innovations may not occur without the appropriate organizational environment and opportunities created by leaders who can help articulate goals for managers and workers.

Second, leaders in innovative organizations must have personal qualities including serious personal commitment and devotion; tolerance and openness to new initiatives, suggestions, and proposals; and a willingness to share power with others, including middle managers and front-line workers. Leaders in innovative organizations need to use realistic strategies developed jointly by managers, workers, union members, and others. Such strategies may be developed through total quality management or similar management tools.

Third, the role of middle managers should be clearly defined. Why are middle managers important in the innovation process? At least three reasons can be offered: (1) through "buying-in" activities, middle managers can have a sense of ownership of innovations; (2) they can create an environment and allocate the resources necessary to implement innovations; and (3) they can help continue and sustain innovations.

Fourth, to create an innovative agency, state policy makers and managers need to redefine roles of front-line workers. Behn (1995) has offered useful "hints" for involving front-line workers in the innovation process:

1. Be immediately responsive to requests for improved working conditions (or when they ask for a new photocopier, produce it).
2. Support mistakes (or sit next to the first honest innovator who is called before a legislative committee).
3. Create an explicit mission and related performance measure (or give people a real reason to be innovative).
4. Broaden job categories (or don't let each individual do only one narrow task).
5. Move people around (or don't let workers think they need learn only one job for life).
6. Reward teams, not individuals (or find ways to beat the formal performance-appraisal and promotion system).
7. Make the hierarchy as unimportant as possible (or at least walk around without an entourage).
8. Break down functional units (or don't let the procurement guys tell everyone "no").

9. Give everyone all the information they need to do the job (or don't let the overhead units hoard the critical data).
10. Tell everyone what innovations are working (or have front-line workers report their successes to their colleagues).

B. Diffusion of Innovations

Most studies on innovation diffusion have focused on horizontal diffusion among the states. Innovation researchers have attempted to explain why some states tend to be more innovative than others. One key question has been, What causes a state government to adopt a new policy or program? Despite many case studies on the question, findings of such studies may be classified into two models: "internal determinants," and "regional diffusion" (Berry and Berry, 1995).

The internal-determinants model posits that causes of adopting innovations may be answered by examining internal characteristics—political, economic, and social—of a state. The classic answer to the question is that the larger, wealthier, more industrialized states adopt new programs somewhat more rapidly than their smaller, less developed neighbors. Other scholars have found, however, that states that are innovators in one policy area are not necessarily innovators in other areas, and that "innovativeness is not a pervasive factor; rather, it is issue- and time-specific." Still, some researchers discounted interaction effects in the innovation diffusion process and claimed that "only the policy itself can be assumed to be invariant over time" (Chi, 1996).

The regional diffusion model, to the contrary, focuses more on the influence of "geographically proximate states" in the innovation adoption process. It has been widely thought that state policy makers and managers look primarily to regional neighbors when contemplating a new venture. There is no question that regionalism plays a major role in innovation diffusion. As mentioned in the previous section, however, innovators in state governments tend to replicate innovations from any states, not necessarily from neighboring states. Today, thanks to communications technology and other factors, state innovators can learn about creative and novel solutions to problems from any jurisdiction without regard to its location or characteristics.

How long did it take for all states to replicate an innovation in a given policy area? This question has been investigated by several political scientists. For example, based on 88 state laws enacted between 1870 and 1966, Walker found that the average elapsed time of innovation diffusion decreased from 52.3 years for all adoptions (or 22.9 years for the first 20 states) in 1870–1899 to 25.6 years for all adoptions (or 18.4 years for the first 20 states) in 1930–1966. And Welch and Thomspon, based on 57 laws, including 52 from the Walker data, found the average diffusion time to be nearly 30 years (Chi, 1996). It is interesting to see if the average diffusion time has further decreased in recent years. It can be assumed that the diffusion time may have drastically shortened in part because of the roles played by third parties, including federal financial agencies with a variety of financial incentives (Welch and Thompson, 1980).

On the other hand, researchers on innovations in state government have paid little attention to vertical diffusion of state innovations, transferring innovations from states to the federal government. Vertical diffusion occurs because of "a search for ideas from within and pressures from below and outside to adopt policy innovations" (Sapart, 1997). Vertical, as well as horizontal, innovations may be diffused through third parties—interest groups, profit and nonprofit organizations, civic organizations, and national and regional organizations of state officials. They can act as information brokers and catalysts by conducting various activities, such as clearinghouses, publications, conferences, and workshops; by offering policy options and recommendations; by providing technical assistance; by giving interstate consulting services; and with recognition and award programs to encourage continuous adoption of innovations. Major national organizations representing state governments include the National Governors' Association, the Council of State Governments, and the National Conference of State Legislatures. Other national organizations of elected state officials are the National Conference of Lieutenant Governors, National Association of State Treasurers, National Association of Attorneys General, and National Association of Secretaries of States. In addition, there exist a number of organizations of appointed state officials that can help states diffuse innovations from one state to another; these include national associations of state budget officers, personnel executives, purchasing officials, state administration and general services, emergency management, parole and probation, and telecommunication and information resources.

V. INNOVATIONS AWARDS PROGRAMS

There exist several innovations awards programs designed to promote innovation diffusion in government. In this section, three awards programs are briefly described, focusing on selection criteria: the Innovations Awards Program conducted by The Council of State Governments, which is the only national program exclusively for state governments; the Innovations in American Government Program by the Ford Foundation and Harvard University's John F. Kennedy School of Government, which is for all three levels of government; and the Exemplary State and Local Awards Program by the National Center for Public Productivity at Rutgers University, which is for state and local governments as well as nonprofit organizations.

Begun in 1975, with seed money from the National Science Foundation, the Council of State Governments' innovations transfer program has given state policy makers opportunities to share with officials in other states information on their new and creative programs and policies. Each year, CSG asks state officials to participate in the innovations program by identifying and submitting information on new initiatives that have been successfully implemented and that have the potential to be adopted by other states. In 1986, the Innovations Awards Program was initiated to give more public visibility to the innovative programs. Only state officials are eligible for the awards program. Four regional panels of state officials each select two programs from the hundreds of applications submitted each year. The eight programs selected every year are formally recognized during special ceremonies at CSG's annual meetings and showcased in CSG publications, such as *State Innovations Briefs, State Trends, and State Government News*. In addition, CSG's States Information Center maintains a clearinghouse of the applications as part of the innovations transfer program (Chi, 1996).

At each stage of the CSG Innovations Awards selection process, the following questions are employed to determine whether the policy or program is eligible for an award:

1. Newness: Has this program been operational for at least eight months but no longer than five years?
2. Creativity: Does it represent a new and creative approach to problem(s) or issue(s)?
3. Effectiveness: Has the program or policy been effective in achieving its stated goals and purposes to this point?
4. Significance: Does the program or policy address significant problem(s) or issue(s) that are regional or national in scope?
5. Applicability: Is the program or policy applicable to other states?
6. Transferability: Could the program or policy be easily transferred to other states?

In 1985, the Ford Foundation and the John F. Kennedy School of Government at Harvard University began an innovations awards program (initially called "Innovations in State and Local Government," now called "Innovations in American Government"). Since its inception, the innovations awards program has recognized more than 115 innovative programs with monetary awards. Each year, 20 programs are chosen as finalists by teams of researchers and practitioners. According to its 1998 application form, the awards program honors "exemplary programs that address important social and economic issues. Another goal was to identify initiatives that might be replicated" (Innovations in American Government, 1998).

At each stage of the selection process, applications are evaluated based on "creativity and effectiveness in responding to important problems of local or national concern, their transferability to other jurisdictions, and the value to their clients." The selection criteria are that programs:

1. Be administered or operated by a government or special authority
2. Take a new approach to a pressing social need, or significantly improve an existing program
3. Have been in operation for at least one year
4. Have a proven record of effectiveness and be able to provide evidence that the program has achieved its goals.

The National Center for Public Productivity at Rutgers University established the Exemplary State and Local Awards Program in 1989 to recognize public initiatives that improve the quality of government services and operations. The program recognizes "innovative projects and programs that have produced measurable increases in quality and productivity, significant cost savings, and improvements in the efficiency and effectiveness of government services." Awards are given to the most creative approaches to problem solving in areas such as administration and management, criminal justice, education, public works, environment, health and human services, housing, public safety, technology, and transportation.

The awards program has broad selection criteria. Awards may be given to innovative "projects and programs which have positive impacts on state and local government operations and the communities served by those entities." Programs must have been in operation for at least one year prior to the application deadline. Nominations can be made by an agency's chief administrative or elected officials in state and local government, as well as school districts, regional authorities, community-based organizations, nonprofit agencies, and public-private partnerships.

VI. BARRIERS TO INNOVATIONS

Innovations are not easy to conceive or replicate because new initiatives usually mean changes and disruptions in an organization. There are institutional barriers as well as employee resistance to innovations, especially from those affected by implementation of new policies or programs. The absence of pressure or incentives is another obstacle in adopting innovations. These barriers and obstacles to innovations in state government may be summarized under the following 10 areas (Altshuler and Zegans, 1997; Behn, 1997).

Bureaucratic Discretion. Traditionally, state managers and administrators have not been encouraged to exercise bureaucratic discretion, since their role is believed to be executing policies crafted by elected legislators. This tradition continues to curtail administrative innovations.

Routines. State managers tend to be reluctant to give up familiar routines in favor of changes with uncertain results unless they are required to do so. Moreover, unlike in private organizations, they rarely face serious competition of threats from other states, thus lacking incentives to abandon traditional ways of managing and delivering services.

Receptivity. State workers are not always receptive to new ideas, however appealing, because of the individual, organizational, or political environment in which they work. In addition, the organization and the broader social context can be unreceptive to new technology.

Measurement. Unlike in private businesses, where company performance can be measured by profits, it is difficult to use a common measure of success, thus making innovations difficult to implement. As a result, very few agencies are eager to depart from current practices no matter how effective innovations may be to realize agency objectives.

Fear of Failures. State leaders and managers tend to be fearful of·unsuccessful innovations. They don't initiate innovative programs for fear of bad media exposures. Old programs may be inadequate, but their familiarity insulates them from much media attention.

Time and Resources. Innovations require state leaders and managers to invest necessary time and resources. State agencies rarely have such resources for research and development. Information costs and the lack of extra funding tend to discourage implementation of new ideas.

Diversity. The variation of social, institutional, and technical context from state to state makes adaptability difficult, and many moving parts do not translate well into other environments. In particular, value-ridden ideas are difficult to replicate.

Results. Many program and management innovations are process oriented. But the public is more concerned about results of policy or programs, not processes. Thus, unless innovations produce radical improvements in client services, it is difficult to justify adopting new and untested programs.

Incentives. Like in the private sector, managers and workers need to be motivated to be innovative. The absence of monetary or nonmonetary incentives makes it difficult for state workers to initiate new programs.

Elected Leaders. Elected leaders of state government, such as governors, elected executives, and legislators, might have debated on innovative ideas during their election campaigns, but not everyone follows up with their campaign promises to improve state government performance.

It is important to keep in mind that one deeply rooted barrier comes from the practice of democracy. The inherent characteristics of American democracy that hinder the creation and preservation of innovative public agencies are several. To mention just a few: election cycles that inevitably result in frequent leadership and management changes, thus voiding or nullifying sustainable policy and program initiatives; public ignorance may result in emotional and prudent policy making as a result of leadership changes rather than innovative policies and programs; and partisan and interest group politics might make innovations in state government more difficult to implement due to conflicting interests and demands. How can state officials overcome such barriers and obstacles? Specific strategies vary widely, but the most salient include the following suggestions (Zegans, 1997):

1. Innovators and supporters should try to alleviate problems that are widely recognized as urgent. They need to convince others that the current system is not working.
2. They should promote the cost-effectiveness as a justification for the innovation.
3. They should proceed with the innovation incrementally.
4. They should try not to divert resources for innovative programs from other deserving programs.
5. They should count on their customers' sending a preponderance of positive messages to political authorities.
6. They should cast their nets widely in search of support, and they should be ingenious in linking their efforts to sources of funding and institutional capacity.
7. They should be skilled at building and sustaining networks that embrace the various centers of authorizing and implementing capacity essential to success.
8. They should try to gain commitment from leadership; achieving recognition in the broader social context (such as with media) facilitates innovations.
9. They should be open to feedback. They should recognize an innovation as a process of continuous learning and adaptation.
10. They should be tenacious, passionately committed, and optimistic. More often than not they might have to experience major setbacks along the way to success and long periods without recognition or apparent progress.

VII. SUSTAINING INNOVATIONS

Do innovations last? One scholar on innovations in government concluded,

Most public innovations do not survive . . . large numbers of innovations perish quickly, usually within five years of launch, easily shucked off by their sponsoring organizations, rarely altering the course of the public organizations to which they are attached. . . . Even innovations that make it to the finals of the Ford Foundation's prestigious award program may have lower survival rates, in spite of the enormous endorsement and $100,000 that each receive (Light, 1992).

Light estimated the "survival rate" to be one in ten. It seems that much more, systematic research is needed to validate this claim. Based on practical experiences with the CSG innovations awards program, however, many innovations appear to survive, often under different labels and in modified forms. While nothing can be sustained permanently in government, efforts need to be made to keep innovations alive for some time so the benefits of innovations can be realized.

Elements needed to sustain innovations include: setting up an ongoing external board to maintain strategic visions; obtaining financial and in-kind support; maintaining media visibility; buy-in by career civil servants; keeping infrastructures, such as innovations awards programs; and strategic experiments to test and refine the quality management process. Additional strategies may include: constituency support (client groups and unions); institutionalization of the quality process through statutes, rules, and regulations; depoliticizing the process; selling the quality process, not the label; courting legislatures and oversight organizations conducting continuous training programs reflecting new culture and long-term changes in the labor force; protecting and nurturing institutional memory; and grooming candidates for succession in elective state offices and emphasizing the quality process in transition documents.

VIII. CONCLUSION

Government innovations have attracted a good deal of attention from academic researchers and practitioners in the past three decades. We know now much more than we did about the administration of innovations in state government. As this chapter reveals, however, there are several areas in need of further research and verification—areas ranging from defining innovations to sustaining innovations. In addition, we have noted that political scientists tended to focus on laws or policy innovations for their research on innovations, while public administration and management researchers have paid attention mostly to program and management innovations. This pattern might not be a surprise to some observers, given the nature of the discipline. What seems to be noteworthy is that there have been no meaningful dialogues between these two groups of scholars regarding their research findings on state government innovations as reflected in the use of citations and reference sources. We all can learn more about innovations if scholars and practitioners communicate more often than in the past.

REFERENCES

Altshuler, A. A., and Zegans, M. (1990). Innovation and creativity: comparisons between public management and private enterprise, *Cities* 7(1):16–20.
Altshuler, A. A. (1997). *Public innovation and political incentives*, A Report of the Inno-

vations in American Government Program, John F. Kennedy School of Government, Harvard University, Cambridge, MA.

Altshuler, A. A. (1997). Bureaucratic innovation, democratic accountability, and political incentives, *Innovation in American Government: Challenges, Opportunities, and Dilemmas*, Altshuler, A. A. and Behn, R. D., eds., Brookings Institution, Washington, DC.

Arnold, D. (1990). Lessons of the innovations program, Ford Foundation's governance and public policy program (unpublished report).

Behn, R. D. (1995). Creating an innovative organization: ten hints for involving front-line workers, *State and Local Government Review 27(3)*: 221–234.

Behn, R. D. (1995). *Creating Innovative Public Agencies: A Challenge for State and Local Government*, Governors Center at Duke University, Terry Sanford Institute of Public Policy, Durham, NC.

Behn, R. D. (1997). The dilemmas of innovation in American government, *Innovations in American Government: Challenges, Opportunities, and Dilemmas*, Altshuler, A. A., and Behn, R. D., eds., Brookings Institution, Washington, DC.

Berry, F. S., and Berry, W. D. (1988). Explaining innovations by American states: the case of taxes, Paper presented at the annual meeting of the American Political Science Association, Washington, DC.

Bingham, R. D. (1976). *The Adoption of Innovation by Local Government*, Lexington Books, Lexington, MA, p. 217.

Chi, K. S., and Grady, D. O. (1990). Innovators in state governments: their organizational and professional environment, *The Book of the States, 1990–91*, Council of State Governments, Lexington, KY, 382–404.

Chi, K. S. (1996). Innovations in state government, *The Book of the States, 1996–97*, Council of State Governments, Lexington, KY, 537–546.

Cox, R. W. (1985). Organizing for innovation, Paper presented at the annual conference of the American Society for Public Administration, Indianapolis, 2.

Downs, G. W. Jr, and Mohr, L. B. (1979). Toward a theory of innovation, *Administration and Society 10(4)*: 379–408.

Eyestone, R. (1977). Confusion, diffusion and innovation, *American Political Science Review 71*, 441–447.

Golden, O. (1990). Innovation in public sector human services programs: the implications of innovation by groping along, *Journal of Policy Analysis and Management 9(2)*: 219–248.

Gray, V. (1973). Innovations in the states: a diffusion study, *American Political Science Review 67*: 1174–1185.

Innovations in American Government: Achieving Excellence and Building Trust (1997), John F. Kennedy School of Government, Harvard University, Cambridge, MA.

Light, P. (1992). Surviving innovation: thoughts on the organizational roots of innovation and change, Paper presented at the Innovations and Organization Conference, University of Minnesota.

Nice, D. C. (1984). *Policy Innovation in State Government*, Iowa State University, Ames.

Polsby, N. W. (1984). *Political Innovation in America: the Politics of Policy Initiation*, Yale University Press, New Haven, CT.

Schall, E. (1991). Why innovate: reflections from the field, Paper delivered at the conference on the Fundamental Questions of Innovation, Duke University, Durham, NC.

Spart, A. (1997). State-federal relations: the vertical diffusion of state policy innovations, Paper delivered at the annual meeting of the American Political Science Association, Washington, DC, Aug. 28–31.

Walker, J. L. (1969). The diffusion of innovations among the American states, *American Political Science Review 63*: 880–899.

Welch, S., and Thompson, K. (1980). The impact of federal incentives on state policy innovations, *Journal of Politics, 24(4)*: 715–729.

11
Productivity Management in State Governments

Evan M. Berman
University of Central Florida, Orlando, Florida

INTRODUCTION

Productivity improvement efforts are being increasingly used to ensure that state agencies are effective, efficient, and responsive. Examples of new improvement strategies are found in many state transportation, social services, corrections, environmental protection, financial management, health, and other agencies. Productivity improvement efforts during the 1990s emphasized performance measurement, partnerships, realignment, empowerment, quality management, and information technology. These strategies help address some key problems of many state agencies because of the need to increase public confidence in public services in an era of tightly constrained resources, heightened public expectations, and demand for services. For example, performance measurement increases public accountability, partnerships enhance the level and efficiency of service delivery, and information technology increases access by users to state government services, and the timeliness of service transactions.

This chapter examines a wide range of productivity improvement strategies in state governments. The first part addresses productivity improvement efforts which improve service outcomes and effectiveness. Citizens, clients, and others who interact with state organizations are increasingly impatient with sloppy or untimely public services. They want results, and many users and vendors are especially impatient with bureaucrats who emphasize rule compliance over effectiveness. The second part discusses strategies for streamlining delivery processes and increasing efficiency. This part focuses on reengineering efforts and traditional uses of productivity improvement tools. It also discusses the use of partnerships. The third part examines new uses of information technology. Rapid improvements and diffusion of this technology created new opportunities for productivity improvement that were scarcely imaginable a decade ago. This chapter does not discuss strategic planning.

Definition. Productivity is defined as the effective and efficient use of resources to achieve outcomes (Berman, 1998; Morley, 1986; Rosen, 1993; Newland, 1972). In this regard, effectiveness is defined as the level of outcomes, for example, as the percentage of vehicle users who travel at safe speeds on state roads, the percentage of welfare recipients who find jobs within six months, the health of the environment, and so on. These outcomes reflect long-term achievements or goals. Efficiency is defined as the ratio of outputs to inputs (e.g., the number of citations issued per inspector). Outputs are defined as the immediate result of activities (e.g., the number of citations issued). Whereas outcomes concern long-term goals, outputs are short-term objectives which, in turn, cause outcomes. The distinction between outputs and outcomes is important in public organizations, because although the public often values effectiveness, public organizations often have more control over outputs than outcomes.

Fundamental differences exist between productivity improvement in public organizations and for-profit corporations. Public organizations, including state governments, often are more concerned with effectiveness than efficiency (Berman, 1998). Citizens care more about the public safety, effective education, environmental safety, health regulation, and other state activities than the efficiency with which these services are provided. For example, consumers often care more about the safety of the food supply than the cost of maintaining that safety. Likewise, parents are foremost concerned about the poor quality of public education, rather than its cost. This is not to say that efficiency is unimportant; proposals for productivity improvement efforts often find greater support when they result in efficiency increases, as well. Yet efficiency is often of greater concern in business because of its singular focus on profitability. It follows that business productivity improvement strategies must be adapted to the different purposes of public organizations.

A second difference is that public organizations and services often affect a greater multitude of stakeholders, and that many stakeholders must be consulted in public decision-making processes. Such broad, public consultative processes slow down improvement efforts but are nevertheless critical to successful implementation. For example, changes in state teacher licensing provisions are apt to generate much public discussion. Public managers who wish to raise teaching standards must provide ample opportunity for input from many stakeholders such as teachers, school districts, and teachers' unions, and managers should probably plan for legal challenges as well. State agencies must also frequently deal with myriad intergovernmental actors, including federal agencies, municipalities and counties, special districts and public authorities (e.g., school districts, airports, water management districts, hospital districts), and other state organizations. Consultative processes are further complicated by the different priorities of various stakeholders. The interests of state regulators, teachers, and school districts are seldom aligned. Consequently, many productivity improvement address a multitude of objectives. By contrast, businesses seldom need to contend with such public and divergent issues. The challenge of productivity improvement is therefore often greater in state agencies than in private corporations.

History of Productivity. The history of productivity spans almost a century (Bouckaert, 1992). Berman (1998) discusses five periods in the development of productivity improvement strategies. Each period is characterized by unique challenges and the development of productivity improvement strategies to address these challenges. Many strategies are still relevant today. The first period of "industrialization" (1900–1939) concerned the challenges of building large organizations. Hierarchical designs were used by many state agencies in developing their functions during this period and thereafter. Procedures were also developed for rationalizing the work processes of large organizations. The second period, World War II (1939–1945), dealt with the challenge of rapid, high-quality production. Processes were developed for quality assurance, including inspection processes which are still used by many regulatory agencies. The third period, "controlled growth" (1945–1965), dealt with the challenge of ensuring controls of large bureaucracies by top managers and elected officials. The "solution" involved program and performance budgeting which, in adapted form, is often the foundation of performance measurement today. The fourth period, "program analysis," provided additional tools for solving problems of resource allocation and strategic planning, which is the focus of another chapter of this book. The present period, "Quality Paradigm," from 1980 onwards, emphasizes effectiveness, efficiency, and public trust through strategic interventions in work processes, human relations, and governance. The backbone of the Quality Paradigm is Total Quality Management (TQM), which is a comprehensive effort of client orientation, performance measurement, empowerment, and reengineering. Often, TQM is followed by specific efforts in each of these areas. In addition, rationalization processes of the first period are finding renewed use, including process analysis. This period further includes efforts in privatization, partnerships, and the use of information technology.

The introduction of new productivity improvement often occurs piecemeal and intermittently. There is some evidence that productivity improvement efforts are most likely to occur in state governments during waves of economic decline. For example, Chackerian (1996) notes that statewide reorganizations are relatively rare events, occurring about once every 25 years, and that they do tend to occur in economic down times. Likewise, Berman (1994) notes that TQM efforts are frequently driven by budget pressures and governor interest in strategic planning and other productivity improvement efforts. In addition, Chackerian notes that statewide reorganizations often occur when governors are in competition with legislatures for control of the executive branch. Chi (1992) and Garnett (1980) also note political motives of governors to increase their control. However, Berman (1994) finds that although governors play an important role in legitimatizing TQM, agency directors and senior managers often lead productivity improvement efforts. These divergent findings about the role of chief executives may reflect the level at which different productivity improvement efforts occur: TQM efforts typically target program-level activities and policies that affect them, whereas reorganizations affect agency-wide organizational structures and policies.

Although some observers believe that productivity improvement efforts are fads, anecdotal evidence suggests that many productivity improvement efforts do produce change and eventually find widespread use (Chi, 1997; Walters, 1996; Lee, 1991). For example, even though at the present time TQM is no longer the "strategy du jour," many state agencies have become more customer oriented in the past decade. Likewise, partnerships evolved from a novelty to a business-as-usual approach, and employee empowerment is no longer a controversial idea but a reality in many workplaces. The result of past productivity improvement efforts is thus an amalgam of various management practices that are part of management education and folklore. Managers are expected to be familiar with the above productivity improvement strategies. Similarly, many states are now promoting performance measurement in their agencies, and managers are expected to be familiar and have expertise in implementing them. Present performance measurement efforts build upon previous efforts which increased accountability and information about program outcomes. As in the past, the new performance measurement efforts are likely to further increase expectations about program information and accountability.

Managers need to know how contemporary productivity improvement efforts can aid them and how they can be made to work. The usefulness of productivity improvement strategies furthers their use and diffusion across organizations. In this regard, a 1993 survey of early TQM efforts in state education, health, transportation, welfare, and corrections agencies found that although one-third of respondents who implemented these improvements felt that it was still to early to tell, among managers who did provide assessments, better than three-quarters agreed that it had had positive impacts on productivity, group decision-making processes, and commitment to stakeholders, as well as increased the availability of information for decision making and the ability of managers to achieve improvements in the presence of resource constraints (Berman, 1994). Such findings show that productivity improvement often helps managers to address their objectives.

I. EMPHASIZING OUTCOMES, NOT EFFORTS

A. Client Orientation

The Quality Paradigm that was developed in the 1980s grew out of client and citizen frustration with the poor quality of services and unnecessary red tape. Public concern followed reports of unsatisfactory outcomes of children who were the recipients of the oversight of state social services, escapes of inmates from state prisons which were commanding high costs per inmate, long delays in state-run programs that sought to resolve traffic congestion, poor oversight of food safety in public schools and restaurants, and graduating students in public high schools who were years behind their reading and science levels. These concerns caused many governors and public managers to ensure that programs produced outcomes that were timely, relevant, without error, cost-effective, and competitive with alternative providers or the practices of other states. Recent productivity improvement efforts often emphasize an increase in client responsiveness.

It should be noted, though, that concerns about client satisfaction are endemic to organizations throughout the United States, not only state agencies. Efforts to increase client satisfaction begun in multinational firms that faced Japanese competition in the 1970s. When U.S. consumers turned away from domestic products that were perceived as substandard, U.S. firms countered with the introduction of new management strategies that aimed to increase customer satisfaction through improved product quality and customer service. Domestic service organizations followed the lead of multinational organizations, including the federal government in the late 1980s. These organizations focused on making services more relevant, timely, and cost-effective for its customers. Since the early 1990s, many state and local governments have also implemented TQM (Berman, 1994). It can be argued that educational and nonprofit organizations are among the last of institutions in the United States to address client satisfaction issues. Client orientation is often the focus of initial TQM efforts, which is a comprehensive strategy of client orientation, performance measurement, empowerment, and reengineering. Typically, initial TQM efforts are followed by detailed customer service initiatives, which are reenforced in subsequent efforts such as performance measurement and reengineering.

Client orientation involves three general questions:

1. Which client (or stakeholder) groups do programs impact?
2. What are the needs of these client groups?
3. To what extent do programs satisfy client needs and expectations?

These question have significant implications for state administration. Many state programs have a multitude of stakeholders including program clients, citizens, legislators, and other public agencies. Often, program managers have only incidental contact with the broad range of stakeholders that are affected by their programs. For example, state transportation planning engineers often work closely with other agencies and counties, more so than with citizens, elected officials, business, and even some cities. However, the support of these groups is increasingly critical, especially in an era of tight resources and heightened environmental consciousness. For this reason, the Minnesota Department of Transportation now seeks community support in early stages of its road proposals. By identifying and involving stakeholders in planning and delivery process, public managers better identify stakeholder needs and concerns. This is critical to stakeholder support, and also results in more responsive programs. Likewise, many state environmental regulators are increasingly involving civic leaders in their environmental planning and decision making (Arrandale, 1997). Clients of corrections departments include communities in which inmates are released. By engaging in dialogue with communities, correction departments better identify community concerns and often avail themselves of community resources that may result in better work-release programs.

Managers learn about stakeholder needs through focus groups, in-depth conversations, and public debate. The emphasis of these interactions should be on stakeholder needs, rather than the state programs. This is because many stakeholders know little about state programs, and what they do know is sometimes stated in terms of complaints rather the than missions, goals, and objectives of programs. Also, knowledge of stakeholder needs helps managers to better assess their programs. Whiteley and Hessan (1996) make a useful distinction about the types of needs that clients have based on their relationship with service providers. Services that require infrequent interactions and which involve little in-depth knowledge often require staff to be courteous and effective. However, when relationships are on-going and involve in-depth expertise by service providers, clients expect staff to be courteous and effective and to have higher commitment to client goals. Service providers must also have a high level of specialized expertise that is relevant to client problems. Thus, expectations and needs vary considerably for these different kinds of relations.

Some clients of state agencies are involuntary and others are internal rather than external. Businesses are voluntary clients of state economic development agencies when they submit grant applications, but they are the involuntary clients of business regulators. Client orientation suggests that regulators should consider their subjects as clients. Involuntary clients have needs, as well. They need to know what information to present, which deadlines exist, what they can do to avoid delays and complications, to whom they should address inquiries, and so on. State regulators avoid problems and reduce often negative perceptions by being responsive to these concerns. State prison inmates have very similar needs. In many instances client orientation reduces costs, as well. By providing accurate and timely information, agencies reduce rework, complaints, and appeals. It should be noted that clients are sometimes internal. Staff offices such as human resources management or purchasing have mainly internal clients, namely, the departments that utilize their services. Applying the concept of internal clients often leads to superior service and minimizes friction among departments and their staff members.

The fact that state agencies have many clients sometimes leads to conflicting priorities. For example, should public health agencies provide increased resources for alleviating the symptoms of AIDS, or should they increase their resources for education and awareness efforts that reduce the spread of this virus? The objectives reflect the priorities of different stakeholder groups. AIDS patients and service providers have an interest in the former, whereas parents of young children may prefer the latter. Examples of conflicting demands are sometimes raised to illustrate a problem of client orientation (Denhardt, 1993; Linden, 1992). These dilemmas must be resolved through processes of consultation and reasoned judgment. In these instances, managers must prioritize competing demands and strike a balance across different needs.

Many state agencies are now routinely undertaking customer satisfaction surveys. In the above-mentioned 1993 survey of state agencies, 73% of respondents report that customer and client surveys are regularly used in their agency, and about 30% of respondents indicate that they are regularly used in more than half of agency units. Also, 79% of agencies identify customer needs, and 60% monitor customer satisfaction (Berman, 1994). Agencies also use other means of feedback from clients and citizens, such as focus groups, client contact reports, toll-free numbers phone numbers and "hot lines," ombudsmen, suggestion boxes, e-mail, and complaint tracking mechanisms. It is important to distinguish between client feedback mechanisms as a form of quality assurance, and sample surveys of client and citizen attitudes. Whereas the former assist in identifying problems and dissatisfaction among individual clients, only sample surveys provide a valid measure of the satisfaction of the client base.

B. Performance Measurement

In recent years, performance measurement is increasingly used. Berman (1994) reports that 71% of state agencies monitor their internal performance and that 46% engage in some form of benchmarking. Performance measurement is a strategy for focusing on outcomes rather than efforts, workloads, and inputs. For example, rather than measuring the workload of processing applications or being responsible for a growing number of inmates, performance measurement requires that employees and managers identify and measure outcomes, such as the percentage of applications that are corrected or processed, or the percentage of functionally illiterate inmates that have been taught to read and write and even use computers. Many agencies that use performance measurement compare their progress over time, but some agencies also compare their performance against that of other organizations, some of which are leading or have "best practices." Such comparisons are referred to as "benchmarking."

Performance measurement is consistent with client orientation because it helps managers focus on client needs. Ammons (1995) also notes some other purposes. Performance measurement increases accountability to citizens and elected officials. Performance measurement further assists in planning, for example, by providing information about trends in service demands or the allowing managers to identify trends in the service costs, including costs per unit. Performance measurement is also used in the oversight of contractors as part of contract management. Contractors are increasingly required to provide evidence of their accomplishments, rather than of mere effort. For example, state billing services that are contracted out are increasingly required to meet a minimum collection rate, and incentives are provided for performing that expectation. This is very different from paying collecting agencies based on their efforts alone.

Statewide performance measurement efforts are often driven by the need to show accountability to citizens. Implementation efforts are frequently overseen by state budgeting offices or governors' offices. A well-known example is Oregon Benchmarks, which provides citizens with a wide range of indicators relevant to their well-being. The governor's office of the State of Florida created a commission on government accountability to the people which since 1993 produces annual reports that cover seven major areas: families and communities; public safety; learning; health; economy; environment; and government. Like other states, Florida created several task forces of citizens, business leaders, and others to identify and design its performance measures. The Florida effort now includes over 225 indicators. For example, indicators of public safety include both public surveys about the perception of safety and objective data about the number of different types of violent crimes. The Florida benchmarks report also includes a measure of public trust in its government (State Legislatures, 1995).

Some states are also making performance measurement part of their budget reforms. Agencies are required to submit annual performance measures which aid budget offices in making allocation decisions. In Arizona, performance measurement is also tied to its state strategic planning efforts. Various state legislatures are showing an interest as well. In Texas and Oregon, legislators are now examining ways in which performance measures can be incorporated in their appropriation processes. At the present time, the outcomes of these accountability and budget reform efforts have not yet been evaluated. However, statewide reports often receive little media coverage and hence probably have little impact on public attitudes. Also, while agency directors provide the requested performance-based information to budget staff and legislators, doing so does not imply that these requests change internal expectations and decision-making processes of agencies. Another problem is that these budget reforms do not supplant budget decision making processes which are often political in nature.

As a tool of productivity improvement, performance measurement must support and reenforce outcome orientations at the program level (Hatry and Fisk, 1992). Performance measurement is but one of several productivity tools to increase outcome orientation, and its effectiveness may lie, first, in increasing awareness about the importance of service outcomes and identifying specific, measurable outcomes and, second, in the axiom that "what gets measured, gets done." To increase the impact of this productivity improvement strategy, program managers are frequently asked by their superiors to focus on key areas of client needs and to monitor progress. Program managers further instill outcome and client orientation by bringing managers together with clients, employees, and others to discuss key issues in responsiveness and measures of accountability. An important operational issue in performance measurement is the extent to which it can be conducted in real time and with few additional resources: as discussed further, information technology facilitates the collection and analysis of program data. Performance measurement conducted on an ongoing basis provides more improvement opportunities for managers than evaluations or client feedback surveys that are conducted on a periodic basis.

An example of program-level performance measurement is Kentucky's Center for Adult Education and Literacy (1997). Some measures concern outcomes of program participants, such as the percentage of program participants in civic or community activities, those who take GED tests and pass GED exams, and the percentage of participants who participate in school-related conferences of their school-age children (grades 1–12). This center has also received a federal grant to coordinate these measures with other providers of adult education. These data are readily collected by program officials on a periodic basis, and are accompanied by benchmarks or standards for future performance. For example, whereas in 1995 only 25% adults with school-age children participate in school-related conference, the program seeks to raise this percentage to be 45% in 2001 and 58% by 2005. Wholey (1994) provides a detailed description of outcomes for Tennessee's prenatal program.

Some criteria for performance measures is that they should be relevant, controllable, and valid. *Relevant* means that they should pertain to the mission of programs, and *controllable* means that managers must be able to shape their programs to increase the attainment of benchmarks. Thus, for example, whereas the "percentage of a population that possesses basic skills required by employers" is a relevant performance measure for policy makers and program advocates, it is not a relevant measure for program managers of adult education efforts because their programs do not provide adequate control over the composition of the population which affects program performance. Macrolevel performance measures often deal with the population as a whole, whereas program-level measures must focus on the client groups that are being served. Program-level performance measurement includes detailed concern for program delivery processes and the need for different outcomes to satisfy the needs of different groups. By focusing on such detailed measures, program managers are able to better address their clients' needs.

Finally, performance measurement is increasingly part of personnel management policies. For example, GeorgiaGain is an improvement effort that began in 1992 and which requires managers to define performance measures for employee rewards and promotion. Managers are required to develop a performance plan for employees and to periodically provide them with feedback about their progress. The attainment of performance standards is linked to merit-based, pay-for-performance policies. An important component of GeorgiaGain is measures of customer satisfaction and the retention of fee-for-service clients. Employees are expected to achieve specific service outcomes rather than merely following rules and procedures. To this end, employees receive considerable training to adapt to their new roles and responsibilities, for example, toward identifying and implementing service improvements. Performance measures are established for these activities, as well (Madler, 1997).

C. Empowerment

Empowerment is increasingly used as a strategy to increase outcome-orientation and accountability. Empowerment is defined as the delegation of decision-making responsibilities to lower units and employees while holding them accountable for producing outcomes. Productivity improvement results lie in the reduced need for sustained supervision by managers of employees and lower units, as they are better able to tailor services to client and stakeholder needs. The result is further cost savings by reducing staff involvement and rework. Although empowerment is used to further outcome orientation among employees, in recent years it has also been used to increase the accountability and responsiveness of district offices. By delegating (i.e., decentralizing) authority and decision making, district managers are held accountable for increasing their responsiveness to their constituencies. Another use of empowerment concerns relations with contractors. State agencies are increasingly giving contractors greater leeway in performing their services, while holding them accountable for performance and compliance with process-based regulations. Such contractor relationships are discussed in a subsequent section on partnerships.

According to Berman (1994), 83% of agencies have some employee empowerment effort. Empowerment increases client orientation because it enables employees to tailor services to the needs of clients. People want to have their differences respected, and the bureaucratic practice of treating everybody fairly often leads to equal and impersonal treatment that produces high levels of dissatisfaction (Johnston, 1993). Empowered employees have greater freedom to determine service objectives and procedures in consultation with clients. Employee empowerment increases timeliness, because it reduces the need for employees to consult with their superiors prior to making service delivery decisions. The basic steps of employee empowerment are to decide what should be delegated and why; who should be empowered; ensure adequate resources; address reducing employee uncertainty over policy, processes, and rewards; creating a pilot effort; monitoring initial results; and make adjustments.

A frequent mistake in employee empowerment efforts is to assume that employees welcome empowerment. Behn (1997) notes that being an accountability holder can be fun, because managers get to check up on others. But being an accountability holdee increases the risk of punishment. Therefore, employee empowerment presupposes a culture of fairness in rewards and punishments, and a tolerance for the innovations and mistakes that often accompany it. Empowerment requires managers to renegotiate with their employees about mutual expectations, rewards, and processes for dealing with changes. These are sometimes called *psychological contracts*, and they concern matters that go beyond legal employment contracts. When employees perceive a culture of fear, they will be reluctant to undertake initiative that gives empowerment its payoff. In these instances, managers must proceed piecemeal to rebuild employee trust in their organizations. Managers must further deal with employees who lack enthusiasm and energy, or who merely want to "go by the rules" and produce no more than minimally necessary to continue collecting their salary. Managers will need to consistently and persistently explain the need for change and provide explicit and simple guidance (Berman, 1995a).

An important concern is also that empowerment does not eliminate safeguards against discrimination and prejudice. Fairness of access, service, treatment, and, in some instances, outcomes, remains important in public organizations. Traditional rules and regulations aim to ensure these outcomes by proscribing certain service procedures and criteria. Empowerment requires less constraining rules and a different, outcome-oriented approach to ensure equality. Restrictive directives are typically replaced by policies that promote increased customer responsiveness, documentation of service efforts and outcomes, choice in service delivery, and mechanisms to address complaints in a fair and timely manner. These alternative strategies provide clients with the means to ensure equality, and consequences for employees who do follow these policies. Likewise, it also helps ensure that employees are treated fairly and equitably by their supervisors. It is important that alternative strategies be clearly identified, because employees, as well as managers, need to know the processes and standards to which they are held accountable.

The concept of empowerment is not limited to employees, and many states have made it part of recent decentralization efforts. For example, during the 1970s, many states consolidated their different welfare services into single agencies or umbrella organizations in order to maximize the efficiency of support services (e.g., central purchasing, centralized training) and to increase the political clout of this state function. However, in recent years the trend has been toward decentralization for increased responsiveness to local populations. Decentralization is made possible in part by increased contracting out, which reduces the need for central support functions. Information technology allows branch operations to access the same information as central offices and to make decisions in the same timely manner. Decentralization also reflects a desire to increase local participation in decision making and funding in efforts that benefit them (Berman, 1995).

The empowerment of district offices is coupled with accountability and expectations that services will be responsive and adequate to meet local needs. Although states vary in the degree that they empower their field offices, the idea is that empowerment should reduce delays by central office participation in decision making. Central office staff, instead, emphasize oversight by holding district offices accountable, for example, through performance measurement, as well as a continuing role in providing support services that are not readily or efficiently decentralized such as legal services, management training, and staff relations with elected officials. Key to successful empowerment of district offices is to ensure that the responsibilities between central offices and district offices are clearly defined. Empowerment of district offices requires a "contract" which specifies the responsibilities and duties of each. Although such contracts are not always written, they are nevertheless key to maintaining workable relationships between district and central offices. For example, many field offices now enjoy greater flexibility in their recruiting and training practices, yet it is important that accountability and oversight for these functions are clearly established with central HRM offices.

II. STREAMLINING DELIVERY PROCESSES, INCREASING EFFICIENCY

A. Reengineering

Reengineering is a comprehensive approach to organizing that examines the entire process of service delivery. It examines the way in which agencies aim to achieve their missions, including specific delivery processes that are used for this purpose. Reengineering is a "blank-slate" approach that typically identifies the best way to organize existing resources to accomplish missions. Reengineering is grounded in organization principles, namely, that (1) delivery processes should be organized around outcomes, not efforts; (2) the number of steps in delivery processes should be reduced whenever possible; (3) information should be captured early and once, and at the source; and (4) processes should be conducted in parallel when this speeds up the delivery process. In addition, reengineering may include a review of existing service objectives to achieve outcomes (Champy and Hammer, 1993; Hyde, 1995).

In many states, welfare reform has involved both mission review and redesign of delivery processes. In the past, many welfare delivery processes were organized around the problem of correctly determining the eligibility of welfare recipients—a main output. As a result, many welfare programs assigned their employees to compliance-related activities, thereby deemphasizing efforts that help people find jobs. Today, limits on the duration of welfare in many states have freed up resources that enable agencies to devote more employees to programs that help people find jobs. For example, Florida and some other states now offer comprehensive counseling programs and job search assistance programs, as well as profiling to better identify workers who might benefit from different levels and types of job retraining and counseling. Driven by public dissatisfaction with the cost and outcomes of existing programs, these reforms reflect a fundamental rethinking of program objectives and activities.

Many new programs also incorporate reengineering principles to increase streamlining and efficiency. Past welfare eligibility processes often required recipients to deal with multiple caseworkers who had little follow-up with recipients. While each employee was held accountable for his or her part of the process, none could be held accountable for ensuring that recipients undertook the steps that were necessary to find new employment. Reengineering suggests that activities should be organized outcomes which is, in this instance, reemployment. Some agencies now provide a single point of contact which brings together all necessary services and regulations to recipients. These caseworkers are held accountable for ensuring that recipients get the services that are available and relevant to produce the result. Recipients are assigned to these caseworkers for the duration of their reemployment efforts; when multiple caseworkers are needed because of unique expertise, teams are created. Likewise, regulatory processes are increasingly organized by providing a single point of contact and accountability that brings together all rules, requirements, processes, and resources to help applicants comply with regulatory requirements.

Another reengineering principle is that information should be captured early and once, at the source. In traditional organizations, information is often captured multiple times; for example, the name, qualifications, needs, and plans of welfare recipients are captured by each separate department or unit as its service is utilized. Consequently, a complete profile of the recipient is difficult to assemble and seldom available. Moreover, welfare recipients benefit by having accurate information about job opportunities, requirements, and future eligibility requirements at the earliest possible moment. Today, information technology makes it possible to capture information once by making it available to all service providers. Likewise, information about employment opportunities can be captured and related to the profile of welfare recipients. Employers can search and scan among profiles of eligible recipients. Information should also be provided to welfare recipients at an early moment, so that they can make better choices about their reemployment strategies.

Reengineering also suggests that processes should be structured to produce timely outcomes. In the above example, rather than delaying reemployment services until various eligibility issues are determined, services should be provided that help unemployed persons "get back on track," such as job skill assessments, access to job banks and referral services, and information about welfare services. Moreover, many of these services should be provided in parallel fashion, rather than sequentially. There is little reason from the perspective of outcomes to delay information about job opportunities until recipients have been duly informed of welfare services and regulations. It is also important to reduce the number of steps that are required for recipients to obtain services, since each step delays the outcome. Reengineering suggests that processes often become lengthier as a result of involving more employees which, in turn, seems to justify more frequent inspections. In this regard, the number of employees is reduced by organizing around outcomes and using single points of client contact. The number of inspections is further decreased by focusing accountability on outcomes rather than compliance with rules and regulations. This is because most processes have fewer outcomes than rules and regulations that might be violated (Edwards et al., 1996).

The quality of processes is important, too. The legacy of early TQM efforts and so-called quality circles is the increased awareness that service mistakes are quite costly because of rework, the accompanying use of more inspection, and customer dissatisfaction, which increases client complaints, grievances, and litigation. This last is undesirable and also increases costs. It follows that efficient service delivery is increased by producing services with zero errors in state agencies and organizations (Berman and West, 1997). Many state agencies have quality teams whose purpose is to (1) examine the quality of service processes, (2) make recommendation for their improvement, and (3) implement improvements. The term "quality" is usually defined as conformance, performance, accuracy, timeliness, and reliability of services. For example, in 1995, the State of Oklahoma had 182 employee teams which examined problems and quality improvement opportunities in 15 agencies. Of these teams, 41% were in the department of health and human services, and others in commerce (15%) and safety and security (12%). Agency savings as a result of 63 earlier projects was $16.7 million (Oklahoma, 1995). Poister and Harris (1997) discuss how TQM efforts in the Pennsylvania department of transportation reduced service backlogs and increased labor productivity. They calculate the return of quality improvement efforts to be about 35% in that agency.

Some quality improvement projects target administrative processes that consume inordinate amounts of staff time. For example, in the mid-1990s, the Michigan department of corrections estimated that it processed monthly 176,000 forms of 1267 different types (Berman, 1994). Employees' suggestions reduced the number and variety of forms. Other quality team activities identify process reasons for customer complaints. By focusing on processes rather than symptoms, organizations can make fundamental improvements in their delivery systems, for example, suggesting single point of contact and other process reengineering approaches mentioned above. Still other efforts involve surveys of customers to generate ideas for quality improvement objectives. For example, business customers often want speedier and clear responses to their inquiries and applications. As a result, many economic development programs now have streamlined processes that provide fast turnaround.

Quality improvement efforts require considerable training in the new approaches. Many training efforts in the early 1990s emphasized statistical techniques for process analysis. For example, Pareto charts are bar charts of the number of problems or complaints that services generate. Pareto bar charts are quite useful tools, because they focus attention on problems that are frequent, rather than infrequent. They also provide a means to evaluate improvements. Tools include cause-and-effect analysis which helps employees and managers think through the causes of poor service delivery processes. Quality improvement is also consistent with empowerment, because it is based on the idea that those who are closest to processes and problems have the greatest knowledge to help identify meaningful improvements.

An important element of quality training is getting employees and their supervisors comfortable with the idea of team-based decision making, and providing employees with necessary power to make and implement various changes. Agencies vary in the extent they have provided such training. Among agencies that had formed a quality council or support team by 1994—a measure of commitment to TQM in the early 1990s—81% of efforts involved employee training in team skills and 85% provided training in quality techniques. However, among agencies that had not formed a quality council, only 44% and 45% had provided such training. Training is usually also provided for managers, and widespread training helps to create an appropriate climate for change. For example, in one recent example, the California department of corrections decided to first emphasize a culture that values and acts on the contributions of each individual. Senior managers and employees engaged in a two-year effort to revise policies and work relations to create an appropriate culture for subsequent change efforts (Battalino et al., 1996). Halachmi (1997) noted that organizations must be willing to embrace the implications of reengineering for undertaking subsequent process improvements and client orientation efforts before they undertake it. It is believed that agencies in which employees receive quality training and which practice empowerment are better prepared to engage in reengineering, as well.

B. Privatization, Partnerships

In recent years, privatization has received much attention as a productivity management tool, albeit with some shifting emphases. In the 1980s, the term "privatization" was often used to denote a general reduction in the role of government, such as through banking and airline deregulation. However, such deregulation led to imprudent risk taking by industry which is now held in disrepute. In the 1990s, privatization has come to mean increased private-sector competition for public services, and subsequent contracting for public services. The rationale for such privatization is that increased competition results in lower costs (Savas, 1992). Privatization is commonly used by many agencies to contract for such services as copying and printing, cafeteria services, cleaning and maintenance functions, and information technology systems maintenance. However, privatization is also used to contract out main services. Some well-known examples of privatization involve state corrections facilities that are run by private companies.

However, by both state and federal law, some public functions are prohibited from being contracted out. When the State of Colorado attempted to privatize its public University Hospital, the state supreme court ruled that this public organization could not abandon its public responsibility for indigent care and policy making; it could only contract for operational tasks. When the State of Texas sought to contract out the entirety of its intake processes for welfare, Medicaid, and other programs, the federal government ruled that eligibility determination must be done by public employees. Since then, other states have contracted out for selected reemployment and other services. In Wisconsin, the performance of district welfare offices is monitored and those that fail to meet performance standards are subject to competition by private service providers. Although few studies exist of cost savings as a result of privatization, the Texas intake proposal was worth about $2 billion over a five-year period and was expected to save the state about $10 million per month (Johnston, 1993; Lemov, 1997).

A concern with privatization is that private-sector providers may underbid contracts in order to obtain them. This may cause private organizations to underperform, as well as cause them to pressure public organizations for contract increases in subsequent years. To minimize these politics of contracting, public agencies are increasingly using performance-based standards for reimbursement of services. In addition, some agencies may choose to privatize no more than one-quarter of eligible services in any given contract period. This allows public agencies to improve service delivery and rebid for contracts in subsequent years.

Doing so also maintains the competition for services: the purpose of privatization is not to replace public monopolies with private ones.

Competition is used to reduce costs, but in some instances, agencies use partnerships to increase services and reduce costs. For example, the department of transportation in Minnesota has proposed new toll roads, run by private companies, to meet its transportation needs. Obviously, many aspects of these roads are coordinated in partnership with the state transportation agency. In similar fashion, the State of Florida has created new, self-supporting special districts that own and operate urban toll roads. While these districts are not privately owned, they behave in many ways as nonprofit, private organizations that must meet their payrolls and debt obligations. In both instances, state agencies attract new, paying constituents to expand service in processes that involve close cooperation. In similar fashion, many state economic development services use public-private partnerships to help plan their programs and, in some instances, support them through contributions for operations, marketing, or training. For example, the Ohio department of development developed a partnership with utility companies to bring their expertise to local companies to achieve energy cost savings. This partnership uses staff, resources, and expertise from a many different sources.

The use of partnerships to increase service is increasingly important. Some partnerships also involve planning and funding as primary objectives. Managing partnerships requires skills different from managing contracts, which often are arms-length transactions. By contrast, effective partnerships involve intensive management of client relations and a clear division of roles and responsibilities. Partnerships require managers to develop win-win relationships that affect significant interests or key missions of participants. Leaders need good negotiation and conflict management skills that are used for the purpose of building trustworthy relationships. Trust is essential to good working relationships, and managers must work toward ensuring that partnerships serve mutual interests in productive ways.

C. Cost-Saving Strategies

Managers continue to look for ways to reduce their expenditures. Many of the above productivity improvements take a strategic perspective on meeting stakeholder needs and providing services in an effective and efficient manner. In addition to these perspectives, managers also use other approaches to increase productivity. These efforts, discussed below, often emphasize cost reduction. Some tactics are traditional efforts that are finding renewed application (Washnis, 1980).

Personnel expenses make up a significant share of total expenditures in many organizations. Consequently, some productivity improvement initiatives focus on improving manpower allocation. A useful tool for this purpose is demand analysis. State agencies often face service demands that very according to time, day, month, or location. For example, many state parks have higher peak loads during weekends and the pleasant seasons of the year (that is, summer in most of the country, but off-summer in the South). By anticipating periods of peak demand, agencies improve their manpower resource allocation. For example, some state parks increase maintenance and preservation efforts during off-peak periods. Some agencies are also able to affect peak demands, which can be costly and often decrease client satisfaction due to backlogs and waiting times. Peak demands are often reduced by requiring or giving incentives to customers to schedule appointments at off-peak hours, as well as by using alternative means of communication. E-mail, the Internet, voice mail and mailed-in service requests allow staff to service these demands in off-peak periods. In selected instances, analytical techniques such as linear programming, queuing, and inventory analysis also used to optimize service schedules.

Agencies also use volunteers, interns, and temporary help to decrease costs. It is estimated that 100 million Americans donate their time each year. Volunteers are often used by nonprofit organizations. Semiretired persons provide an increasing pool of volunteers. Although volunteers are often used to save money, they can also be used to build bridges with constituents and clients. Some volunteers bring specialized expertise to agencies; others provide routine, low-skilled tasks. Volunteers are not a free resource, however. They require considerable recruitment, training, development, management, and evaluation, and agencies must address liability issues, as well. Moreover, because volunteers do not receive compensation, the quality of the job experience must be sufficient for them to want to serve. Interns are also used to reduce personnel costs. Interns look for opportunities that provide exposure and which are a springboard for career development. To further reduce personnel costs, many agencies also use temporary employees for incidental, clerical needs.

Agencies further reduce personnel costs by controlling the growth of benefits and salaries. In some states, salary adjustments are minimal and increasingly linked to merit performance rather than cost-of-living indices. From the perspective of productivity, the problem with low salary growth is that compensation may be too low to retain productive employees and attract top graduates. Thus, productivity suffers in the long term. In Florida, the problem of low salary increases is somewhat reduced by the attractiveness of the location (year-round warm weather) and a 10-year vesting period for retirement benefits: employees who leave employment prior to this period lose most of their retirement benefits. This policy gives underpaid employees an incentive to work for at least 10 years before leaving the state system.

State agencies also use nonpersonnel strategies to reduce costs. For example, state agencies sometimes reduce expenditures by leasing rather than purchasing. The legal issue in leasing is usually that they must be treated as current obligations rather than long-term debt. To this end, many leases contain nonap-propriation clauses which terminate the lease in the event that states fail to pro-vide funding for the lease (Wallison, 1996). Other strategies involve ongoing audits of operating expenses, such as photocopying, telephone, travel, energy, and rents. These expenses can be quite substantial, and cost savings are some-times possible through alternative providers or plans. Travel costs are also some-times reduced through better planning. Computer purchases and maintenance are increasingly important, too, as discussed in the following section.

Finally, some states use comprehensive reorganizations and agency down-sizing to try to control costs. These efforts help governors increase their control over executive agencies by streamlining decision-making processes and reducing senior decision makers (Chi, 1992; Conant, 1993). In theory, comprehensive reor-ganizations save costs by combining disparate organizations into fewer agencies that have economies of scale for some staff functions. However, increased em-powerment and use of information technology suggests that such mega-depart-ments may in fact slow down service delivery and create new problems. Thus, according to Chi (1992), less than 25% of reorganization attempts actually result in cost savings, in part because reorganizations are often incomplete due to politi-cal pressures, drawn out over many years, and because savings are reinvested in new programs. Agency downsizing produces many of the same results, as well as increased client dissatisfaction due to service disruptions. Therefore, many experts now advise state governments to pursue cost savings by focusing on agen-cies on their core missions and by using reengineering, empowerment, and pro-ductivity improvement strategies to improve the cost-effectiveness of service de-livery.

III. INFORMATION TECHNOLOGY

Many state agencies have significant investments in information technology (IT). Although many applications of IT involve traditional uses such as word pro-cessing, spreadsheet applications for budgeting, and interoffice e-mail, state agen-cies are increasingly making strategic uses of IT for productivity improvement, as well. IT is increasingly used to help clients better access state agency services. For example, Oregon's department of consumer and business services web site offers 24-hour access to department information. Internet use also provides easy access to myriad forms and regulations which can be electronically submitted and processed. E-mail speeds up communication between agency staff and cli-ents, and continuing improvements in encryption technology suggest that many clients will be able to access their personal, confidential information, as well, such as tax payments and traffic violations. In addition, in recent years many new IT applications connect or integrate different data bases. For example, California's office of emergency services (OES) developed a regional information management system (RIMS) that connects offices throughout California and which enables OES to track and direct EMS personnel to disasters in different locations. In Massachusetts, police officers are able to access an integrated network of law enforcement data bases from remote locations. Outstanding court orders, parole violations, unpaid parking tickets, and other information is automatically brought up within minutes upon entering a person's identification (Kittower, 1997).

These new IT applications increase productivity by reducing processing time and costs. However, they build upon the lessons of previous efforts as well as the presence of increasingly professional information technology staff and planning processes. In this regard, many states, as well as agencies, have developed information technology policies and budgets. Some states have chief information officers (CIOs) whose job is to ensure that agencies use IT resources in coordinated and efficient ways. This is necessary because information technology increasingly requires extensive integration. About 36 states have a CIO (Gurwitt, 1996). It should be noted that although state and local governments spent $34.5 billion on IT in 1996 (Enos, 1997), many productivity-enhancing applications of IT are increasingly inexpensive: for example, creating RIMS, mentioned above, cost less than $500,000 because of already existing computers and networks.

IT planning often results in a vision for state IT resources. For example, Texas has formulated an information technology vision that regards technology as an essential support structure for services, and which is committed to using it in innovative ways. The Texas effort seeks to coordinate services to citizens in efficient and effective ways, and bring electronic services to citizens in ways that meet their needs, while protecting individual privacy rights and making information technology easily available. Texas recognizes that while unit costs for information technology have continued to decrease, total expenditures rise as a result of new applications. To further its vision, the Texas department of information resources emphasizes the development of standards and guidelines to facilitate the interoperation and interconnection of various information systems; the development of structures to share information and access data networks; providing support to agencies in developing strategic plans for their information technology that are aligned with their visions; eliminating duplication in information technology; helping agencies to adopt cost savings measures by replacing paper forms and postal mail by electronic forms and communication; ensuring that new information technology projects are implemented in a timely and efficient manner; and developing equitable access to information that protects privacy rights.

Central, statewide IT organizations support agency information technology development and implementation, but agencies must engage in their own planning for information technology. Indeed, even within agencies, divisions and programs find that they must often develop their own technology efforts. The planning process for information technology requires a coherent vision of core agency missions, how agencies interact with clients and citizens, and delivery processes that can be improved through information technology applications. For example, although agencies sometimes pursue information technology in response to growing case loads and paperwork, creating a "paperless" office is but one application of information technology. Welfare agencies can also use IT to coordinate services to clients, monitor compliance, integrate with other data bases, and provide a point of access to employers. These applications are consistent with focusing on the needs of clients, rather than overburdened managers. They also require strategic thinking, rather than bandage approaches to management.

Ideas for new information technology projects are often simultaneously developed by different agencies throughout the country. Many agencies face similar challenges. IT managers in public organizations are increasingly organized and many share their experiences. Likewise, innovation networks of public managers help diffuse innovations. Though some managers learn of new innovation by participating in professional meetings and reading professional journals, others link to Internet web sites that are repositories of successful new innovations. One such example is the web site of the National Center for Public Productivity at Rutgers University.

In recent years, several lessons from past experiences have become increasingly important. In the past, IT applications were often designed for the use of senior managers and policy makers who used a larger mainframe to aggregate data. Today, information technology applications are designed bottom-up, from the perspective of employees and clients. For example, the Wisconsin department of transportation developed an expert IT system to analyze pavement treatment strategies. The developers failed to consult with engineers who would use the system and, as one consequence, the expert system required information that was unavailable to the engineers. The system quickly fell in disuse. Such errors can be avoided by involving users in the design and operation of system. Other problems occur when systems are designed that are complex and encompassing. Such systems require pilot testing and application, careful phase-in, and much training. By contrast, Oregon pulled the plug on an ambitious $48 million driver vehicle registration project after costs soared to $123 million. This project was designed to replace an antiquated mainframe. However, it was implemented during reengineering and downsizing, with little pilot testing and training. The lack of phase-in and small-scale testing resulted in great client dissatisfaction and eventual disuse. Agencies should replace their systems in a deliberate, piecemeal fashion with trail phases to reduce costs and frustration (Cohodas, 1997).

As state agencies continue to invest in information technology, expectations increase for evaluating the cost-effectiveness of information technology applications. However, it is often very difficult to show that information technology reduces total costs to agencies, because often information technology improves the quality of service and enables staff to handle more service transactions. Also, hardware and software often make up less than 40% of total investment costs, because other costs include training, conversion, maintenance, modification, installation, and consulting. Thus, even unit costs sometimes fail to decrease as a result of information technology.

In addition, expectations about the productivity and client orientation of IT staff increase. Many IT personnel have a technical training and orientation that does not always result in high levels of client satisfaction. IT staff must be trained to be client oriented, that is, be effective and courteous in dealing with client needs. End user satisfaction is key acceptance of IT services and application. In addition, as information technology units become more professional, so too does the need for them to use management tools that increase timeliness, efficiency, and accountability. Project management tools include accurate assessment of client needs, work charts that identify services and time frame for completion, and cost and accountability charts which show the cost of each activity and staff that is assigned to complete them. By applying these productivity improvement tools, as well as other productivity improvement strategies mentioned in this chapter, information technology units increase their effectiveness and efficiency.

IV. SUMMARY

Productivity improvement strategies help state agencies to become more effective, more efficient, and more responsive. Managers who wish to increase the productivity of their organizations should (1) identify core missions that respond to the needs of stakeholders and clients; (2) develop delivery processes that address these needs in the most timely, efficient, and effective manner using strategies of empowerment, reengineering, quality management, and information technology; and (3) provide accountability through performance measurement. In addition, managers who use the above strategies should inform themselves of implementation strategies and exemplary applications. Productivity improvement requires commitment from top management and input from employees, clients, and lower managers to ensure that they are used effectively.

REFERENCES

Ammons, D. (1995). *Accountability for Performance*, International City/County Managers Association, Washington, DC.

Arrandale, T. (1997). Brownfield blues, *Governing*, *10(10)*: 20–28.

Battalino, J., Beutler, L., and Shani, A. (1996). Large-system change initiative: transformation in progress at the California department of correction, *Public Productivity and Management Review*, *20(1)*, 24–44.

Behn, R. (1997). Holding people accountable, *Governing*, *10(10)*: 70.

Berman, E. (1998). *Productivity in Public and Nonprofit Organizations*, Sage Publications, Thousand Oaks, CA.

Berman, E. (1995). Implementing TQM in state welfare agencies, *Administration in Social Work*, *19(1)*: 55–72.

Berman, E. (1995a). Empowering employees in state agencies: a survey of progress, *International Journal of Public Administration*, *18(5)*: 833–850.

Berman, E. (1994). Implementing TQM in state governments: a survey, *State and Local Government Review*, *26(1)*: 46–53.

Berman, E., and West, J. (1997). Total quality management in local government, *Handbook of Local Government Administration* (J. Gargan, ed.), Marcel Dekker, New York, 213–238.

Bouckaert, G. (1992). Public productivity in retrospective, *Public Productivity Handbook* (M. Holzer, ed.), Marcel Dekker, New York, 15–45.

Cohodas, M. (1997). When it's best to pull the plug, *Governing 10(9)*: 64–65.

Conant, J. (1993). Executive branch reorganization, *The Book of The States 1992–1993* (Council of State Governments, ed.), Author: Lexington, KY, 64–73.

Chackerian, R. (1996). Reorganization of state governments: 1900–1985, *Journal of Public Administration research and Theory*, *6(1)*: 25–47.

Champy, J., and Hammer, M. (1993). *Reengineering the Corporation*, Nicholas Brady: London.

Chi, K. (1997). Innovations in state government, *The Book of The States 1996–1997* (Council of State Governments, ed.), Author: Lexington, KY, 537–544.

Chi. K. (1992). Trends in executive reorganization, *Spectrum: The Council of State Governments*, *65(2)*: 33–40.

Denhardt, R. (1993). *The Pursuit of Significance*, Wadsworth, Belmont, CA.

Edwards, R., Cook, P., and Reid, P. (1996). Social work management in an era of diminishing federal responsibility, *Social Work 41(5)*: 468–479.

Enos, G. (1996). Technology mega-deals, *Governing 10(4)*: 51–56.

Garnett, J. (1980). *Reorganizing State Government: The Executive Branch*, Westview Press, Boulder, CO.

Gurwitt, R. (1996). The new data czars, *Governing*, *10(3)*: 52–57.

Halachmi, A., and Bovaird, T. (1997). Process re-engineering in the public sector: learning some private sector lessons. *Technovation*, *17(5)*: 227–235.

Hatry, H, and Fisk, D. (1992). Measuring productivity in the public sector, *Public Productivity Handbook* (M. Holzer, ed.), Marcel Dekker, New York, 139–160.

Hyde, A. (1995). A primer on process reengineering, *Public Manager*, *24(1)*: 55–68.

Johnston, K. (1993). *Beyond Bureaucracy*, Business One Irwin, Homewood, IL.

Johnston, V. (1993). *Entrepreneurial Government: Privatization's Contributions Toward Re-Inventing Partnerships for Progress*. Paper presented at the American Association for Public Administration National Conference, San Francisco, July 17–21.

Kentucky Center for Adult Education and Literacy. (1997). Performance measurement initiative, Frankfort, KY, Oct 12.

Kittower, D. (1997). Winners that work, *Governing*, *10(11)*: 57–64.

Lee, R. (1991). Developments in state budgeting: trends of two decades, *Public Administration Review 3*: 257.

Lemov, P. (1997). The rocky road to privatizing welfare, *Governing, 10(10)*: 36–39.

Linden, R. (1992). Meeting which customers' needs?, *Public Manager, 21(4)*: 49–52.

Madler, L. (1997). Overview of GeorgiaGain and the performance measurement process, *Journal of Environmental Health, 59(9)*: 6–9.

Morley, E. (1986). *A Practitioner's Guide to Public Sector Productivity Improvement*, Van Nostrand Reinhold, New York.

Newland, C. (1972). Symposium on productivity in government, *Public Administration Review, 32(6)*: 739–850.

Oklahoma. (1995). *Quality Oklahoma Activities Report*, Office of Personnel Management, Quality Oklahoma Office.

Poister, T., and Harris, H. (1997). The impact of TQM on highway maintenance: benefit/cost implications, *Public Administration Review, 57(4)*: 294–302.

Rosen, E. (1993). *Improving Public Sector Productivity*, Sage Publications, Newbury Park, CA.

Savas, E. (1992). Privatization and productivity, *Public Productivity Handbook* (M. Holzer, ed.), Marcel Dekker, New York, 79–98.

State Legislatures. (1995). Six states show feds how to manage for results, *Author, 20* (May): 8.

Walters, J. (1996). Management by fad, *Governing, 9(12)*: 48–53.

Washnis, G. (1980). *Productivity Improvement Handbook for State and Local Government*, Wiley-Interscience, New York.

Wallison, F. (1996). The leasing option, *Governing, 9(12)*: 67–73.

Whiteley, R., and Hessan, D. (1996). *Customer Centered Growth*, Addison-Wesley, Reading, MA.

Wholey, J. (1994). Assessing the feasibility and likely useful of evaluation, *Handbook of Practical Program Evaluation* (J. Wholey, H. Hatry, and K. Newcomer, eds.), San Francisco, Jossey-Bass, 15–39.

12
Policy Research in State Government

Peter J. Haas
San José State University, San José, California

Like all governments, state governments in the United States operate with imperfect, incomplete information about the policies they seek to implement (Dye, 1984). Whereas most state government agencies and other institutions generally have fairly accurate information about how much money they are spending for a given policy or program, levels of awareness about many other aspects of public policy may be quite limited. State government has grown in size and complexity such that important details about the management, organization, and operation of a given policy area may be less than apparent to key decision makers.

Consider, for example, state policies toward the mentally ill. Most state governments have moved from the relatively simple (if inhumane) practice of essentially warehousing the chronically mentally ill to "deinsitutionalizing" such individuals to community-based treatment settings (Bardach, 1977). Although it represents a clear improvement in policy, deinstitutionalization also creates a potentially extremely complex administrative challenge: one state agency needs to supervise the transitioning of clients from state hospitals to communities; an-

I would like to thank the following individuals for their assistance in preparing this chapter: Bruce Gartner, Fiscal Policy Analyst for the Maryland Department of Transportation; Dr. Richard C. Elling, Dr. Lyke Thompson, and Roger Kempa of Wayne St. University; Robert Rotz, Senior Division Chief for the Virginia Joint Legislative Audit and Review Commission; Donna Crane, Director of Congressional Affairs for the American Public Health Association; and Joël Phillips, President of Evaluation, Management, and Training, Inc. Data from the American State Administrator Project were supplied by Deil S. Wright, University of North Carolina at Chapel, with the support of the Earhart Foundation, Ann Arbor, Michigan.

other may need to provide housing placements or ensure that existing housing is safe and appropriate; and yet another may be needed to provide vocational training and rehabilitation. Local governments and nonprofit agencies may also be involved in providing outpatient treatment and counseling to the mentally ill, and the federal government may be involved by means of various entitlement programs that benefit mentally disabled persons.

Such a complex policy arena may be difficult if not impossible for any one individual or agency to monitor at a meaningful level of detail. Moreover, state officials may lack fundamental information about even relatively simple and straightforward state policies. Decision makers may want to know how effective given policies or programs are, whether they are worth the costs to state taxpayers, if they could not be even better organized and more efficiently delivered. Faced with an array of policy options, they may want systematic analysis to help them make the best decision, or they may need forecasts about future conditions they can use to guide the policies of the present. They nearly always lack ready access to this sort of information (Dye, 1984).

This chapter explores various dimensions of the use of *policy research* to meet the information needs of state governments. Unfortunately, very little scholarly attention has been focused on the prevalence, context, and use of various forms of research in American government generally and in state government particularly. Existing work tends to address the methodology of policy research at the expense of describing and analyzing the actual context in which research activities occur (Haas and Springer, 1998).

I. WHAT IS POLICY RESEARCH?

To address the information needs noted, decision makers at all levels of government turn to various forms of research. Traditionally, two specific forms of research—policy analysis and program evaluation—have received special emphasis among scholars of public administration and public policy. Typically, "policy analysis" refers to prospective research that informs decisions yet to be made, whereas "program evaluation" is aimed retrospectively on assessing past policies and programs (Meltsner, 1976; Rist, 1990; Patton and Sawicki, 1993). To further complicate matters, closely related terms like "policy evaluation," "program analysis," and "policy studies" are frequently invoked to describe very similar if not identical policy research activities (Rist, 1990:4). Additionally, the term "audit" (and particularly "performance audit") is frequently used in the state government context to connote related research activities (Davis, 1990).

Whereas theoretical distinctions exist between these various forms of research, in practice they tend to blur because decision makers typically require policy-related information during all phases of the policy process, i.e., both prospectively and retrospectively—as well as amid implementation efforts (Dunn, 1994; Lee and Johnson, 1994; Haas and Springer, 1998). Moreover, decision makers frequently want more than one type of information and the same organization or individual may supply different types (Haas and Springer, 1998). As Meltsner (1976:72) comments, "the evaluator examining a particular program is a policy analyst in disguise."

A state legislative research agency might conduct a study of the state prison system that includes both program evaluation information (how well the prisons are being run, for example) and policy analysis (such as an assessment of options to improve the prison system). Such a study might also include other, more descriptive kinds of analysis as well as audit-oriented information. The various specific forms of research contained in the report stemming from this study would probably be transparent to its intended audience of state legislators and other decision-makers.

A more inclusive way of talking about the role of research for policy-related purposes is appropriate. *Policy research* is a general term that embraces the many information-gathering and processing activities that public agencies and their agents engage in to facilitate decision making (Putt and Springer, 1989; Haas and Springer, 1998). Policy research in its various forms is an increasingly important part of the ongoing effort to increase the efficiency and accountability of government (Lee and Johnson, 1994; Newcomer, 1996).

There are many specific forms of policy research and each research project may entail a unique form of research (Lee and Johnson, 1994:143). Bearing in mind the frequent blurring of distinctions among the more specific forms of policy research, those typically pursued by and for state governments include:

A. Program or Policy Evaluation

Program evaluation activities are generally intended to identify the impact, outcomes, or effectiveness of specific public programs. As one theorist states it, "the crux of [program evaluation] is a comparison of what did happen after implementing the program with what would have happened had the program never been implemented" (Mohr 1988:2–3). However, innumerable kinds of specific research activities are conducted under the rubric of program evaluation (Davis 1990:40).

B. Policy or Program Analysis

Policy analysis is particularly difficult to peg to a specific set of activities (Lee and Johnson, 1994). MacRae and Wilde (1979) define it as the "the use of reason and evidence to make the best decision." Some scholars link policy analysis to a specific "rational" model of decision making (MacRae and Wilde, 1979; Carley, 1980; Patton and Sawicki, 1993; Dunn, 1994); others liken it an art or craft, emphasizing the necessity for a more creative approach (Wildavsky, 1979). Most scholars, however, tend to agree that policy analysis involves research that supports the selection of the best policy or decision from a number of alternatives. Program analysis typically focuses on a narrower, program-based scope of alternatives (Carley, 1980; Hatry et al., 1987).

C. Performance Audits

Performance audits assess the economy, efficiency, and effectiveness of government organizations, programs, activities, and functions, and their compliance with state laws and regulations. Performance audits tend to focus on management control issues and must conform to Generally Accepted Government Auditing Standards (GAGAS) established by the U.S. General Accounting Office. However, performance audits are frequently confused with other forms of policy research (Davis, 1990).

II. LOCI OF POLICY RESEARCH IN STATE GOVERNMENT

Because the need for policy-related information is widespread, policy research is ubiquitous in state government. It springs from various institutions in and around state government; additionally, different kinds of individuals—including those from outside of state government—actually conduct policy research.

A. Institutions (Internal)

Policy research is conducted in a wide variety of settings and contexts in state government. However, its practice and presence are probably less institutionalized than at the federal level (Guston et al., 1998). As a rule, the national government has (1) more resources available to staff and fund policy research (Hatry et al., 1987; Davis, 1990), and (2) more programs of sufficient size to warrant the costs associated with policy research. Among the institutions of state government typically involved with policy research are:

> Gubernatorial and agency executive staff
> Legislative and legislative committee staff
> Legislative research agencies
> Consulting firms and consultants
> Universities/think tanks

Table 1 State Administrators Reporting an
Evaluation Unit in Their Agencies: 1978 and 1984
Surveys of State Administrators

	1978 (N = 1393)	1984 (N = 1191)
Percentage of responding agencies with evaluation units	40.5%	37.8%

1. Gubernatorial and Agency Staff

Most governors and high-level agency executives have staff dedicated to various
forms of policy research; in addition to small personal staffs, agency heads may
have policy research-oriented offices reporting directly to them. Such offices have
a variety of names in different states and different organizations, but they often
include words like "evaluation" or "analysis" (Weimer and Vining, 1992:11).
These offices may be involved in a variety of staff activities, of which policy
research is only a portion (Benveniste, 1972). In smaller states and agencies,
policy research may be the responsibility of a handful of individuals within an
agency, or even delegated to a single (overworked) research "expert." Because
they frequently lack the capacity to conduct their own policy research, many state
agencies contract policy research projects to outside organizations (see below).

Results from a series of surveys of top-level state administrators (Wright,
1986) suggest that in-house policy research shops are quite common, though
hardly ubiquitous, among state agencies. In both 1978 and 1984, approximately
40% of responding state agency executives reported the existence of an evaluation
unit within their agency (Table 1). The analysis of the 1984 responses in Table
2 suggests a strong relationship between the existence of such an "in-house"
evaluation unit and agency size (in terms of number of employees). Clearly, larger

Table 2 Cross-Tabulation of Existence of Evaluation Unit with Agency Size: 1984
Survey of State Administrators

Is there an evaluation unit?	Agency size (number of employees)			
	50 or less	51–100	101–250	251 or more
Yes	26.4%	36.4%	35.6%	51.2%
No	73.6%	63.6%	63.1%	48.8%
No	390	140	149	404

agencies are more likely to possess the resources necessary to support a formal research-oriented unit. The larger agencies (i.e., those with 251 or more employees) are nearly twice as likely as the smallest agencies to boast such a unit.

These data, however, raise questions about the adequacy of evaluation and other forms of policy research in the remaining majority of agencies that do not report in-house units. Of course, other state-level agencies and services, along with consultants and other forms of outside assistance, may serve to shore up the supply of necessary expertise. But it is also likely that many agencies rely on "back of the envelope" techniques to fill in the gaps.

2. Legislative and Legislative Committee Staff

To the extent that a state legislature commits funds to staff itself, legislative committees as well as individual legislators may have staff devoted to policy research activities. The trend toward enhanced legislative professionalism during the 1970s made professional staff more numerous across the nation, particularly in states that were already highly professionalized. However, in many if not most states, legislators share staff assistants or have staff assistance only during legislative sessions. All states provide at least some staff assistance to legislative committees (Patterson, 1983). In California, the number of legislative staff was drastically reduced in 1992 by a provision of Proposition 140, which also created legislative term limits. This episode represents a rare instance in which voters apparently acted on the sentiment that a "legislature had become too professionalized for its own good" (Gerston and Christensen, 1995:43).

The extent to which legislative staff actually engage in policy research in highly variable. Many legislative staffs are confined to relatively narrow matters of information gathering, while others act in more political roles as the "eyes and ears" of their respective legislative masters. In all likelihood, few state legislative staffs have the capacity and the ability to conduct formal, structured policy research.

3. Legislative Research Agencies

In 1970, the State of New York created the Legislative Committee on Expenditure Review, the first state agency established to conduct legislative program evaluations and related policy research. This innovation spread quickly to other state governments; by 1984, 34 states had either expanded existing agencies or created new ones to evaluate the effectiveness and/or efficiency of state policies and programs (Brown, 1984). At present every state is represented in the National Legislative Program Evaluation Society (NLPES), although some lack freestanding legislative research agencies. The precise institutional arrangements for such agencies vary from state to state. In Michigan, for example, a fiscal agency associated with each house of the state legislature is involved in policy research. In

Virginia, the Joint Legislative Audit and Review Commission (JLARC) serves both houses of the state legislature. In Illinois, legislative policy research is conducted by the Office of the Auditor General (Green, 1984).

Whatever the exact institutional setting, legislative research agencies tend to share the following characteristics:

1. They are staffed by professional researchers with diverse academic backgrounds and qualifications, although social scientists are frequently important contributors.
2. They are politically independent, and seek to maintain an objective viewpoint despite their close ties to one or both houses of the state legislature.
3. Their work is conducted with a legislative, policy-oriented focus.

Despite the ubiquity of legislature-based research agencies, they tend to lack a shared professional identity, due perhaps in part to the diverse backgrounds of their staff and attendant diversity of methodological approaches (Brown, 1984). In noting the lack of professional identity among legislative research agencies, Funkhouser (1984:261) argued that "program evaluation has become too generic a term to be used to define what we do. It seems primarily to be used by academics . . . to describe an activity more related to scholarly research than to legislative oversight." The blurring among the various forms of policy research information requested by legislatures may also contribute to this state of affairs.

Guston et al. (1998) note that the demand for information and analysis in technically complex policy areas is widespread and increasing. Their survey of state legislators, staff, and other professionals in 11 states found "legislative research staff" to be the single most important source of technical information and analysis (Guston et al., 1998:456).

4. Auditing Agencies

As discussed earlier, most state auditing agencies conduct "performance audits" and occasionally participate in other, less fiscally anchored forms of policy research. According to a survey conducted by the National State Auditors Association (1996), 39 state auditor agencies perform "economy and efficiency audits," and 35 conduct " comprehensive performance audits." Additionally, 10 state auditor agencies report that they participate in audits prescribed by sunset legislation.

Although it is generally associated with a narrower, accounting-based approach, the policy research role fulfilled by auditing agencies can easily be confused with that of other agencies that conduct research (Davis, 1990). Occasionally this overlap creates tension between "performance auditors," typically based in auditing agencies and "program evaluators," who are usually based in freestanding evaluation organizations (Funkhouser, 1984). Most states have both. Wye and Sonnichchsen (1992:6), in reference to the national government, note that "the line between audit and evaluation functions may be clear in theory, but in practice it has become blurred."

B. Institutions (External)

Like the national government, state governments rely heavily on outside institutions to conduct policy research. Such research is frequently contracted out to consulting agencies, colleges and universities, and associated "think tank" organizations. The impetus for contracting out may stem from one or both of two primary reasons:(1) many state line agencies lack adequate and technically capable internal staff and other resources to design and implement their own policy research;(2) agencies may desire the additional objectivity presumed to exist among those outside of state government. Additionally, external interest groups and associations may also sponsor policy research activities.

1. Consulting Agencies

The extensive participation of consulting firms in conducting policy research at the national level (including the so-called Beltway bandits) is relatively well documented (Meltsner, 1976). Much less has been written about the extent to which state governments rely on consulting firms and other outside organizations that contract for policy research work. Anecdotal information suggests that such firms often develop long-term relationships with various state agencies and, over time, come to rely heavily on their expertise in conducting policy research.

Typically, a state agency will circulate a request for proposals (RFP), also known as a request for assistance (RFA), that specifies the parameters and goals for a given project. Ideally, the agency selects from a number of bidders to determine which firm is best prepared to conduct the research. However, in some cases certain firms and consultants are repeatedly selected by the same agency, in part because they gain familiarity and expertise with a given agency's policy arena, available data, and information needs.

2. Universities/Think Tanks

Many state agencies make frequent use of the resources available at their respective state universities, or "think tanks" (policy institutes, etc.) that are housed within universities. Typically, state universities maintain policy-oriented research organizations that exist primarily to obtain contracts for research with state and local governments. In many if not most instances, use of university faculty and other staff is a logical outgrowth of the university's role of serving the state. However, in some cases, state universities are excluded from competitive bidding requirements, enabling state agencies to "sole-source" contracts for policy research without a time-consuming (and competitive) bidding procedure. In any event, many state agencies develop long-standing relationships with university-based policy research organizations. Respondents to the survey by Guston et al. ranked public colleges and university fairly highly as an "important source of technical information and analysis"(Guston et al., 1998:458).

3. Interest Groups and Associations

Other policy actors may be involved in policy research activities on an ad hoc basis. Interest groups, both privately and publicly based, frequently sponsor studies of issues that concern them. For example, the National Council of State Legislatures, the National Governors' Association, and the Council of State Governments occasionally initiate studies of interest to their respective memberships. Additionally, associations of line agency officials, such as the National State Health Directors Association, the Association of State and Territorial Health Officials, and the National Association of Attorneys General, also sponsor policy-related research.

4. National Government

State governments can sometimes take advantage of relevant research efforts of national government agencies, although the lines of exploitation frequently run in the opposite direction. That is because the national government relies upon state agencies for information pertaining to compliance with the myriad of regulations associated with acceptance of national grants-in-aid to state government (Ingram, 1977). In fact, significant amounts of state policy research arise from national requirements to produce such research (see previous section). Respondents to the survey of state legislative officials by Guston et al. did not rank the national government very highly as a source of technical information and analysis (Guston et al., 1998:458).

C. Individuals in Policy Research

Just as policy research is conducted by many kinds of institutions, the persons who "do" policy research hold a variety of job titles (Meltsner, 1976). Typically, policy researchers within state government hold titles like program analyst, management analyst, legislative analyst, or policy analyst. However, even policy generalists may participate in policy research activities (Putt and Springer, 1989). Policy researchers tend to come from a variety of academic backgrounds, although many are trained in a social science discipline.

D. Policy Research in the Context of State Government

Policy research in state government is perhaps best described in comparison to that at the national level. The use, or at least the commitment to the funding, of policy research in the federal government is far-reaching and institutionalized (Meltsner, 1976; Derlien, 1990; Newcomer, 1996). By contrast, state policy research is typically conducted in a context of relatively fewer resources, including fewer staff members, and less expertise. Even the national government has been criticized for its shortfalls and cutbacks in policy research activities (Havens, 1992; Lee and Johnson, 1994; Newcomer, 1996), begging the question of the adequacy of state efforts. Despite their constraints, some state efforts have been lauded as innovative; for example, Florida's Department of Children, Youth and Family Services has been cited for its efforts in performance-monitoring programs (Newcomer, 1996:559). State legislative policy research units have gained national prominence (Lee and Johnson, 1994:160). On the other hand, many state policy research efforts—particularly those undertaken by line agencies—occur only because they are mandated by federal grant regulations (Mangun, 1997).

It is extremely difficult to generalize about the policy research productivity of state governments, and there is apparently little interest or incentive to piece together existing state policy research into a well-documented whole (Havens, 1992:24). The following sections, based on limited existing information, provide a suggestion of the range of state policy research efforts.

1. Environmental Policy

Mangun (1997) provides an overview and assessment of state efforts to support environmental management with program evaluation that may serve to exemplify state policy research generally. As in many policy areas, environmental management is an intergovernmental affair: state and local governments develop and implement environmental legislation to help implement federal policies. State governments are required to develop evaluations of their own efforts to implement federal standards.

Mangun's review of state evaluation efforts includes the following observations:

1. State evaluations tend to emphasize measurement of process (e.g., number of enforcement actions taken) rather than outcomes (e.g., actual impact on environmental quality) due to the complexity of environmental policy as well as the demands of state budgeting procedures.
2. Federal (EPA) policy also serves to emphasize compliance with regulations, rather than measurement of policy objectives.
3. The extent to which each state is involved with implementing various

federal environmental regulations varies, and evaluation activity varies accordingly.

4. No single method or system of collecting data about environmental effectiveness exists from one state to another, confounding comparative analysis.

5. A few states (notably Oregon and Washington) "are taking new and innovative approaches to . . . environmental program evaluation" (Mangun, 1997:103).

Mangun associates inadequate evaluation activities with a long-term, national failure of state governments to enhance environmental conditions. The extent to which policy research in other state policy arenas resembles the situation in environmental management cannot be readily ascertained. However, it is likely that among policies with a strong intergovernmental component—in most policy areas, in other words—these patterns may repeat themselves.

2. Legislative Program Evaluation

Legislative program evaluation agencies engage in a wide variety of policy research activities. The variety ensues in part from the fact that their activities are typically prescribed by their respective legislatures. Table 3 contains a list of the

Table 3 Selected Publications of the Virginia Joint Legislative Audit and Review Commission, 1996–June 1997

Review of the Department of Environmental Quality (Interim Report)
Minority-Owned Business Participation in State Contracts
Virginia Retirement System Oversight Report: Semi-Annual VRS Investment Report
Legislator's Guide to the Virginia Retirement System, First Edition
Virginia Retirement System Oversight Report: Biennial Status Report on the Virginia Retirement System
Review of the ADAPT System at the Department of Social Services (Special Report)
Review of the Medicaid Forecasting Methodology (Technical Report)
Review of the Magistrate System in Virginia
Review of the Virginia Liaison Office
Virginia Retirement System Oversight Report: Review of VRS Fiduciary Responsibility and Liability
Feasibility of Consolidating Virginia's Wildlife Resource Functions
Operation and Impact of Juvenile Corrections Services in Virginia
Secretarial System in Virginia (Interim Report)
Review of the Department of Environmental Quality
Feasibility of Modernizing Land Records in Virginia
Review of the Department of Corrections' Inmate Telephone System
Virginia's Progress Toward Chesapeake Bay Nutrient Reduction Goals

studies completed by Virginia's JLARC between 1996 and June of 1997. That JLARC engages in different forms of policy research under the rubric of evaluation is evident from the titles of these studies: some imply policy analysis (e.g., "Feasibility of Consolidating Virginia's Wildlife Resource Functions"); others imply program evaluation ("Virginia's Progress Toward Chesapeake Bay Nutrient Reduction Goals"). Other projects suggest more of an emphasis on descriptive research (e.g., Legislator's Guide to the Virginia Retirement System). However, as stated earlier, most of these studies probably contain a combination of types of policy research, unique to the information needs they were intended to address.

3. Budget Analysis

The advent of planning-programming-budgeting (PPB) in the 1960s helped promote the use of policy research in state budget systems. Robert Lee has monitored the prevalence of policy research in the state budget processes (Lee and Staffeldt, 1977; Lee, 1991; Lee and Johnson, 1994). Lee's surveys of state budget offices reveal that policy research has become widespread: whereas in 1970 fewer than 20% of state budget offices reported that they conducted "effectiveness program analysis," by 1990, 66% reported such activity. Similar increases in the use of "productivity analysis" are also reported in these surveys over the same time period (Lee and Johnson, 1994:160). Lee also found that states with budget offices that conduct "effectiveness analysis" were also much more likely to have legislative staff engaged in the same activity, suggesting that these branches of state government engage in policy research as a means of "self-defense" (Lee, 1991:258).

III. USE OF POLICY RESEARCH BY STATE GOVERNMENTS

To what extent is the vast collective policy research generated on behalf of state governments actually used? Answering this question requires brief consideration of what is meant by "use" of policy research. Traditionally, use is associated with an "obvious, direct, and immediate application of findings and recommendations to specific decision" (Put and Springer, 1989:63). However, in the context of state government policies—one that is open, diffuse, fluid, and responsive to many exogenous and endogenous forces—this view is too restrictive. Rarely are the findings and recommendations of state policy research translated directly into specific policy actions; state policy arenas are far too sluggish, and policy research must compete with a myriad of other policy queues.

However, contemporary theorists of utilization of policy research (Weiss and Bucuvalas, 1977; Bulmer, 1982; Sabatier and Jenkins-Smith, 1988; Putt and Springer, 1989) suggest a broadened definition of research utilization, one that acknowledges the complexity of the policy process. Included in this broader view are the following kinds of potential impact:

Altering the ways in which decision makers view issues

Enhancing the understanding of issues and facilitating enlightened discussions

Correcting incorrect assumptions about policies and procedures

Promoting administrative and legislative introspection about policies and procedures

Advocating long-term policy change.

Viewed from this perspective, policy research can and frequently does exhibit significant levels of utilization—although that utilization may be difficult to measure accurately.

Studies of the utilization of policy research by state officials tend to confirm that research is an important factor in the creation and implementation of state programs and policies. Decades ago, Lee and Staffeldt (1977) conducted a survey of state budget offices that demonstrated that policy analysis was commonly used by both executive and legislative officials in the budget process. However, the results also suggested that executive agencies were more likely to *conduct* analysis than to actually *use* it. More recently, Webber (1985) found that use of policy research information by state legislators are influenced by legislators' "job images." Legislators who focus on either the "constituent activities" or "elections" objectives were more likely to report use of policy research information.

A more recent study by Lester (1993) focused on the use of policy analysis by state agency officials. The study, which involved a survey of officials working in state hazardous waste, economic development, welfare, and education agencies, found that these officials:

do *not* appear to reply heavily on policy analysis from research organizations or from university faculty; instead they rely principally on policy advice from their peers in other state agencies, newspapers, their counterparts in federal agencies, and staff from the governor's office (Lester, 1993: 267).

The study also found that officials in "wealthier, more conservative, moralistic states" were more likely to use policy research than those in "poorer, more traditional, liberal states." Additionally, "more experienced and better educated officials" were also more likely to use research (Lester, 1993:267). However, this study was designed to measure only the direct use of policy research compared with other sources of information, and therefore could not determine the more diffuse and long-range impact of policy research among state officials.

IV. SUMMARY

This chapter has provided an overview of the nature and role of policy research in contemporary state government. "Policy research" is a general, inclusive term that refers to the many information gathering and processing activities that public agencies engage in to facilitate decision making. State governments engage in a wide variety of policy research activities, including policy analysis, program evaluation, performance evaluation and auditing, and other forms of research.

The growing size and complexity of state government have increased the need for such research, although states' officials vary in their ability to create and use it. Policy research emerges from a variety of sources both within and outside of state government.

Within state government, common sources of research information are gubernatorial and agency executive staff, legislative and legislative committee staff, and legislative research agencies. Outside sources may include other governments, private think tanks and consultants, interest groups, and universities. However, the resources available for formal, rigorous policy research are thought to be fewer among states than at the national level.

The extent to which state officials actually create and use policy research information is largely unknown. Survey and anecdotal evidence suggest that the creation of policy research is fairly ubiquitous, but not universally present in state government agencies. Determining the actual *utilization* of policy research information is perhaps even more problematic and depends in part on what is meant by "utilization." In all likelihood, policy research is at best one of a crowded field of competing sources seeking to influence state governments.

REFERENCES

Bardach, E. (1977). *The Implementation Game*, MIT Press, Cambridge, MA.

Benveniste, G. (1972). *The Politics of Expertise*, Glendessary Press, Berkeley, CA.

Brown, J. R. (1984). Legislative program evaluation: defining a legislative service and a profession, *Public Administration Review 44(3)*: 258–260.

Bulmer, M. (1982). *The Use of Social Research*, Allen and Unwin, Boston.

Carley, M. (1980). *Rational Techniques In Policy Analysis*, Policy Studies Institute, London.

Gerston, L. N., and Christensen, T. (1995). *California Politics and Government: A Practical Approach*, Wadsworth, New York.

Davis, D. F. (1990). Do you want a performance audit or a program evaluation?, *Public Administration Review 50(1)*: 35–41.

Derlien, H.-U. (1990). Genesis and structure of evaluation efforts in comparative perspective, *Program Evaluation and the Management of Government: Patterns and Pros-*

pects across Eight Nations R. C. Rist, (ed.), Transaction Publishers, New Brunswick, NJ, pp. 147–175.

Dunn, W. N. (1994). *Public Policy Analysis* (2d ed.), Prentice-Hall, Englewood Cliffs, NJ.

Dye, T. R. (1984). *Understanding Public Policy*, Prentice-Hall, Englewood Cliffs, NJ.

Funkhouser, M. (1984). Current issues in legislative program evaluation, *Public Administration Review 44(3)*: 261–263.

Green, A. (1984). The role of evaluation in executive decision making, *Public Administration Review 44(3)*: 265–267.

Guston, D. H., Jones, M., and Branscomb, L. M. (1998). The demand for and supply of technical information and analysis in state legislatures, *Policy Studies Journal 25(3)*: 451–469.

Haas, P. J., and Springer, J. F. (1998). *Applied Policy Research: Concepts and Cases*, Garland Publishing Co., New York.

Hatry, H. P., Blair, L., Fisk, D., and Kimmel, W. (1987). *Program Analysis for State and Local Governments*, Urban Institute, Washington, DC.

Havens, H. S. (1992). The erosion of federal program evaluation, *Evaluation in the Federal Government: Changes, Trends and Opportunities*, C. G. Wye and R. C. Sonnichsen, eds., Jossey-Bass, San Francisco; pp. 21–29.

Ingram, H. (1977). Policy implementation through bargaining: the case of federal grants-in-aid, *Public Policy 25*: 499–526.

Lee, R. D. (1991). Developments of state budgeting: trends of two decades, *Public Administration Review 51(3)*: 254–262.

Lee, R. D. Jr., and Staffeld, R. J. (1977). Executive and legislative use of policy analysis in the state budgetary process: survey results, *Policy Analysis 3(3)*: 395–405.

Lee, R. D. Jr., and Johnson, R. W. (1994). *Public Budgeting Systems (5th ed)*. Aspen Publishers, Gaithersburg, MD.

Lester, J. P. (1993). The utilization of policy analysis by state agency officials, *Knowledge: Creation, Diffusion, Utilization 14(3)*: 267–290.

MacRae D. Jr., and Wilde, J. (1979). *Policy Analysis for Public Decisions*, Duxbury Press, North Scituate, MA.

Magnun, W. R. (1997). Environmental program evaluation in an intergovernmental context, *Environmental Program Evaluation: A Primer* (G. Knapp and T. Kim, eds.), University of Illinois Press, Champaign-Urbana, IL. pp. 86–125.

Meier, K. J. (1984). The limits of cost-benefit analysis, *Decision-Making in the Public Sector* (L. G. Nigro, ed.), Marcel Dekker, New York.

Meltsner, A. J. (1976). *Policy Analysts in the Bureaucracy*. University of California Press, Berkeley, CA.

National State Auditors Association. (1996). *Auditing in the States: A Summary*, National Association of State Auditors, Comptrollers, and Treasurers, Lexington, KY.

Newcomer, K. E. (1996). Evaluating public programs, *Handbook of Public Administration (2d ed.)* (J. L. Perry, ed.), Jossey-Bass, San Francisco, pp. 555–573.

Patterson, S. C. (1983). Legislators and legislatures in the American states, *Politics in the American States* (4th ed.) (V. Gray, H. Jacob, and K. N. Vines, eds.), Little, Brown, Boston.

Patton, C. V., and Sawicki, D. S. (1993). *Policy Analysis and Planning: Theory and Practice* (2nd ed.), Prentice-Hall, Englewood Cliffs, NJ.

Putt, A. D., and Springer, J. F. (1989). *Policy Research: Concepts, Methods, and Applications*, Prentice-Hall, Englewood Cliffs, NJ.

Rist, R. C. (1990). Managing of evaluations or managing by evaluations: choices and consequences, *Program Evaluation and the Management of Government: Patterns and Prospects Across Eight Nations* (R. C. Rist, ed.), Transaction Publishers, New Brunswick, NJ. pp. 5–17.

Rogers, J. M. (1988). *The Impact of Policy Analysis*, University of Pittsburgh Press, Pittsburgh.

Sabatier, P. A., and Jenkins-Smith, H. C. (1988). Symposium on policy change: editors' introduction, *Policy Sciences 21*: 123–127.

Stevens, J. M., and Lee, R. D. Jr. (1981). Patterns of policy analysis use for state governments: a contingency and demand perspective, *Public Administration Review 41(6)*: 636–644.

Weimer, D. L., and Vining, A. R. (1992). *Policy Analysis: Concepts and Practice* (2d ed.), Prentice-Hall, Englewood Cliffs.

Webber, D. J. (1985). State legislators' use of policy information: the importance of legislative goals, *State and Local Government Review 17*: 213–218.

Weiss, C., and Bucuvalas, M. J. 1977. The challenge of social research to decisionmaking, *Using Social Research in Public Policymaking* (C. Weiss, ed.), Lexington Books, Lexington, MA.

Wildavsky, A. (1979). *Speaking Truth to Power: The Art and Craft of Policy Analysis*, Little, Brown, Boston.

Wright, D. S. (1986). *American State Administrators Project*. Institute for Research in the Social Sciences, University of North Carolina, Chapel Hill, NC.

Wye, C. G., and Sonnichsen, R. C. (1992). Editors' notes, *Evaluation in the Federal Government: Changes, Trends and Opportunities*, Jossey-Bass, San Francisco, pp. 1–10.

13
Measuring Performance in State Government

Maria P. Aristigueta
University of Delaware, Newark, Delaware

There has recently been a great deal of interest in government for performance information (Bavon, 1995). In 1990, Congress passed the Chief Financial Officers Act requiring the timely reporting of performance information. Also in 1990, the National Academy of State Budget Officers created a task force to help states develop performance measures. In addition, the Government Accounting Standards Board in 1990 outlined the measures for major state and local government functions. In 1991, the National Academy of Public Administration adopted a resolution endorsing and encouraging the development and use of performance monitoring at all levels of government. Congress passed the Governmental Performance and Results Act (GPRA) in July 1993 requiring all federal agencies to develop strategic plans, set agreed-upon goals and objectives, and measure their progress toward these goals. In September 1993, President Clinton unveiled the results of the National Performance Review, strongly encouraging the use of performance measures as one of the several recommendations to improve government.

Performance measurement is not new. More than a half century ago, Clarence Ridley teamed with Herbert Simon to write a book urging local governments to measure their performance and offering guidelines for doing just that (Ridley and Simon, 1943). The Hoover Commission, a few years later, recommended performance budgeting using a similar rationale. Alan Ehrenhalt recently drew attention to the resilience of performance measurement as a management strategy, noting that a common strand of management thoughts links the planning-programming-budgeting systems (PPBS) of the 1960s, zero-based budgeting (ZBB) of the 1970s, and management by objectives (MBO) of the 1980s to the current enthusiasm for measures. As noted by Ehrenhalt, "it is a good idea. It was a good idea in 1943. It is basically the same idea . . . it just keeps getting renamed" (Ehrenhalt, 1994:9). More than just renaming, performance measures have undergone fine-tuning.

Performance measurement may be described as the gathering of information about the work effectiveness and productivity of individuals, groups, and larger organizational units (Larsen and Callahan, 1990). These measures are commonly defined by objectives established to support organizational goals. Performance measurement systems have at least four purposes: (1) to improve or sustain organizational performance; (2) to improve accountability; (3) to enhance motivation; and (4) to improve communication (Greiner, 1996). Grizzle (1981) views the essence of performance measurement systems to be the reduction of uncertainty in programs. This includes reducing the uncertainty involved in planning future courses of action, and summarizing the consequences of past actions in ways useful to a variety of decision makers.

Program performance indicators specify the types of evidence, qualitative and quantitative, used to assess program performance and results. These will include indicators of program productivity, effectiveness, cost-effectiveness, quality, timeliness, and responsiveness (Wholey, 1983).

Another term used in the literature is *outcome monitoring*. Affholter (1994: 97) describes outcome monitoring as "outcome-focused or results-oriented; it is built into the routines of data reporting within program operations; it provides frequent and public feedback of performance; and it is not explanatory in itself, nor does it produce corrective action plans."

State governments use the term *benchmarks* to refer to statewide performance indicators. These measures are typically social indicators and not attributable to a single program. The practice of quantifying societal phenomena for public decision making dates back to the 17th century. Indeed, the term *statistics* refers to "matters of the state," and the earliest were simply outputs of governmental record-keeping systems (Innes, 1990). More recently, social indicators are used by states as benchmarks providing information to the public.

I. RECOMMENDED STRATEGIES AND SUPPORT FOR MEASURING PERFORMANCE

Strategies for a results-oriented, comprehensive planning, goal-setting, and measurement system have long been advocated by Peter Drucker (1974) and Joseph Wholey (1983). Drucker argues that government agencies should take steps to manage for performance and results. He blames the inefficiencies in government to budget allocations, as opposed to payments for results. Drucker (1974) recommends the following processes:

1. Define agency and program objectives by the outcomes achieved
2. Establish priorities
3. Define qualitative and quantitative performance measures and performance targets
4. Assess performance and results
5. Use performance information to improve performance and results
6. Identify and abandon unproductive activities.

Wholey agrees with Drucker and makes recommendations to deal with policy-making and management environments that may hinder progress in managing for results. The hindrances include "program goals that tend to be vague or unachievable; program performance is often hard to define and measure; political and bureaucratic constraints often make it difficult to use program performance information to improve program or agency performance" (Wholey, 1983:4). He considers the foundations to results-oriented management in government as:

> (1) agreement on a set of program outcome objectives and outcome indicators in terms of which the program will be assessed and managed; (2) development of systems for assessing program performance in terms of those outcome objectives; (3) use of program outcome information to achieve improved program performance; and (4) communication of program performance and results to policy levels and to the public (Wholey, 1983: 4–8).

Although Drucker and Wholey's descriptions of managing for results most closely resemble what is being used in organizations today, it is difficult to ignore management by objectives (MBO) as a foundation. MBO incorporates the features of three processes that are known to constitute good management practice and are found in the most recent models: participation in decision making, goal setting, and objective feedback (Rogers and Hunter, 1992). In 1976, Newland was asking, "Why would such a theoretically sound management system that had received such high marks from surveys and longstanding support from social science theory have been 'pronounced stillborn?'" (Rodgers and Hunter, 1992: 36). The answer may be that MBO has undergone a rebirth. MBO is a necessary component for today's performance management systems.

In 1983, Wholey's question is whether, and to what extent, results-oriented management exists or should exist, in government agencies and programs. As this chapter demonstrates, results-oriented data are collected in states; these data are used for internal management and other uses are starting to surface.

Major institutions have participated in work on results-oriented management. The U.S. General Accounting Office (GAO) took an active role in making recommendations to Congress for what would later be the Government Performance and Results Act (GPRA). The National Academy of Public Administration (NAPA) and the Governmental Accounting Standards Board (GASB) publicly supported performance monitoring and reporting by public organizations. GAO also examined state experiences and experiences abroad with "managing for results," to assist national agencies with the implementation of GPRA.

In 1992, Charles Bowsher, Comptroller General of the United States, provided information to Congress on the steps that could be taken to improve accountability for program results (GAO/TGGD 92-35). Bowsher had three major recommendations: (1) agencies should clearly articulate their mission in the context of statuary objectives and with regard to services and citizen expectations; (2) agencies should develop implementation plans for the goals and objectives and specific measures for progress towards achieving them; and (3) agencies should report annually on their progress. He finally recommended that the national government start with pilot projects, build on successes, and learn from mistakes.

Additional support for performance measurement was provided by Wholey and Hatry (1992:604) as they referred to regular monitoring of service quality and program results as a "key component of informed public management and the identification of opportunities for improved public-sector performance" and additionally, advocated multiple indicators. Their article also contained the resolution adopted by NAPA in 1991 for the encouragement of performance monitoring and reporting by units of government at all levels.

On August 3, 1993, the Government Performance and Results Act (GPRA) was passed by Congress. This act addressed the implementation of strategic planning and performance measures in the national government and included a plan to initiate program performance reforms with a series of pilot projects in fiscal years 1994, 1995, and 1996. The GAO studied the pilot projects and identified a series of practices that yield successful implementation (GAO/GGD-96-118):

1. In defining mission and desired outcomes, (a) involve stakeholders, (b) assess the environment, and (c) align activities, core processes, and resources

2. In measuring performance, (a) produce a set of performance measures at each organizational level that demonstrate results, respond to multiple priorities, and link to responsible programs; in addition (b) collect sufficiently complete, accurate, and consistent data

3. In use of performance information, (a) identify performance gaps, (b) report performance information, and (c) use performance information to support mission.

GAO concludes that leadership practices reinforce the implementation of GPRA and that the effective leader develops decision making with accountability, creates incentives, builds expertise, and integrates management reforms. Figure 1 displays GAO's recommendations. The steps and critical practices for successful implementation listed in Figure 1 are expanded upon in Section V of this chapter

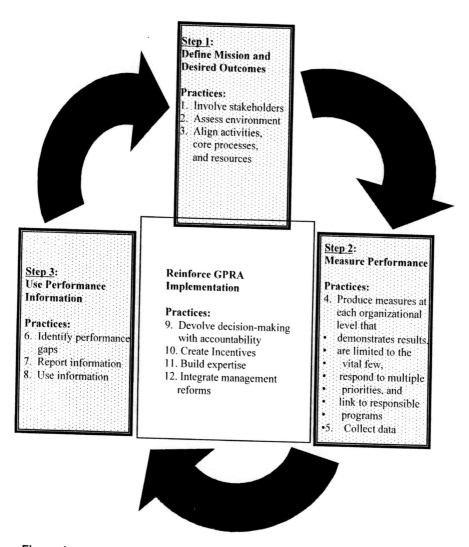

Figure 1 GAO's model for effective implementation of the government performance and results act. (From *U.S. General Accounting Office*, 1996.)

to gauge accomplishments in states identified by GAO as front-runners in these efforts: Florida, Minnesota, North Carolina, Oregon, Texas, and Virginia.

The Government Accounting Standards Board (GASB), in an exposure draft (GASB 1993), recommended service efforts and accomplishment (SEA) reporting for state and local governments. The SEA is again a form of performance measurement with its focus on results, accountability, and dissemination of information. The SEA was adopted by GASB in 1994.

II. STATES' USE OF RESULTS-ORIENTED MANAGEMENT

Limited information is available on states' initiatives. Some of the national associations, such as the Council of State Governments, the National Governors' Association, and the National State Budget Officers' Association, have conducted surveys. The fourth National Public Sector Productivity Conference published its proceedings on new approaches to productivity in the winter 1991 issue of *Public Productivity and Management Review*. This provided a few case studies of selected states. The GASB reported the results of their survey in the *Public Administration Times* (Fountain, 1997). The preliminary analysis of 800 responses to 5000 surveys (a 17% response rate) indicates that the "use of performance measures is fairly widespread, with states more likely to be involved in their use than local governments" (Fountain, 1997:8). A comprehensive study of state government reforms was published by GAO in 1995. This report responded to a congressional request to study success stories in implementing management reforms at the state level (GAO/GGD-95-22).

The states studied by GAO were Florida, Minnesota, North Carolina, Oregon, Texas, and Virginia. These states were found to have utilized requirements similar to those outlined in the GPRA. Results-oriented management in these states included strategic planning, performance measurement, and the linking of management systems (such as information and human resource systems) with mission-related goals. The states' experiences suggest that implementing reforms is a long-term effort requiring that the executive and legislative branches work together for implementation (GAO/GGD-95-22).

A recent study by Aristigueta (1999) found the following components in these states:

1. Florida engages in citizen-based goal setting for benchmarks, agency strategic planning, performance measurement, performance-based budgets, and performance evaluations.

2. Minnesota uses citizen-based goal setting for milestones, agency performance measurement, performance-based budgets, and performance evaluations.

3. North Carolina uses citizen-based goal setting for benchmarks (indicators are not yet available) and agency performance measurement. Performance-based program budget is undergoing revisions.

4. Oregon uses citizen-based goal setting for benchmarks, but it has no requirement for strategic planning or performance budgeting for state agencies. Pilot studies link agency programs to benchmarks.

5. Texas uses goal setting for benchmarks without assigned indicators. Agency strategic planning, performance measurement, and budgeting are fully integrated. Performance evaluations, including validation of measures, are part of the system in Texas.

6. Virginia does not use benchmarks. Agency citizen-based strategic planning, performance measurement, performance-based budgets, and performance evaluations are used.

III. GOAL OF THE PROGRAM AND MEASUREMENT MODEL

Measurement models in the states studied included agency performance indicators, generally comprising input, output, and outcome measures; and statewide benchmarks or milestones (as referred to in Minnesota). The benchmarks found in Florida, Oregon, and Minnesota included input, output, and outcome measures. Hatry and Kirlin (1994:5) found that, outside Oregon, "the term benchmark is usually applied to the targets and not the indicators" such as those for the years 2000 and 2010. In Oregon, the term benchmark applies simultaneously to both indicators and targets.

The goal of performance measurement models found in the states included two primary, yet distinct, purposes: accountability to stakeholders to improve perceptions of government; and management, which through the collection of performance information, aims to improve government. Internal to state governments, this distinction is not apparent. State officials discussed the dual purposes of all performance measurement systems as accountability and management improvements. Indeed, in Virginia, where benchmarks are not utilized, state officials discussed the problematic situation that benchmarks would present: not being able to hold any one program accountable for the specific measure. In Virginia, the legislative auditor's office recommended benchmarking based on individual agency measures, as opposed to statewide benchmarks.

"Holding an agency accountable for performance" continues to be the primary function of the agency performance measurement in state government. This is a separate goal from the two previously stated, but it is the basis most often found for utilization of performance measures. The unintended consequences resulting from this type of use includes goal displacement, "whereby organizational behavior reacts over time to maximize performance on those dimensions emphasized by the system at the expense of other equally more important objectives" (Poister, 1992:201).

IV. USES AND IMPACT OF PERFORMANCE INFORMATION

Performance information is used for purposes of internal management at the agency level. The managing-for-results systems in states include strategic planning, performance-based budgeting, and performance evaluations. Uses of these systems most often reflect internal controls and accountability to the public. Detailed descriptions of these findings are reported in the book by Aristigueta (1999), containing individual case studies of the six states. Performance information infrequently affected the budget allocations (as in Texas and Minnesota). The performance information has also had limited use in program evaluations (as in Florida), policy decision-making and community projects (as in Florida and Texas), and improved effectiveness, most clearly demonstrated by the pilot studies in Oregon. Expanding on Hatry and Kirlin's (1995) observations of the Oregon benchmarks, benchmarks and agency performance information provide opportunities through the use of strategic planning for social learning and integration of what is currently a fragmented system.

"Benchmarks offer the possibility of achieving two difficult objectives: social learning, and integrated action in fragmented systems" (Hatry and Kirlin, 1995:1). Social learning includes at a minimum, educating the public on the capacity and limitations of government. The argument is presented that when the public is involved in the process of agency performance measures, as in Virginia; agency performance information may also be utilized for social learning.

Social learning is related to the public's perceptions of government and to the desirable outcome for these initiatives. In a public perception of local government survey, Glaser and Denhardt (1997) found that the public's perceptions of government improved with information available. Most clearly, benchmarks, and in some cases agency performance measures, used in state government provided the opportunity to communicate with the public on issues that in most cases have been identified by the community to be of importance. This is accomplished through community-based strategic planning efforts or community-based goal setting. For example, Virginia and Oregon engaged in community-based strategic planning through focus groups all over the state to identify issues of importance. Florida and Minnesota used a similar format for goal setting. Following the logic demonstrated by Glaser and Denhardt, it would follow that if benchmarks and/ or agency performance measures engage the public in the process, and the information is readily available, then the public's perception of government will improve. However, agency performance measures do not alleviate fragmentation of the system.

V. STEPS AND CRITICAL PRACTICES FOR SUCCESSFUL IMPLEMENTATION

GAO bases its formula for best practices in findings in a number of leading public organizations including the states studied (GAO/GGD-96-118). GAO warns that each organization has its own agenda for management reform according to its own environment, needs, and capabilities. Regardless of the approach, GAO found three key steps in managing-for-results: (1) define clear missions and desired outcomes; (2) measure performance to gauge progress; and (3) use performance information as a basis for decision making. Figure 2 summarizes how states are meeting these requirements.

In defining clear missions and desired outcomes, GAO found three critical practices; and five important criteria (4–8 below) for performance measures. These are followed by findings in the states.

1. *Involve stakeholders*—stakeholders are defined as the public for the purpose of this chapter. Florida, Minnesota, North Carolina, and Oregon included the public in their statewide benchmark efforts to define goals and desired outcomes. Texas and Virginia involved the public in the desired outcomes for agency performance measures.

2. *Assess the internal and external environments*—North Carolina assessed the internal and external environments for the statewide benchmarks. Florida, Virginia, and Texas assessed the environment (usually referred to as trends and conditions) for agency performance measures.   .

3. *Align activities, core processes, and resources to support mission-related outcomes*—In Florida the benchmarks are aligned with the state comprehensive plan. Florida, Minnesota, Virginia, and Texas link budgeting and performance measurement in agencies. Florida, Virginia, and Texas also include strategic planning in the agency level linkages.

4. In measuring performance, GAO found a need for performance measures to meet the following criteria, at each organizational level:

a. *Demonstrating results*—Requires that "performance measures tell each organizational level how well it is achieving its goal" (p. 24). Florida, Minnesota, and Oregon are demonstrating results through benchmark indicators. Virginia, on a limited basis, and Florida, Minnesota, and Texas are demonstrating results through agency performance measures.

b. *Limit to the vital few per goal*—Virginia has limited to two measures per goal and two to five goals per program. None of the other states have specific

				FL	MN	NC	OR	TX	VA
Define Mission Outcomes	1.	Involve Stakeholders		Some	No	*ne	No	Some	Yes
	2.	Assess Environment		Yes	No	*ne	No	Some	Yes
	3.	Align Activities		Yes	Yes	*ne	No	Some	Yes
Measure Performance	4.	Measure at Each Organizational Level	A. Demonstrate Results	Yes	Yes	*ne	Yes	Yes	Yes
			B. Limited to Vital Few per Goal	Yes	No	*ne	Yes	Yes	Yes
			C. Respond to Multiple Priorities	Yes	Yes	*ne	Yes	Yes	Yes
			D. Link to Responsible Programs	Yes	Yes	*ne	Yes	Yes	Yes
	5.	Collect Data		Yes	Yes	*ne	Yes	Yes	Yes
Use Performance Information	6.	Identify Performance Gaps		Yes	Yes	*ne	Yes	Yes	Yes
	7.	Report Information		Yes	Yes	*ne	Yes	Yes	Yes
	8.	Use Information	A. Policy Decision Making	Yes	No	*ne	No	Yes	No
			B. Management	Yes	Yes	*ne	Some	Yes	Yes
			C. Accountability to Public	Yes	Yes	*ne	Some	Yes	Yes
			D. Community Projects	No	No	*ne	No	Some	No
			E. Improved Effectiveness	Some	No	*ne	Some	Some	Some
Reinforce Implementation	9.	Devolve Decision Making		Some	No	*ne	No	Some	No
	10.	Create Incentives		No	No	*ne	No	No	Some
	11.	Build Expertise		Yes	Yes	*ne	No	Yes	Yes
	12.	Integrate Management Reforms		Some	Some	*ne	No	Some	Some

Figure 2 Key steps and critical practices for successful implementation in agency performance measures. (From U.S. General Accounting Office, 1996; Aristigueta, 1999.) (*ne, no evidence.)

limits; indeed, one of the Minnesota legislative auditor's criticisms of the agency performance measures is the number of measures.

    c. *Respond to multiple priorities*—Florida, Minnesota, Oregon, Texas, and Virginia respond to priorities established by the citizens, and the executive and legislative branches of government. Florida has identified "critical benchmarks" for prioritizing.

    d. *Link to responsible programs*—Agency performance measures are linked to programs in all states utilizing them. However, this is not the case with the benchmarks. This remains a criticism of those studying the systems. For example, Hatry and Kirlin recommended improving linkages of state agency performance measures to benchmarks in their assessment of the Oregon benchmarks (Hatry and Kirlin, 1995). The Minnesota legislative auditors recommended more effective linkages between the performance reports and the biennial budget proposals (Minnesota, 1995). Linking has been most comprehensive in Texas with the ABEST management information system.

    5. *Collect data*—Florida, Minnesota, and Oregon are collecting data for benchmark indicators. Florida, Minnesota, Texas, and Virginia are collecting data for agency performance measures.

In addition, GAO recommends the use of performance information to:

    6. *Identify performance gaps*—Florida, Minnesota, and Oregon identify performance gaps through benchmarks. Florida, Minnesota, Texas, and Virginia identify performance gaps by the agency performance measures.

    7. *Report information*—Florida, Minnesota, and Oregon report benchmark information. Florida, Minnesota, Texas, and Virginia report agency performance measures.

    8. *Use information*—Broader uses include:

    a. *Policy decision making*—This is difficult to document. Florida and texas claim that the agency performance measures are utilized for funding decisions. Although it is intended in the other states, there is no evidence.

    b. *Management*—The strength of these programs appear to be in their use for internal management. Florida, Minnesota, Texas, and Virginia all stated that the measures were being used internally. Oregon has documented impressive accomplishments through their pilot studies. A Texas official emphasized the importance of the use of measures for internal management, as opposed to focusing on their use for policy decision making.

    c. *Accountability to the public*—Florida, Minnesota, and Oregon, through public involvement in the goal setting process and published reports, are providing information to the public. Virginia follows a similar process of citizen involvement for the agency strategic planning process. Florida, Minnesota, Texas, and Virginia publish agency performance measures. In Minnesota, the entire performance report may be accessed via the Internet.

    d. *Community projects*—These were not recommended by GAO but have been added by the author after studying the states. Community projects provide opportunities through other governments or non-profit organizations for partnerships, greater accomplishments, and understanding of the workings of government. Community projects are encouraged in the Florida, Minnesota, and Oregon benchmarks.

     e. *Improve effectiveness*—This area is also an addition to GAO's criteria. Improved effectiveness is a desired outcome of the measurement systems and was notably demonstrated by the pilot programs in Oregon.

To reinforce implementation, GAO recommends the following:

     9. *Devolve decision making*—This requires allowing managers to bring their judgment to bear in meeting their responsibilities, rather than mere compliance. Texas and Florida were the only two states with limited use of this practice. In Texas, allowances are made for budget flexibility to accomplish targets. Florida in conducting pilot studies allowing for flexibility in spending and hiring in agencies.

     10. *Create incentives*—Virginia is the only state with pilot studies of bonus programs for accomplishments in agencies.

     11. *Build expertise*—This requires the staff at all levels to be skilled in strategic planning, performance measurement, and the use of performance information in decision making. Florida, Minnesota, North Carolina, Texas, and Virginia all emphasized the need for training. North Carolina has discontinued its performance measurement systems, and Virginia has limited the number of measures in part due to the need for training.

     12. *Integrate management reform*—Integration of management reform is occurring on a limited basis. Agency performance measures are integrated with budget processes and the management information system in Florida, Minnesota, Texas, and Virginia. Florida, Texas, and Virginia integrate agency strategic plans. Florida, Minnesota, Texas, and Virginia integrate performance evaluations. Oregon, Florida, Minnesota, and to a limited extent Texas, also integrate the use of statewide goal setting and benchmarks.

     In summary, all of the necessary practices for successful implementation identified by GAO and others referenced in this chapter were found in some states, particularly at the agency level. These practices are best geared to the agency, as the recommendations are tailored to the implementation of the Government Performance and Results Act, more closely resembling the agency performance measurement efforts than the statewide benchmarks.

VI. RECENT RESISTANCE TO MEASURES

Sound management which allows for accountability and communication to policy makers and to the public is of critical importance at a time of tight fiscal constraints for many state governments. Implementation of managing for results is meeting resistance although work in states demonstrates the utility of rational models for sound management practices. Thus, for example, since the writing of this chapter, the Florida benchmarks have been eliminated for the 1998 fiscal year through the legislative budget process. The Florida benchmarks were a series of quantitative indicators describing the well-being of the public in Florida across seven areas of concern: families and communities, safety, learning, health, economy, environment, and government. In a companion publication, *Critical Benchmark Goals*, 60 of the most important indicators are used to set goals for Florida to reach in the years 2000 and 2010. The Florida program was modeled after the Oregon benchmarks and the Minnesota milestones and has been hailed as the best of its kind in its organization, reading ease, and comprehensiveness. What could make it disappear?

According to the executive director of the government accountability to the people commission, the benchmarks were well received by government in Florida. The opposition came when an attempt was made to tie outcomes to the performance measures at the program level. Opposition was also found among those who control the budget process (Stanford, 1998). This points to the difficulties involved in the near-simultaneous use of performance indicators for the purposes of accountability and budgeting in state government.

Problems are also surfacing in Minnesota where the legislative auditor's office is recommending the repeal of Minnesota's 1993 Performance Reporting Law. Though the law requires agencies to develop performance measures, the measures are scarcely "looked at by the legislature." According to Michael Q. Patton (1997), Jim Nobles, the Minnesota legislative auditor, attributes the failures to four primary problems: (1) lack of honesty about the challenges at the outset; (2) overreaching in promises and overburdening agencies with paperwork; (3) failure to build capacity prior to implementation; and (4) failure to understand that performance data has limited use in public decision-making.

Nobles makes the following recommendations with regard to the effectiveness of performance measures (Patton, 1997): (1) be more honest about the challenges; (2) stop mandating uniform, across-the-board reporting systems and allow agencies to design meaningful systems; (3) rely on capacity building and good management; and (4) rely more on periodic in-depth evaluations to inform priority policy discussions.

VII. SUMMARY AND CONCLUSION

Coupled with resistance to measures are high hopes for the use of performance information. In expanding Greiner's (1996) earlier list, these hopes include but are not limited to (1) improved perception of government by the public, (2) improved program efficiency and effectiveness, (3) improved decision making, (4) improved service delivery, (5) more accountable internal management, (6) enhanced motivation, and (7) reduction in program uncertainty.

For now, important lessons may be learned from the current systems:

1. Consistent with Glaser's (1991) earlier findings, greater benefit is to be gained from germane, as opposed to generic measures.

2. The greatest use for measures may be internal to the organization, as in Texas (Aristigueta, 1999).

3. Holding an agency accountable for performance remains an important priority for use of these systems yet may have the unintended consequence of goal displacement (see Poister, 1992).

4. Performance information lends itself to community partnerships to address issues as in Oregon (Aristigueta, 1999).

What the future holds for the use of performance measurement is uncertain at this point, and important lessons are yet to be learned. For example, will including the public in the process and sharing performance information serve the purpose of improving the public's perception of government? Will legislating measures lead to their stability? Future evaluations will lead to answers in this area and other measures of lasting impact.

REFERENCES

Affholter, D. P. (1994). Outcome monitoring, *Handbook of Practical Program Evaluation*, J. Wholey, H. Hatry, and K. Newcomer, eds., Jossey-Bass, San Francisco, pp. 96–118.

Aristigueta, M. P. (1999). *Managing for Results in State Government*, Quorum, Westport, CT.

Bavon, A. (1995). Innovations in performance measurement systems: a comparative perspective, *International Journal of Public Administration 18*: 491–519.

Drucker, P. F. (1974). *Management: Tasks, Responsibilities, Practices*, Harper and Row, New York.

Ehrenhalt, A. (1994). Performance budgeting, thy name is . . ., *Governing, 8*: 9.

Fountain, J. R. (1997). Are state and local governments using performance measures?, *Public Administration Times 20*: PM-2.

Glaser, M. A. (1991). Tailoring performance measurement to fit the organization: from generic to germane, *Public Productivity and Management Review XIV(3)*: 303–319.

Glaser, M. A., and Denhardt, R. B. (1997). Local government performance through the eyes of citizens, Presented at the American Society for Public Administration, 58th National Conference, Philadephia, PA.

Governmental Accounting Standards Board (1993). Proposed statement on concepts related to service efforts and accomplishment reporting, Exposure Draft.

Government Performance and Results Act, Public Law 103-62, [S20]. (1993). 107 Statute 285 (Aug.).

Greiner, J. M. (1996). Positioning Performance measurement for the twenty-first century, *Organizational Performance and Measurement in the Public Sector* (A. Halachmi and G. Bouckaert, eds.), Quorum Books, Westport, CT, pp. 11–50.

Grizzle, G. (1981). A manger's guide to the meaning and uses of performance measurement, *American Review of Public Administration 15*: 16–28.

Hatry, H. P., and Kirlin, J. J. (1994). An assessment of the Oregon benchmarks: a report to the Oregon progress board. Unpublished document.

Innes, J. E. (1990). *Knowledge and Public Policy: The Search for Meaningful Indicators,* Transaction Publishers, New Brunswick, NJ.

Larsen, J. R., and Callahan, C. (1990). Performance monitoring: how it affects work productivity, *Journal of Applied Psychology 75*: 530–538.

Minnesota, Office of the Legislative Auditor, Program Evaluation Division (1995). *Development and Use of the 1994 Agency Performance Reports,* Saint Paul, MN.

Poister, T. H. (1992). Productivity monitoring: systems, indicators, and analysis, *Public Productivity Handbook* (M. Holzer, ed.), Marcel Dekker, New York, pp. 195–211.

Patton, M. Q. (1997). E-mail communication, Nov. 27.

Ridley, C. E., and Simon, H. A. (1943). *Measuring Municipal Activities: A Survey of Suggested Criteria for Appraising Administration,* International City Managers' Association, Chicago.

Rodgers, R., and Hunter, J. (1992). A foundation of good management practice in government: management by objectives, *Public Administration Review 52(1)*: 27–39.

Stanford, K. (1998). E-mail communication, April 20.

U.S. General Accounting Office. (1992). *Performance Measurement: An Important Tool in the Managing for Results,* U.S. Government Printing Office, Washington, DC. (GAO/T-GGD-92-35.)

U.S. General Accounting Office. (1996). *Executive Guide: Effectively Implementing the Government Performance and Results Act.* U.S. Government Printing Office, Washington, DC. (GAO/GGD-96-118.).

Wholey, J. S. (1983). *Evaluation and Effective Public Management,* Little, Brown, Boston.

Wholey, J. S., and Harry H. (1992). The case for performance monitoring, *Public Administration Review 52(6)*: 604–610.

14
Administration of State Economic Development Policy

Keith Boeckelman
Western Illinois University, Macomb, Illinois

Beginning in the 1970s, economic development emerged as a top agenda item for state governments (Herzik, 1983). One sign of the issue's importance is that activities in policy areas ranging from higher education to welfare to prison construction are justified on economic development grounds. A side effect of this increasing prominence is that administration has become more complex. Traditional economic development departments must manage more and more programs, while new, semiautonomous agencies, less dependent on direct financial support from legislatures, have emerged to administer complementary and competing initiatives. The proliferation of agencies and programs involved in economic development has rendered even more difficult the already weighty task of evaluation.

This chapter focuses on policy delivery and evaluation in economic development administration. After a brief historical overview, I discuss three basic approaches to improving state economies. The first focuses on attracting businesses to a state, and the second tries to enhance local productivity, and the third emphasizes general "capacity building." Following this discussion, I examine research evaluating the impact of economic development policies and consider what guidance it provides for state officials. Before concluding the chapter, I consider how welfare reform and possible changes in intergovernmental relations are likely to shape the future of economic development administration.

I. HISTORICAL BACKGROUND ON ECONOMIC DEVELOPMENT

States have played a key role in economic development throughout much of U.S. history (Schreiber, 1987). Even before the Revolutionary War, the colonies competed against one another to maximize immigration, develop trade, and encourage investment and growth. Land grants, loans, and tax exemptions subsidized industries ranging from iron and nail manufacturing to woolen and cotton mills (Brace, 1993:18). During the 19th century intervention continued as states developed their infrastructure, chartered banks, and subsidized private business ventures (Fosler, 1988:12). Massive projects such as the Erie Canal in New York characterized this era of economic development, and resulted in significant advantages for states capable of making such investments.

During the post–Civil War era, however, the relative importance of state-level economic development policies began to decline for a number of reasons (Schreiber, 1987). First, the federal government became increasingly active in economic regulation, particularly during the Progressive Era. In addition, the rise of large-scale corporations with wide-ranging operations lessened the impact of states' efforts, as it became increasingly difficult to contain economic activities within the boundaries of one state. Finally, the U.S. Supreme Court struck down many state attempts at intervention, favoring a nation-centered interpretation of the Commerce clause (Brace, 1993:21).

From the New Deal until the 1960s, the national government dominated economic policy. Federal programs such as the Community Development Block Grant and the Urban Development Action Grant funded economic development efforts targeted at urban areas and the poor (Kossy, 1996). Large northern cities benefited from this intergovernmental aid, while federal defense spending acted as a *de facto* federal development program for at least parts of the South (Brace, 1993). During this period, state-level economic development programs were most evident in lower-income, Southern states, such as Arkansas, Louisiana, and Mississippi. Beginning in the 1970s, however, a number of factors, including a struggling national economy, the apparent failure of macroeconomic policy, and a growing interest in devolving federal responsibilities, converged to make economic development a top state priority.

II. CONTEMPORARY ECONOMIC DEVELOPMENT POLICY

Contemporary economic development policies fall into three basic types, or "waves." Classifying programs in this way is useful for understanding the economic premises that underlie them. The wave metaphor is misleading, however, in that it implies that successive policies replaced their predecessors. In many states all three approaches now operate simultaneously, and in most at least two of the three are present. Furthermore, experimentation and the demands of politics, rather than a desire for theoretical coherence, often shape actual policy choices.

A. First Wave

The "first wave" of policies is also known as the "supply-side" approach (Eisinger, 1988) "locational policies" (Clarke and Saiz 1996), or, more pejoratively, "smokestack chasing." The basic idea is to entice businesses to move their branch plants from one state to another by minimizing taxes, wage rates, or other costs. While every state has engaged in plant attraction strategies over the past 25 years, the roots of the policy are in the economically troubled South of the 1920s and 1930s. During this era, Southern states adopted three basic approaches to recruiting business (Cobb, 1993). The first involved offering tax exemptions to relocating industries. Arkansas first adopted this approach in 1926. Industrial development bonds, which finance the construction or purchase of industrial buildings with public funds, are the second early supply-side policy. Mississippi's "Balance Industry with Agriculture Program," created in 1936, was the pioneering effort. The third policy initiative of this era, right-to-work laws, appeared slightly later. Essentially these statutes outlawed the closed shop requirement that workers join a union as a condition of employment. Arkansas and Florida were the first states to adopt, in 1944, but all of the members of the former Confederacy had followed this lead by 1954. Complementing explicit first-wave strategies, Southern states acted to create favorable "business climates" through lax environmental and worker protection standards.

Local governments played a key role in administering and financing many of the early tax incentive and industrial development bond efforts. As early as the 1920s, however, Southern states created economic development agencies to promote and, in some cases, oversee local efforts. Despite almost immediate questions about their effectiveness, the agencies and their influence in state government, grew rapidly, especially after World War II (Cobb, 1993).

Although the Southern states pioneered first-wave policies, the use of tax incentives and other business subsidies had "gone national" by the 1970s, as Northeastern and Midwestern states began to outpace the South in the number of programs they offered (Eisinger, 1988:62). Especially hard hit by the decade's economic crises, rust belt policy makers discarded earlier reservations about "smokestack chasing." By the late 1970s, when states began to compete for foreign investment in auto plants and related industries, Northern states such as Pennsylvania and Ohio were among the fiercest combatants. At this point, economic development policy had begun to resemble an "arms race" where fear of becoming "uncompetitive" drove states to adopt the incentive programs of their neighbors (Wilson, 1993:7). Annual "business climate" reports by the Fantus Corporation and the Alexander Grant accounting firm (later Grant-Thornton) stoked the arms race mentality. These studies awarded high rankings to states with low taxes, cheap labor, minimal worker protections, and lax environmental regulations, thereby legitimizing the connection between cost factors and economic performance (Brace, 1993).

As first-wave policies became more universal, they also began to appear less effective. Diligent, long-run efforts to attract businesses by offering tax incentives and related concessions failed to reverse economic stagnation and outright decline in some regions (Eisinger, 1988:81). High-profile industrial recruitment efforts, such as Pennsylvania's successful bid to attract Volkswagen, failed to produce the expected job benefits. Critics charged that the success of the Sunbelt stemmed more from federal defense expenditures than state-level policies (Brace, 1993).

These doubts about the effectiveness of existing first-wave approaches led many states to experiment with alternatives. Some fit the second-wave model, discussed in more depth below. Others were variations on old themes. For example, enterprise zones offer targeted tax incentives to attract businesses to putatively depressed areas. In the end, however, first-wave policies remain popular into the 1990s. Widely publicized incentive packages, most notably Alabama's successful bid of $300 million to attract Mercedes-Benz and 1500 jobs, illustrate this point. More systematic evidence comes from a survey conducted by the Council of State Governments, which revealed that between 1992 and 1997, 35 states offered more business incentives, while only three offered fewer (Chi and Leatherby, 1997). This study also showed that the number of states offering each of 15 tax incentives increased between 1986 and 1996. By some estimates, states spend more on tax incentives (in the form of forgone revenue) than on all other economic development programs combined (Lynch, 1996).

The continuing popularity of tax incentives coexists with increasing concerns about their possible misuse. In particular, state officials worry about balancing potential economic gains with actual revenue losses and ensuring accountability. To address this issue, some states use cost-benefit analyses before awarding incentives, while others restrict their use to attracting high-quality jobs, and a few deny incentives to businesses that are downsizing elsewhere in the state (Peirce, 1995). Somewhat more widespread are "clawback laws" that require payback of all or part of subsidies in cases where the number of jobs created does not meet initial promises (Mahtesian, 1994). Administering these policies has been difficult, however. Public officials are often unwilling to antagonize local industries, especially those that appear to be in financial trouble (Mahtesian, 1994). For example, in the early 1990s, when Northwest Airlines was facing possible bankruptcy, Minnesota was reluctant to punish it for reneging on a deal to site repair facilities in a depressed part of the state.

A more comprehensive approach encourages state cooperation to limit interstate bidding wars that drive incenitve packages to levels exceeding $100,000 per job, as illustrated in the Alabama example cited above. So far, however, these efforts seem to have had little success. For example, a 1991 nonaggression pact among Connecticut, New York, and New Jersey lasted only a few months (Mahtiesen, 1994). A 1993 National Governors Assoication agreement to voluntarily reduce the use of incentives also appears toothless.

B. Second Wave

Second-wave policies, also designated "demand-side" (Eisinger, 1988) and "entrepreneurial" (Clarke and Saiz, 1996), emerged in the 1980s to supplement the first wave. In short, the second wave favors improving the productivity of existing industries and promoting local entrepreneurship, rather than trying to attract businesses. Before examining the specifics, it is useful to understand the economic context in which the new policies emerged. The second wave was, in part, a response to increasing awareness of global competition, a phenomenon that existing programs seemed unable to address.

In the early 1980s, the U.S. economy appeared to face challenges on two fronts. On the one hand, improved communications and transportation technology allowed firms to locate routine production throughout the world, wherever costs were lowest. Thus, many manufacturers who had moved to the U.S. South during the 1950s and 1960s to cut expenses left for developing world locations during the 1970s and 1980s (Eisinger, 1988:40). In this environment, first-wave policies focused on lowering business costs began to make less sense, as competing with Third World nations on this basis would require drastic reductions in U.S. living standards.

On the other hand, a challenge stemmed from the higher quality of many goods produced by advanced industrial competitors of the United States, such as Japan and Germany. Their increasing dominance of technologically sophisticated "high-end" manufacturing seemed to pose a serious threat to well-paying domestic jobs. Furthermore, German and Japanese success appeared to stem from "industrial policies," which featured public-private cooperation to assist particular industries and promote collaborative research and development spending within various sectors (Corporation for Enterprise Development, 1987). First-wave efforts, by contrast, did nothing to encourage domestic manufacturers to innovate or improve product quality and ignored issues such as inadequate R&D. While Japanese and German policies appeared to help firms complete effectively in the global marketplace, those of the U.S. states seemed to reward businesses that came up with the most innovative ways to demand tax concessions.

Growing awareness of these trends, combined with the rejection of an explicit national industrial policy during the Reagan era, led to the second wave of economic development in the states. Key themes of the second wave include public-private partnerships, increasing research and development spending, strategic planning, geographic and industry targeting, promoting entrepreneurship, and a concern with creating quality jobs in "high-value" industries. In a 1992 speech, Governor Zell Miller of Georgia (1992:6) summarized the elements of second wave as "identifying high-value-added clusters of industry and technology, analyzing our regional needs, pulling together state agencies and weaving all of the factors into a strategic plan built on public-private partnerships." Perhaps the most prominent policies, existing in all 50 states, emphasize high technology development. Venture capital financing schemes and export promotion programs have also been widely used (Eisinger, 1988). Each of these three major initiatives is discussed in more depth below.

High-technology initiatives rest on two somewhat related premises. The first is that this sector is an "industry of the future." The obvious, although not necessarily proven, corollary of this thesis is that states without a strong high-technology presence face a grim economic outlook. The second basic premise is that applied technological innovation is the only way to preserve the competitiveness of traditional industries ranging from food processing to automobile manufacturing.

Actual state programs reflect these two basic emphases. North Carolina's Research Triangle Park is a very early example of an effort to promote technology-intensive industries. Texas' Advanced Research Program and Advanced Technology Program also emphasize basic research in the hope that it will enhance long-run productivity (Feller, 1992). This approach is becoming less common, however, owing to fears that the results will be diffused to other states (Berglund and Coburn, 1995). Business incubators are another way to promote technology-based industries. With these programs state or local governments provide space and shared services, ranging from secretarial help to accounting and marketing advice, to entrepreneurs who lack business experience.

A number of high-profile state programs also fit the applied model. The Ben Franklin Partnership in Pennsylvania emphasizes spinoff product development. The New Jersey Advanced Technology Centers and Ohio's Thomas Edison Program target research tailored to particular industries, such as food or ceramics (Feller, 1992). The Michigan Modernization Service is an industrial extension program for traditional industries, particularly small firms that supply automobile manufacturers. Services it offers include applying technology to the workplace, retraining workers, and providing advice on topics such as marketing (Osborne, 1988:165–167). Falling somewhere in between the basic and applied models are biotechnology initiatives. Thirty states had created centers to promote research, funding, and business development in this area by the late 1980s (Webber, 1995).

Many states run high-technology programs through their public research universities, in order to draw on the expertise of science and engineering faculty.

Actual administrative structures, however, reflect fears that the universities will divert funds toward basic research, rather than that with an economic payoff for the state. Thus, programs such as the Ben Franklin Partnership require a partial business match of any state funding for university projects (Osborne, 1988). To further ensure that projects focus on economic development, many states administer technology programs through outside boards, rather than the normal higher-education bureaucracy (Feller, 1992). Still, states vary widely in the extent to which universities or industry control the research agendas of high-technology programs (Berglund and Coburn, 1995).

Venture capital programs rest on the premise that small businesses are critical to promoting economic growth through new product development, and that traditional institutions for providing private capital, such as banks or the stock market, fail this sector. Even private firms that specialize in venture capital are often undercapitalized, and may ignore projects that have the greatest economic development payoffs. To fill this gap, states have used their own resources, such as pension funds, to finance new business start-ups. The mechanics of the programs differ, but common tactics include loan programs for first-time entrepreneurs, and product development corporations that finance new products in return for a royalty or a share of the profits (Eisinger, 1988:249–261).

The third major second-wave initiative, export development programs, are in a sense successors to first-wave efforts to attract direct foreign investment. These programs focus on financing, developing markets through personal contact, and assisting firms, particularly small businesses, attempting to sell products in a foreign country (Eisinger, 1988:302). About 40 states maintain offices abroad to administer these efforts, and spending increased sharply during the 1980s (Donahue, 1997:84). More recently, however, export development programs have faced something of a backlash. Unlike other second-wave initiatives, export promotion programs have received explicit backing from the federal government, especially through Department of Commerce programs (Eisinger, 1988:299).

Programs that most closely resemble Japanese-style industrial policy, such as restructuring labor-management relations, or targeting specific industries, have not been implemented as widely, except as regards the technology-focused programs described above. Oregon's attempt to promote two or three key industries in each region of the state is perhaps the most ambitious example of targeting (Roberts, 1993). Like earlier efforts, however, this policy was relatively short-lived (Slavin and Adler, 1996). Programs to adopt less conflicting labor-management relations along the lines of the Japanese model have been even more rare. Those that do exist have been criticized as shallow and cosmetic (Osborne, 1988).

For several reasons, second-wave policies never achieved the levels of political support that the first wave enjoyed. To begin with, potential beneficiaries tend to be unorganized, so strong interest group support is lacking (Wilson, 1993). Second, the benefits of second-wave policies are not always clearly visible, so it is often difficult to draw a cause-effect relationship in the public's mind between policy and economic outcome. By contrast, when a plant moves to a state after receiving tax incentives, the causal connection appears to be clear, even if it is actually absent. Third, many citizens view second-wave policies as elitist (Silver and Burton, 1986).

Specific second-wave policies have also encountered barriers to political success. Support for technology initiatives often erodes when the governor who created the program leaves office (Feller, 1992). Compounding this problem is the fact that well-organized working class constituencies tend to oppose technology development programs, because they see few benefits accruing to relatively uneducated production workers (Osborne, 1988). Implementation problems have eroded support for venture capital programs. The long-time horizon and high risk inherent in such efforts conflict with the electoral cycle and the fear of scandal if taxpayers lost money in investment schemes (Eisinger, 1993a). Finally, efforts to target particular regions have encountered opposition from legislators whose districts are slighted (Slavin and Adler, 1996).

C. Third Wave

The political weaknesses of second wave approaches, combined with growing doubts about their effectiveness, led to another reassessment of economic development in the early 1990s. The result, according to at least some observers, was a "third wave" of policies. Focused on developing human capital, promoting education, investing in distressed communities, encouraging cooperation between businesses and local governments, and general "capacity building," this approach signaled a retreat from direct economic management (Pilcher, 1991).

In general, proponents of the third wave accept the second-wave premise that economic growth is a result of productivity improvements. The key philosophical difference is that the third wave is less directly interventionist, and rejects the idea of patterning state government behavior on Japanese-style industrial policy. Instead, the third wave emphasizes the need to focus on fundamentals such as infrastructure, education, and job training while allowing the market to work out the details of which specific industries will succeed or fail. The lines between second- and third-wave approaches are not always clear in terms of specific policies, however (Eisinger, 1993b; Donahue, 1997). For example, job training programs or community-targeting efforts could fall into either or both categories. In terms of policy delivery, the third wave emphasizes cutting back on direct spending and turning some responsibilities over to nonprofits.

At this point, it is difficult to determine the extent to which states have actually embraced the third wave. Eisinger (1993b:14) contends that although states may be experimenting, there is little evidence of a "sea change" in policy making. A recent analysis of state economic development budgets supports this view. While a minority of states spent slightly more on third-wave approaches in the mid-1990s than during the mid-1980s, more increased economic development spending (as a percentage of their budgets) than decreased it during this period (Boeckelman, 1997b). Also, the newest state initiatives reflect second-wave thinking. Specifically, these policies emphasize promoting industrial "clusters," which encourage small manufacturers in the same industry to share ideas and personnel in ways that will improve productivity (Berglund and Coburn, 1995).

D. The Three Waves: Patterns of Policy Adoption

As suggested above, most states combine different elements of the three waves, adopting a "mix-and-match" approach to economic development. Furthermore, states in economic straits tend to offer more policies of all types (Boeckelman, 1991). Nevertheless, states do differ in their relative preferences for first- and second-wave policies. These variations reflect political differences, especially regarding the roles of interest groups and governors.

   States with powerful business interest groups are most likely to adopt first-wave programs, particularly tax incentives (Ambrosius, 1989). Support may result more from direct benefits received than from the belief that the policies actually have an economic impact. In Louisiana, for example, political support for tax incentives stems from the fact that 80% of the beneficiaries of a major exemption program already operate in the state (Nauth, 1992). By contrast, second-wave policies are more common in states with weak interest groups, largely because potential opponents are neutralized (Gray and Lowery, 1990).

   States where governors have strong formal powers are also likely to adopt second-wave policies (Clarke and Saiz, 1996). On the other hand, in states with relatively weak governors, legislatures can subvert second-wave programs in favor of policies that provide more opportunities for pork-barreling and credit claiming (Slavin and Adler, 1996). Republican governors tend to favor first-wave policies, while Democrats generally support second-wave (Boeckelman, 1996). Although some moderate Republicans, such as Richard Thornburgh in Pennsylvania, were among the leaders in promoting second-wave policies, there seems to be a backlash among more conservative contemporary governors. For example, John Engler in Michigan and George Pataki in New York have attacked technology programs in their states (Feller, 1997). Governors of both parties find it difficult to resist offering big tax incentives when their neighbors do, however (Clarke and Saiz, 1996). As Eisinger (1988:138) argues, "No political leader wishes to be accused of acting in such a way as to lower a state's business climate. In state politics, this is tantamount to the presidential sin of losing Central America to the communists."

III. THE IMPACT OF ECONOMIC DEVELOPMENT PROGRAMS

Efforts to evaluate state economic development programs have focused on both overall effort and the impact of specific initiatives. Before reviewing the findings, however, it is necessary to point out that assessing the impact of these policies is difficult. To begin with, there are a number of methodological problems that hamper evaluation research in economic development (Bartik, 1991). Key policy variables such as tax rates and the level of tax incentives are hard to operationalize, especially because state officials sometimes resist attempts at objective evaluation (Fosler, 1988:315). Measuring the magnitude of resources devoted to tax exemption or loan programs is often particularly difficult because so many operate "off budget." The sheer number of variables affecting economic performance also complicates attempts to specify a model correctly and achieve adequate control (Bartik, 1991). In addition, variables that are supposed to affect levels of economic development, such as labor costs, are in turn affected by levels of economic development, making it difficult to isolate causal relationships. Finally, states have open economies, subject to vast national and international forces beyond their control. Measuring the impact of many small programs, typical of the second wave, is particularly vexing given the magnitude of outside economic forces at play.

Compounding these problems is a lack of consensus about what the goal of economic development is, and how it should be measured. This absence of agreement is important because there may be trade-offs between different development policy outcomes, such as raising per capita incomes or promoting job growth. As Brace (1993:111) puts it, "By succeeding in one area, the states may set themselves up to fail in another by pricing themselves out of the labor market. This is the fundamental bind that the states find themselves in." As a result, studies of the same program may reach very different conclusions, depending on whether effectiveness is measured in terms of income growth, jobs created, or something else.

A. Impact of Overall Economic Development Effort

Studies of the impact of overall economic development effort yield contradictory results that appear to depend, at least in part, on the time period under study, the definition of economic development in use, and the measure of policy effort. One measure of commitment is resources. Goss and Phillips (1997) find that agency spending had a positive impact on state income growth but an indeterminate impact on job growth between 1986 and 1994. Examining the 1986–1988 period, however, Bingham and Bowen (1994) conclude that economic development expenditure has no impact on the change in gross state product.

An alternative measure of effort is the number of programs a state offers. Based on a sum of tax incentives, financial assistance programs, and industry support initiatives that each state offers, Brace (1993) concludes that greater activity raises per-capita income, but only under certain conditions. First, a state's efforts only matter if its economy is relatively independent of the national economy. When, on the other hand, national factors drive a state's performance, state-level policy efforts are useless. Second, state policies seem to have had more of an impact during the 1980s than during the 1970s.

B. Impact of First-Wave Programs

Other studies have looked at the impact of more narrowly defined policy initiatives. Perhaps the most widely studied question concerns the impact of tax policy, including incentives. The methods and conclusions of this research have shifted significantly over time, with many early studies based on survey research concluding that tax factors had little impact on location decisions, although more recent research has challenged this conclusion (Donahue, 1997).

Surveys and interviews of corporate decision makers have generally shown that tax factors, particularly tax incentives, play a relatively small role in determining where businesses locate. According to Kieschnick (1981:84), "Tax incentives do appear to influence some firms, but very few. For the great majority, the reduced taxes represent a pleasant windfall." Based on interviews with key location decision makers, Schmenner (1982:46–50) concurs that taxes were a "minor consideration, capable of altering the decision in favor of a particular site only if almost all other factors are equal." Another analysis, by Schmenner et al. (1987), found a two-stage decision-making process in locating plants. In the first stage, when decision makers narrow down which states to consider directly, tax factors, particularly overall tax rates, seem to have an impact. In the final decision stage, when a specific location is selected, tax factors seem to be less important.

Studies using econometric techniques conclude that taxes, especially tax rates, have a greater impact on state economies than the earlier location studies suggest, in part due to changing conditions. Goss and Phillips (1997) argue that, in contrast to the past, "recent reductions in relative transportation costs and improvements in communications technology may have . . . encouraged decision makers to become even more sensitive to even small tax differentials among states in evaluating alternative locations for firm location or relocation." Bartik (1991:43) reviews a number of studies on the impact of business taxes on location choices and concludes that a 10% state tax increase reduces business activity between 1% and 6%, all else equal. A more recent review by Wasylenko (1997) suggests that high business taxes and high overall taxes negatively affect employment levels, gross state product, levels of manufacturing investment, and location choices of manufacturers. The impact of taxes on income levels is less clear, however.

Econometric studes of the impact of taxes on state economies, particularly those focused on tax incentives, suffer from difficulties in collecting accurate data on the programs in question. As a result, some of the most recent studies in this area have adopted simulation techniques to model the behavior of businesses. In general, these studies suggest that incetives affect business behavior, at least for certain industries, particularly capital-intensive manufacturers (Donahue, 1997; Wasylenko, 1997).

Although there is an increasing consensus, then, that tax factors have some impact on state economies, existing research also suggests several important caveats. First, businesses look at the overall tax benefit picture and the fiscal health of the state in determining where to locate, rather than tax factors alone. Thus, state and local tax increases that fund particular public services may encourage more business activity (Bartik, 1991:48). Second, fiscal distress, such as high debt, is a disincentive to business location, even if the borrowing is used to fund tax incentives (Grant and Hutchinson, 1996). Third, while much attention has focused on the impact of tax rates and incentives, the incidence of taxation also shapes a state's economy. Specifically, regressive tax systems that limit the burdens of corporations appear to promote manufacturing investment, and have a weak, but positive, impact on state growth (Grant and Hutchinson, 1996; Chernick, 1997). Finally, statistical significance in econometric studies can disguise the fact that the overall policy impact of tax factors may be small. By one estimate, for example, a 1% cut in state and local taxes would create a mere 975 jobs annually in New York and 44 in Montana (Lynch, 1996).

Enterprise zones have also received extensive evaluation. A review of this research by Dowall (1996) suggests that their overall impact is modest, at best. Most tax breaks that enterprise zones provide go to businesses that would operate there anyway (Porter, 1997). Furthermore, the few businesses that are attracted to the area rarely hire neighborhood residents. In sum, the tax incentives offered in enterprise zones are typically too modest to offset more serious barriers to economic development, such as lack of skilled labor or capital financing (Dowall, 1996).

Other first-wave policies have received less attention. Available evidence, however, suggests that labor-oriented polices, such as right-to-work laws, affect plant location, particularly for relatively "footloose" plants that do not need to be located near specific markets or suppliers (Schmenner et al., 1987). States with high workers compensation costs also tend to lose out on such businesses (Tannenwald, 1997). Bingham and Bowen (1994) find that states that aggressively use industrial revenue bonds had stronger manufacturing sectors. Grant (1996) finds that the use of loan guarantee programs is positively associated with levels of new business formation.

C. Impact of Second-Wave Programs

Because they appeared on the scene relatively recently, there are fewer outside evaluations of second-wave policies than was true of their predecessors. In-house evaluations are more numerous. For various methodological and political reasons, however, they are often poorly designed and of limited usefulness (Feller, 1992). One of the few evaluations of the aggregate impact of the second wave suggests that offering a mix of policies, including capital financing, technology assistance, and job training, enhances state economic performance (Bingham and Bowen, 1994). The time period for this study was relatively brief, however.

Independent evaluations of individual second-wave policies are sparse and show mixed results. Analyses of university-based technology programs show little evidence of a direct economic impact (Feller, 1992, 1996). Their greatest contribution may be indirectly enhancing government-business relations, improving academic programs that train high technology workers, or increasing small business efficiency. While these accomplishments may have an economic impact in the long run, existing evaluation methods have a hard time discerning it. Geographic targeting and venture capital initiatives also appear to have little direct effect, although the latter may have a symbolic appeal to business interests and engender public-private cooperation (Grant, 1996; Ferguson and Ladd, 1988).

On the other hand, some second-wave efforts show more direct evidence of program effectiveness. A study of incubator programs found that they create a modest number of jobs at a relatively low cost, at least compared to tax incentives, while increasing state income and sales tax revenues (Markley and McNamara, 1996). This research also suggests that incubators have the greatest chance of success when the businesses they nurture complement or serve as suppliers to existing industries. Evaluations of export promotion programs also tend to show that they are effective, a somewhat ironic finding, given recent state cutbacks in this area (Bartik, 1991; Bingham and Bowen, 1994).

D. Impact of Third-Wave Programs

In terms of third-wave approaches, efforts to improve infrastructure appear to have the greatest economic effect. Fisher (1997) reviews a number of studies on the impact of highways, and concludes that spending raises income levels and manufacturing investment, but has no apparent effect on overall employment. Krol (1995), however, argues that maintaining existing roads may yield a greater payoff. He also finds that investing in sewer and water systems promotes economic development. Fisher (1997) finds little evidence that educational spending affects a state's economy, although he acknowledges that dollars may not be the best measure of quality. States with a better-educated population attract more domestic investment, however (Grant and Hutchinson, 1996).

E. National Impacts and Unintended Consequences

The studies discussed above concern the effect of economic development policy
on an individual state's economy. A broader evaluation issue concerns their impact on other states and on national well-being. A common view is that tax incentives are a negative-sum game (Lynch, 1996). According to this outlook, the
forgone revenues states spend on attracting businesses are a waste of national
resources, since the plants would locate somewhere in the United States. If all
states respond to external competition by increasing incentives, they only lose
more revenue, but create no new competitive advantage. Bartik (1991) challenges
this line of reasoning, however. He argues that competition among states may
lead to more regionally balanced patterns of economic development, which, in
turn, may promote national goals such as reducing inflation and increasing overall
productivity. Of course, these benefits will only occur if the policies in question
actually work, which is not always the case. In any event, empirical evidence on
this question is sparse at this time.

Recent studies have begun to consider unintended consequences of economic development programs. Perhaps the most dramatic involve distortions of
a state's tax system through the use of incentives (Brunori, 1997). To begin with,
tax exemptions violate the principle of horizontal equity, because similarly situated businesses pay different tax bills. Second, their use can create a regressive
tax system, as the largest and most profitable companies receive the lion's share
of tax incentives. Third, widespread use of incentives also complicates tax administration, because laws are likely to change more frequently.

Unintended consequences accompany other programs as well. In decreasing the bargaining power of unions, right-to-work laws may be partly responsible
for recent increases in income inequality (Bradbury et al., 1996). Enterprise zones
may discourage entrepreneurship in the areas so designated (Porter, 1997). Programs that actually do create jobs for an area may result in service costs that
exceed the economic benefits, especially since a substantial majority of jobs created by conventional development programs go to in-migrants (Wasylenko, 1997:
48). Finally, educational spending and job training programs may enable skilled
workers to leave the area that paid for these skills (Loveridge, 1996).

F. Discussion

While informative, the studies discussed above hardly provide crystal-clear guidance to those whose job is to design programs to improve a state's economy.
Even if the results were more definite and concrete, it is important to keep in
mind that evaluation research in this area continues to evolve, and new studies
are likely to produce new findings, some of which will contradict today's knowledge. It is probably worth noting that 30 years after President Johnson's Great

Society, debate over the effectiveness of its programs continues, fueled by new rounds of evaluation research.

That said, some important themes do emerge from the studies discussed above. In terms of the "big picture," states should adopt a reasonable tax system that is not too far out of line with their neighbors, in terms of either overall bite or the relative share that businesses pay. Adequate spending for some infrastructure programs also appears to pay off. More targeted programs, whether incentives or various second-wave programs, need to be used carefully. In making decisions on incentives, cost-benefit criteria, and consideration of whether the offerings will really affect a corporate decision should be more important than what other states are promising. Second-wave policies that build on existing economic strengths, such as export promotion and incubators, are probably a better bet for most states than university-based high-technology policies, particularly for those without strong research institutions to begin with. Since the economic benefits of some programs appear only in the long term, patience is often necessary (Markely and McNamara, 1996).

States also need to be aware that economic development presents many trade-offs. Programs that create jobs may depress wages, while those that raise incomes may heighten unemployment. Tax incentives funded through service cutbacks or deficit financing may backfire. Finally, it is important to keep in mind that many factors affecting economic development, such as climate, energy costs, and accessibility to markets, are outside a state's direct control (Bradbury et al., 1997).

For all the problems of evaluation discussed above, states do learn from some of their mistakes (Berglund and Coburn, 1995:32). Still, better in-house program evaluation may improve outcomes, or at least place states in a better position to judge the effectiveness of their policies. To achieve such improvements, a number of steps are necessary. First, it is important to set clear performance standards when economic development programs are created or expenditures occur (Bingham and Bowen, 1994). Second, these standards must be objectively measurable, unlike common measures such as jobs created, which are easy to manipulate. Third, evaluation strategies should be tailored to the type of program in question (Bartik, 1991). For programs large enough to have a detectable economic impact, it is crucial to choose several states as controls, based on different assumptions about the role of outside economic forces. For smaller programs that are unlikely to have a measurable impact on aggregate economic indicators, micro-level data on businesses affected by the program and a comparable control group are appropriate (Bartik, 1991). For example, surveys of hiring patterns in enterprises under both conditions would provide useful information on program success.

Of course, all of this advice ignores the political context of policy. It will perhaps come as no surprise that the most effective programs are often the least politically popular, and vice versa (Dewar, 1998). Thus, policies that work, such as export promotion, need to be presented such that voters don't perceive them as junkets for governors and bureaucrats. Dealing with politically popular but economically questionable programs, such as tax incentives or high-technology initiatives, is more difficult. Lobbying the federal government to take a greater role in overseeing state policies is one possibility, but not an extremely promising one in the current climate of devolution.

IV. OTHER ISSUES IN ECONOMIC DEVELOPMENT

A. Economic Development and Welfare Reform

In 1996 Congress passed the Personal Responsibility and Work Opportunity Act, which replaces Aid to Families with Dependent Children (AFDC) with a new program called Temporary Assistance for Needy Families (TANF). A major feature of this law is a block grant financing system that enhances state flexibility in designing programs. Most discussion of the plan has focused on how it will impact benefit levels that states provide (Lurie, 1997). Less remarked upon, but more significant for our purposes, the flexibility in the welfare reform law may lead to a partial merger of welfare and economic development functions.

A few states have already begun to overhaul their welfare agencies to emphasize economic development functions such as job training, development, and counseling (Tweedie, 1998). Illinois, for example, exempts potential entrepreneurs from work requirements and allows them to continue to receive welfare benefits while they start their own businesses. The other side of the coin is that economic development agencies may become more focused on welfare issues. The new law differs from AFDC in allowing states to administer programs through a number of agencies, rather than a single welfare bureaucracy (Lurie, 1997). As a result some, including Florida and Arkansas, have already begun to enlist their economic development agencies to help implement TANF (Tweedie, 1997).

At this point, it is impossible to predict the extent to which distributive concerns will drive states' development policy agendas. An inescabable conclusion, however, is that an increasing focus on redistribution will complicate efforts to adminster programs and heighten the conflict surrounding them (Ripley and Franklin, 1982). Ironically, current programs often benefit areas and people that are already well off (Dewar, 1998; Boeckelman, 1997a). To cite a recent example, North Carolina agreed to incentives of $272 million to induce Federal Express to locate a sorting hub in the prosperous Greensboro area, despite that fact that the more economically troubled eastern section of the state also sought the facility. The fact that economic development policies are associated with a positive image (i.e., ''growth'') and with a constituency that the public views favorably (i.e., business) keeps conflict over such policy decisions to a minimum (Lindblom, 1982). Economic development programs designed explicitly to help the poor or to promote income equality are unlikely to enjoy such legitimacy.

B. Intergovernmental Aspects of Economic Development Administration

Economic development administration operates in a complex intergovernmental environment. Despite cutbacks, federal grants, especially in the areas of job training and urban redevelopment, account for the majority of funds in most state development agencies' budgets. States also use intergovernmental aid to finance local economic development activities ranging from job training to incubators. In light of continuing interest in reassigning policy responsibilities among levels of government, it is pertinent to ask whether the current division is ideal. Put another way, is the state role too large, too small, or just right?

Some have argued for more national involvement in economic development, or at least greater oversight (Donahue, 1997). This argument reflects the idea that economic development policies create externalities or spillovers that lead states to overuse some policies and underuse others. On the one hand, offering tax incentives to attract industry creates pressures on neighboring states to "bid" more than they otherwise might, leading to overspending in this area. On the other hand, states may underinvest in second-wave policies, because, to the extent that they work, some economic benefits will accrue to nearby states as well. The continuing popularity of tax incentives in the face of severe criticisms of their cumulative impact and the scaling back of second-wave policies in some states are consistent with this scenario. The federal government could deal with this problem by developing its own industrial policy and by imposing curbs on the use of tax incentives, or even challenging their constitutionality on Commerce Clause grounds (Bradbury et al., 1997). Currently, such changes appear unlikely. The Clinton Administration has a more activist economic development agenda than its predecessors, and is less hostile to industrial policy. Still, its specific initiatives, such as empowerment zones, overlay, rather than replace or oversee, existing policies.

A contrasting view holds that local governments should be more responsible for economic development. A basic rationale for state, rather than federal, responsibility in this area is that states are more flexible in the face of rapid economic change, and more sensitive to local variation. Thus, they are better able to target policies to real needs (Rivlin, 1992). Pushing this logic one step further, however, implies that cities and counties could handle economic development administration better than states. The impact, if any, of many state programs ranging from university-based technology programs to incubators to tax incentives tends to be more local than statewide. In fact, not only do local governments offer policies that parallel many of the state initiatives outlines earlier, there is some evidence that the local versions work better. For example, tax incentives tend to be more important in shaping business location decisions among cities within a state or region, rather than among states (Wasylenko, 1997).

If it is appropriate to devolve direct administration of some policies to local governments, then the state role may come to focus more on coordination and ovesight. States may want to expand the use of intergovernmental grants to support productive local efforts, as many already do in areas ranging from incubators to job training. In the oversight realm, states could ensure that programs don't threaten local fiscal health and the abiltiy to provide public services such as infrastrucutre and public safety that support economic development. In effect, states would be perfomring a role similar to that outlined for the federal government above.

V. CONCLUSION

The high profile of economic development issues over the past 25 years stems directly from the fact that the economy has performed poorly during much of this period, at least by post–World War II standards. Given the centrality of economic issues in American politics generally, state officials have faced great pressures to "do something" to improve the situation. As discussed above, however, it is often unclear what works, and policies that help fix some problems often make others worse. In these circumstances, economic development policy administration involves claiming credit and avoiding blame in a climate of "uncertainty, ambiguity, and turbulence" (Wolman and Spitzey, 1996:129).

The future of economic development administration depends on economic context. The prosperous environment of the late 1990s has led to a shift of emphasis in some states' efforts. For example, the focus of policy in some areas is changing to deal with labor shortages, rather than job shortages (Berry, 1998). This shift has already led to new types of concessions. Kentucky recently agreed to create a new university for students working the night shift at United Parcel Service in order to keep the company in Louisville (Jaffe and Blackmon, 1998).

Other economic forces likely to shape development administration in the future include continuing global integration and the evolution of an information-based economy. The former trend is leading border states to develop cooperative economic development institutions with Mexican states and Canadian provinces. As a result, direct marketing activities may become less important for economic development administrators, while regional planning and coordination may become more central to their role.

The increasing importance of a knowledge-based economy is also likely to lead to changes in the focus of economic development activities. Some states are already creating agencies and commissions that respond to and promote the needs of the information industry. For example, California has formed an "Electronic Commerce Council" to advise state government on commercial issues related to the Internet (Wilson, 1998). This trend may require economic-development officials to develop more in-depth knowledge of the industries they are promoting than was true in the past.

Notwithstanding these changes, scrutiny and oversight are likely to increase. In the 1998 gubernatorial campaigns, candidates in various states have called for greater auditing of state economic development expenditures and for budget cuts in some programs. In this climate, divisions of development agencies that can produce easily measurable results may be in the best position to survive cutbacks. Increased oversight and the possibility of budget cuts and downsizing obviously create a more difficult climate for administrators in some respects. In the long run, however, it could lead to better programs and a more appropriate balance between economic development and other state functions.

REFERENCES

Ambrosius, M. M. (1989). The role of occupational interests in state economic development policy-making, *Western Political Quarterly* 42: 53–68.

Bartik, T. (1991). *Who Benefits from State and Local Economic Development Policies?*, W. E. Upjohn Institute for Employment Research, Kalamazoo, MI.

Berglund, D., and Coburn, C. (1995). *Partnerships: A Compendium of State and Federal Cooperative Technology Programs*, Battelle, Columbus.

Berry, D. E. (1998). The jobs and workforce initiative: northeast Ohio employers plan for workforce development, *Economic Development Quarterly* 12: 41–53.

Bingham, R. E., and Bowen, W. M. (1994). The performance of state economic development programs, *Policy Studies Journal* 22: 501–513.

Boeckelman, K. (1997a). Issue definition in state economic development policy, *Policy Studies Journal* 25: 286–298.

Boeckelman, K. (1997b). The evolution of state economic development policies: evidence from state budgets, Paper presented at the annual meeting of the Southern Political Science Association, Atlanta, GA.

Boeckelman, K. (1996). Governors, economic theory, and development policy, *State and Local Government Review* 10: 342–351.

Boeckelman, K. (1991). Political culture and state development policy, *Publius: The Journal of Federalism* 21 (#2): 49–62.

Brace, P. (1993). *State Government and Economic Performance*, Johns-Hopkins University Press, Baltimore, MD.

Bradbury, K. L., Kodrzycki, Y. K., and Tannenwald, R. (1997). The effects of state and local public policies on economic development: an overview, *New England Economic Review* (March/April): 1–12.

Bradbury, K. L., Kodrzycki, Y. K., and Mayer, C. J. (1996). Spatial and labor market contributions to inequality: an overview, *New England Economic Review* (May/June): 1–10.

Brunori, D. (1997). Principles of tax policy and targeted incentives, *State and Local Government Review 29*: 50–61.

Chernick, H. (1997). Tax progressivity and state economic performance, *Economic Development Quarterly 11*: 249–267.

Chi, K. S., and Leatherby, D. (1997). *State Business Incentives: Trends and Options for the Future*, Council of State Governments, Lexington, KY.

Clarke, S. E., and Saiz, M. R. (1996). Economic development and infrastructure policy, *Politics in the American States* (Virginia Gray and Herbert Jacob, eds.), CQ Press, Washington.

Cobb, J. (1993). *The Selling of the South* (2nd ed.), University of Illinois Press, Urbana.

Corporation for Enterprise Development. (1987). *Making the Grade: The Development Report Card for the States*, Corporation for Enterprise Development, Washington.

Dewar, M. W. (1998). Why state and local economic development programs cause so little economic development, *Economic Development Quarterly 12*: 68–87.

Donahue, J. D. (1997). *Disunited States*, Basic Books, New York.

Dowall, D. E. (1996). An evaluation of California's enterprise zone program, *Economic Development Quarterly 10*: 352–368.

Eisinger, P. (1993a). State venture capitalism, state politics, and the world of high-risk investment, *Economic Development Quarterly 7*: 131–139.

Eisinger, P. (1993b). *State Economic Development in the 1990s*, LaFollette Institute of Public Affairs, Madison, WI.

Eisinger, P. (1988). *The Rise of the Entrepreneurial State: State and Local Economic Development Policy in the U.S.*, University of Wisconsin Press, Madison.

Feller, I. (1997). Federal and state government roles in science and technology, *Economic Development Quarterly 11*: 283–295.

Feller, I. (1992). American state governments as models for national science policy, *Journal of Policy Analysis and Management 11*: 288–309.

Ferguson, R. F., and Ladd, H. F. (1988). *Massachusetts, The New Economic Role of the American States* (R. S. Fosler, ed.), Oxford University Press, New York.

Fisher, R. C. (1997). The effects of state and local public services on economic development, *New England Economic Review* March/April: 53–65.

Fosler, R. S. (1988). *The New Economic Role of the American States*, Oxford University Press, New York.

Goss, E. P., and Phillips, J. M. (1997). The effect of state economic development agency spending on income and employment growth, *Economic Development Quarterly 11*: 88–96.

Grant, D. S. (1996). The political economy of new business formation across the American states, *Social Science Quarterly 77*: 28–42.

Grant, D. S., and Hutchinson, R. (1996). Global smokestack chasing: a comparison of the state-level determinants of foreign and domestic manufacturing investment, *Social Forces 43*: 21–38.

Gray, V., and Lowery, D. (1990). The corporatist foundations of state industrial policy, *Social Science Quarterly 71*: 3–24.

Herzik. E. (1983). The governors and issues: a typology of concerns, *State Government 51*: 58–62.

Jaffe, G., and Bjlackmon, D. A. (1998). Even in a strong economy, Kentucky wasn't willing to lose a big employer, *Wall Street Journal* (April 24): 1.

Kienschick, M. (1981). *Taxes and Growth: Business Incentives and Economic Development*, Council of State Planning Agencies, Washington.

Kossy, J. A. (1996). Economic restructuring and the restructuring of economic development practice: a New York perspective, 1985–1995, *Economic Development Quarterly 10*: 300–314.

Krol, R. (1995). Public infrastructure and state economic development, *Economic Development Quarterly 9*: 331–338.

Lindblom, C. (1982). The market as prison, *Journal of Politics 44*: 324–336.

Loveridge, S. (1996). On the continuing popularity of industrial recruitment, *Economic Development Quarterly 10*: 151–158.

Lurie, I. (1997). Temporary assistance for needy families: a green light for the states, *Publius: The Journal of Federalism 27(#2)*: 73–87.

Lynch, R. G. (1996). *Do State and Local Tax Incentive Work?*, Economic Policy Institute, Washington.

Mahtesian, C. (1994). Romancing the smokestack, *Governing* (Nov.): 36–40.

Markley, D. M., and McNamara, K. T. (1996). Local economic development and state fiscal impacts of business incubators, *State and Local Government Review 28*: 17–27.

Miller, Z. (1992). Remarks to the Georgia economic development association, Atlanta, GA (Nov. 23).

Nauth, Z. (1992). *The Great Louisiana Tax Giveaway*, Louisiana Coalition for Tax Justice, Baton Rouge.

Osborne, D. (1988). *Laboratories of Democracy*, Harvard Business School Press, Boston.

Peirce, N. R. (1995). The gold in them thar states, *National Journal* (Nov.): 2820.

Peters, A. H., and Fisher, P. S. (1997). Do high unemployment states offer the biggest business incentives?, *Economic Development Quarterly 11*: 107–122.

Pilcher, D. (1991). The third wave of economic development, *State Legislatures* (Nov.): 34–37.

Porter, M. E. (1997). New strategies for inner-city economic development, *Economic Development Quarterly 11*: 11–27.

Ripley, R. B., and Franklin, G. A. (1982). *Bureaucracy and Policy Implementation*, Dorsey Press, Homewood, IL.

Rivlin, A. M. (1992). *Reviving the American Dream*, Brookings Institution, Washington.

Roberts, B. (1993). Governor's keynote address to challenge of change dinner, Eugene, OR (June 2).

Schmenner, R. (1982). *Making Business Location Decisions*, Prentice-Hall, Englewood Cliffs, NJ.

Schmenner, R., Huber, J. C., and Cook, R. L. (1987). Geographic differences and the location of new manufacturing facilities, *Journal of Urban Economics, 21*: 83–104.

Schreiber, H. N. (1987). State law and industrial policy in American development: 1790–1987, *California Law Review 75*: 415–444.

Silver, H., and Burton, D. (1986). The politics of state-local industrial policy, *Journal of the American Planning Association 52*: 277–288.

Slavin, M. I., and Adler, S. (1996). Legislative constraints on gubernatorial capacity for state industrial policy, *Economic Development Quarterly 10*: 224–238.

Tannenwald, R. (1997). State regulatory policy and economic development, *New England Economic Review* (March/April): 83–99.

Tweedie, J. (1998). Building a foundation for change in welfare, *State Legislatures* (Jan.): 26–33.

Tweedie, J. (1997). Building a better bootstrap, *State Legislatures* (May): 30–31.

Wasylenko, M. (1997). Taxation and economic development: the state of the economic literature, *New England Economic Review* (March/April): 37–52.

Webber, D. J. (1995). The emerging federalism of U.S. biotechnology policy, *Politics and the Life Sciences 14*: 65–72.

Wilson, P. (1998). State of the State Address, Sacramento, CA (Jan. 7).

Wilson, R. H. (1993). *States and the Economy*, Praeger, Westport, CT.

Wolman, H., and Spitzey, D. (1996). The politics of local economic development, *Economic Development Quarterly 10*: 115–150.

15
Administration of State Government Rural Development Policy

Robert Agranoff
Indiana University, Bloomington, Indiana

Michael McGuire
University of North Texas, Denton, Texas

Rural communities face challenges related to structural changes in economic and social life: low skill and resource densities, lack of specialized expertise and information, isolation and limited access to urban amenities, and an overspecialization of local economies. These internal forces, coupled with a transition to a service-based economy and simultaneous declines in agricultural and natural-resource bases, have contributed to dwindling populations, relatively low wages, above-average incidences of poverty, and a declining institutional infrastructure in cities located outside of metropolitan areas. Counteracting or adapting to trends within this rapidly changing environment requires new governing relationships. State governments can make a difference in the development of rural areas.

Rural development is a policy arena in which the federal government traditionally played the leading role, although the focus of federal rural policy was typically on the functional area of agriculture rather than on the cross-cutting issues of rural development. In response to federal disengagement and resource deficiencies across all levels of governments, most states have only recently sought to broaden their economic development focus to include the revitalization of rural cities and regions. Although the central debate in most policy arenas concerns which *policy* tools and approaches are best suited to address societal problems, states face a unique set of *administrative* challenges in rural policies that rarely exist in other policy arenas. To a greater degree than in most policy arenas, the effectiveness of state rural development policy activity is tied closely to the effectiveness of administrative activity. That is, policy design and public management are so tightly linked that public management in state rural development policy may in fact be more consequential than in other arenas. A greater understanding of rural development administration in the states is thus warranted.

The intent of this chapter is to demonstrate how states work with communities in meeting the daunting challenges associated with rural survival and growth and to suggest how the unique characteristics of rural development policy contribute to distinct administrative challenges for state governments. It is about state government activities in rural policy—present and future—from a multiorganizational administrative perspective. Adequate understanding of rural development policy at the state level requires an understanding of the unique structures and processes through which policy is formulated and administered. We show that state government administrators work through a host of networks involving officials from federal government, local governments, the private sector, and nongovernmental organizations as co–policy makers and as project partners. The resources and capabilities of all of these entities are an important part of the administrative equation. We offer a descriptive framework upon which to link rural development policy with state administration by suggesting that the form and content of administrative strategies is a significant determinant of policy effectiveness. That is, policy effectiveness is tied inextricably to network effectiveness.

I. WHY STATES?

Why are states assuming primary responsibility for rural development, especially given the policy and administrative challenges associated with this policy area? There are several justifications for state involvement in rural development. First, most scholars and practitioners argue that long-run success in preserving rural communities must rest on genuine local preferences orchestrated through coordinated collective action. These actions are increasingly coupled with such new means of operation as intercommunity collaboration, new relationships between rural and urban areas, and cooperative ventures with state and federal governments (Bradshaw, 1993; Cooper, 1993; Galston and Bahler, 1995). From this federalism perspective, state governments are in the best position to help communities. States have the flexibility to tailor policies to specific local circumstances, to provide assistance to communities seeking to take charge of their future, and to design policy responses around local plans and strategies (John, 1991; Ross and Friedman, 1991). This combination of top-down and bottom-up connections stand in sharp contrast to the federal government experience in rural policy, which has traditionally been focused on broad economic patterns and policy responses designed to raise overall levels of performance, not always with the participation and cooperation of the rural communities being affected by the policy. Furthermore, there has not been a concerted effort to establish rural (or urban) development policy by the federal government since the Carter Administration. States working with local governments cannot reverse broad economic trends, but they do work at reversing local decline on a targeted basis.

Second, states are able to affect the relationship between rural and urban areas. In some states, taxes from more prosperous or more populated urban areas are reallocated to rural areas. Financial and technical assistance from states can improve equity between the two areas. States can also build on the strong social and economic linkages between rural and urban areas. States recognize that "rural problems of low skill levels and high unemployment" often manifest as "urban problems through migration from the state's rural to its urban areas" (Sears et al., 1992). Market failures in rural economies affect metropolitan areas and consequently the entire state economy. Efficiencies within the state economy as a whole can be gained by devoting sufficient attention to rural development activities.

The third justification for state involvement in rural development policy is based on the notion of preservation. The people of each state, through their elected officials and their governments, are in the best position to decide whether the rural way of life is worth preserving or, alternatively, whether the notion of a rural lifestyle is outdated and unnecessary. This argument raises the same issues as the public policy debate of whether to save or redevelop downtowns in central cities. Should we save the small rural towns that serve only the lowest of economic functions? Or should the areas with inefficiencies and low productivity be eradicated so that the state, regional, national, and international economy can operate at a higher capacity? Unlike natural resources, individual human resources—the people of a community—are mobile. The collective human resources of a community are less mobile but tend to change over time as individuals move in and out of a community. The ability of a community to retain, develop, or attract the quantity and quality of human resources needed to sustain local development will depend largely on the quality of life available in the community. One of the primary attraction-and-retention advantages that rural communities have over urban and suburban areas is the perception of the rural lifestyle: the slower, friendlier, and more family-oriented community. Neither the federal government nor the community itself is able to effectively address and resolve the preservation issue.

II. DISTINCTIVENESS OF RURAL DEVELOPMENT POLICY

Part of the rural development effort by states includes a search for the most appropriate administrative structures to carry out policy activity. Determining *what* works for rural development, the policy question, has in many ways been

Table 1 Distinctiveness of State Rural Development

Distinct characteristics of state rural development policy
1. Varies along geographical rather than purely socioeconomic lines.
2. Is a policy area without a home.
3. Is largely information-based.
4. Is designed and administered across organizations and sectors.

exceeded in importance by the need to determine *how* to make it work, the managerial question. Analysis of state activity in development issues during this decade has focused on constructing the proper public technology for delivering goods and services to communities (Fosler, 1992; Ross and Friedman, 1991). While this analytical soul-searching has helped redirect general economic development efforts in states, a more specific focus on development issues for rural areas has been difficult. As a possible explanation for this difficulty, we can look to four characteristics of state rural development policy that distinguish it from other policy activity. These four characteristics, listed in Table 1, accurately depict the challenges faced by state administrators. They also frame our description of state rural development policy administration.

A. Geographical vs. Socioeconomic Emphasis

The first unique quality of state rural development policy is the way in which geographical rather than socioeconomic conditions determine the content of and emphasis on rural policy in the states. What constitutes rural development is only partially a function of poverty or education levels; some states dedicate more resources and energy to rural development activities simply because there are more rural areas in that state. However, while deciding what constitutes a "rural area" and what a definition of this term means for policy making and administration remains an important task, it is also a difficult task. Many people across the country have an intuitive but mistaken notion of ruralness—grazing cows, blowing wheat fields, or miles of neatly planted rows of corn. Homey restaurant-based but no more accurate definitions have been heard in rural communities. One small-town native mentioned only half-mockingly that rural is "where people eat, not dine." Another rural resident told us that rural is "where the table is set with only one fork." A rural development scholar has even offered a restaurant-based definition: using his "McDonald's criterion," Cooper (1993) states that an area is truly rural if it is still without a McDonald's restaurant (p. 36). It is no surprise then that most people still associate the term rural exclusively with sparse amenities, the farm or with areas of natural resource extraction.

There is also a tendency in economic research to equate the term rural with a poor or struggling economy. Scholars and practitioners alike know that particular features of ruralness include small scale, low density of population, isolation, specialization of local economies, and the relative lack of human and financial resources (Deavers, 1992; Lapping et al., 1989). And to be sure, many rural places are characterized by particularly weak economies, as measured by many different socioeconomic indicators. Job growth, yearly earnings, and education attainment are, on average, lower in rural places than in urban or suburban places, whereas tax burden, poverty rates, and mortality rates are, on average, higher. Rural areas have experienced declines in population over the past few decades, and a loss of schools and hospitals has contributed to a declining institutional base. However, utilizing these indicators as the primary means to differentiate between rural and urban places is misleading because this practice presumes that all rural places are comparable. The true condition of rural America is not nearly so homogeneous: rural areas include not just farmlands, but mines, oil wells, woodlands, industrial centers, commercial centers, resorts, and retirement communities (Sears et al., 1992). A small, poor suburb is not at all like a large, prosperous suburb; these two communities share the suburban classification and little else. The same is true for rural places. Some rural places are poor, but some are not. Some rural places are inhabited by just a few hundred persons, while many others have more than 20,000 people. Some rural places are located ''in the middle of nowhere,'' whereas others are relatively close to thriving metropolitan areas. While rural is often used as an all-encompassing term, such a blanket descriptor of communities is an inadequate guide for development policy.

The standard and simplest definition of rural, as used by the Census Bureau, is adopted in this chapter. Rural simply refers to any community—incorporated as a municipality or not—that is not located within a metropolitan statistical area. The more accurate term for rural is ''nonmetropolitan.'' States and the federal government designate counties as metropolitan or nonmetropolitan and then generally refer to the cities and towns within these counties as urban or rural when targeting assistance programs. The metro/nonmetro distinction encompasses all cities, the latter of which includes small to medium-size independent towns of up to 25,000 in population, as well as the majority of towns that are inhabited by fewer than 10,000 persons. This simple definition yields varying and sometimes nonintuitive notions of ruralness throughout the country. For example, states like New Hampshire, Idaho, Kentucky, and Arkansas have a larger rural population than states like Kansas, Iowa, or Nebraska that are located in the corn belt, although the latter have a higher proportion of rural land dedicated to farming. The northeastern state of Vermont, in fact, has a larger percentage of its population living in rural areas than any state in the nation.

A coupling of the place-based concept of ''rural'' with the equally ambiguous term ''development'' presents an even greater policy challenge. Development has been defined by rural specialists as "fundamental and sustainable increases in the productivity of individuals and institutions, leading to higher per capita incomes for individuals" (Sears and Reid, 1995:2). Although the goal of development may be to increase incomes and to improve the quality of life, Ferguson and John (1992) argue that development often destroys old options even as it creates new ones, and it harms interests while it helps others. Therefore, far from being based solely in business development and economic growth, rural development is a broad, community-level process. The importance of geography in the development of rural areas is sometimes framed as a choice between people or places. While obviously interlinked, the most successful state efforts in developing rural communities have been place-oriented to the extent that activities are designed to facilitate the ability of communities to plan and implement development programs on their own. These efforts involve not only the development of the local economy, but also improvement of local physical infrastructure, strengthening of local institutions, and enhancement of the social and organizational infrastructures (Bradshaw, 1993:171). Moreover, providing financial resources does not constitute the totality of state efforts. As we discuss later, programs also emphasize the provision of information as a means to develop the community's capacity to develop on its own.

State administrators do not "do rural development," but rather they undertake activities and tasks as a means to affect the development process in rural *communities*. The importance of this place-oriented approach to policy lies in the fact that an overarching economic trend applying to all rural communities simply does not exist. As economic research indicates, much of what affects the development of rural communities is geographical—location in relation to urban areas, proximity to transportation, natural resource availability. The culture of a particular area is also in some part geographically as well as historically determined. The key to success in rural areas thus lies in significant measure inside the rural community, making geography an important component of rural development.

B. Policy Without a Home

Rural development is a policy area without a home. Unlike many state policy sectors, including most of those examined in this volume, such as education, welfare, and criminal justice, the responsibility for developing rural communities does not rest with any single agency, department, or office or even a single set of designated agencies. One cannot readily point to a rural program or agency that administers rural policy. Although related closely to state economic development policy, which is typically located in its own office or as a major part of a larger office, rural development policy is but one targeted component of state economic development. To be sure, many states have responded to the difficult times in rural areas over the last decade and established offices or coordinator's positions for rural affairs in their economic development department. A recent survey conducted by the Corporation for Enterprise Development (CfED) found that state efforts devoted to rural development vary considerably in size, structure, activities, funding, and location in state government. The CfED study found that 32 states have assigned some responsibility for rural concerns to a coordinator unit within a branch of government or to a quasi-public entity. Of these, 22 have created a specific office or organization with singular rural responsibilities within state agencies, offices within the governor's office, or quasi-public nonprofit organizations. However, the development of rural communities involves more than economic-based programs.

Many factors contribute to the orphan status of state rural development policy. The primary challenges to the American economy simply have not affected rural areas. The American economy as a whole—metropolitan and non-metropolitan—has experienced shifts in its economic base, a geographical redistribution of persons and wealth from the Northeast and Midwest regions to the South and the West, and rapidly changing responsibilities within the worldwide economy. Although constrained in part by internal factors such as low density and relatively low levels of development capacity, rural communities face the same external constraints as any other city, nonmetropolitan or otherwise. Scholars and policy makers continue to debate whether the condition of rural communities warrants the designing of new policies and programs for rural areas, or if merely applying existing policies and programs to these areas is the proper course of action. Commenting on this fact, Gillis (1991) suggests that in a "rising tide lifts all boats theme, state policy makers have tended to assume that rural areas could benefit automatically from an improvement in the economic health of the state, as have federal policy makers" (p. 123).

Another factor contributing to the varying administrative location of rural development policy in the states is the nature of the policies that actually affect rural communities. A state's rural development policy is the package of goals, strategies, policies, and programs that in some way or another promote the growth and development of rural communities. However, it is difficult to unravel the part of these strategies and programs that specifically benefit rural areas. In addition to the more *targeted* activities that comprise what most people refer to as development policies are those *cross-cutting* public functions that significantly but not exclusively affect rural communities. When the federal government was in the business of designing and implementing policies specifically designed for rural America, the efforts were focused on just four primary policy arenas: the distribution and management of land, development of human resources and physical infrastructure, financial support for farmers, and the alleviation of poverty in peripheral regions (Lapping et al., 1989). Since states returned in earnest to local economic development in the 1980s, policy development for localities has been plentiful and includes various targeted approaches. John (1991) places them in three categories: entrepreneurship, technology, and human resources.

Influenced by research indicating that the vast majority of new jobs are created by innovative small firms rather than large corporations, states employ a number of targeted activities designed to improve business conditions, business finance, and the local rural business climate. The commonly used expression was that states switched from ''smokestack chasing'' and the ''buffalo hunt'' (attracting branch plants) to growing their own businesses and nurturing small firms. States continue to engage in recruiting for rural areas—witness the rural locations of new automobile plants in the South—but increased competition has led them to such small-firm efforts as business incubators, entrepreneurship training, microenterprise programs, encouraging flexible networks of small manufactures who share marketing, and a multitude of support services. Innovative rural-specific targeted activities include developing small and home-based business, agricultural products processing, and fiber-optic telecommunications.

Since the growth and expansion that occur in small communities are associated largely with those firms that quickly applied new technologies to products and processes, many states and communities have directed their services and products focus to attracting high-technology firms and in bringing new technologies to other industries. States have invested in applied research at their universities, invested in technology transfer and industrial extension centers, and helped firms train workers and/or made other work force adjustments to assure that new technologies can be adapted successfully. The rural community has not been a primary recipient of these efforts by state government, but efforts have been undertaken in some states to improve the production processes of firms in rural communities.

Targeted activites in human resources involve efforts by states to ensure that the work force is at a skill level commensurate with the demands placed on it by the global exonomy. Unlike most federal government efforts, states have experimented with development programs that are not targeted on the basis of income. States have led the efforts to upgrade skills by reforming public education. Many states have created customized job training programs, normally as an inducement for industrial recruitment. State welfare reform efforts that included training as a condition of receiving aid have also been a component of these human resource efforts.

In addition to these targeted development activities, cross-cutting policies such as taxation, education, regulation, health care, and arts and culture are standard functions of state government that are not explicitly directed to but still significantly impact rural communities. These functions are spread across several state departments that administer programs having a bearing on rural development. For example, rural communities are affected by the nontargeted (in terms of place) nature of activities in the state's department of agriculture. Although commonly thought of as a "weights-and-measures" operation, agricultural departments also operate innovative agriculture and new farmer loan programs, promote value-added agricultural products manufacturing, and engage in a wide range of agricultural products marketing programs. Transportation departments in the state administer federal-state highway programs and fund roads for rural communities and for industrial access. State housing authorities acquire, construct, reconstruct, and rehabilitate housing for low- and moderate-income citizens, which affects some citizens in rural communities. Departments of human services provide benefits to persons in rural communities by administering income and social services programs for low- and moderate-income persons, including welfare, Medicaid, weatherization, elderly services, and many other programs. Departments of environment and natural resources administer federal-state and state programs involving environmental regulation, permit issuance, and infrastructure funding, including wastewater projects and solid waste generation and disposal. States also assist rural communities through their participation in a federal-state network of assistance agencies known as small-business development centers, usually co-located at universities, colleges, and community colleges.

From within this policy milieu, states must choose whether to pursue a single overarching goal, such as to advance the rural economy to the same rate of economic activity and job growth as the urban economy, or to set more modest goals. In the early 1990s, Iowa's Rural Policy Academy established five midlevel goals to support the rural sector. The academy team felt that these midrange goals were useful for mobilizing different interests in the state to take specific actions to enhance these aims. The goals involved both targeted and cross-cutting policies, and they provide a good example of how both types of policies, some of which are rural-specific and others not, are important components of a state rural development policy. Table 2 lists these goals.

State administrators in some way involve the work of these various departments and policies as they work to apply generic programs for the benefit of rural areas or to forge special rural initiatives. Because of the questionable economic and social distinctions between metropolitan and nonmetropolitan areas and the minimal guidance it provides to state policy makers, and because of the many targeted and cross-cutting policies affecting rural communities, state rural development policy is truly a policy area without a home.

C. Information-Based Nature of State Rural Policy

A significant portion of the goods and services provided by the states are information-based, as opposed to tangible, goods. Many of the most important tasks undertaken by state agencies include developing leadership in rural communities, helping a community develop an understanding of its local economy, conducting

Table 2   Example of Multiple Policy Types in State Rural Development

Iowa Rural Policy Academy goals

Improve business development and retention in rural Iowa by strengthening and expanding the competitive position of existing business.

Enhance agricultural production and related value adding activities by strenghtening and expanding the competitive position of producers and business.

Develop local leaders and organizations designed to improve the capacity of rural communities to grow and provide services.

Maintain a viable rural health care system, which sustains itself on available resources and is accessible to residents.

Assist local communities in developing new innovative ways to provide quality and affordable public infrastructure.

institutional and environmental evaluations, and assisting a community in establishing priorities for the purposes of designing and implementing strategic development plans (Luke et al., 1988). Even in programs providing financial assistance to rural communities, there is a large information-based, technical assistance component. Table 3 illustrates a number of Iowa's development programs targeted to communities. It displays descriptions of the explicitly labeled rural development programs offered by the Division of Community and Rural Development in Iowa's Department of Economic Development. It also displays more general division programs targeted to communities, of which rural communities are benefactors. Both the rural-targeted and the general community development programs are highly information-based. As demonstrated in these programs descriptions, administrators working in the rural development area not only must be knowledgeable of financial and managerial processes, but also understand profoundly the policy challenges facing rural communities.

One of the most essential tasks performed by state administrators in the rural development policy area is to gather information about the conditions of rural communities and to assess the capacities of the institutions and people in these communities. Through community assessment, administrators attempt to reduce uncertainty felt by communities and to raise the level of information about the applicability and merit of rural development activities. State policy makers and administrators provide information so that local administrators are able to more capably fit development policy activities with the problems and objectives of the community. An administrator can pursue one of two mechanisms in attempting to match strategies and activities with communities (Sears and Reid, 1995). The first mechanism, the *program-centered* approach, seeks to determine the "best" or most effective policy activity or strategy. This approach emphasizes the way in which the myriad policy tools and instruments at the disposal of state and local government are manipulated, combined, and packaged into policies without explicit consideration for their applicability in a specific type of community. Critical information is arrived at through analysis of policy decisions, and the "best" package of policy tools is made available to all communities.

The second policy mechanism is the *community-centered* approach, which starts with a particular community's strengths and weaknesses and then seeks to determine what activity or strategy would work best in that community. This approach requires a two-way information exchange between state administrators and community officials. Community officials help state administrators assess the conditions and capacities of the community, whereas state administrators provide information to community officials regarding how to effectively plan, design, and implement development policy strategies. State administrators act as planners, assisting rural communities in particular planning efforts, which often are based on a vision of what the community should look like. An important information-based function of state rural development policy is to help jurisdictions to adapt to turbulence and capitalize on opportunities that appear. Thus, state and local actors work together to establish which aspects of the community should be preserved and which should be altered.

Building community capacity is consistent with a community-centered approach. Capacity has long been identified as an important correlate of effective governance, and nowhere is the issue of insufficient development capacity more prevalent than in rural communities (Reeder, 1989; Hustedde, 1991; Reed and Paulsen, 1987; Reed and Paulsen, 1991; Walzer and Gruidl, 1991; Sears et al., 1992; McGuire et al., 1994), where there is a "disconnectedness" to outside resource bases and opportunities. These communities usually lack the political will and skill of larger governments (Reid, 1986), are less well off according to the usual standards of organizational and managerial capacity (Sokolow, 1989), and seldom possess the scale to implement the kinds of development projects demanded in the larger economic environment (Brown and Glasgow, 1991; Mead, 1986). Additionally, traditional concerns with administrative efficiency and effective service delivery in rural communities have been supplanted by the demands placed on communities for new jobs, higher personal incomes, and new infrastructure. Capacity and rural development are thus closely linked.

Community capacity is understood to be the ability of a community (and its local government(s)) to anticipate and influence change; make informed and intelligent policy and program decisions; attract, absorb, and manage resources; and evaluate current activities in order to guide future action (Honadle, 1981). Capacity is an *intermediate* and direct outcome of development planning processes, which, in turn, should lead to specific development efforts in the community. Scholars and practitioners have attempted to establish some operational baseline of what capacity actually means in the real world, but, as Gargan (1981) argued several years ago, the concepts of capacity and capacity building have

Table 3 Information-Based Component of Iowa's Rural Development Programs (1997)

	Description
Rural Enterprise Fund	Provides grants and *technical assistance* to multicommunity economic development groups to *build staff capacity* and expand programs.
Rural Leadership Program	Provides grants and *technical assistance* to multi-community development groups to implement sustainable leadership programs. Seeks to *develop individual leadership skills, integrate new leaders,* encourage multi-community development initiatives, and *mentoring.*
Housing Assessment/Action Planning	Provides grants to communities to complete housing needs *assessments and action plans* in developing housing strategies.
Government Services Sharing Program	Provides grants and *technical assistance* to government entities to *study* and implement sharing strategies between governments.
Rural Action	Provides grants and *technical assistance* to development groups to *study* and implement agricultural development projects.
Rural Innovation Grants Program	Provides *study, training,* or planning project grants to community and economic development groups for the purchase of services to further local development initiatives. Includes purchase of *consultative services* for *study, training, or planning* on projects.

Nontargeted Programs	
Industrial Development Community/Economic Preparedness Program	Certification process involving *needs assessment*, developing a contact team, developing a business call program, conducting *team training*, and packaging financial incentives for industry.
Community Development/Community Economic Preparedness Program	Certification process involving building design, recognition and retention activities, development of *marketing* materials, and retail *sales analysis*.
Tourism Development Community Economic Preparedness Program	Provides *assessment of tourism impact, education, marketing*, and builds a strong organization to enhance tourism opportunities.
Community Consultants	Staff that provides assistance to organizations in the form of *suggestions* for hiring and managing staff, managing organizations, and *facilitation of board retreats and* community meetings.
Iowa Community Betterment Program	Provides technical support to volunteers, who *identify needs* and complete community projects.
Governmental Enterprise Fund	Provides seed money to governmental entities to design, develop and implement innovative approaches to delivering governmental services. *Technical assistance* is provided by multiple partners.
Main Street Iowa/Rural Main Street Program	Assists in development and implementation of a downtown revitalization strategy. Provides extensive *technical support* in organizational development, *marketing* activities, commercial business assistance, and design improvements in the historic center.

Note: Italics inserted by authors to highlight information-based activities.

come to be used in rhetorical rather than scientific terms. One of the more useful indices of rural community capacity, developed and field-tested in several rural communities, is derived from an evaluation of a large-scale rural development project (Agranoff et al., 1994; McGuire et al., 1994).

Three dimensions of capacity are identified: citizen participation, community structure, and development instruments. The first factor addresses issues dealing with community input and the strength of the local political institutions. The second factor of capacity, community structure, addresses management in governmental institutions, formal linkages with other communities and higher levels of government, and participation in development activities. The third factor, development instruments, measures the degree to which appropriate and effective policy tools are used by the community. Research has revealed that greater levels of capacity were present in 12 rural communities that had received external planning assistance compared to the same number of "control" communities that had not received any external planning assistance (McGuire et al., 1994). Table 4 displays the thirteen items within these dimensions that were actually tested.

State government efforts in capacity development include programs in leadership training, community assessment, institution-building, and certified communities. The focus of leadership training is normally on organizing skills, specific subject matter (e.g., economic development), exposure to "best practices" or experiences in other communities, and practical exercises in applying new skills. In addition to state government, the W. K. Kellogg foundation has financed many start-up leadership programs, particularly through state extension services, for 3- to 5-year periods. Community assessment focuses on how a group of leaders can develop the skills to engage in a traditional planning process—environmental needs assessment, goal-setting, consensus-building—geared to developing visions, strategic plans and working partnerships. In addition to states and extension services, private consulting firms, rural electric cooperatives and state associations (e.g., Chamber of Commerce, United Way) are also involved in this activity. Institution-building is normally conducted by small grant programs to support local nonprofit development agencies, often to obtain professional services. These seed funds can help rural communities with assistance that can boost local efforts. Certified community programs recognize towns that have been through a planning process and/or have adequate social and physical infrastructure to support growth. Some certified community programs are entirely linked to industrial recruitment, whereas others look comprehensively at social and economic development (John, 1991). These capacity programs are generally operated out of state economic and community development departments.

The greatest single shortcoming with capacity building programs is that they generally end where they really need to begin—in implementation. Programs generally bring communities only to the plan-making or primary decision

Table 4 Community Capacity Index

Citizen participation

A. Acceptance of change/controversy/conflict: Does the community accept the potential need for economic and/or social change in the face of worldwide economic restructuring, and do they resolve the controversies and conflicts often associated with this change in a productive manner?

B. Acceptance of community strengths and weaknesses: Has the community undergone an honest assessment of its strengths and weaknesses, allowing this to guide its development effort?

C. Effective mechanisms for direct community input: Are town hall meetings or community-wide meetings and discussions a normal part of the political process?

Community structure

D. Dispersed leadership roles: Are leadership roles in organizations that address development issues divided among many different persons?

E. Vertical linkages: Does the community actively and aggressively seek out external resources from the state and federal levels of government?

F. Horizontal linkages: Is the community involved in development efforts with other communities, either formally through partnerships or by seeking knowledge from other successful communities?

G. Shared vision or direction: Does the community have a clear, shared vision for development?

H. Project-oriented involvement: Does the community have many different groups working on development projects?

I. Lead agency: Is there a single core organization for coordinating and implementing development?

Development instruments

J. Community spirit activities: Does the community hold and continue to promote regular community appreciation activities, such as festivals and other annual events?

K. Infrastructure: Does the community dedicate financial resources and effort to improving the physical (e.g., roads and sewers) and institutional (e.g., schools and medical facilities) infrastructure?

L. Appropriate development focus: Does the community avoid, for the most part, expensive industrial attraction efforts and concentrate instead on indigenous development efforts?

M. Major business developments: Has the community recently experienced any major expansions in jobs or business?

point. For example, in both leadership and strategic planning exercises, communities are often told about the importance of accessing external resources from foundations, corporations, and state and federal government, but are rarely provided assistance in *obtaining* these resources. Similarly, in certified community programs, towns are encouraged to make their communities attractive to prospective businesses by improving site locations or infrastructure, but are not helped with the basics of actually recruiting firms. As a result, a gap develops between state services and programs and learning how to work within existing policy contexts for local advantage (Agranoff, 1994). States need to help communities combine their investment and will to change with timely external assistance.

D. Multiorganizational Policy Making and Administration

Rural development is not a specific service designed and administered directly by government personnel. Rural development, like the broader economic development policy sector of which it is a part, is carried out by all levels of government and across both private and public sectors—it is multibureaucratic. The intergovernmental linkages that are required for formulating and implementing economic policy have resulted in a public administration based in networks rather than hierarchies. Bureaucratic structures still characterize the multiple agencies and organizations involved in rural development, but these bureaucracies do not act alone. Instead, multiple bureaucracies collaborate on projects, design policy together, and implement policy in a coordinated and cooperative fashion.

The development policy sector in the states was once characterized by a paradigm that viewed prevailing economic forces as a given, only to be affected by national policy or larger economic trends. This limited view enabled state economic development policy to be conceived as merely a government function with administrative responsibilities being consigned to a traditional government agency such as a department of economic development or commerce (Fosler, 1992). Very little organizational interdependencies existed in this sector; agencies did the recruitment while localities occasionally lobbied the agency or marketed their community for consideration by the state. All policy-making resources (e.g., legal authority, organization, information, expertise, and funding) were held by the dominant state agency, although even these resources were used in only limited ways. In the emerging state rural development area, the recognition that dependencies exist among a host of private and public organizations for scarce economic resources has induced a new set of governing responsibilities for affecting the process of development. The administrative and institutional arrangements required by this policy paradigm are no longer predominantly functional and agency-driven, but instead are often based in public-private and state-local linkages. The emphasis on resource dependencies among private organizations have given way to a new kind of strategic interdependence among private, governmental, and paragovernmental organizations.

Faced with the need to provide financial resources to enhance local revenues, as well as information and expertise to compensate for the complexity and uncertainty inherent in the policy area, the state rural development administrator has become dependent on many other actors in and outside of the community. The governance instruments through which states and rural communities cities now plan, design, and execute development policy are complex multiorganizational networks. Multiorganizational arrangements like the variety that characterize development policy making in rural communities are intersectoral and built upon the idea of collaborative problem solving (Radin et al., 1996). Such networks are not merely mechanisms for coordination, but arrangements for solving interorganizational problems that cannot be achieved by single organizations.

One of the unique characteristics of state rural development policy lies not simply in the extent to which networks are the primary organizational setting for designing and executing policy, but, coupled with the various targeted and cross-cutting policies that comprise the development policy inventory, in the *number* and *type* of networks that exist within the policy making realm of a single city (Agranoff and McGuire, 1998). Many states have rural policies that include numerous strategies such as business attraction, business expansion, agriculture expansion, infrastructure development, community development, and enhancement of health care and public services. Each of these strategies involve many programs comprising different policy instruments like grants, loans, credit buydowns, technical assistance, capacity building, and direct provision. These programs may be configured as national government pass-through programs and some as state programs. For each of these programs, state executives are involved in different strategies and network configurations in order to deliver the policy.

State and rural development managers attend to multiple strategic tasks within the context of designing and executing development policy. As a result, even the fundamental, routine tasks of the development manager, such as building organizations, designing strategies, marketing the area, seeking out finances, or organizing numerous development projects (Blakely, 1994; Levy, 1990), cannot be carried out alone or with the same set of actors. Managers in networks are continually faced with problems that can lead to instability (Milward, 1996), and these concerns are compounded by the number of networks that constitute local economic policy making. Rural communities pursuing development aims must design their own strategies and mobilize public support while seeking assistance from the many relevant agencies in state government involved in development. As they engage in such activity, these local actors also face different network

Table 5 Four Distinctive Characteristics of State Rural Development Policy

Program areas	Geography-based	Without a home (state agencies)	Information-based (policy component)	Multibureaucratic (network members)
Recruitment	Place-oriented Rural and nonrural	ED CD division Environment Transportation Secretary of State	Planning Analysis Assessment Feasibility studies	State: ED; CD divison Local: county; city; school district Other: dev. groups; private sector; credit institutions
Capacity building	Place-oriented Rural and nonrural Some rural targeting	ED CD division Cooperative extension service	Education Planning Training	State: ED; CD division regional plan dist. Local: city Other: dev. groups
Enterprise zone	Place-oriented Rural and nonrural	ED Labor Revenue	Planning	State: ED; Labor Local: city Other: dev. groups; EZ board, private sector

Job training	People-oriented Rural and nonrural	ED Labor SBDC Vocational rehab.	Training Education Planning	Federal: labor State: ED; labor reg: SBDC, PIC Local: city Other: dev. groups; private sector
Housing	Place-oriented Rural and nonrural	CD division Housing Financing authority	Planning Analysis Assessment Feasibility studies	Federal: HUD State: CD division; housing authority; financing authority Regional plan dist. Local: county; city Other: developers; credit institutions
Infrastructure	Place-oriented Rural and nonrural	ED CD division Transportation Natural resources Agriculture	Planning Feasibility studies	Federal: HUD; Trans. State: ED; CD division; Trans.; Nat. resources; agriculture Regional plan dist. Local: city
Regulatory policy	Place-oriented People-oriented Rural and nonrural	Transportation Natural resources Agriculture Labor Environment	Analysis Assessment Education	State: all Local: county; city Other: dev. groups

configurations within the rural policy area. Insofar as the performance of a particular policy sector is dependent on the effectiveness of organizational and network design, developing the capacity to organize and manage these processes is critical to policy performance.

The multibureaucratic nature of rural development is one important characteristic that distinguishes state administration of rural development from some other policy areas. Unlike a single organization that can capitalize on a familiar culture, operating procedures, and relatively formal divisions of labor, administrative operations in rural development networks involve multiple cultures, procedures, and divisions of labor. The parties need to develop strategy, mechanisms for operation and implementation, and some means for determining whether expected results are being accomplished (Agranoff, 1998). The linkages that comprise the networks designed for one particular strategic purpose are often not the same as those in networks addressing another purpose. As a result, questions regarding what configuration of organizations is needed to perform a particular function place a significant burden on the manager to recognize the complex of entities and interests best suited to achieve a particular purpose (Wise, 1990).

States assist their rural communities economies through networks because of the increasing organizational interdependence faced by the two levels of jurisdictions. States seek to decrease the uncertainty and increase the level of information in the rural community to enable these communities to seek out partners that will jointly develop policy with the city, work together on development efforts and projects, jointly finance, and so on. Such tasks are clearly not the same as, say, ordering a water hook-up, sequencing a street project, preparing a land use plan, or negotiating a loan program under CDBG. Networking requires knowledge of joint financing arrangements, negotiation of joint strategies, complementary implementation of projects through a sequence of organizations, writing of interagency agreements, contract management and assessment, and more. Through complex networks of agencies, organizations, and interests, states provide this important assistance.

Rural development policy in the states possesses characteristics that distinguish it from many other policy areas. Table 5 summarizes these distinctions by exploring seven common program areas within the rural development policy. We show that the majority of these seven program areas are place-oriented but applicable to either rural or urban areas; that rural development policy as a whole is homeless, in that programs are designed and implemented through several different state agencies; that information is a major component of state rural development policy; and that the policy making and administrative networks associated with rural development policy are complex and vary across each program area. The administrative challenge of rural development policy in the states is obvious.

III. MANAGING IN THE STATE RURAL POLICY SECTOR

A. Linkages with Other Governments

A major part of the work of state rural development administrators is managing relationships among governments, including the federal government and regional, county, city, and special district governments. Federal contact begins with federal-state programs administered by the states such as Small Cities Community Development Block Grants. Federal programs that assist rural communities include those involved in the reorganized Rural Development office of the U.S. Department of Agriculture (USDA) and from other USDA offices, but also from the Small Business Administration, Economic Development Administration in the Department of Commerce, the Environmental Protection Agency, Department of Housing and Urban Development, Department of Health and Human Services, and the Army Corps of Engineers.

The challenge to state administrators is to help local government officials, community leaders, and prospective business investors work through the network of federal and nonfederal entities to help implement a program. In most cases the potential set of resources is so great that state officials have to provide a road map and guide local officials through the bewildering maze. Effective state development agents guide prospective lenders to the right sources, make contacts, help in preparation of applications, advocate on behalf of communities, and follow through on the progress of local activity. This brokering activity is the state administrators' intergovernmental role of the implementation process. Table 6 illustrates this point by providing a listing of the potential loan and credit programs and business assistance that exist *in addition to* state assistance.

State administrators also interact with communities on behalf of the programs administered for other state agencies. For example, a rural coordinator in an economic development agency will find that communities may seek basic information and an interpretation, or attempt to make a program adjustment, regarding a specific funding program. The coordinator will work with both the loan and grant program officer and the community representative. Similarly, a community request may be external to the development agency, for example, for road funding from the state highway department or for a construction permit from the state environment agency. The state rural coordinator would again help make the contact, assist in applications, advocate, and follow through.

B. Working in Partnerships and Networks

An increasing amount of the work of state rural administrators entails working with other entities—government and nongovernmental—to identify rural strategies and programs. State governments do not go it alone in rural development but team up with other entities to tackle selected rural problems. Although part-

Table 6   Financing Programs Available in Addition to State Assistance

Business planning and credit assistance
   Small-business development centers
   Regional field staff of state development department
   Services Corps of Retired Executives

Major federal financing programs
   EDA: Generally construction projects (e.g., industrial parks for disadvantaged areas)
   SBA 504 Certified Development Company: loans for nonprofit development compa-
      nies
   SBA Low Doc: business development loans for small businesses
   USDA Business and Industrial Guaranteed Loan Program: used for working capital,
      machinery and equipment, buildings, and real estate
   USDA Intermediary Relending Loan Program: allows local entities to establish re-
      volving loan funds for businesses and community development projects in rural
      areas
   USDA Rural Business Enterprise Grants: grants to facilitate development of small
      and emerging business enterprises in rural areas
   USDA Rural Economic Development Loan and Grant Program: loans and grants to
      rural electric and telephone cooperatives who then lend to business and commu-
      nity development organizations

Local and regional sources
   Banks and other financial institutions
   City and county government direct and revolving loans
   Chambers of commerce and local economic development groups
   Councils of governments and other regional planning commissions
   Rural electric cooperatives and cooperative telephone companies
   Community development cooperatives
   Private capital funds and individual venture investors

nerships have been important factors of public administration for some time, they became most prominent through the "reinventing government" movement (Osborne and Gaebler, 1992) and have become a key feature of the National Performance Review (1997) facilitated in the federal government at the behest of the Vice President. Such an emphasis on partnerships signifies the widespread acceptance by the public sector of the need to reach beyond its traditional bound-aries and strike new relationships with other parties (Radin, 1997).

   In the early 1990s, the Council of State Planning Agencies and the National Governor's Association sponsored a series of 10 state rural policy academies to strategically plan for rural development. With the lead of governors' offices, each state built a policy team composed of state administrative officials, state legisla-tures, business leaders, agricultural business leaders, banking industry representatives, interest groups, and the extension service to conduct a strategic planning process. In North Dakota, the policy academy team's work was combined with a business-driven group, North Dakota 2000, to form a new strategy presented to the governor and legislature, *Growing North Dakota* (Office of the Governor, 1990). The report contained a number of proposals to enhance a four-sector economy featuring agriculture, energy, manufacturing, and exported services. Proposals included creation of a Primary Sector Development Fund, a Science and Technology Corporation, Agricultural Vision 2000 (expansion of this sector of the economy) Fund, five new agricultural support funds, technical assistance, capacity-building programs, and an entrepreneurship development program. This agenda was largely adopted by the 1991 session of the legislature, with funds for the non-agricultural portions of the program earmarked for rural areas. Most of the programs were financed out of the earnings of the Bank of North Dakota, a state-owned bank devoted to enhancing development in the state.

A Nebraska-based network grew out of its Rural Development Commission in 1992 involving state government, regional government, nonprofit service providers, and the private sector. A forum of participation governs the rural network organizations that are chaired by the Lieutenant Governor and administered by a network office inside the Department of Development. The network also operates with a policy and management group, which focuses on long-term issues. Among other accomplishments the network has established: eight regional groups of rural services providers; a Nebraska Development Academy to coordinate, organize, and conduct educational and training programs; Nebraska Online, a computerized interactive information and communications vehicle among rural communities and services providers; Nebraska Intelligence System, which provides usable economic intelligence to communities and regional groups; and a variety of working groups to explore new programs and development tools (Corporation for Enterprise Development, 1993). The network is a high-profile arrangement that pulls together diverse rural interests while focusing on specific projects.

Other rural partnerships are the Federal-State Rural Development Councils (SRDC). Begun with eight pilot councils in 1990, nearly 40 councils now operate in the United States. Each SRDC involves representatives from federal, state, and local government; tribal governments; and nonprofit and for-profit organizations. Council partners join together voluntarily to identify and remove intergovernmental barriers and to generally improve rural development programs within the state. SRDCs receive small operating budgets from the federal government, and state in-kind matches provide for a very small staff. Research on the councils has indicated that within the limits of their mission, they have been able to deal with a broad range of rural issues, changed many attitudes and working relationships, and provided a setting for collaboration (Radin et al., 1996).

States are also active in promoting business-related networks. A number of Midwest states have been active in promoting networks of small firms or home-based business networks, which are often the core of business activity in many rural areas (Agranoff, 1998). The Michigan Jobs Commission, a comprehensive economic development and work force agency, has a "targeted business networks" program consisting of trade groups, professional associations, and education and research organizations to strengthen the competitiveness of key industries. These industry-driven networks, many of which are in rural Michigan, promote business-to-business collaboration, and develop cooperation strategies. The Jobs Commission has provided seed funding for a number of these networks. Iowa's Department of Economic Development and its Science and Technology Corporation have supported the formation of small-firm producer networks in plastics, metallurgy, graphic arts, and wood products. In addition, Iowa is building a data base of these small producers and is creating a producer's organization. In North Dakota, a full-blown home-based products production and marketing network existed that had numerous state government, nonprofit, and private-sector partners (Agranoff, 1998).

State rural administration involves promoting and working in such networks. It involves providing some seed resources and a great deal of information sharing, technical assistance, and provision of services. The administrator no longer simply runs an internal program or works with other state officials. He/she also collaborates in partnerships and networks. State officials encourage local governments and nongovernmental organizations to collaborate among themselves and within their communities. Intergovernmental activity for state program officials increasingly means establishing linkages among resources and programs through task forces, partnerships, and networks comprised of both state and non-state employers.

C. Joint Policy Development

State officials also regularly work with one another and with external leaders to develop rural policies. One example involves an effort in Iowa by state officials, state legislators, the research community, and nongovernmental organizations to create demonstration projects and raise public awareness regarding the impact of agricultural chemicals in groundwater. The consortium effort led to several enacted bills and other efforts to reduce chemical use (John, 1994). A joint policy effort by state and nonstate officials was conducted in 1997 in Indiana by the Lieutenant Governor, who also heads the Departments of Commerce and Agriculture. The council's rural policy recommended changes including (1) infrastructure (farmland conservation, site-building inventory, identification of environmental regulatory impediments); (2) technical assistance (targeted industry program, promotion of agricultural-business partnering, funding of Indiana SRDC); (3) tools, grants, loans (new funding criteria, rural enterprise zones); (4) work force and training (school-business programs, rural industry retention support); and (5) regulatory environment (state agency, education and outreach, enhanced state role as rural business partner) (Office of Lt. Governor, 1997).

As in the case of partnering and networking, state administrators now sit down with staff from other agencies, state legislators, interest groups, and other association representatives to hammer out agreed courses of action. Policy making is no longer exclusive to the bureaucracy. Petitioners are not only heard, but are now among the participants in policy development. The state agency member and the state legislator share their traditional policy-making role with a host of external actors (Sabatier and Jenkins-Smith, 1993).

D. Collaborative Projects with the Private Sector

Like their local government counterparts, state governments often enter into combined development projects with the private sector. David Osborne (1989) has written about the new joint efforts in technology development and technology transfer in the general economic development efforts of Pennsylvania, Michigan, and other states. In the rural sector, the same type of technology-related effort has occurred. An Ohio effort by a private corporation, a nonprofit business incubator, the Ohio Agriculture Department, and the Ohio Nature Conservancy has developed an innovative hay-drying process that uses less land and fewer chemicals and brings highest-quality hay at considerably higher market prices. An Iowa combine, spearheaded by the state's Department of Economic Development, is working with several large livestock producers, the Iowa Livestock Association, meat processors, and Iowa State University researchers to find an environmentally sound method of disposing of animal waste as livestock production increases. Finally, the Kentucky Education Department is working with its rural-based automobile assembly plants, community colleges, and vocational and technical schools to develop work force–ready manufacturing employees.

The nonprofit state-chartered corporation is another mode of public-private collaboration. Minnesota created an independent nonprofit organization charged with stimulating development in rural Minnesota, particularly through technological development. Following several controversial and difficult years, the Minnesota legislature restructured the corporation in July 1991 as Minnesota Technology, Incorporated (MTI). Under new leadership, the corporation is now charged with modernizing the state's industrial base and introducing new technology throughout Minnesota. Rather than being established as a state office or a partnership with a university, MTI has been structured as a public nonprofit entity so that firms will perceive it as part of the business community, rather than as a typical state agency. This approach could face a considerable barrier to success, since MTI still depends largely on the legislature for its funding. With a budget of about $6 million augmented by federal technology development funds, MTI's 65-person staff provides services through six regional offices. MTI focuses on strategic planning and education services, information services, and early-stage capital. It places special emphasis on four strategic industries: computers, metals fabrication, polymer composites, and nonelectrical machinery.

Each of these examples demonstrates that joint public and private investment projects begun as demonstrations can lead to widespread adoption and provide a benefit to the rural sector. The state administrative role is to participate as a catalyst in getting the parties together, securing the state's portion of resources needed, offering technical assistance, and often assistance in marketing the effort. In the process, the efficacy of sector joint venturing is demonstrated.

E. Leveraging and Engagement of Nonpublic Resources

One new role for government is to create demand for goods and services over the long run rather than simply subsidize their production. This entrepreneurial development strategy can be accomplished in part by attracting private nonprofit and for-profit resources. Such a leverage strategy has been the core of the collaborative applied science and technology projects previously identified. Pennsylvania's Ben Franklin Partnership program funds a number of advanced technology centers throughout the state, basing its dollar commitments on the financial match provided by a consortium of business and universities. By the early 1990s the match was four dollars of external funds for every public dollar, with nearly three of these matching dollars from private business contributions (Ross and Friedman, 1991). Similarly, the Georgia Economic Development Laboratory (EDL) is an example of a state trying to spread the benefits of manufacturing to nonmetropolitan areas by stimulating the creation of a private market for services by stimulating companies' interest in services and their willingness to pay for them. Started in 1950, the EDL has a budget of approximately $12 million and a staff of about 100 to provide a comprehensive array of services. Most of the services are delivered through Georgia Tech's industrial extension service, the largest in the country with its 12 field offices located across the state, but projects often draw in faculty and private sector providers.

In the arena of natural resource-based development, the Oregon Wood Products Competitiveness Corporation (WPCC) was created in 1991 to fill a gap in service support to the secondary wood products industry. The corporation is an independent agency committed to making Oregon a major processor of its timber resources and the future home of a world-class secondary wood products industry. It uses a range of tools that include finance programs, work force preparation, and manufacturing networks. The program was funded initially from a state lottery and had a biennial budget of about $2 million. WPPC is now privatized and its designers expect it to become self-sufficient through industry contributions and sale of services. It is governed by a board of directors composed of industry representatives.

There are other moves that states can undertake to leverage and engage private investment. A number of states promote private-sector institution-building by providing small challenge grants to organizations to support up-front training. Also, many of the state and federal business loan programs identified earlier require formula matches that include a combination of government funds, private credit, and investments by the applicant. As a result of these activities, state administrators find themselves active in stimulating private investment.

F. Fostering Sustainable Development

There is increasing concern for balancing economic growth with sustainability—the ability to produce food, fiber, and other natural resource-based products—well into the future without compromising the underlying resource base. For example, part of the crisis in Oregon's wood products industry was created by poor forest management practices in the past, as well as current stricter regulations, the most famous being protection of the spotted owl. A survey of rural leaders by the Council of State Governments (McBeth, 1996) identified the "need for balancing the environment and the economy, environmental preservation" as the most important issue/problem facing rural communities. It even slightly exceeded the item, "Job creation, capital investment, increase in salaries, link to global economy."

Natural resource-based strategies must consider best management practices. The Maryland Aquaculture Office (MAO) was created in 1988 to promote Maryland's aquaculture industry, including the commercial raising of finfish, shellfish, and aquatic plants for sale, barter, or shipment. MAO, supported primarily through general tax revenues and with a budget of about $700,000, finances new wastewater treatment processes for fish farms as one step in the direction of sustainability. It also coordinates policies across a variety of state agencies, and designs, tests, and constructs environmentally sound wastewater treatment for fish farm operations. As in other rural development areas, state officials work with communities as they develop their own approaches to sustainability. Wild rice harvesters in nonreservation areas of Minnesota have learned from reservation Native Americans that mechanical harvesting reduces long-term yields. Where they have returned to traditional manual methods, they have been able to preserve their crops over the long haul.

In the long run, sustainability requires investments in education, research, and demonstration projects (John, 1994). Sustainable agriculture and natural resource industries require growth-from-within approaches to rural development, where human capital is more highly valued than financial capital. The value of intellectual and human experience capital and other resources is enhanced when employed in the community. It is the "virtuous cycle" of education, increased innovation, increased investment, increased value, and higher wages.

G. Transparency: Dealing with Publics

State rural administrators deal with the various publics that bring resources and support to problem solutions. Such activity includes contacts with state legislators, local officials, community leaders and groups, agribusiness, rural cooperatives, statewide trade associations, and state civic associations—for example, municipal leagues and associations of counties. It also includes contacts with the communications media, educational community, health community, and others who influence policy. While some of this contact involves advocacy or lobbying for new legislation, considerably more time can be spent in informing publics concerning rural problems and enlisting them in projects that involve solutions.

The Corporation for Enterprise Development (1993:19) identified five roles for rural development offices, which appear to be widely applicable to the transparency role of all state officials working on rural development. First, as *entrepreneur*, state administrators exercise leadership in a strategic fashion, constantly exploring new approaches with external publics. Second, as *research and demonstration laboratories*, administrators tap the talents of innovative leaders at state and local levels. Third, as *builders of institutions*, administrators create bridges with associations and leaders, often resulting in new groups that can garner more political support than a state bureaucrat. Fourth, administrators act as *clearinghouses* of information useful to other organizations in their projects and state legislative and program efforts. Fifth, as *conveners*, administrators focus attention on critical issues and serve as catalysts for action on the agendas that result from these efforts. In the final analysis, activists from these publics possess the support needed to build important agendas and to take action.

H.   Promoting Administrative Modernization/Change

As noted earlier, studies of small-town planning and development skills reveal that many mayors and other officials lack the skills to work with state government in acquiring the services of their programs (Reed and Paulsen, 1991; Walzer and Gruidl, 1991). State leaders therefore work with local leaders in promoting better administrative skills among small-town officials. There are a number of strategies that can be utilized to bridge this gap.

First, formal training offered free of charge for financially hard-pressed small governments can enhance professionalization. If planned and executed collaboratively with peer trainers and best practices, it may avoid any "top-down" perceptions. Among the skills that are usually addressed are management methods, grant writing, negotiation, team management, effective communication, and conflict resolution.

Second, communities need accurate information on social and economic trends in order to plan, seek resources, and foster a course of development. While census and other information is available, it is not readily usable or apparently useful for the local official. State agencies can encourage extension economists or other technical experts to evaluate the feasibility of various courses of action.

Third, organizational solutions can be encouraged, such as seeking and finding a full-time or part-time professional administrator. While few communities can afford a city manager, multicommunity partnerships may be able to achieve quality administration through a circuit-riding administrative officer. Another organizational approach is to help communities find and utilize the services of part-time consultants.

Fourth, regional approaches previously identified in relation to development strategies could be extended to services such as water and wastewater treatment, fire protection, libraries, jails, and other public facilities. For example, regional water treatment plants are becoming more common, to take advantage of scale and multisource financing. A number of states are now encouraging intermunicipal clustering where the capital and professional costs are shared.

Fifth, a state may be able to help declining towns manage their fate by recommending effective economic development tools and providing planning tools. Iowa Department of Economic Development programs identified in Table 3 address this issue. Many of the programs may also provide support in coping with this reality instead of raising local expectations.

Sixth, innovative governance techniques can be encouraged by state administrators to face the problems of scale. An example already mentioned would be consolidation and sharing of public facilities. Other examples include taking advantage of telecommunication methods to extend the reach of services; making greater use of volunteers, such as retired people, for technical skills; and the use of innovative methods such as action research where residents work with specialists in all aspects of planning, conducting, analyzing, and utilizing research (Agranoff et al., 1992, 1994; Brown and Glasgow, 1991; McGuire et al., 1994; Reed and Paulsen, 1991; Sokolow, 1989).

IV. ANALYSIS OF ADMINISTRATIVE STRATEGIES

The agendas facing state administrators are broad and nontraditional. Administering policies within the rural development policy sector requires more than following the standard models of management in single-organization, compartmentalized, bounded, command-and-control operations. Public administration strategies also vary across rural development programs. Clearly, the way in which administration unfolds in each program is an empirical question. In any policy sector, but especially in a unique sector like rural development policy, particular factors are essential to administration. One important factor of administration in any policy sector is the commitment within the sector to a particular set of policy options. We have shown that rural development policy is carried out with many different policy instruments: subsidies, capacity building tools, regulations, directly provided services, and many others. Second, we have also emphasized the importance of knowing the organizations involved in the extensive administrative networks and of developing an understanding of which organizations are the focus of administrative control. Third, the distribution of policy-making resources is also an important variable of state rural development administration. In multiorganizational administrative settings the involved parties need each other, and the resources of policy making—legal authority, funding, organization, expertise, and information—are at the disposal of many different organizations (Franz, 1991). Each party possesses some level of the resources that make a policy work.

These administrative factors are interrelated in a way such that a change in one often produces changes in the others. Different combinations of these factors lead to different administrative strategies. We illustrate the various administrative challenges of state rural development policy by examining three rural program areas that have become a standard component of a state's overall rural development policy: the portion of the Small Cities Community Development Block Grant (CDBG) program used for infrastructure and community services; assistance for leadership development and capacity building; and grants for business development activities such as start-up, marketing, and promotion. These three program areas operate within the rural policy sector, but are administered through very different mechanisms. The Small Cities CDBG program is a state's component of the national program. Community leadership programs, aimed at leaders in small communities, focus on building the skills of persons to engage in strategic planning for the purposes of building the capacity to undertake a development effort in the community. Grant programs used for business development typically provide small grants, technical assistance, and training to rural communities in order to help achieve various economic goals, primarily business promotion and start-up, product development and marketing, and the development of local business/community resources (e.g., day care or health and living facilities for the elderly).

Substantial differences exist in the administrative structures associated with each program. Table 7 summarizes the differences in the administration of these program areas. All three are administered in some form of multiorganizational setting, and each is involved in some way in the provision of development, but they display very different administrative characteristics. The policy instrument used to affect program goals, for example, differs across the programs. The Small Cities CDBG is a subsidy that transfers money to communities in return for the performance of specific short-term actions. These place-oriented project grants are not large scale, but are significantly better funded than most state development programs. On the other hand, community leadership programs utilizes capacity-building tools with investments made in human as well as material resources.

Table 7 Properties of Systemic Networks and Managerial Strategies in Three
Development Programs

	Small Cities CDBG	Community leadership	Business development
Policy instrument	Subsidy	Capacity building	Combination
Membership	Federal HUD	External contractor	State departments
	State departments	State departments	Local boards
	Local governments	Extension offices	State boards
	Private contractors	Community colleges	LDOs
		Local trainers	Private entrepreneurs
		Local leaders	
Authority	State department	State, extension	State, boards
Funding	HUD, state, local	Contractor, state	State department
Information	State department	contractor	Local, state, boards
Organization	Local, state	State, contractor	Local, state
Expertise	Local	State, contractor	Local, boards
Focus of control	State department	External contractor	Mixed
Administrative	Top-down planning	Strategic planning	Direct contracting
strategy	Information exchange	Capacity building	Network development

Business development grants programs are typically based in both of these kinds
of instruments: subsidies in the form of project grants that are much smaller than
the CDBG grants, and capacity building through technical assistance and training.

Membership in the administrative network associated with the Small Cities
CDBG is comprised predominantly of public organizations, namely the three
levels of government. The federal Department of Housing and Urban Development works in conjunction with the equivalent of the state department of economic or community development and with local general-purpose governments.
The state administrative department possesses most of the policy-making resources in the network as state officials make discretionary decisions based on
their status as the primary repository of funding, legal authority, and information.
Some organizational and expertise resources are held by local governments, as
well as those building and construction contractors who carry out projects that
implement the final steps of the grant. The focus of control and central player
in program delivery is clearly the state department, but the effectiveness of the
CDBG program depends as much on the local organizational and professional
skills of the recipients as it does on the funding capabilities of the state.

Community leadership programs are delivered through a network where,
in many cases, the predominant player for shaping the program is an interest
outside of state government. For example, in Iowa the community development

division of the Iowa State University Extension Service operates the program for both the Kellogg Foundation and the state Department of Economic Development. Administrative collaboration involves both public agencies and quasi-public organizations as well. A Wisconsin program administered by the University of Wisconsin Cooperative Extension is jointly funded by the U.S. Department of Agriculture, the State of Wisconsin, and county governments (Shaffer and Pulver, 1995). Similarly, the University of Nebraska is an important contributor to that state's rural capacity-building efforts. The university operates the Community Development Block Grant certification program for the state, which includes training on CDBG regulations as well as continuing education training in areas such as housing, economic development, and finance administration. Such programs are directed toward the local leaders receiving the training and expertise, but the delivery agent (i.e., the extension service providing the training) or "contractor" is the real focus of the network. Funding is both externally and state provided, while authority is shared among the state development department, the external contractor, and the trainers. As with many rural development programs, the focus of control is outside of a particular state government agency.

Grant programs for business development are administered in complex setting with both public and private, state and local representatives playing an active role in program management. Despite funding control by the state department of development, resources are sometimes distributed by agreement of a separate board or steering committee of volunteer community-level and state association leaders. Legal authority rests officially with the state development department, but since such funds involve small seed capital or demonstration grants that have political implications (i.e., for communities not funded), control is shifted somewhat by sharing decision making responsibility with the voluntary committee. Authority is thus shared among all the members of the network. Information and expertise is distributed relatively equally between the state agency, the separate board, and the community organizations charged with accessing the assistance, whereas the organizational responsibilities rest largely with the community organizations. As a result, the focus of control does not rest with a single organization or agency.

The differing administrative settings of the rural development policy sector require different managerial strategies. Programs involving Small Cities CDBG funds primarily involve top-down planning, or the attempt to make national and state program purposes work locally. Conditional transfers of funding are exchanged for local actions in improving local conditions. Government control of most policy making resources ensures this top-down control through the production network. In contrast, community leadership programs necessarily employ strategic planning and management as its primary administrative strategy, reflecting the objective of transmitting leadership skills to local interests. Since such programs place emphasis on building clusters of capable local leaders, the development of effective networks of interaction is the primary approach to public management. The expectation is that through such capacity-building activity, local leaders will enhance their capability to plan and manage subsequent governmental efforts (McGuire et al., 1994). Finally, the primary administrative strategy in business development assistance programs involve direct contacts by state administrators as they work to develop experimental programs and launch new ventures that traditional lending institutions are reluctant to engage. Strategic emphasis is on building administrative structures that result in effective processes of interaction. Because the program encourages demonstration, negotiations also occur over model program efforts. Transactionally, the administrator is working more directly with entrepreneurs, trade associations, or local economic development corporations.

V. CONCLUSION

Scholarly fascination with the types of economic policy instruments that can be applied to rural communities has provided a vast inventory of knowledge about *what* works for rural communities. This chapter is intended to correct the virtual neglect of the rural policy management and administration by providing knowledge about *how* such policy is designed and carried out. Agriculture-based policy making of the recent past was relatively simple and direct in scope. Design and management of local development policy was centralized, functionally based, and hierarchically organized through rarely more than one government agency. One need only observe rural development policy making and administration in any state in America to realize that the administrative environment of rural development is complex, strategic, and often collaborative. Unitary policy goals and a stable flow of intergovernmental assistance have given way to stiff competition for limited resources possessed by multiple sources and policy demands from a multiplicity of rural interests. As states have intensified their involvement in economic policy making in general and rural development specifically, the number of actors that have a stake in economic matters and thus must be mobilized has proliferated. Such changes in the policy and institutional context of rural development have resulted in changes in the role and operation of the state administrator.

The challenges of rural development for state administrators are daunting and "postmodern." If the modern era is highlighted by hierarchical bureaucracy, where information, resources, and service delivery are within the single organization, the postmodern administrative organization is the opposite, that is, less hierarchical in policy with operations that are diffused among a number of public and nonpublic organizations (Clegg, 1990). Rural development at the state level represents this postmodern challenge, in that its geographic orientation is distinctive but it involves a policy arena with several administering agencies, based largely on information strategies and invoking numerous organizations and sectors. As a result, rural development leaders at the state level find themselves working with and through other agents to help communities help themselves. Increasingly, the efforts of state administrators include orchestrating multiagency policy, working in partnerships and networks, working collaboratively with the private sector, leveraging nonpublic resources, promoting sustainable development, dealing with a variety of internal and external publics, and fostering administrative modernization at the community level. Different rural programs involve variegated policy tools, administrative networks, and resource configurations, which in turn lead to different administrative strategies. The rural development agenda facing state administrators continues to move far from conventional bureaucratic work.

ACKNOWLEDGMENTS

The authors would like to thank B. J. Reed and DeWitt John for their very helpful comments on this chapter.

REFERENCES

Agranoff, R. (1994). Intergovernmental management for community economic development, *Managing Municipal Change* (C. F. Bonser, ed.), Institute for Development Strategies, Bloomington, IN.

Agranoff, R. (1998). Rural enterprise alliances: challenges to public management, *International Journal of Public Administration 21*: 1533–1575.

Agranoff, R., and McGuire, M (1998). Multi-network management: collaboration and the hollow state in local economic policy, *Journal of Public Administration Research and Theory 8*: 67–91.

Agranoff, R., McGuire, M., Richards, C., and Rubin, B. (1994). *Round Two Pioneer Search Communities Evaluation Report*, School of Public and Environmental Affairs, Indiana University, Bloomington.

Agranoff, R., Richards, C., McGuire, M., Mandel, J., Wise, L., and Radin, B. A. (1992). *Year One Pioneer Search Communities Evaluation Report*, School of Public and Environmental Affairs, Indiana University, Bloomington.

Blakely, E. J. (1994). *Planning Local Economic Development*, 2nd ed., Sage Publications, Newbury Park, CA.

Bradshaw, T. K. (1993). Multicommunity networks: a rural transition, *Annals of the American Academy of Political and Social Science 529*: 164–175.

Brown, D. L., and Glasgow, N. (1991). Capacity-building and rural government adaptation to population change, *Rural Policies for the 1990s* (C. B. Flora and J. A. Christensen, eds.), Westview Press, Boulder, CO.

Clegg, S. R. (1990). *Modern Organizations: Organization Studies in the Postmodern World*, SAGE, London.

Cooper, R. S. (1993). The new economic regionalism: a rural policy framework, *Annals of the American Academy of Political and Social Science 529*: 34–47.

Corporation for Enterprise Development. (1993). *Rethinking Rural Development*, Corporation for Enterprise Development, Washington.

Deavers, K. (1992). What is rural?, *Policy Studies Journal 20*: 184–189.

Ferguson, R. F., and John, D. (1992). Making the right distinctions: basic ideas for the rural development movement at the state level, unpublished manuscript.

Fosler, R. S. (1988). *The New Economic Role of States*, Oxford University Press, New York.

Fosler, R. S. (1992). State economic policy: the emerging paradigm, *Economic Development Quarterly 6*: 3–13.

Franz, H.-J. (1991). Interorganizational policy coordination: arrangements of shared government, *The Public Sector—Challenge for Coordination and Learning* (F.-X. Kaufmann, ed.), Walter de Gruyter, Berlin, pp. 469–499.

Galston, W. A., and Bahler, K. J. (1995). *Rural Development in the United States*, Island Press, Washington.

Gargan, J. J. (1981). Consideration of local government capacity, *Public Administration Review 41*: 649–658.

Gillis, W. R. (1991). Encouraging economic development in rural america, *The Future of Rural America* (K. E. Pigg, ed.), Westview Press, Boulder, CO, pp. 119–136.

Honadle, B. W. (1981). A capacity-building framework: a search for concept and purpose, *Public Administration Review 41*: 575–580.

Hustedde, R. J. (1991). Developing leadership to address rural problems, *Rural Community Economic Development* (N. Walzer, ed.), Praeger, New York, pp. 111–123.

John, D. (1991). When does a state need a rural development policy?, Unpublished paper, Aspen Institute.

John, D. (1994). *Civic Environmentalism: Alternatives to Regulation in States and Communities*, Congressional Quarterly Press, Washington.

Lapping, M. B., Daniels, T., and Keller, J. (1989). *Rural Planning and Development in the United States*, Guilford Press, New York.

Levy, J. (1990). What economic developers actually do: location quotients versus press releases, *Journal of the American Planning Association 56*: 153–160.

Luke, J. S., Ventriss, C., Reed, B. J., and Reed, C. (1988). *Managing Economic Development: A Guide to State and Local Leadership Strategies*, Jossey-Bass, San Francisco.

McBeth, M. K. (1996). Attitudes of state rural development officials, SPECTRUM: *The Journal of State Government 69*: 17–25.

McGuire, M., Rubin, B., Agranoff, R., and Richards, C. (1994). Building development capacity in nonmetropolitan communities, *Public Administration Review 54*: 426–433.

Mead, T. D. (1986). Issues in defining local management capacity, *Perspectives on Management Capacity Building* (B. W. Honadle and A. M. Howitt, eds.), State University of New York Press, Albany, pp. 24–46.

Milward, H. B. (1996). Symposium on the hollow state: capacity, control, and performance in interorganizational settings, *Journal of Public Administration Research and Theory 6*: 193–195.

National Performance Review. (1997). *Performance-Based Organizations*, National Performance Review Press, Washington.

Office of the Governor. (1990). *Growing North Dakota, Report of Rural Development Academy/North Dakota 2000*, Bismark.

Office of Lieutenant Governor (1997). *Lt. Governor's Jobs Council Subcommittee Reports*, Indianapolis, IN.

Osborne, D. (1988). *Laboratories of Democracy*, Harvard University Press, Boston.

Osborne, D., and Gaebler, T. (1992). *Reinventing Government*, Addison-Wesley, Reading, MA.

Paulsen, D. F., and Reed, B. J. (1987). Nebraska's small towns and their capacity for economic development, *Nebraska Policy Choices—1987*, University of Nebraska, Omaha, pp. 43–77.

Radin, B. A. (1997). *Partnerships as a New Institutional Form: Expectations, Evidence, and Effectiveness*, Paper delivered at the 1997 Annual meeting of the American Political Science Association, Washington.

Radin, B. A., Agranoff, R., O'Mera-Bowman, A., Buntz, G. C., Ott, S. J., Romzek, B. S., and Wilson, R. H. (1996). *New Governance for Rural America: Creating Intergovernmental Partnerships*, University Press of Kansas, Lawrence.

Reed, B. J., and Paulsen, D. F. (1991). Small towns lack capacity for successful development efforts, *Occasional Paper 91-1* (February), University of Nebraska, Center for Public Affairs Research, Omaha.

Reeder, R. J. (1989). Targeting state aid to distressed rural communities, *Publius: The Journal of Federalism 19*: 143–160.

Reid, J. N. (1986). Building capacity in rural places: local views on needs, *Perspectives on Management Capacity Building* (B. W. Honadle and A. M. Howitt, eds.), State University of New York Press, Albany, pp. 66–83.

Ross, D., and Friedman, R. E. (1991). The emerging third wave: new economic development strategies, *Local Economic Development: Strategies for a Changing Economy* (R. S. Fosler, ed.), International City Management Association, Washington.

Sabatier, P. A., and Jenkins-Smith, H. C., eds. (1993). *Policy Change and Learning: An Advocacy Coalition Approach*, Westview Press, Boulder, CO.

Sears, D. W., and Reid, J. N. (1995). Successfully matching development strategies and tactics with rural communities: two approaches, *Rural Development Strategies* (D. W. Sears and J. N. Reid, eds.), Nelson-Hall Press, Chicago, pp. 282–296.

Sears, D. W., Redman, J. M., Gardner, R. L., and Adams, S. J. (1992). *Gearing Up for Success: Organizing a State for Rural Development*, Aspen Institute, State Policy Program, Washington.

Shaffer, R., and Pulver, G. C. (1995). Building local economic development strategies, *Rural Development Strategies* (D. W. Sears and J. N. Reid, eds.), Nelson-Hall Press, Chicago, pp. 9–28.

Sokolow, A. D. (1989). Small local governments as community builders, *National Civic Review 78*: 362–370.

Walzer, N., and Gruidl, J. (1991). Local economic development: perceptions and actions of small city officials in Illinois, *Rural Community Economic Development* (N. Walzer, ed.), Praeger, New York, pp. 97–110.

Wise, C. R. (1990). Public service configurations and public organizations: public organization design in the post-privatization era, *Public Administrative Review 50*: 141–155.

16

Administration of State Economic Development: Decision Making Under Uncertainty

Karen Mossberger
Kent State University, Kent, Ohio

In the past few decades, economic development activity has expanded rapidly across the states. It has now been institutionalized as an important policy function. Yet observers still describe an "emerging paradigm" in the states (Fosler, 1992) and an "emerging profession" employing many methods that are still experimental (Iannone, 1997:159). This may be due in part to the relatively brief period since the ascendance of the field, but also to the inherent complexity of the problems it addresses, the relative lack of control governments face in this issue area, and uncertainty about how to achieve results. Prior research, conducted mostly at the local level, has indicated that practitioners cope with uncertainty in a variety of ways. Some of these strategies may produce undesirable effects, including goal displacement (Reese, 1997:84), symbolism (Rubin, 1990; Wolman, 1988), and policy "lock-in" (Jones, 1994:171). It is possible, however, that some of these strategies may also lay a foundation for gathering more information or applying experience in new ways.

This chapter examines complexity and uncertainty in economic development policy, and the way in which state practitioners responded to these problems in a particular case—the formulation of the state enterprise zones. State administrators play a critical role in formulating economic development policy because of the expertise they contribute in a complex policy domain (Eisinger, 1988:6). Moreover, the way in which administrators cope with complexity, uncertainty, and environmental "turbulence" in economic development policy (Rubin, 1988,

1990) may have implications for other complex issues in which the states bear responsibility for innovation—for example, welfare reform and school reform.

First, this chapter reviews the problems of complexity and uncertainty in state economic development policy generally, and the research on administrative decision making in this issue area. Most of the existing literature focuses on the role of administrators at the local level, although some authors have addressed this issue at the state level. The remainder of this chapter focuses on evidence drawn from a five-state comparative case study of the adoption of state enterprise zone programs as an example of complexity and uncertainty in economic development.

I. NATURE OF ECONOMIC DEVELOPMENT POLICY

Theories of decision making have long pointed to problem complexity, causal ambiguity, and uncertainty of outcomes as barriers to rational decision making (Cohen et al., 1972; Lindblom, 1959; Simon, 1982). "Problem complexity" refers to multiple causes and their interdependence, and may lead to ambiguity, or a lack of clarity, regarding causal mechanisms. Complex and ambiguous problems increase the potential for uncertainty, or inability to predict outcomes.

States (and the cities and rural areas within their boundaries) experience growth and decline through complex, often poorly understood processes. Phrases like *elusive, capricious*, and *unpredictable* (Osborne, 1988:249) feature prominently in descriptions of state economic development policy. In the past few decades almost every state has developed its own "little industrial policy" (Eisinger, 1988:6; Gray and Lowery, 1990), but causal theories and technology remain unclear. How effective, for example, are the much-lauded "demand-side," or entrepreneurial, strategies—such as state-supported research and development, venture capital funds, and promotion of trade? Fosler has argued that the states have been charting a new course without much recourse to theory. Traditional economic theories have limited utility in defining the role of the public sector, for example, in fostering entrepreneurialism and the development of new products (Fosler, 1992). States have been forced to forge a new paradigm, that "in some ways has leapfrogged conventional economic theory" (Fosler, 1992:4). Uncertainty about efficacy has also surrounded some of these interventions. Eisinger, who first chronicled the "rise of the entrepreneurial state" in 1988, was by 1995 describing a decline of entrepreneurialism in many states. He ascribed the retreat to recessionary pressures, budget woes, the uncertainty of evaluation, and the lengthy time period required to show results (versus short electoral cycles).

There are other examples. Despite location theory and extensive research on business location decisions, the number of factors involved complicates prediction. The effectiveness of tax incentives is perhaps the most famous controversy in economic development. Early research on business location decisions showed that taxes played a marginal role in attracting firms, in comparison to proximity to markets, suppliers, and labor (Schmenner, 1982). Taxes, however, are more easily controlled by states than these other factors. More recent research demonstrates that tax rates may indeed have some effect on business location decisions. One summary of 57 studies conducted between 1979 and 1991 revealed that in 70% of these studies, higher state and local taxes influenced businesses negatively (Bartik, 1992). The effect was fairly minor, however, and it ranged greatly among the different studies. Differences in taxation mattered more within metropolitan areas, but the differences were not confined to intrametropolitan location decisions (Bartik, 1992; Brace, 1997).

Taxes illustrate the uncertainty that reigns more broadly in economic development policy. Difficulty in evaluating programs, interdependence with national and global economies, interstate competition, and the need for collaboration with the private sector are factors that lead to complexity and uncertainty in outcomes.

The measurement of outcomes in economic development programs is problematic because the effect of any single intervention is difficult to isolate (Bartik and Bingham, 1997; Eisinger, 1995; James, 1991; Persky et al., 1997). It is therefore often difficult to establish whether or not development would have occurred "but for the incentives." Proper evaluation involves complex modeling for expected investment and employment patterns in the absence of the program, and unintended consequences such as displacement effects (Persky et al., 1997). "Evaluation has always been the central difficulty in economic development policy," according to Eisinger (1995:149). "Establishing a causal link between state development incentives and job-creating investment is rarely simple."

Inability to control outcomes also provokes uncertainty. State economies are of course permeable to the movement of capital and people across state lines; they are highly vulnerable to the external vagaries of national and international markets. States lack even the limited tools available to national governments in coping with recessions. Moreover, states often find themselves competing for investment with other states. This competition heightens their policy interdependence.

The very character of economic development in a capitalist economy introduces dependence upon private sector decisions (Lindblom, 1977). Fosler characterizes economic development as a "a process rooted in the private sector but supported by public actions," rather than a government function. States, therefore, provide a "legal, regulatory, and policy framework" for what is essentially "a market-driven private-sector activity" (Fosler, 1992:4). This introduces the complexity of implementation with multiple actors (Pressman and Wildavsky, 1984). Moreover, governments often suffer from an information asymmetry in their dealings with private sector actors. Businesses may extract a "corporate surplus" in their negotiations with government officials (Jones and Bachelor, 1993). When governments bargain over incentive packages with businesses, they are unable to gauge the minimum package necessary to retain or attract an employer. It is in the interest of businesses, of course, to demand more than this minimal amount. As a result, corporations may obtain a "surplus" exceeding what was actually needed to secure their cooperation. Businesses may encourage intergovernmental competition, driving the stakes higher and enlarging their corporate surplus.

Finally, state governments intervene in cases of market failure—instances where private firms are unwilling to absorb the risk of underwriting research and development of a new product, or capitalizing new and risky concerns. State governments also extend assistance to small businesses and to projects in distressed communities—again, because the private sector has shunned these higher-risk investments.

II. HOW ADMINISTRATORS COPE WITH UNCERTAINTY

How, then, do administrators cope with complexity and uncertainty? This question has been addressed more thoroughly in research on local rather than state economic development. These descriptions, however, may parallel the experiences of state administrators. As demonstrated above, uncertainty characterizes state-level economic development policy as well.

According to Rubin, local practitioners often

> saw only a weak relationship between their efforts and resulting changes, between action and consequence. . . . This problem was compounded by doubts about whether or not municipalities had the wherewithal to effect major economic changes, the value of the information on which decisions might be made and, more generally, the efficacy of the techniques and tools used in economic development (Rubin, 1988:237).

The reaction to such a decision environment was to "shoot anything that flies, and claim anything that falls" (Rubin, 1988). In a more recent study, local administrators compared their economic development activities to "throwing spaghetti at the wall to see if it is properly cooked—we try everything and anything and eventually something will stick" (Reese, 1997:3). Reese found, as Rubin did, that lack of planning wasn't due to unfamiliarity with planning techniques and tools such as cost-benefit analysis, but that it seemed futile in the face of great uncertainty (Reese, 1997:83, 91; Rubin, 1988, 1990). Case studies of local economic development have also revealed "an element of rational analysis, but a considerable amount of political conflict, negotiating among interests, symbolic appeal, incomplete information, and snap decisions" (Jones and Bachelor, 1986: 200; cf. Reese, 1997:83).

When local development officials perceive their task environment as "turbulent" (characterized by complexity and a lack of adequate tools), they emphasize symbolic actions (Rubin, 1990). These include "showcase projects," such as highly visible downtown development, and promotional campaigns. Some degree of political symbolism is present in economic development policy more generally. Particularly when economic distress, crises, or competition are present, governments strive to be seen as "doing something". Political incentives favor programs with short-term, visible results, such as business attraction through tax incentives (Eisinger, 1995; Wolman, 1988, 1996). Long-term planning, and programs that require many years of investment before producing results (such as venture capital programs and research and development) may suffer in comparison to the "quick fix" (Eisinger, 1995; Wolman, 1988, 1996).

Administrators also employ strategies to simplify the complexity of decision making and to introduce some control or certainty into the policy environment. Rubin describes a certain "proceduralism" in his respondents. They emphasize process rather than results—following appropriate "procedures and routines that provide a checklist of activities that they can accomplish" (1988: 249). Maintaining a data base of employers was one example of the procedural approach. Decision rules, or "routinized procedures" dominated decision making in Reese's survey of local economic development officials (1997:84). Adherence to decision rules, while simplifying the task of administrators, carries the possibility of goal displacement. "Going by the book" becomes more important than accomplishing organizational goals.

Decision makers may simplify their task by employing "solution sets" or "both regularized ways of doing things and consensual definitions of the problems" (Jones and Bachelor, 1993:217). In a study of Detroit, the authors found "characteristic solution-sets to economic development problems, which are then applied almost routinely to superficially similar situations. What were once adaptive and creative policy initiatives become routine, and may not work as intended" (Jones and Bachelor, 1993:xi–xii). The use of solution sets, according to Jones, promotes conservatism and rigidity through policy "lock-in" or "path dependency" (1994:171).

Prior research indicates that uncertainty and a turbulent decision environment produce policy that is symbolic, or fettered to bureaucratic routines or solution sets that replace deliberation. How well do these descriptions depict decision making in the formulation of the state enterprise zones?

III. ENTERPRISE ZONES

The remainder of this chapter discusses the history of the state enterprise zones, and comparative case studies of the adoption of the enterprise zones in five states: Virginia, Indiana, Michigan, New York, and Massachusetts. Examining the way in which state administrators contributed toward formulation yields some insights into bureaucratic responses to uncertainty and complexity. Adoption of a new program always presents some risk of the unknown, and this was increased by the characteristics of the idea itself.

The sample of five states included both early and late adopters. Virginia enacted its enterprise zone program in 1982, followed by Indiana in 1983, Michigan in 1985, New York in 1986, and Massachusetts in 1993. Later policy adoption could be expected to involve less uncertainty, due to the more widespread experience of other states. While this is not necessarily a "representative" sample of states, the experience of administrators in these five states may suggest some comparisons to the research on local economic development officials. I conducted 55 semistructured interviews in these five states in 1995 and 1996. I supplemented interviews with written records whenever possible, using copies of legislation, newspaper accounts, legislative histories, transcripts, meeting minutes, reports, letters, and memoranda.

At the heart of the enterprise zone concept lay the notion that cutting taxes and government regulations in a defined geographic area would reverse urban decline. Shortly after the Thatcher government began to experiment with enterprise zones in 1979, Stuart Butler of the Heritage Foundation advocated the idea on this side of the Atlantic. At about the same time, enterprise bills began to appear in state legislatures and in Congress. Federal legislation stalled on Capitol Hill, despite repeated efforts during the Reagan and Bush administrations. Yet, 40 states enacted some type of enterprise zone legislation between 1981 and 1993.

The state zones boast a diverse array of programs. There are urban, rural, suburban, and border enterprise zones (New York Chapter 686 of 1986; U.S. Department of Housing and Urban Development 1986, 191–93; Wolf 1991). The number of enterprise zones ranges from one in Michigan to 1,422 in Louisiana (U.S. Department of Housing and Urban Development 1995, 43). State zone programs vary in terms of their incentives, amount of deregulation, criteria for designation, objectives, coordination of resources, and management styles (Brintnall and Green 1988, 1991: Elling and Sheldon 1991; Erickson, Friedman, and McCluskey 1989, 26; Gunn 1993). Most state programs depart substantially from Butler's supply-side approach, as few of them offer any substantive regulatory relief, and many of them involve government activism in the form of loan programs, job training, infrastructure improvements, and other support services (Cowden 1995; Erickson and Friedman 1991; Gunn 1993). While tax incentives are the single most common feature of enterprise zone programs, even this was not a universal characteristic. One state, Pennsylvania, avoided the use of tax incentives in its enterprise zones until recently (Erickson and Friedman 1991; Underhill 1995). The enterprise zones diffused as a policy label, or as a loose category of geographically targeted policies for distressed areas (Mossberger forthcoming).

A. Enterprise Zone Characteristics: Problem Complexity and Uncertainty

A major reason for diffusion as a generic label was the loosely bundled character of the concept. The fundamental mechanisms proposed in Butler's conceptualization and the early federal bills were tax incentives and regulatory reform. Unemployment, disinvestment, and neighborhood decline have multiple and interdependent causes, not all of which may be easily addressed by tax incentives or regulatory relief. Recent research had fomented controversy over the use of tax incentives, and there was no evidence that deregulation would stimulate investment. The relationships between the incentives and the policy's purported goals were unclear at best, leading state policymakers to tinker with the concept. In other words, the diversification and transformation of the enterprise zones was at least in part a response to uncertainty on the part of state policymakers.

Uncertainty about the effects of the enterprise zones continued later, even when evaluation results became available. The evidence provided by enterprise zone research has been mixed, owing to differences between the enterprise zones, and to differences in research methodology (James, 1991). Early studies on the state programs reported increased activity in the zones, without being able to definitively attribute such growth to the enterprise zone incentives (Jones et al., 1985; Sabre Foundation, 1983; U.S. Department of Housing and Urban Development, 1986). Impact evaluations began to appear mid-decade, and participants in Michigan, New York, and Massachusetts were aware of these at the time of adoption. Many of these studies concluded that the enterprise zones had little or no effect on investment or job growth (U.S. General Accounting Office, 1988; Jones, 1987; Papke, 1990), although some portrayed the enterprise zones in a more favorable light (B. Rubin and Wilder, 1989; M. Rubin, 1991). Many of the impact studies used survey data or other methods that tended to inflate the estimated effect of the project. Even so, the overall picture has been "not highly flattering" (James, 1991:225). The largest comparative study undertaken found that employment and investment increased on average, although the authors could not attribute this growth directly to the zone programs. The state programs with the most investment were those with a broad array of incentives and coordination of other programs, such as financing. One of the most successful programs, according to the study, was the Pennsylvania program which avoided tax incentives entirely (Erickson et al., 1989:73–74).

B. Response in the States

As might be expected, state decision makers confronted many uncertainties in the process of designing their programs. The reaction of some administrators and policy experts resembled "shooting anything that flies" or "throwing spaghetti."

An Indiana administrator wondered, "Were we [just] moving jobs around? We were not sure, but we did it anyway. We comforted ourselves in the belief that any government support makes it easier for business to invest." According to one Massachusetts respondent, the enterprise zones were "like religion," Proponents "just believe it." States feel, he said, "At the very least, this can't hurt. Communities are desperate to find the right key" to economic growth. These sentiments were echoed in Michigan, despite skepticism about the concept. "Benton Harbor resembled Berlin after the war," said one participant. "We were wanting to try almost anything that might conceivably jump-start it."

C. Analysis and Tax Incentives

Formulating programs that require one to predict the behavior of firms is clearly a risky endeavor. A respondent in one of the states recalled that policy design was "just a bunch of guesses." Administrators in all five states complained about the difficulty of performing cost-benefit analysis or budget projections, although each state required one or the other. In such an atmosphere, a cost-benefit analysis can become a political act as much as an analytical tool. Some proponents talked about being fortunate in getting a "neutral assessment" that showed no large impact on the budget either way. All respondents agreed that it was difficult to truly project what the effect of the program would be.

Designing the tax incentives involved considerable uncertainty. Adopters wrestled with how deep the incentives should be to make the zones attractive without incurring large revenue losses. The task of devising incentives often fell to administrators who assisted with drafting legislation. A senior policy analyst for Virginia's Department of Housing and Community Development explained, "The issue was also, to what degree will credits [on taxes] affect the behavior of businesses? . . . We were trying to put something in the code that shows good faith, but doesn't give away the store or provide a windfall." This same policy analyst described Virginia's early effort, as one of the first adopters, as "flying blind."

A decade later, after much more state experience with tax incentives and other economic development programs, an administrator in the Massachusetts Executive Office of Economic Affairs approached the same problem of striking a difficult balance between enticing business and protecting the public coffers:

> There is a dynamic to the public getting involved in private development. The business community forgets Adam Smith. . . . [Our] biggest concern, since the program had built-in safeguards—would it be used? [You might] hold the party, and nobody comes.

D. Administrators and Proceduralism

In Virginia and Indiana, where administration officials had significant responsibility for designing the new programs, they used professional techniques, information search, and consultation as a way to reduce uncertainty. In other words, proceduralism became important. Bureaucrats could be expected to emphasize process concerns, compared to elected officials. But it was clear from the comments of respondents that attention to process was an attempt to control uncertainty. One example was Virginia, an early adopter. In Virginia, the Department of Housing and Community Development (DHCD) had responsibility for developing many of the details of policy, since the legislation was sparse. The administrator who directed the team writing the regulations explained, "This was a new concept. There was not a whole lot of information, . . . [including] information . . . from other states. . . . The only thing available at the federal level were drafts of legislation."

The implementing agency responded first with systematic analysis. A team of DHCD staff met regularly. "We went through the Virginia legislation point by point, analyzed it, decided what we had to deal with, knew the concept before we started," said the associate director. One of the other participants joked about the team leader, saying he had "flow charts coming out of his ears—massive rolls of the stuff."

Although the legislation did not require any advisory committees, the department established two—a policy committee and a technical committee. Lacking outside guidance in designing the program, they marshalled resources from within Virginia. The policy group served a more "philosophical" role, providing expertise on the appropriate commercial-residential blend, size, geographic distribution, and the application process. This committee included members of the General Assembly, the Department of Economic Development, and representatives from local government. The technical advisory committee worked out the details for implementing incentives and marketing. This committee included the Department of Taxation, local economic development specialists, the Department of Social Services, Department of Highways and Transportation, and Division of Engineering and Buildings.

The department also held six public hearings around the state, and incorporated 14 of the 22 suggestions made during the period for public comment. Building consensus for the program at the local level was an important goal of this participatory process; but department officials clearly sought input because they were charting new territory.

Indiana offers another example of proceduralism. After an initial enterprise zone bill failed, the state legislature set up a study commission on the issue in 1981. The Department of Commerce assumed responsibility for coordinating the commission's work. Administrative staff on the commission approached their task through a vigorous information search, drawing upon expert testimony and the experience of the other states. Commission staff examined and analyzed the programs in each of the states that had adopted a program. They kept in touch with zone administrators in other states and hosted public meetings featuring a number of experts. Among these were an urban planning professor who shared his research on the British enterprise zones, an organizer from a Louisville community development program, a state legislator from Kentucky (which had just passed its own enterprise zone legislation), and officials from the U.S. Department of Housing and Urban Development. The study commission split into subcommittees that considered issues such as neighborhood development, regulatory relief, taxes, and administration of the zones. Minutes for these subcommittees show that many alternatives were presented and debated. The decision to award abatements on the inventory tax resulted from a survey of the Indiana membership of the National Federation of Independent Businesses. Again, in the face of uncertainty, administrators emphasized the quality of the decision-making process in whatever way they could.

The extensive information-gathering effort in Indiana was largely due to the efforts of an energetic staff person on the study commission. Other respondents credited her with guiding the process and the formulation of much of the legislation. One reason for this individual's enthusiasm and comprehensive approach may have been her recent experience in graduate school. But uncertainty influenced the extent of the search, too. The staff person talked about feeling isolated, and gaining support from the individuals she contacted in other states.

Compared to the other three states, administrators in Indiana and Virginia played a larger role in policy formulation. In all five states, however, bureaucrats were important actors in policy formulation. Because more controversy erupted over the zone legislation in the other states—over the desirability of the program, the intended beneficiaries, or partisan politics—much of the process consisted of political debate and bargaining. Administrators still sought information and tried to analyze alternatives, but the overall decision processes were political rather than technical. (See Mossberger, forthcoming, for a fuller account.) Indiana and Virginia, therefore, represent clearer examples of the way in which bureaucrats coped with complexity and uncertainty. They utilized bureaucratic routines and techniques such as consultation, surveys, flow charts, public hearings, and expert testimony. They also strove to create an appropriate process, bringing in stakeholders and seeking fairly comprehensive information.

What effect did proceduralism have on policy making? Concern for process enables participants to dodge the larger questions about the effectiveness of what they are doing, instead concentrating on the mechanisms for doing it. But there was no way that participants could predict the effectiveness of the enterprise zones, or adopt guaranteed techniques for attracting businesses. By opening the process, participants in these two states enlarged the available information on which to base their decisions. Attention to procedure in the face of complexity and uncertainty is a hallmark of bounded rationality, according to Simon. (See for example, Simon, 1982.)

IV. UNCERTAINTY AND ADAPTATION

While pioneering states like Indiana and Virginia felt they were breaking new ground, many of the administrators in Michigan, New York, and Massachusetts confronted their task with a keen awareness of the negative research on the impact of taxes, and a sense that the early evaluation studies weren't producing much hard evidence of success. In two states, Michigan and New York, at least some of the legislative and administrative staff harbored serious doubts about the zone programs, and pointed to the research on tax incentives and the early zone evaluations. One New York administrator explained, "No one could quantify how it made a difference." As a result, "the political will existed beyond the inclination of professional staff." Uncertainty led to adaptation. Administrators and Democratic legislative staff in New York tried to supplement tax breaks within their budgetary limitations. The Department of Economic Development staff sought ways to prioritize existing programs and to add money for women- and minority-owned businesses. According to one of the key negotiators from the administration, the Governor would have preferred direct assistance rather than tax incentives, had the money been available. Economic development experts on staff in the New York State Assembly pushed for the addition of capital incentives, not willing to rely on tax incentives to stimulate new investment.

New York's adaptation of the enterprise zone idea was not unique. Indiana and Massachusetts administrators modified the idea as well. Like many other states, they provided job training and other economic development programs in the zones.

A. Applying Solution Sets

The modifications in these states belie a more general trend in the diffusion of the enterprise zones. Adaptation of the enterprise zone program represented a way of "hedging bets" against the possibility that tax incentives would not produce much investment in the zones. The way in which states adapted the idea provides some support for the idea that administrators turn to "solution sets" to approach new problems. Despite the supply-side origins of the enterprise zone concept, the state enterprise zones "have become one more tool for fostering economic development, often in combination with other traditional and cutting-edge state and local programs" (Wolf, 1990:7).

Most states offered common economic development programs in unison with the enterprise zones, such as low-interest loans, tax increment financing, bonds, and infrastructure improvements (Erickson and Friedman, 1991; Gunn, 1993). States also tended to employ the economic development incentives with which they had experience (Green and Brintnall, 1987).

Bureaucrats and politicians often pointed to analogies that influenced program design. Indiana's Lieutenant Governor, who headed the Department of Commerce, emphasized the potential for community development and local governance in the zones. The Lieutenant Governor's experience in the state legislature colored his thinking about the potential of enterprise zones. When the legislature consolidated the Indianapolis area under "unigov" in 1969, they also defeated a "minigov" bill to decentralize some decisions to the neighborhoods. But the idea of community development and neighborhood governance influenced his later thinking about the zones. Both the Lieutenant Governor and the full-time member of the commission staff referred to community development corporations as their point of reference for the administrative structure of the zones, and for the later requirement that businesses contribute part of their tax savings for neighborhood development.

There were other examples of the way in which administrators used analogies. The Massachusetts administrator who crafted the flexible and negotiable incentives for that state's "Economic Opportunity Areas" sought a way to give municipalities some leverage with firms. The program's three-tier design focused on specific projects rather than automatic benefits. He cited his own experience as a former local development official, and the project-oriented nature of local development, as his primary influences. New York administrators and legislative staff raised the Bedford-Stuyvesant Restoration Corporation launched by Robert Kennedy as an analogy for the enterprise zones. One official characterized the administration's thinking as "The same kind of ideas as Model Cities, but reworked. There is not anything new under the sun."

The New York and Massachusetts analogies more closely fit the definition of a "regularized way of doing things" than the Indiana example. Indiana decision makers used the community development corporation analogy to import solutions that were different from previous routines. New York administrators drew upon solution sets for urban development in their adaptation of the zones, and the Massachusetts administrator applied a solution set from project-oriented local development. But administrators and legislative staff in New York looked for new ways in which to assist placed-based revitalization, partly because of budget constraints, and partly because of the emphasis that economic development places on inducing private-sector activity. The New York program aimed to coordinate existing resources for job training, social services, and technical assistance. This represented a new way of delivering services. New York participants, including assembly staff, sought new ideas to induce private sector investment from both fledgling businesses and major manufacturers. A linked deposit program and special utility rates for the zones also appeared in New York's program. While both New York and Massachusetts used existing solution sets, they applied them in new ways, or combined them with different approaches.

Respondents in Virginia also indicated that solution sets are institutionalized. This supports Jones' contention that different solution sets reside in different policy venues (Jones, 1994:172; Baumgartner and Jones, 1993:216). At the time of enactment, Virginia administrators saw the enterprise zones as targeted assistance rather than economic development per se:

> Economic development people [at the state and local level in Virginia] were not real interested in the idea. They were not focused on targeting to geographic areas. They were concerned with development of the state or locality in general. Geographic targeting was foreign. Support came from the community development area. They had experience with targeted programs. People at the local level in distressed areas had experience with Model Cities.

This explained why the Department of Housing and Community Development rather than the Department of Economic Development assisted with drafting legislation, and became the implementing agency. During the early 1980s, the solution set employed by economic development officials in a low-tax southern state was to market the tax advantages of the state overall. Housing and community development officials, on the other hand, had experience with targeted programs, and were more receptive to the idea.

The phrase "solution set" implies an unchanging, unimaginative approach to policy. "Analogy" might be a more precise way to express the way in which participants in these five states used previous experiences. Analogies helped respondents to categorize a problem, or to frame it in a way that was more bounded and therefore more manageable. Using analogies helped participants to highlight possible solutions from their own experience (or the experience of others, such as community development corporations). Simon argues that bounded rationality consists of using experience to define problems and to limit the otherwise unmanageable number of potential solutions (1982). Risk and uncertainty cause policy makers to search for ideas either from other places, or from experience, argues Rose (1991).

Is the use of analogies from experience a hide-bound response to policy problems? Policy lock-in could certainly be expected as one result. For supply-side purists, the enterprise zones are an example that existing solution sets prevent the triumph of new ideas. Stuart Butler has complained that in some cases the term was "used merely as a fashionable catch phrase to repackage old urban development ideas" (Butler, 1991:28). He viewed previous urban programs, such as Model Cities, as antithetical to his concept of the enterprise zones. Butler's observations also suggest "garbage can" or opportunistic decision-making. The New York administrator's comments about reworking Model Cities because there is nothing new under the sun eerily echoes the policy streams or garbage can model (Cohen et al., 1972; Kingdon, 1995).

But it is also possible to use previous ideas in new ways, to use them as "inspiration" rather than exact models, or to combine ideas to form new hybrids (Rose, 1991). Such combinations can produce innovation. Experimentation with nongovernmental organizations, coordination of programs, and negotiated incentives in the zones were innovative twists that resulted from existing solution sets or prior experiences in community or economic development.

B. Networks

Professional organizations (especially those with a state focus) encouraged the diffusion of the enterprise zones and served as a source of information for states (Beaumont, 1991; Mossberger, forthcoming). The intergovernmental network which developed around the issue brought together officials from various states. All five states had some contact with organizations in the enterprise zone network, including the U.S. Department of Housing and Urban Development, the National Association of State Development Agencies (NASDA) the National Conference of State Legislatures (NCSL), the National Governors Association (NGA), the National Council for Urban Economic Development (CUED), the Council of State Community Action Agencies (COSCAA),[1] the American Association of Enterprise Zones (AAEZ), and many others.

The network helped administrators cope with the uncertainty of formulating and implementing a new program. First, these organizations published information about various city and state programs. Second, they provided opportunities to share ideas and gain support at round tables and workshops at national conferences. After the first round table held by NASDA, Virginia participants began to correspond with state enterprise zone staff in Kentucky and Indiana. The Indiana study commission's staff member emphasized the importance of such a network in the early days. She spoke about her feeling of isolation, and her efforts to build a personal network: "I contacted other states for copies of legislation. Just talking on the phone was helpful. What I got from contact with others was their support. It was not so much borrowing [from their legislation]." This individual later became a key figure in formalizing a broader network through her participation in NASDA, CUED, and the AAEZ.

The comments from this administrator recall Rubin's interviews with local economic development practitioners, who linked uncertainty with feelings of isolation. Perhaps networks can reinforce professional commitment in the face of challenges, as well as offer concrete advice.

Michael Allan Wolf, an academic and enterprise zone consultant, was also

---

[1] The organization has since changed its name to the Council of State Community Development Agencies (COSCDA).

a participant in the network. He recalled one of the roundtables NASDA held on enterprise zones:

> I had never seen anything like it. This was at a time of great competition between the states (for example, the competition over the Saturn plant). These same people sat down and listened to each other and shared ideas. They were friendly, and anxious to talk about their programs.

Administrators who attended such conferences shared problems. "This was instrumental to implementation," Wolf believed, "and to changes in programs."

Networks of practitioners may be another way in which administrators try to reduce problems of uncertainty, particularly in issue areas where problems are complex. Specialized organizations such as NASDA and the AAEZ, and more generalist organizations like NCSL and the NGA have long been recognized by scholars as agents of policy diffusion (Walker, 1969). Evidence exists that professional and state organizations have helped to spread other economic development ideas as well. Gray and Lowery assert that "One reason for increased policy activity [in economic development] is the presence of stronger professional networks among bureaucrats and among public officials. The National Governor's Association is a particularly good example" (1990:7). Osborne documents the spread of economic development ideas during the 1980s, through the efforts of the NGA and the Council of State Planning Agencies (1988:33). (See also chapters on Pennsylvania, Arkansas, and Michigan.)

C. Symbolism and Politics

A degree of political symbolism existed in the adoption of the enterprise zones in all of these states. The importance of the program's symbolism (as well as anticipation of federal incentives) often overcame uncertainty about the results. Election campaigns and economic crises featured prominently as reasons for the ascendance of the issue on state agendas. Respondents also explained their state's interest in the program as a way of "doing something" for distressed areas. The official who said that Benton Harbor resembled Berlin after the war also pointed out that the administration didn't have alternative programs for the area.

Enterprise zone policy sometimes resulted from political conflict and negotiating among interests, as Jones and Bachelor argue is common in economic development (cf. Reese 1997:83). In three of the states—Michigan, New York, and Massachusetts—political considerations and bargaining dominated the decision processes. Credit claiming, logrolling, struggles over the name of the program, and the distribution of benefits among geographic constituencies featured more prominently in these states. But there was less conflict or competition over the issue in Virginia and Indiana,[2] giving administrative staff more discretion in decision making.

D. Comparing the Enterprise Zones to Prior Research

These case studies confirm many of the findings of earlier studies, with some modifications and additions. Although rational analysis was difficult because of search, consultation, surveys, and public hearings, states frequently adapted the concept, grafting on other economic development programs, and applying solution sets from closely related or analogous policies.

Did proceduralism mean that administrators engaged in meaningless activity? The procedures emphasized by administrators (in at least two of the states) aimed at providing additional information upon which to base decisions: the expertise of people in different policy areas; the desires of local governments; the experiences of the other state or British programs; and the preferences of small businesses. In the absence of reliable information upon which to predict the behavior of firms, administrators "satisficed" by garnering what was available. All of these activities could reasonably have some bearing on informed decision making, although they could not produce any real certainty. There may well be instances of futile proceduralism, but bureaucratic adherence to standards or routines is not always dysfunctional.

Did the application of solution sets merely preserve the status quo? The use of solution sets certainly explains the results of the diffusion of the enterprise zones—their similarity to other economic development programs at the time, and their use as focal points for other targeted assistance to the area. It is also true that the enterprise zones departed less from existing policy than had been envisioned by its original advocates. Yet, the solution sets that were applied differed somewhat from state to state, creating experimentation through a variety of enterprise zone programs. Some states used existing ideas in new ways, creating quasi-governmental administration of the zones, for example, or devising flexible and negotiable incentives. Solution sets can serve as a resource for innovation, and don't automatically rule out creativity and change.

Another resource that state administrators used was an intergovernmental information network that developed around the issue. While the existence of these professional networks has been documented before, they have not been noted as

---

[2] Indiana was the only state in this study that experienced organized protests against the enterprise zone legislation. These protests were organized by labor unions, community activists, and consumer advocates. Although respondents noted that the dissidents' concerns caused some changes in the legislation, the enactment of the bill was never seriously threatened. With a Republican administration and majority in both houses, policy formulation took place primarily within the commission rather than in legislative negotiations.

a strategy for coping with the uncertainties of economic development policy. This would seem to be a logical role. The activism of professional networks in other types of economic development policy strengthens the possibility that networks perform this type of function for practitioners.

Symbolism appeared as a factor in every state, particularly as a way that states could express concern about distressed areas. This didn't necessarily mean, however, that the program was merely symbolic, with no concrete assistance offered to local zones. But the symbolic appeal overrode concerns about the program's potential effectiveness. It was a powerful political argument for adoption in the face of uncertainty. As Rubin argues, policymakers want to be viewed as doing something to address problems.

Political competition and bargaining dominated decision processes in three of the states, lending some credence to Jones and Bachelor's contention about political rather than "rational" decision processes frequently characterizing this policy area. In the two states that demonstrated less competition or conflict over the program within state government, decision-making was more oriented toward administrative proceduralism.

These five case studies, confined to a single policy, can only suggest some ways in which state administrators grapple with uncertainty. There are also questions left unanswered in this study. None of the cases supported Reese's argument that administrators rely upon decision rules, risking goal displacement. Because this research examined the formulation of new legislation and new regulations, there were few existing decision rules. A study of the problems encountered in implementation, however, may have produced such results.

The ways in which administrators handle uncertainty merit a closer look. Economic development is just one major policy area riddled with complexity and uncertainty. In an era of devolution, when states are experimenting with new approaches to health care, education, and welfare reform, administrators may need to be more conscious of the strategies they use, and more aware of potential resources, such as professional networks.

ACKNOWLEDGMENTS

This research was made possible by support from the College of Urban, Labor, and Metropolitan Affairs at Wayne State University, and the Graduate School and Department of Political Science, Wayne State University.

REFERENCES

Bartik, T. J. (1992). The effects of state and local taxes on economic development: a review of recent research, *Economic Development Quarterly 6(1)*: 102–110.

Bartik, T. J., and Bingham, R. D. (1997). Can economic development programs be evaluated?, *Dilemmas of Urban Economic Development: Issues in Theory and Practice* (R. D. Bingham and R. Mier, eds.), Sage Publications, Thousand Oaks, CA, pp. 246–277.

Baumgartner, F. R., and Jones, B. D. (1993). *Agendas and Instability in American Politics*, University of Chicago Press, Chicago.

Beaumont, E. (1991). Enterprise zones and federalism, *Enterprise Zones: New Directions in Economic Development* (Roy E. Green, ed.), 41–57. Sage Publications, Newbury Park, CA, pp. 41–57.

Brace, P. (1997). Taxes and economic development in the American states: persistent issues and notes for a model, *Dilemmas of Urban Economic Development: Issues in Theory and Practice* (R. D. Bingham and R. Mier, eds.), Sage Publications, Thousand Oaks, CA, pp. 140–161.

Brintnall, M., and Green, R. E. (1988). Comparing state enterprise zone programs: variations in structure and coverage, *Economic Development Quarterly 2(1)*: 50–68.

Brintnall, M., and Green, R. (1991). Framework for a comparative analysis of state-administered enterprise zone programs, *Enterprise Zones: New Directions in Economic Development* (R. E. Green, ed.), Sage Publications, Newbury Park, CA, pp. 75–88.

Butler, S. (1991). The conceptual evolution of enterprise zones, *Enterprise Zones: New Directions in Economic Development* (R. E. Green, ed.), Sage Publications, Newbury Park, CA, pp. 27–40.

Cohen, M. D., March, J. G. and Olsen, J. P. (1972). A garbage can model of organizational choice, *Administrative Science Quarterly 17*: 1–25.

Cowden, D., Executive Director of the American Association of Enterprise Zones. (1995). Interview by author 9 October, Washington.

Eisinger, P. (1988). *The Rise of the Entrepreneurial State: State and Local Economic Development Policy in the United States*, University of Wisconsin Press, Madison.

Eisinger, P. (1995). State economic development in the 1990's: politics and policy learning, *Economic Development Quarterly 9(2)*: 146–158.

Elling, R. C., and Sheldon, A. W. (1991). Determinants of enterprise zone success: a four state perspective, *Enterprise Zones: New Directions in Economic Development* (R. E. Green, ed.), Sage Publications, Newbury Park, CA, pp. 136–154.

Erickson, R. A., and Friedman, S. (1991). Comparative dimensions of state enterprise zone policies, *Enterprise Zones: New Directions in Economic Development* (R. E. Green, ed.), Sage Publications, Newbury Park, CA, pp. 155–176.

Erickson, R. A., and Friedman, S., with McCluskey, R. E. (1989). *Enterprise Zones: An Evaluation of State Government Policies*, Prepared for U.S. Department of Commerce, Economic Development Administration, Pennsylvania State University, University Park, PA.

Fosler, R. S. (1992). State economic policy: the emerging paradigm, *Economic Development Quarterly 6(1)*: 3–13.

Gray, V., and Lowery, D. (1990). The corporatist foundations of state industrial policy, *Social Science Quarterly 71*: 3–24.

Green, R. E., and Brintnall, M. (1987). Reconnoitering state-administered enterprise zones: What's in a name? *Journal of Urban Affairs 9(2)*: 159–70.

Gunn, E. M. (1993). The growth of enterprise zones: a policy transformation, *Policy Studies Journal 21*: 432–439.

Iannone, D. T. (1997). Commentary on industry targeting, *Dilemmas of Urban Economic Development: Issues in Theory and Practice* (R. D. Bingham and R. Mier, eds.), Sage Publications, Thousand Oaks, CA, pp. 95–96.

James, F. J. (1991). The evaluation of enterprise zone programs, *Enterprise Zones: New Directions in Economic Development* (R. E. Green, ed.), Sage Publications, Newbury Park, CA, pp. 225–240.

Jones, B. D. (1994). *Reconceiving Decision-Making in Democratic Politics: Attention Choice, and Public Policy*, University of Chicago Press, Chicago.

Jones, B. D., and Bachelor, L. (1993). *The Sustaining Hand: Community Leadership and Corporate Power*, 2d ed., University Press of Kansas, Lawrence.

Jones, E. R. (1987). Enterprise zones for the black community. Promise or product: a case study, *Western Journal of Black Studies 11*: 1–10.

Jones, S. A., Marshall, A. R., and Weisbrod, G. E. (1985). *Business Impacts of State Enterprise Zones*, Systematics, Inc, Cambridge, MA.

Kingdon, J. W. (1995). *Agendas, Alternatives and Public Policies*, 2d ed., HarperCollins, New York.

Lindblom, C. E. (1959). The science of "muddling through," *Public Administration Review 19(2)*: 79–88.

Lindblom, C. E. (1977). *Politics and Markets: The World's Political Economic System*, Basic Books, New York.

Mossberger, K. (Forthcoming). *Diffusion and decision-making: The enterprise zones and the politics of ideas.* Georgetown University Press, Washington, D.C.

Osborne, D. (1988). *Laboratories of Democracy*, Harvard Business School Press, Boston.

Papke, J. A. (1990). *The Role of Market-Based Public Policy in Economic Development and Urban Revitalization: A Retrospective Analysis and Appraisal of the Indiana Enterprise Zone Program, Year Three Report*, Purdue University, West Lafayette, IN.

Persky, J., Felsenstein, D., and Wiewel, W. (1997). How do we know that "but for the incentives" the development would not have occurred?, *Dilemmas of Urban Economic Development: Issues in Theory and Practice* (R. D. Bingham and R. Mier, eds.), Sage Publications, Thousand Oaks, CA, pp. 28–45.

Pressman, J. L., and Wildavsky, A. (1984). *Implementation*, 3d ed., University of California Press, Berkeley.

Reese, L. A. (1997). *Local Economic Development Policy: The United States and Canada*, Garland Publishing, New York.

Rose, R. (1991). What is lesson-drawing?, *Journal of Public Policy 11*: 3–30.

Rubin, H. J. (1988). Shoot anything that flies; claim anything that falls: conversations with economic development practitioners, *Economic Development Quarterly 2(3)*: 236–251.

Rubin, H. J. (1990). Working in a turbulent environment: perspectives of economic development practitioners, *Economic Development Quarterly 4(2)*: 113–127.

Rubin, B. M., and Wilder, M. G. (1989). Urban enterprise zones: employment impacts and fiscal incentives, *Journal of the American Planning Association* Autumn: 418–432.

Rubin, M. M. (1991). Urban enterprise zones in New Jersey: have they made a difference?, *Enterprise Zones: New Directions in Economic Development* (R. E. Green, ed.), Sage Publications, Newbury Park, CA, pp. 105–121.

Sabre Foundation. (1983). *Enterprise Zone Activity in the States*, Author, Washington, DC.

Schmenner, R. (1982). *Making Business Location Decisions*, Prentice-Hall, Englewood Cliffs, NJ.

Simon, H. A. (1982). From substantive to procedural rationality, *Decision Making: Approaches and Analysis* (A. G. McGrew and M. J. Wilson, eds.), Manchester University Press, Manchester, pp. 87–96.

Underhill, J., U.S. Department of Housing and Urban Development, Office of Community Planning and Development. (1995). Interview by author, 10 October, Washington.

U.S. Department of Housing and Urban Development. Office of Community Planning and Development. (1986). *State-Designated Enterprise Zones: Ten Case Studies*, Author, Washington.

U.S. Department of Housing and Urban Development. Office of Community Planning and Development. (1995). *State Enterprise Zone Update*, Author, Washington.

U.S. General Accounting Office. (1988). *Enterprise Zones: Lessons from the Maryland Experience*, Author, Washington.

Walker, J. L. (1969). The diffusion of innovations among the American states, *American Political Science Review 67*: 880–899.

Wolf, M. A. (1990). Enterprise zones: a decade of diversity, *Economic Development Quarterly 4*: 3–14.

Wolf, M. A. (1991). Enterprise zones: through the legal looking glass, *Enterprise Zones: New Directions in Economic Development* (R. E. Green, ed.), Sage Publications, Newbury Park, CA, pp. 58–74.

Wolf, M. A., Director, EZ Project. (1995). Interview by author, 12 October, Richmond, VA.

Wolman, H. (1988). Local economic development policy: what explains the divergence between policy analysis and political behavior?, *Journal of Urban Affairs 10*: 19–28.

Wolman, H., with Spitzley, D. (1996). The politics of local economic development, *Economic Development Quarterly 10(2)*: 115–150.

17

Administration of Developmental-Disabilities Services in State Government

Paul J. Castellani
New York State Office of Mental Retardation and Developmental Disabilities, and The University of New York at Albany, Albany, New York

Developmental-disabilities service is an important area of state responsibility that is unfamiliar to many outside the field, but which presents new and complex challenges to state administrators. The changes in the area of developmental disabilities that affected local government administration have been discussed elsewhere (Castellani, 1997). These included the closure and downsizing of large state-operated institutions; the creation of a large number of community programs to accommodate both the people moving from institutions as well as those previously living at home; an expansion in the numbers and types of individuals served by these community programs; the emergence of new kinds of services and types of provider agencies; and the challenges for local administrators as they managed a disparate and fluid variety of services and clientele in many types of public and private organizations. This chapter is an overview of the features of the field of developmental disabilities that have importance for administration and management of state programs.

I. SCOPE OF STATE ADMINISTRATIVE RESPONSIBILITY

The numbers of people affected by developmental disabilities, the costs of services for these people, and the lifelong nature of the disabilities are key features affecting the scope of state administrative responsibility.

A. Numbers and Definitions

The prevalence of severe mental retardation in society (approximately 0.7% of the population) means that states must administer developmental-disabilities services for large numbers of individuals and their families. However, the number of people within a state's responsibility varies with the definition of developmental disability. Traditionally, mental retardation has been the most prominent disability within the range of developmental disabilities. However, the term developmental disabilities can include other disabilities such as cerebral palsy, epilepsy, autism, and a large number of other neurological impairments. In several states, mental retardation is the only disability addressed by the major state developmental-disabilities agency. Responsibility for other developmental disabilities falls to mental health, health, and other human services agencies. The implications can be substantial. For example, New York State's Office of Mental Retardation and Developmental Disabilities is responsible for a broad range of developmental disabilities, and only 80.9% of the people served in core residential and day programs have mental retardation as their primary disability. In all programs including family supports, mental retardation is the primary disability for only 76.7% of the individuals (OMRDD, 1990). Consequently, a state developmental-disabilities agency, in states with a broad scope, may be responsible for 20–25% more individuals than in states such as Connecticut, Maryland, Massachusetts, Pennsylvania, and Texas, where the lead agency serves only those with mental retardation (Braddock et al., 1998). In some of these latter states, other developmental disabilities are the responsibility of separate units, bureaus, or offices within larger umbrella agencies, and the issue of dealing with the full range of disabilities is one of coordination within one large agency. However, in several states, the responsibility for substantial numbers of individuals, those with cerebral palsy or traumatic brain injury, for example, is widely dispersed throughout the state administration.

A second feature of this definitional issue is whether a state's responsibility is for serving individuals with categorical diagnoses of a disability and whether this extends to functional disabilities. The traditional categorical definition of developmental disabilities involved a diagnosis of severe and chronic mental retardation, cerebral palsy, epilepsy, and autism. In the 1978 amendments to the Developmental Disabilities Services and Facilities Construction Act, the federal government embraced a functional definition of developmental disabilities that included the presence of three or more substantial functional limitations in seven major life activities (self-care, receptive and expressive language, learning, mobility, self-direction, capacity for independent living, and economic self-sufficiency). Despite the federal model, many states continued to restrict eligibility to individuals with mental retardation and the other categorical disabilities. The debate over a functional vis-à-vis categorical definition intensified in the early

1990s with the promulgation by the American Association on Mental Retardation of an approach that went beyond the individual's functional limitations to encompass environmental, familial, social, and situational limitations (Luckasson et al., 1992).

Within the past few years, clinical, administrative, judicial, and legislative approaches to these questions have competed as the substantial implications of expansion in the numbers and characteristics of clientele have become apparent. This was the core of the U.S. Supreme Court's 1990 decision in the *Sullivan v. Zebley* in which the Court held that the Social Security Administration had to establish a functional test for children, and the ability to participate in age-appropriate activities as the equivalent to employability for adults was the standard adopted (Derthick, 1990). From 1990 to 1995, about 400,000 new recipients of Supplemental Security Income (SSI) resulted from the *Zebley* decision (Cedarbaum, 1995). The debate continues within the field, but it is clear that functional and situational definitions of developmental disability are likely to increase the numbers and types of individuals within the scope of a state's responsibility in this area (Reiss, 1994).

B. Costs of Developmental-Services Programs

The closure and downsizing of large state-operated institutions and creation of community-based residential and day programs has been the most prominent change in the field in the past thirty years. Medicaid funding underwrote much of the costs of this transition, supporting the remaining large institutions as well financing a substantial proportion of the community programs: the former as large Intermediate Care Facilities for the Mentally Retarded (ICFs/MR) and the latter as small ICFs/MR, as well as day treatment facilities, clinics, and other programs qualifying for federal financial participation (Boggs et al., 1985; Castellani, 1987). More recently, this federal funding has shifted from the ICF/MR program to the Home and Community Based Services (HCBS) waiver. Medicaid became the primary source of funding for developmental services, and its share of the overall costs of Medicaid is large and growing. Of the approximately 36 million people in Medicaid, about 1.7 million are those with developmental disabilities— 4.9% of the total—and triple the approximately 506,000 people with developmental disabilities receiving Medicaid in 1975—2.3% of the 1975 total (Hemp et al. 1998; Smith and Ashbaugh, 1995). Moreover, the recipients with developmental disabilities (4.9% of the total) account for 15.7% of total federal-state Medicaid spending (Hemp et al., 1998). Medicaid's contribution to federal and state budget deficits drew attention of funders from both parties at all levels of government, and the costs of developmental services became an important issue in states' consideration of the scope of administrative responsibility.

C. Age and the Implications of the Lifelong Disabilities

The lifelong and often severe nature of developmental disability is another important feature of this area. State developmental disabilities agencies typically provide and finance services to adults. However, developmental disabilities usually
become manifest at birth or infancy and are lifelong. Children born with severe
disabilities are more likely to survive than was the case even 20 years ago, and
people with developmental disabilities are living longer. Age is an important
factor determining who is served, and there is wide variation among states in the
administration of services for children and elderly people with developmental
disabilities.

From a broad state perspective, responsibility for developmental disabilities
usually falls to health providers in infancy; shifts to a variety of preschool and
developmental service agencies until the child reaches school age; and is within
the primary and secondary education arena until an individual "ages out," usually around age 21. From the perspective of the affected individual and his/her
family, getting services is a struggle to deal with widely different and changing
eligibility criteria, financing, service type, and provider agency from birth to
school age. (Bird et al., 1990)

In the early years of a child's life, not only does the administrative framework shift from the uncertain boundaries of the health care arena to the school
district, but this has important management implications. Financing of early
childhood services is often a patchwork of Medicaid, private insurance, and various state funding and eligibility criteria and arrangements. Once a child comes
within the pre-school, primary, and secondary education area, primary funding
shifts to school districts and administrative responsibility shifts to local school
districts, albeit operating under a variety of state special education mandates. For
most individuals, the major state developmental services agency plays a secondary role: certifying early intervention providers, sometimes providing funding,
delivering or funding family support services, and playing a role in coordinating
services for children under age 21.

When an individual with a developmental disability "ages out" of school,
another distinct panoply of eligibility criteria, funding mechanisms, provider organizations, and services comes into play. The mandates of the federal Individuals with Disabilities Education Act cease; waiting lists are encountered; funding
mechanisms change; and services fall within a new state administrative framework: the various state-level departments, divisions, offices, and programs. From
the perspective of the state developmental services agency, the individual who
seeks access to adult services is likely to have a 20-year service history or more.
State developmental services agencies must deal with parents with experience
with mandated educational services, eligibility based on age, and other entitle-

ments and expectations that may not be part of a state's adult developmental services program.

The second aspect of the lifelong nature of developmental disabilities affects the political context within which developmental services agencies function. Parent and advocacy organizations and interest groups develop and maintain continual and intensive involvement in policy. Parents often become involved in organized advocacy from the birth of a child with a disability. Interest groups such as Arc (formerly, Association for Retarded Citizens), United Cerebral Palsy Association, and others that focus on specific disabilities assist parents and lobby policy makers, administrators, and service providers on the many issues of access to and use of developmental services. State developmental services agencies operate within a context of powerful interest groups, made up largely of parents with lifelong involvement and political acumen honed from encounters with a variety of health, education, and human service agencies from the birth of their children.

D. Capacity and Commitment

The states' capacity and commitment to developmental services is not a definitional issue but is, nonetheless, an important one affecting the scope of responsibility in administration of these services. There is wide variation among states in the rates with which people with developmental disabilities are served and the fiscal commitment of states to developmental services. In virtually every category of the numbers of individuals served and the amounts states spend, there are wide variations that are not explained by measures of a state's wealth (Braddock et al., 1998). Braddock and colleagues have attempted to explain variations in spending for community services with a civil rights and advocacy model rooted largely in class action suits brought against state operation of large institutions. However, the wide variations in the patterns of utilization and expenditure in states' overall service systems is largely unexplained. More recently, attention has shifted to wide variations in waiting lists as indicative of substantial differences in states' commitment to serving people with developmental disabilities (Arc, 1997). As one looks across the states, there are virtually no consistent models of service system capacity, fiscal effort, and scope of administrative responsibility.

II. ADMINISTRATIVE STRUCTURES

There is a great deal of restructuring of the administration of developmental services under way in the states. This is going on at the statewide level, in state-local arrangements, and in local administration of these services.

A. State-Level Administrative Arrangements

At the state level, almost all of the restructuring is in the direction of consolidation. In the late 1970s and early 1980s advocates for people with developmental disabilities were successful in several states in getting separate agencies created to administer developmental services. However, the majority of state developmental services programs are submerged within larger administrative agencies. In many states, the developmental disabilities bureau, office, or division is linked to a mental health unit and occasionally units dealing with aging, substance abuse, children, and people with other disabilities. These administrative units are embedded in various departments of mental health/mental retardation; health; and social and human services and often at the second or third levels within the organizational hierarchy. Despite the large numbers of people served in developmental services programs and the relatively substantial costs of these services, in most states developmental disabilities does not have the cabinet status of programs serving many fewer people and having less substantial operational and fiscal consequence.

Although administration of developmental services began the 1990s largely submerged within other administrative structures, the combination of the changeover to Republican governors who promised to streamline state bureaucracies as well as the wider enthusiasm for reinventing government and reengineering organizations resulted in further consolidations. In every state reorganization proposed or undertaken in the past few years, developmental services were rearranged or subsumed within larger administrative structures: Department of Community Health (Michigan), Department of Health and Social Services (Wisconsin), and Department of Human Services (Illinois). The bureaucratic location of developmental services appears to be a signal of less specialization of funding, service approach, and management for developmental services.

Another feature of state administration is the location of responsibility for Medicaid financing. This is often difficult to discern from general reviews of state administration of developmental services. Sparer (1996) argues that centralized control of Medicaid rate-setting in long term care in California led to lower costs than in New York's decentralized approach. In several states, Utah and Virginia, for example, the primary developmental disabilities agency operates the state's large institutions and publicly funded community services, but oversight and funding of private ICFs/MR are the responsibility of health care finance agency–type organizations. In other states, responsibility for Medicaid may be consolidated or disaggregated within the developmental services agency and/or split along institutional-community, public-private, long-term/acute, or other dimensions. While much of the attention of developmental services advocates and consumers has been on the bureaucratic location of the developmental disability agency, the consolidation of responsibility for Medicaid rate setting and administration has been a less noticed but important feature in recent reorganizations (e.g., Michigan and Wisconsin).

B. Intergovernmental Management

Other important features of state administration of developmental services are state-local fiscal and administrative arrangements and new forms of local administration. Key issues here are relative fiscal burden, administration of contracts for services, governance, and control of access to services.

The state and federal governments are the source of the overwhelming proportion of the costs of developmental services. In 37 of the 51 state (and District of Columbia) jurisdictions, local governments bear none of the direct costs of these services. In the 14 states with a local government contribution, only four have substantial local shares (Iowa, 23.6%; Missouri, 23.8%; Ohio 33.6%; Virginia, 17.0%), and the others are all under 10%, with most making negligible contributions (Braddock et al., 1998). Local governments in the states with large fiscal contributions play important roles in decisions about funding, access to services, and operation of community developmental services. However, county governments that make no, or negligible, contributions still play important roles in many states, often passing state and federal funding through contracts and making key decisions about which agencies get funding, what services are funded, and who gets access to services. This results in wide variations within many states in the availability and accessibility of developmental services, and this is often not evident from the formal state-local funding or structural arrangements (Castellani et al., 1993). A clearer picture of the relative roles of state and local governments in this area requires a closer examination of traditional roles of local government as well as the impact of the changes in the financing and organization of developmental services. For example, as more community developmental services are delivered outside congregate settings, individuals with disabilities get direct access to so-called generic Medicaid-funded services. The costs are not easily linked to developmental services and often not reported in national surveys. However, in many states these costs have an impact on state-local negotiations on how services are to be delivered and financed. It is important to remember that developmental services for individuals under 21 years of age are largely the responsibility of schools, and state-local relations on such issues as funding formulas for education costs (of which special education is a significant element), student-teacher ratios for special education, and related costs are important aspects of intergovernmental relations in this area.

In addition to local governments, substate specialized developmental services agencies play important roles in several states. In some states, (e.g., Connecticut, New York, and Massachusetts), *state* regional offices play important roles in decisions about which agencies get funded, what services are funded, and who gets access to services.

In other states, local or regional organizations are nonprofit (e.g., California) or hybrid (e.g., Colorado and New Hampshire) organizations. They represent an interesting phenomenon as state and local governments share some governance power with formal parent, advocacy group, and consumer representation. In New Hampshire, the state's division of developmental services contracts with 12 private, not-for-profit regional area agencies, governed by citizen boards, to oversee community services and to provide case management and family support services. These area agencies may provide other services or contract with local service provider agencies. The area agencies also act as a single point of entry into the service system, which is a key element of local control. In many states, this is loosely controlled, with local provider agencies making decisions from their own waiting lists. In other states, this is tightly controlled by the local government, the state regional office, or the substate governance organization.

The New Hampshire experience is being closely watched as other states struggle with new structures of substate administration of developmental services. Colorado has had a strong substate system with its community center boards (CCBs): 20 nonprofit organizations that operated noninstitutional services by acting as case management agencies, contracting with provider agencies, or providing community developmental services themselves. In the mid-1990s, Colorado undertook an in-depth review of its services and proposed a restructuring in which a key feature was to be the elimination of categorical funding of services in favor of block grant allocations of state and federal Medicaid funds to the CCBs (Colorado, 1995). The CCBs were to become "managed care organizations" which would have wide latitude to "reengineer" the system by negotiating payments with provider agencies as well as being able to offer individuals with disabilities and their families vouchers for services and supports. The blueprint was withdrawn in the face of strong opposition from virtually the entire spectrum of consumers and providers.

Wisconsin attempted another, more radical approach to local administration of developmental services. The state proposed to establish a single, consolidated program for people with long-term care needs, including those with developmental disabilities, under the aegis of local aging and disability resource centers. These local resource centers were to be responsible for screening, eligibility determination, and assistance in enrolling individuals in "care management organizations." (NASDDDS, 1997). Consumers, advocates, and providers in the developmental disabilities field were concerned that a unified system with a single, capitated payment would underfund developmental services and relegate people with disabilities to medically oriented long-term services. County officials fought to retain their traditional role as hubs for Wisconsin's service system for people with chronic disabilities (NASDDDS, 1997). In 1997, Wisconsin withdrew the plan.

Michigan is also undergoing a significant shift in the management of its community developmental services. Michigan was one of the first states to begin deinstitutionalization and development of community services, and its network of community mental health boards that operated in single- or multiple-county frameworks, with a 90/10 state-local split in funding, and shared governance among state government, county government, consumers, and providers, has been a model of state-local governance. In the mid-1990s, Michigan's consolidation of developmental services into a department of human services at the state level also involved significant devolution of responsibility for funding, operation, and administration of community services. The county and multicounty community health boards are being reorganized into nonprofit managed care organizations which are expected to compete with private managed care organizations for the state contracts to operate developmental and other services.

In many respects, many of these changes in state, state-local, and local administrative arrangements have been epiphenomena of various aspects of the new managerialism as state governments reinvented and reengineered in an attempt to achieve operational and fiscal efficiencies. The administration of developmental services was also affected by pressures for Medicaid reform, managed care, and reform of long-term care. The progress and outcomes of reorganizations in several states can be viewed in these larger contexts, affected as much or more by state and federal budget surpluses, waning enthusiasm for managed care, and the chronic uncertainties of long-term care reform. These factors coming from outside the developmental services field have, nonetheless, had a substantial impact on states' administration of these programs.

III. SHIFTING PARADIGMS AND ADMINISTRATION

Within the past few years, the notions of shifting and shattering paradigms have been prominent in the developmental services field (Bradley, et al., 1994; President's Committee, 1994). An important issue for state administration is the consequences of several distinct approaches to providing developmental services.

A. Supported Living

Concern about the large and growing costs of Medicaid for people with developmental disabilities, managed care, as well as the pressures of reinvention, devolution, cost-savings, and consolidations were important forces largely from outside the field of developmental disabilities that resulted in changes in states' administration of developmental services. These external forces were made more potent because they were consistent with demands for change from within the field.

As policy makers and funders grew concerned about the rapidly rising costs of Medicaid for developmental services, advocates in the field pointed out that although Medicaid was funding more group homes and community-based services, these were largely professionalized, medically oriented programs. Demands for less clinical and more personal supports, direct supports to consumers and families, and more self-direction were central in the approach that became known as supported living or self-determination. Dovetailing with policy makers and funders desires for cost constraints, more funding was shifted from the Medicaid ICF/MR program to the Medicaid home and community-based waivers (HCBS). HCBS waivers have been used to fund independent case managers, job coaches, personal care attendants, home modifications, cash subsidies, rent and housing subsidies, and other direct supports to individuals and their natural care givers.

In addition to new kinds of services in supported living, consumers are expected to get those supports from their family and neighbors, the market, and generic rather than specialized agencies. In fact, there is an antithesis toward traditional provider agencies, and creation of new agencies that are smaller and less clinically oriented is an important part of supported living (O'Brien and O'Brien, 1994; Taylor et al., 1991). For state administrators, this means oversight of more provider agencies, and agencies with different standards for staffing and service than in traditional agencies.

B. Managed Care

At the same time supported living was being proposed as the new paradigm, managed care was being proffered as a comprehensive solution for state administration of developmental services (e.g., Rhode Island, Michigan, and Connecticut). In fact, some of the same advocates proposing supported living were simultaneously recommending managed care as a strategy for reform of Medicaid funded congregate care programs (Smith and Ashbaugh, 1995). While these advocates saw the capitation mechanisms of managed care as a potential vehicle for reforming the service system, state executives and legislators saw managed care as a strategy for Medicaid reform, cutting the size and growth of costs in an area that had grown disproportionately expensive to the size of the clientele, had remained largely immune to the cost-cutting in the generic health arena, and was a potentially lucrative opportunity for managed care organizations facing diminishing returns from efficiencies in the generic health arena. The enthusiasm for managed care has cooled among advocates (Ashbaugh and Smith, 1996; NYArc, 1998), but several states had already begun reorganization of developmental services with a managed care approach.

C. Long-Term Care

Long-term care is not a prominent reform theme in this field, but it does point to the fact that despite the closure and downsizing of large state-operated institutions in the past 30 years, large congregate settings are still a major locus of service for people with developmental disabilities. In 1996, there were 59,726 individuals residing in large state-operated institutions, and 79,441 people with developmental disabilities were living in other institutions: 38,438 in nursing homes, and 41,003 in private and other large institutions (Braddock et al., 1998; Prouty and Lakin, 1997; Wagner, 1995).

While the focus has been on large state-operated institutions, in a number of states (e.g., Indiana, Kentucky, Michigan, Minnesota, and Ohio) more people resided in nursing homes than in state institutions, and in many states, Massachusetts, for example, the numbers are close. Indeed, some states such as New Hampshire have been lauded for closing all its large state-operated institutions, but from 1992 to 1996, at the time this closure was under way, New Hampshire's nursing home population of people with developmental disabilities more than quadrupled (Braddock et al., 1998).

In addition to nursing homes, many states use other large private facilities for people with developmental disabilities. For example, in Wisconsin, 1214 individuals reside in three large state-operated institutions, and no plans have been announced to close these facilities. Moreover, 664 individuals reside in nursing homes, 2241 in large private ICF/MRs, and 957 in other large facilities, including ICFs operated by county governments and "child caring institutions" (Braddock et al., 1998).

The issue of institutional vis-à-vis community programs is much more complex than often portrayed. In many states, there has been a long-standing pattern of the use of nursing homes for people with developmental disabilities independent of changes along the large institution–small community program dimension. In other instances, there seems to be some transinstitutionalization under way, with at least some diversion or transfer of individuals from large state-operated institutions into nursing homes and other large private institutions.

D. Forensic Services

Throughout the era of the shift from large state institutions to community programs, opposition to this trend was largely centered around parents and public employees in those large facilities who raised issues of safety, the availability of medical care, as well as job security (Castellani, 1992). In the mid-1990s, the issue of safety reemerged from the perspective of the community. Megan's Law in New Jersey and the 1997 Supreme Court ruling in *Henricks v. Kansas* that upheld the Kansas Sexually Violent Predator Act, which allowed predatory sex offenders to be paroled from jail to mental hospitals or kept in mental hospitals, refocused attention on individuals who had "challenging behaviors." New York, for example, is increasing the size and building new "secure units" within its developmental services program as well as enhancing other programs to deal with this issue. This increased forensic responsibility is another distinct approach to states' administration of developmental services.

E. Current Institutional and Community-Based System

These new paradigms and alternative approaches to developmental services must be considered in the context of the existing service system in most states. With a handful of exceptions, most states still operate large institutions which house almost 60,000 individuals (Braddock et al., 1998). The institutional model remains substantial and may be revitalized with the renewed attention to "special populations" and forensic concerns. Moreover, despite the advocacy for supported living, the overwhelming majority of individuals served by state developmental service agencies get their services from community-based organizations, financed through various rate and contract mechanisms based on enrollment, attendance, certification of provider, qualifications of staff, conformity of services with state Medicaid plans, and all the other fiscal, operational, and regulatory arrangements governing this large and complex industry.

F. New Paradigms or Boutiques?

Supporting living, managed care, long-term care, forensics, and the current institutional and community-based service system are distinct approaches to providing developmental services. There is not a new paradigm in developmental services which forms an overarching framework for delivering and managing developmental services. Instead, the earlier state institutional framework which was supplemented by the group home–community program model has evolved into a plurality of approaches, each with a distinct clientele, its own approach to services, separate types of financing, and distinct types of service providers. This has important, and largely unacknowledged, ramifications for administration of developmental services.

IV. ORGANIZATION AND IMPLICATIONS FOR ADMINISTRATION

The locus of services has been a major issue in the field for the past 30 years as services have moved from large state-operated institutions to group homes, community-based day programs, and to supported living agencies and informal and open-market arrangements. Despite some movement toward informal, generic, and market sources of support, the overwhelming majority of services to developmentally disabled adults in states is provided by public and private agencies specializing in developmental services. In every state, there is some version of the following organizational landscape: state agency-operated large institutions; state or local government agency-operated community services; and private nonprofit and for-profit agencies operating large institutions, group homes, community day programs, and family and individual support programs. The mix varies widely from state to state, represents a combination of strategic or incremental policy choices and private practices, and is undergoing substantial changes in some states. Despite the wide variations and changes, the impact of the sector, size, and structure of these various organizational types on the availability and accessibility of services and how states administer developmental services programs is largely unexamined. There are, nonetheless, indications of how the ways developmental services programs are organized in states affect administration of these programs.

A. Sector Choice

Many states privatized large segments of developmental services programs as they downsized and closed large institutions and established group homes and community-based services. In most states, these private agencies are nonprofit organizations often operated by or affiliated with parent and advocacy groups such as United Cerebral Palsy or Arc. There has been debate about whether nonprofit organizations are inherently superior to government agencies in the quality of services, but most of the discussion focuses on the lower costs of nonprofit agencies with lower pay and fewer benefits than are typical of government agencies. There is little evidence of substantial differences in comparable government operated and nonprofit agency-operated community programs. Nonetheless, as programs are privatized, budgeting, rate setting, contract administration, quality assurance, and outcome measurement for private agency contracting represent substantial administrative changes from the mechanisms and procedures of direct government operation (Castellani, 1997; Kettl, 1993).

Most of the attention to these problems has been on the nonprofit sector. Here, the administrative problems of contracting with a fragile nonprofit sector as well as the entrepreneurial growth of some nonprofit agencies have been the focus (Castellani, 1997; Smith and Lipsky, 1993). A more recent phenomenon in the developmental disabilities field has been the growth and entry of large for-profit corporations. Some of these corporations, Res-Care and VOCA, for example, operate hundreds of group homes and day programs in several states and specialize in developmental services. The growth of managed care has brought a number of generic managed care organizations into the field, and while the overall penetration remains low, developmental disability advocacy and provider organizations see these corporations as having the potential to effect substantial changes in the organizational landscape of developmental services (NYArc, 1998). From the standpoint of state administration, the challenges of managing networks of small, often fragile provider agencies are obviously different from dealing with large, multistate, multiprogram nonprofit organizations and for-profit corporations.

B. Number, Size, and Structure of Provider Agencies

Whether public or private, variations in the number, size, and structure of developmental-services agencies present challenges for state administration of these services. In some states these organizations vary from small agencies providing one type of service to large and highly complex organizations serving thousands of individuals with hundreds, sometimes thousands, of employees and tens of millions of dollars a year in revenues. The extent of horizontal and vertical integration of services in these agencies is also important. In some states, multiprogram agencies provide individuals with an all-encompassing array of residential, day, recreation, transportation, clinic, and other services. Many of these large agencies are also vertically integrated, with children entering early intervention and preschool programs, school programs, after-school programs, family support programs, and other services leading to the multiprogram adult services and involve the person with the disability and family virtually from birth to death within the same agency. In other states, horizontal integration of day, residential, and ancillary services as well as vertical integration by age is discouraged. The organizational mix in locales and across states presents myriad problems for state administrators. The experience of the past thirty years has been one of managing highly regulated networks: certifying providers, shoring up fiscally fragile agencies (large and small), attempting to ensure some equity in availability of services within and among locales, and managing access of individuals into provider organizations. The simultaneous growth of small supported-living agencies, access of consumers to private-market and generic sources of support, large multistate developmental services corporations, and managed care organizations presents an exponential increase in complexity for state administration in budgeting, rate setting, contract administration, quality assurance, constituency relations, and policy making.

V. COURTS AND THE ADMINISTRATION OF SERVICES

Adversarial legalism is a feature of administration of virtually every program, as statutes, regulations, and practices are constantly litigated (Kagan, 1991). Judicial decisions have also had strategic implications for the administration of state programs. In the developmental-disabilities policy area, court decisions had a significant impact in three areas: cases challenging the operation of large state-run institutions (Castellani, 1987); challenges to SSI eligibility (*Sullivan v. Zebley*), and most recently, challenges to establish an entitlement to Medicaid funded developmental services (*Doe v. Chiles*). The impact of the first two were discussed in Castellani (1997). The third is a recent case that is likely to have broad, strategic impact on state administration of developmental services programs. In fact, it may have broad implications for states' Medicaid-funded long-term care programs.

A. *Doe v. Chiles* and Restructuring of State Programs

In early 1998, a three-judge panel of the 11th U.S. Circuit Court of Appeals upheld a lower-court order directing the State of Florida to make ICF/MR services available to all qualified Medicaid recipients within 90 days of determining that they need such services. In their original suit (*John/Jane Does v. Chiles et al.*), plaintiffs, all of whom were on waiting lists for admission to private ICFs/MR, challenged the decision of the Florida legislature to place a moratorium on the certification of additional ICF/MR beds. The plaintiffs claimed that the State of Florida was violating their rights, contending that the state was failing to meet its obligations under federal statutes to furnish services covered under its Medicaid plan "with reasonable promptness to all eligible individuals" (42 USC 1396(a)(8).

Florida conceded the existence of lengthy waiting lists. In 1996, the Florida Department of Children and Families had a waiting list of over 8000 individuals awaiting developmental services statewide, of whom 1700 were in need of ICF/MR placements. The state argued (as have all other states) that it was not obligated to make Medicaid services available on the basis of open-ended funding, citing the bed capacity limit and the subsequent moratorium imposed by the legislature.

In many ways this case represents the implications of the fundamental inconsistency in the federal Medicaid statute and states' use of this funding for long-term care services. The original federal statute focused primarily on the delivery of acute medical services to low-income recipients. Consequently, states had to agree to provide those services *promptly* to all qualified individuals without respect to state funding limitations. However, as states used Medicaid funding for long-term care services where they traditionally regulated access on the basis of available appropriations and regulated supply and maintained waiting lists, the potential for conflict between federal and state statutes and practices grew.

Over the years, states avoided conflict with the issue of Medicaid entitlement for long-term care services by limiting optional services in their Medicaid plans and imposing amount, duration, and scope restrictions on existing services. States also used Medicaid-funded home and community-based waivers to provide services to people with developmental disabilities, the frail elderly, persons with physical disabilities, and persons with severe and persistent mental illnesses outside general and psychiatric hospitals, nursing homes, and ICF/MR beds. Over the years, Congress and HCFA acquiesced to these state strategies by repealing or watering down certificate-of-need requirements and encouraging expansion of waiver programs.

The *Does v. Chiles* suit has been active since 1992, but Florida's enactment of a so-called Cut Law (H.R. 1621) eliminated coverage of private ICF/MR services from the state's Title XIX plan and required transfer of the 2176 individuals then residing in private ICFs/MR to the state's home- and community-based waiver programs. This precipitated a new class-action suit (*Cramer v. Chiles*) which challenged the legality of the statute. The federal district court ruled in *Cramer* that the plaintiffs had an enforceable civil rights action, that the state's Title XIX plan must provide that *all* individuals wishing to make application for medical assistance under the plan shall have the opportunity to do so, and such assistance shall be furnished *with reasonable promptness* to *all eligible individuals*. The time standards for determining eligibility may not exceed 90 days for applicants who apply on the basis of disability, and 45 days for all other applicants.

As of early 1998, Florida officials were examining the impact of the ruling. Preliminary estimates indicated that the state would have to spend at least an additional $1 billion annually on specialized developmental disabilities services to ensure that all qualified Medicaid recipients are served within the time frame specified in the court order. In 1996, Florida's total expenditures for all developmental services was $491 million (Braddock et al., 1998).

The impact of the decision is substantial for several reasons. First, because of the comprehensive nature of ICF/MR services, states cannot easily apply amount, duration, and scope limitations without placing the certification of provider facilities in jeopardy. Second, states cannot tighten ICF/MR admission criteria without disenfranchising large numbers of current participants through level-of-care determinations. Finally, states cannot decline ICF/MR and HCBS funding without losing 35–60% of the total expenditures for state developmental services.

Florida and other states are examining the immediate implications of the decision. For states, the major consequences seem obvious: an entitlement to ICF/MR services rather than capped appropriations and waiting lists, substantial expansion of ICF/MR and Medicaid-funded services, and implementation of procedures for eligibility determination and access within much shorter time frames than currently in place.

Thirty years ago, federal courts began playing critical roles initiating the downsizing and closure of large state-operated institutions. Since then, courts have continued to be important, but federal Medicaid funding through the ICF/MR program and later the HCBS waiver has been the most significant factor in states' overall developmental services programs. The *Chiles* case has the potential of bringing federal courts back to the center of policy making in this area. The initial impact of the implementation of this ruling may be expansion in states' developmental services programs. It may also lead to greater equity among states as courts move beyond a focus on states' widely varying waiting lists to variations in states' fiscal commitment and capacity unrelated to the underlying similarities in prevalence and need.

VI. CONCLUSION

Variation, complexity, and change are the salient features of state administration of developmental services that emerge from this review. States have widely varying capacity in their developmental service systems in the numbers of individuals served, the amounts expended for services, and the willingness to address waiting lists. Differences in what disabilities are covered by the developmental services agency, how disability is defined, and how eligibility for services is determined also create substantial differences among states and often large changes over short periods of time. State developmental-services agencies are largely submerged within other human services structures, and the experience with initiatives in new state-local and local governance arrangements has been uncertain and difficult. The so-called shattering of institutional and community-based paradigms of services has not led to a new, single, overarching model of service delivery but rather a plurality of approaches, with distinct clienteles and provider organizations. The ways in which services are organized in states also vary widely, often within as well as among states, and substantial changes are under way as large corporations and managed care organizations enter this market. Finally, federal courts, which have played important roles in the past, may again have strategic impact on states' developmental services programs. This diversity, variation, and change provides an interesting area of study in an important area of human services and public policy. However, there are two consequences for state administration of developmental services programs that may be unsettling to those in the field.

The first is whether state administrations have the capacity to manage this complexity (Gargan, 1995). The changes in developmental services programs have been taking place at the same time states have trimmed the size of their administration. The results of consolidations and reinvention initiatives may have made the remaining administrative structures, processes, and staffs more efficient and capable of dealing with this multiplicity, complexity, and change. Administration of distinct types of services (institutional long-term care, community-based congregate care, forensics, medical managed care, and supported living) delivered by a variety of public and private agencies and available from generic and market sources is a daunting task. The creation and operation of separate mechanisms and processes for budgeting, rate setting, fiscal management, contracting, quality assurance, and other administrative functions may overwhelm the management capacity in many states' developmental services agencies.

If states' management capacity is deficient, then the centrifugal forces already underway in developmental services may accelerate. The plurality and diversity of approaches and structures of developmental services along with the absence of the capacity to manage it within existing arrangements may lead to the disintegration of developmental disabilities as a framework for administration of developmental services. Managed care, long-term care, foster care, income maintenance, and welfare/workfare are alternative, existing frameworks within which developmental services could be administered. Consolidation of developmental services within larger human services agencies is increasing. The capacity to successfully manage the myriad streams emerging in developmental disabilities may be the critical factor in the continuation of this field as a distinct area of state administration.

REFERENCES

Arc. (1997). *A Status Report to the Nation on People with Mental Retardation Waiting for Community Services*, Arc. Arlington, TX.

Ashbaugh, J., and Smith, G. (1996). Beware the managed health-care companies, *Mental Retardation 34(3)*: 189–193.

Bird, W. A., Castellani, P. J., and Nemeth, C. (1990). Access to early intervention services in New York State, *Journal of Disability Policy Studies 1(2)*: 65–84.

Boggs, E., Lakin, K. C., and Clauser, S. (1985). Medicaid coverage of residential services, *An Analysis of Medicaid's Intermediate Care Facility for the Mentally Retarded (ICF/MR) Program* (K. C. Lakin, ed.), University of Minnesota Center for Residential and Community Services, Minneapolis.

Braddock, D., Hemp, R., Parish, S., and Westrich, J. (1998). *The State of the States in Developmental Disabilities*, 5th ed. American Association on Mental Retardation, Washington, DC.

Bradley, V. J., Ashbaugh, J. W., and Blaney, B. C., eds. (1994). *Creating Individual Supports for People with Developmental Disabilities: A Mandate for Change at Many Levels*, Paul H. Brookes, Baltimore.

Castellani, P. J. (1997). Managing alternate approaches to the provision and production of public goods: public, private, and nonprofit, *Handbook of Local Government Administration* (J. Gargan, ed), Marcel Dekker, New York.

Castellani, P. J., Bird, W. A., and Manning, B. L. (1993). *Supporting Individuals with Developmental Disabilities in the Community*, New York State Office of Mental Retardation and Developmental Disabilities, Albany.

Castellani, P. J. (1992). Closing institutions in New York State: implementation and management lessons, *Journal of Policy Analysis & Management 11*: 593–611.

Castellani, P. J. (1987). *The Political Economy of Developmental Disabilities*, Paul Brookes, Baltimore.

Cedarbaum, J. G. (1995). *Policies for Children with Disabilities: Connecticut, Virginia and Some National Trends*, National Academy for Social Insurance, Washington. DC.

Colorado Division for Developmental Disabilities. (1995). *Blueprint for Change*, Author, Denver, CO.

Derthick, M. (1990). *Agency Under Stress: The Social Security Administration in American Government*, Brookings Institution, Washington, DC.

Gargan, J. J. (1995). Professionalism and the public sector, *Handbook of Public Personnel Administration* (J. Rabin et al. eds.), Marcel Dekker, New York.

Kagan, R. A. (1991). Adversarial legalism and American government, *Journal of Policy Analysis and Management, 10(3)*: 369–406.

Kettl, D. F. (1993). The myths, realities, and challenges of privatization, *Revitalizing State and Local Public Service* (F. J. Thompson. ed.), Jossey-Bass, San Francisco.

Hemp, R., Braddock, D., and Westrich, J. (1998). Medicaid, managed care, and developmental disabilities, *The State of the States in Developmental Disabilities*, 5th ed. (D. Braddock, R. Hemp. S. Parish, and J. Westrich, eds.), American Association on Mental Retardation, Washington, DC, pp. 67–89.

Luckasson, R., Coulter, D. L., Polloway, E. A., Reiss, S., Schalock, R. L., Spitalnick, D. M., and Stark, J. A. (1992). *Mental Retardation: Definitions, Classification, and Systems of Support*, American Association on Mental Retardation, Washington, DC.

National Association of State Directors of Developmental Disabilities Services. (1997). Wisconsin set sights on integrated health/LTC system, *Perspectives 2(6)*: 2.

New York State ARC. (1998). *Medicaid Managed Care: Can Managed Care Manage the Risk of People with Developmental Disabilities?*, Author, Delmar, NY.

New York State Office of Mental Retardation and Developmental Disabilities. (1990). *The Community Challenge: A Partnership with Families, Consumers, and Providers*, Author, Albany, NY.

O'Brien, J., and O'Brien, C. L. (1994). More than just a new address: images of organization for supported living agencies, *Creating Individual Supports for People with Developmental Disabilities: A Mandate for Change at Many Levels* (V. J. Bradley et al., eds.), Paul Brookes, Baltimore.

President's Commission on Mental Retardation. (1994). *The National Reform Agenda and People with Mental Retardation: Putting People First*, U.S. Department of Health and Human Services, Washington, DC.

Prouty, R., and Lakin, K. C. (1997). *Residential Services for Persons with Developmental Disabilities: Status and Trends Through 1996*, University of Minnesota, Research and Training Center on Community Living, Institute on Community Integration, Minneapolis.

Reiss, S. (1994). Issues in defining mental retardation, *American Journal on Mental Retardation 99:1*, 1–7.

Smith, S. R., and Lipsky, M. (1993). *Nonprofits for Hire: The Welfare State in the Age of Contracting*, Harvard University Press. Cambridge, MA.

Smith, G., and Ashbaugh, J. (1995). *Managed Care and People with Developmental Disabilities: A Guidebook*, National Association of State Directors of Developmental Disabilities Services and Human Services Research Institute, Alexandria, VA.

Sparer, M. S. (1996). *Medicaid and the Limits of State Health Reform*, Temple University Press, Philadelphia.

Taylor, S. J., Bogdan, R., and Racino, J. A., eds. (1991). *Life in the Community: Case Studies of Organizations Supporting People with Disabilities*, Paul H. Brookes, Baltimore.

Wagner, B. R., Long, D. F., Reynolds, M., and Taylor, J. R. (1995). Voluntary transformation from an institutionally based to a community-based service system, *Mental Retardation 33(5)*: 317–321.

Wisconsin Department of Health and Family Services. (1997). *Redesigning Wisconsin's Long Term Care System*, Author, Madison, WI.

18
Administration and Management of State Human Service Agencies

Lawrence L. Martin
Columbia University, New York, New York

Other chapters of this book deal with the topics of welfare, welfare reform, and Medicaid. These topics are of critical importance to the administration and management of state human service agencies today and deserve to be singled out for special attention and discussion. However, state human service agencies are engaged in variety of programs, services, and activities in addition to welfare and Medicaid. As a general rule, state human services agencies tend to be some of the largest and most complex agencies in each of the 50 states. For example, in fiscal year 1996–97 the Florida Department of Children and Families (Florida DCF) had 27,000 employees and a budget of $3 billion (Florida DCF, 1996).

This chapter looks at the structure and functions of the designated state human service agencies in each of the 50 states. The discussion takes a comparative approach (both cross-sectionally and longitudinally) by examining the structure and functions of the 50 designated state human services agencies today, as well as the changes that have occurred over the past decade. As the analysis will show, when it comes to the administration and management of the 50 designated state human service agencies, *diversity* is the order of the day. The data presented in this chapter are taken primarily from the *1997/98 Public Welfare Directory* and the *1986/87 Public Welfare Directory*, both compiled and published by the American Public Welfare Association (APWA, 1997, 1986). The annual APWA directory is arguably the best source of up-to-date information about the structure and functions of state human service agencies.

I. WHAT ARE THE HUMAN SERVICES?

No universally agreed-upon definition exists as to what constitutes "human services." This definitional difficulty arises because the human services encompass a variety of related, yet disparate, programs, services, and activities. As Table 1 illustrates, some human services are directed toward individuals at a particular stage of the life cycle: children, adults, and the elderly. Other human services attempt to address the needs of individuals who possess a physical or mental disability. Some human services provide financial assistance and services to people based on economic need (e.g., unemployment insurance; food stamps; general assistance, which is usually state funded; and Temporary Assistance to Needy

Table 1   Types of Human Services

Adult corrections
Adult protective services
Child day care services
Child protective services
Child support enforcement services
Child welfare services
Employment services
Energy assistance services
Food stamps
General assistance
Health
Housing
Job training services
Medicaid
Mental health
Probation and community control
Services to adults
Services to the developmentally disabled
    and the mentally retarded
Services to older americans
Services to persons with disabilities
Public assistance
Public health
Temporary assistance for needy families
Unemployment insurance
Vocational rehabilitation services
Youth facilities

Note: This list is meant to be illustrative, not exhaustive.

Families [TANF], the new federal welfare program; and others). Still other human services are available to anyone seeking employment or in need of job training or retraining (e.g., a variety of employment and job training services). Finally, some human services are targeted at "involuntary clients" including adults and juveniles confined to jails, prisons, or mental health facilities or who are on probation or in alternative community control programs.

The diversity of the programs, services, and activities identified in Table 1 serves to illustrate both the definitional and complexity issues surrounding the human services. Nevertheless, these disparate programs, services, and activities are generally recognized as comprising what can be called the human services (e.g., Chi, 1987; Mehr, 1995).

II. DESIGNATED STATE HUMAN SERVICE AGENCIES

Any organization that provides at least one of the human services identified in Table 1 can rightfully be called a human service agency. In many states, the human services shown in Table 1 are the responsibility of two or more different state agencies. This division of responsibility presents a classification problem. Which agency in each state should be called the "state human service agency" or should all state agencies that have responsibility for at least one human service be referred to generically as state human service agencies? In preparing its annual *Public Welfare Directory*, the APWA identifies and designates the single agency in each state that has *primary* responsibility for both public assistance and social services. Following this convention, Table 2 identifies the 50 APWA designated state human service agencies in 1997.

How important is the name, or title, given to a designated state human service agency? An argument can be made that an agency's name says a great deal about how the organization views itself and how it wants stakeholders, including taxpayers, to view it. For example, including the term "welfare" in the name of designated state human service agencies has not been popular in recent years. Table 2 reveals that in 1997 only three of the 50 designated state human service agencies still included the term welfare in their titles: the California Health & Welfare Agency, the Idaho Department of Health & Welfare, and the Pennsylvania Department of Public Welfare.

The preferred name for designated state human service agencies is, not surprisingly, departments of human services. As Table 2 illustrates, 22 (44%) of the 50 designated state human service agencies refer to themselves as departments of human services, including 18 agencies that use this title exclusively and an additional four (Massachusetts, Montana, Nebraska, New Hampshire) that include either health or public health together with human services in their titles. The second and third most popular names for designated state human services

Table 2 The 50 Designated State Human Service Agencies in 1997

Alabama Department of Human Resources
Alaska Department of Health & Social Services
Arizona Department of Economic Security
Arkansas Department of Human Services
California Health & Welfare Agency
Colorado Department of Human Services
Connecticut Department of Social Services
Delaware Department of Health & Social Services
Florida Department of Children & Families[a]
Georgia Department of Human Resources
Hawaii Department of Human Services[a]
Idaho Department of Health & Welfare
Illinois Department of Human Services[a]
Indiana Family & Social Services Administration[a]
Iowa Department of Human Services
Kansas Department of Social & Rehabilitative Services
Kentucky Cabinet for Families & Children[a]
Louisiana Department of Social Services[a]
Maine Department of Human Services
Maryland Department of Human Resources
Massachusetts Executive Office of Health & Human Services
Michigan Family Independence Agency[a]
Minnesota Department of Human Services
Mississippi Department of Human Services[a]
Missouri Department of Social Services
Montana Department of Public Health & Human Services[a]
Nebraska Department of Health & Human Services[a]
Nevada Department of Human Resources
New Hampshire Department of Health & Human Services[a]
New Jersey Department of Human Services
New Mexico Department of Human Services
New York Department of Family Assistance[a]
North Carolina Department of Human Resources
North Dakota Department of Human Services
Ohio Department of Human Services
Oklahoma Department of Human Services
Oregon Department of Human Resources
Pennsylvania Department of Public Welfare
Rhode Island Department of Human Services
South Carolina Department of Social Services
South Dakota Department of Social Services
Tennessee Department of Human Services
Texas Department of Human Services
Utah Department of Human Services[a]
Vermont Agency of Human Services
Virginia Department of Social Services[a]
Washington Department of Social & Health Services
West Virginia Department of Health & Human Resources[a]
Wisconsin Department of Health & Family Services[a]
Wyoming Department of Family Services[a]

[a] State human service agencies with name changes since 1986.
Source: AWPA, 1997.

agencies are departments of social services and departments of human resources. The term social services is used either exclusively or in combination with health by a total of 10 (20%) designated state human service agencies, while human resources is used either exclusively or in combination with health by a total of seven (14%).

The importance associated with the name, or title, used to identify a designated state human service agency is made even more apparent when recent name changes are examined. Some 17 designated state human service agencies changed their names during the last decade. When the current names are compared with those of a decade ago (see Table 3), some interesting observations can be made. Seven of the 17 (41%) designated state human service agencies with name changes during the last decade (Hawaii, Mississippi, Montana, Nebraska, New Hampshire, West Virginia, Utah) now include the term human services in their titles. During this same period, two states (Indiana, Mississippi) dropped the terms public welfare and social welfare respectively from their titles. None of the 17 designated state human service agencies with name changes opted to include the term welfare in their new titles. An obvious conclusion is that the term human services is considered less controversial and perhaps less objectionable today than is the term welfare.

Several designated state human service agencies with name changes during the last decade now include terms like children and families in their titles. Seven of the 17 (41%) designated state human services agencies with name changes (Florida, Indiana, Kentucky, Michigan, New York, Wisconsin, Wyoming) have taken this approach. These designated state human service agencies appear to be signaling their stakeholders that children and families are considered priorities. This contention is given added support when the mission/vision statements (see Table 4) of four of these designated state human services agencies are examined. For example, the Florida Department of Children & Families proposes to help people become self-sufficient and live in stable families. The Indiana Family & Social Services Agency has the goal of strengthening the ability of families to succeed. The Michigan Family Independence Agency helps strengthen individuals and families through mutual respect and mutual responsibility. And the Wisconsin Department of Health & Family Services fosters healthy self-reliant individuals and families.

III. FUNCTIONS OF DESIGNATED STATE HUMAN SERVICE AGENCIES

As noted earlier, not all human services in the 50 states are the responsibility of the 50 designated state human services agencies. What services, then, are the responsibility of the 50 designated state human service agencies? In an effort to

Table 3 State Human Service Agency Name Changes (1986–1997)

State	Old name	New name
Connecticut	Department of Human Resources	Department of Social Services
Florida	Department of Health & Rehabilitative Services	Department of Children & Families
Hawaii	Department of Social Services & Housing	Department of Human Services
Indiana	Department of Public Welfare	Family & Social Services Administration
Kentucky	Cabinet for Human Resources	Cabinet for Children & Families
Louisiana	Department of Social Services	Department of Health & Human Resources
Michigan	Department of Social Services	Family Independence Agency
Mississippi	Department of Social Welfare	Department of Human Services
Montana	Department of Social & Social & Rehabilitative Services	Department of Health & Human Services
Nebraska	Department of Social Services	Department of Health & Human Services
New Hampshire	Department of Human Resources	Department of Health & Human Services
New York	Department of Social Services	Department of Family Assistance
Utah	Department of Health	Department of Human Services
Virginia	Department of Human Resources	Department of Social Services
West Virginia	Department of Human Resources	Department of Health & Human Services
Wisconsin	Department of Health & Social Services	Department of Health & Family Services
Wyoming	Department of Health & Social Services	Department of Family Services

Source: APWA, 1986, 1997.

answer this question, the Council of State Governments (Chi, 1987) has devised a useful approach. Building upon the work of the APWA, the Council of State Governments has identified nine major human service functions: public assistance (PA), social services (SS), public health (PH), mental health (MH), mental retardation (MR), adult corrections (AC), youth facilities (YF), vocational rehabilitation (VR), and employment services (ES). Table 5 presents data on the number of functions that are the responsibility of each of the 50 designated human service

Table 4 Mission/Vision Statements of Designated State Human Service Agencies 1997

Florida Department of Children & Families (Florida DCF)
—To work in partnership with local communities to help people be self-sufficient and live in stable families and communities.
Indiana Family & Social Services Administration (Indiana FSA)
—To help strengthen the ability of families to succeed.
Michigan Family Independence Agency (Michigan FIA)
—We strengthen individuals and families through mutual respect and mutual responsibility.
Wisconsin Department of Health & Family Services (Wisconsin DHFS)
—To lead the nation in fostering healthy, self-reliant individuals and families.

Sources: Florida DCF ⟨http://sun6.dms.state.fl.us/cf_web?⟩ 12/17/97; Indiana FSA ⟨http://www.ai.org/fssa/HTML/PROGRAMS/overview.html⟩ 12/17/97; Michigan FIA ⟨http://www.mfia.state.mi/us/1996fact.html#a1⟩ 12/17/97; Wisconsin DHFS ⟨http:www.dhfs.state.wi.us⟩ 12/17/97.

agencies. One additional function (services to older Americans) has been added to this list. The addition of services to older Americans (OA) recognizes the increasing importance of this human service function.

The mean average number of functions that a single designated state human service agency had responsibility for in 1997 was 4.7, with the range being between one and eight. The designated state human service agency in New Mexico was responsible for only one function (public assistance). At the other extreme, the designated state human service agencies in Vermont and California were responsible for nine and eight functions, respectively. In 1997, the 50 designated state human service agencies were responsible, in order of frequency, for social services (49), public assistance (48), mental retardation (29), mental health (28), and services to older Americans (27). Only three designated state human service agencies (Arizona, California West Virginia) were responsible for employment services in 1997, while only one designated state human service agency (Vermont) was responsible for adult corrections.

An interesting feature of Table 5 is the finding that in three states (New Mexico, Utah, Wisconsin) the responsibility for the functions of public assistance and social services have been divided among different state agencies, with public assistance being placed in one state agency and social services in another. The actions of New Mexico, Utah, and Wisconsin reverse a long-standing tradition of having a single state agency responsible for both of these functions. The actions of New Mexico, Utah, and Wisconsin also have implications for the classification systems developed by the APWA and the Council of State Governments. No longer can it be said that New Mexico, Utah, and Wisconsin truly have a single

Table 5   Major Functions of Designated State Human Service Agencies 1997

	PA	SS	PH	MH	MR	AC	YF	VR	ES	OA
Alabama (2)	X	X								
Alaska (5)	X	X	X					X		X
Arizona (7)	X	X	X	X	X				X	X
Arkansas (6)	X	X		X	X		X			X
California (8)	X	X	X	X	X			X	X	X
Colorado (7)	X	X		X	X		X	X		X
Connecticut (4)	X	X						X		X
Delaware (6)	X	X	X	X	X			X		
Florida (4)	X	X		X	X					
Georgia (7)	X	X	X	X	X			X		X
Hawaii (4)	X	X					X	X		
Idaho (5)	X	X	X	X	X					
Illinois (6)	X	X	X	X	X			X		
Indiana (6)	X	X		X	X			X		X
Iowa (5)	X	X		X	X		X			
Kansas (6)	X	X		X	X		X	X		
Kentucky (3)	X	X								X
Louisiana (3)	X	X						X		
Maine (4)	X	X	X							X
Maryland (2)	X	X								
Massachusetts (7)	X	X	X	X	X		X	X		
Michigan (3)	X	X					X			
Minnesota (5)	X	X	X	X			X			
Mississippi (4)	X	X					X			X
Missouri (4)	X	X					X			X

	PA	SS	PH	MH	MR	AC	YF	VR	ES	OA
Montana (7)	X	X	X	X	X			X		X
Nebraska (6)	X	X	X	X	X					X
Nevada (7)	X	X	X	X	X		X			X
New Hampshire (6)	X	X	X	X	X					X
New Jersey (4)	X	X		X	X					X
New Mexico (1)	X									
New York (2)	X	X								
North Carolina (7)	X	X		X	X		X	X		X
North Dakota (6)	X	X		X	X			X		X
Ohio (2)	X	X								
Oklahoma (4)	X	X		X	X					X
Oregon (7)	X	X	X	X	X			X		X
Pennsylvania (5)	X	X		X	X		X			
Rhode Island (3)	X	X						X		X
South Carolina (2)	X	X								
South Dakota (3)	X	X								
Tennessee (3)	X	X								X
Texas (2)	X	X								
Utah (5)	X	X		X	X		X	X		X
Vermont (9)	X	X	X	X	X	X	X	X		X
Virginia (2)	X	X								
Washington (7)	X	X		X	X		X	X		X
West Virginia (7)	X	X	X	X	X				X	
Wisconsin (3)	X	X	X							
Wyoming (3)	X	X	X							
Totals (236)	48	49	17	28	29	1	15	19	3	27

PA = public assistance, SS = social services, PH = public health, MH = mental health, MR = mental retardation, AC = adult corrections, YF = youth facilities, VR = vocational rehabilitation, ES = employment services, OA = older Americans.
Source: APWA, 1997.

Table 6 Major Functions of Designated State Human Service Agencies 1986

	PA	SS	PH	MH	MR	AC	YF	VR	ES	OA
Alabama (2)	X	X								
Alaska (6)	X	X		X	X		X			X
Arizona (7)	X	X	X	X	X			X		X
Arkansas (7)	X	X		X	X		X	X		X
California (8)	X	X	X	X	X			X	X	X
Colorado (5)	X	X					X	X	X	
Connecticut (4)	X	X						X	X	
Delaware (6)	X	X	X	X	X		X			X
Florida (7)	X	X	X	X	X		X	X		X
Georgia (8)	X	X	X	X	X		X	X		X
Hawaii (5)	X	X				X				
Idaho (5)	X	X		X	X	X				
Illinois (2)	X	X								
Indiana (2)	X	X								
Iowa (5)	X	X		X	X		X	X		
Kansas (6)	X	X		X	X		X	X		
Kentucky (8)	X	X	X	X	X		X	X		X
Louisiana (6)	X	X	X	X	X		X	X		
Maine (5)	X	X	X	X				X		X
Maryland (2)	X	X								
Massachusetts (8)	X	X	X	X	X	X	X	X		
Michigan (2)	X	X								
Minnesota (5)	X	X		X	X					X
Mississippi (2)	X	X								
Missouri (4)	X	X					X			X
Montana (5)	X	X			X			X		X

State	PA	SS	PH	MH	MR	AC	YF	VR	ES	OA
Nebraska (2)	X	X								
Nevada (8)	X	X	X	X	X			X	X	X
New Hampshire (6)	X	X	X	X				X		X
New Jersey (4)	X	X	X	X						
New Mexico (2)	X	X								
New York (2)	X	X								
North Carolina (8)	X	X	X	X	X			X	X	X
North Dakota (6)	X	X	X	X				X		X
Ohio (2)	X	X								
Oklahoma (6)	X	X	X	X	X					X
Oregon (10)	X	X	X	X	X	X	X	X	X	X
Pennsylvania (5)	X	X	X	X				X		
Rhode Island (3)	X	X						X		
South Carolina (2)	X	X								
South Dakota (5)	X	X	X	X						X
Tennessee (4)	X	X	X	X						
Texas (2)	X	X								
Utah (6)	X	X	X	X				X		X
Vermont (9)	X	X	X	X	X	X		X	X	X
Virginia (2)	X	X								
Washington (8)	X	X	X	X	X			X	X	X
West Virginia (2)	X	X								
Wisconsin (9)	X	X	X	X	X	X		X	X	X
Wyoming (6)	X	X	X	X				X		X
Totals (251)	50	50	29	27	24	5	4	23	17	22

PA = public assistance, SS = social services, PH = public health, MH = mental health, MR = mental retardation, AC = adult corrections, YF = youth facilities, VR = vocational rehabilitation, ES = employment services, OA = older Americans.

Source: APWA, 1986: Chi, 1987.

designated state human service agency. Because this chapter is based on an analysis of the 50 designated state human service agencies in both 1997 and 1986, a decision was made to identify as the designated state human service agency in these three states in 1997, the same agency that provided both the functions of public assistance and social services in 1986. While this approach is somewhat arbitrary and has its drawbacks, the alternative course of action would be to exclude New Mexico, Utah, and Wisconsin from the analysis, an even less satisfactory solution.

Table 6 presents the data on total number of human service functions that the 50 designated state human service agencies had responsibility for a decade earlier, in 1986. The mean average number of functions a single designated state human service agency had responsibility for in 1986 was 5.0, with the range being between two and ten. The designated state human service agencies in 13 states (Alabama, Illinois, Indiana, Maryland, Mississippi, Nebraska, New Mexico, New York, Ohio, South Carolina, Texas, Virginia, West Virginia) were responsible for only two functions: public assistance and social services. At the other end of the range, the designated state human service agency in Oregon had responsibility for all 10 functions, while in Vermont the number was nine, excluding only employment services.

In 1986, the 50 designated state human service agencies had responsibility, in order of frequency, for public assistance (50), social services (50), mental retardation (29), mental health (27), youth facilities (23), vocational rehabilitation (24), and services to older Americans (22). Two particularly interesting features of Table 6 are the findings that five designated state human service agencies (Hawaii, Massachusetts, Oregon, Vermont, Wisconsin) were responsible for adult corrections in 1986, while four designated state human service agencies (Arizona, California, Connecticut, Oregon) were responsible for employment services.

When Tables 6 and 7 are compared, some interesting findings emerge in terms of both stability and changes in the functional mixes of the 50 state human service agencies between 1986 and 1997. Some 31 (62%) designated state human service agencies changed their functional mixes between 1986 and 1997. However, the total number of functions performed by all 50 designated state human service agencies declined only slightly, from 251 in 1986 to 236 in 1997, a decline of less than 1%. Some functions (public assistance, social services, mental health, mental retardation) demonstrate remarkable stability between 1986 and 1997. From a policy perspective, it appears that the functions of mental health and mental retardation (like the functions of public assistance and social services) tend to be the responsibility of the same state agency.

In terms of overall changes in the functional mixes of the 50 designated state human service agencies between 1986 and 1997, decreases are observed in four functions: Adult corrections declined from five to one (-80%); youth authorities declined from 23 to 15 (-35%), vocational rehabilitation declined from 24 to 19 (-22%), and employment services declined from four to three (-25%).

Table 7 State-Supervised/County-Administered Welfare Systems 1997

Alabama	State supervision and county administration by 67 county departments of human resources
California	State supervision and county administration by 58 county departments of social services
Colorado	State supervision and county administration by 63 county departments of social services
Georgia	State supervision and county administration by 159 county departments of family and children services
Minnesota	State supervision and county administration by 86 county social services and human services agencies
New York	State supervision and administration by 57 county departments of social services and the City of New York
North Carolina	State supervision and county administration by 100 county departments of social services
Ohio	State supervision and partial county administration by 88 county departments of human services
South Carolina	State supervision and county administration by 46 county departments of social services
Virginia	State supervision and administration by 34 independent cites (city/county consolidations) and some 102 county social service agencies
Wisconsin	State supervision and county administration by 72 county social/human services offices

Sources: APWA, 1997; ICMA, 1993.

Only the function of services to older Americans demonstrated an increase during the period, rising from 22 to 27 (+23%). From a policy perspective, it would appear that the majority of states have decided that the functions of corrections and employment services (and to a lesser extent youth facilities) should no longer be the responsibility of their designated state human service agencies. Only the designated state human service agency in Vermont continued to be responsible for adult corrections in 1997. And only four designated state human service agencies (Arizona, California, Connecticut, Oregon) continued to be responsible for employment services in 1997.

IV. STRUCTURE OF DESIGNATED STATE HUMAN SERVICE AGENCIES

In terms of structure, the 50 designated state human service agencies are generally classified in two ways: (1) by type of state welfare system (state-administered, state-supervised/county-administered, or mixed), and (2) by type of organizational structure (comprehensive or noncomprehensive).

A. Type of Welfare System

Counties in the United States have historically played a major role in the administration and management of the human services. The origins of American county government can be traced back some 1000 years to the days of the old English shire. English shires were responsible for poor relief, the functional equivalent of today's public assistance. Following tradition, when the original 13 Colonies were settled, poor relief or public assistance was generally made a county responsibility. Only with the beginning of the "Progressive Era" (1900s–1920s) did states truly begin to play major roles in the administration and management of the human services (Martin, 1993; Martin and Nyhan, 1994).

The legacy of the English shire is such that in many states today, county governments continue to play important roles in the administration and management of the human services, particularly in states with state-supervised/county-administered welfare systems. In terms of the actual administration and management of the human services, states operate as: (1) state-supervised/county-administered welfare systems, (2) state-administered welfare systems, or (3) mixed systems.

1. State-Supervised/County-Administered Welfare Systems

Eleven states (See Table 7) can be classified as state-supervised/county-administered welfare systems. In these 11 states, the designated state human service agencies establish overall policy direction and provide managerial supervision and oversight, but the actual day-to-day administration of the human services is carried out by county governments. The states of California, New York, and Virginia are examples of supervised/county administered welfare systems. In California, the California Health and Welfare Agency supervises 58 county departments of social services that are charged with the day-to-day administration of human services in the state. In New York, the New York Department of Family Assistance oversees the work of 57 county departments of social services and the City of New York. And in Virginia, the Department of Social Services monitors the activities of 102 counties and 34 independent cities. In Virginia, when independent cities are formed they essentially secede from their county government. Consequently, Virginia's independent cities provide basic county services in addition to traditional municipal services.

Five of the 11 states (46%) with state-supervised/county-administered welfare systems (Alabama, Georgia, North Carolina, South Carolina, Virginia) are located in the South of the United States. The other six state-supervised/county-administered welfare systems are scattered randomly across the county. The high concentration of state-supervised/county-administered welfare systems in the South is most likely attributable to the influences of both history and political culture (Elazar, 1972; Martin, 1993; Salant and Martin, 1993). Historically, counties were generally the first local governments to be organized in the South and, in keeping with the tradition of the English shire, were assigned the primary responsibility for poor relief or public assistance (Martin, 1993). Political culture probably explains why the South continues to possess such a disproportionate share of all state-supervised/county-administered welfare systems. Political culture can be thought of as the particular orientation to political action that is embedded in a state's political system (Elazar, 1972). The political culture of the South is said to be "traditional" in nature and characterized by a desire to maintain historical patterns of political behavior (Elazar, 1972:9).

2. State-Administered Welfare Systems

Thirty-six states (see Table 8) can be classified as state-administered welfare systems. In these states, the designated state human service agencies have direct administrative responsibility for human services which they usually provide through a series of regional, district, or local offices. The states of Arizona, Nebraska, and Florida are examples of state-administered welfare systems. In Arizona, the Department of Economic Security provides human services through six district offices. In Florida, the Department of Children and Families provides human services through 15 regional offices. And in Kansas, the Department of Health and Rehabilitative Services provides human services through 12 area offices.

Even in states with state-administered welfare systems, counties (in the geographical sense) continue to be important in the provision of human services. In at least eight states (Arkansas, Indiana, Iowa, Maryland, Michigan, Missouri, New York, Tennessee), the county is still a basic service unit. In these states, the designated state human service agencies have direct responsibility for the administration of human services, but they chose to provide them through a series of substate offices that are generally coterminous with county boundaries.

3. Mixed Welfare Systems

Three states (Montana, New Jersey, North Dakota) can be classified as mixed welfare systems. In these three states, the function of public assistance is administered differently than the other human service functions. In Montana, New Jersey, and North Dakota, public assistance is directly administered by counties under the supervision of the designated human service agency. All other human services in Montana, New Jersey, and North Dakota are the direct administrative responsibility of the designated state human service agencies. No obvious rationale exists

Table 8 State-Administered Welfare Systems 1997

Alaska	State administered through 35 field offices
Arizona	State administered through six district offices
Arkansas	State administered through 80 county offices
Connecticut	State administered through 16 regional offices
Delaware	State administered through three regional offices
Florida	State administered through 15 district offices
Hawaii	State administered through four branch offices
Idaho	State administered through seven regional offices
Illinois	State administered through 131 local offices
Indiana	State administered through 92 county offices
Iowa	State administered through 99 county offices
Kansas	State administered through 12 area offices
Kentucky	State administered through 16 district offices
Louisiana	State administered through 10 regional offices
Maine	State administered through 16 regional offices
Maryland	State administered through 24 local departments
Massachusetts	State administered through 26 area offices
Michigan	State administered through 83 county offices
Mississippi	State administered through some 90 county and branch offices
Missouri	State administered through 114 county offices and the City of St. Louis
Nebraska	State administered through eight district offices
Nevada	State administered through 18 field offices
New Hampshire	State administered through 12 district offices
New Mexico	State administered through 33 county offices
Oklahoma	State administered through some 77 county offices
Oregon	State administered through a variety of district and regional offices
Pennsylvania	State administered through 67 county offices
Rhode Island	State administered through 19 district offices
South Dakota	State administered through four district offices
Tennessee	State administered through 95 county offices
Texas	State administered through 254 county offices
Utah	State administered through four regional offices
Vermont	State administered through 12 district offices
Washington	State administered through six regional offices
West Virginia	State administered through 37 local offices
Wyoming	State administered through 23 field offices

Source: APWA, 1997.

to explain the mixed welfare systems of Montana, New Jersey, and North Dakota other than history.

B. Comprehensive and Noncomprehensive Agencies

Another way of thinking about the administration and management of the 50 state human service agencies is the extent to which states have attempted to use organizational structure as a form of services integration. Services integration can be broadly defined as any systematic attempt to resolve the problems of service fragmentation and the lack of fit between the needs of individuals and the categorical nature of many human service programs (Kahn and Kamerman, 1992). One approach to services integration by organizational structure is to place as many human service functions as possible into one "comprehensive" state human service agency, sometimes referred to as an "umbrella" agency.

During the 1970s, several states experimented with services integration by organizational restructuring either for their own reasons or as the result of encouragement by the federal government that funded many of the experiments (Ezel and Patti, 1990; Frumkin et al., 1987). Recent actions by the federal government (e.g., welfare reform, block grants, and increased decentralization of decision making to the states) have fueled speculation that states might again begin experimenting with services integration by organizational structure (Yessian, 1995; *Governing*, 1997).

Referring again to the Council of State Governments' study (Chi. 1987), the 50 designated state human service agencies can be classified as being either comprehensive (umbrella) or noncomprehensive (See Table 9), depending on the number of human service functions they provide. To be classified as a comprehensive, or umbrella, agency using the Council of State Governments' criteria, an individual designated state human service agency must provide the functions of public assistance and social services and at least three other functions. Table 9 shows the 50 designated state human service agencies and their classifications (comprehensive or noncomprehensive) in 1986 and again in 1997. Because the 1986 Council of State Governments' study did not include services to older Americans as a function, it is not included in the count of the minimum number of functions required to classify a state human service agency as comprehensive in either 1986 or 1997.

In terms of the overall picture, Table 9 demonstrates that a 50/50 split exists between comprehensive and noncomprehensive designated state human service agencies. In 1986, 26 of the 50 designated state human service agencies (52%) could be classified as comprehensive, or umbrella, agencies. In 1997 just the reverse was true; 26 of the 50 designated state human service agencies (52%) could be classified as noncomprehensive. The status of 14 designated state human service agencies changed from noncomprehensive to comprehensive or vice versa

Table 9 Comprehensive and Noncomprehensive Designated State Human
Service Agencies 1986 and 1997

	1986	1997
Alabama	Non-Comprehensive	Non-Comprehensive
Alaska	Comprehensive	Comprehensive
Arizona	Comprehensive	Comprehensive
Arkansas	Comprehensive	Comprehensive
California	Comprehensive	Comprehensive
Colorado[a]	*Non-Comprehensive*	*Comprehensive*
Connecticut	Non-Comprehensive	Non-Comprehensive
Delaware	Comprehensive	Comprehensive
Florida[a]	*Comprehensive*	*Non-Comprehensive*
Georgia	Comprehensive	Comprehensive
Hawaii[a]	*Comprehensive*	*Non-Comprehensive*
Idaho	Comprehensive	Comprehensive
Illinois[a]	*Non-Comprehensive*	*Comprehensive*
Indiana[a]	*Non-Comprehensive*	*Comprehensive*
Iowa	Comprehensive	Comprehensive
Kansas	Comprehensive	Comprehensive
Kentucky[a]	*Comprehensive*	*Non-Comprehensive*
Louisiana[a]	*Comprehensive*	*Non-Comprehensive*
Maine	Non-Comprehensive	Non-Comprehensive
Maryland	Non-Comprehensive	Non-Comprehensive
Massachusetts	Comprehensive	Comprehensive
Michigan	Non-Comprehensive	Non-Comprehensive
Minnesota	Non-Comprehensive	Non-Comprehensive
Mississippi	Non-Comprehensive	Non-Comprehensive
Missouri	Non-Comprehensive	Non-Comprehensive
Montana[a]	*Non-Comprehensive*	*Comprehensive*
Nebraska[a]	*Non-Comprehensive*	*Comprehensive*
Nevada	Comprehensive	Comprehensive
New Hampshire	Comprehensive	Comprehensive
New Jersey	Non-Comprehensive	Non-Comprehensive
New Mexico	Non-Comprehensive	Non-Comprehensive
New York	Non-Comprehensive	Non-Comprehensive
North Carolina	Comprehensive	Comprehensive
North Dakota	Comprehensive	Comprehensive
Ohio	Non-Comprehensive	Non-Comprehensive
Oklahoma[a]	*Comprehensive*	*Non-Comprehensive*
Oregon	Comprehensive	Comprehensive
Pennsylvania	Comprehensive	Comprehensive
Rhode Island	Non-Comprehensive	Non-Comprehensive
South Carolina	Non-Comprehensive	Non-Comprehensive
South Dakota	Non-Comprehensive	Non-Comprehensive
Tennessee	Non-Comprehensive	Non-Comprehensive
Texas	Non-Comprehensive	Non-Comprehensive
Utah[a]	*Comprehensive*	*Non-Comprehensive*
Vermont	Comprehensive	Comprehensive
Virginia	Non-Comprehensive	Non-Comprehensive
Washington	Comprehensive	Comprehensive
West Virginia[a]	*Non-Comprehensive*	*Comprehensive*
Wisconsin[a]	*Comprehensive*	*Non-Comprehensive*
Wyoming[a]	*Comprehensive*	*Non-Comprehensive*

[a] Indicates state has switched from one system to the other.
Sources: APWA, 1986, 1996; Chi, 1987.

during the period 1986 to 1997. The status of the designated state human service agencies in six states (Colorado, Illinois, Indiana, Montana, Nebraska, West Virginia) changed from noncomprehensive to comprehensive. However, the status of the designated state human service agencies in eight states (Florida, Hawaii, Kentucky, Louisiana, Oklahoma, Utah, Wisconsin, Wyoming) changed in the opposite direction from comprehensive to noncomprehensive.

The reason for status changes from non-comprehensive to comprehensive during the period 1986 to 1997 does appear related to attempts by states to promote services integration by organizational structure. Status changes from comprehensive to noncomprehensive during the same period appear to be more reflective of regional differences that are themselves again most likely the result of history and political culture. When all 14 designated state human service agencies undergoing status changes are grouped into regions (using standard Census Bureau categories), some evidence of regional clustering begins to emerge. As Table 10 demonstrates, none of the designated state human service agencies in the Northeast region changed their status between 1986 and 1997. Four designated state human service agencies in the South did change their status, including three states (Florida, Kentucky, Louisiana) that changed from comprehensive to noncomprehensive. The remaining two regions (North Central and West) present a mixed picture.

Table 10 Designated State Human Service Agencies
Changing Status Between 1986 and 1997

	To comprehensive agency	To noncomprehensive agency
Northeast		
	(0)	(0)
North Central	Illinois	Oklahoma
	Indiana	Wisconsin
	Nebraska	(2)
	(3)	
South	West Virginia	Florida
	(1)	Kentucky
		Louisiana
		(3)
West	Colorado	Hawaii
	Montana	Utah
	(2)	Wyoming
		(3)

Source: APWA, 1997.

When all 50 designated state human service agencies in 1997 are grouped into Census Bureau regions (see Table 11), stronger evidence of regional clustering is apparent. As Table 11 illustrates, the designated state human service agencies in the Northeast and the North Central region are well balanced in terms of their status (comprehensive or noncomprehensive). The Northeast region had four comprehensive agencies in 1997 and five noncomprehensive agencies, while the North Central region had five comprehensive agencies and seven noncomprehensive agencies. The major differences in Table 11 are between the South and the West. In the South region, noncomprehensive agencies (11) outnumbered comprehensive agencies (5) in 1997 by a ratio of more than 2:1. In the West, the reverse situation existed with comprehensive agencies (9) outnumbering noncomprehensive agencies (4) by a ratio of more than 2:1. Again, the differences between the South and the West are probably due to a combination of historical forces and political culture.

V. SUMMARY AND CONCLUSION

From a policy perspective, some sorting out of human service functions appears to have occurred over the last decade. The functions of corrections, employment services, and to a lesser extent youth facilities have been removed by states from their designated state human service agencies and located elsewhere. While not a major trend, the fact that three states have placed the functions of public assistance and social services in different state agencies could be a harbinger of changes to come in the state administration and management of the human services.

A small but significant number of designated state human service agencies have changed their status from noncomprehensive to comprehensive organizations over the last decade, a phenomenon referred to as services integration by organizational structure. However, a larger number of designated state human service agencies have gone in the opposite direction, changing their status from comprehensive to noncomprehensive. Thus, it appears that there are both centralizing influences and decentralizing influences at work in terms of state administration and management of the human services. The centralizing influences are found primarily in the West of the United States, while the decentralizing influences are most prevalent in the South.

What is most clear from this analysis of the structure and functions of the 50 designated state human service agencies is that the search by states for the best way to administer and manage the human services is ongoing. Diversity continues to be the watchword in state administration and management of the human services and will probably continue to be so for the foreseeable future.

Table 11 Comprehensive and Noncomprehensive Designated
State Human Service Agencies by Region 1997

	Comprehensive state agency	Noncomprehensive state agency
Northeast	New Hampshire Vermont Pennsylvania Massachusetts (4)	Connecticut Maine New Jersey New York Rhode Island (5)
North Central	North Dakota Illinois Iowa Nebraska Kansas (5)	Minnesota South Dakota Wisconsin Michigan Ohio Indiana Missouri (7)
South	Virginia West Virginia North Carolina Georgia Arkansas (5)	Maryland Delaware Alabama South Carolina Kentucky Louisiana Mississippi Tennessee Florida Oklahoma Texas (11)
West	Alaska Arizona California Oregon Washington Nevada Montana Idaho Colorado (9)	Hawaii Wyoming Utah New Mexico (4)

Source: APWA, 1997.

REFERENCES

American Public Welfare Association (APWA). (1997). *1997/98 Public Welfare Directory*, APWA, Washington, DC.

American Public Welfare Association (APA). (1986). *1986/87 Public Welfare Directory*, APA, Washington, DC.

Chi, K. (1987). What has happened to the comprehensive human services agency? *New England Journal of Human Services 8*: 24–30.

Elazar, D. (1972). *American Federalism—A View From the States*, Thomas Y. Cromwell, New York.

Ezel, M., and Patti, R. (1990). State human service agencies: structure and organization, *Social Service Review* 64(March): 22–45.

Florida Department of Children and Families (Florida DCF). (1996). *Florida Department of Children and Families Target Budget*, Florida DCF, Tallahassee.

Frumkin, M., Martin, P., and Page, W. (1987). The future of large public human service organizations, *New England Journal of Human Services 8*: 15–23.

Governing. (1997). Management—devolution drives a mega merger, October. p. 78.

International City/County Management Association (ICMA). (1993). *The Municipal Year Book—1993*. ICMA, Washington, DC.

International City/County Management Association (ICMA). (1993). *The Municipal Year Book—1991*, ICMA, Washington, DC.

Kahn, A., and Kamerman, S. (1992). *Integrating Services Integration: An Overview of Initiatives, Issues, and Possibilities*, National Center for Children in Poverty, Washington, DC.

Martin, L. (1993). American county government: an historical perspective, *County Government in An Era of Change* (D. Berman, ed.), Greenwood Press, Westport, CT, pp. 1–13.

Martin, L., and Nyhan, R. (1994). Determinants of county charter home rule, *International Journal of Public Administration 17*: 955–970.

Mehr, J. (1995). *Human Services: Concepts And Intervention Strategies*, Prentice-Hall, Englewood Cliffs, NJ.

Salant, T., and Martin, L. (1993). County constitutional officers: a preliminary investigation, *State and Local Government Review 25*: 164–172.

Yessian, M. (1995). Learning from experience: integrating human services, *Public Welfare 53*: 34–42.

19
Administration of Welfare Reform in the States

Edward T. Jennings, Jr.
University of Kentucky, Lexington, Kentucky

Gary Locke came to office as Washington's new governor in January 1997 determined to transform the state's welfare system. Like many governors of the 1980s and 1990s, he believed the existing welfare system to be dysfunctional and saw political and policy opportunities for change. A new welfare law, adopted by the national government in 1996, eased his task. Congress adopted and the President signed the Personal Responsibility and Work Opportunity Reconciliation Act (PRWORA) in August 1996. The Personal Responsibility Act includes the Temporary Assistance to Needy Families (TANF) program, which imposes limits on the length of time that recipients can receive benefits, and requires most recipients to participate in work programs within two years of their entry on the rolls.

Most welfare programs in the United States are intergovernmental in nature. The national government sets basic policy and provides a major share of the funding. Because of this, state actions have been shaped and constrained by national policy since the 1930s, when President Roosevelt's New Deal included a public assistance program under the umbrella of the Social Security Act. That program evolved as Aid to Families with Dependent Children (AFDC), which became the focal point of concern about the welfare system in the 1980s and 1990s.

During the 1980s and early 1990s, many states, led by their governors, began to experiment with welfare reforms through waivers to federal law approved by the U.S. Department of Health and Social Services under Presidents Reagan, Bush, and Clinton (Gueron and Pauley, 1991; Greenberg and Wiseman, 1992). These experiments, typically called welfare-to-work programs, focused on efforts to reduce welfare dependency by moving welfare recipients to self-sufficiency through compensated work. They often relied on a human capital strategy that provided education to prepare clients for work and support, like child care, to make it possible for single mothers to work. Both early and later experiments fueled further demands for reform and provided models for transforming the welfare system. In fact, scholars maintained that the experiments of the 1980s provided an information base consistent with the Family Support Act (Wiseman, 1991; Baum, 1991; Haskins, 1991; Szanton, 1991). A report issued by one group of analysts a year before Congressional action makes clear that the Personal Responsibility Act did not enjoy the same base of research support (Weaver and Dickens, 1995), although Mead's (1997) findings based on administrative data suggest that it is on the right track.

When Congress adopted the Personal Responsibility act in 1996, it replaced AFDC with the Temprary Assistance for Needy Families program. The major features of this program will be discussed in detail later in this chapter. For now, we need only note that it represents a dramatic departure from the past. It sets stiff requirements for states to meet, including high levels of mandatory welfare client participation in work activites. The law gives the states the opportunity ot continue waiver experiment programs that they had put in place prior to the adoption of the legislation. That gives some states the opportunity to continue programs that diverge from requirements of the Personal Responsibility Act.

In fact, five days before Governor Locke took office, his predecessor submitted a proposal to the state legislature that would have continued Washington's program as it operated under the waiver. That program was less stringent in its work requirements and was built around an education and service strategy. The program was designed by policy makers who believed that many welfare recipients needed education, training, and supportive services if they were to succeed in leaving the rolls. Governor Locke believed that this approach would not succeed in moving welfare recipients to self-sufficiency, and certainly not quickly enough. Like many observers of the welfare system, he believed that the service approach was making welfare more attractive and leading individuals to apply for benefits, thus increasing the welfare rolls (Mead, 1997).

The governor proposed WorkFirst, a program that stresses immediate engagement in job search activites for public assistance applicants. The program requires virtually all recipients of public assistance to seek work at any wage and to participate in work preparation activities or community service work if they do not find a job. The legislature adopted WorkFirst, and the Washington Department of Social and Health Services began to implement it in August 1997.

The waves of welfare reform that gathered energy and momentum in the United States in the 1980s and culminated in a major transformation of the welfare system in the 1990s placed considerable demands on welfare administrators to manage systemic change. Policy initiatives created the need for changes in service delivery systems, organizational behavior, management processes, and accountability standards. Policy makers sought nothing less than wholesale change in the culture of the welfare system. Public administrators have played critical roles in this process of change and will continue to do so as the evolution of welfare continues.

Public policies are seldom self-executing (Bardach, 1977; Goggin et al., 1990; Elmore, 1982). Attainment of their goals depends on successful implementation. As studies of welfare reform have demonstrated, effective management is essential to successful implementation. Behn (1991), Nathan (1993), Mead (1996), Meyers and colleagues (1998), and others have called attention to the need for managers who can marshal resources, evoke a vision of change, guide administrative systems, and provide leadership in the transformation of systems. In the welfare arena, Jennings and Krane (1994, 1998) have demonstrated the importance of interorganizational networks and the need to coordinate activities for program success.

This chapter portrays the array of programs that constitute the welfare system, reviews the nature of the reforms that have transformed welfare over the past 18 years, describes the policy options that have been put in place, assesses state responses to the challenge of reform, and analyzes the management challenges routinely faced by public administrators as they implement change. The analysis will illustrate that the goals and designs of policy shape the management challenges. At the same time, it will demonstrate that effective administration is a key to the success of welfare reform.

Case studies of two states' welfare reform efforts will be used to illustrate the pace of change and variations in the management challenges of welfare reform. These cases are the early effort of Massachusetts, with its ET Choices program in the 1980s, and the recent moves by Washington to respond to the Personal Responsibility Act with its WorkFirst program. The case study of ET Choices draws on Behn's (1991) fine portrayal and analysis in *Leadership Counts* and a series of interviews with officials and managers carried out in 1991. The Washington case study is based on interviews of managers and documentary information, as well as an account by Lahr-Vivaz (1997). I also draw on a brief survey of state welfare directors that identifies their perceptions of the management challenges of reform.

I. TRANSFORMATION OF WELFARE POLICY

Debates over the role, place, and nature of welfare policy animated public policy conflict from the 1960s through the 1990s (Mead, 1992; Nathan, 1993; Norris and Thompson, 1995). Contenders in this debate framed it largely in terms of core American values—equity, rights, meeting basic human needs, work, and family. The debate was highly charged, characterized by compelling rhetoric and symbols on both sides of the issue. While the conflict over welfare has divided political activists, largely along traditional liberal/conservative lines, those lines blurred over time. Conservative Republicans have championed the safety net, and many moderate and liberal Democrats have become advocates of work requirements. In a policy-making world characterized by think tanks, university research centers, and scholarship, much of decision making was informed by extensive studies of poverty and welfare (Gueron and Pauly, 1991; Baum, 1991; Haskins, 1991; Wiseman, 1991).

In the 1960s, the debate largely centered on the question of how to more adequately meet the needs of the poor. Benefit levels varied dramatically among the states, as did eligibility criteria. Many of the poor were not eligible for any support, and those who were eligible for benefits often found it difficult to get on the rolls (Piven and Cloward, 1971). This led to (1) efforts to increase benefit levels; (2) the initiation of new programs, like food stamps to meet nutrition needs and legal aid programs to help the poor assert their rights; (3) the creation of community action agencies that mobilized and represented the poor in their dealings with public agencies; and (4) the nationalization of some elements of welfare policy, such as programs of aid to the elderly, blind, and disabled (Haveman, 1977).

Even during that period of welfare expansion, however, there were concerns about the effects of welfare on work and family structure. In those early years of reform, these concerns were addressed by the introduction of modest incentives to work and weak initiatives to require welfare recipients to take part in job search and job training activites. Because taking a job at a low wage often left a family little better off than it was on welfare, policy makers considered the introduction of negative income taxes that would gradually reduce welfare benefits as earnings from work increased. This focus on an income strategy dominated reform discussions in the 1970s (Moynihan, 1973; Mead, 1992).

Growth in the welfare roles combined with social and economic change to produce increasing levels of concern about the welfare system. Many social commentators and conservative political activists perceived that welfare fostered dependency and undermined the family (Mead, 1992; Murray, 1984). These beliefs paralleled changes in the work force and the family in America. We can understand this by taking a look at some basic trends.

First, welfare rolls, which had grown gradually in the 1950s and early 1960s, exploded in the late 1960s and early 1970s. This was a result of federal policy changes, relaxed eligibility rules, court decisions, social turmoil, mobilization of the poor, and the initiation of new programs to help the poor. The rolls stabilized following that period of expansion, but it set the stage for demands for reform. A later spurt of growth in response to the recession of the early 1990s and the liberalization of program services greatly expanded the welfare population and led to renewed demands for change. The growth and contraction of welfare rolls is depicted in Figure 1, which portrays the annual number of families receiving AFDC.

At the same time that the welfare rolls were expanding, women were entering the work force in growing numbers. This feminization of the work force had profound implications for American attitudes towards the family and the role of women in society. As more and more mothers entered the workforce, a variety of child-rearing arrangements began to emerge. While there is continuing controversy about working mothers and child rearing, most Americans accepted it as a reality. This social change weakened the claim of welfare mothers that they needed to stay home with their children. Many scholars and activists believe that it made the existing welfare system untenable.

The increasing role of women in the workforce is depicted in Figure 2. As can be seen, labor force participation of women increased from 34% in 1950 to almost 60% in 1997. During that same time span, the labor force participation of men declined from almost 87% to 75%.

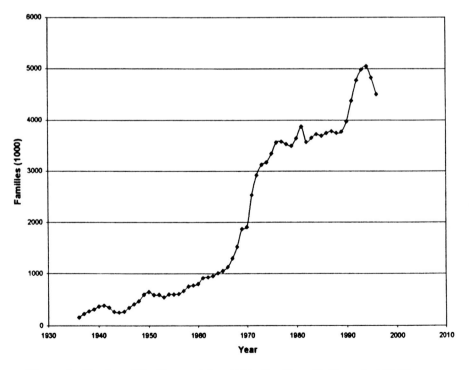

Figure 1   Number of families receiving Aid to Families with Dependent Children.

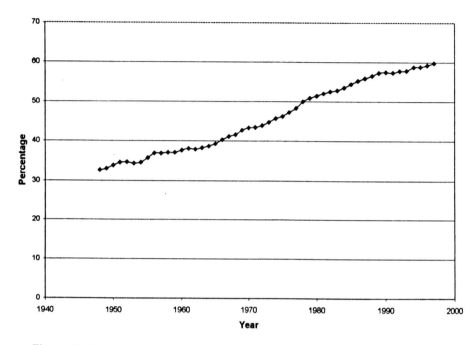

Figure 2 Labor force participation rate of working-age women.

When Congress created the AFDC program in the 1930s, it did so with the understanding that it was providing help largely for widows. Indeed, in the early years of the program, the mothers who sought benefits for their children and themselves were typically widowed or divorced. In 1940, 40% of mothers in the program were widows. By the mid-1970s, this figure was down to 2.5%. Additionally, in the 1970s and 1980s observers began to note an increasing number of children born to out-of-wedlock mothers. This was true in the population at large, but it carried over to the welfare system, where unwed mothers came to represent a large portion of the recipients. Critics of the welfare system argued that the system encouraged young, unmarried women to have children by providing a guarantee of financial support. Others argued that the design of the welfare system encouraged fathers to abandon their families.

In fact, as Figure 3 demonstrates, there has been a substantial increase in the proportion of children born to unwed mothers over the last five decades. In 1940, about 5% of births were to unwed mothers. By 1994, this was up to almost one-third of all births. Clearly not all of this can be attributed to the welfare system, since many unwed mothers are not on welfare and never go on welfare. Since this phenomenon was happening in society as a whole, it is difficult to say

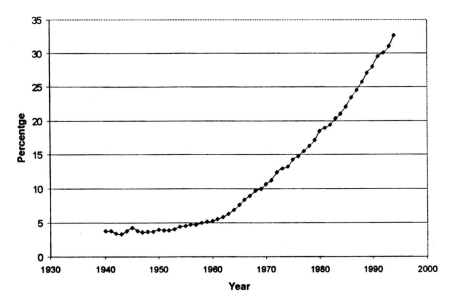

Figure 3   Unmarried mothers' percentage of all births.

how much, if any, is attributable to welfare. There are mixed findings on the subject, as is reflected in recent reviews and assessments by Moffitt (1997) and Hoynes (1997).

II.   STATE RESPONSES TO REFORM PRESSURES AND OPPORTUNITIES

The evolution of demands for reform and the federal response to those demands created numerous pressures and opportunities for states to modify their welfare programs. Although some states, like Michigan, responded to those pressures by changing their programs of general assistance, most of the action has centered on AFDC and TANF. Consequently, our examination of state administration of welfare reform will focus on the transformation of AFDC into TANF and the implementation of the reforms involved in that transformation. The analysis will describe the patterns of change, portray the policy choices made by the states, and examine central issues in the administration of reform. To do this, it is helpful to think about four stages of welfare.

A. AFDC in the 1970s

The first is the AFDC program largely as it existed in the 1970s. The second stage is the experimentation that began in the early 1980s. During this period, change was limited to a few states and the extent of change within any one state was limited. Nonetheless, it was a precursor of things to come. The third stage ran from 1988 to 1996, when the Family Support Act was implemented and widespread experimentation continued. These changes made major, but limited, demands on states. The fourth stage is the period since 1996, during which states have been implementing TANF and the Personal Responsibility Act. The implementation of TANF has called for fundamental policy and administrative changes by the states.

The 1970s provided little pressure for change compared to the most recent period. The most significant federal legislative initiative was Supplemental Security Income (SSI), but this was a nationalization of a set of welfare programs that posed no special administrative challenges for the states. The Nixon Administration authorized and carried out significant experiments with negative income tax or guaranteed income as a way to ensure that basic needs of the poor are met, while providing an incentive for work (Pechman and Timpane, 1975). Proposals of the Nixon and Carter Administrations made little headway in Congress (Moynihan, 1973; Lynn and Whitman, 1981; Califano, 1981).

B. 1981–1988: Early State Experiments with Welfare-to-Work Programs

The growing belief that the welfare system fostered dependency, undermined American values of work and family, left poor families incapable of supporting themselves, and placed a significant drain on the public budget led to three significant stages of reform from 1981 to the present (Cammisa, 1998; Nathan, 1993; Mead, 1992, 1996; Wiseman, 1996). The first stage began with President Reagan and carried through the Reagan and Bush administrations. It included a tightening of the rules that led to the removal of some working poor from the rolls as a result of the Omnibus Budget Reconciliation Act of 1981. More significantly, the Reagan Administration provided an opportunity for states to initiate so-called welfare-to-work experiments by obtaining waivers to rules that regulated the AFDC program.

States like California and Massachusetts led the way with reform initiatives carried out under waivers to federal AFDC rules and regulations made possible by the Omnibus Budget Reconciliation Act of 1981. California initiated Greater Avenues to Independence (GAIN), while Massachusetts implemented ET (Employment and Training) choices. Both of these programs, like initiatives to follow in other states, sought to promote self-sufficiency among welfare recipients. They were, in the phrase that came to dominate the reform movement, welfare-to-work programs.

Despite that similarity, those initial efforts at welfare-to-work programs varied in their plicies, design, and execution. GAIN was mandatory for covered California participants, but never reached a substantial portion of the welfare population. ET in Massachusetts was completely voluntary, based on the belief that welfare recipients would take advantage of services and opportunities if they were offered. Like other experiments of the 1980s, these two programs offered an array of services, including job preparation, job search, basic education, skills training, and advanced education, that were intended to help people obtain and keep jobs. The experiments typically included support services, such as childcare, to remove barriers to work.

GAIN and ET Choices typified the two models that states would experiment with in the 1980s and early 1990s—human capital and work first. California's program was mandatory and explicitly experimental in design. The program in Massachusetts was voluntary and did not include an experimental design. California's program was more consistent with the conservative belief that welfare recipients will avoid work unless it is required, whereas the Massachusetts program conformed to liberal expectations that welfare recipients were eager to work if given the opportunity (Mead, 1992).

C. 1988–1996: Increased Work Requirements Through JOBS

That first stage of reform provided a platform for the emergence of the second stage, which began with the Family Support Act of 1988. The Family Support Act represented a significant departure from the existing AFDC program. It incorporated the Job Opportunities and Basic Skills (JOBS) program, which required the states to involve an increasing percentage of their adult recipients in welfare-to-work activities. Although earlier initiatives, like the Work Incentive (WIN) program, had tried to encourage work, they were largely ineffective. The new JOBS program mandated that states develop systematic programs to encourage self-sufficiency. The legislation built on the welfare experiments of the 1980s.

Although many referred to the experiments of states like California and the activities developed through JOBS as "workfare," the states actually required very few recipients to work for their benefits. While some state programs under JOBS emphasized job preparation and job search activities, most took a human capital approach. Under the human capital approach, welfare agencies sought to increase the knowledge and skills of welfare recipients to prepare them for success in the labor market. This included an emphasis on basic education, high school equivalency examinations, vocational and technical education, and even higher education. The philosophy underlying this approach was that welfare recipients were ill-prepared to support themselves. Without improved knowledge and skills, they would not be able to obtain jobs that would support their families and allow them to do without welfare benefits.

Despite the substantial shift brought about by the Family Support Act, the ferment for reform continued. Policy makers and political activists pressed for more substantial change. States were leaders in this movement for change (Nathan, 1993; Wiseman, 1996; Norris and Thompson, 1995). Governors such as Tommy Thompson of Wisconsin, John Engler of Michigan, and then-Governor Bill Clinton of Arkansas instituted an array of reform efforts in their own states. More than 40 states initiated reform experiments through waivers of AFDC rules and regulations so they could experiment with new approaches (Ewalt, 1996). Catchy labels captured some of the central elements of these experiments. Family caps, for example, prohibited parents from receiving increased benefits for children conceived and born after they entered the welfare rolls. "Learnfare" required teenage welfare mothers and the children of welfare recipients to attend school or the benefits of the family would be reduced or eliminated. Workfare required recipients to work for their benefits or participate in job-seeking activities.

This reform experimentation at the state level was not enough to satisfy the critics of welfare. Governors like Mike Leavitt of Utah led the National Governors Association to advocate more dramatic changes in Congress that would provide a substantial devolution of authority to alter the welfare system. The fervor for reform was epitomized by Presidential candidate Bill Clinton's pledge to "end welfare as we know it." While President Clinton put that pledge on the back burner to pursue his agenda for health care reform, he did appoint a task force to develop proposals. Those proposals would have moved the welfare system in the direction of more extensive work requirements and would have put in place lifetime limits on benefits. The Republican Party's "Contract with America" in the 1994 Congressional campaigns promised even sharper breaks with the past (Cammisa, 1998).

Not everyone believed that the system required changes like these. Many critics argued that systematic data contradicted many claims of the proponents of reform. The Center on Hunger, Poverty, and Nutrition Policy (1995) issued a statement citing dozens of academic studies to support its claims that the reformers were wrong on central issues of the debate. Their evidence suggested that welfare is not the cause of the growth of single-parent families in the United States, that welfare has little if any effect on out-of-wedlock births among AFDC recipients, and that single-parent families are not the cause of the growth of poverty. A group of scholars sponsored by the Brookings Institution also urged caution (Weaver and Dickens, 1995). Despite Weaver's (1995) cautionary assessment of the political possibilities for dramatic change, the forces of reform held the upper hand. Resistance proved to be futile, in the end.

D. 1996: The Personal Responsibility Act

Political ferment and policy experimentation led to the Personal Responsibility Act, which dramatically changed American welfare policy. That act, with its Temporary Assistance for Needy Families provisions, sets a five-year lifetime limit on the length of time recipients can receive welfare benefits. It requires that all recipients be placed in a work program within two years of beginning to receive benefits and mandates that teen parents live in a household headed by an adult or in a group care setting. It also allows states to impose family caps, permits states to treat migrants from other states differently, and converts federal welfare assistance from an entitlement to a block grant. These changes represented much more than incremental adaptations of welfare policy. As we will see, states have moved aggressively to implement TANF.

III. DIMENSIONS OF POLICY

The design of welfare reform strategies turns on a series of issues. These issues include voluntary versus mandatory participation, immediate employment versus human capital investment, short-term versus long-term perspective, sanctions versus incentives, and the definition of sucess.

A. Voluntary Versus Mandatory

In the design of welfare reform, a major issue has been whether participation in welfare-to-work programs should be voluntary or required. Proponents of voluntary participation generally believe that welfare recipients want to work and will take advantage of opportunities if they are offered. They believe that voluntary programs are more likely to succeed because they attract clients who want to succeed.

Proponents of mandatory participation have a very different perspective. They believe that the welfare rolls contain a large number of individuals who would rather not work. As long as they can have their basic needs met through public generosity, they will avoid work. If this perspective is correct, then mandatory welfare-to-work activities are critical to the effort to treat clients equitably and ensure that everyone pursues the opportunity to be self-sufficient.

B. Immediate Employment Versus Human Capital Investment

A second major design issue revolves around the question of whether agencies should encourage or require clients to first seek work or to enhance their work readiness, education, and skills before sending them into the workplace. Some proponents of the work-first perspective believe that clients need to assume some immediate responsibility for their own well-being, and that the way to do this is by obtaining a job. Others believe that many welfare recipients have not succeeded in educational activities in the past and are better served by programs that get them into a job so they can enjoy success. They also believe that human capital programs that encourage work only after clients receive education, training, and other services provide an inducement for more people to pursue welfare benefits and provide an incentive for recipients to remain on welfare rather than going to work.

Proponents of human capital strategies believe that many welfare recipients are ill-prepared to go to work. They lack the literacy, work habits, education, job skills, and training to succeed in most jobs. Even if they can get a job, the jobs they are qualified to hold provide little prospect for self-sufficiency. Since minimum-wage jobs offer little opportunity to lift recipients out of poverty, welfare-to-work programs should focus on raising education and skills to levels that will allow clients to obtain jobs that can support them at wages above poverty levels.

C. Short-Term Versus Long-Term Perspective

Proponents of a short-term perspective believe that progress and achievement have to come quickly. Clients need to enjoy success in the short run in order to see the possibilities of long-term improvement. Indeed, it is possible for clients to obtain jobs and succeed in the short run, according to this perspective. Further, proponents of this viewpoint tend to believe that welfare clients are present-oriented, so efforts to get them to look to the future are not likely to succeed.

Advocates of a long-term view believe that success in reducing welfare rolls cannot be achieved in the short run. They see the opportunities for recipients as being limited or the recipients themselves as being poorly prepared for success. From this perspective, complex programs to address multiple barriers to success need to be developed and implemented. This alone requires a long-term perspective. Furthermore, jobs are few and have to be developed and matched with clients.

D. Participation Requirements and Limits on Benefits

Proponents of stringent reform measures believe that states must be required to meet high levels of participation in welfare-to-work activities and that there should be limits on the length of time that recipients can receive welfare benefits. Otherwise, according to this perspective, participants will not actively engage themselves in the process of finding and retaining jobs. Advocates of the poor maintain that high participation rates and time limits on benefits will create undue hardship for welfare recipients, particularly children.

E. Sanctions Versus Incentives

Contending positions on sanctions and incentives animate much of the welfare reform struggle. On the one hand are those who believe that welfare recipients typically do not want to work and avoid assuming responsibility for their own well-being. The only way to change this is to invoke sanctions. Sanctions send a clear message that dependency is no longer acceptable. Sufficiently strong sanctions make it impossible for clients to rely on welfare to meet their basic needs for food, clothing, and shelter.

On the other hand are those who believe that welfare clients would like to work and take care of their own needs, but are financially punished by the welfare system when they try to do so. From this perspective, the design of the welfare system has undermined efforts to promote self-sufficiency by ensuring that people were financially better off if they received benefits than if they worked. The key to promoting work and self-sufficiency is to make sure that people are better off when they go to work by gradually reducing benefits and continuing to provide supportive services.

F. Definition of Success

There are many criteria by which actors judge the success of reform. For some, the critical measure of success is reduction in the rolls. As long as policy and program changes can reduce the number of welfare recipients, it is a success. For others, the central criterion of success is whether it promotes self-sufficiency, leaving families better off than they were under traditional welfare. For still others, the criteria might be more extensive participation in employment, a reduction in the welfare budget, improved child well-being, or any of a dozen other objectives. The goals of reform determine the definition of success, and that definition, in turn, has significant implications for program policy, design, and implementation.

IV. JOBS AND TANF DIFFERENCES

JOBS and TANF differed in their treatment of these issues, as is reflected in Table 1. JOBS was oriented toward a human capital investment strategy, set modest participation targets, and placed no time limits on benefits. It was silent on the topics of teen pregnancy and births to welfare mothers. It was an entitlement that offered unlimited support for state determined benefits. States could

Table 1 Key Features of JOBS and TANF

	JOBS	TANF
Emphasis	Human capital development	Immediate labor force participation
Participation requirement	25%	50% for one-parent families 90% for two-parent families
Time limits	None	5 years
Teen mothers	No provisions	Mandatory education; live in home headed by adult or in group care setting
Family caps	None	Allowed
Work requirement	Weak	Mandatory within 2 years of entry

emphasize a work-first approach if they chose, but few did so. They could require higher levels of participation, but most did not. They could request waivers to impose time limits, but mostly they did not. Indeed, states typically followed a human capital investment approach that exempted many mothers from mandatory participation. Some did the minimum that was required under JOBS regulations.

The Personal Responsibility Act structures TANF quite differently. It imposes a time limit on benefits to any recipients. It requires that recipients be enrolled in work activities within 24 months after coming on the rolls. It sets high participation requirements. It transforms welfare from an entitlement to a block grant. There are limits on how much money states will receive. Within this framework of restrictions, it sets states free to pursue their own course of action. They design the strategies to move clients into the work force. They decide if family caps will apply. They can provide lower benefits to migrants from other states for their first year of residency. They can exempt a portion of the caseload from program requirements. The specific provisions are as follows.

> Recipients may not receive benefits for more than five years total.
> Unmarried teen parents must participate in educational activities.
> Unmarried teen parents must live with an adult or in a group home setting.
> Adults in families receiving assistance must participate in work activities after receiving assistance for 24 months.
> States must achieve a 90% participation rate for two-parent families by FY 1999. They must achieve a 35% participation rate for all families by FY 1999 and a 50% rate by FY 2000.
> For two-parent families, the minimum hours worked each week is 35. For single-parent families, the requirement is 20 hours in FY 1997–1998, 25 hours in FY 1999, and 30 hours in FY 2000.

The Personal Responsibility Act comes down squarely on the high participation/short time limits side of this debate. While the Personal Responsibility Act sets participation mandates and time limits on benefits, states had to make decisions on their own with respect to these matters. Would they set more stringent participation requirements than those mandated by law? Would they place stricter time limits on benefits? Would they take advantage of exceptions permitted under federal law? These issues have a critical bearing on program design and implementation.

States vary in the ways they have responded to these questions (Gallagher et al., 1998). Two, Michigan and Oregon, allow the possibility of a family receiving more than five years of lifetime benefits, the limit set by TANF. Ten states set lifetime limits of less than five years, typically 36 months. Connecticut has the shortest time limit—21 months. Some states set limits on the number of months in a fixed time period that a family can receive benefits. For example, Florida limits benefits to 24 months in a five-year time period, with a lifetime benefit of 48 months. Illinois sets a 24-month limit with reeligibility after another 24 months.

Some states are setting much higher participation requirements. Wisconsin has moved to require all recipients to work for their benefits. In addition, Wisconsin expects recipients to work 40 hours a week. Washington and other states are setting goals for 100% participation.

Many of the states provide exemptions or extensions to the limits. These are based on such factors as extra time needed to complete education, inability to find employment with good cause, making a good-faith effort to find employment, victims of domestic violence, agency inability to provide needed services, making a good-faith effort to find a job or fulfill work requirements, disability, need to care for disabled or ill family member, or other factors.

Under AFDC, a family automatically received an increase in benefits when a new child was born into the family. During the JOBS era, some states obtained waivers to adopt family caps, which reduce or eliminate the additional benefit for a child conceived while the mother was receiving welfare. The Personal Responsibility Act leaves decisions about this in the hands of the states. Twenty-two states have opted to impose caps that limit benefits in this way. Seventeen states provide no additional benefit to a family for a child born 10 months after the family begins receiving assistance. Five states provide some support for these children.

The first major study of the early stages of TANF implementation suggests that states are moving aggressively to incorporate its emphasis in their policies and practices. The General Accounting Office (GAO, 1998:26–72) study of seven states reports that they have strengthened their focus on work by requiring more recipients to participate in their welfare-to-work programs, requiring them to participate in activities tied to employment, requiring earlier participation, and invoking stronger sanctions for nonparticipation. According to the GAO study, states have changed their policies to encourage self-sufficiency by providing incentives to increase the financial return to work. They also are trying to reduce the need for welfare by diverting clients, increasing child support, and initiating programs to reduce out-of-wedlock pregnancies.

V. MANAGEMENT CHALLENGES

Welfare reform generates a whole series of challenges for managers (Brodkin, 1995; Corbett, 1994; Jennings, 1998; Lurie, 1996; Mead, 1997; Nathan, 1993). The breadth and depth of the challenges depend in part of the nature of reform. Incremental changes pose fewer challenges than wholesale reform. In addition, the nature of the challenge depends on how the design issues are answered. For example, voluntary programs pose different challenges from mandatory programs. A major challenge is to design a delivery system that is compatible with the goals of reform. This often involves mediating competing priorities. Among the many issues that managers have to address are:

Designing a client process
Determining the necessary services
Identifying service providers and creating a service delivery network
Locating, allocating, and using financial resources
Mediating the intergovernmental system
Managing contracts
Information system design and use
Changing the organization
Measuring results

While it is difficult to say which of these are most critical for the success of welfare reform, it seems clear that the more extensive the change required, the greater the importance of organizational change. In discussions of welfare reform, this is typically identified as changing the culture of the organization. Welfare managers themselves identify this as their most important task. This is reflected in a recent survey that asked state welfare agency directors to identify the most important administrative challenges they face (Jennings, 1998). The three challenges that they cited most frequently are, in order of mention:

1. Transforming the culture of welfare
2. Development of information system technology and information management
3. Partnerships building, coordination, and collaboration

They also mentioned a variety of other administrative challenges that affect their success. These included monitoring and evaluation, meeting legal control or benchmark obligations, staff development, program design, efficient use of funds, and development of legislative support.

A. Linking Design and Operations to Policy and Priorities

The design and management requirements of a program depend on policy goals and underlying beliefs about what is necessary to achieve those goals. This is reflected in ET Choices and WorkFirst, both of which represented dramatic departures for their states, but which also differed in critical ways from each other.

Behn (1991:9–15) argues that ET Choices was based on an idea of reform that had eight critical components:

Welfare recipients want to work.
The Department of Public Welfare needs to help recipients find a way out of poverty.
The department has to help recipients become self-sufficient by providing basic education, job skills training, and placement services.
Recipients need support services, especially day care for their children and transportation.
The department needs a long-term perspective.
A welfare-to-work program has to be voluntary if it is to be effective.
Each recipient has to make her own critical choices.
Other organizations are more capable of providing education, training, placement, and support services.

These ideas were central to the design of the program. They meant that welfare recipients would not be forced to take jobs, although they would be required to sign up for the program. Beyond the initial sign-up, participation would be voluntary. This was a critical decision; it is the decision that distinguishes ET Choices from WorkFirst in Washington. The name of the program, of course, reflects this idea that participants should make decisions for themselves. These design characteristics shaped the management challenges.

Governor Locke and the Washington legislature identified three goals for WorkFirst:

1. Reducing poverty by helping people get jobs
2. Sustaining independence by helping people keep jobs
3. Protecting children and other vulnerable residents

In support of these goals, state officials identified a set of guiding principles that emphasizes the importance of work, the responsibilities of welfare parents, and the provision of services to help clients become self-supporting.

Underlying the program goals and supporting principles are two central beliefs. First, welfare recipients and their families will be better off if they work, no matter the kind of work or the wage. Second, some clients, if not most, will not voluntarily participate.

Michael Masten, director of the WorkFirst Division of the Washington Department of Social and Health Services is quick to identify five major differences between WorkFirst and everything that preceded it in Washington:

1. WorkFirst is temporary, incorporating the five-year limit established by TANF with few exceptions.
2. Everyone is expected to participate, with few exceptions. Under the previous program, less than half of their clients were expected to participate.
3. The first step for most clients is job search. This is a sharp contrast to the prior program which emphasized human capital investment and made training available to everyone.
4. Clients are expected to accept any bona fide offer. They have to go to work even if it is a minimum wage job.
5. The program is designed to ensure that work pays. To do this, there are significant income disregards to guarantee that people are better off if they work. The program subsidizes health care and child care for people who work. In addition, once people are working at least 20 hours a week, they have opportunities for training and education to help them advance in their work.

Beyond this, Washington will not hesitate to use sanctions to encourage participation and self-sufficiency.

It is evident that Washington's policy choices led to a program significantly different from ET Choices, a difference that is captured well by the WorkFirst appellation. Those choices also led to some different management issues.

B. Designing a Client Process

In the 1970s, the major focus of welfare reform was on processing clients for benefits. The goal was to make sure that clients received benefits to which they were entitled, while avoiding fraud and abuse. The major activity of welfare offices was eligibility determination and redetermination. Client processing focused on obtaining information necessary to determine eligibility and benefit levels.

The welfare-to-work programs have a different focus and require different types of client processing. In fact, if the processes are not designed to support the goals of the program, the program is unlikely to succeed, as pointed out by Meyers et al. (1998) and Nathan (1993). Client flows in the ET Choices program of Massachusetts and the Washington WorkFirst program illustrate this point. Because ET emphasized the development of employability plans for individual clients, that is a major focus of the early steps in the process. Only when the client's skills and needs have been assessed is it possible for case managers to determine the appropriate next step. That might be career planning, education and training, supported work, or job development and placement, depending on the individual. In Washington's WorkFirst program, on the other hand, the priority is work as quickly as possible. Thus, applicants are almost immediately placed in job preparation and job search activities. Only if those activities fail are more extensive plans developed and training made available.

One of the critical issues in the design of process is where to locate eligibility determination and how to link it to welfare-to-work activities. Under AFDC, where delivery of benefits was the priority, an immediate focus on eligibility determination made sense. When the goal is to place the highest priority on work, as states are doing under TANF, it may make sense to delay or deemphasize benefit related activities. A side effect, of course, is that some people will not receive financial assistance as quickly as they need it.

One of the important questions facing managers of reform is how to stage the workload. Each state welfare system has two components to its workload—new applicants and continuing recipients. Decisions have to be made about how to process each of these groups. States can process new applicants consistent with new rules and procedures. This is what Washington decided to do. Unless exempt from participation or eligible for diversion, case managers assign each new applicant to job preparation. For most applicants, this means job search. Case managers put individuals from the preexisting caseload into the new process as they come up for reeligibility determination. Thus, one-twelfth of the preexisting caseload enters the new program each month. According to program managers who were interviewed, early indications are that it will be more difficult to get them involved in WorkFirst activities.

Related to process design is the question of who will manage the client's movement through that process. The solution that has emerged in the transformation of public assistance from a cash benefit to a self-sufficiency orientation is the case management position. Case managers replace the traditional caseworker, whose primary role was eligibility determination. Case managers are responsible for overseeing the client's movement through the system, working with the client to formulate an employment or personal development plan.

Policy makers insisted that case management be a central feature of ET Choices. Case managers would follow clients through all phases of their participation in the program. They would oversee the development of the employment plan, direct the client to appropriate services, and monitor the movement of the client from program entry to self-sufficiency. As the department of public welfare's case management guide put it (Behn, 1991:46), ''In addition to determining financial eligibility for entitlement programs, the Case Manager and the client plan and secure those services available through the Department necessary to help the client and his or her family become independent." A similar approach is found in Washington, where 700 eligibility workers were retrained to fill the case management positions.

C. Determining Necessary Services

Welfare-to-work programs typically provide a range of services to ease the transition to self-sufficiency. Some of these services are designed to help clients seek out and obtain jobs. Others are designed to help clients obtain knowledge and skills required by employers. Still others are supportive services designed to make it possible for a client to meet family responsibilities while working: child care and health care are prime examples. A final set of services supports employment by removing or reducing other barriers to work. Examples would be mental health and substance abuse treatment.

Administrators have to determine the mix and extent of services necessary to support the welfare-to-work effort. Plans for the service mix depend on the goals and priorities of the program, the characteristics of the client population, and resources. While program goals and client needs should drive the provision of services, it is possible, if not likely, that case manager proclivities and the availability of service providers are key determinants of what happens (Ewalt, 1998).

Many discussions of welfare reform have pointed out the difficulties in arranging the appropriate services. Analysts have suggested that child care will be a major barrier to TANF implementation in many settings. In fact, when regional offices in the state of Washington developed their first plans for WorkFirst, they typically cited child care as a problem. Managers have to go further than this, however. They have to decide what kind of problem it is and develop a strategy for addressing the problem. With child care, the problem could be cost, quality, accessibility, time of availability, or willingness to accept disabled children or children who are ill. Each of these problems with child care requires a different kind of solution.

D. Creating a Service Delivery Network

Whatever services are needed, managers have to develop a network of providers to deliver those services. While it is conceivable that the welfare agency could deliver all necessary services itself, it is neither practicable, effective, nor politically feasible to do so. When welfare encompassed little more than the delivery of cash benefits and vouchers, with perhaps a bit of social work, it was practical and reasonable for welfare programs to be self-contained. Once the shift to a welfare-to-work approach began to take place, this no longer made sense. In the first place, many other agencies already had expertise in the services clients required. The employment service was a ready source of job training activities; school systems provided basic education; community colleges and technical schools were prepared to offer vocational training; private industry councils offered skills training. As the designers of ET Choices recognized, this meant that they did not have to re-create the wheel. They could call on others who had already done it and not waste resources on the start-up costs necessary to develop new capacities to deliver these services. Because other agencies had expertise, the welfare office was unlikely to be as effective in delivering the service, so the reasoning went.

Second, because other agencies had a stake in providing many of the services, they were a ready source of opposition should the agency choose to develop services on its own. They wanted access to new resources made available by the reform effort, and they wanted recognition of their authority and competence within their realm of expertise.

Finally, new doctrines in public administration recognized the gains in efficiency and effectiveness that could be obtained by contracting out services (Rehfuss, 1979; Wolf, 1988). Those gains, of course, depend on the degree of competition among service providers (Kettl, 1993). If there is no competition, most of the gains from contracting will be lost. In fact, because the agency loses some degree of control, it may lose some flexibility and effectiveness under conditions of sole source contracting.

The challenge for managers, then, is first to decide what services and activities are better handled within the agency and which are better provided by other entities. These entities might be other government agencies, not-for-profit organizations, or private businesses. Although welfare was long considered an unlikely target for profit-seeking businesses (indeed, some activists, analysts, and policy makers consider it immoral for anyone to make a profit on the poor), that conception has rapidly fallen by the wayside. Welfare reform involves large sums of money, and large parts of it have been contracted out in recent years. One of the considerations here is what array of organizations is available with what kinds of expertise.

E. Locating, Allocating, and Using Financial Resources

Although one of the long-term goals of welfare reform is to reduce the public cost of welfare, in the short run it requires resources. Indeed, under the JOBS program, many states had trouble finding the resources they needed to run their programs effectively. States often failed to draw down the full amount of available federal funding, either because they lacked sufficient state matching money or because they were moving slowly with reform. As the discussion to this point makes clear, TANF requires considerable resources if it is to be effective. Supporting services like transportation, child care, and health care have to be made available. State programs require direct services in the form of job placement, job preparation, education, and training.

Under JOBS, states often did not have sufficient funds available in the program itself to provide all of the needed services. For that reason, welfare reform managers looked for other sources of funding. They found it in Job Training Partnership Act funds, state education agencies, Medicaid, and separate child care programs. Managers had to take care to draw on these resources in ways that would maximize available funding.

Because AFDC and JOBS were entitlement programs, states could increase federal contributions by increasing state funding. The federal match reduced the amount of state funds needed to provide services. In fact, some critics have argued that the matching and entitlement nature of the program led to expansions of services that encouraged dependency. Under the Personal Responsibility Act, this changes. Each state receives a block grant based on the amount of funding it was receiving under AFDC. That amount cannot be increased by increasing the amount of state spending.

There was concern that this funding arrangement would lead states without sufficient resources to fail to fulfill the legislative mandates of the law. That has not been the case, however, as a vigorous economy and substantial drops in welfare rolls have left states in a solid financial position. At least in the short run, most state managers are not casting about for additional money. Instead, they are looking for ways to spend their money most effectively. GAO (1998) indicates that states have experienced surpluses under TANF and have been using the money to provide additional services.

States are required under TANF to maintain their spending of state funds at the level they were spending in 1994. There are strategic considerations with respect to how they do this (Savner and Greenberg, 1997). They can commingle state and federal funds in a single TANF program so that each family's assistance consists of a mixture of federal and state funds. In this case, all TANF rules apply to all families. They can segregate state and federal funds so that some families receive federal support and others do not. In this case, some federal rules, such as time limits, will not apply to the family. They can spend state funds in a separate program or programs that receive no federal TANF funds. In this case, federal rules would not apply, but the money would not count toward maintenance of effort requirements. These choices will become more important as states start to work with harder-to-serve clients.

F. Coordinating the System

Over the past 50 years, policy developments, programmatic additions, and administrative choices have led to considerable complexity in the social welfare system

(Jennings and Zank, 1993). This carries over to the arena of reform, where a host of potential providers are eager participants in service delivery. While this opens the possibility of tailoring services to local conditions and obtaining gains in efficiency and effectiveness, it also creates a considerable need for coordination (Agranoff, 1991; Jennings and Zank, 1993). As O'Toole (1997) and Provan and Milward (1995) have made clear, management in networks calls on a different set of skills and strategies than management in a self-contained organization. The ability to sort responsibilities, recognize unique competencies and contributions, and effectively link activities is critical to success in this environment.

For welfare reform, network coordination means identifying the responsibilities of different agencies, sorting out resource acquisition and allocation, developing management information systems that allow efficient collection and sharing of information by and among agencies, and effectively sequencing the contact of clients with relevant agencies. Coordination does not have to mean consolidation of activities within an agency; nor does is necessarily involve conflicts among agencies. As Grubb (1996) found in his study of vocational education programs, agencies can effectively create a division of labor and link their activities to pursue common purposes. Chisholm (1989) presents a powerful theoretical and empirical analysis of transportation services in the San Franciso Bay area that suggests considerable possibilities for mutual adjustment among agencies to coordinate services effectively.

There are several dimensions to coordination. Welfare reform requires it with respect to policy, planning, operations, finances, client information, and administrative functions. It can occur through formal or informal means.

The Job Training Partnership Act of 1981 required states and their service delivery areas to create formal bodies to coordinate policy and programs. While such interagency coordinating bodies have been used extensively in human services, the Personal Responsibility Act does not require such a mechanism. Despite this, most states have drawn on interagency committees to coordinate policy and action.

Washington provides a good example of this. The governor assigned four state agencies a role in the WorkFirst program. The Department of Social and Health Services has lead responsibility for the program. It operates the case management system and is responsible for eligibility determination, grant diversion, participant orientation, establishment of individual responsibility plans, and other activities. The Employment Security Department provides job preparation services for clients, operating a placement service and preparing the clients to seek work. The Board of Technical and Community Colleges is responsible for coordinating education and training services through the state's 32 technical and community colleges. The Department of Community, Trade, and Economic Development links state economic development policies with WorkFirst strategies. It is to work with private and public sector entities to create incentives for businesses to hire WorkFirst participants.

To coordinate the department's activities, committees operate at several levels. The Department of Social and Health Services convened a statewide committee to help plan the implementaion of WorkFirst. During the implementation phase, a high-level committee composed of deputy directors or assistant secretaries of four major departments has met weekly to resolve policy issues. Beneath them, a committee composed of the directors of divisions responsible for Work-First activites in the four major departments has also met weekly to work out operational issues and coordinate activities.

Washington has a state-administered welfare system, meaning that the state sets policies and administers programs through local offices of the Department of Social and Health Services. The state is divided into six regions, and each of those regions was charged with development of a regional WorkFirst plan. To prepare those plans, the regional offices convened meetings involving the other lead agencies, local governments, not-for-profit organizations, service providers, and advocates of the poor. The regional plans are supposed to tailor WorkFirst to local conditions and opportunities. Doing that requires considerable coordination of the activities of a variety of contributing organizations.

Massachusetts faced similar issues with ET Choices, which required extensive coordination because of the array of services and organizations involved. Consistent with the idea that the Department of Public Welfare should rely on other agencies to provide services in their areas of expertise, most services were provided outside of the Department. The Division of Employment Security provided job placement. The Office of Training and Employment Policy offered job training through the Job Training Partnership Act programs offered by private industry councils and service delivery areas. School systems and other education providers offered educational services. Outside vocational counseling services helped with client assessments. The Department of Social Services arranged child care. Thus, there was a complex, multiorganizational network of partners in the program.

There are multiple mechanisms for formal coordination, including coordinating bodies, rule and regulations, memoranda of agreement, and contracts. Formalized processes are often put in place to link activities. This is the case, for example, in the process by which Social and Health Services refers clients to Employment Security in Washington. In addition to the formal mechanisms, however, effective coordination requires competent use of interpersonal skills (Jennings and Krane, 1994). The informal, or interpersonal, aspect of coordination helps create a shared set of expectations and communication networks that help resolve difficulties.

G. Managing Contracts

Contracts are a major mechanism by which welfare agencies acquire the range of services required to make reform work. Many of these contracts are for services to clients: job preparation, job development, job placement, basic education, skills training, and child care referral. Others are for various aspects of the management of the system. Management information system design is a management function for which states often contract. Some states, however, are contracting for case management, a traditional core activity of the welfare agency.

Contracting is a well-established tool of contemporary public management (Rehfuss, 1989). It is a useful and effective way to acquire expert services. It is a device by which agencies can turn to each other for help and by which agencies can seek the effort of not-for-profit organizations or profit-seeking firms. While many observers continue to find it unsettling that profit might be made on the plight of the poor, it is clear that profit-seeking organizations will turn their talent and effort to a wide variety of tasks. How successful they are, remains an open question.

Many factors will shape the effectiveness of contracted services, but four dimensions of the arrangement are particularly critical. First, the agency has to be able to clearly specify what the contractor will provide. Second, contracting depends on competition for its effectiveness. When sole-source providers are the only source for contracting, there is much less incentive for the contractor to perform effectively. When competitors are not available, the third critical factor may help. This is the use of performance-based contracts in which the payments to the contractor depend, at least in part, on delivering specified outcomes. In other words, it is not sufficient for the job preparation and placement provider to put participants through a workshop and send them out to apply for jobs. The participants have to acquire jobs in order for the contractor to receive full payment. The fourth factor that can be critical is the ability of the agency to monitor the contract. A clearly written contract with specific performance measures facilitates monitoring, but the agency has to establish effective processes to do the monitoring. It also has to have trained, skilled personnel to carry out that function.

H. Changing the Culture

Welfare managers report that the single most critical management challenge they face is changing the culture of welfare. What they mean by this is changing the attitudes, orientations, and behaviors of case managers and other service providers in the system. Corbett (1994:1) expresses this quite effectively: "Ultimately, the culture of welfare is defined by what clients experience when they interact with welfare agencies and with people who run those agencies." In their study of welfare reform in California, Meyers and colleagues (1998) found that there were two critical shortcomings. First, the organization's processes had not been changed sufficiently to reflect the new mission. Process was inconsistent with the priorities. Second, case managers were not communicating the welfare-to-work message through their words and actions. They continued to focus on the financial needs of clients and failed to place priority on work. This is similar to Hagen and Lurie's (1992) finding that a failure to make case manager behavior consistent with the priorities of the JOBS program reduced the attainment of program goals. Ewalt (1998) found a pattern of case manager behavior in Kentucky counties that reflected a failure to adapt the organization's culture to new realities.

Changing the culture is not easy, as any number of policy makers and managers have discovered when they tried to reorient an organization or a service delivery system. A variety of tools are available, but they must be deployed effectively to work. Managers who responded to the survey of welfare reform management challenges indicated that they were doing a number of things to change the culture. These included developing and clearly communicating the message of change and the new priorities of the program, changing the processing of clients and arrangements in the office to be consistent with the new priorities, redefining the roles of case managers, providing extensive staff training, and modeling the culture change themselves.

Mike Masten, the director of WorkFirst in Washington, models the change in his state. He has a clear and consistent message that he articulates effectively. When asked what Washington is doing to change the culture, his response was consistent with these points:

> We are fond around here of saying we have a plan and we're sticking to it. In the field, of all the comments we get back, the one they seem to value the most is "You have a plan and you are sticking to it. We know the message and it isn't changing every day. You have a set of goals, you've articulated them, you're trying to support us to deliver them today more than ever, and to get out of our way so we can try to deliver."

Washington also communicates the message in the way that it has redesigned its offices. As Lahr-Vivaz (1997:22) puts it, "the department's recent changes in organization and operation have made it difficult for some citizens to identify the 'welfare' office they once knew." The work message is communicated in a variety of ways when clients enter offices—bulletin boards full of job notices, digital message boards that ask how the agency can help the person find a job, and attractive posters that communicate the respect and dignity that come with work and self-sufficiency. Although these symbols of change are targeted at welfare recipients and applicants, they also send a message to agency staff— "It's a new world, and our job has changed."

Symbols are important because they communicate the message of renewal efficiently. In many states, this has been done through the labeling of programs. ET Choices, GAIN, and WorkFirst are examples. Another example is in the renaming of agencies responsible for welfare. Washington no longer has a welfare agency; it now has a WorkFirst division. This has carried over to the major professional association for welfare. The American Public Welfare Association has changed its name to the American Public Human Services Association.

One way to produce culture change, of course, is to create a new organization or assign the responsibility to a different agency. In fact, some states have moved responsibility for welfare reform from traditional welfare agencies to employment agencies. Washington may have followed this strategy, in part, when it shifted case management of welfare-to-work activities to staff in the WorkFirst division, removing that responsibility from the state's employment service, which had handled case management for the JOBS program. Other states, apparently lacking confidence in their ability to change the culture, are opting to contract out case management to the private sector. This brings in a completely different organization that has no ties to the old way of doing business.

Another approach is to involve staff in the design of service delivery strategies. Typical organizational development approaches suggest a bottom-up approach to change that relies on the members of the organization to design and implement the change. While effective, this approach is often at odds with the top-down nature of welfare reform. It can be particularly difficult if the values and beliefs of the workers contradict the direction of reform.

While many reformers talk about using sanctions and incentives to change the behavior of welfare recipients, none of the managers I have surveyed or interviewed talked about using sanctions or incentives to change the culture of the organization. Besides the irony of this, it is surprising, given the emphasis in recent years on performance rewards for public employees. Despite this failure to consider the use of incentive and sanctions with individual employees, they are being used through contracts and interagency agreements. Performance-based contracting has become a common feature of welfare reform, carrying over from the employment and training arena. With a performance-based contract, a contractor's payment depends on the level of outcomes achieved. The performance contracts focus on actual outcomes, not service or activity levels. Thus, a not-for-profit contractor for placement services might receive a base of payment depending on the number of clients it serves, but the remainder of the payment might depend on the number successfully placed in jobs, their average wages, or the number who retain jobs after a set period of time. This gives the organization an incentive to perform.

In its study of TANF implementation, GAO reports that states are changing worker roles and altering local offices to support the work focus of their programs (GAO, 1998:73–76). In the seven states it studied, GAO found that states had expanded the caseworker's role, assigning new responsibilities that focus on moving clients to work. This effort to change the caseworker's role is supported by training, but undermined by continuing responsibility for eligibility determination and other demands on their time. The states reorganized local offices to consolidate service delivery.

I. Information Systems and Use

Welfare reform requires the creation, processing, and use of considerable amounts of information. The Personal Responsibility Act mandates that states report certain types of information to the U.S. Department of Health and Human Services. Time limits imposed by the Act mean that states have to be able to track individuals to make sure they do not exceed the limits. This is relatively easy, but not guaranteed, for the typical case in which the state has to make sure that recipients are placed in a work activity within 24 months after beginning to receive benefits. Less certain, however, is how states will be able to track the five-year lifetime limit on benefits for recipients who receive benefits in more than one state over time.

Performance management, of course, requires that states be able to generate data on performance. If job placements, wages, earnings increases, retention in employment, and reduction in benefit payments are measures of performance, the state needs an information system that will report that information to managers. The use of this information will allow the state to make accurate payments to service providers whose contracts are based on performance. It also allows managers to make programmatic adjustments in response to fluctuations or trends in performance levels. The states also must report performance information to HHS, and management information systems provide the means to do this.

Management information is required for more than simply gauging and reporting on performance. Case managers need information to allow them to work effectively with clients. They have to know details about the client's background, needs, and services. They need to know whether clients are participating in program activities. They have to be able to share client information with service providers. The network of case managers and service providers who work with clients in a typical welfare-to-work system has to share information about the client. While this could be done with paper, telephone, and face-to-face discussions, electronic management information systems greatly facilitate the needed information exchange. Designers need to base the systems on the information needs of individuals who deal with clients, but they also need to incorporate important safeguards to insure that information is secure and is not released to unauthorized individuals. The information system also has to provide data required by local, regional, and state office managers to allow them to monitor the welfare-to-work system and guide its performance.

There are data determination, technical, and human sides to the design of information systems to meet these needs. Decisions have to be made about who needs what kind of information, the form in which they need the information, and when they need the information. Designers have to determine who is best situated to provide the information for the system and how it can be entered in the system. With this information, designers and managers can make hardware and software decisions. Effective system design requires that architects take into account the capabilities of different actors to enter and retrieve data. They have to consider how the demands on the time of individuals will affect their ability to do this. Training is a must if people are to use the system effectively.

J. Measuring Results

The discussions of culture change, contract management, and information systems suggested the importance of measurable results. Not only has the federal government established performance expectations, but actors throughout the system have demanded that performance measurement systems be put in place. If we are to judge the effectiveness of reform, we have to know the goals and priorities and be able to sort out their attainment. This is consistent with the public's broader demands for performance and accountability in government (Newcomer, 1997). Those demands are reflected in the National Performance Review (Gore, 1994) and countless state and local efforts to reinvent government (Osborne and Gaebler, 1992).

A group of policy makers and managers in the Midwest participated in a project to identify an appropriate set of measures of the success of welfare-to-work programs. The Midwest Welfare Peer Assistance Network (WELPLAN, 1998) is a group of senior welfare officials from seven Midwestern states brought together by the Institute for Research on Poverty of the University of Wisconsin and the Family Impact Seminar of Washington, D.C., to discuss issues related to welfare reform. The group recognized that the success of welfare reform involves much more than a reduction in the rolls. While the experiments of the 1980s and 1990s had pursued multiple goals, including increased wages, increased employment, and a reduction in welfare payments, WELPLAN suggested a systematic array of measures, some of which relate to short-term goals and others of which relate to long-term goals. That time dimension is important to keep in mind while thinking about the accomplishments or failures of reform. The range of measures suggested by WELPLAN is indicative of the enormous depth and breadth of outcomes that various actors expect from welfare reform.

This group of knowledgeable participants identified four areas of initial concern for which they believe they will be held most directly accountable (WELPLAN, 1998): welfare dependency, self-sufficiency, economic well-being, and parental responsibility. For each of these, they suggested examples of relevant measures, as indicated in Table 2.

These welfare officials also identified six ultimate areas of concern that they believe states will use to measure progress under welfare reform (WELPLAN, 1998). These capture outcomes that are less direct, but which WELPLAN

Table 2 Sample Measures for Initial Outcome Areas for Welfare Reform

Area of concern	Sample measures
Welfare dependency—Families' use of public assistance programs to meet their basic economic needs	Caseload counts Reasons for exit Reentry counts Average grant amounts Average duration of welfare spell Use of other public services
Self-sufficiency—Welfare clients' attachment to the work force	Job entry Type of work (paid, subsidized, community) Enrollment in training Job retention/turnover
Economic well-being—family income and other sources of financial well-being	Income Wages Job benefits
Parental responsibility—parents' fulfillment of their financial responsibilities toward their children	Paternity establishment rates; child support systems

members assert to be the broader concerns motivating welfare reform. The six ultimate areas of concern are child well-being, adult/parent well-being, family well-being, community involvement, economic development, and family formation. Table 3 suggests potential measures of each of these dimensions.

Formal studies of TANF outcomes are not available yet, but there has been considerable excitement surrounding the substantial decline in welfare roles that has accompanied its implementation. From the adoption of the Personal Responsibility Act in August 1996 to March 1998, caseloads declined by 27% nationally, reducing the number of families receiving benefits from 4.4 million to 3.2 million. All states except Hawaii and Nebraska experienced a decline, with the most dramatic reductions occurring in Idaho (80%), Wyoming (74%), and Wisconsin (68%). These are extraordinary reductions. While proponents of reform are quick to credit TANF and other welfare reforms with these reductions, the downward movement had begun before TANF was adopted, and much of its is clearly attributable to the expanding economy (Council of Economic Advisers, 1997; Martini and Wiseman, 1997; Blank, 1997; GAO, 1998). As GAO (1998:105–108) points our, little is known about TANF's impacts on the well-being of children and families.

Table 3 Sample Measures for Ultimate Outcomes of Welfare Reform

Ultimate area of concern	Sample outcome measures
Child well-being—Child health, education, social development	Health—immunization rates Child care—availability, quality Education—academic achievement, absenteeism, and dropout rates Juvenile justice system contacts
Adult/parent well-being—Parent health, education, job skills	Health—receiving alcohol, drug, or mental health treatment Enrollment in higher education, receipt of degree of certificate
Family well-being—families' ability to provide a healthy, supportive, safe environment	Medical insurance/managed care Child abuse and neglect Spouse/partner abuse Housing/homelessness Residential stability/mobility
Community involvement—Communities' support of welfare reform	Public attitudes toward welfare Business/community partnerships, safety-net services Community safety/violence
Economic development—accessibility of jobs that encourage self-sufficiency	Changes in low-wage labor market Job creation Creation of new types of support services
Family formation—for participants and the general population, individuals' ability to form and maintain stable family bonds	Marriage/divorce rates Cohabitation rates Additional, postprogram entry births Out-of-wedlock births

VI. LEADERSHIP FOR REFORM

Welfare reform does not happen by itself. It requires both political and managerial leadership. Governors, in fact, have been the keys to welfare reform in the American states. Several governors have gained considerable visibility because of their welfare reform initiatives. These would include Tommy Thompson of Wisconsin, Michael Dukakis of Massachusetts, John Engler of Michigan, Bill Clinton of Arkansas, and Mike Leavitt of Utah. The first three received attention because of pioneering efforts to foster change in their states. The last two were visible proponents of change through their activities in the National Governors' Association.

Gubernatorial leadership has focused on broad issues of agenda setting, issue definition, coalition building, policy intent, and policy design. Dukakis,

Engler, and Thompson epitomize these leadership activities. Dukakis was an early leader in welfare reform (Behn, 1991). He helped focus attention on the issue in his state. He worked to build support for initiatives to change the system. As Behn puts it, "Governor Dukakis became an enthusiastic champion of ET Choices" (Behn, 1991:211). He gave managers the support they needed to implement change. Behn points out that "Dukakis' support for ET was important. When a manager's governor regularly participates in his various awards ceremonies and brags about the manager's program on national television, it helps in many ways: it convinces people inside the agency that their work is important, and it helps gain cooperation from those outside" (Behn, 1991:213). A panel of the National Academy of Public Administration concluded, "A strong commitment from the governor is necessary to make a cross-cutting (welfare-to-work) program like this work" (Behn, 1991:211).

Engler of Michigan took the lead in abolishing his state's General Assistance program and developing alternative services for some of its recipients (Thompson, 1995). Persistent effort over an extended period of time was necessary for the governor to produce the type of change he sought. He faced considerable opposition from advocates for the poor. He was able to overcome that opposition by successfully framing the issue and building a coalition of support among Republicans and suburban Democrats whose constituents were not beneficiaries of general assistance.

Thompson of Wisconsin has become the most visible gubernatorial leader of welfare reform, transforming the Wisconsin system over a period of years through programmatic experiments and policy changes (Corbett, 1995; Wiseman, 1996). Like other leaders of reform, he achieved his objectives, at least in part, by framing the issue in terms of the deleterious effects of the welfare system on the poor. By emphasizing the idea that the welfare system encourages dependency and makes it hard for the recipients to care for themselves, he was able to build support for dramatic change in a state with an extraordinary progressive tradition and a generous system of support.

Beyond the governors, however, we can see the importance of managerial leadership. This critical component is emphasized in Behn's account of ET Choices. Managers have to exploit opportunities, build cooperation among organizations and individual workers, and structure a multifaceted strategy that reflects the mission to be achieved and the goals to be met (Behn, 1991:215). Mangers have to develop organizations, structure processes, motivate workers, foster culture change, monitor performance, mediate disputes, and build links with political leaders.

This is proving to be the case in Washington and other states implementing the Personal Responsibility Act. Although many of their agencies had already begun a process of transformation under the Family Support Act and JOBS, most are moving in distinctly new directions (GAO, 1998). This is certainly the case in Washington with its shift from human capital improvement to a work-first approach. Managers under these circumstances face enormous challenges in moving the organization in new directions.

Behn (1991:67–79) argues that successful management of ET involved six distinct aspects: establishing an overall mission; setting specific goals; personally monitoring results; rewarding success; watching carefully for distortions; and modifying mission, goals, monitoring, or rewards to correct defects.

These are likely to be central to successful managerial leadership of welfare reform today. Two things are striking about this. One is the emphasis on personal attention by the manager. It is not sufficient to have a system to monitor performance. The manager has to personally monitor the results, call attention to the results, meet with staff to discuss them, offer praise for results, and regularly communicate about the results.

The second striking aspect of the management challenge is an ongoing process involving shifting goals and constant modifications of processes. Goals should change over time to reflect achievements of the organization, changes in the environment, and new priorities. When oversight reveals failures of process or attainment, managers must take steps to motivate workers, modify processes, adjust structures, or alter the program.

It is tempting to try to sum up the vast policy, leadership, and management challenges of welfare reform that are addressed in this chapter. Redundancy, after all, is often a virtue. It's one that we've discovered to be important in administrative systems (Landau, 1969). Rather than reiterate the ground we have covered, however, it is perhaps instructive to conclude with this section's discussion of leadership. While technical and organizational capacity clearly are critical to the success of welfare reform, both political and managerial leadership will be necessary to convert those capacities to effective action.

ACKNOWLEDGMENTS

Jo Ann Ewalt offered invaluable comments and suggestions on this chapter. It also benefited considerably from the long-term collaboration that Dale Krane and I have carried out on welfare-to-work programs.

REFERENCES

Agranoff, R. (1991). Human services integration: past and present challenges in public administration, *Public Administration Review 51*: 531–542.
Bardach, E. (1977). *The implementation Game: What Happens When a Bill Becomes a Law*, MIT Press, Cambridge.

Baum, E. B. (1991). When the witch doctors agree: the Family Support Act and social science research, *Journal of Policy Analysis and Management 10*: 601–615.

Behn, R. (1991). *Leadership Counts: Lessons for Public Managers from the Massachusetts Welfare, Training, and Employment Program*, Harvard University Press, Cambridge.

Blank, R. M. (1997). What causes public assistance caseloads to grow? (working paper), Joint Center for Poverty Research, *http://www.jcpr.org/caseloads.html*.

Brodkin, E. Z. (1995). Administrative capacity and welfare reform, *Looking Before We Leap*: *Social Science and Welfare Reform* (R. Kent Weaver and W. T. Dickens, eds.), Brookings Institution, Washington.

Califano, J. A. Jr. (1981). *Governing America: An Insider's Report from the White House and the Cabinet*, Simon and Schuster, New York.

Cammisa, A. M. (1998). *From Rhetoric to Reform? Welfare Policy in American Politics*, Westview Press, Boulder, CO.

Center on Hunger, Poverty, and Nutrition. (1995). *Statement on Key Welfare Reform Issues*: *The Empirical Evidence*, Tufts University, Medford, MA.

Chisholm, D. (1989). *Coordination Without Hierarchy*: *Informal Structures in Multiorganizational Systems*. University of California Press, Berkeley.

Corbett, T. J. (1994). Changing the culture of welfare, *Focus 16*.

Corbett, T. J. (1995). Welfare reform in Wisconsin: the rhetoric and the reality, *The Politics of Welfare Reform* (Norris and Thompson, eds.), Sage Publications, Thousand Oaks, CA.

Council of Economic Advisers. (1997). *Explaining the Decline in Welfare Receipt, 1993–1996*, Council of Economic Advisers, Washington, DC.

Elmore, R. (1982). Backward mapping: implementation research and policy decisions, *Studying Implementation* (W. Williams, ed.), Chatham House Publishers, New York.

Ewalt, J. A. G. (1998). *An Analysis of the Job Opportunities and Basic Skills Program in Kentucky*: *Determinants of Component Choice*, Dissertation, University of Kentucky, Lexington.

Ewalt, J. A. G. (1996). The "content" of welfare policy: the states and Section 1115 waivers, Presented at the Southeastern Conference of Public Administration, September, Miami.

Gallagher, L. J., Gallagher, M., Perese, K., Schreiber, S., and Watson, K. (1998). *One Year After Federal Welfare Reform*: *A Description of State Temporary Assistance for Needy Families (TANF) Decisions as of October 1997*, Urban Institute, Washington, DC.

GAO. (1998). *Welfare Reform*: *States Are Restructuring Programs to Reduce Dependence on Welfare*, U.S. General Accounting Office, Washington, DC.

Goggin, M. L., Bowman, A. O., Lester, J. P., and O'Toole, L. J. Jr. (1990). *Implementation Theory and Practice*: *Toward a Third Generation*, Harper Collins, New York.

Gore, A. (1994). *Creating a Government That Works Better & Costs Less*: *Report of the National Performance Review*, U.S. Government Printing Office, Washington, DC.

Greenberg, D., and Wiseman, M. (1992). What Did the OBRA Demonstrations Do? *Evaluating Welfare and Training Programs* (C. F. Manski and Irwin Garfinkel, eds.), Harvard University Press, Cambridge.

Grubb, W. N., and McDonnell, L. M. (1996). Combating program fragmentation: local systems of vocational education and job training, *Journal of Policy Analysis and Management 15*: 252–270.

Gueron, J. M., and Pauly, E. (1991). *From Welfare to Work*, Russell Sage Foundation, New York.

Hagen, J. L. (1989). Income maintenance workers: technicians or service providers?, *Social Service Review 61*: 261–271.

Hagen, J. L., and Lurie, I. (1995). Implementing JOBS: from the Rose Garden to reality, *Social Work 40(4)*.

Hagen, J. L., and Lurie, I. (1992). *Implementing JOBS: Progress and Promise*, State University of New York at Albany, Rockefeller Institute of Government, Albany.

Haskins, R. (1991). Congress writes a law: research and welfare reform, *Journal of Policy Analysis and Management 10*: 617–632.

Haveman, R. H. (1977). *A Decade of Federal Antipoverty Programs: Achievements, Failures, and Lessons*, Academic Press, New York.

Hoynes, H. W. (1997). Does welfare play any role in female headship decisions?, *Journal of Public Economics 65*: 89–117.

Jennings, E. T. Jr. (1998). *Management Challenges in the Implementation of the Personal Responsibility and Work Opportunity Act*, James W. Martin School of Public Policy and Administration, University of Kentucky, Lexington.

Jennings, E. T. Jr., and Krane, D. (1994). Coordination and welfare reform: the quest for the philosopher's stone, *Public Administration Review 54*: 341–348.

Jennings, E. T. Jr., and Krane, D. (1998). Interorganizational cooperation and the implementation of welfare reform: public service employment in welfare reform programs, *Policy Studies Review 15*: 170–201.

Jennings, E. T. Jr., and Ewalt, J. A. G. (1998). Interorganizational coordination, administrative consolidation, and policy performance, *Public Administration Review 57*: 417–428.

Jennings, E. T. Jr., and Zank, N. S., eds. (1993). *Welfare System Reform: Coordinating Federal, State, and Local Public Assistance*, Greenwood Press, Westport, CT.

Kettl, D. (1993). *Sharing Power: Public Governance and Private Markets*, Brookings Institution, Washington, DC.

Lahr-Vivaz, E. (1997). Putting work first in Washington state, *Public Welfare* (Fall): 22–30.

Landau, M. (1969). Redundancy, rationality, and the problem of duplication and overlap, *Public Administration Review 29(4)*: 346–358.

Lurie, I. (1996). A lesson from the JOBS program: reforming welfare must be both dazzling and dull, *Journal of Policy Analysis and Management 15*: 572–586.

Lynn, L. E. Jr., and Whitman, D. deF. (1981). *The President as Policymaker: Jimmy Carter and Welfare Reform*, Temple University Press, Philadelphia.

Martini, A., and Wiseman, M. (1997). *Explaining the Recent Decline in Welfare Caseloads: Is the Council of Economic Advisers Right?*, Urban Institute. Washington, DC.

Mead, L. M. (1992). *The New Politics of Poverty: The Nonworking Poor in America*, Basic Books, New York.

Mead, L. M. (1996). Welfare policy: the administrative frontier,'' *Journal of Policy Analysis and Management 15*: 587–600.

Mead, L. M. (1997). Optimizing JOBS: evaluation versus administration, *Public Administration Review 57*: 113–123.

Meyers, M. K., Glaser, B., and MacDonald, K. (1998). On the front lines of welfare delivery: are workers implementing policy reforms?, *Journal of Policy Analysis and Management 17*: 1–22.

Moffitt, R. A. (1997). The effect of welfare on marriage and fertility: what do we know and what do we need to know?, Discussion paper No. 1153–97, Institute for Research on Poverty, Madison, WI.

Moynihan, D. P. (1973). *The Politics of a Guaranteed Income: The Nixon Administration and the Family Assistance Plan*, Random House, New York.

Murray, C. (1984). *Losing Ground: American Social Policy, 1950–1980*, Basic Books, New York.

Nathan, R. P. (1993). *Turning Promises into Performance: The Management Challenge of Implementing Workfare*, Columbia University Press, New York.

Newcomer, K., ed. (1997). *Using Performance Measurement to Strengthen Public and Nonprofit Programs*, Jossey-Bass, San Francisco.

Norris, D., and Thompson, L., eds. (1995). *The Politics of Welfare Reform*, Sage Publications, Thousand Oaks, CA.

Osborne, D., and Gaebler, T. (1992). *Reinventing Government: How the Entrepreneurial Spirit Is Transforming the Public Sector*, Addison-Wesley, Reading, MA.

O'Toole, L. Jr. (1997). Treating networks seriously: practical and research-based agendas in public administration, *Public Administration Review 57* (Jan./Feb.).

Pechman, J. A., and Timpane, P. M., eds. (1975). *Work Incentives and Income Guarantees: The New Jersey Negative Income Tax Experiment*, Brookings Institution, Washington, DC.

Provan, K. G., and Milward, H. B. (1995). A preliminary theory of interorganizational network effectiveness: a comparative study of four community mental health systems, *Administrative Science Quarterly 40*: 1–33.

Rehfuss, J. A. (1989). *Contracting Out in Government*, Jossey-Bass, San Francisco.

Savner, S., and Greenberg, M. (1997). *The New Framework: Alternative State Funding Choices Under TANF*, Center for Law and Social Policy, Washington, DC.

Szanton, P. L. (1991). The remarkable "Quango": knowledge, politics, and welfare reform, *Journal of Policy Analysis and Management 10*: 591–602.

Thompson, L. (1995). The death of general assistance in michigan, *The Politics of Welfare Reform* (Norris and Thompson, eds.), Sage Publications, Thousand Oaks, CA.

Weaver, K. (1995). The politics of welfare reform, *Looking Before We Leap*, (Weaver and Dickens, eds.), Sage Publications, Thousand Oaks, CA.

Weaver, R. K., and Dickens, W. T. (1995). *Looking Before We Leap: Social Science and Welfare Reform*, Brookings Institution, Washington, DC.

WELPLAN. (1998). Welfare reform: how will we know if it works?, Midwest Peer Assistance Network, Family Impact Seminar, January, Washington, DC.

Wiseman, M. (1991). Research and policy: a symposium on the Family Support Act of 1988, *Journal of Policy Analysis and Management 10*: 588–589.

Wiseman, M. (1996). State strategies for welfare reform: the Wisconsin story, *Journal of Policy Analysis and Management 15*: 515–546.

Wolf, C. Jr. (1988). *Markets or Governments: Choosing Between Imperfect Alternatives*, MIT Press, Cambridge.

20
Medicaid in the States: Administrative Reforms Under Devolution

Joseph Drew
Kent State University, Kent, Ohio

Thomas E. Yatsco
U.S. General Accounting Office, Washington, D.C.

I. A FRAMEWORK FOR VIEWING ADMINISTRATIVE REFORM

This chapter addresses the major administrative reforms adopted by state Medicaid programs during the 1990s. These reforms have come about in response to continuing federal devolution, combined with pressures already existing in states to deliver health care services to their poor.

These pressures are (1) federal and state desires to expand access to health insurance coverage for the uninsured; (2) demographic growth in the number of elderly requiring long-term care services; (3) disproportionate growth of state Medicaid budgets; and (4) concerns over the quality of care under the current institutional structure of health care delivery. To a great extent, these issues mirror the mutually conflicting policy concerns of health care in the United States in general: how to expand access to health care while simultaneously containing costs, but not reducing the quality of health care services (Aaron, 1991:1–2).

In 1965 Title XIX amended the Social Security Act of 1935. The resulting program, Medicaid, was first implemented in 1966. Administered by the states, with federal oversight, as one of the United States' major programs in federalism, Medicaid is, in actuality, 55 distinct programs. This total includes the District of

Columbia and the American protectorates of Guam, Puerto Rico, Virgin Islands, and American Samoa, in addition to the 50 states (Health Care Financing Administration, 1999b).

As Medicaid is constituted under federalism, within broad federal guidelines each program is unique relative to implementation and the reforms adopted by states in response to coping with their respective problems. Devolution has compounded this variation. Attempting to review the programs and reforms on a state-by-state basis, while important, would be both redundant and overwhelming (Urban Institute, 1999). Instead, in this chapter a conceptual *policy template* is employed, under which the majority of state administrative programs and subsequent reforms may be classified. The programs and reforms adopted by state Medicaid programs may be described within the context of the following three dimensions: *eligibility determination*; *financing structure*; and *organization of service delivery*.

A. Eligibility Determination

The dimension of eligibility is a precondition of access to service provision. Decisions about eligibility determine who the intended beneficiaries of the largesse of the state or market will be, or conversely, who they will not be. The significance of eligibility for Medicaid (or any policy) can be demonstrated by contrasting two extremes of eligibility: universal entitlement versus market-driven eligibility. Under universal entitlement, service provision is mandated for all persons and the state is responsible for financing services. With the latter, provision and financing of services would be a function of individual's capacity to pay. Within these extremes, federal mandates and/or state desires to provide services to citizens becomes a decision of eligibility determination. Eligibility in turn is one of the most critical drivers of financing and service delivery provision.

B. Financing Structure

The structure of financing arrangements is critical for any policy area. The key decisions regarding financing relate to the dollar magnitude of the burden and who pays for goods and services rendered. In this respect, the issue of who pays is analogous to the incidence of a tax. Under Medicaid, the incidence falls twice on individual taxpayers: once as a state taxpayer, and then again as a federal taxpayer. The dollar magnitude of the Medicaid burden is driven by the interaction of eligibility determination, type of medical category for which services are provided, levels of reimbursement to providers for services rendered within each medical category, and medical care inflation. States with different combinations of each of the above items incur differential financial obligations.

C. Organization of Service Delivery

Conceptually, decisions about how service delivery is organized are decisions of the highest level of public policy: decisions addressing *property rights* within the *state* and the *allocation of resources* (Lindberg and Campbell, 1991:361–363). Decisions about property rights inform us of the decisions made by legislators as to who has access to the largesse of the state and, critically, who controls the supply of that largesse.

Illustrating the extremes that can occur in the determination of property rights is a decision permitting private sector entities to produce and control the delivery of goods or services versus a centralized government entity (e.g., government corporation) being given the right to do so.

Within the domain of health care, these rights have been given to two segments of the private sector: health care providers (physicians, hospitals, medical supply companies, etc.) and private sector insurance companies. Both of these sectors are regulated by the state and federal governments, as well as their respective professional associations.

Under federalism, the organization of service delivery within Medicaid is a shared responsibility among the federal government, the states, and private sector health care providers. The latter deliver health care to Medicaid eligibles on a contractual and voluntary basis to the states. With devolution, the combination of greater responsibility for eligibility and financing of Medicaid has forced states to shift the nature of property rights within their respective domains. States have reconfigured contractual relationships with providers and have increased their regulation and oversight of those same providers. Again, this has been variable across the states.

II. THE CURRENT POLICY STRUCTURE OF MEDICAID

A. Eligibility Determination

The Medicaid program is one of the largest providers of health insurance in the United States. In 1996, Medicaid provided eligibility (i.e., potential access) to some 41.3 million persons, or roughly 1 in 7 Americans (Kaiser Family Foundation, 1998a:1). This large number, however, constitutes only a subset of the poor in America, the *deserving* poor. The deserving poor, in contrast to others, are individuals deemed unable to fend for themselves economically through no fault of their own (Wilensky and Lebeaux, 1965:33–36, 41–42). These persons include children in low-income families, persons with permanent disabilities preventing them from seeking gainful employment (e.g., persons with mentally retardation, nursing home patients who are poor, and low-income women who are pregnant).

By contrast, the *nondeserving poor* are purposely not covered by Medicaid. Rather they are segregated out on neoclassical economic grounds: their marginal contribution (to their employers) does not outweigh their marginal benefits to those same employers. As such, the *nondeserving* poor include most of the working poor and contrary to popular misconception are not persons who are indolent. Relatedly, employer-funded health insurance has fallen steadily during the past decade. The proportion of nonelderly workers covered by employers has fallen from 66% to 61% in the period 1989 to 1993 (Brown and Wyn, 1996:49). The nondeserving poor are subject to this shift in private coverage.

This market-driven distinction within the ranks of the poor is the fundamental reason why in America some persons have insurance coverage under Medicaid and others do not. Empirically, this facilitates the understanding of Medicaid as an economic benefit program rather than an exclusive health care program for the poor. The reason some citizens do not have health insurance coverage is not justifiable from either an ethical or clinical-medical perspective. Rather, the lack of coverage is best understood from an economic perspective.

The economic understanding of eligibility within the Medicaid program is verified by three fundamental facts. First, and related to federalism, is that states set their respective Medicaid eligibility requirements based on their internally generated income and asset criteria. The result is that eligibility for Medicaid for individuals residing in different states, but with similar health conditions vary. If program eligilibity were driven by clinical health status, this would not be the case. Second, Medicaid programs across most states are almost universally located and administered by state human services (i.e., welfare) departments, not health or insurance departments as is typically the case for non-Medicaid populations. This policy decision is both symbolic and instrumental in keeping Medicaid distinct from non-Medicaid health care programs even though coordination for purposes of efficiency and effectiveness would be enhanced. Third, despite covering some 41 million persons, if one uses the official federal poverty level, 50% of the poor in America remain uncovered (Bodenheimer and Grumbach, 1998: 25). The official poverty level, referred to as the 100% federal poverty level (FPL), was $8050 for one person in 1998 (Department of Health and Human Services, 1999:1).

1.   Federal Eligibility: Categorically Needy

Due to the nature of federalism, eligibility to Medicaid may occur under a combination of federal and state requirements. Federal eligibility includes persons classified as *categorically needy* (CN). CN population are individuals eligible for several categorical federal programs: the Supplemental Security Income program, the (former) Aid to Families with Dependent Children (AFDC) program, or disabled and elderly persons below the federal poverty level.

Of these, the most complex and significant for Medicaid is the former AFDC program. Under the former AFDC program, a monthly cash assistance grant to families deemed poor by a state's poverty criteria carried an automatic federal requirement that the state provide Medicaid coverage to families receiving cash assistance.

In 1996, Congress passed the Personal Responsibility and Work Opportunity Reconciliation Act (PRWORA). Under PRWORA, AFDC was replaced with a new program called Temporary Aid to Needy Families (TANF). PROWRA effectively separated the linkage between cash assistance for children and the simultaneous issuance of Medicaid eligibility. To prevent states from severely restricting Medicaid enrollment, states were still required to maintain eligibility for Medicaid based on the 1996 income eligibility standards utilized in their state under the former AFDC program.

This new requirement maintains the current flexibility and related complexity and inequities in health care provision under Medicaid. To understand this point more completely it is necessary to understand how eligibility was determined under the former AFDC law in 1996. AFDC eligibility for Medicaid required the comparison of an individual's income and resources (e.g., bank account, stocks) with federally set income exemptions and disregards, then applied the remaining (countable) income to state determined income thresholds (*need standards*). Individuals then falling below a state's need standard became eligible for Medicaid.[1]

Once these AFDC federal criteria were met, each state then compared an

---

[1] *Federal Income and Resource Standards.* The total of income and resources (including exemptions listed below) could not exceed the resource standard of $1000. The following resources were exempted: the home and its contents; $1500 equity in one automobile; $1500 in funeral/burial agreements per person; one burial plot; trust funds where income from the fund is not available on demand; educational assistance; home produce; bona fide loans; nine-month housing exemption while family makes good faith effort to sell home; self-employment/business assets directly related to and essential for producing goods and services.

Income was divided into earned and unearned income. Additionally, under each of these categories there were exemptions, plus income that was not counted (i.e., disregards).

Earned Income Exemptions included: $30 plus 1/3 of income for four months; $30 for eight months; $90 work expense; child care $200 under age 2, child care $175 children over 2; other dependents $175; 100% of child's income under JPTA for six months, and 100% of child's income if child is student after six months.

Unearned Income Exemptions included: gifts less than or equal to $30 per person per quarter; first $50 of child support payment; bona fide loans; travel and training allowances; value of food stamp and WIC vouchers; payments for energy assistance; educational assistance and college work study; and unearned in-kind income.

individual's remaining income and resources, the countable income, to three need standards—a *state-specified need* standard, a 185% *gross income* test, and a *state payment standard*.

The state-determined need standard was the minimum dollar amount the state determined was necessary to provide for a family's living needs (adjusted for family size). By illustration, in 1996, New Hampshire's need standard was $2034 per month, while Delaware's was $338.

The 185% gross income test determined whether an individual's gross income exceed 185% of the above-noted state need standard. If the applicant's income exceeded 185% of the state's need standard, then AFDC and Medicaid were denied. New Hampshire's gross income standard would be $3763, and Delaware's would be $625.

The state payment standard was the amount of cash an individual could receive based on the net difference between their countable income (i.e., income minus the exemptions and disregards) and the state's payment standard. New Hampshire's standard was $550 and Delaware's was $338, equal to its need standard (Peller and Shaner, 1999:1–6).

In 1995, over 3 million children were eligible for Medicaid but were not enrolled in the program. As noted, AFDC income thresholds varied by states, independent of health status. This will change by the year 2002, when all children below the age of 19 whose families meet the federal 100% poverty threshold become uniformly eligible for Medicaid services across the United States. However, eligibility should not be confused with enrollment (Thompson, 1998:280–286).

The separation of Medicaid from welfare payments under the new welfare law PRWORA, may negatively alter even more the enrollment of children eligible for Medicaid. Data indicate that children in families not receiving cash assistance through welfare are much less likely to enroll in the Medicaid program. Indeed, in 1994, only 38% of eligible children under age 11 who did not receive cash assistance were enrolled in Medicaid. Alternatively, two-thirds of these children were uninsured, and half of these were totally without insurance. Critically, under PRWORA, children will probably not have health insurance coverage under Medicaid once their parents find employment. The reason, to repeat, is that low-wage employees are viewed as the nondeserving poor and typically do not have health insurance coverage.

The Supplemental Security Income program exists under Title XVI of the Social Security Act of 1935. This program, which provides monthly cash payments, has the following eligibility requirements: an individual must either be blind or have a medical condition, physical or mental impairment at a level prohibiting the individual from engaging in any substantial work; countable income below $484 a month for an individual, resources below $2000 for an individual; and be either a citizen, legal permanent resident of granted asylee (University of

Buffalo Libraries, 1998:1). As in other categories of welfare, the notion of limiting assistance only to the *deserving poor* is embodied in the SSI program through eligibility requirements based on one's ability to do substantial work. To reinforce this latter point, eligibility under SSI for children required that a child's impairment level had to be comparable to that of an adult relative to the substantial work criteria. This was liberalized under the United State Supreme Court's decision in *Sullivan* v. *Zebley* (493 U.S. 521, 1990).

The states are also required to provide Medicaid services to pregnant women at or below the official federal poverty level. Additionally, states at their discretion could provide Medicaid eligibility to pregnant women up to 185% of the federal poverty threshold, but on a sliding fee schedule. Under new federal regulations, states are permitted to provide coverage to this same cohort with eligibility income levels up to 185% of the federal poverty level (Kaiser Family Foundation, 1998b:6).

2. State Determined Eligibility: Medically Needy

States may provide Medicaid services to other citizens who have incurred catastrophic health care bills, and thereby reduced their relatively high incomes to the point where they meet the poverty income threshold set by their respective state. These populations termed *medically needy* (MN), are heavily represented by the disabled and nursing home populations. The Medicaid nursing home population constitutes approximately 50% of the total nursing home population in the United States (Halfon, 1996: 234).

Additional state eligibility for Medicaid coverage during the 1990s has been enabled by federal legislation. Chief among these are Title XXI of the Social Security Act, known as the Children's Health Insurance Program (CHIP), and various programs waiving or amending sections of the Medicaid program as specified in the original legislation of 1965. These waivers include Sections 1115 and 1915(a), 1915(b), and 1915(c) waivers. These will be discussed further later in this chapter.

To summarize these various conditions of eligibility, Table 1 provides a matrix of Medicaid eligibility criteria by demographic/clinical status by variations in poverty levels permitted across states. Aggregating across these criteria yields the numbers of persons served by the current Medicaid program (Table 2).

B. Financing Structure

1. Fiscal Federalism Plus Private Sector Subcontracting

As a component of fiscal federalism, Medicaid is a joint federal-state funded health care insurance program. During fiscal year 1998, total Medicaid expenditures approximated $165 billion. Of this total, $102 billion, or 62%, came from

Table 1 Summary of Medicaid Eligibility Criteria: Demographic and Clinical Status by Permissible State Variations in Poverty Levels

Category	State ranges as pct. of FPL	Mode(s)
Children in poverty:		
Ages covered:		
<6	133–185%	133%
6–15	100–185%	100%
16–20	≤100%	100%
All Title IV-E foster care children		
All Title IV-E adopted assistance children		
All children in welfare-to-work families		
Pregnant women	133–185%	133/185%
Supplemental Security	41–75%	
Income recipients		
Medically needy:	23–72%	Mean = 49.5%
(includes elderly in nursing homes)		

Source: Kaiser Family Foundation (1998d).

federal contributions; the remainder, $63 billion, or 38%, came from state contributions (Smith et al., 1998:129). Operationally, financing of the Medicaid program works as follows. Each state first determines the extent of state dollars it will expend on its deserving poor. The state's determination of expenditure level is a function of six components:

1. *Federally mandated* eligibility requirements (i.e., CN populations such as SSI)
2. The *need standard* (i.e., the state's poverty threshold or floor), below which persons may be considered eligible

Table 2 Medicaid Beneficiaries by Enrollment Group

Eligibility group	Number	Percent
Children <21 years	21,300,000	52%
Adults ages 21–64	9,200,000	22
Blind and disabled	6,700,000	16
Elderly (65+)	4,100,000	10
Total	41,300,000	100%

Source: Kaiser Family Foundation (1998a).

3. Expansion of access to persons beyond the floor, as permitted by federal enabling legislation
4. The *categories* of medical services provided beyond the 11 core service categories mandated by the federal government
5. The levels (or limits) of service units to be provided within each medical service category
6. The payment levels made to health care providers for the units of services rendered.

Once states calculate their respective dollar expenditure levels, the federal government calculates the per capita income for each state and ranks the states inversely, based on their relative per capita income. Federal dollar matching funds are then allocated to each state. The federal matching amount, referred to as the Federal Matching Assistance Percentage (FMAP), is provided on a sliding scale percentage ranging approximately from 50% to 83% (Boyd, 1998, p. 64). Poorer states receive the higher levels of FMAP. By illustration, Ohio, a wealthy state, estimates its fiscal year Medicaid expenditures will total $8 billion. Since it is a wealthy state, its FMAP is close to 50%. In this instance, Ohio taxpayers will contribute $4 billion, with the federal government providing the residual $4 billion. By contrast, Arkansas, a poor state, will spend $400 million on Medicaid; Arkansas' FMAP is 80%. Therefore, the federal government contributes 80% of $400 million, or $320 million, and the state taxpayers finance the remaining $80 million. In some states, counties share the state's share of the Medicaid budgetary liability with the state. Parenthetically, administrative costs of Medicaid, including computer upgrades and software systems, are supported almost entirely by the federal government.

States contract with health care providers to deliver health services to Medicaid eligible populations. States pay health care providers *directly* from the combined revenues received from their respective federal and state contributions. Typically, reimbursement of providers is not under the aegis of the county welfare departments. Instead, health providers generally submit bills to the state human services/welfare department, which reimburses providers directly.

C. Organization of Service Delivery

The federal government requires each state to submit a plan for administering its Medicaid program. The plan, in addition to specifying eligibility and financial arrangements between providers and the state, requires extensive information on the administration and management operations a state plans to implement. Almost all states administer their Medicaid programs through their state welfare/human services departments. Few states have Medicaid programs administered by state health departments or insurance departments.

State-determined eligibility requirements are implemented by county welfare/human services offices. At the county level, caseworkers process incoming persons according to federal and state eligibility criteria, as well as beginning a recertification of eligibility process on a monthly or quarterly basis.

In turn, state welfare departments contract with health care providers, physicians/physician groups, hospitals, nursing homes, laboratories, and increasingly, managed care organizations (MCOs) to provide services to Medicaid-eligible persons. The providers with whom Medicaid contracts are not a unique group providing health services to Medicaid enrollees only. They are in fact the same providers treating the general population and receiving reimbursement from private sector insurance plans and private pay patients.

When the Medicaid program was initially constructed in 1966, Medicaid emulated the private sector provision of health care. Specifically, there was a structural reliance on the same cohort of health care providers and payment mechanisms as existed in the private sector. This meant that the nature of service delivery in Medicaid emulated the contractual and market-based relationships between health care providers and insurance firms in the non-Medicaid population. The only difference was that given the inability of Medicaid eligibles to pay premiums, it was left to the *state*, acting as the insurer/payer of health care services to reimburse health care providers. This relationship is present today. Figure 1 depicts the intergovernmental administrative structure of the Medicaid programs in the United States.

Cementing the federal, state, and private sector together under Medicaid

Figure 1 Intergovernmental Administrative Structure of Medicaid Program(s)

Medicaid: Title XIX; Social Security Act of 1935
↓
Department of Health and Human Services (DHHS)
Health Care Financing Administration (HCFA)
↓
State departments of human services
County departments of human services
↓
Private/public subcontractors
|

MCOs	Physicians	Hospitals	Nursing homes	Home health agencies	Labs	Pharmacies

↓
Medicaid-eligible citizens

is the flow of payments (reimbursement). Providers generate a bill which is in turn submitted to the respective state human services department. This is termed *retrospective reimbursement*. In the case of managed care organizations, the state enters into contracts with MCOs and purchases a service plan from particular providers to provide a predetermined set of services to eligible individuals for a fixed period of time, at a predetermined and fixed annual dollar amounts.[2] In either case, state human services departments pay providers for services rendered.

III. PARALLEL PROBLEMS RESULTING FROM THE CURRENT POLICY STRUCTURE

Medicaid is imbedded in the institutional structure of private sector health care policy. As such, the most critical problems affecting Medicaid parallel those of the private sector health care system. These problems are threefold: *expanding access* to health insurance coverage—an issue of eligibility; containing *spiraling health care expenditures—an issue of financing structure*; and restructuring health care delivery systems to find more effective treatment arrangements and assure *quality of service* emanating from the current organization of service delivery (Aaron, 1991:1–3).

A. Eligibility Determination

Medicaid enrollment from the early 1990s rose quickly, from some 29 million persons through 1995 to some 42 million persons (Kaiser Family Foundation, 1998a:5). This growth has been attributable to expanded coverage to low-income pregnant women and young children, and increases in the numbers of blind and disabled beneficiaries. Among the disabled there has been an increase in the AIDS population (Cunningham et al., 1996:204–205), actions expanding the SSI eligibility for disabled children (*Sullivan v. Zebley*), and demographic increases in the number of aged dependent persons (Weissert, 1985:88–89).

---

[2] Briefly, MCOs take on various organizational forms and may be viewed on a continuum. At one end of the continuum is case management or primary care case management (PCCM). Here the state contracts with a given provider (usually a physician) who for a set fee acts as the initial gatekeeper and referral agent to specialized care or services for any Medicaid eligible (Hurley and Freund, 1993:10–16). At the other end of the continuum are Health Maintenance Organizations (HMOs). This latter form of MCO is generally organized by insurance companies, although providers may organize them as well. Groups of physicians, hospitals, labs, indeed an entire network of providers are contracted with to provide services for all eligibles in the HMO on a set, predetermined monthly/yearly fee. Within the network, HMOs may be organized as employees in a single or multiple facility, or as a group of providers (e.g., a physician group practice in internal medicine) who then contract with the insurance company.

This is not to say that eligibility for Medicaid is not still constrained. Despite federal enabling legislation and cost sharing, Medicaid does not cover all of the poor. Less than one-half of all persons below 150% of the federal poverty level, the near-poor, are covered (Bodenheimer and Grumbach, 1998:29). In its analysis of children's eligibility under Medicaid, estimates of uninsured children in the United States ranged from 7.6 million to 10.6 million in 1995. More than half of these children lived in homes with incomes below 200% of the federal poverty level (Ullman et al., 1998: 7).

The Urban Institute has classified states into three classes of coverage with respect to children: *broad-coverage, low-coverage*, and *middle-of-the-road* states (Bruen and Ullman, 1999:2–3). *Broad-coverage* states have income and age thresholds for eligibility much higher than Medicaid minimum standards. States in this category are Minnesota, Rhode Island, Tennessee, Vermont and Washington. *Low-coverage* states provide Medicaid coverage that complies with federal standards, but offer little or no coverage beyond that point. These states are Alabama, Arkansas, Colorado, Idaho, Illinois, Indiana, Louisiana, Montana, Nevada, Ohio, Oklahoma, and Wyoming. Several of these latter states are seeking to expand coverage to children. Another group of states offer benefits that barely exceed the minimum federal mandated levels. These states are Arizona, Iowa, Mississippi, Nebraska, Oklahoma, South Carolina, Texas, and the District of Columbia. The remainder of the states are somewhere in between with varying levels of eligibility (Bruen and Ullman, 1999:2–3).

Moreover, despite an improving economy during the 1990s, employer-sponsored health insurance has continued to decrease (U.S. General Accounting Office, 1997). Were it not for this growth in the economy during the decade of the 1990s, Medicaid enrollment would have been much greater.

The combination of these factors are the reasons why access to health insurance coverage for the poor has been declining and has placed additional pressure on state Medicaid programs (Anderson and Davidson, 1996:26–27, 31). It is *not*, as some authors have posited, the result of intentional state strategies to throw people off the Medicaid rolls (Leichter, 1997:19–20). Table 3 displays the result of the growth in Medicaid enrollees resulting from federal and state enabling legislation.

Table 3 demonstrates that the federal and state governments have expanded coverage to an additional 12 million persons in 6 years. The decreasing percentages during this same period is expected to reverse due to shifts in population demographics among the elderly and periodic downturns in the economy.

These figures do not include the expected increases in coverage by the year 2002, when all children under the 100% federal poverty level will be included under Medicaid. If all children who were eligible to enroll were in fact enrolled by the states, some 3 million children would be added to the Medicaid program (Thompson, 1998:280–281).

Table 3 Medicaid Enrollee Growth by
Enrollment Group 1990–96

Year	Millions	% annual increase
1990	28.9	—
1991	32.3	12
1992	35.8	11
1993	38.8	8
1994	40.9	5
1995	41.7	2
1996	41.3	−1

Source: Kaiser Family Foundation (1995a).

Another impending problem with Medicaid will come from growth in the numbers of elderly, medically dependent citizens requiring institutionalization. Demographic projections for this group have been done by Weissert. Weissert predicted that the institutionalized elderly in America will jump from 4.7 million persons in 1985 to 6.3 million in 2000 (Weissert, 1985:89). These numbers do not include Weissert's estimates of the noninstitutionalized dependent elderly. These elderly will not only be more numerous, but due to medical advances will live longer. The implications of this for Medicaid financing and service provision are profound. With elderly growth rates not peaking until the year 2030, failure to address this cohort's needs could be catastrophic. At issue here is the necessity of providing chronic long-term care services, whether in the home, congregate home sites, assisted-living sites, or nursing homes.

For state Medicaid agencies, the combination of these factors results in the Medicaid program bearing the burden for providing health care for the indigent almost exclusively by itself. This is despite the fact that demographic shifts, income disparities, and the overall costs of medical service provision are driven by forces common to all health care segments in the United States. Yet Medicaid, structurally separated from other health programs through its designation as a welfare program, has borne the brunt of financing health care for the needy almost exclusively. This is a subject to which we now turn.

B. Financing Structure

In the financing of Medicaid the central problem faced by the states has been escalating pressures on state budgets. These pressures have been driven by three factors: contradictory health legislation inherent in federalism; the general rise in health care inflation; and the open-ended nature of the Medicaid program.

1. Contradictory Health Legislation Under Federalism

Federalism has created contradictory sets of problems for state Medicaid programs. For example, enabling federal legislation has mandated and permitted expansion. Other legislation embedded in federalism has prevented states from obtaining financial support to expand coverage for persons who are uninsured (Spitz, 1998:153). The result is these persons typically find their way to the Medicaid roles.

In 1974, Congress passed the Employee Retirement Income Security Act (ERISA). ERISA was supported by two powerful constituencies—multistate companies and labor unions. The original intent of ERISA was to encourage employer pension plans. Moreover, companies deciding to self-insure, rather than use insurance companies, were exempted from all taxes and regulations governing health insurance in a given state. Under ERISA, self-insured companies were required to establish funds to pay health benefits. Monies in these funds were invested and benefits were paid from the interest. Companies and unions favored ERISA's federal preemption of state regulation because any health contracts negotiated would not be susceptible to state by state manipulation (Fox, 1997:39–41; Well et al., 1998:163).

Despite its original intent, companies discovered that by self-insuring they could not only avoid state regulation regarding minimal coverage benefits for their employees, but they would also be exempted from making state-mandated contributions to help finance care for uninsured workers. This would not have presented a budgetary problem for states, except for one seldom addressed fact: some 40% of all privately employed persons are in now self-insured company health plans (Spitz, 1998:153).

With ERISA, most states have been left with two options for providing health care to the uninsured: insurance reform for non-ERISA plans, and Medicaid. Insurance reform efforts that have been tried by states to expand eligibility, such as subsidizing insurance, risk pools, and community rating, have failed to expand coverage (Sloan and Conover, 1998:287–289). The result is that the burden of financing of health care for the uninsured (employed or not) falls on state Medicaid programs—the result of federalism in health care.

2. Inflation in Health Care

In addition to expanded eligibility, the expenditure growth in Medicaid during the 1990s was attributable to the general rise in medical inflation. As measured by the medical component of the Consumers Price Index (CPI-Medical), medical care inflation during the decade has run consistently at an average of double the rate of inflation in the general economy. This was so even when inflation was decreasing, as it has during this past decade. When general inflation in 1990–91 was 4.2%, the rate of medical care inflation was 8.7%. In 1992–93, when general inflation was 3%, medical care inflation ran 5.9%. During 1998–99, when there was almost no general inflation in the economy (1%), the rate of medical care inflation was 3% (Rice, 1996:71; Bureau of Labor Statistics, 1999:1, 2).

3. Open-Ended Fiscal Federalism

The combination of eligibility determination, contradictory legislation, and medical inflation has resulted in ever-increasing expenditures for the Medicaid program at the federal and state levels. While the rate of growth has diminished, the absolute dollar magnitude has not and will not. The overall level of Medicaid expenditure growth from 1990 through 1996 went from $70.6 billion to approximately $156 billion (Kaiser Family Foundation, 1998a:5).

The percentage distribution of these funds in 1996, in descending order, were as follows: nursing homes received 20% of all funds; inpatient hospitals 18%; physicians (outpatient) 13%; payments to MCOs totaled and home health care agencies were 8% each; and the mentally retarded in intermediate care facilities was 6%, as was the expenditure for pharmaceuticals. An additional 10% went to payments to hospitals for taking care of excessive numbers of indigent through Disproportionate Share Payments (DSH).[3] Expenditures for overall administration of the Medicaid program totaled 4% (Kaiser Family Foundation, 1998a:3).

Expenditure levels in the Medicaid program have been troubling for state budget policy executives. In the private sector, pressures on expenditure growth are felt initially through insurance premium rises on private employers. In the public sector, this pressure is seen on the state budgets. The result has been that Medicaid currently constitutes the single largest expenditure component in virtually every state budget, averaging some 20.4%. While Wyoming, a rural, low-population state spent only 8% of its budget on Medicaid, Louisiana, a poor state, spent 38%. The net effect of these levels of expenditures on state budgets is to crowd out spending on other funding necessities, especially during periods of economic downturn (Kaiser Commission on the Future of Medicaid, 1995e).

During the later 1990s, Medicaid expenditure rates have slowed. Reasons for the slowdown include (1) lower rates of enrollment growth because of decreases in the absolute number of eligibles; (2) lower rates of unemployment due to an improved economy resulting in fewer persons needing assistance; and (3) mandated restrictions on DSH payments (Kaiser Family Foundation, 1998c:5).

Despite this, projections for Medicaid spending for the years 1998 and 2000 (in real dollars) will increase to $166 billion and $203 billion, respectively. This

---

[3] Disproportionate Share Hospital Payments. Medicaid hospitals providing disproportionately higher levels of services to Medicaid beneficiaries receive additional revenues form the state Medicaid program. Funds come from the federal and state governments. This expenditure category has been the source of state-based illegalities during the 1990s.

translates into Medicaid expenditures increasing to 8% for the federal government and 7% for the state governments *annually* in each of the three years from 1998 to 2000 (Smith et al., 1998:129). The Urban Institute estimates that despite recent slowdown, spending will increase by 7.5% *per year* until 2002 (Kaiser Family Foundation, September, 1998c:5).

A related fiscal problem is that of redistribution across the states. The Medicaid program is intended to be highly redistributive across the states from the input side, through the utilization of the FMAP. However, the precise amount of redistribution is another matter. Because states have wide flexibility in their eligibility and financing decisions, the true extent of redistribution across the United States is not known. The potential for redistribution is constrained by the fact that five states alone consume 41% of all Medicaid spending in the United States. New York spends 15% of the U.S. total, California spends 11%, Texas 6%, Pennsylvania 5%, and Ohio 4% (Kaiser Family Foundation, 1998e).

There is a final financial problem looming on the horizon for Medicaid—an intergenerational problem driven by the demographic composition among the poor. This is already evident in the current distribution of Medicaid expenditures by age cohort, which is anything but proportional to enrollees. While children of the poor constitute slightly over one half of all Medicaid eligibles, they only receive 16% of all Medicaid dollars. By contrast, the elderly and disabled, comprising slightly less than 25% of the Medicaid-eligible population, account for almost two-thirds of Medicaid expenditures. Most of these funds are committed to long-term care services, predominantly nursing homes (Kaiser Family Foundation, 1998a:2).

The future demographic composition of Medicaid eligibles will include larger numbers of elderly persons. It is questionable whether MCOs will save as much money as projected. The majority of persons in MCOs enrolled by the states have been children and young adults. Yet the elderly and disabled, the most expensive patients to treat, have with the exception of limited demonstration programs been exempted from enrolling in MCOs (Holahan et al., 1998:43, 59–60). The net effect is projected increased expenditures and heightened competition for funding between elderly poor and the young poor. The intergenerational pressure among the ranks of the *deserving poor* will constitute a major policy issue during the first quarter of the 21st century.

The future of Medicaid's capacity to finance health care does not bode well. Several proposals now before Congress seek to block grant Medicaid (Twentieth Century Fund, 1999:1). Should the Medicaid program be block-granted and capped, the financial implications of such proposals for the states would be profound. The range of projected dollar losses in FMAP funds to the states are $24 billion in 1999, $33 billion in 2000, and $43 billion in 2001 (Mann and Kogan, 1995:2). Dollar losses to states of this magnitude would need to be made up through some combination of service cuts, eligibility cuts, reduction in reimbursement rates, reorganization of service delivery arrangements, and/or increased pressures on state tax coffers.

C. Organization of Service Delivery

The delivery of Medicaid services relies on the same set of health care providers delivering services to the non-Medicaid population. Despite this single set of providers, service delivery under Medicaid has resulted in (1) a *two-market system*, where providers are often unwilling to serve Medicaid populations, and (2) quality of care delivered to Medicaid patients not being effectively regulated (Hurley and Freund, 1993:26).

1. The Two-Market System in Medicaid

The decision to utilize the same health care providers treating the general population has presented Medicaid with a serious problem of service deficits and provider attrition. The driving forces behind this are twofold: (1) most health care providers are embedded in the context of a market approach to medicine; and (2) many health care providers cannot relate to and often disapprove of the behaviors of their Medicaid clients.

As to markets, it is easily demonstrated that health care providers follow insurance markets. Since insurance for health care is structurally related to one's position in the economy, lucrative insurance markets and providers tend to be in geographic areas where employment is middle class or above, and where individuals receive coverage through their employers.

One of the negative outcomes of this rational market response is a geographic maldistribution of Medicaid providers. This is more so the case under managed care. A review of managed care in 50 states as late as 1997 reported that less than 12% of rural counties were covered by fully capitated managed care programs, compared to almost 29% in urbanized counties (Slifkin et al., 1998: 219). Physicians and other providers compete to find population densities of the most lucrative payers and customers.

Known as the *two-market economic demand model*, providers are viewed as operating in a price-setting market in which they set fees, and simultaneously operating in a price-taking market in which they accept predetermined fees as payment in full (Perloff et al., 1997:145). Since Medicaid typically reimburses at rates far below those of other payers, Medicaid is the least preferable payer for providers. Therefore, physicians, as a class of providers, tend to have lower percentages of Medicaid enrollees as patients, even within a given metropolitan area (Perloff et al., 1997: 149).

It is therefore not uncommon to see a subset of physicians who are unable to access the more lucrative insurance markets servicing the Medicaid market. By illustration, Medicaid physicians tend to have the following characteristics: they are primarily African-American or Asian; are foreign medical school graduates; are not board certified; and have their practices in geographic areas where Medicaid eligibles reside (Perloff et al., 1997: 153–155).

A related issue is the health behavior and utilization patterns of the Medicaid enrollees. From the perspective of the providers, most of whom are highly educated and grew up in middle- to upper-middle-class families, dealing with clients not sharing similar value orientations to health care is difficult. The resulting differences in expectations surrounding health behaviors have added to commonly noted problems of access to Medicaid eligibles (Perloff et al., 1997: 142–157; Rowland and Salganicoff, 1994: 550–552). The empirical evidence of underutilization of health services by the poor is a case in point. By illustration, pregnant women under Medicaid tend to delay or not keep obstetrical appointments in contrast to those with private insurance (Bodenheimer and Grumbach, 1998:30). This is so despite their having health insurance through Medicaid. The reasons for underutilization of health services is complex. Yet it is clear that not all of the burden on health outcomes of the poor rests with providers or the Medicaid program.

Nonetheless, a significant portion of problems in service delivery for Medicaid eligibles are attributable to the manner in which the organization of service delivery has been constructed. This has serious implications for the quality of care delivered to Medicaid patients.

2. Problems in Quality of Care

As noted, one of the major changes in the states' control of service delivery has been the movement toward managed care by state Medicaid agencies. As state Medicaid agencies have become purchasers of health care, they, like health care purchasers in the private sector, are beginning to inquire as to the value of the produce they are receiving for their money. In contemporary health care, value for money translates as quality in the control of service delivery.

The concerns with quality were driven in large part by an ever-growing body of literature examining the relative efficacy of different medical treatments (Aday et al., 1993:61–66). In addition to problems with the efficacy of treatment, evidence was building that *organizational structure* resulted in variances both in medical practices and medical outcomes for patients. Despite the once sacrosanct view that the physician always knows best, data indicated that across solo practices, physicians often treat patients with similar maladies and similar acuity levels, with different procedures (Roos and Roos, 1994:231–252). The problem is similar within smaller group practices and managed care organizations, many of which have developed their own treatment protocols.

Even the size and experience of the organization was found to be significant for patient outcomes. It is empirically demonstrated that lower mortality rates are associated with larger institutions (i.e., hospitals) with greater experience in performing certain procedures (Luft et al., 1990). In 1990, New York State's Department of Health published mortality figures that were risk adjusted for coronary artery bypass graft surgery (CABGS) by hospital. In 1992 the same data were published for cardiac surgeons practicing in the state (Bodenheimer and Grumbach, 1998:205). The results of the findings were that 27 physicians who performed low numbers of CABGS and who had high (risk-adjusted) mortalities, stopped performing these procedures. In four years, risk-adjusted mortality dropped by 41% in New York (Bodenheimer and Grumbach, 1998:204).

Organizational structure, particularly with regard to MCOs, was also found to affect outcomes for specific populations. While Arizona's statewide Medicaid managed care program found no major differences in outcomes compared to private insurance plans for patients with minor/acute problems, this was not true for children or other persons with multiple handicaps or needs, such as the mentally ill (Birenbaum, 1997:52, 58–59). Indeed, the combined data over the past decade reinforce the finding that outcomes for persons with higher levels of acuity, whether children or the elderly, indicates a less than sanguine picture for individuals in managed care (Birenbaum, 1997:68–69).

In sum, a portion of the variance in patient outcomes is associated with differences in clinical practices (Aday et al., 1993:59). Given these findings, it is clear how quality becomes linked to control over service delivery. Quality of care is a function of policy structure.

The concern with quality of care for Medicaid managed care has been compounded for two reasons: (1) capitation provides incentives to decrease care, and (2) the Medicaid population has been shown to be highly vulnerable due to illiteracy, inadequate social supports, poor nutrition, and problems with transportation and communication. As such, Medicaid beneficiaries generally have more trouble negotiating complex bureaucratic arrangements (Landon et al., 1998:211).

IV. STATE ADMINISTRATIVE REFORMS

During the decade of the 1990s, states have adopted administrative reforms in response to the problems that have been discussed. These administrative reforms corresponding to each of the three dimensions of policy structure are summarized in Table 4.

A. Eligibility Determination

The primary method states have utilized to expand access to health care for their indigent populations has been to increase insurance coverage for the uninsured.

Table 4 Administrative Reforms in the States: Dimensions of Policy Structure

Dimension I: Eligibility Determination
  (1) Expansion of coverage using enabling legislation
Dimension II: Financing Structure
  (2) Reorganization of insurer to provider reimbursement mechanisms managed care
       for Medicaid clients
Dimension III: Organization of Service Delivery
  (3) Utilization of waivers
  (4) Implementing Title XXI, Children's Health Plan
  (5) Reorganization of the providers and Medicaid eligibles into Medicaid managed
       care organizations
  (6) Assuring quality of care: increased regulation and reporting

States' efforts have primarily been through the use of federal enabling legislation, specifically, Medicaid Waivers: *Section 1115* and *1915b* and *1915c* waivers; the *Balanced Budget Act* of 1997; and *Title XXI*—the Children's Health Insurance Program (CHIP).

1. Medicaid Waiver Options: Section 1115

Medicaid Section 1115 waivers are *statewide demonstration* projects aimed at reconfiguring the policy structure of a state's Medicaid program. As such, Medicaid 1115 waivers permit a state to change the mix of eligibility, financing, and control of service delivery not previously covered or specified under the original federal Title XIX rules. Each demonstration waiver can last for up to five years and as demonstration projects, requires the establishment of formal control groups and external evaluations. At the end of that period, states and the federal government make a decision as to whether to retain the 1115 demonstration waiver beyond the five-year period, or to include it as a permanent shift in a state's Medicaid program.

The Section 1115 waiver requirements under Title XIX, permit states to undertake changes in the following seven categories:

  1. *Statewideness*: permits variations across different geographic areas of a state. By illustration, Ohio has Section 1115 waivers for 17 of its 88 counties; Alabama's waiver covers only one county (Mobile), and Illinois' waiver is statewide (Health care Financing Administration Fact Sheet, 1999:1)

  2. *Comparability*: allows variation in benefit structure and or eligibility across groups

  3. *Eligibility*: permits states to revise Medicaid eligibility and standards

4. *Freedom of choice*: allows restrictions on Medicaid enrollees in the selection of providers and permits states to require mandatory enrollment in managed care plans
5. *Medicaid managed care organization (MMCO)*: permits states to contract with MCOs that have Medicaid enrollments beyond the 75%/25% mix; may limit times within the year when Medicaid enrollees may withdraw from a given MMCO to once per year
6. *Reimbursement*: allows changes in Medicaid payment requirements from retrospective fee for service to prospective and capitated
7. *Benefits*: allows state to expand benefits beyond those traditionally covered under Medicaid (American Public Human Services Association, 1999b:1)

All waivers to date have included expansion in eligible populations under the 1996 AFDC and AFDC-related criteria. Except for the most recent 1115 waivers, all 1115 waivers have included expansions to the SSI-related elderly and disabled beneficiaries. Practically every state has requested a waiver of the 75/25 Medicaid rule to expand utilization of MCOs exclusively for Medicaid clients. This is no longer necessary because the 75/25 requirement was eliminated under the Balanced Budget Amendment of 1997 (Health Care Financing Administration, 1999:3). Finally, there is every expectation that health outcomes for 1115 waivers will be examined closely as there is very little experience with elderly and disabled persons in managed care (America Public Human Services Organization, 1999b:2) (Table 5).

2. Medicaid Waiver Options: Section 1915(b)

Section 1915(b) of the Title XIX of the Social Security Act is designed to permit states to restructure service delivery operations. Specifically, Section 1915(b) waivers limit Medicaid enrollees' freedom of choice by permitting states to require their enrollees to obtain their health care from a single provider or health

Table 5 Status of Section 1115 Waivers: December 1997

Submitted:	29	
Withdrawn		1 (KS)
Under review	8	
Approved:	19	
Implemented		16
Denied		2 (MO, LA)

Source: Kaiser Family Foundation (1998f).

plan. Section 1915(b) waivers are intended to both save money for the state through rationing of Medicaid services and provide continuity of care to enrolled Medicaid eligibles.

Section 1915(b) service delivery options are generally of two types, a Primary Care Case Manager (PCCM) or a Health Maintenance Organization (HMO), although permutations exist. However, 1915(b) waivers differ from 1115 waivers in three ways: (1) application for a 1915(b) waiver must be submitted to the Health Care Financing Administration (HCFA); (2) 1915(b) waivers may be employed on a statewide basis or restricted to a few counties; and (3) 1915(b) waivers are not demonstration programs and therefore do not require control groups and external evaluations. The 1915(b) waivers are granted for a period of two years, with the possibility of a two-year extension. In short, the relative attractiveness of 1915(b) waivers is that they permit states to explore different policy structures in a limited setting, before making comprehensive changes to their Medicaid programs.

Section 1915(b) is composed of four subsections: (1) a *Freedom of Choice* section permits states to require beneficiaries to choose a primary care provider; (2) *an Enrollment Brokers* section allows states to contract with organizations assist Medicaid eligibles in selecting from competing HMOs; (3) an *Expanded Care Through Savings section* permits states to utilize any savings to be spent on expanded services for its current Medicaid eligibles; and (4) a *Selective Contracting* subsection permits states to selectively issue contracts only to vendors the state has deemed effective or efficient in the delivery of services.[4] Since 1993, 35 states have implemented a total of 63 Section 1915(b) waivers (American Public Human Services Association, 1999c:2).

3. Medicaid Waiver Options: Section 1915(c)

As with the Section 1915(b) waiver program, Section 1915(c) waivers are designed to reconfigure the policy structure of the Medicaid program. The primary

---

[4] Section 1915(b) is composed of four subsections: (1) *Freedom of Choice*: Section 1915(b)(1) permits states to require all Medicaid enrollees to choose a primary care case manager (PCCM), generally a physician acting as a gatekeeper and traffic cop, or Medicaid eligibles may select an HMO. Section 1915(b) waivers limit freedom of choice by allowing states to require beneficiaries to choose a primary care provider and continue with that provider for more than one month (Birenbaum, 1997: 53). (2) *Enrollment Brokers*: Subsection 1915(b)(2) permits localities to act as brokers in assisting Medicaid eligibles in selecting from competing single provider health plans, normally competing HMOs. States may contract with organizations to act as local enrollment brokers. (3) *Expanded Care Through Savings*: Subsection 1915(b)(3) permits states to utilize any savings obtained from Subsections 1915(b)(1) and (2), savings from shifting the control of service delivery to managed care, to be spent on expanded services for its current Medicaid eligibles. (4) *Selective Contracting*: Subsection 1915(b)(4) permits states to utilize a subset of health care vendors (i.e., providers) who meet the general provider eligibility rules under the Medicaid program. Under subsection 1915(b)(4)

objective of this waiver is to shift the control of service delivery for the elderly requiring long term care, away from nursing homes and toward community-based providers. Referred to as *home and community based waivers*, the service mix under 1915c waivers typically consists of case management, assessment, and primary and ancillary health services to the homebound elderly.

The genesis of this waiver program was driven by both budgetary concerns associated with nursing home costs and humanitarian considerations of keeping the elderly in their own homes. From the inception of Medicaid in 1965 until the Reagan presidency in 1981, the dominant form of long-term care was institutionalization, primarily in nursing homes. Medicaid as originally structured created an institutional bias toward expensive nursing home care. Yet most elderly and nonelderly are chronically ill and do not require higher and integrated levels of health care. Health care could be provided less expensively in these elderly person's own homes or in community-based facilities such as assisted-living complexes than in nursing homes. Home care could be provided by home health agencies funded by Medicare. Ancillary services such as health assessment and referral, homemaker and chore services, minor home repair, and home-delivered meals could be provided and funded through Title III of the Older Americans Act, and Title XX of the Social Security Act of 1935, as amended.

The Reagan Administration, eager to reduce expenditures for social services, helped to push through the Omnibus and Budget Reconciliation Act of 1981 (OBRA 81). OBRA 81 permitted states to apply for two types of waivers for their Medicaid population. These waivers were designated as Section 2176 or 1915c and permitted states to provide home based community services rather than institutionalized services for persons requiring long term care (Thompson, 1998:25).[5]

1915c waivers are granted by HCFA for three years initially, with continuous five-year renewals. These waivers were typically applied to specific segments of the Medicaid-eligible population, and could be applied in selected geographic areas (Thompson, 1998:26).[6] States did not automatically receive FMAP for their

states may selectively issue contracts only to vendors the state has deemed effective or efficient in the delivery of services.

[5] Section 2176 of OBRA 81 created section 1915c of the Social Security Act 5.

[6] (1) *Statewideness waiver*: 1915c waivers may be created in only certain geographic regions. (2) *Service flexibility* in both levels of services and categories of services: (a) under 1915c categories of required Medicaid services (e.g., inpatient hospital) previously required to be delivered in every county of a state, if that state offered such categories of service, may vary in levels and duration provided to Medicaid eligibles; and (b) *provision of ancillary social services* critical to maintaining persons in their homes, including case management, homemaker services, home health care, personal care, adult day care, minor home repair, and respite care. (3) *Eligibility*: more liberal financial eligibility requirements comparable to those utilized for persons being placed in nursing homes. APSHA maintains an updated database of all current and pending 1915c waivers (i.e., regular and model).

home and community-based waivers. States had to make special application to the Secretary of Health and Human Services for each of the specific programs they wished to implement. A primary stipulation of any application was that any 1915(c) waiver must demonstrate that home and community-based services would be no more expensive than the current level of Medicaid spending for nursing home care. However, the Secretary of DHHS may waive several significant normal Medicaid rules relating to statewideness, services, and eligibility. Under contract to HCFA, the American Public Human Services Association (APHSA) maintains a data base on home and community-based waiver programs. As of 1996, there were 216 home and community-based waiver programs across the United States (American Public Human Services Association, 1999d:2–3).

4. Title XXI: Children's Health Insurance Program (CHIP)

The Balanced Budget Act of 1997 provided $24 billion in federal funds over the next five years for expansion of children's health care coverage. The states' share of the Children's Health Insurance Program (CHIP) accounts for over $20 billion of these funds. Established as Title XXI of the Social Security Act, this program entitled states to block grants intended to help create and expand insurance programs for children in low-income families (Bruen and Ullman, 1999:1). Funds are allocated to each state based on its share of the nation's uninsured children whose family incomes are below 200% of the federal poverty level and allow for adjustments for differences in health care costs across states. While the CHIP funds may be used for children in families up to 200% of the FPL, exceptions are made for states that already increased their eligibility levels beyond 150% of poverty prior to CHIP. These latter states may raise their eligibility thresholds another 50% above their existing Medicaid thresholds (Ullman et al., 1998:4). Title XXI is a block grant program to the states offering *enhanced cost sharing* beyond that paid by the federal government to the states under Medicaid. This cost sharing essentially reduces the state's additional matching requirement by 30% (Mann and Guyer, 1997:4–5; Ullman et al., 1998:2–3).

States may elect to utilize the block grant to add to, but not subsidize, their existing Medicaid program. Conversely, states may expand health care to children through another existing non-Medicaid program, or begin a new program. In the event of selecting a new program, states are free to use an existing state agency or contract with a private organization. Whatever option states select, there is the requirement that if states do expand their existing Medicaid program, they may not do so by lowering eligibility levels for Medicaid (Ullman and Bruen, 1999:3).

As of July 1996, there were 219 1915c waivers programs in place across the states (American Public Human Services Association, 1999d:1–4).

States must also coordinate any enrollees eligible for Medicaid into Medicaid or any other existing health care programs prior to utilizing CHIP funds for expansion (Mann and Guyer, 1997:3–4). In essence, then, CHIP provides states with the flexibility and encouragement to expand coverage for children, but not to use those funds to supplant existing Medicaid budgetary outlays.

As of February 1999, 53 Medicaid programs have expanded eligibility beyond the required minimum levels through the CHIP program. Twenty-eight states have expanded their Medicaid programs, 15 states have created exclusive Title XXI programs, and 10 states have developed combination programs (American Public Human Services Association 1999a:1; ASTHO, 1999:1–2).

B. Financing Structure

Despite the increase in absolute expenditure levels on a yearly basis during the 1990s, states have had little incentive of late to initiate reforms to control spending. In part this is attributable to an overall Medicaid spending *rate* decline since 1992, combined with a robust national economy during most of the decade. After Medicaid expenditure increases that averaged an incredible 27% per year between 1990 and 1992, Medicaid spending rates fell to approximately 9% to 10% from 1992 through 1995, a decrease of two-thirds. From 1995 through 1997, it appears the rate of spending growth decreased even further, to an average of 2.3% per year (Holahan et al., 1998:1).

This reduction in the rate of spending has been attributable to three reasons: (1) an enormous decrease in the Disproportionate Share Payments (DSH) due to federal limitations on cost sharing, (2) decreases in the rate of medical care inflation which helped to decrase expenditures per beneficiary; and (3) a slowdown in the rates of new Medicaid enrollees (Holahan et al., 1998:2; Boyd, 1998:62).

Despite the slowdown in the rate of expenditure growth, medical care utilization has increased, resulting in absolute dollar expenditures also increasing. In 1990 total Medicaid expenditures were $73.7 billion, but by 1996 grew to $161 billion (Holahan et al., 1998:1–2).

Aside from enrolling more Medicaid persons in MCOs, major state efforts to decrease expenditures are focused in two areas: long-term care, and prospective payments for ambulatory care for non-MCO Medicaid enrollees. In long-term care, states are experimenting with two strategies. First, an increased reliance on privatization. The major thrust would be through expanding the insurance market for long-term care to help offset Medicaid expenditures (Wiener, 1998:209). Such an expansion would require tax incentives either at the state or federal level or both. A second strategy for controlling long-term care costs would be reducing per diem payments to nursing homes. The primary tactic here relies on a federal initiative to develop a prospective payment system for nursing homes. Referred to as *Resource Utilization Groups III* (RUGs), system development and funding are through a contract with HCFA (Health Care Financing Administration, 1998: 1–7). RUGS payments to a given nursing home are based on the clinical and functional status of residents plus staff time spent on services utilized for each resident and overall. Currently RUGS is being field tested and evaluated by six states: Kansas, Maine, Mississippi, New York, South Dakota, and Texas and involves approximately 700 nursing homes (Reilly, 1999:1).

The emerging strategy for reducing payment rates for ambulatory non-MCO Medicaid enrollees is through development of a prospective payment system analogous to that used for inpatient hospital care (diagnostic-related groups; DRGs). Congress mandated such a system be developed after the implementation of DRGs. Presumably this mandate was intended to counter cost-shifting strategies by hospitals. Hospitals, whenever possible, transfer their surgical patients to outpatient facilities (ambulatory care clinics), many of which are owned and operated by and adjacent to hospitals. In so doing, hospitals can bill on a fee-for-service basis rather than being constrained by DRGs, the result being that health care costs increase despite regulatory efforts to control a portion of the system. While directed at ambulatory care in general, the implications for Medicaid expenditures are significant.

Having won the competitive bid process from HCFA, the 3M Corporation is currently under contract to develop a prospective payment for outpatient care. Known as *Ambulatory Patient Groupings* (APGs), this system pays providers on the basis of an *office visit*. Office visits are classified as either a medical procedure, ancillary medical procedure, or consultative-diagnostic. Costs of related procedures during the visit are bundled together and heavily discounted (3M, 1999:1–7). The program is currently being piloted and evaluated in Iowa and California.

C. Organization of Service Delivery

Nowhere have administrative reforms adopted by the states in response to devolution been as significant as in their overhauling the organization of service delivery. These administrative reforms have occurred in three areas: (1) the shift to managed care organizations to deliver Medicaid services; (2) extending public private linkages, primarily through the CHIP program; and (3) regulating the quality of care.

1. The Medicaid Shift to Managed Care

With the passage of the 1997 Balanced Budget Act and subsequent waivers, states have responded aggressively to reorganizing their control over service delivery. States have been moving both to restructure their service delivery arrangements and to restrict from whom Medicaid enrollees may receive services. The way they have done this is through shifting the majority of their beneficiaries into MCOs. Exempted from this shift in the control of service delivery were certain children with special needs, Medicare beneficiaries whose incomes are below the federal poverty level, elderly and poor individuals in nursing homes, and Native Americans.

Medicaid eligibles, for their part, are required to enter one of the MCOs within their geographic area. Selection as to which MCO to join is left to the Medicaid enrollee. In many states, Medicaid agencies have contracted with independent organizations located in each geographic area of the state where Medicaid eligibles may go to seek information about the quality and focus of a specific MMCO.

In 1996, there were 11 million Medicaid eligibles enrolled in some form of MCO. Only one year later, by June 1997, 15.3 million Medicaid beneficiaries were enrolled in managed care (Health Care Financing Administration, 1997:1–2). In general, state strategies have targeted low-income individuals for enrollment in managed care, not the aged or disabled. In 1997, the use of managed care in Medicaid encompassed approximately 15 million enrollees. Of these, fully one-half were in full-risk HMOs (Kaiser Family Foundation, 1998: 1, 3). The rate of MMCO utilization across states has varied, as demonstrated in Table 6.

Nor has this trend reversed or slowed down. In fact, it is increasing. Again, this should not be surprising given the reality that Medicaid is embedded in the larger institutional context of economic governance. In the private sector, MCOs have been increasing to the point where now over 60 million persons in the United States receive their care through managed care organizations (Bodenheimer and Grumbach, 1998:5).

2. Extending Public-Private Linkages

For the standalone CHIP programs and the combined programs, states have leveraged their CHIP grant dollars. States have done this through changes in the orga-

Table 6 Percent of Medicaid Eligibles in Full-Risk HMOs by State

Percentage	Number of states
<5%	21
6–24%	9
25–50%	10
51–75%	5 (CT, KY, RI, UT, WA)
75–100%	5 (TN, OR, DE, HA, AZ)

Source: Kaiser Family Foundation (1995c).

nization of service delivery by (1) subsidizing individuals directly to purchase private sector insurance policies, and (2) public-private partnerships.

Examples of the first are California's Access for Infants and Mothers (AIM). AIM is available to women with family incomes between 200% and 300% of the federal poverty level. Qualified eligibles contribute a maximum of 2% of their annual gross income to the program. In Florida, *Healthy Kids* serves over 39,000 children from kindergarten through age 12 regardless of income. The *Children's Medical Security Plan* in Massachusetts is available to youth under 18 whose incomes fall at or below 200% of the FPL but who are not on Medicaid. Indeed, children in families between 200% and 400% of the FPL pay a $10.50 per month premium. Many states require cost sharing from patients (National Conference of State Legislatures, 1998:1–5).

A second strategy adopted by states has been to employ public-private partnerships in the provision of health care. These program options can vary from alliances to the formal exchange of goods and services and finances. There are several examples of public-private partnerships currently in existence. The largest is the *Caring Program for Children*. Covering children in 26 states, Caring for Children pools Blue Cross and Blue Shield administrative services and matching funds with private donations from philanthropic agencies to provide subsidized preventive and primary care insurance for uninsured children living below 235% of the federal poverty level (National Governor's Association, 1999).

In California, Kaiser Permanente has donated $100 million to provide subsidized health insurance for up to 50,000 children from low-income families. Through its Kaiser Permanente Cares for Kids program all kids receive benefits equivalent to other plan members. Subsidies range from 25% to 75% of the premium. The program will also work with state officials to enroll children in Medicaid. The Child Health Plan in Colorado targets children who are below age 13 and ineligible for Medicaid in families with incomes below 185% of FPL (National Governor's Association, 1999).

What these approaches have in common are two things: (1) They further expand reliance on the private sector notion of indemnity insurance as the mainstay of health care provision. Specifically, states contract with private insurance companies to provide coverage to children. (2) They are gap-fillers, between what Medicaid covers and what private insurance does not. As such, they continue the long tradition of constraining health coverage for the poor in America.

3. Regulating Quality of Care

State efforts to assure quality of care for their respective Medicaid programs has in part been attributable to inducing competition among plans where feasible. The main thrust of the administrative reform efforts, however, has been a regulatory strategy. This strategy has been dependent on the *integration of federal and private sector* quality-of-care criteria developed over two decades. States have utilized these criteria for generating comparative quality of care data on MMCOs in their states and disseminating this data (Gosfeld, 1997:30–33).

Unfortunately, the development of quality-of-care standards has been and continues to be a politically contentious process. A conceptual definition of quality is problematic. As a result, regulation where introduced has resulted in conflicts between providers and regulators regarding which regulatory standards are legitimate and should be implemented.

Conceptually, Bodenheimer and Grumbach have defined quality of care as consisting of five interrelated and somewhat conflicting dimensions: access; adequate scientific knowledge; competent health care providers; separation of financial and clinical decisions; and organization of health care institutions to maximize quality (Bodenheimer and Grumbach, 1998:193–196).

Donabedian's theoretical work in the 1960s has provided a conceptual framework for quality assessment based on *systems theory* and consisting of three stages: *structure, process,* and *outcomes* (Aday et al., 1993:26–27). This trichotomy remains in place today and provides a coherent framework for quality of care measures.

Structure refers to health care organization and characteristics, provider characteristics, community population health status, and socioeconomic variation. *Process* refers to technical competence of providers as they relate to maladies and patients—specifically, appropriateness of interventions, adherence to practice guidelines, practice profiling, and consumer ratings (McGlynn and Brook, 1996:146–51). *Outcomes* refers to temporal changes in health status and utilizes three set of measures: *condition-specific/tracer measures, generic measures,* and *adverse measures. Tracer* measures or outcomes refers to the results for individuals for specific maladies. *Generic* refers to outcomes assessed on all individuals regardless of health problems; examples include mortality, general functional status, and patient satisfaction *measures. Adverse* or *sentinel* outcomes refers to events such as mortality, complications from surgery, nosocomial infections, suicide, adverse drug reactions, and early readmission to hospitals (McGlynn and Brook, 1996:162–163).

The potential for administrative and political complexity at this point should be apparent: different advocates stress different dimensions of quality. This results in a matrix of options in which each of Donabedian's stages are crosstabulated with those specified by Bodenheim and Grumbach. Add to this the problem of controlling for acuity levels of presenting patients as well as their respective health histories and one begins to appreciate the demands placed on regulators desirous of producing legitimate and valid standards.

4. State Reliance on Federal Legislative and Private Sector Efforts to Regulate Quality of Care in Medicaid

Concerns with quality of care in Medicaid have been dealt with through legislation for over 20 years. The HMO Act of 1973 required quality assurance programs for inpatient and outpatients (Bodenheimer and Grumbach, 1998:203). In an effort to assure that managed care plans, primarily HMOs, would not discriminate against Medicaid clients, HMOs were prohibited from enrolling Medicaid clients exclusively. Therefore, at least three-quarters of any HMO's population had to be non-Medicaid-eligibles. Relatedly, Congress mandated that Medicaid eligibles be permitted to disenroll from any HMO within a short period of their initial entry into the HMO (Thompson, 1998:28).

In 1982 Peer Review Organizations (PROs) were established. PROs are essentially medical review organizations under contract to HCFA in each state and may be either proprietary or nonproprietary. PROs may initiate a hierarchy of sanctions against providers who are not providing quality services, providing services that are unnecessary, or billing inaccurately. However, outpatient services do not fall under the aegis of PROs in physician's offices where the majority of ambulatory care occurs. Overall, peer review has proved an ineffective mechanism due to a failure to educate rather than discipline, reluctance to find peers at fault, suits by physicians, and questions of whether there are improvements in the quality of care (Bodenheimer and Grumbach, 1998:203–204).

In the fall of 1986, the Joint Commission on Accreditation of Healthcare Organizations (JCAHO), a private, nonprofit organization responsible for the accreditation of institutional health care providers nationwide, applied the systems orientation to the facilities (hospitals and nursing homes) it accredits. In its *Agenda for Change*, the change was stated: ''Health care quality is monitored using measures related to structures, processes, and outcomes of diagnoses and treatments, as well as their interrelationships'' (JCAHO, 1988:13).

Specific to nursing homes, Congress approved legislation in 1987 aimed at regulating nursing homes, largely in response to numerous complaints concerning nursing home quality across the United States. Under OBRA 87, federal requirements for regulating quality and medical procedures in nursing homes were to be reviewed on an annual basis by each state's department of health. Included in these regulations were requirements that each nursing home develop a quality assurance committee comprising the director of nursing services, staff members at the nursing home, and a physician. Quality assurance committees were required to assure that functional levels of each resident were periodically reassessed. Moreover, using retrospective reviews of case records, combined with on-site field assessments, state health inspectors visited nursing homes and conducted reviews. Reports were then submitted back to the Secretary of Health and Human Services for evaluation and sanctions where and if necessary (Thompson, 1998: 28–29).

In contrast to regulation by PROs, there is substantial evidence that the quality standards imposed by OBRA 87 have improved the quality of care in nursing homes. An evaluation led by the Research Triangle Institute demonstrated the decreased use of chemical and physical restraints, indwelling catheters, and numbers of dehydrated patients. Conversely, participation and activity levels of residents increased (Wiener, 1998:204–205).

In 1989 the federal government established the Agency for Health Care Policy Research (AHCPR) within the Department of Health and Human Services. The goal of AHCPR is to evaluate common treatment protocols utilized by health care providers and organizations as to the efficacy of those protocols. The objectives are twofold: (1) to support research designed to improve the quality of health care, and (2) to disseminate this information to practitioners (Agency for Health Care Policy Research, 1999:1).

In 1990, the Institute of Medicine (IOM) made a distinction between quality *assessment* and quality *assurance*. IOM defined quality assessment as measuring quality of care, detecting problems of quality, or finding examples of good performance. *Quality assurance*, by contrast, includes quality assessment, verification, isolation of what can be corrected, interventions, and continuous monitoring to ensure that the original problem or unintended consequences do not exist (Birenbaum, 1997:88).

Specific to MCOs, the Health Care Financing Administration in conjunction with the National Committee for Quality Assurance (NCQA) have developed what will most likely be the standard for comparative evaluation and accreditation of managed care plans used across the United States. NCQA, an industry-sponsored association, is the creation of the American Association of Health Plans (AAHP), which represents managed care plans in the United States. NCQA has developed 50 standards for quality assurance of MCOs. NCQA has applied these standards to MCOs and with this data set, titled the *Health Plan Employer Data and Information Set, or* HEDIS, provides comparative data on MCOs and makes a determination as to which MCOs should be accredited (NCQA, 1995a:1).

With the increased market penetration of HMOs into general health care, the purpose of these quality measures are not only to assure the public and payers of the quality of HMO services, but to assure the providers contracting and or referring to the plans as to the quality of those plans. First reported in 1995, original versions of HEDIS focused on services provided, the quality of inputs and process indicators, and requirements for compliance rather than outcomes (Thompson, 1998:28–29).

Heavily criticized for its input and process focus, a third major revision of these standards, HEDIS 3.0, is currently in place. HEDIS 3.0 is focused more on outcomes and provides standardized measures of clinical results, access to and satisfaction with service encounters, and critically, a process for evaluating future measures to evaluate ongoing improvement (NCQA, 1995b:2).[7] While

---

[7] HEDIS 3.0 examines eight domains used to address each plan. These domains are effectiveness of care, access/availability of care, satisfaction with experience, health plan stability, use of services, costs of care, informed health care choice, and health plan descriptive information (NCQA, 1995b:

NCQA is refining its methodology, HCFA has developed its own set of guide-lines, exclusively for the Medicaid population, using HEDIS. This latter data set is known as the Health Care Quality Improvement Systems (HCQIS) (Fossett, 1998:142–43).

The Health Insurance and Portability Act of 1996 (HIPA) provided addi-tional enabling legislation to states in regulating quality of care. Specifically, the HIPA established standards and requirements for the electronic transmission of certain health information. Many of these requirements are designed to permit the development of integrated health care systems. States are already involved in considerable activity of this sort. Indeed, California is expanding its Medicaid Management Information System (MMIS) to track patterns of treatment and health care outcomes (Mendelson and Salinsky, 1997:108).

Finally, in 1997, the federal government, as a full partner in the Medicaid program, gave states the ability to monitor the quality of care in managed care through the Balanced Budget Act of 1997. The Balanced Budget Act of 1997 requires states to develop standards for assessing care and collecting data (Health Care Financing Administration, 1999e:5). Unfortunately, the costs of developing these standards both for the plans and for the states will be weighed against the objective of getting everyone into managed care quickly.

Despite all of these efforts, current state regulation of quality of care is moving slowly. One should not be overly optimistic that all states will aggres-sively pursue compliance and evaluation (Fossett, 1998:142–144).

In the studies on the regulation of quality in managed care, in both the private and Medicaid sectors, the data are very limited. Even in the Urban Insti-tute's in-depth coverage of long-term care and Medicaid, which utilizes in-depth case studies of 13 states, substantive information on quality of care is provided only for one state—Texas. In that section of the report, the discussion was limited to legislative proposals (Wiener and Stevenson, 1999:47). The few studies avail-able indicate the regulation of quality of care is fragmented.

In a comparative state review of the existing quality monitoring practices

---

3–4). In addition, every HMO volunteering to be evaluated by NCQA must submit a profile of the credentials of providers and scope of providers available (Birenbaum, 1997:90–91). HEDIS is being further developed to assess whether practice guidelines were adhered to for serious health problems prevalent in the population such as diabetes, coronary conditions, and chronic disabilities, especially those with complications (Birenbaum, 1997:92). Furthermore, HEDIS 3.0 requires HMOs to identify and report how patients with complicated illnesses (comorbidities) are taken care of under each plan (Birenbaum, 1997:93). As for risk adjusting of patients, the assignment of acuity levels is difficult at best and is currently not being undertaken as part of HEDIS. Finally, NCQA provides a monthly updated list of HMOs that are accredited, provisional-accredited, under review, and denied accreditation (NCQA, 1995a:2).

undertaken by states, Landon et al. (1998) surveyed all 50 state Medicaid agencies relative to six common measures of quality and four common measures of access. As late as 1996, the results were first and foremost that collection and provision of data by states was both varied and nascent. Second, state Medicaid agencies provided comparative quality data on Medicaid MCOs (MMCOs) more than they did for either Medicaid fee for service or the commercially insured population. Third, state strategies have been directed at providing comparative MCO quality data primarily to MMCOs rather than directly to beneficiaries. Fourth, the rate of state Medicaid agencies *planning* to increase their quality assurance reporting to MMCOs was to double from 1996 to 1997 (Landon et al., 1998, Table 2, p. 213). Presumably this latter initiative has been spurred on by Section 1932 of the Balanced Budget Act of 1997. This section mandated states to provide both quality assurance indicators to patients and MMCOs, and significantly, an annual external review of access and quality of care (Health Care Financing Administration, 1999e:5).

The National Governor's Association (NGA) developed a *Center for Best Practices* dedicated to assembling information on the performance and quality of MCOs by the states. The center acts as a clearing house of state efforts to monitor performance and quality of managed care plans and reports out lists of states where there is comparative data on health plans.[8] Currently, only nine states list 13 comparative reports (Center for Best Practices, 1999:3).

The *Alpha Center*, which monitors current state-level reform initiatives, has reported on Florida's Agency for Health Care Administration (AHCA) efforts in developing standardized report cards on all HMO plans within the state (Alpha Center, 1999:2).

Moreover, at the state agency level, where states have implemented quality measures, regulation has been fragmented and inconsistent. Riley assessed the extent of regulation of quality control of MCOs by states. In a survey of all 50 states, that included insurance departments, Medicaid agencies, and health departments, Riley found that insurance departments do little in the way of assess-

---

[8] Additionally, the NGA's Center for Best Practices provides information on other quality of care agencies at the federal level collecting and disseminating information on the quality of care. These include AHCPR, HCFA Quality of Care and Managed Care Information (QISMC), HCFA-Medicare Compare, the Presidential Advisory Commission on Consumer Protection and Quality in the Health Care Industry, Substance Abuse and Mental Health Administration, Maternal and Child Health Bureau, and the Institute for Child Health Policy—Purchaser's Tool (Center for Best Practices, 1999: 2). Also listed are consumer guides both by states, such as Maine-Bureau of Insurance Consumer Information and nationwide data sets such as IPRO Inc.'s Nationwide Analysis of Medicaid HMO Performance Data (Center for Best Practices, 1999:3).

ing quality, their focus being primarily on financial regulation (Riley, 1997:41). As to health departments, only half of state health departments have a role in regulating quality among MMCOs. A further 18 states reported that no one public agency in their state monitors health plan quality standards. Overall, state Medicaid agencies, acting as both purchaser and regulator of Medicaid MCOs, tend to be the most aggressive relative to both financial and quality oversight (Riley, 1997:42). Although not systematically evaluated, state capacity to regulate the quality of managed care is very uneven and fragmented across agencies within states (Fossett, 1998:142).

Minnesota disseminates measures of HMO performance using a combination of the following: three sets of NCQA's HEDIS, the Foundation for Accountability (FACCT) quality measures, and the Agency for Health Care Policy Research, hospital quality indicators. Pennsylvania's Health Care Cost-Containment Council utilizes an automated system to provide outcome data to the public via the Internet (Mendelson and Salinsky, 1997:109). This is commendable, but empirical studies of reports given to citizens have demonstrated that, for Medicaid enrollees in particular, reports have not proven to be effective. This is primarily due to the inability of the Medicaid population to comprehend what they are reading in these reports (Jewett and Hibbard, 1996:83–87).

The assemblage of quality-of-care data has been problematic for states. Epstein notes that the conversion to Medicaid managed care contracting has required states to focus on program management. The states have had to identify health plans, oversee enrollment, manage the assignment of payment, develop procedures to prevent cost overruns. Monitoring of quality of care and developing programs for state oversight may be of lower priority for states.

Additionally, there are limitations on states' ability to manage quality of care. States often lack the financial resources, trained administrative staff, and data systems required for quality oversight. Even where states have this capacity, the data from MMCOs encounters between patients and the plans are not available or systematically classified (Epstein, 1997:1619).

Implementing such oversight for state Medicaid agencies is made all the more difficult for special Medicaid populations, primarily the disabled and the disabled elderly. Despite the large proportion of Medicaid funds provided to this group, MMCOs have little experience caring for the elderly and other persons with disabilities such as AIDS or mental illness. Complicating this is the issue of acuity levels, or measuring plan performance relative to risk-adjusted illness measures. This level of quality control measures at yet does not exist (Epstein, 1997:1619).

The Quality Assurance Reform Initiative (QARI), a demonstration project, was developed in 1991. Designed as a comprehensive state-based system for assuring quality of care in Medicaid Managed Care, the program is currently in place in Minnesota, Ohio, and Washington. The results of the QARI demonstration project are mixed. Relative to coordination between plans and states in addressing quality improvement issues, QARI reinforced state's decisions to move from a regulatory approach to a partnership approach with health plans and sharing of information. QARI also provided a greater role for Medicaid enrollees to participate in each state's system because of the implementation of a beneficiary satisfaction component within QARI. QARI succeeded in aligning the quality improvement programs of the Medicaid plans with industry standards. However, the QARI component requiring states to monitor their health plans' compliance with standards for internal quality improvement failed. Specifically, the ability of plans to identify problems and assess overall effectiveness varied by state (Felt-Lisk, 1997:248–250)

Taken together, the reports on state efforts at regulating quality of care in their Medicaid programs are not encouraging. This is especially the case with MMCO. Failure to invest in oversight may result in the advantages of managed care as a delivery system not materializing. Managed care has provided states the opportunity to realize budgetary savings in the short term, coordinate care for the indigent, and simplify their administrative control and payments to providers. However, absent any consensus on which quality of care standards to employ or how to develop collaborative relationships with providers could derail significant attempts at improving quality of care for Medicaid enrollees.

V. CONCLUSION

This chapter has focused on the administrative reforms undertaken by state Medicaid programs in response to devolution. The Medicaid program is without question a complex program operating in one of the most complex policy domains (health care) in the United States. To facilitate an understanding of this complexity, a policy template was employed in which three dimensions constitute and determine the policy and structure of a given program. This template permitted the discussion of the current Medicaid program and a description of the reforms adopted by the states corresponding to each dimension.

Today's administrative reforms are tomorrow's administrative structures. It is not known what reforms will take place in the future of the Medicaid program. If devolution continues, the resulting implementation structures and reforms will generate even greater variation and complexity. This complexity needs to be systematically and comparatively understood. One technique to such an understanding of administrative reforms is to evaluate them in the context of the dimensions of policy structure.

REFERENCES

3M. (1999). Ambulatory patient grouping software. 3M health information systems. Retrieved from the World Wide Web on Jan. 7, 1999. [http://www.mmm.com/market/healthcare/his/product/apg/brochure/menu.htm]

Aaton, H. J. (1991). *Serious and Unstable Condition: Financing America's Health Care*, Brookings Institution, Washington, D.C.

Aday, L., Begley, C. E., Lairson, D. R., and Slater, C. H. (1993). *Evaluating the Medical Care System: Effectiveness, Efficiency, and Equity*, Health Administration Press, Ann Arbor, MI.

Agency for Health Care Policy Research (AHCPR). (1999). *AHCPR overview*. Retrieved from the World Wide Web on May 3, 1999. [http://ww.ahcpr.gov/about/overview.htm]

Alpha Center. State information, *State Update—Florida*. Retrieved from the World Wide Web on Feb. 10, 1999. [http://www.ac.org/httpdocs/updatef197.htm]

American Public Human Services Association. (1999a). National Association of State Medicaid Directors. *CHIP Update—February 1999*. Retrieved from the World Wide Web on March 4, 1999. [http://medicaid.aphsa.org/chipupdate2-99.html]

American Public Human Services Association. (1999b). National Association of State Medicaid Directors. *Medicaid 1115 Waivers*, Retrieved from the World Wide Web on Feb. 14, 1999. [http:medicaid.aphsa.org/1115waivers.htm]

American Public Human Services Association. (1999c). National Association of State Medicaid Directors. *1915(b) Waivers*. Retrieved from the World Wide Web on February 14, 1999. [http:medicaid.aphsa.org/1915(b)waivers.htm].

American Public Human Services Association. (1999d). National Association of State Medicaid Directors, *Medicaid Home and Community-Based Services Waivers*. Retrieved from the World Wide Web on Feb. 14, 1999. [http:medicaid.aphsa.org/1915ctext.htm]

Andersen, R. M. and Davidson, P. L. (1996). Measuring access and trends. *Changing the U.S. Health Care System: Key Issues in Health Service, Policy, and Management* (R. M. Andersen, T. Rice, and G. Kaminski (eds.), Jossey-Bass, San Francisco.

Association of State and Territorial Health Officials. (1999). *State Plans*. Retrieved from the World Wide Web. [Internet: www.astho.org/html/boody_state_plans.html]

Birenbaum, A. (1997). *Managed Care: Made in America*. Praeger, Westport CT.

Boyd, D. J. (1998). Medicaid devolution: a fiscal perspective, *Medicaid and Devolution: A View From the States* (F. J. Thompson and J. J. DiIulio) (eds.), Brookings, Washington.

Bodenheimer, T. S. and Grumbach, K. (1998). *Understanding Health Policy: A Clinical Approach. 2nd Edition*. Appleton and Lange, Stamford, CT.

Brown, R. E. and Wyn, R. (1996). Public policies to extend health care coverage, *Changing the U.S. Health Care System: Key Issues in Health Service, Policy, and Management* (R. M. Andersen, T. Rice, and G. Kaminski (eds.), Jossey-Bass, San Francisco.

Brown, R. E., and Wyn, R. (1996). Public policies to extend health care coverage, *Changing the U.S. Health Care System: Key Issues in Health Services, Policy, and Man-

agement R. M. Andersen, T. H. Rice, and G. F. Kominski (eds.), Jossey-Bass, San Francisco.

Bruen, B. K. and Ullman, F. (1998). *Children's health insurance programs: Where states are, where they are headed.* Retrieved from the World Wide Web on Feb. 16, 1999. [http://newfederalism.urban.org/html/anf20.html]

Bureau of Labor Statistics. (1999). *Table 1, Consumer Price Index for All Urban Consumers (CPI-U): U.S. City Average, by Expenditure Category and Commodity and Service Group,* U.S. Department of Labor. Retrieved from the World Wide Web on March 8, 1999. [http//stats.bls.gov/news.release/cpi.t01.htm]

Lindberg, L. N. and Campbell, J. L. (1991). The state and the organization of economic activity, *Governance of the American Economy (Structural Analysis in the Social Sciences)* J. L. Campbell, J. Hollingsworth, Rogers, and L. N. Lindberg, eds., Cambridge University Press, Cambridge.

Center for Best Practices. *Managed care,* National Governor's Association. Retrieved from the World Wide Web, March 11, 1999. [http://www.nga.org/CBP/Activities/ManagedCare.asp]

Center for Health Policy Research. George Washington University Medical Center, *Negotiating the New Health Care System, A Nationwide Study of Medicaid Managed Care Contracts,* 2nd ed. Retrieved from the World Wide Web, Feb. 16, 1999. [http://ww.chcsl.org/oview.htm#Exe]

Cunningham, W. E., Beaudin, C. L., and Panarites, C. J. (1996). *AIDS in transition, changing the U.S. health care system, Key Issues in Health Services, Policy, and Management* (R. M. Andersen, T. Rice, and G. Kaminski (eds.), Jossey-Bass, San Francisco.

Department of Health and Human Services. (1998). Federal Poverty Guidelines. Retrieved from the World Wide Web on Feb. 23, 1999. [http://aspe.os.dhhs.gov/poverty/98poverty.htm]

Epstein, A. M. (1997). Department of Health Policy and Management, Harvard School of Public Health, Policy perspectives: Medicaid managed care and high quality, *JAMA* 278(19): 1617–1621.

Felt-Lisk, S. and St. Peter, R. (1997). Quality assurance for medicaid managed care, *Health Affairs May/June.*

Fox, D. M. (1997). The competence of the states and the health of the public, *Health Policy Reform in America: Innovation from the States, 2nd ed.* (H. M. Leichter, ed.), M. E. Sharpe, Armonk, NY.

Fossett, J. W. (1998). Managed care and devolution, *Medicaid and Devolution: A View from the States* (Thompson, F. J. and DiIulio (eds.), Brookings Institution, Washington.

General Accounting Office. (1997). *Report: Declines in Employer-Based Coverage Leave Millions Uninsured: State and Private Programs Offer New Approaches,* GAO/T HEHS-97-105, Government Printing Office, Washington, DC.

Gosfeld, A. G. (1997). Who is holding whom accountable for quality?, *Health Affairs* 16(3): 26–40.

Halfon, N., Inkelas, M., Wood, D. L., and Schuster, M. A. (1996). Health care reform for children and families, *Changing the U.S. Health Care System: Key Issues in Health Services, Policy, and Management* (R. M. Andersen et al., eds.), Jossey-Bass, San Francisco.

Health Care Financing Administration. (1999). *Ohio Statewide Health Reform Demonstration Fact Sheet.* Retrieved from the World Wide Web, Feb. 15, 1999. [HCFA: http://www.hcfa.gov/medicaid/ohfact.htm]

Health Care Financing Administration. (1999a). *Alabama Mobile County Health Reform Demonstration Fact Sheet.* Retrieved from the World Wide Web, Feb. 15, 1999. [HCFA: http://www.hcfa.gov/medicaid/alfact.htm]

Health Care Financing Administration. (1999b). *HCFA Regional office officials.* Retrieved from the World Wide Web on April 30, 1999. [http://www.hcfa.gov.medicaid/rcontact.htm]

Health Care Financing Administration. (1999c). *Illinois Statewide Health Reform Demonstration Fact Sheet.* Retrieved from the World Wide Web, Feb. 15, 1999. [HCFA: http://www.hcfa.gov/medicaid/ilfact.htm]

Health Care Financing Administration. (1999d). *Medicaid Managed Care State Enrollment: June 30, 1997.* Department of Health and Human Services. Retrieved from the World Wide Web on Feb. 23, 1999. [http://www.hcfa.gov/medicaid/plantyp7.htm]

Health Care Financing Administration. (1999e). *Subtitle H—BBA 1997.* Retrieved from the World Wide Web on Feb. 16, 1999. [http://www.HCFA.GOV/regs/subt_h.htm]

Holahan, J., Bruen, B., and Liska, D. (1998). *The Decline in Medicaid Spending Growth in 1996: Why Did It Happen?* Retrieved from the World Wide Web on May 3, 1999. [http://www.urban.org/health/decline_spending.html]

Holahan, J., Zuckerman, S., Evans A., and Rangarajan, S. (1998). Medicaid managed care in thirteen states, *Health Affairs, 17*(1): 43–61.

Hurley, R. E., Freund, D. A., and Paul, J. E. (1993). *Managed Care in Medicaid: Lessons for Policy and Program Design,* Health Administration Press, Ann Arbor, MI.

Jewett, J. J., and Hibbard, J. H. (1996). Comprehension of quality of care indicators: differences among privately insured, publicly insured, and uninsured. *Health Care Financing Review, 18*(1): 75–94.

Joint Commission on Accreditation of Healthcare Organizations (1988). *The Joint Commission Guide to Quality Assurance,* Joint Commission, Chicago, IL.

Kaiser Family Foundation. (1998a). Kaiser Commission on the Future of Medicaid, *Medicaid at a Glance.* Retrieved from the World Wide Web on May 5, 1999. [kff.org/archive/health_policy/kcfm/glance/glance.html]

Kaiser Family Foundation. (1998b). Kaiser Commission on the Future of Medicaid, *Reasons for Cost Explosion.* Retrieved from the World Wide Web. [kff.org/archive/health_policy/kcfm/spending/enroll.html]

Kaiser Family Foundation. (1998c). Kaiser Commission on the Future of Medicaid, *States Sheet: Table 15.* Retrieved from the World Wide Web. [kff.org/state_health/factsheets/statesheet_t1j.html]

Kaiser Family Foundation. (1998d). Kaiser Commission on the Future of Medicaid, *States Sheet: Table 16.* Retrieved from the World Wide Web. [kff.org/state_health/factsheets/statesheet_t16.html]

Kaiser Family Foundation. (1998e). Kaiser Commission on the Future of Medicaid, *States*

Sheet: Table 17. Retrieved from the World Wide Web. [kff.org/state_health/factsheets/statesheet_t17.html]

Kaiser Family Foundation. (1998f). Kaiser Commission on the Future of Medicaid, *States Sheet: Table 18.* Retrieved from the World Wide Web. [kff.org/state_health/factsheets/statesheet_t18.html]

Landon, B. E., Tobias, C., and Epstein, A. M. (1998). Quality management by state medicaid agencies converting to managed care, *JAMA* 279(3): 211–216.

Leichter, H. M. (1997). Health care reform in America: back to the laboratories, *Health Policy Reform in America: Innovation from the States*, 2nd ed. (H. M. Leichter, ed.), M. E. Sharpe, Armonk, NY.

Mann, C. and Guyer, J. (1997). *Overview of the New Child Health Block Grant, Center on Budget and Policy Priorities.* Retrieved from the World Wide Web *on March 14, 1999.* [http://www.cpbb.org/chhlth.htm]

Mann, C. and Kogan, R. (1995). *State Impacts of the Reduction in Federal Medicaid Spending Called For in the Budget Resolution,* Center on Budget and Policy Priorities. Retrieved from the World Wide Web, April 15, 1999. [http://www.epn.org/cbpp/cbstat.htm]

McGlynn, E. A. and Brook, R. H. (1996). Ensuring quality of care, *Changing the U.S. Health Care System: Key Issues in Health Services, Policy and Administration* (R. M. Andersen, T. Rice, and G. Kaminski, eds.), Jossey-Bass, San Francisco.

Mendelson, D. M. and Salinsky, E. M. (1997). Health information systems and the role of state government, *Health Affairs, May/June* 1997.

National Committee for Quality Assurance. (1995a). *NCQA Accreditation Status List.* Retrieved from the World Wide Web, June 29, 1998. [http://www.ncqa.org/hedis/30exsum.htm#whatmeasures]

National Committee for Quality Assurance. (1995b). *HEDIS 3.0. Executive Summary.* Retrieved from the World Wide Web, June 29, 1998. [http://www.ncqa.org/hedis/30exsum.htm#whatmeasures]

National Conference of State Legislatures. (1998). *CHIP and Cost-Sharing: As of October, 1998.* Retrieved from the World Wide Web on Feb. 16, 1999. [http://www.ncsl.org/programs/health/chipcost.htm]

National Governor's Association. (1999). *Fact Sheet: State Designed Progams to Provide Health Insurance for Children.* Retrieved from the World Wide Web, Feb. 10, 1999. [http://www.nga.org/MCH/StateDesignedPro.htm]

Peller, J. and Shaner, H. (1996). *Medicaid Eligibility Standards for Low-Income Families and Children: State Implementation of the Personal Responsibility and Work Opportunity Reconciliation Act of 1996,* American Public Works Association (APWA). Retrieved from the World Wide Web, Feb. 10, 1999. [http://medicaid.apwa.org/tanfmedicaid2.html]

Perloff, J. D., Kletke P. R., Fossett, J. W., and Banks, S. (1997). Medicaid participation among urban primary care physicians, *Medical Care 35*: 142–157.

Personal Responsibility and Work Opportunity Reconciliation Act (P.L. 104–193).

Reilly, K. (1999). Multistate nursing home case-mix payment and quality demonstration. Retrieved from the World Wide Web on Jan. 9, 1999. [http://www.alliedtech.com/research/Hproject1/index.html]

Rice, T. (1996). Measuring health care costs and trends, *Changing the U.S. Health Care*

System: Key Issues in Health Services, Policy, and Management (R. M. Andersen, T. Rice, and G. Kaminsky, eds., Jossey-Bass, San Francisco.

Riley, T. (1997). The National Academy for State Health Policy (NASHP), the role of states in accountability for quality, *Health Affairs May/June*.

Roos, N. P. and Roos, L. L. (1994). Small area variations, practice style, and quality of care, *Why Some People Are Healthy and Others Not: The Determinants of Health of Populations* (R. G. Evans, M. L. Barer, and T. Marmor, eds.), Aldine de Gruyter, New York.

Rowland, D., and Salagnicoff, A. (1994). Controversy: lessons from Medicaid—improving access to office based physician care for the low income population, *American Journal of Public Health 84*: 550–552.

Slifkin, R. T., Hoag, S. D., Silberman, P., Felt-Lisk, S., and Pokin, B. (1998). Medicaid managed care programs in rural areas: a fifty state overview, *Health Affairs 17*(6).

Sloan, F., and Conover, C. J. (1998). Effects of state reforms on health insurance coverage of adults, *Inquiry 35*: 280–293.

Smith, S., Freeland, M., Heffler, S., McKusick, D., and Health Expenditures Project Team. (1998). *The next ten years of health spending: what does the future hold?, Health Affairs 17*(5): 128–140.

Spitz, B. (1998). The elusive new federalism, *Health Affairs 17*(6): 150–161.

Sullivan v. Zebley, 493, U.S. 521 (1990).

Thompson, F. J. (1998). The faces of devolution, *Medicaid and Devolution: A Review from the States* (F. J. Thompson and DiIulio, eds.), Brookings Institution, Washington.

Thompson, F. J. (1998). Federalism and the Medicaid challenge, *Medicaid and Devolution: A View from the States*. (F. J. Thompson and DiIulio, eds.), Brookings Institution, Washington.

Twentieth Century Fund. (1999). *The Risks of Congressional Reforms*. Retrieved from the World Wide Web on Feb. 10, 1999. [http://www.tcf.org/Publications/Basics/Medicaid/Reform_Risks.html]

Ullman, F., Bruen, B., and Holahan, J. (1998). *The State Children's Health Insurance Program: A Look at the Numbers*, Urban Institute. Retrieved from the World Wide Web on Feb. 16, 1999. [http://newfederalism.urban/org/html/occ4.html#medi]

United States General Accounting Office. (1997). *Declines in Employment-Based Coverage Leave Millions Uninsured: State and Private Programs Offer New Approaches*, GAO/T-HEHS-97-105, Government Printing Office, Washington, D.C.

University of Buffalo Libraries. *A Desktop Guide to SSI Eligibility Requirements*. Retrieved from the World Wide Web, June 15, 1998. [http://ublib.buffalo.edu/libraries/e-resources/ebooks/records/765.html]

Urban Institute. (1999). *Assessing the New Federalism: An Urban Institute Project*. Retrieved from the World Wide Web on April 30, 1999. [http://newfederalism.urban.org]

Well, A., Wiener, J. M., and Holahan, J. (1998). Perspective: assessing the new federalism, *Health Affairs 17*(6): 162–164.

Weissert, W. (1985). Estimating the long-term care population: prevalence rates and selected characteristics, *Health Care Financing Review 6*(4): 83–90.

Wiener, J. M. (1998). Long term care and devolution, *Medicaid and Devolution: A View from the States.* (Thompson, F. J. and DiIulio, eds.), Brookings Institution, Washington.

Wiener, J. M. and Stevenson, D. G. (1999). Long-term care of the elderly: profiles of thirteen states, Urban Institute, Washington, D.C. Retrieved from the World Wide Web on Feb. 10, 1999. [http://newfederalism.urban.org/html/occal2.html]

Wilensky, H. L. and Lebeaux, C. N. (1965). Capitalism and American culture, *Industrial Society and Social Welfare*, Free Press, New York.

21
Management of State Corrections Policies: Consequences of Getting Tough on Crime

Betsy Fulton
Eastern Kentucky University, Richmond, Kentucky

For 25 years the United States has engaged in a social war on crime that is characterized by ''get-tough'' policies including ''three strikes'' laws, mandatory sentencing, the reinstatement of the death penalty, and harsh community-based sanctions. By 1996 the rate of incarceration had climbed to 519 per 100,000 persons, a rate five times that of any other industrialized country (Cullen et al., 1996). If the get-tough mantra heard from current political candidates is any indication, these punitive criminal justice policies are likely to continue.

Despite the apparent political support for get-tough policies, recent public opinion polls indicate that many citizens support rehabilitation as a goal of corrections (Applegate et al., 1997). These contradicting sentiments lead some to suggest that current correctional practices suffer from the lack of a ''coherent conscience or ideology'' (Cullen et al., 1996:36). Without any organizing theory or philosophy to guide rational decision making, decisions about crime control strategies are driven by political motives and more immediate operational considerations (Rothman, 1980). Clear (1994) argues that get-tough policies reflect a ''penal harm'' movement that has resulted from arbitrary policy decisions in judicial, executive, and legislative branches of government. Feeley and Simon (1992) contend that the ''traditional objectives of rehabilitation and crime control'' have given way to a ''new penology'' that emphasizes the ''efficient control of internal system processes'' (p. 450). Whether they resulted from mean-spirited decision making or from a bid for efficiency, get-tough policies have created insurmountable challenges for the American correctional system.

What is needed to counteract these challenges is an organizing philosophy for the future of state correctional policy. This requires learning from past experiences and raising the level of debate from one of political pontification to one that focuses on empirical evidence regarding what works to control crime. Within this context, this chapter examines the antecedents of the get-tough movement, its strategies and consequences, promising alternatives for reducing crime, and critical issues in the management of correctional organizations.

I. ANTECEDENTS OF THE GET-TOUGH MOVEMENT

A. Evolution of Correctional Policy

Correctional history in the United States is strewn with examples of well-intentioned policies that have been corrupted by organizational and political pressures (Cullen and Gilbert, 1982; Rothman, 1980). The American prison, for example, was founded on the idea of rehabilitation (Cullen and Gilbert, 1982). Penitentiaries were introduced in the 1800s as a rational alternative to the barbaric forms of corporal punishment used in colonial times (Newman, 1978). Developed under Quaker influence, penitentiaries were designed to isolate offenders from the bad influences in society and to give them time to reflect and repent on their sins (Newman, 1978). Because of prison crowding and a lack of incentives for good behavior among inmates, however, the fervor for prisoner reform gave way to prisoner abuse as a means for maintaining control within the prison walls (Rothman, 1971). Crowding and coercive control of offenders continue today as common ailments of the modern prison system.

The determinate sentence is an example of a well-intended policy that succumbed to political pressure and gave rise to harsh criminal penalties. According to Cullen and Gilbert (1982), the determinate sentence emerged from an unusual moment of agreement among liberals and conservatives in the mid-1970s. Having experienced the turbulent 1960s, both political parties were dissatisfied with the manner in which criminal offenders were being punished. Conservatives viewed the indeterminate sentence and other prominent rehabilitation strategies as signs of a permissive society. They believed that the criminal justice system was coddling offenders and decreasing the costs of crime by releasing offenders early from prison. They called for determinate sentences aimed at minimizing discretion and tougher sentencing practices designed to restore social order. Believing that the government was using the mask of benevolence to inflict suffering on offenders, liberals agreed that discretion must be limited through the use of determinate sentences. Liberals, however, wanted to reduce the length of sentences to minimize the harm caused by the coercive prison environment. In the end, punishment won out (Rothman, 1980) and the get-tough movement was set into motion.

B. Ideological Basis for Getting Tough

The get-tough movement is characterized by deterrence and incapacitation-based strategies. Deterrence has served as justification for stiffer penalties since the late 1700s and the emergence of the classical school of thought (Beccaria, 1963). Deterrence predicts that as the severity, swiftness, and certainty of punishment increase, crime will go down. "Tough-on-crime" policies such as mandatory sentences, truth in sentencing, and three-strikes legislation are designed to create special deterrence for the individual experiencing the punishment and general deterrence for others who observe the punishment (Shichor, 1992).

It is only in the past 18 years that incapacitation has emerged as the principle justification for criminal sentencing (Zimring and Hawkins, 1995). Incapacitation is designed to prevent crime through the physical constraint of individuals. Advocates of incapacitation make no claims of offender reform; they simply assert that offenders will not be able to commit crime against society while incarcerated or otherwise restrained (Wilson, 1983; Zimring and Hawkins, 1995). Together, incapacitative and deterrent ideologies have contributed to correctional policies and practices that are increasingly punitive in nature.

II. GETTING TOUGH—STRATEGIES AND CONSEQUENCES

Although discussions about the get-tough movement focus on its implications for the American prison system, adult probation and parole and juvenile justice systems are equally vulnerable to the political pressures for tough crime control strategies. Both have relinquished their traditional emphasis on rehabilitation in order to compete for correctional dollars that are allocated by legislators interested in getting tough on crime. This section of the chapter discusses the implications of the get-tough movement for prisons, community corrections, and juvenile justice.

A. A Nation's Obsession with Imprisonment

The state and federal prison systems in the United States have experienced a precipitous growth in the inmate population since 1970. Recent statistics from the Bureau of Justice Statistics give no indication of this trend abating (Gilliard and Beck, 1998). By midyear 1997, 1.7 million people were incarcerated in local jails or state and Federal prisons. This was an increase of 5.2% over the previous year.

It often is assumed that the growth in the prison population reflects increased crime rates. Comparisons of changes in the crime rates and changes in the prison population, however, have revealed that these trends are loosely matched over time (Clear, 1994; Zimring and Hawkins, 1991). Several studies have attributed the growth to the introduction of tough legislation such as mandatory sentences, truth in sentencing, and three-strikes legislation (Parent et al., 1997a; Tonry, 1987; Wooldredge, 1996). Langan (1991) argued that this new legislation has played a modest role and that the primary source of growth in the prison population was judges' increased willingness to imprison convicted felons. Regardless of its cause, the growing prison population is wreaking havoc on correctional systems and communities.

On December 31, 1997, state and federal prisons were operating between 15% and 24% above capacity (Gilliard and Beck, 1998). This situation creates management nightmares within the prison walls. Prison crowding has been found to contribute to negative psychological and physical reactions among inmates (Paulus et al., 1985) and to increased rates of violence (Gaes and McGuire, 1985). Crowding puts such a drain on prison resources that vocational, educational, and counseling programs are extremely limited and sometimes discontinued altogether (Gottfredson, 1984; Joyce, 1992). Even if such programming were available, the fear and health problems created by crowding interfere with inmates' rehabilitation (Goodstein et al., 1984; Paulus et al., 1985).

Perhaps more disturbing than the strained prison system is the impact that high incarceration rates have on families and communities. Applying standard life table techniques used by demographers and actuaries, Bonczar and Beck (1997) estimated the lifetime likelihood of incarceration for U.S. citizens. Based on 1991 rates of incarceration, the lifetime likelihood of serving time in a state or federal prison is 5.1%, or one of every 20 persons. This likelihood increases dramatically for black males—"a black male in the United States today has greater than a 1 in 4 chance of going to prison during his lifetime" (Bonczar and Beck, 1997:1). Feeley and Simon (1992) suggest that these high rates of imprisonment have created "permanent marginality" for the black male population and relinquished any hope for their transformation.

Women and children are also negatively affected by these high rates of imprisonment. As "survivors" of the incarceration of their spouses, many women struggle to keep their homes and support their children (Danner, 1998). As recipients of get-tough strategies themselves, more women offenders are being sent to prison. Since 1990, the increase in the female prison population has averaged 8.8% annually (Gilliard and Beck, 1998). Over two-thirds of these female prisoners have children under the age of 18 (Morash et al., 1998). Because most states only have one women's facility, female inmates often are incarcerated far away from their children and other family members. This breaks social bonds that may have insulated them from future criminal behavior, and makes readjustment more difficult upon release (Pollock-Byrne, 1990). In turn, children suffer from parental separation and inadequate childcare provided by family members who often are struggling themselves (Danner, 1998).

Although these social costs of get-tough strategies are often overlooked, the direct financial costs are creating concern for state policy makers. Correctional expenditures amount to $25 billion annually (Bureau of Justice Statistics, 1992), with corrections being the fastest-growing item in state budgets (National Conference of State Legislatures, 1994). These exorbitant costs provide fodder for a healthy debate about whether or not get-tough strategies are worth the cost.

Two recent studies compare the cost of additional crimes that would be committed by offenders had they not been incarcerated ($46,072) with the cost of their incarceration per year ($25,000 per prisoner) and conclude that "prison pays" (DiIulio and Piehl, 1991; Piehl and DiIulio, 1995). The cost estimates were based on the average costs of property crime and self-report data that suggests that offenders commit a median of 12 crimes per year. These studies overlook two important considerations when assessing the cost-effectiveness of imprisonment. First, they do not compare the effects of prison with the effects of other less costly forms of punishment (DiIulio and Piehl, 1991). Second, they overlook opportunity costs; that is, they do not assess how much crime might have been saved had the money spent on incarceration been allocated to other types of social programs (Cullen et al., 1996). Whether or not prison pays, rising costs have forced states to develop alternative forms of punishment.

B. Beyond Imprisonment—Getting Tough in Communities

Probation and parole agencies across the nation have instituted various forms of intermediate sanctions including intensive supervision programs, day reporting centers, and electronic monitoring programs. Each of these programs avows to meet a new and pressing need in probation and parole. In reality, they all represent a variation of the same strategy—watching offenders closely and responding swiftly and harshly to technical violations or new criminal behavior. These tough new programs were well received by the public, politicians, and practitioners because they "shared the rhetoric of punishment but offered to accomplish crime control at a reduced cost" (Cullen et al., 1996:73). As demonstrated below, available research challenges the extent to which these programs are achieving their stated objectives.

1. Intensive Supervision Programs

Intensive supervision programs (ISP) date back to the early 1960s, when they were implemented as a management tool to examine the effectiveness of various caseload sizes (Neithercutt and Gottfredson, 1975; Carter and Wilkins, 1976;

Banks et al., 1977). Results of this experimentation found that intensive supervision was difficult to achieve, and that when it was achieved it did not guarantee greater success—offenders in ISP had similar arrest rates and more technical violations. These findings led to the demise of this early model of ISP.

In 1982, the Georgia Department of Corrections reintroduced the concept of ISP as an alternative sanction for offenders who would have otherwise gone to prison. Most states followed suit throughout the 1980s. The defining characteristics of ISP are small caseloads (e.g., 25–40 offenders) and an emphasis on controlling offenders in the community through increased contact, drug testing, curfews, electronic monitoring, and stringent responses to technical violations. Treatment and services are not a primary focus of these ISPs.

Most studies of ISP have revealed an increase in technical violations (i.e., violations of the rules of probation/parole) for ISP offenders as compared to offenders placed in other sentencing options, but no significant differences in the rates of new arrests (Erwin, 1987; Petersilia and Turner, 1993; Wagner, 1989). Furthermore, offenders in ISP are more likely to be sent to prison for a technical violation than are offenders in regular probation or parole (Tonry, 1990; Turner and Petersilia, 1992). Several authors have argued that an increase in technical violations and revocations is indicative of an ISP that is doing its job. That is, by catching offenders in violation of their supervisory conditions and removing them from the streets, ISPs are preempting future criminal behavior and thus protecting the public (Nidorf, 1991; Wagner, 1989). Others argue, however, that this focus on technical noncompliance at best produces short-term in-program crime control and, at worst, limits the extent to which ISPs can divert offenders from prison, and relatedly, save money (Harland and Rosen, 1987).

Another consistent finding from studies of ISP is that there appears to be a relationship between greater participation in rehabilitative programming and a reduction in recidivism (Byrne and Kelly, 1989; Paparozzi, *n.d.*; Petersilia and Turner, 1993). Based on this finding, a prototypical model of ISP was developed that incorporated intensive levels of surveillance and treatment (Fulton et al., 1994). Results of a recent study on this model suggest that the intensity of treatment is not as important to the reduction of recidivism as the quality of the treatment that is provided (University of Cincinnati, 1997). More definitive analyses of the specific type and quality of program components is required to fully assess the effectiveness of this prototypical ISP.

2. Electronic Monitoring/Home Confinement

Electronic monitoring (EM) is another popular intermediate sanction used in all 50 states. It involves the electronic surveillance of offenders to assure compliance with home confinement. There are two primary types of EM equipment (Bureau of Justice Assistance, 1989). One type involves random calls to the offenders' homes at which time they must verify their presence with a coded wristlet/anklet or voice verification. The second type involves the emission of a continuous signal from a miniaturized transmitter that is strapped to the offender's ankle or wrist. If the offender leaves his/her home a receiver dials a central computer, and a violation is recorded. Various technological problems have been noted including tampering with the wristlets/anklets, false positives (a signal alerting officials of a violation when one has not occurred), and false negatives (the failure of the equipment to alert officials of a violation) (Baumer and Mendelsohn, 1992). Additionally, the suggestion that EM would provide a less labor-intensive option to manual surveillance has been refuted. Although EM may relieve some of the burden of field work for probation and parole officers, it introduces other labor intensive duties such as program installation and maintenance, offender scheduling, coordination with the EM service provider, and the verification and responses to violations (Baumer et al., 1990).

EM has been largely used for nonviolent offenders, drug offenders, drunk drivers, and those who commit crimes against property. Recidivism rates for these programs are generally low, ranging from 10% to 30% (Brown and Roy, 1995; Petersilia, 1988). Studies available on EM programs that target high-risk offenders report no significant differences in rates of recidivism between the EM group and a matched comparison group of offenders who were not subjected to EM (Smith and Akers, 1993; Jolin and Stipak, 1992). As with ISP, better results have been found for those offenders who participated in treatment in conjunction with EM (Jolin and Stipak, 1992). Baumer and Mendelsohn (1992) suggest that EM offers the most promise as a means to stabilize offenders while providing them with necessary treatment. More methodologically sound evaluations of EM programs are needed to guide its future applications.

3. Day Reporting Centers

The first known day reporting center (DRC) was implemented in Massachusetts in 1986 (McDevitt and Miliano, 1992). By the end of 1994, 114 DRCs were operating in 22 states (Parent et al., 1995). Although day reporting programs differ in structure and purpose, the most common model serves both treatment and surveillance functions. DRC participants generally live at home and continue to work or go to school. They are offered a variety of treatment and support services, are required to report to the center daily, and are closely monitored at night through telephone calls, drug testing, curfews, and electronic monitoring (McDevitt and Miliano, 1992; Parent et al., 1995). Although low-risk offenders are most likely to be targeted for participation in DRCs, an increasing number are accepting offenders convicted of serious or violent crimes (Parent et al., 1995).

From their survey of DRCs, Parent et al. (1995) found that negative termination rates range from 14% to 86% with an average of 50 percent. An evaluation of DRCs operating in Ohio found that a slightly higher percentage of DRC participants were rearrested (52.8%) than comparison groups of offenders on regular probation (45.7%), intensive supervision (49.1%), and prison (50.5%) (Latessa et al., 1998). Further analysis revealed that those offenders who completed the day reporting program were 16% less likely to be rearrested than those who were unsuccessfully terminated. The evaluators cautioned that the quality of the DRCs studied was less than adequate, and proposed that improved outcomes might be expected from DRCs with more programmatic integrity.

In sum, there is no evidence to suggest that increased surveillance of offenders reduces recidivism. In fact, a meta-analysis of studies on these control-oriented intermediate sanctions revealed that they produce a slight increase in recidivism (Gendreau and Little, 1993). As a result, more offenders in these specialized programs are returned to prison, thus limiting the extent to which any diversionary effect can be achieved. Ironically, it is the rehabilitative aspect of these programs that seems to be positively impacting recidivism. This finding has been used to suggest that perhaps the provision of intensive treatment is a more meaningful form of crime control.

C. Tough Policies in Juvenile Justice

The current level of violent juvenile crime is 60% above the level recorded in 1987 (Snyder, 1997). Recent responses to juvenile crime have revolved around treating juvenile offenders more like adult offenders. Legislative changes have authorized the opening of juvenile criminal records, allowed fingerprints and photographs to be taken of juveniles who allegedly commit misdemeanor or felony crimes, and granted victims of juvenile crime the right to notification of case status and the right to address the court (Lyons, 1995). Recent trends in the sentencing of juvenile offenders include stricter determinant sentences for younger juveniles who commit serious violent crimes and the increased use of secure correctional facilities (DeComo et al., 1993). By far, however, the most popular change in juvenile legislation has revolved around the transfer of juveniles to adult courts.

All states have some mechanism in place for transferring juveniles to adult court (Sickmund, 1994). Recent legislative changes related to juvenile waivers have lowered the age at which juveniles are eligible for transfers, expanded the list of crimes for which juveniles can be transferred, and changed the process for transfer hearings (Parent et al., 1997b). These changes have contributed to a 71% increase in the number of juvenile waivers from 1985 to 1994 (Butts, 1997).

The intention of juvenile waivers is to protect the public and deter other youth from criminal behavior by imposing more severe sanctions on youth than is possible in juvenile court (Greenwood, 1996). Early studies of juvenile waivers, however, found that the majority of transferred cases received probation or some other community-based option (Hamparian et al., 1982; Bortner, 1986). More recently, the majority of these juvenile offenders have been sentenced to prison (GAO, 1995), introducing a host of problems for both juvenile and adult facilities. According to Parent et al. (1997b), several states hold these offenders in juvenile training schools until they reach the age of majority, at which time they are transferred to adult prisons. With nothing to lose, these juveniles engage in frequent misconduct and present serious management problems for juvenile facilities. Once they get to adult prisons, housing and programming become issues: housing these juveniles with adult inmates raises concerns about their safety, and few prisons have the resources to develop educational or other programs that meet the specialized needs of these young inmates.

Although we have a good idea of the problems created by the increase in juvenile waivers, as of yet there is no indication as to their effect on rates of delinquency. The next section of this chapter tackles this difficult issue within the context of the entire get-tough era.

III. ARE GET-TOUGH POLICIES REDUCING CRIME?

The value of crime control strategies is typically assessed through an examination of recidivism rates and crime rates. Recidivism rates generally refer to the proportion of offenders who are arrested or convicted for a new crime. As previously reported, studies of ISP, electronic monitoring, and day reporting centers found no significant differences in the rates of recidivism between offenders placed in these programs and offenders placed in traditional probation and parole supervision. Additionally, a study of a representative sample of prisoners released from prisons in 11 states during 1983 revealed that 46.8% were convicted for a new offense within three years (Beck and Shipley, 1989). These recidivism rates show that a substantial proportion of those people most directly affected by get-tough strategies is not deterred from future crime.

Crime rates offer a more complex indicator of the effectiveness of crime control policies. According to the Uniform Crime Reports (UCR), preliminary 1997 statistics show a 4% decline in serious reported crime (FBI, 1998). This represents the sixth consecutive annual decline. Statistics from the National Crime Victimization Survey (NCVS) reveal a similar downward trend since 1994. And for the second year in a row, there was a decline in the number of juvenile arrests for violent crime (Snyder, 1997).

Several researchers use these reported declines in serious crime as support for get-tough strategies. Langan (1991:1573), for example, uses the rising incarceration rates from 1973 to 1986 and a concomitant decline in crime rates as measured by the NCVS to suggest that prisons could be "responsible for sizable reductions in crime." What Langan could not foresee, however, was the subsequent increase in violent crime from 1986 to 1993 to nearly peak levels (Rand et al., 1997), while the incarceration rate continued its upward trend. The National

Center for Policy Analysis (NCPA) also credits higher rates of imprisonment for declining crime rates. A recent report by NCPA concludes that the recent reduction in crime can be attributed to an increase in "expected punishment" (i.e., an increase in the likelihood of going to prison and the median sentence length) (Reynolds, 1997).

Other researchers challenge the role of imprisonment and other get-tough strategies in reducing crime. "Clearly, imprisonment has an incapacitative effect on the individual offender. The key issue, however, is whether increased imprisonment results in an overall decrease in crime and at what cost" (Campaign for an Effective Crime Policy, 1995:2). Visher (1987) examined several studies on the effect of incapacitation and concluded that despite a doubling of the prison population crime reductions were limited to 10–30%. Similarly, Reiss and Roth (1993) report that violent crime rates remained stable despite a tripling in the average prison time served per crime. Clear (1994:62–63), uses such findings to argue that the "punishment experiment" in which the United States has engaged over the past two decades "did not produce a commensurate reduction in the amount of crime."

Several factors may account for these disparate views on the effects of get-tough legislation. First, the selected method of crime measurement may bias conclusions. The two primary methods of crime measurement, the UCR and NCVS, examine crime from very different perspectives. The UCR includes only those crimes reported to the police. The NCVS estimates crime rates based on interviews with members of a nationally representative sample of households in the United States about victimization they have experienced in the past year. A comparison of the UCR and NCVS shows very different patterns in crime rates over time (DiMascio, 1997). Second, it has been argued that misleading snapshots of crime trends can muddle the truth about the relationship between imprisonment and crime rates (Austin and Irwin, 1993; Campaign for an Effective Crime Policy, 1995; DiMascio, 1997). For example, 10-year increments of UCR data reveal a decrease in the crime rate of 2.2% from 1980 to 1990, while masking an increase in the crime rate of 11.8% from 1985 to 1990 (DiMascio, 1997). Third, since 15- to 24-year-old males commit most crime, fluctuations in this population can be expected to produce changes in the crime rate (Austin and Irwin, 1993). The failure to consider the influence of demographic shifts on crime rates often leads researchers to falsely attribute reductions in crime to the increased use of imprisonment (Austin and Irwin, 1993; DiMascio, 1997). Given the complexities surrounding the interpretation of crime statistics, an examination of what is known about crime and a return to the theoretical basis underlying get-tough strategies may better illuminate their likely effect on crime.

Although many questions regarding the causes and nature of crime remain, a substantial amount of evidence suggests consensus in two main areas. First, there is a high degree of consensus in the literature regarding the continuity of behavior, with childhood conduct problems being the best predictor of later delinquency and criminality (Gottfredson and Hirschi, 1990; Greenwood et al., 1996; Yoshikawa, 1994). Chronic juvenile offenders are characterized by an early age of onset, with their first conviction occurring between the ages of 10 and 15 (Yoshikawa, 1994). Second, it has been empirically demonstrated that delinquency is the product of multiple forces. An early study found that, as a group, delinquents could be distinguished from nondelinquents based on physical, temperamental, attitudinal, psychological, and sociocultural factors (Glueck and Glueck, 1950). Family processes such as poor parental supervision, erratic child-rearing behavior, and parental rejection of the child are consistently found to be associated with delinquency (Glueck and Glueck, 1950; Laub and Sampson, 1988; Greenwood et al., 1996). Individual characteristics that are strongly and consistently correlated with criminality include weak self-control, extraversion, risk taking, and possession of antisocial values (Andrews and Bonta, 1994). Considering the early onset and multiple forces of chronic criminality, why would strategies rooted in deterrence and incapacitation be expected to reduce crime?

Clearly, offenders are prevented from committing crime against society during their incarceration. By the time offenders are incarcerated, however, it is late in their criminal careers and their criminal activity is beginning to decline (Petersilia, 1992). Combine this with the fact that those in prison are immediately replaced by new recruits and the marginal effect of incapacitative strategies becomes more clear (Petersilia, 1992).

The known correlates of crime challenge the basic assumption of deterrence. Deterrence assumes that people are rational—that they weigh the costs and benefits before acting, and if the costs of crime are high enough people will be deterred from committing criminal acts. The literature on offenders' temperament and antisocial attitudes suggests, however, that offenders are characterized by impulsivity (Glueck and Glueck, 1950; Gottfredson and Hirschi, 1990; Gendreau et al., 1992). Given this, it is unlikely that offenders take the time to engage in a rational examination of the costs of crime. Thus, the ability of deterrent strategies to reduce crime is questionable.

Logan and DiIulio (1992) argue that punishment affirms morals and cultural values regardless of whether it upholds the social order. Although many American citizens may agree with the expressive value of punishment, few would be willing to sacrifice their personal and community safety to policies that do not reduce crime. Given this, it is time to counteract these past 25 years of get-tough strategies with strategies proven effective in reducing crime.

IV. STRATEGIES FOR REDUCING CRIME

Although incapacitative strategies may prevent crime during the offender's period of incarceration, such strategies do nothing about the multiple forces that lead young, inner-city youth to engage in crime (Clear, 1994; Greenwood et al., 1996).

Currie (1985) argues that current government policies regarding the punishment of criminal offenders perpetuate and expand racial and economic inequalities. He believes that answers to crime lie not with increased control inherent in deterrence and incapacitation-based strategies, but with government policies which invest in poverty-stricken communities by providing support in the form of welfare, health care, child care, and early-childhood intervention programs. In line with Currie's suggestions, corrections role should be to develop correctional programs that target the multiple contributors to crime and that prevent the escalation of delinquent and criminal behavior and further penetration into the criminal justice system. The following section explores promising approaches for diverting an offender from a life of crime.

A. Promising Programs

One of the first questions asked when considering correctional policy is, "How much does it cost?" The second question asked is, "Is it worth it?" A recent study found that early intervention programs are more cost-effective than get-tough strategies. Greenwood et al. (1996) compared the projected costs and effects of two early-intervention programs with that of California's three-strikes legislation and concluded that the early-intervention programs are more cost-effective. Graduation incentives and parent-training interventions together were projected to reduce serious crime by 22% at a combined annual cost of less than $1 billion; the three-strikes legislation was projected to achieve a 21% reduction in crime at the cost of $5.5 billion per year. In addition to being more cost-effective, there is mounting evidence that correctional interventions that target known correlates of crime are capable of reducing recidivism.

The National Institute of Justice sponsored a comprehensive review of prevention programs for the purpose of identifying programs that work to prevent crime. Despite research limitations, researchers from the University of Maryland were able to differentiate between programs that work, programs that don't work, and programs that are promising (Sherman et al., 1998). The authors defined prevention in broad terms: "any practice shown to result in less crime than would occur without the practice" (p. 2). Programs were classified as "working" if positive results were found in at least two evaluations that employed quasi-experimental designs. Among those correctional programs that "worked" were family therapy and parent training on delinquent and at-risk behavior, life skills training in schools, training in cognitive skills for at-risk youth, rehabilitation programs for adult and juvenile offenders that are appropriate for their level of risk, and therapeutic communities for the drug treatment of offenders in prisons. Programs were classified as "promising" if they were found to be effective in at least one quasi-experimental evaluation. Among those correctional programs identified as promising were mentoring programs, after-school recreation programs, prison-based vocational education, drug courts, intensive supervision and aftercare of serious juvenile offenders, and fines for criminal acts. Following are brief overviews of two of the more popular and promising correctional programs: drug courts and cognitive programs.

1. Drug Courts

Drug courts emerged in the 1980s as a means to improve the flow of drug-related cases through backlogged court systems and to better address the treatment needs of drug-involved offenders (NIJ, 1995). Since its inception in Miami, Florida, in 1989, the drug court concept has been implemented in over 100 jurisdictions nationwide. Although early drug courts were designed for adult offenders, the concept has recently been implemented within juvenile courts.

Drug courts differ from traditional court models in several ways. First, drug courts downplay the adversarial process in favor of a collaborative process that recognizes the need to address the underlying problem of drug abuse (National Association of Drug Court Professionals [NADCP], 1996). Prosecutors, defense counselors, judges, treatment professionals, and probation officers work together to achieve a case outcome that provides the best opportunity for the offender's success in treatment. Second, judges are key players in the treatment and supervision of drug-involved offenders. This differs remarkably from traditional models where judges simply hear the case and hand down a sentence, hardly getting to know the offender (Wager, 1992). Third, drug courts make provisions for intervention to occur immediately after arrest. Prompt identification of drug-involved offenders and immediate intervention capitalizes on the crisis of arrest, making it difficult for offenders to deny their problem. Furthermore, minimizing the time from arrest to disposition is believed to maximize an offender's motivation for change (NADCP, 1996).

Research substantiates the role that the criminal justice system can play in treatment success. People coerced into treatment are found to do just as well as voluntary participants; and the coercive process may facilitate longer involvement in treatment, which is a key factor in success (Center for Substance Abuse Treatment, 1995). A review of drug court evaluations by American University revealed that 70% of drug court participants either successfully completed the program or were still active in the program. An evaluation of Miami's Drug Court Program found that 60% of the program participants had favorable treatment outcomes and that drug court participants had lower rates of rearrests than comparison groups of felony drug and nondrug offenders participating in other programs (Goldkamp, 1994). These early results led to the replication of Miami's program in many jurisdictions.

2. Cognitive Restructuring and Skills Training

Cognitive interventions are popular strategies for both juvenile and adult offenders within community-based and institutional settings. They are based on research

indicating that offenders are characterized by cognitive skills deficits (e.g., problem solving, critical reasoning) and internalized antisocial values (Ross and Fabiano, 1985; Goldstein and Glick, 1995). According to Lester and Van Voorhis
(1997) there are two primary types of cognitive interventions: cognitive restructuring, and cognitive skills training.

Cognitive restructuring interventions are designed to challenge and modify
the content of the offender's thinking. That is, they focus on changing the attitudes, values, and beliefs of offenders that excuse, support, and reinforce criminal
behavior (Lester and Van Voorhis, 1997). Two examples of cognitive restructuring paradigms are Ellis' Rational Emotive Therapy (RET) (Ellis, 1973) and
Yochelson and Samenow's (1976) Criminal Thinking Errors. RET is based on
the idea that criminal and other problem behaviors are the result of unhealthy
thought sequences. These sequences begin with an activating event (e.g., flunked
a test) and are followed by an irrational thought or belief (e.g., I'm stupid, a
failure) and a behavioral consequence of that belief (e.g., drop out of school).
RET involves confronting offenders' irrational thoughts, helping them identify
objective factors leading to the activating event, and assisting them in developing
rational, healthy thoughts which lead to a more positive consequence. RET can
be delivered in individual or group sessions.

Yochelson and Samenow (1976) introduced the idea of criminal thinking
errors that are used to excuse and support criminal behavior. Common thinking
errors include the externalization of blame, an ''I can't'' attitude, and a sense of
entitlement. Samenow (1984, 1989) proposes that these thinking errors need to
be challenged by accepting no excuses, confronting the thinking errors when
expressed, and refocusing blame and responsibility on the offender. This approach to cognitive restructuring is often incorporated into residential programs
for youth that use peer pressure to attack thinking errors (Gibbs et al., 1995).

Cognitive skills training is designed to enhance cognitive deficiencies by
changing the form and process of thinking (Lester and Van Voorhis, 1997). According to Ross and Fabiano (1985), offenders are impulsive, concrete thinkers,
conceptually rigid, egocentric, and lack critical reasoning skills. Several models
of cognitive skills training programs have been developed to address these deficits. The programs are more educational than therapeutic, and therefore probation, parole, and correctional officers can be trained to facilitate the educational
groups. The groups are designed to be experiential to allow offenders to practice
new skills and get feedback on their behavior. Additionally, offenders are instructed to complete homework assignments that require them to practice the new
skills in more natural settings.

The research on cognitive programs is promising. An evaluation involving
the random assignment of adult offenders to regular probation, ISP, and ISP with
a cognitive skills training component found that offenders who participated in
the cognitive component had lower rates of recidivism than both comparison

groups (Johnson and Hunter, 1992). Two juvenile programs that combine cognitive skills training, anger control training, and moral education have revealed equally positive results. Positive program outcomes include enhanced social skills, improved anger control, reduced unexcused school absences, and reduced recidivism (Gibbs et al, 1995; Goldstein and Glick, 1995).

Drug courts and cognitive programs are promising strategies for promoting long-term behavioral change among adult and juvenile offenders. Even within these programs, however, there are several criteria that must be met to enhance the likelihood of success.

B. Developing Research-Based Intervention Programs

Over the past two decades, numerous authors have conducted literature reviews and meta-analyses to examine the effectiveness of various correctional interventions. Despite the inclusion of different studies and the variety of techniques used in these analyses, the conclusions drawn by these authors are strikingly similar: those programs that lead to a reduction in recidivism possess several common characteristics (Andrews et al., 1990; Gendreau and Andrews, 1990; Izzo and Ross, 1990; Lipsey and Wilson, 1998). The most effective programs were conducted in the community (Izzo and Ross, 1990; Lipsey and Wilson, 1998; Palmer, 1974; Whitehead and Lab, 1989), included multimodal programming (Clements, 1988; Lipsey, 1992; Lipsey and Wilson, 1998; Palmer, 1992, 1996), and involved the family in the offender's treatment (Clements, 1988; Gendreau and Ross, 1987; Palmer, 1996).

Other, more specific characteristics that have been identified have been referred to as "the principles of effective intervention" (Andrews et al., 1990; Gendreau and Andrews, 1990; Gendreau, 1996). They include:

1. Effective interventions are behavioral in nature. A well-designed behavioral program combines a system of reinforcement with modeling by the treatment provider to teach and motivate offenders to perform prosocial behaviors. Additionally, problem solving and self-instructional training may be used to change the offender's cognitions, attitudes, and values that maintain antisocial behavior.

2. Levels of service should be matched to the risk level of the offender. Intensive services are necessary for a significant reduction of recidivism among high-risk offenders, but, when applied to low-risk offenders, intensive services produce a minimal or negative effect.

3. Offenders should be matched to services designed to improve their specific criminogenic needs such as antisocial attitudes, substance abuse, family communication, and peer associations. Improvements in these areas will contribute to a reduced likelihood of recidivism.

4. Treatment approaches and service providers are matched to the learn-

ing style or personality of the offender. For example, high anxiety offenders do not generally respond well to confrontation (Warren, 1983), and offenders with below-average intellectual abilities do not respond to cognitive skills programs as well as offenders with above-average or high intellectual abilities (Fabiano et al., 1991).

5. Services for high-risk offenders should be intensive, occupying 40–70% of the offenders' time over a 3-to-9-month period.

6. The program is highly structured, and contingencies are enforced in a firm but fair way: Staff design, maintain, and enforce contingencies; internal controls are established to detect possible antisocial activities; program activities disrupt the criminal network and prevent negative peers from taking over the program.

7. Staff relate to offenders in interpersonally sensitive and constructive ways and are trained and supervised appropriately.

8. Staff monitor offender change on intermediate targets of treatment.

9. Relapse prevention is employed in the community to monitor and anticipate problem situations, and to train offenders to rehearse alternative behavior.

10. High levels of advocacy and brokerage occur if community services are appropriate.

Meta-analyses of correctional interventions have found that programs that meet these principles are achieving, on average, a recidivism reduction of 30–50% (Andrews et al., 1990). This research on "what works" in correctional interventions provides a powerful agenda for correctional programming. It suggests that public safety interests may be better served by shifting the emphasis of popular intermediate sanction programs from deterrence-based strategies to the provision of intensive, research-based treatment. It also suggests that the current obsession with imprisonment is misplaced—given the appropriate intervention, many offenders can be managed safely within the community and can achieve long-term behavioral change that surpasses the incapacitation effect of prison. Even the best programs, however, cannot survive without management strategies that support and direct their activities. The remainder of this chapter will focus on four recent trends in the management of correctional policy.

V. MANAGEMENT ISSUES

Keeping pace with the growing correctional populations and managing constant change is no easy task. Proposed solutions often are nothing more than stopgap approaches that ultimately perpetuate the very problems they are trying to resolve. Four recent management trends, however, represent a sincere effort to find long-term answers and to interject rationality and accountability into the system. Following are brief discussions on how case classification, performance-based measurement, privatization, and the localization of corrections are being used to improve services and decision making in correctional systems.

A. Case Classification

Shrinking resources and a demand for equitable and appropriate decision making have led to an increased interest in case classification in institutional and community-based corrections (Jones, 1996). Classification systems are designed to categorize offenders based on specific behavioral or psychological dimensions (Van Voorhis, 1997). A well-designed classification system can assist agencies in managing offenders' risk of recidivism during supervision, in planning for more effective interventions to reduce the probability of recidivism, and in making more efficient use of limited correctional resources (Andrews and Bonta, 1995).

The dominant focus of classification is on predicting offenders' risk of recidivism or their risk to institutional security (Clements, 1996). The methods of risk prediction have evolved over the years from a more subjective form of clinical assessment based on professional judgment to actuarial risk assessment based on objective and standardized factors (Jones, 1996). Although no form of risk prediction is perfect, empirical evidence suggests that actuarial methods are more accurate at predicting risk than clinical methods (Gottfredson, 1987).

Burgess (1928) was the first to develop the actuarial, or statistical, approach to risk assessment. He based it on a study of 3000 parolees through which he identified 21 factors that differentiated successful and unsuccessful offenders. Since that time several variations of actuarial risk assessment instruments have emerged, including the Salient Factor Score (SFS; Hoffman, 1983) and the Statistical Index on Recidivism (SIR; Nuffield, 1982). These instruments consist of several common variables predictive of future criminality including the number of prior convictions, number of prior incarcerations, age at first arrest, and number of prior probation or parole revocations. The SFS and SIR consist of seven and 15 items, respectively, most of which are historical, static factors. Both instruments have proven predictive validity and provide a strong basis for the separation of offenders according to their security and supervision needs (Bonta, 1996; Van Voorhis, 1997). Because of their exclusive focus on factors that cannot be changed, however, neither instrument provides any direction for the provision of treatment services.

Recent developments in risk assessment have addressed this deficiency with the addition of items designed to measure dynamic factors that are known correlates of crime. The Wisconsin Classification System (Baird, 1981) includes single measures of attitude, drug use, alcohol use, employment, and residential stability. The Level of Services Inventory (LSI; Andrews and Bonta, 1994) includes multiple items to measure antisocial attitudes, peer associations, drug and alcohol use, employment, residential stability, family characteristics, use of leisure time, and antisocial personality characteristics. By measuring these dynamic factors, or criminogenic needs, corrections agencies can identify those factors most strongly associated with an offender's criminal behavior and target them for change through the provision of appropriate treatment and services.

The best classification systems are characterized by four key elements (Van Voorhis, 1997). First, they include both static and dynamic factors that are known correlates of crime. Second, they involve periodic reassessment of offenders as a means to measure offender change and program effectiveness. Third, they are validated on the local population to identify the base rate of recidivism, to establish proper cut-off scores for assigning cases to various supervision or custody levels, and to assure that the predictors are valid. Fourth, they include comprehensive staff training to ensure high interrater reliability. Given the benefits of case classification it is a worthy investment for correctional systems.

B. Promoting Accountability Through Performance Measures

Hiding behind their expressive function, get-tough strategies have held their ground as the backbone of correctional policy. This reign may end, however, with the movement toward results-based decision making in state and local government. Heightened competition for limited public funds is forcing government agencies to demonstrate their worth by achieving bottom-line results. According to Friedman (1996:2), "They [results] are about the fundamental desires of citizens and the fundamental purposes of government." Public opinion polls have repeatedly revealed that what the public wants from corrections is to be safe from crime (Doble, 1987; Cullen et al., 1988; Tilow, 1992; Applegate et al., 1997). Citizens are becoming less tolerant of policies and programs that are not capable of meeting this utilitarian challenge.

A system of performance-based measurement is a robust management tool for keeping organizations focused on achieving desired results. It assists agencies in answering four key questions (Boone and Fulton, 1995; Friedman, 1996):

1. What are desired outcomes for offenders, families, and communities?
2. What works to achieve the desired outcomes?
3. How will the agency determine if the elements of the strategy are being performed as well as possible?
4. How will the agency determine if the desired outcomes have been achieved?

Many correctional agencies have evaded these commonsense questions for far too long. They have masked their failure to achieve meaningful outcomes with reports on system outputs (e.g., the number of people served, the number of service hours provided) rather than reports on results. In several states, however, legislators faced with the challenge of appropriating state funds are demanding more. For example, a 1994 letter from the House Appropriations and Senate Ways and Means Committees in Kansas informed all state funded agencies of an impending performance-based budgeting system that would hold agencies "accountable for accomplishments through the use of performance measurements and not for how much will be spent buying paper clips." Since that time, the Kansas Department of Corrections has developed a comprehensive system of performance-based measurements. Other states (e.g., Texas, New Jersey, Arizona) have followed suit, developing performance-based measures as part of good business practice.

In addition to positioning agencies to compete for limited public funds, performance-based measurements offer other important benefits (Boone and Fulton, 1995):

1. They provide an alternative to recidivism as the sole measure of effectiveness. Recidivism measures provide little insight for policy modifications. By measuring intermediate outcomes (e.g., number of offenders obtaining their GED, number of days drug-free) in addition to recidivism, agencies can begin to disentangle the effects of specific program activities and components and to determine what it is that leads to the ultimate outcomes of behavioral change and reduced recidivism.

2. Performance-based measures enhance cost-benefit analysis by providing a mechanism for incorporating performance into cost considerations. A program with lower up-front costs may be more costly in the long run because of poor performance.

3. Performance-based measures assist agencies in differentiating success from failure (Osborne and Gaebler, 1993). This allows managers to encourage desired performance through rewards and corrective techniques (e.g., training).

4. Performance-based measures assist agencies in creating a learning environment that contributes to organizational growth through structured feedback and continuous monitoring and evaluation.

C. Privatization

Complaints about ineffective practices, crowding, and rising correctional costs have led policymakers to turn to the private sector for solutions. The private sector is involved in corrections in several ways, including the complete operation and management of prison facilities, contracting for specific programs or services, and operating prison industries (Kinkade and Leone, 1992; LIS, Inc., 1996).

Private involvement in the full-scale operation of prisons began in 1983 when the Corrections Corporation of America was awarded a contract from the Immigration and Naturalization Services to design, build, and manage a 350-bed, minimum-security facility (Singal, 1998). A survey sponsored by the National

Institute of Corrections found that, as of December 1995, privately run prisons were in operation in six states and Puerto Rico, and under development in five additional states (LIS, Inc., 1996). By 1996, privately managed adult secure beds accounted for 2.9% of the prison beds in the United States (Singal, 1998). Although limited in scope and methodology, the results of recent studies favor privately managed correctional facilities over their public counterparts. Two studies have found that the privately run facilities were more cost-effective (Archambeault and Policy Research Institute as cited in Singal, 1998). A study that compared private and public female prisons on eight dimensions of quality (care, safety, security, justice, activity, order, conditions, and management) found that private prisons outperformed the publicly run facilities on most dimensions (Logan, 1992). Despite these findings, there continues to be resistance to the full-scale privatization of prisons. Kinkade and Leone (1992) found that this lack of acceptance for the private management of prisons is driven by concerns that the profit motive would take precedence over quality and contribute to deteriorating conditions of confinement. Another source of resistance surrounds the ethical concerns about the delegation of the use of deadly force to the private sector (Kinkade and Leone, 1992; LIS, Inc., 1996).

Contracting for services is a common form of privatization. All state departments of corrections except for Colorado and Puerto Rico contract for some type of program or service including medical care, mental health care, offender programming (e.g., educational, vocational, sex offender treatment), and food services (LIS, Inc., 1996). Cullen (1986) identifies several potential dangers associated with contracting for treatment services. First, there may be resistance from existing correctional employees regarding territorial issues and threatened security. Second, the push to meet performance criteria specified in the contract may lead to coercive methods of treatment. Third, states may turn to private vendors to get cheaper services rather than to get more effective services. On the positive side, Cullen (1986) suggests that contracting for treatment services may provide a means for overcoming the often-cited chasm between the custody and security roles of prison employees.

The third major type of privatization is prison industries which involves the use of prisoners in the manufacturing or marketing of made-for-profit goods or services (Kinkade and Leone, 1992). Over 4000 prisoners work for the private sector making and marketing products and servicing hotels, airlines, and catalog merchandisers (Cohen, 1996). Opposition to prison industries focuses on job stealing (i.e., prisoners are paid less than the union wages for the same types of jobs) and interference with institution schedules and security (Kinkade and Leone, 1992). Support for prison industries focuses on increased postrelease employment opportunities, a reduction in inmates' idle time and misconduct, and a reduction in prison operating costs through the garnishment of prisoners' wages (Kinkade and Leone, 1992). Additionally, Guynes and Grieser (1986) suggest that prison work may reduce an offender's likelihood of recidivism by providing him/her with funds that facilitate reintegration.

Clearly, privatization has both benefits and drawbacks. As of this date, the data do not clearly support or oppose the value of privatization (Secrest and Shichor, 1996). At the very least, privatization is providing an alternative way of looking at current practices, and is introducing new ideas into the prison system (Cullen, 1988; Mays and Gray, 1996). Given the continuing growth of the correctional industry, the private sector is likely to play an expanding role in resolving the prison crisis.

D. Localizing Corrections

As an extension of the intermediate sanctions movement, several states have introduced legislation designed to shift the burden of housing offenders from state-level systems to local criminal justice systems. Ohio's 1995 Senate Bill 2 created a fifth level of felony and downgraded some offenses previously classified as felonies to misdemeanors. Offenders convicted of these new low-level felony and misdemeanor offenses must now be sentenced to jail or other community-based sanctions rather than prison. This legislation encourages the use of noninstitutional sanctions by taking advantage of the fact that judges are more concerned about exceeding the capacities of their county-supported jails than they are the state-supported prisons. To assist counties in bearing this burden, Senate Bill 2 extends an earlier Community Corrections Act by providing additional funding to local criminal justice systems for the creation of a broader range of alternatives to prison. To be eligible for this funding, counties must create a community corrections planning board and develop a comprehensive plan for community corrections that coordinates all correctional services in the county and reduces the number of people committed to state prisons or local jails.

Oregon's Senate bill 1145 is similar to Ohio's bill. The law states that counties will provide sanctions for a specified group of less serious felony offenders while the state will incarcerate violent or more serious felony offenders. All sentences of less than one year must be served in the county that has jurisdiction over the case. Furthermore, the responsibility for the operation of the community corrections offices was shifted from the state to county government. State assistance was provided to local governments for jails and the development of alternative sanctions.

A new program in Ohio is designed to promote accountability for sentencing practices in juvenile court. Specifically, RECLAIM Ohio is designed to discourage juvenile courts from overreliance on state training schools and to encourage the creation of community-based options (Latessa et al., 1998). Each juvenile court is allotted a specified amount of money that may be used to buy treatment services for delinquent youths. However, when judges send youths to state-run institutions, the local treatment fund is charged approximately $75/day for the cost of the youth's treatment by the state. The pilot of RECLAIM in nine counties resulted in a 43% reduction in commitments to the Department of Youth Services (DYS) and the provision of community-based treatment to nearly 1000 adjudicated offenders. Based on these positive results, the program was expanded to all Ohio counties in January 1995. A recent evaluation reveals that in 1997, despite a rise in adjudications, the nonpilot counties reduced the number of youths committed to DYS institutions by 36% and the pilot counties reduced commitments by 42% (Latessa et al., 1998). It appears that Ohio has found an effective way to control the state budget and to encourage the community-based treatment of juvenile offenders.

VI. CONCLUSION

Correctional history suggests that continued infatuation with get-tough policies will have costly ramifications for all components of the criminal justice system with marginal effects on the rates of crime. A major shift in correctional policy is needed if states hope to fulfill the public expectations regarding community protection. This shift should be guided by empirical evidence regarding what works to reduce crime. A large body of research has been amassed on the correlates of crime and the characteristics of effective intervention. This research directs correctional policy makers to begin investing in early-intervention programs designed to counteract the individual, familial, and environmental forces that contribute to criminal behavior. The intervention process can be effectively managed through a well-designed case classification system that increases consistency and fairness in decision making, targets high-risk offenders for more intensive services, and identifies offenders' individual treatment needs.

Correctional policy makers with a vested interest in enhancing public safety will earmark funds for the ongoing evaluation of programs and practices. Performance-based measures provide agencies with continuous feedback that drives program improvements. More sophisticated evaluation designs also are needed to more clearly distinguish program effects. Investing in research-based policies and engaging in evaluation will promote a rational approach to managing state corrections policy in the 21st century.

REFERENCES

Andrews, D., and Bonta, J. (1994). *The Psychology of Criminal Conduct*, Anderson Publishing Co., Cincinnati, OH.
Andrews, D., Zinger, I., Hoge, R., Bonta, J., Gendreau, P., and Cullen F. (1990). Does

correctional treatment work? A clinically relevant and psychologically informed meta-analysis. *Criminology 28*:369–404.

Applegate, B. K., Cullen, F. T., and Fisher, B. S. (1997). Public support for correctional treatment: the continuing appeal of the rehabilitative ideal. *Prison Journal 77*:237–58.

Austin, J., and Irwin, J. (1993). *Does Imprisonment Reduce Crime? A Critique of "Voodoo Criminology,"* National Council on Crime and Delinquency, Washington, DC.

Baird, C. (1981). Probation and parole classification: the Wisconsin model, *Corrections Today 43*:36–41.

Banks, J., Porter, A., Rardin, R., Sider, R., and Unger, V. (1977). *Evaluation of Intensive Special Probation Projects: Phase I Report* (grant No. 76 NI-99-0045), U.S. Department of Justice, Washington, DC.

Baumer, T., and Mendelsohn, R. (1992). Electronically monitored home confinement: does it work?" *Smart Sentencing: The Emergence of Intermediate Sanctions* (J. Byrne, A. Lurigio, and J. Petersilia, eds.), Sage, Newbury Park, CA, pp. 54–67.

Baumer, T., Mendelsohn, R., and Rhine, E. (1990). *Executive Summary—The Electronic Monitoring of Non-Violent Convicted Felons: An Experiment in Home Detention*, National Institute of Justice, Washington, DC.

Beccaria, C. (1963) [1764]. *On Crimes and Punishments*, Bobbs-Merrill, Indianapolis.

Beck, A., and Shipley, B. E. (1989). Recidivism of prisoners released in 1983, Bureau of Justice Statistics, April.

Bonczar, T. P., and Beck, A. J. (1997). Lifetime likelihood of going to state or federal prison, Bureau of Justice Statistics Special Report, March.

Bonta, J. (1996). Risk-needs assessment and treatment, *Choosing Correctional Options That Work: Defining the Demand and Evaluating the Supply* (A. T. Harland, ed.), Sage, Thousand Oaks, CA. pp. 18–32.

Boone, H., and Fulton, B. (1995). *Results-Driven Management: Implementing Performance-Based Measures in Community Corrections*, American Probation and Parole Association, Lexington, KY.

Bortner, M. A. (1986). Traditional rhetoric, organizational realities: remand of juveniles to adult court. *Crime and Delinquency 32*:53–73.

Brown, M., and Roy, S. (1995). Manual and electronic house arrest: an evaluation of factors related to failure, *Intermediate Sanctions: Sentencing in the 90s* (J. Smykla and W. Selke, eds.), Anderson, Cincinnati, pp. 37–53.

Bureau of Justice Assistance. (1989). *Electronic Monitoring in Intensive Probation and Parole Programs*, U.S. Department of Justice, Washington, DC.

Bureau of Justice Statistics. (1992). Expenditure and employment, 1990. (September).

Burgess, E. (1928). Factors determining success or failure on parole, *The Workings of the Indeterminate Sentence Law and the Parole System in Illinois* (E. Burgess and J. Landesco, eds.), State Board of Parole, Springfield, Il.

Butts, J. A. (1997). Delinquency cases waived to criminal court, 1985–1994, Office of Juvenile Justice and Delinquency Prevention Fact Sheet (February).

Byrne, J., and Kelly, L. (1989). Restructuring probation as an intermediate sanction: an evaluation of the massachusetts intensive probation supervision program, Final report to the National Institute of Justice, Research Program of the Punishment and Control of Offenders, U.S. Department of Justice, Washington, DC.

Campaign for an Effective Crime Policy. (1995). *What Every Policymaker Should Know About Imprisonment and the Crime Rate*, Author, Washington, DC.

Carter, R., and Wilkins, L. (1976). Caseloads: some conceptual models, *Probation, Parole and Community Corrections* (R. Carter and L. Wilkins, eds.), Wiley and Sons, New York, pp. 391–401.

Center for Substance Abuse Treatment. (1995). Planning for alcohol and other drug abuse treatment for adults in the criminal justice system, *Treatment Improvement Protocol* (Series 17).

Clear, T. R. (1994). *Harm in American Penology: Offenders, Victims, and Their Communities*, State University of New York Press, Albany.

Clements, C. (1988). Delinquency prevention and treatment: a community-centered perspective, *Criminal Justice and Behavior 15*:286–305.

Clements, C. (1996). Offender classification: two decades of progress, *Criminal Justice and Behavior 23(1)*:212–143.

Cohen, W. (1996). Need work: go to jail, *U.S. News and World Report* Dec.: 66–67.

Cullen, F. T. (1986). The privatization of treatment: prison reform in the 1980s, *Federal Probation* 8–16.

Cullen, F. T., Cullen, J. B., and Wozniak, J. F. (1988). Is rehabilitation dead? The myth of the punitive public, *Journal of Criminal Justice 16*:303–317.

Cullen, F. T., and Gilbert, K. E. (1982). *Reaffirming Rehabilitation*, Anderson, Cincinnati.

Cullen, F. T., Van Voorhis, P., and Sundt, J. L. (1996). Prisons in crisis: the American experience, *Prisons 2000: An International Perspective on the Current State and Future of Imprisonment* (R. Matthews and P. Francis, eds.), Martin's Press, New York, pp. 21–52.

Cullen, F. T., Wright, J. P., and Applegate, B. K. (1996). Control in the community: the limits of reform, *Choosing Correctional Interventions That Work: Defining the Demand and Evaluating the Supply* (A. T. Harland, ed.), Sage, Newbury Park, CA.

Currie, E. (1985). *Confronting Crime: An American Challenge*, Pantheon, New York.

Danner, M. (1998). Three strikes and it's women who are out: the hidden consequences for women of criminal justice policy reforms, *Crime Control and Women: Feminist Implications of Criminal Justice Policy* (S. L. Miller, ed.), Sage, Thousand Oaks, CA, pp. 1–14.

Decomo, R., Tunis, S., Krisberg, B., and Herrera, N. (1993). *Juveniles Taken into Custody Research Program: FY1992 Annual Report*, Office of Juvenile Justice and Delinquency Prevention, U.S. Department of Justice, Washington, DC.

DiIulio, J., and Piehl, A. M. (1991). Does prison pay? The stormy national debate over the cost-effectiveness of imprisonment, *Brookings Review 9*:28–35.

DiMascio, W. M. (1997). *Seeking Justice: Crime and Punishment in America*, Edna McConnell Clark Foundation, New York.

Doble, J. (1987). *Crime and Punishment: The Public's View*, Public Agenda Foundation, New York.

Ellis, A. (1973). *Humanistic Psychotherapy*, Julian, New York.

Erwin, B. (1987). Evaluation of intensive probation supervision in Georgia: final report, Georgia Department of Corrections, Athens.

Fabiano, E., Porporino, F., and Robinson, D. (1991). *Corrections Today* Aug.:102–108.

Federal Bureau of Investigation. (1998). UCR press release—preliminary figures 1997, U.S. Department of Justice, Washington.

Feeley, M., and Simon, D. (1992). The new penology: notes on the emerging strategy of corrections and its implications, *Criminology 30*:449–474.

Friedman, M. (1996). Moving toward results: an emerging approach to community accountability for child and family well-being, *Georgia Academy Journal* Winter: 2–5.

Fulton, B., Stone, S., and Gendreau, P. (1994). *Restructuring Intensive Supervision Programs: Applying "What Works,"* American Probation and Parole Association, Lexington, KY.

Gaes, G., and McGuire, W. (1985). Prison violence: the contribution of crowding versus other determinants of prison assault rates, *Journal of Research in Crime and Delinquency 23*:41–65.

Gendreau, P. (1996). The principles of effective intervention with offenders, *Choosing Correctional Options That Work* (A. T. Harland, ed.), Sage, Thousand Oaks, CA, pp. 117–130.

Gendreau, P., and Andrews, D. (1990). Tertiary prevention: what the meta-analyses of the offender treatment literature tell us about "what works," *Canadian Journal of Criminology 32*:173–184.

Gendreau, P., and Little, T. 1993. A meta-analysis of the effectiveness of sanctions on offender recidivism, Unpublished manuscript, Department of Psychology, University of New Brunswick, Saint John.

Gendreau, P., and Ross, R. (1987). Revivication of rehabilitation: evidence from the 1980s, *Justice Quarterly 4*:349–407.

Gendreau, P., Andrews, D., Coggin, C., and Chanteloupe, F. (1992). The development of clinical and policy guidelines for the prediction of criminal behavior in criminal justice settings, Unpublished manuscript, Department of Psychology, University of New Brunswick, St. John.

Gibbs, J. C., Potter, G. B., and Goldstein, A. P. (1995). *The EQUIP Program: Teaching Youth to Think and Act Responsibly Through a Peer-Helping Approach*, Research Press, Champaign, Il.

Gilliard, D. K., and Beck, A. (1998). Prisoners in 1997. Bureau of Justice Statistics Bulletin, August.

Glueck, S., and Glueck, E. (1950). *Unraveling Juvenile Delinquency*, Commonwealth Fund, New York.

Goldkamp, J. S. (1994). Miami's treatment drug court for felony defendants: some implications of assessment findings. *Prison Journal 73(2)*:110–166.

Goldstein, A., and Glick, B., eds. (1995). *Managing Delinquency Programs That Work*, American Correctional Association, Laurel, MD.

Goodstein, L., MacKenzie, D. L., and Shotland, L. R. (1984). Personal control and inmate adjustment to prison, *Criminology 22*:343–369.

Gottfredson, S. (1984). Institutional responses to prison overcrowding, *Review of Law and Social Change 12*:29–273.

Gottfredson, S. (1987). Prediction and classification, *Prediction and Classification: Criminal Justice Decision Making* (D. Gottfredson and M. Tonry, eds.), University of Chicago Press, Chicago, pp. 1–20.

Gottfredson, M. R., and Hirschi, T. A. (1990). *General Theory of Crime*, Stanford University Press, Stanford, CA.

Greenwood, P. (1996). Responding to juvenile crime: lessons learned, *Juvenile Court 6(3)*: 75–85.

Greenwood, R. W., Model, K. E., Rydell, C. P., and Chiesa, J. (1996). Diverting children from a life of crime: measuring costs and benefits, Final report for the University of California, Berkeley.

Guynes, R. G., and Grieser, R. C. (1986). Contemporary prison industry goals, *A Study of Prison Industry: History, Components, and Goals*, National Institute of Corrections, Washington, DC.

Hamparian, D., Estep, L., Muntean, S., Pristino, R., Swisher, R., Wallace, P., and White, J. (1982). *Youth in Adult Courts: Between Two Worlds*, U.S. Department of Justice, Office of Juvenile Justice and Delinquency Prevention, Washington, DC.

Harland, A. T., and Rosen, C. J. (1987). Sentencing theory and intensive supervision probation, *Federal Probation 51(4)*:3–42.

Hoffman, P. (1983). Screening for risk: a revised salient factor score (SFS 81), *Journal of Criminal Justice 11*:539–547.

Izzo, R., and Ross, R. (1990). Meta-analysis of rehabilitation programs for juvenile delinquents: a brief report, *Criminal Justice and Behavior 17*:134–42.

Jolin, A., and Stipak, B. (1992). Drug treatment and electronically monitored home confinement: an evaluation of a community-based sentencing option, *Crime and Delinquency 38*:158–170.

Johnson, G., and Hunter, T. (1992). Evaluation of the specialized drug offender program for the Colorado Judicial Department, Unpublished report, Center for Action Research, University of Colorado, Boulder.

Jones, P. (1996). Risk prediction in criminal justice, *Choosing Correctional Options That Work: Defining the Demand and Evaluating the Supply* (A. T. Harland, ed.), Sage, Thousand Oaks, CA, pp. 33–69.

Joyce, N. M. (1992). A view of the future: the effect of policy on prison population growth, *Crime and Delinquency 38*:357–368.

Kinkade, P. T., and Leone, M. C. Issues and answers: prison administrators' responses to controversies surrounding privatization, *Prison Journal 72*:57–76.

Langan, P. A. (1991). America's soaring prison population, *Science 251*:1568–1573.

Latessa, E., Travis, L, Holsinger, A., and Hartman, J. (1998). Evaluation of Ohio's pilot day reporting program: final report, Submitted to the Ohio Office of Criminal Justice Services, Columbus.

Latessa, E., Turner, M., Moon, M., and Applegate, B. (1998). A statewide evaluation of the RECLAIM Ohio initiative, Unpublished report for the Ohio Department of Youth Services, Columbus.

Laub, J. H., and Sampson, R. J. (1988). Unraveling families and delinquency: a reanalysis of the Gluecks' data, *Criminology 26*:355–380.

Lester, D., and Van Voorhis, P. (1997). Cognitive therapies, *Correctional Counseling and Rehabilitation, 3rd ed.*, (P. Van Voorhis, M. Braswell, and D. Lester, eds.), Anderson, Cincinnati, OH, pp. 163–185.

Lipsey, M. (1992). Juvenile delinquency treatment: a meta-analytic inquiry into the variability of effects, *Meta-Analysis for Explanation* (T. Cook et al., eds.), Russell Sage, New York, pp. 83–127.

Lipsey, M., and Wilson, D. (1998). Effective intervention for serious juvenile offenders: a synthesis of research, *Serious and Violent Juvenile Offenders: Risk Factors and Successful Interventions* (R. Loeber and D. P. Farrington, eds.), Sage Thousand Oaks, CA, pp. 313–345.

LIS, Inc. (1996). Privatization and contracting in corrections: results of an NIC survey, *Correction* February.

Logan, C. H. (1992). Well kept: comparing quality of confinement in private and public prisons, *Journal of Criminal Law and Criminology 83:*577–613.

Logan, C. H., and DiIulio, J. (1992). Ten deadly myths about crime and punishment in the U.S., *Wisconsin Interest 1(1):*21–35.

Lyons, D. (1995). Juvenile crime and justice state enactments. (1995). *State Legislative Report 20(17)*.

Mays, G. L., and Gray, T., eds. (1996). *Privatization and the Provision of Correctional Services: Context and Consequences*, Anderson, Cincinnati.

McDevitt, J., and Miliano, R. (1992). Day reporting centers: an innovative concept in intermediate sanctions, *Smart Sentencing: The Emergence of Intermediate Sanctions*, (J. Byrne, A. Lurigio, and J. Petersilia, eds.), Sage, Newbury Park, CA, pp. 152–181.

Morash, M. T., Bynum, S., and Koons, B. A. (1998). Women offenders: programming needs and promising approaches, *National Institute of Justice Research in Brief*, August.

National Association of Drug Court Professionals. (1996). *Standards for Drug Courts*, National Institute of Justice, grant No. 96-DC-MX-K001.

National Conference of State Legislatures. (1994). State Budget Actions 1994.

National Institute of Justice. (1995). The drug court movement, *NIJ Update*.

Neithercutt, M., and Gottfredson, D. (1974). Caseload size variation and differences in probation/parole performance (grant No. 75-DF-99-0014), National Center for Juvenile Justice, Washington, DC.

Newman, G. (1978). *The Punishment Response*, Lippincott, New York.

Nidorf, B. (1991). Nothing works revisited, *Perspectives 3:*12–13.

Nueffield, J. (1982). *Parole Decision-Making in Canada*, Solicitor General of Canada, Ottawa.

Osborne, D., and Gaebler, T. (1993). *Reinventing Government*, Plume, New York.

Palmer, T. (1974). The youth authority's community treatment project, *Federal Probation 38(1):*3–14.

Palmer, T. (1992). *The Re-Emergence of Correctional Intervention*, Sage, Newbury Park, CA.

Palmer, T. (1996). Programmatic and nonprogrammatic aspects of successful intervention, *Choosing Correctional Options That Work* (A. T. Harland, ed.), Sage, Thousand Oaks, CA, pp. 131–182.

Papparozzi, M. (*n.d.*). An evaluation of the New Jersey board of parole's intensive supervision Program, Unpublished report.

Parent, D., Byrne, J., Tsarfaty, V., Valade, L., and Esselman, J. (1995). *Day Reporting Centers*, National Institute of Justice, Washington, DC.

Parent, D., Dunworth, T., McDonald, D., and Rhodes, W. (1997a). Key legislative issues in criminal justice: mandatory sentencing, National Institute of Justice Research in Action, January.

Parent, D., Dunworth, T., McDonald, D., and Rhodes, W. (1997b). Key legislative issues in criminal justice: transferring serious juvenile offenders to adult courts, National Institute of Justice Research in Action, January.

Paulus, P., McCain, G., and Cox, V. (1985). The effects of crowding in prisons and jails, *Reactions to Crime: The Public, Courts, and Prisons* (D. Farrington and J. Gunn, eds.), John Wiley, New York, pp. 113–134.

Petersilia, J. (1988). House arrest, *Crime File*, National Institute of Justice, Washington, DC.

Petersilia, J. (1992). California's prison policy: causes, costs, and consequences, *Prison Journal* 72:8–36.

Petersilia, J., and Turner, S. (1993). Evaluating intensive supervision probation/parole: results of a nationwide experiment, National Institute of Justice Research in Brief, May.

Piehl, A. M., and DiIulio, J. (Fall 1995). Does prison pay? Revisited, *Brookings Review* 21–25.

Pollack-Byrne, J. (1990). *Women, Prison, and Crime*, Brooks/Cole, Pacific Grove.

Rand, M. R., Lynch, J. P., and Cantor, D. (1997). Criminal victimization, 1973–95, Bureau of Justice Statistics National Crime Victimization Survey, April.

Reiss, A. J., and J. A. Roth, eds. (1993). *Understanding and Preventing Violence*, National Academy Press, Washington, DC.

Reynolds, M. O. (1997). Crime and punishment in America: 1997 update, NCPA policy report No. 209. National Center for Policy Analysis, September.

Ross, R. R., and Fabiano, E. A. (1985). *Time to Think: A Cognitive Model of Delinquency Prevention and Offender Rehabilitation*, Institute of Social Science and Arts, Johnson City, TN.

Rothman, D. J. (1971). *The Discovery of the Asylum: Social Order and Disorder in the New Republic*, Little, Brown, Boston.

Rothman, D. J. (1980). *Conscience and Convenience: The Asylum and Its Alternatives in Progressive America*, Little, Brown, Boston.

Samenow, S. (1984). *Inside the Criminal Mind*, Times Books, New York.

Samenow, S. (1989). *Before It's Too Late*, Times Books, New York.

Sechrest, D., and Shichor, D. (1996). Comparing public and private correctional facilities in California: an exploratory study, *Privatization and the Provision of Correctional Services: Context and Consequences* (G. L. Mays and T. Gray, eds.), Anderson, Cincinnati.

Sherman, L. W., Gottfredson, D. C., MacKenzie, D. L., Eck, J., Reuter, P., and Bushway, S. D. (1998). Preventing crime: what works, what doesn't, what's promising. National Institute of Justice Research in Brief, July.

Shichor, D. (1992). Following the penological pendulum: the survival of rehabilitation, *Federal Probation* 2:19–25.

Sickmund, M. (1994). How juveniles get to criminal court. Office of Juvenile Justice and Delinquency Prevention Update on Statistics, October.

Singal, A. (1998). The private prison industry: a statistical and historical analysis of privatization, *Corrections Compendium* 23(1):1–18.

Smith, L., and Akers, R. (1993). A comparison of recidivism of Florida's community control program: a five-year survival analysis, *Journal of Research in Crime and Delinquency* 30:267–292.

Snyder, H. N. (1997). Juvenile arrests 1996. *OJJDP Juvenile Justice Bulletin*, November.

Tilow, N. (1992). New public opinion poll cites support for intermediate punishment programs, *Perspectives 1*:44–46.

Tonry, M. (1987). *Sentencing Reform Impacts*, U.S. Department of Justice, National Institute of Justice, Washington, DC.

Tonry, M. (1990). Stated and latent functions of ISP, *Crime and Delinquency 36*:174–191.

Turner, S., and Petersilia, J. (1992). Focusing on high-risk parolees: an experiment to reduce commitments to the Texas department of corrections, *Journal of Research in Crime and Delinquency 29(1)*:34–61.

U.S. General Accounting Office. (1995). *Juveniles Processed in Criminal Courts and Case Dispositions*, U.S. Government Printing Office, Washington, DC.

University of Cincinnati (1997.). Should we admit defeat? Evaluating the prototypical model of ISP, Paper presented at the 1997 Academy of Criminal Justice Sciences, Albuquerque, NM.

Van Voorhis, P. (1997). An overview of offender classification systems, *Correctional Counseling and Rehabilitation, 3rd ed.* (P. Van Voorhis, M. Braswell, and D. Lester, eds.). Anderson Publishing, Cincinnati, OH.

Visher, C. (1987). Incapacitation and crime control: does a "lock 'em up" strategy reduce crime? *Justice Quarterly 4(4)*:513–543.

Wager, L. (1992). Fighting crack with speed, *State Government News 35(11)*:30–34.

Wagner, D. (1989). An evaluation of the high risk offender intensive supervision project, *Perspectives 3*:22–27.

Warren, M. (1983). Application of interpersonal maturity theory to offender populations, *Personality Theory, Moral Development, and Criminal Behavior* (W. Laufer and J. Day, eds.), Lexington, MA, Lexington Books, pp. 23–49.

Whitehead, J., and Lab, S. (1989). A meta-analysis of juvenile correctional treatment, *Journal of Research in Crime and Delinquency 26(3)*:276–295.

Wilson, J. Q. (1983). *Crime and Public Policy*, Institute of Contemporary Studies, San Francisco.

Wooldredge, J. (1996). Research note: a state-level analysis of sentencing policies and inmate crowding in state prisons, *Crime and Delinquency 42*:456–466.

Yochelson, S., and Samenow, S. (1976). *The Criminal Personality, Vol. 1: A Profile for Change*, Jason Aronson, New York.

Yoshikawa, H. (1994). Prevention as cumulative protection: effects of early family support and education on chronic delinquency and its risks, *Psychological Bulletin 115(1)*: 28–54.

Zimring, F. E., and Hawkins, G. (1991). *The Scale of Imprisonment*, University of Chicago Press, Chicago.

Zimring, F.E., and Hawkins, G. (1995). *Incapacitation: Penal Confinement and the Restraint of Crime*, Oxford University Press, New York.

22

Administration of State Environmental Policies

A. Hunter Bacot
University of North Carolina, Charlotte, North Carolina

Roy A. Dawes
Gettysburg College, Gettysburg, Pennsylvania

Environmental program administration changed dramatically in the 1980s as states witnessed the return of many national programmatic efforts to the state level for execution. This return of programmatic responsibility, called primacy (Crotty, 1987), placed states at center stage of environmental management at a time when public support for environmental activities was among its highest levels (Dunlap, 1991). Devolvement of national initiatives to state governments for implementation creates tremendous interest in environmental program management and administration.

Scholarly research on comparative state government environmental management and administration has steadily increased in the past two decades as states have borne greater responsibilities for these programs (e.g., see Lowry, 1992; Ringquist, 1992; Scheberle, 1997). Attention by nongovernmental organizations and think tanks with an interest in states' environmental disposition has increased as well (Ridley, 1987; Council of State Governments, 1992, 1996; Hall and Kerr, 1992). Furthermore, understanding the success of national and state programs aimed at curbing environmental degradation throughout the nation, while gaining newfound attention, is increasingly complex as analysis and review must devote attention to the progress of at least 50 different environmental agencies across the states. Also, federal legislation and initiatives (e.g., USEPA's termination of data gathering; right-to-know legislation that gave us the Toxic Release Inventory; citizen participation in planning; requiring environmental justice considerations; etc.) spurred many actions on behalf of states and nongovernmental

591

organizations to indulge state environmental activities more closely. Consequently, state environmental program administration acquired newfound significance in the 1980s and 1990s that placed states at the forefront of environmental
protection in the United States.

In this chapter, we provide an overview of the scholarly research for several
issues on comparative state environmental management and administration. Following this overview, we describe a few of the environmental programmatic responsibilities that states have inherited from the national government as well as
the concurrent administrative duties inherent in accepting these responsibilities.
Finally, we close with a section discussing some of the current efforts on behalf
of the USEPA and states to make environmental administration in the United States
much more cooperative and much less complex.

I. OVERVIEW OF RECENT LITERATURE

Although research in state environmental policy is still in relatively early stages
of development, a body of literature examining its importance has grown impres-
sively. Rather than provide a comprehensive and exhaustive inventory of this
literature, this section highlights some of the more recent developments, findings,
and research directions. This section is organized around major stages of the
policy process—enactment, implementation, and evaluation—and concludes
with a section on environmental equity and justice in the United States.

A. Policy Enactment

1. Acceptable Risk, Risk Assessment, and Comparative Risk

The assessment of acceptable risk plays a prominent role at this stage of the
policy process. Definitions of acceptable risk in environmental regulations are
usually by statutory standards, which are "standards written into law to guide
regulators in determining when to regulate a substance" (Rosenbaum, 1995:176).
There is little consistency in these standards across legislation on environmental
policy (Cohrssen and Covello, 1989).

If state legislators use risk and the risk assessment process in their decision
making calculus in setting environmental policy, it is sensible to understand how
well they grasp these concepts. A survey of state legislators and their staffs found
strong support for the use of risk assessment by most state legislators (Cohen,
1997). However, significant gender and party differences are discovered concerning the perceptions of the risks from chemical releases, the importance of risk
assessment for enacting environmental legislation, and the environmental hazards
encountered by ethnic and racial minorities.

State comparative risk projects provide an ideal opportunity to study procedural and substantive fairness in risk-based policy making. An early state comparative risk project, "Environment 2010," in Washington, tried to expand the field of actors to locate, measure, and produce optimum administrative options for a number of environmental dangers. Paterson and Andrews (1995) evaluate this project and indicate that comparative risk projects can be procedurally fair, but do not necessarily produce greater substantive fairness. They suggest that more attention be paid to the processes that translate the consensus gained on risk priorities (by comparative risk projects) into policy.

2. Environmental Interest Groups: Activities, Objectives, and Outcomes

As the responsibility for environmental policy devolved to the states, so too has the battleground where environmental interest groups fight to attain their respective goals (Ingram and Mann, 1989). Variations in interest group structures and dynamics have an impact on state environmental policy making. Different types of social movement organizations may produce different results in the policy process. Centralized groups with modest goals are more likely to achieve policy success than are groups that rely on more unruly tactics (Shaffer, 1995). No matter the type of organization, it appears that environmental interest groups have better organized industrial interests at the state level; industrial groups may be reduced to (at least for the time being) playing a game of catch-up in the field of competing interests (Bacot and Dawes, 1996). Salazar (1996) surveys 73 environmental groups in the state of Washington to examine a similar type of distinction—institutionalized groups that regularly testify at the state legislature and grassroots groups that do not. Institutionalized groups have larger memberships and paid staff, receive greater funding from outside organizations, and are more bureaucratized. Institutionalized groups utilize mobilization resources and expertise more than organizational assets in their political activities, while grassroots groups are heavily dependent upon mobilization resources. Mobilization resources are positively related to public outreach activities, and expertise and organizational assets are positively related to conventional political action.

Another division among interest groups relevant to the environmental movement is between rural and urban interests, especially in the intermountain West. While Westerners want to keep the benefits associated with their great natural environment, they would also like to encourage economic development along environmentally unorthodox lines—agriculture, logging, mining, and tourism. Although conventional wisdom insists that this is a rural-urban conflict, Alm and Witt (1995) present convincing evidence that rural and urban residents of the intermountain West share similar environmental opinions than is commonly thought to be the case.

B. Policy Implementation

1. Privatization, Market-Based Incentives, and Governmental Regulation

The impact of privatization on environmental programs varies based on how these programs are implemented. Morris (1997) argues that it depends on the distinction between "formal" and "informal" privatization. Formal privatization possesses accountability mechanisms absent from informal privatization formats. He analyzes data from state revolving loan fund programs in an effort to understand the effects of privatization on the distribution of loans to types of applicant communities. Private sector involvement in this program leads to significantly different patterns of resource distribution in the program; informal privatization is associated with a lower likelihood that the national policy objectives of the program are met.

Conventional, assertive enforcement activities by states improve environmental outcomes. Nonregulatory market-based incentives used outside of traditional enforcement actions, such as permits and inspections, may not be particularly effective in protecting air and water quality. However, in combination, incentives with standard regulatory practices result in a general improvement in environmental conditions (Reams, 1995).

2. Legislative-Bureaucratic Oversight

What influences the oversight decisions of federal bureaucrats on environmental programs? Using pooled time-series analysis, Hedge and Scicchitano (1994) examine the interaction of national and state influence on the U.S. Office of Surface Mining (OSM; Department of the Interior) from 1985 to 1989. They suggest the states' and the nation's political climate and their entrepreneurial activities influence decisions by individual members of Congress. National policy makers can direct the oversight activities of bureaucratic underlings, but are limited by subnational concerns. According to O'Leary (1994), however, lower and middle-level bureaucrats are able to mold their own working conditions. O'Leary documents the surreptitious activities of officials in the U.S. Department of Interior and the Nevada Department of Wildlife that led to legislation counter to their superiors' interests. Lessons learned from these bureaucratic deviants are also outlined in this chapter.

A potential problem associated with the delegation of authority from Congress to administrators is that it creates the opportunity for Congress to change the orders given to administrators. On the other hand, this creates incentives for administrators to disregard the first set of instructions and wait for alterations Congress may yet impose. Hill and Weissert show that "this irony of delegation is part of a dynamic process between federal and state governments and outline the conditions under which states can strategically use noncompliance to alter the terms of policies that they have been directed to implement'' (1995:344). Further, Hill and Weissert (1995) develop a model of the decision process created by the federal Low-Level Radioactive Waste Policy Act, then examine how this model explains state implementation actions in general, and specifically in the state of Michigan.

3. Experimentation and Innovation

One outcome of shifting environmental policy making to the state level is the proliferation of state experimentation and innovation, in both policy enactment and implementation (Council of State Governments, 1992). These initiatives are distinguished by their willingness to forgo traditional regulatory practices for behavior modification through public education and economic and operation incentives (Geller et al., 1982; John, 1994; Portney, 1985). Scholarly research in this area has proceeded along several fronts.

Appointed public officials experiment during program implementation with scant planning and evaluation—innovation by "groping along" (Deyle, 1994). Deyle's (1994) analysis of two cases of environmental regulatory policy innovation on coastal erosion management in North Carolina indicates that agencies are more likely to display typical policy behavior when conflict is high. Still, uncertainty about problems and their potential solutions leads to continued state experimentation and innovation.

Another example of experimentation involves a trade-off between increased permit flexibility and emissions reductions. An examination of developments in Minnesota and New Jersey indicates that traditional patterns of fragmented, single-medium programs are not necessarily administratively and politically inevitable. These initiatives may prove to act as viable models for additional state experimentation (Rabe, 1995a). Fragmentation has serious environmental consequences, because single-medium programs shift pollutants from medium to medium. The initiatives in New Jersey and other states have the potential to decrease cross-media transfers, enhance pollution prevention, and promote regulatory efficiency. Although these examples display great promise, the vast majority of state-level permitting remains single-medium permitting (Rabe, 1995b).

4. Environmental Federalism

States are more likely to respond positively to environmental initiatives when implementation is federal than when it is national. Wood (1991) uses impact assessment models to compare political responses from state and local clean air enforcement programs with responses from his earlier study of EPA enforcement.

He discovers responsiveness varies widely depending on whether implementation is federal or national in nature.

Striking a balance between uniform national standards on one hand, and state autonomy on the other, produces persistent conflict (Weiland and O'Leary, 1997). Courts, however, appear to be the places not to look for guidance or direction in regards to proper levels of state autonomy. While court actions have an impact on the environmental administration functions of federal and state governments, the courts fail to rule consistently on environmental federalism. Sometimes the courts favor state autonomy, and sometimes they do not. It is clear that the federal courts are *not* offering messages that favor a national policy of state supremacy in environmental policy (Wise and O'Leary, 1997).

The Coastal Zone Management Act makes state governments (instead of the national or local governments) the locus of power for planning and managing coastal zones. Recognizing that variation exists in coastal states' abilities to manage their coastal zones, Malysa (1996) conducts a comparative case study of tidal wetlands protection in Virginia and Maryland. Through in-depth, elite interviews with state and local politicians, bureaucrats, and interested stakeholders, this researcher develops a capacity ranking system to assess their (Virginia and Maryland) ability to manage coastal zones over time. Institutional, organizational, and state evaluation capacities have all been enhanced since the early 1970s, as has overall state planning and management capacity in both Virginia and Maryland. The only exception is in the area of economic capacity, where, in the time period under study, weak state economies hamper economic capacity to plan and manage for wetlands protection.

5. Citizen and Group Participation in State Environmental Administration

Participation of nongovernmental actors in state environmental management broadly assumes two forms—individual citizens and interested stakeholders. The level of state support for these types of programs conditions the impact of citizen participation. States with right-to-sue laws, or that provide significant funding for right-to-know programs, have discernibly lower rates of toxic emissions over time. States that fail to provide citizens with resources to mobilize their interests are engaging only in symbolic politics when they enact this type of legislation (Grant, 1997).

Preferences for resource management options depend on whether policies are perceived as regulatory or distributive. A study of water conservation strategies in the Ogallala East region of New Mexico examines support and opposition to voluntary conservation, mandatory regulation, and water importation. Avalos and De Young (1995) find that the least effective option—voluntary conservation—is most supported by water users, while the most effective option for conservation—mandatory regulatory policies—generates the most opposition.

6. Comparative State Environmental Policy Outputs

One approach to analyzing variation in state commitment to environmental protection relies on general measures of state environmental commitment. Hays et al. (1996) develop a causal model integrating six major explanatory approaches to state environmental policy. They are able to show that liberal citizens, strong environmental interest groups, and liberal and professional legislatures are most committed to environmental protection, while states' manufacturing interests, economic means, environmental conditions, and federal government influence exhibit little to no affect on environmental commitment.

Another perspective on analyzing state environmental commitment relies on fiscal measures of environmental effort. This approach often yields different results. A fiscally based examination of state effort finds that pollution and environmental interest group activity are the strongest determinants of state effort (Bacot and Dawes, 1996). Upon more detailed examination, it appears that these two differing operationalizations of a similar concept have more in common than originally thought. It should not be considered surprising that each may be better suited for certain types of studies, but in general the fiscal measure produces more precise results. Whatever measure is used, pollution continues to be the most consistent and dominant explanatory factor of state environmental effort (Bacot and Dawes, 1997).

7. Regional Variation in Comparative State Environmental Policy Outputs

Clear regional differences persist in the distribution of environmental externalities across the American states (Bacot et al., 1996). This analysis of environmental effort of the Southern states utilizes nontraditional measures of pollution, organizational capacity, and state fiscal health. Pollution levels and fiscal health are found to be significant estimators of environmental effort, while organizational capacity is not.

A focus on a specific policy area (acid rain) produced broadly comparable results. Alm (1994) finds a strong relationship between region and environmental policy, even while controlling for total pollution emissions, coal production, and precipitation pH. Significant determinants of policy activity regarding acid rain are a state's commitment to environmental protection, total pollution emissions, and region.

C. Policy Evaluation

1. Obstacles to Evaluation

Calls for economic evaluations of environmental programs spring largely from local governments and industry, although the impact of this movement cannot be considered either pro-environmental or pro-industrial. One reason that uniform evaluation methods remain a pipe dream is disciplinary walls between the natural and social sciences. At least in part, the purpose of evaluations (ranging from the political to the scientific), can explain variation in methods—process, impact, and efficiency (Knapp and Kim, 1998). The preoccupation with the success or failure of environmental initiatives dates back to the early 1980s. Before a program can be evaluated, an assessment must be made of how ready an agency is to be evaluated. Even when programs are evaluated, the methods of practical evaluation "employ modes of inquiry and methods of data collection that violate the assumptions of the traditional approach" (Rich, 1998:35).

2. Practical Impact of Evaluation

What does all of this mean for the evaluation of environmental programs in practice? Mangun (1998) addressed the issue of EPA evaluation of state responses to federal environmental initiatives as well as states' evaluation of their own programs through questionnaires and interviews of state and EPA officials. Despite considerable variation in state responses to federal initiatives, the "EPA doesn't conduct specific program evaluations of individual state programs" (Mangun, 1998:88). However, this lack of uniformity creates an atmosphere ripe for innovation. Examples from states such as Oregon and Washington lead to "the prospects for environmental program evaluation to evolve from bean counting into a vigorous and richly diverse field" (Mangun, 1998:103).

In contrast to the command-and-control methods of the federal government, state governments depend on the voluntary cooperation of industry in hazardous waste regulation and reduction. While most companies are committed to voluntarily reducing their hazardous waste, it is not because of state pollution prevention reporting requirements. Instead, most corporations are more concerned with reducing hazardous waste because they wish to minimize possible cleanup and legal costs that accompany persistent production of high levels of hazardous waste (Folz and Peretz, 1997).

D. Environmental Equity

A thriving subfield of its own revolves around issues of environmental equity and environmental justice. This literature deals broadly with questions about how class and race influence the distribution of pollution. The standard claim is that communities of color and poor communities receive a disproportionate share of pollution. Just as states must deal with almost all environmental problems in this time of devolution, they must also deal with problems arising from environmental equity and/or racism.

Pollock and Vittes (1995) investigate the relative impact of racial/ethnic, economic, and occupational characteristics in explaining proximity to possibly toxic release. They find that racial and ethnic subgroups—especially African-Americans—live closer to potentially hazardous sources. This relationship persists, however diluted, when controlling for other socioeconomic characteristics.

A similar study of siting patterns in Texas produces somewhat different findings. Yandle and Burton (1996a) conclude that the siting of hazardous waste landfills is associated with poor, white communities, a finding that does not persist over time. Poverty remains important, but race does not, suggesting a changing ethnic composition (Yandle and Burton, 1996a). Yandle and Burton's article precipitated a minor maelstrom with three commentaries on their work. Bullard (1996) claims they fail to place their study in the proper sociohistorical context. He further suggests that they make false assumptions and inaccurate generalizations about environmental equity. Bullard (1996) concludes that their findings buttress the ideas of environmental justice advocates and scholars: that not all communities are the same.

Barkenbus et al. (1996) are more gentle in their commentary, complimenting the authors for their contribution to the field. Their criticism centers on the limited scope and treatment of the original question. Yandle and Burton's (1996b) reply acknowledges some of the criticism as valid, but they claim that they simply wanted to keep their topic manageable.

Bowman and Crews-Meyer (1997) develop a measure of locally unwanted land uses (LULUs) to test potential explanations for the siting of hazardous waste facilities in southern counties. While the standard environmental justice model has modest explanatory power, the class variable is opposite the expected direction. In addition, race is discernible in high-income counties, but further examination shows that population size is the strongest predictor of hazardous waste location in southern counties.

The two types of politics practiced by the environmental justice movement—identity politics and disinterested politics—are at odds with each other. Identity politics emphasizes appeals grounded in the experiences of its members, while disinterested politics relies on the expertise of scientists. Because each differs fundamentally on its perspective of the proper role of scientific knowledge, these two types of politics decrease the probability of attaining their objectives. Reconciliation between the two is necessary and possible by expressing social constructionist views of knowledge highlighting the relationship between values and facts (Tesh and Williams, 1996).

While scholarly research informs us on how states fare in their effort to administer national environmental priorities, a further understanding of states' efforts requires us to explore their administrative responsibilities. States assume significant administrative duties for several national environmental policies. Discerning the role of states in environmental management begins with a discussion of the various programmatic responsibilities as prescribed in national legislation.

II. ENVIRONMENTAL ADMINISTRATION IN THE STATES

The federal structure in which programmatic administration is shared in the United States creates a complex system of managing many national priorities through states; environmental affairs is one national priority that relies on the states for implementation. Given our federal arrangement, environmental protection may be more complex owing to different environmental media that require varied policy approaches depending on the unique needs and requirements of distinct regions and states.

Environmental administration in the United States is generally distinguished according to media; air, water, and waste (solid, hazardous, and toxic) are the three generally accepted environmental arenas. Each environmental medium presents its own unique set of challenges to state governments. However, to ensure that they are combating environmental problems deemed national in scope, state administrators are never void of federal oversight. Accordingly, the management of environmental problems is further confounded through the federal administration of these programs. To acquire an appreciation of the challenges states face, major provisions of national environmental legislation that states administer is discussed by environmental media—air, water, and waste.[1]

A. Air Quality Regulations

Cooperation on policies affecting air quality in the United States is essentially guided by provisions in the Clean Air Act (CAA), which was originally passed in 1972 and subsequently reauthorized. In the name of protecting the public health and welfare, the CAA initially regulated air quality standards of pollutants that threaten public health and are considered hazardous. With changes in the CAA amendments, the USEPA was further charged with addressing, via the states, previously overlooked threats to air quality. For example, by regulating air toxins and acid rain, and becoming more vigorously involved in local air quality attainment, the agency's responsibility for improving air quality expanded incredibly. The original CAA listed only a few contaminants, now regarded as rather common

---

[1] In addition to the public laws detailing these responsibilities, much of the following discussion draws generally from a host of excellent sources discussing the administration of environmental programs; see ACIR (1992), Jessup (1994), Council of State Governments (1996), Brownell (1997), Case (1997), Gallagher (1997), Halbleib (1997), Lee (1997), Mangum (1997), Nardi (1997), Scagnelli (1997), Scheberle (1997), Rabe (1997), and Williams (1997).

(e.g., lead and carbon monoxide), as the focus of the Act. The original Act also established national emissions standards for hazardous air pollutants (NESHAP); NESHAP expanded the realm of air quality regulations, though not too extensively, by including elements long used in commercial and industrial processes (e.g., asbestos, mercury, and benzene).

Subsequent amendments to the CAA in 1990, however, greatly enhanced the responsibilities of environmental agencies across levels of government, but particularly for states, where fundamental administration of environmental programs resides. Amendments to the CAA required states to prepare state implementation plans (SIPS), which force states to submit to the USEPA an "inventory" of their progress in reducing pollution (per media) as specified by national standards (that are set by Congress and implemented by the EPA). In this same Act, Congress significantly expanded the list of pollutants to be regulated, which, because of most states' primacy status, endowed states with primary regulatory (and administrative) responsibility for air pollution. The CAA Amendments identify approximately 200 chemicals released into the air across the United States; the amendments also identify new areas of regulation to control releases contributing to acid rain and ozone depletion as well as define urban nonattainment areas. These provisions identify a host of chemicals, based on "technological benchmarks" that essentially identify acceptable emission levels for each chemical source.

Urban nonattainment areas are areas that fail to meet preestablished pollution levels for a geographically defined area; in essence, while entire states have defined attainment levels, metropolitan areas within states receive the strictest attainment levels. In an effort to reduce the byproduct of vehicular fuel emissions, e.g., carbon monoxide, areas are defined and pollution emission levels set; these areas, which are generally metropolitan areas, are those in which vehicular concentration and use is pronounced. Upon determining areas and levels, limits are set on the number of days pollution emission levels may exceed the predetermined level; exceeding the defined number of days is referred to as nonattainment.[2]

Generally, states are given reasonable responsibility for establishing acceptable emission levels (in their SIPs). States must account for their performance by periodically tracking the emission levels of these chemical sources, as well as other new sources identified through increased technological capacity. In essence, the new emission regulations determine which areas have poor air quality, as well as the areas that meet ambient air recommendations, which are established

---

[2] This effort is integrative and, in addition to the governments of the defined metropolitan area, requires more than a concerted effort from, for example, the auto manufacturing, fuel, and transportation industries.

using technologically driven analysis (based on "best available technology" [BAT] or other technology-based criteria). Merely meeting the set criteria, however, does not automatically mean success for states' air pollution program efforts. As technological capacity constantly improves detection of previously undetectable elements, states that meet their specified standards must continually monitor the status of air pollutants.

As is evident of testing standards and monitoring responsibilities, states' assumption of programmatic responsibility for air quality is an arduous assignment. Environmental management of ambient air quality is a continuous, challenging task and is but one of the primary environmental media demanding attention by state environmental agencies.

B. Water Quality Regulations

An equally demanding area of emphasis for state environmental administrators is surface water quality (e.g., rivers, lakes, etc.) and groundwater quality (e.g., underground discharge, aquifers, etc.) in the United States. Like air quality, water quality standards are determined by national legislation, the Clean Water Act (CWA) and subsequent amendments, and generally implemented at the state level. Water quality standards represent efforts to regulate discharges of effluents from industrial, commercial, and municipal facilities (ICM facilities) as well as on-point sources (generally runoff from an area into regulated waters, e.g., agricultural runoff) and storm water systems (both municipal and commercial operations that use water drainage systems).

Like air quality guidelines regulating emissions, states must also develop guidelines for controlling effluents discharged into regulated waters. Over time, modifications to the CWA, similar to the CAA, include increases in the number of regulated chemicals and greater devolution of programmatic responsibilities to states. For example, amendments to the CWA in 1987 established a list of nearly 70 toxins and increased state programmatic responsibilities for permit programs (a state's ability to issue permits to ICM facilities and regulate their discharges). Through treatment standards and effluent lists, states create ambient water quality standards for ICM facilities that discharge pollutants into surface waters for conventional (e.g., discharges that deplete or disturb natural elements and/or the balance of elements) and nonconventional pollutants (e.g., airborne pollutants that originate elsewhere settling in bodies of water).

The CWA endows the USEPA in concert with state agencies, the responsibility for managing water quality in the United States. Sections of the CWA provide specific guidelines to the USEPA for managing water quality and administering directives to the states. Under the purview of the USEPA, final implementation of many of the provisions set forth in the CWA is the responsibility of state agencies. The CWA also specifies water quality standards according to the type and use of waters, whether recreational, sporting (fishing and hunting), serving as a water supply, etc.[3] States have extended management and administration responsibilities for classifying bodies of water based on the water quality essential for maintaining the classified use. Under the CWA four classifications are required, but common among states are classifications that exceed the specified minimum of four categories, further complement or refine these national definitions, and designate certain pristine waters as protected. Groundwater protection (which includes aquifer protection) is another area of significant responsibility for state agencies. Primary threats to groundwater quality are leachates from landfills and hazardous wastes facilities and underground storage tanks (e.g., tanks storing petroleum products). States accept responsibility for protecting groundwater and commit to regulating threats to groundwater quality by (1) establishing quality standards within national parameters; (2) classifying groundwater sources according to current and potential uses (e.g., uses include to service people, agriculture, or other bodies of water); and (3) attempting to control the migration of nonpoint sources and managing water extraction practices.

With these responsibilities, determination of groundwater regulations essentially becomes a state-administered program as these water sources, uses, and threats vary widely among the states.

Another important provision of the CWA amendments is one enabling states responsibility of the permitting process for the National Pollutant Discharge Elimination System (NPDES). This permit responsibility lay primarily with the USEPA until 1987, when permission to determine effluent levels and grant permits transferred principally to the states. Provisions of the NPDES regulate direct discharges, or point source discharges (as opposed to nonpoint source discharges discussed previously), by industrial, commercial, and government facilities into surface waters. Discharge regulations provide guidelines for determining the amount of allowable discharges and the relative quality of the water to which these discharges are directed. According to the type of activity in which the industry, commercial, or government facility is engaged and quality of the receiving surface waters, a permit is issued granting the facilities permission to discharge the specified waste into specific bodies of water.

Permission to regulate and permit effluent discharges into surface waters transfers only when states can demonstrate capacity to manage the program; these functions, however, never transfer completely, as USEPA always reserves final responsibility through oversight. Thus, while most states currently administer their "own" state program, administration of NPDES provisions, like most envi-

---

[3] Categories are classified based on water quality that supports recreational uses by people (class A), ecological integrity and promotes natural habitation (class B), water supplies for public consumption (class C), and uses by industrial, commercial, and agricultural activities (not intended to consumption) (class D).

ronmental acts, depends on a state's administrative capacity to accept this responsibility.

With the amendments to the CWA in 1987, states assume (with USEPA guidance, of course) responsibility for another pollution concern—nonpoint source pollution. Nonpoint source elements are introduced to surface waters or groundwaters indirectly; in essence, these sources originate from activities that use or generate waste but eventually get into protected water bodies. Common culprits are pesticides used in urban lawn maintenance. For example, when people in a neighborhood treat their lawns with chemicals to eradicate weeds, these chemicals are washed from lawns by rain or sprinkler systems and migrate to groundwater or surface waters naturally through soil drainage or drain into a body of water. These chemicals are not directly discharged into surface or groundwaters, but are introduced indirectly, making it difficult to detect their origin and manage their introduction or application. Thus, unless environmental agencies are able to locate chemical sources (or origins), management of nonpoint pollution sources becomes "ends-oriented"; i.e., agencies must manage pollution levels of the surface waters into which these pollutants flow.

Over time, states have demonstrated the ability to manage water quality programs. In fact, approximately half of the 50 states administer comprehensive water protection programs. While difficult, states are proving quite diligent in assuming responsibilities for administering programs to protect and preserve water quality.

C. Waste Regulations

Waste management in the United States is regulated by several acts that address the different dispositions of waste (solid, hazardous, and toxic) produced and disposed of in the United States.[4] The Resources Conservation and Recovery Act (RCRA) provides regulations for hazardous and solid waste. The Comprehensive Environmental Response, Compensation, and Liability Act (CERCLA, and commonly referred to as "Superfund"), and subsequent amendments in the Superfund Amendments and Reauthorization Act (SARA), and the Emergency Planning and Community Right-To-Know Act (referred to as the "Right-to-Know Act) are national Acts legislated to deal with toxic wastes, spills, and contamination. These laws provide directives and guidance for regulating the disposition of waste in the states.

Responsibility for managing hazardous, toxic, and solid waste at the state level is initiated in the RCRA. This law provides guidelines for managing solid and hazardous wastes "from the cradle to the grave"; i.e., the RCRA establishes

---

[4] Nuclear waste comes under federal jurisdiction, and thus is not discussed here.

provisions for determining which materials are classified as hazardous or solid (referred to in the act as nonhazardous)[5] and how these materials are handled from generation to final disposal.[6] The RCRA promulgates provisions for disposing of wastes, whether hazardous or solid; the law provides guidance for establishing environmentally suitable regulations on the method of disposal for specific materials. The regulations for disposal provide comprehensive standards for disposal facilities that include provisions regulating the design (requiring liners), location (recognizing environmental justice concerns), monitoring (leachate systems and methane gas monitoring devices), and postclosure planning (viable land uses after facility closes and/or bond guarantees for restoration).

Another provision of this law is to require waste reduction plans, i.e., reuse or recycling, of government that in turn encourage and promote such plans to commercial operations. Waste reduction mandates require states to facilitate plans for reducing materials traditionally disposed of in sanitary landfills. These mandates include municipal recycling plans, commercial oil recycling facilities, municipal or state mulch facilities (through the reuse of yard waste), and household hazardous waste disposal days (where communities accept hazardous materials used in households, e.g., paints, pesticides, cleaning agents, etc.).

It is through the aforementioned Acts that states acquire much responsibility for regulating waste within their borders. The Right-to-Know Act requires industrial and manufacturing companies to report annually the pounds of toxic materials released into the air, water, and ground. Though self-reported by firms with 10 or more employees, states use this information to assist their efforts at regulating each environmental media according to the type and amount of toxins released into the environment by these firms. Business and industry use this information for making decision about a facility's continued operation, efforts to reduce emissions and effluents, etc.

Similar to the reporting requirement of the Right-to-Know Act regulating toxic chemicals, companies that use or manufacture chemicals are regulated by the SARA. The SARA establishes provisions for states to monitor the disposition of chemicals within their borders. To encourage the identification, location, and disposition of such facilities, states were ordered to implement methods of compliance. The SARA forces states to form emergency commissions that oversee the implementation of these provisions throughout the state. Based on provisions contained in the SARA, emergency response agencies are established throughout

---

[5] Though hazardous waste is discussed separately from solid waste, technically it is a solid waste. In this discussion, hazardous waste refers to waste materials that causes, contributes, or threatens people's health as well as the environment (e.g., dioxins), while solid waste refers to common household waste materials.

[6] Medical or infectious waste is not addressed specifically in this discussion as many of the provisions regulating this type of waste lie with solid waste disposal regulations.

a state with directives to ensure that proper notification, response, and evacuation plans are adopted for at risk areas.

Another aspect of the SARA requires states to ensure that provisions exist for dealing with the disposal of hazardous wastes. States must monitor companies with facilities handling toxic or hazardous materials; strict regulations force states to issue permits to companies wishing to operate facilities that treat, store, or dispose of hazardous or toxic materials. The USEPA yields responsibility to states for granting facility permits, but states must adhere to stringent federal guidelines in their administrative efforts to regulate facilities falling within the purview of SARA. Toxic and hazardous waste regulations appear to embody more national oversight provisions and less state autonomy than the other laws discussed previously. But, as with the other environmental areas, toxic, hazardous, and solid wastes regulations provide states with amplified responsibilities for protecting and ensuring the integrity of our environment.

III. MOVING FORWARD: COOPERATIVE ENVIRONMENTAL ADMINISTRATION

As can be expected from the environmental administration responsibilities discussed, state administration of environmental programs is complex and challenging, with per-state management decisions affecting the disposition of the national environmental situation. Evident in the provisions of national environmental laws is a tremendous devolvement of environmental responsibilities to states. Equally empowering to states is the recognition that the USEPA generally only ensures that states are establishing and implementing these programs as directed, which bestows states with tremendous accountability in the national effort to promote and maintain a clean environment and protect human health. As most states received permission for managing their own comprehensive environmental programs in the 1980s, new controversies will continue to emerge and challenge state environmental program administrators.

As environmental matters elicit federal legislation and executive directives, many disparate and sometime conflicting commands are issued by various federal agencies; such a morass of directives from different agencies makes cooperation among federal and state officials crucial to successful environmental administration. The complexity of environmental administration for states is recognized (see Scheberle, 1997); several recent initiatives, at both the national and state levels, attempt to address the administration of environmental policies.

In an effort to move toward cooperation, environmental administrative decisions first had to undergo severe challenges; foremost among these challenges is the *multiple* approval at both levels of government required of many policy decisions. In addition, environmental policy decisions were forced to endure review and approval processes from more than one agency at each level, as well as the varying political dispositions of state and national governing bodies. This inherent procedural conflict characteristic of environmental legislation in 1980s, however, did not go unnoticed by public officials from the two levels of government. Neither was this observation lost on researchers interested in intergovernmental/comparative state environmental policy, as scholarly research in this area had begun to develop during this time period. Though difficult, the experience of the 1980s proved educational as the USEPA, in cooperation with comparable state government agencies and informed by current research, made significant efforts to resolve conflicts and make environmental administration in our federal system less complex for all.

Given the recent changes and current direction of the USEPA to devolve programmatic responsibility to the states, it appears that scholarly research informed current policy direction. Many of the aforementioned findings are apparently permeating environmental policy. For example, as Wood (1991) suggests, states are more conducive to environmental policy that is administered federally as opposed to nationally, which is the direction the USEPA is currently pursuing rather vigorously. Rabe's (1995b) research provides another example of scholarship informing policy. He provides evidence that permits flexibility across intrastate environmental programs and that has the potential to reduce pollution (using cross media and prevention strategies) and promote regulatory efficiency. It appears the USEPA efforts to provide states with increased flexibility in permitting across environmental media is informed by this research as it allows selected states to innovate with their permit programs.

In the mid-1990s, state administrators and the administrator of the USEPA identified several areas in which relations between state agencies and the USEPA could improve. These areas of cooperation signaled a new era of collaboration between the states and the national USEPA; the relationship between the USEPA and the states is being redefined to recognize the relative responsibilities for each level of government. For example, roles are being recast to emphasize a partnership between levels of government; states are recognized as "stewards of the environment" (Scheberle, 1997), while the USEPA is accepting a facilitator role by providing technical assistance, setting standards, and reviewing program performance (USEPA, 1994). States, serving the role of primary environmental program administrators in the United States, acquire significant responsibility to accommodate their unique environmental conditions and direct their resources to specific intrastate challenges without abdicating their national responsibility to promote and protect the environment.

Though the current climate of cooperation benefits environmental administration in the states, challenges abound. As technology continues to improve scientists' ability to detect increased levels of chemical concentrations, adjustments to environmental legislation will continue, which will force state environmental agencies to change, if they have not already, and keep abreast of changes in technologies and techniques. Such investment may be difficult for many states that face challenges believed by their citizens to be more important than environmental protection. Another confounding factor in state environmental administration is how the national performance standards imposed at the federal level affect states' accountability in environmental program administration. Questions abound over the implications these performance requirements hold for state environmental agencies. One potential implication for state agencies is an increase in reporting requirements that demand more detailed information about state programmatic efforts, which counters recent efforts to significantly reduce these requirements (Hagevik, 1997).

Emboldened with newfound importance, state environmental agencies are at a pivotal administrative crossroads. States can use this opportunity of expressed trust by the federal government to excel at environmental management or to promote "token environmentalism." Token environmentalism is when state officials, for whatever reasons, do not recognize the importance of environment protection and relegate environmental affairs to secondary status to combat more pressing state problems; in essence, state officials give it a token existence to meet federal requirements. While current administrative roles are such that the USEPA "establishes national standards . . ., while state environmental agencies establish and implement control programs designed to ensure that federal standards are achieved" (Mangun, 1997:88), states' acceptance of programmatic responsibility is easy; ensuring responsible action is difficult, particularly for resource-challenged states.

As this newfound environmental program responsibility for states appears competent policy, it could prove disastrous if not managed carefully. Given that the USEPA is in no position to revoke primacy status of states (Arrandale, 1993), and recognizing that it does little "to determine whether individual state programs generate improvements in environmental quality" (Mangun, 1997:88), these comprehensive responsibility devolutions could damage, rather than improve, environmental situations in the states. For example, "struggler states" (Lester, 1994) do not perform well under centralized national direction, allowing these states greater responsibility to command their own fortunes may prove disastrous administratively as well as environmentally. Though these latest initiatives are being embraced enthusiastically by states, token environmentalism could flourish in states void of requisite resources or motivation to establish and implement such programs. Moreover, states can practice token environmentalism with little threat of reprisal from the USEPA.

Exacerbating the threat of token environmentalism by state officials is the solidification of Republican leadership in states during the 1990s. According to Rabe (1997:47), devolving environmental program responsibility to states under Republican political control places control in the hands of "leaders firmly committed to substantial reduction of overall tax burden, state spending, and regulatory activity." In general, such spending and tax reduction proposals are popular, but from an environmental program perspective these proposals are alarming. Given current intrastate conditions in Republican-dominated states, environmental agencies are likely to bear a disproportionate share of efforts to reduce revenue and restrict regulatory activities across state agencies.

If executed properly, the pronounced effort at intergovernmental management of environmental affairs by the USEPA can mitigate any adverse consequences to the devolvement of environmental responsibilities. In offering a typology of state and national working relationships, Scheberle (1997) provides a framework that promotes intensive intergovernmental cooperation. If her caveats and recommendations are recognized as the USEPA and state environmental agencies embark on a path of partnership, successful intergovernmental environmental administration appears achievable. Scheberle suggests, and provides examples of, how national and state agencies must "pull together" and recommends that agencies must address "the nature of working relationships, levels of trust, and interactions among participants" if intergovernmental cooperation is to be successful (Scheberle, 1997:197). Ultimately, if state environmental administration is to succeed under this cooperative relationship structure, there must be mutual understanding of, and adherence to, determined roles as well as a true balance of authority. Emphasis must be placed on striking a true balance of program authority. Too much centralization at the national level, or too much devolution to state agencies, will condemn this cooperative approach before it is ever implemented. After all, protecting and improving environmental conditions in the United States can only be realized if there is a genuine effort by all involved to develop and sustain a sensible, balanced "cooperative partnership" characterized by trust, respect, and flexibility.

REFERENCES

Alm, L. R. (1994). Regional influences and environmental policymaking: a study of acid rain, *Policy Studies Journal* 21:638–650.

Alm, L. R., and Witt, S. L. (1995). Environmental policy in the intermountain West: the rural-urban linkage, *State and Local Government Review* 27:127–136.

Arrandale, T. (1993). Environmental giveback fever: will there be an epidemic, *Governing* 7:70.

Avalos, M., and De Young, T. (1995). Preferences for water policy in the Ogallala region of New Mexico: distributive vs. regulatory solutions, *Policy Studies Journal* 23: 668–685.

Bacot, A. H., and Dawes, R. A. (1996). Responses to federal devolution: measuring state environmental efforts, *State and Local Government Review* 28:124–135.

Bacot, A. H., and Dawes, R. A. (1997). State expenditures and policy outcomes in environmental program management, *Policy Studies Journal 25*:355–370.

Bacot, A. H. Dawes, R. A., and Sawtelle, A. (1996). A preliminary analysis of environmental management in the Southern states, *Public Administration Quarterly 19*: 389–403.

Barkenbus, J. N., Peretz, J. H., and Rubin, J. D. (1996). More on the agenda (comment on T. Yandle and D. Burton), *Social Science Quarterly 77*:516–519.

Bowman, A. O., and Crews-Meyer, K. A. (1997). Locating Southern LULUs: race, class, and environmental justice, *State and Local Government Review 29*:110–119.

Brownell, F. W. (1997). Clean Air Act, *Environmental Law Handbook*, 14th ed. (T. F. P. Sullivan, ed.), Government Institutes Rockville, MD, pp. 72–108.

Bullard, R. D. (1996). Environmental justice: it's more than waste facility siting (comment on T. Yandle and D. Burton), *Social Science Quarterly 77*:493–499.

Case, D. R. (1997). Resource Conservation and Recovery Act, *Environmental Law Handbook*, 14th ed. (Thomas F. P. Sullivan, ed.), Government Institutes, Rockville, MD, pp. 328–359.

Cohen, N. (1997). The politics of environmental risk: perceptions of risk assessment in the state legislatures, *Policy Studies Journal 25*:470–484.

Cohrssen, J. J., and Covello, V. T. (1989). *Risk Analysis: A Guide to Principles and Methods for Analyzing Health and Environmental Risks*, Council on Environmental Quality, Washington.

Council of State Governments. (1996). *Resource Guide to State Environmental Management*, Council of State Governments, Lexington, KY.

Council of State Governments. (1992). *Innovative State Environmental Programs and Legislation, 1990–1992*, Council of State Governments, Lexington, KY.

Deyle, R. E. (1994). Conflict, uncertainty, and the role of planning and analysis in public policy innovation, *Policy Studies Journal 22*:457–473.

Folz, D. H., and Peretz, J. H. (1997). Evaluating state hazardous waste reduction policy, *State and Local Government Review 29*:134–146.

Gallagher, L. M. (1997). Clean water act, *Environmental Law Handbook*, 14th ed. (Thomas F. P. Sullivan, ed.), Government Institutes, Rockville, MD, pp. 109–160.

Geller, E. S. Winett, R. A., and Everett, P. B. (1982). *Preserving the Environment: New Strategies for Behavior Change*, Pergamon Press, New York.

Grant, D. S. II. (1997). Allowing citizen participation in environmental regulation: an empirical analysis of the effects of right-to-sue and right-to-know provisions on industry's toxic emissions, *Social Science Quarterly 78*:859–873.

Halbleib, W. T. (1997). Emergency planning and community Right-to-Know Act, *Environmental Law Handbook*, 14th ed. (Thomas F. P. Sullivan, ed.), Government Institutes, Rockville, MD, pp. 481–509.

Hagevik, G. (1997). New way to measure results, *State Legislatures*, ⟨http://www.ncsl.org/programs.esnr/results.htm⟩

Hall, B., and Kerr, M. L. (1992). *1991–1992 Environmental Index: A State by State Guide to the Nation's Environmental Health*, Island Press, Washington, DC.

Hays, S. P., Esler, M., and Hays, C. E. (1996). Environmental commitment among the states: integrating alternative approaches to state environmental policy, *Publius 26*: 41–58.

Hedge, D. M., and Scicchitano, M. J. (1994). Regulating in space and time: the case of regulatory federalism, *Journal of Politics 56*:134–153.

Hill, J. S., and Weissert, C. S. (1995). Implementation and the irony of delegation: the politics of low-level radioactive waste disposal, *Journal of Politics 57*:344–369.

Ingram, H. M., and Mann, D. E. (1989). Interest groups and environmental policy, *Environmental Politics and Policy* (J. P. Lester, ed.), Duke University Press, Durham, NC.

John, D. (1994). *Civic Environmentalism: Alternatives to Regulation in States and Communities*, CQ Press, Washington.

Knapp, G. J., and Kim, T. J. (1998). Environmental program evaluation: framing the subject, identifying issues, *Environmental Program Evaluation: A Primer* (Gerrit J. Knapp and Tschango John Kim, eds.), University of Illinois Press, Urbana.

Lee, R. T. (1997). Comprehensive Environmental Response, Compensation, and Liability Act, *Environmental Law Handbook*, 14th ed. (Thomas F. P. Sullivan, ed.), Government Institutes, Rockville, MD, pp. 430–480.

Lester, J. P. (1994). A new federalism? Environmental policy in the states, *Environmental Policy in the 1990s* (Norman J. Vig and Michael E. Kraft, eds.), CQ Press, Washington, pp. 51–68.

Lowry, W. R. (1992). *The Dimensions of Federalism: State Governments and Pollution Control Policies*, Duke University Press, Durham.

Malysa, L. L. (1996). A comparative assessment of state planning and management capacity: tidal wetlands protection in Virginia and Maryland, *State and Local Government Review 28*:205–218.

Mangun, W. R. (1998). Environmental program evaluation in an intergovernmental context, *Environmental Program Evaluation: A Primer* (Gerrit J. Knapp and Tshango John Kim, eds.), University of Illinois Press, Urbana.

Morris, J. C. (1997). The distributional impacts of privatization in national water-quality policy, *Journal of Politics 59*:56–72.

Nardi, K. J. (1997). Underground storage tanks, *Environmental Law Handbook*, 14th ed. (Thomas F. P. Sullivan, ed.); Government Institutes, Rockville, MD, pp. 360–384.

O'Leary, R. (1994). The bureaucratic politics paradox: the case of wetlands legislation in Nevada, *Journal of Public Administration Research and Theory 4*:443–467.

Paterson, C. J., and Andrews, R. N. L. (1995). Procedural and substantive fairness in risk decisions: comparative risk assessment procedures, *Policy Studies Journal 23*:85–95.

Pollock, P. H. III, and Vittes, M. E. (1995). Who bears the burdens of environmental pollution? Race, ethnicity, and environmental equity in Florida, *Social Science Quarterly 76*:294–310.

Portney, K. E. (1985). The potential of the theory of compensation for mitigating public opposition in hazardous waste treatment facility siting, *Hazardous Waste 1*:411–421.

Rabe, B. G. (1997). Power to the states: the promise and pitfalls of decentralization, *Environmental Policies in the 1990s: Reform or Reaction* (Norman J. Vig and Michael E. Kraft, eds.), CQ Press, Washington, DC, pp. 31–52.

Rabe, B. G. (1995a). Integrating environmental regulation: permitting innovation at the state level, *Journal of Policy Analysis and Management 14*:467–472.

Rabe, B. G. (1995b). Integrated environmental permitting: experience and innovation at the state level, *State and Local Government Review* 27:209–220.

Reams, M. A. (1995). Incentive-based vs. command-and-control approaches to improving environmental quality, *Spectrum* 68:6–18.

Rich, R. F. (1998). Program evaluation and environmental policy: the state of the art, *Environmental Program Evaluation: A Primer* (Gerrit J. Knapp and Tschango John Kim, eds.), University of Illinois Press, Urbana.

Ridley, S. (1987). *The State of the States*, Fund for Renewable Energy and the Environment, Washington, DC.

Ringuist, E. J. (1993). *Environmental Protection at the State Level: Politics and Progress in Controlling Pollution*, ME Sharpe, Armonk, NY.

Rosenbaum, W. A. (1995). *Environmental Politics and Policy*, 3rd ed., CQ Press, Washington.

Salazar, D. J. (1996). The mainstream-grassroots divide in the environmental movement: environmental groups in Washington State, *Social Science Quarterly* 77:626–643.

Scagnelli, J. M. (1997). Pollution Prevention Act, *Environmental Law Handbook*, 14th ed. (Thomas F. P. Sullivan, ed.), Government Institutes, Rockville, MD, pp. 510–521.

Shaffer, M. B. (1995). The internal dynamics of environmental organizations: movement interest groups, communal advocacy groups, and the policy process, *Policy Studies Review* 14:183–194.

Scheberle, D. (1997). *Federalism and Environmental Policy: Trust and the Politics of Implementation*, Georgetown University Press, Washington, DC.

Tesh, S. N., and Williams, B. A. (1996). "Identity politics, disinterested politics, and environmental justice, *Polity* 18:285–305.

U.S. Advisory Commission on Intergovernmental Relations. (1992). *Intergovernmental Decisionmaking for Environmental Protection and Public Works* (A-122), Author, Washington, DC.

U.S. Environmental Protection Agency. (1994). *Joint Policy Statement on State/EPA Relations*, ⟨http://www.epa.gov/docs/JPS_State_EPA/jps.txt.html⟩

Williams, S. E. (1997). Safe Drinking Water Act, *Environmental Law Handbook*, 14th ed. (Thomas F. P. Sullivan, ed.), Government Institutes, Rockville, MD, pp. 196–225.

Weiland, P., and O'Leary, R. (1997). Federalism and environmental policy: the case of solid waste management, *American Review of Public Administration* 27:211–227.

Wise, C., and O'Leary, R. (1997). Intergovernmental relations and federalism in environmental management and policy: the role of the courts, *Public Administration Review* 57:150–159.

Wood, B. D. (1991). Federalism and policy responsiveness: the clean air case, *Journal of Politics* 53:851–859.

Yandle, T., and Burton, D. (1996a). Reexamining environmental justice: a statistical analysis of historical hazardous waste landfill siting patterns in metropolitan Texas, *Social Science Quarterly* 77:477–492.

Yandle, T., and Burton, D. (1996b). Methodological approaches to environmental justice: a rejoinder (reply to Comments), *Social Science Quarterly* 77:520–527.

23
Organization and Management of Public Works in State Government

Claire L. Felbinger
American University, Washington, D.C.

Willard T. Price
University of the Pacific, Stockton, California

Public works are an array of physical infrastructure, owned by the public and serving their needs for mobility, access, safety, and security. In all, public works provide the essential platform for public and commercial activity using common facilities. More specifically, public works agencies are responsible for convenience and safety while traveling and using public buildings; avoiding damage or injury from natural disasters; receiving the essential resources of water, energy, and air; facilitating communications via public rights-of-way; and protecting public and environmental health. The American Public Works Association (APWA) provides this definition of public works:

> Public Works is a generic term used to describe the physical structures and facilities required for the delivery of various . . . services provided, directly and indirectly, by federal, state and local governments. The types of services provided by different levels of governments . . . are determined by the voters and elected representatives. These services are usually provided by local government (Felbinger, 1996).

The public works array of infrastructure includes the following functions or services (Price, 1997):

1. Water resource systems
   a. Water supply, storage, treatment, distribution
   b. Wastewater collection, treatment, discharge, reuse

    c. Storm water collection, storage, discharge
    d. Groundwater management
2. Transportation systems
    a. Highways, streets, bridges, tollways
    b. Traffic safety management
    c. Mass transit, public railroads
    d. Airports, seaports, spaceports, other terminals
    e. Waterborne vehicles, ferries
3. Waste management systems
    a. Solid waste collection, recycling, disposal
    b. Toxic and hazardous waste collection, treatment, recycling, disposal
    c. Organic waste collection, composting, disposal
4. Other public facilities and services
    a. Public buildings, parking structures, housing
    b. Parks, pathways, open space
    c. Public vehicles, equipment
    d. Public power systems
    e. Planning, development, environmental regulation

Public infrastructure systems exit under, on, and above the ground surface and appear (1) in "corridors"—strips of public land which cross and connect communities and contain multiple structures and pipes; (2) within "sheds"—watersheds or air sheds that contain the resource, be it surface and groundwater flows or geographically separated bodies of air; or (3) in "places/spaces"—public lands with buildings, open space, and wilderness areas for common use, including airspace and space itself. There are private lands which may serve commerce and the public directly as with railroads or telecommunications channels. For any society the term *infrastructure* certainly involves other public and private assets like schools, hospitals, universities, nonprofit facilities, factories, distribution centers, commercial centers, utilities, communications, and transportation modes. It is an infrastructure industry, with traditional public works functions as well as a growing presence of private participation in ownership, development, and operation of these systems. Infrastructure provides the common platform any developed society must have for economic growth. One main question is how the public and private sectors intertwine for delivering the various services demanded by the economy and the public.

I. PUBLIC WORKS VS. PUBLIC INFRASTRUCTURE

The best single term to capture the governmental role is *public infrastructure*, yet it remains useful to make a distinction of "public works" as the agencies responsible for the various infrastructure systems and the protection of the "public interest." Public works is a term that has been used since the earliest days of the republic (Felbinger, 1995). Called "civil works" by the Army Corps of Engineers, the technical foundation is civil and environmental engineering. Infrastructure is a word initially used to describe the beginning needs of developing nations as they urbanize and industrialize their societies. For reasons not entirely known, it is quite popular among political leadership, the press, and the public to use the name infrastructure to capture attention to the condition of public works facilities.

II. PUBLIC WORKS LIFE CYCLE

Another classification for comprehending infrastructure is the development life cycle from the inception of an idea for a solution to a community need, through the creation of the facility and finally to strategies about its decay and renewal. These are physical, engineered systems, which go through a deliberate order of action. The following is a model of stages in this life cycle:

1. *Planning*: Capabilities/capacities, goals and standards, preliminary design and analysis, laboratory experiments/demonstrations, environmental planning for use and mitigation.

2. *Design*: System performance objectives, trial designs, environmental impacts, community acceptance, final design (plans/specifications), project analysis (benefit-cost).

3. *Construction*: Site, utilities and transportation, foundation, structure and systems, project inspection and acceptance, contract disputes and payments.

4. *Operation*: Usage and decay with time and weather, reliability and downtime (repair), preventive maintenance (optimal funding), rehabilitation options and replacement.

III. FEDERALISM AND PRIVATIZATION

Different levels of government and both public and private resources can participate in each stage of the infrastructure life cycle. Centralized planning and design are common at a headquarters or higher level of government. Historically, private consultants or constructors engage in one or more of these stages. Design has been balanced between the two sectors, but construction of any significant projects has always been the purview of private companies, often because local or state law required private conduct of such work.

What is new today is the private assumption of more stages of the life cycle, in partnerships with public works agencies and in collaborations of multiple companies for design-build-operation (DBO) agreements (Haskins et al.,

1998). This does extend the role of the private sector, effecting a privatization policy. Even the stage of planning (and ownership) is being considered a viable alternative for some public works assets.

A. Federalism and Public Works

Public works services involve all levels of government in various roles of planning, finance, delivery, or regulation. Yet the vast majority of public works are owned and operated by local governments, i.e., cities, counties, or special districts. Many of these functions are structured across a region, serving multiple cities and counties and beginning the aggregation of public works to wider levels of governance. Regions are more natural boundaries, or sheds, and deserve a centralized organization. Water or air sheds are logically managed across the entire shed, rather than face the attempt to rely on coordinated decisions on capital investment and service delivery across jurisdictions.

Some state levels of government are small enough to act as a region by themselves or choose to provide a deeper involvement across several regions through a state highway or waterway system. In some cases, state boundaries do not make much sense from a regional perspective and multiple state compacts may be the most rational structure for some infrastructure systems. One significant example of bi-state compacts is the New York–New Jersey Port Authority, owning and operating several airports, seaport terminals, and a transit line. The natural aggregation of these transportation systems is obviously desirable, even if the systems cross over state boundaries.

Some state boundaries in the United States are inappropriate for the reasonable management of some public works systems, necessitating such compacts. Some international boundaries may not make infrastructure sense and treaties for the St. Lawrence Seaway and water treatment on the Colorado river at Mexico are necessitated. The federal government does own and operate a few public works. The Tennessee Valley Authority and the Bonneville Power Authority, on the Columbia River, are systems having multiple state impacts where the government maintains control. But there has been consideration of selling these assets to eliminate a federal role. A bistate compact or even a private takeover is possible.

The role of states in the conduct of public infrastructure involves more than just logical boundaries. Like the federal government, states often influence plans, provide funding, and regulate the behavior of public works within their boundaries. This traditional role of federalism in the United States, where the greatest contribution to the development of infrastructure over the last 50 years has been the huge federal largess, provides both state and local public works with substantial capital grants, some operating subsidies, yet extracting compliance to national policies on development plans and regulatory outcomes. No doubt the financial support of local public works was readily accepted, even necessary, for rapid development across the nation.

In a serious attempt to examine the nation's public works, the National Council on Public Works Improvement completed *Fragile Foundations* in 1988. This significant study made the following statement regarding the fit of public works in the federalism hierarchy (Felbinger, 1996):

> . . . policy should support local self-sufficiency to the greatest extent possible, all levels of government should share some degree of accountability for infrastructure as a whole, since the effects of most public works are not neatly locked within the boundaries for any given jurisdiction. Primary responsibility for infrastructure can be assigned as follows:
>
> Federal: highways of national significance; air traffic control; inland waterways; environmental standards; hazardous waste cleanup; flood control
>
> State: highways of statewide significance; wastewater treatment capital outlays; airport planning; waste disposal siting; dam safety
>
> Local: local roads; mass transit; airports; ports and harbors; water supply; wastewater treatment operations maintenance; solid waste disposal'' (Felbinger, 1996)

This distribution shows a distinction that may not be surviving 10 years later. The continued devolution of programs and funds to the states, and decentralization to local governments for funding priorities and operations are changing the above model.

B. Justifying Federal Investment

Federal investment in infrastructure was justified, first, as fiscal stimulus to ensure economic growth in regions and the nation, if you agree that infrastructure investment is an effective or the best stimulus for economic development (Gordon, 1997). Second, it is argued as policy to provide equity across regions and states which could not or would not provide the public works service level that are received in other, more affluent regions or states. Whether defensible or not, thirdly, infrastructure investment is no doubt delivered by a federal government that historically has been able to afford to serve their local constituents, across every region, with what has become know as an unkindly term—public works ''pork.'' That is, federal representatives cannot resist serving the electorate with a highly visible and useful piece of infrastructure, be it the desired dam, needed freeway, secured flood protection levee, or required sewage treatment facility to meet environmental standards.

This is not to say that pork barrel politics suggest waste, but in the legislative haste to serve they create a large macro demand on the federal budget along with an inability to resist the federal generosity. Local system support may well be justified on the basis of economic stimulus, equity, safety, and health objectives. The difficulty of prioritizing each region is lessened by a large federal contribution. The need to conduct a benefit-cost comparison is decreased if sufficient dollars are available to avoid discriminating between regions (Pagano, 1996).

Federal involvement in local public works has been almost constant over our history, but has come at a price to the national economy. Given other demands, limited ability to raise revenues, and a political mandate to eliminate the intolerable deficits and balance the national budget, the federal government now places public works in a new predicament. One would expect infrastructure to be less likely to end up in a balanced federal budget because social entitlements, national defense, international security, education, criminal justice, and other programs with louder interest groups would clearly dominate public works in a balanced-budget fight. Infrastructure systems serve more local or regional users, who ought to pay for benefits largely accruing to themselves. Externalities, solved by larger aggregation of funding bases, may be less prevalent or certainly considered less consequential in this current political environment. Federal participation is less defensible economically and politically, thus creating the movement toward devolution and decentralization.

Devolution implies that decision making on infrastructure systems should be sent down to lower levels of governments, to the states and even local entities. It is defended mostly on the basis of ideology (it just sounds good to us), but it is rational if we see the boundary of a system as local or regional where benefits remain local and revenues can be raised locally. For infrastructure, many systems are truly regional in terms of a rational management strategy to capture benefits and provide funding. Yet local government remains a powerful influence on public works decisions, often overwhelming the logical regional view of these systems and making policy choices on a decentralized local government basis. There is no intent here to suggest the ideal level of government to own, finance, and operate each of the myriad public works functions. Instead the goal is to present the alternative models and to indicate the opportunity for state governments to be involved in public works. The question is whether they will gain influence with the federal decline or they too will lose power with decentralization of public works to the regional/local level.

In spite of these arguments, the federal government has a great resiliency in its ability to support public infrastructure. The recent passage of the Transportation Equity Act of 1998 (TEA 21) continues to demonstrate their appetite for funding state and local government (Lomax, 1998; Fahey, 1998). Certainly not complete devolution, with a remaining focus on federal funding of intermodal transportation systems, TEA 21 is a major investment in transportation. There is no doubt some pork is in this legislation if we examine the political debate. It also makes the budget balancing act a greater challenge, yet even conservative politicians need to help locals and produce payoffs for the public works industry. The term *public works industry* implies roles for both the public and private sectors. For a long time the private contribution to infrastructure development has been substantial, delivering services and supplies by contracts or leases with public owner-agencies.

C. Private Sector Contributions

The history of private contributions to public works is immense. Private firms have conducted a large share of infrastructure design and environmental planning, produced essentially all of the construction, provided all materials and equipment, and delivered a portion of the operations and maintenance. Yet provision decisions and ownership commonly remain in the hands of public entities. In terms of the total dollars in public works capital and operating budgets, the private sector likely receives 75% or more of all expenditures.

Public works managers and employees must retain leadership, policy and planning responsibilities, unless the public is willing to have the market make allocation decisions on essential infrastructure resources. Public works agencies do keep a share of the engineering design, surveying and testing as well as a majority of the maintenance and operations of existing systems. For over 25 years there has been a national movement to test this balance and increase the private role in government activities. This privatization movement has targeted public works in particular, even with the substantial share the private sector currently experiences. The extent of private involvement continues to increase by using consultants and operators in place of public employees and by contractors engaging in more complex arrangements across the public works life cycle.

Privatization is defended ideologically as being the preferred alternative per se: "If we can privatize, we should." Another common defense is the "efficient allocation of economic resources," suggesting that private firms can produce a more efficient service. The authors have argued elsewhere that the "per se" argument is not convincing, and the jury is still out on "efficient allocation" (Felbinger and Price, 1998). Continuing study must be accomplished to test the hypothesis that privatization is in the public interest.

It remains the responsibility of public works managers to ensure comprehensive information is at hand to address the challenge of privatization. Decisions need to be rational, ensuring the demand for new private roles can achieve objectives set for public works functions. In absence of good analysis the privatization tide will flood this public policy decision and public works managers may have failed to protect the public interest. These managers remain responsible for ensuring beneficial infrastructure and for representing the public in agreements with private entities. While there is more room for increased privatization, there is a limit to this movement. It is not clear that the sale of all assets and a total market response are expected for any public works function.

Recent evidence shows that private companies may be hesitant to go it alone because they need to share investment and risk with a public partner (Giglio, 1998; Poole, 1998). Public private partnerships may be the norm as we examine new private roles in public works, providing the public sector an ability to contain privatization to ensure public objectives are met. Opportunities for infrastructure systems can operate just as efficiently when performed by public agencies. Is there any reason the public should be denied the chance to reap the net benefits for public works? When the public cannot raise capital, when they do not have comparable expertise and experience and are unwilling to take risks, then the private sector may have advantage. If no one is willing to take a chance on public works, then essential service is denied without a public works agency.

D. Public Works Enterprise

When a public works agency is able to become autonomous from parent governments in the conduct of their function, they most likely do so with the ability to raise capital, receive revenues, and retain earnings. Essentially, a public agency is acting like a private enterprise and reaping the benefit of independence for the citizen-consumer. This condition would lessen the need for private involvement, yet these situations may be the most attractive opportunities for the private sector. Examples of such public enterprise include airports and seaports, water and energy purveyors, and some transit operations (Price, 1981). A privatization push is underway for the nation's airports, but seaports remain firmly in the hands of the public sector in the United States (Comptroller General, November 1996). Water agencies, with steady revenue streams, are under the challenge of private takeover, yet two major energy retailers in California are public agencies (Sacramento Municipal Utility District and Los Angeles Water and Power). At this point some transit operations are generating enough revenues to be attractive to private interests.

While public enterprise can act as efficiently as private companies, there also can be savings for customers in public agencies through less executive costs, no taxation to be paid and no profits to be made. Less pressure on the cost side should result in lower fees for services. So what is in the public interest? Do public enterprises provide an alternative to privatization for the most financially successful public works functions? These and other questions can be addressed by observing what states are actually doing with public infrastructure.

IV. OBSERVING STATE PRACTICE IN PUBLIC WORKS

The observation of public works practice begins with a review of the functions for which a state has responsibility, drawn from the list of public works introduced before. In addition, the state role in the life cycle of infrastructure development is determined. For each function, are they engaged in: (1) Provision of services by ownership, planning, or financing? (2) Production of services by design, construction, or operations? and (3) Regulation of services by safety, health, and environmental protection standards?

Given the dual trends to devolution of federal responsibility to the states and the preference for decentralization of development decisions to local regions, what public works functions and influence remain for states? Local and regional governments look for help but not control from the state. The state can provide resources to ensure equity between localities and may provide a logical and an efficient jurisdiction for some infrastructure systems. Of course, geography, size, history, and politics may explain the State's balance of influence.

This study examines the placement of public works functions in the organizational structure of the state, identifies the division of these functions among senior administrators and addresses integration under common leadership with a single policy umbrella. The extent of disintegration or fragmentation is observed and explained, but integration is defended and means of integration shown.

The purpose of this chapter is not an in-depth case study of any one state or a comparison across the nation. Rather the intent is to test this model of observation with an examination of one state. To provide further insights for public works professionals and academics, significant policy issues and management challenges facing the state are presented. The conclusion of the chapter synthesizes policy solutions and management innovations, suggesting further study to address remaining questions.

A. The California Case

This case is built on survey responses from managers in transportation and water resources as well an interview with a policy staff member.[1] In addition, local public works managers have contributed ideas to this study.

California is a large state ranging north-south for 800 miles and east-west for 200 miles, with a population of over 30 million. While part of the western states, it is isolated from the north by sparsely populated forests and mountains,

---

[1] Interviews were conducted with Roy Nagy of Caltrans, James Bailey of Water Resources, and Del Pierce of the Business, Transportation, and Housing Secretary's Policy Office.

from the east by the Sierra Nevada and eastern deserts, and on the south by the border with Mexico. At the southeast, the Colorado river and the boundary with Arizona creates a significant public works issue across state and national borders. Water resource systems and the air shed in San Diego and Tijuana require international cooperation. The proximity of Las Vegas to the southern California metropolis provides an opportunity for rapid rail connections, likely to require a bistate compact. Lake Tahoe and the Truckee River involve cooperation between California and Nevada. Otherwise, the main river systems all flow within the state, other air sheds are contained, and transportation connections out of state are part of the federal or private systems. Within the state is another matter!

Two of the nation's biggest public works provide connections between the regions. As usual, the interstate highway/freeway system is owned and operated by the State, though much authority for its urban character is decentralized in the regions. One of the most "unnatural" public works is the California Water Project, transporting huge water supplies 400 miles from the Sacramento–San Joaquin Delta to the Metropolitan Water District of greater Los Angeles. It is one state in its isolation, but two or three states when it comes to decisions about infrastructure. Let us identify the three states as Northern California and Southern California, plus Upper California as the mountainous region north of Sacramento, where bold natural resources are located including much of the State's water supply.

Major metropolitan cities exit with San Francisco, Oakland, San Jose, Sacramento, Fresno, Los Angeles, and San Diego. As commonly seen in other states, many smaller local governments occur in coastal regions of San Francisco–Monterey Bays and the Santa Barbara–Los Angeles–San Diego corridor and the growing Sacramento and San Joaquin Valley region. A desert community surrounding Palm Springs is also being "greened," creating an agriculture and population concentration.

California's extensive display of small local governments in close proximity entices regional consolidation of public works on regional planning and efficiency grounds. While only San Diego has truly created a metropolitan government by expanding its boundary to consume most of the county, the councils of government known as the Association of Bay Area Governments (ABAG) and the Southern California Association of Governments (SCAG) do not provide the extensive consolidation of public works that could be justified on a regional basis. Some significant public works agencies have a wide regional jurisdiction, including the Metropolitan Water District, and the Regional Transit District in Southern California, San Francisco Bay Conservation and Development Commission, East Bay Municipal Utility District (water and sewer), Bay Area Rapid Transit District, and the Sacramento Municipal Utility District (electricity) in northern California.

All of these regional entities are publicly owned and operated with little direct state influence over planning or operations, though they may receive state funding. The State, through its Public Utility Commission, has more power over infrastructure privately held, such as private gas and electric and water companies, than it does over publicly owned utilities like Los Angeles Department of Water and Power. The transportation functions of seaports and airports are attached to cities or special districts. Only the City of Oakland and the San Diego Port District involve both sea and air functions.

In California, most public works functions are owned, planned, developed, and operated at the local and regional level. This is certainly more likely in a large state with dispersed geographic regions. Yet the State does have influence through regional planning requirements, funding, and regulation, predicting the model for the new federalism. The State's principal role of ownership and operations is concentrated on the statewide highway system and the state water project. The remainder of its impact is primarily planning, funding, and regulating.

By examining California's comprehensive organization structure, all public works functions are identified along with their chain of command. The purpose is to discover the extent of integration or fragmentation of public works and the type of parent structure that exists. Public works functions ultimately report to the Governor, as shown in Figure 1.

B. Integration or Disintegration (Fragmentation)

The initial question for observing state public works is the extent of functional integration. Integration is measured by the share of the total functions reporting

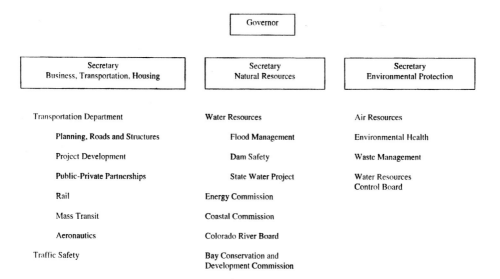

Figure 1 Organization structure for California public works functions.

to a single line of authority or public works administrator. For California there are three senior secretarial positions responsible for public works programs, distributed among the resource secretariats shown in Figure 1.

1. The superagency Secretary for Business, Transportation, and Housing contains the multiple modes of transportation, including a traffic safety regulatory activity. This arrangement suggests the importance of transportation to commercial and residential development. It identifies transportation as a driving force for economic development, one of the public works objectives.

2. The superagency Secretary for Natural Resources captures the water resource multiple activities as well as energy, coastal management, San Francisco Bay conservation, and Colorado River management. No doubt water and natural geography are considered important to sustaining essential resources for human life and is distinctive from economic development strategy. In addition, regional and local delivery of water resource services, common across the nation, limits state involvement. Yet California, due to its unique geography and large size, is in the water wholesale business, transporting huge volumes of supply from the water-richer north to the water-poorer south.

3. The superagency Secretary for Environmental Protection performs a traditional environmental regulation objective, with no ownership or operation of public works assets. They are protecting the air, environmental health, waste disposal hazards, and water quality and quantitative adjudication. Notice that the Water Resources Control Board does not report to the Natural Resource Secretary, suggesting an independent control responsibility. While there is some concern about delaying decision making and causing additional expenditures in a confrontational regulatory model, we apparently do not trust public works administrators to have both infrastructure and environmental responsibilities.

The California, like most other states, owns only a few but significant assets. They do own and operate the interstate and state highway systems, although a portion of those assets are being privatized (Giglio, 1998; Poole, 1998) and devolved to regional/local entities (Peters and Hidalgo, 1997). Examples are provided below where two local authorities have developed major highway projects.

The State owns and operates a major water diversion project, carrying the precious water resource over 600 miles from Lake Shasta in the far north to Los Angeles and San Diego. The California Water Project, completed in the 1950s, is one of largest public works projects ever conducted by the transfer from the great Sacramento and San Joaquin Valley watershed to the Southern Basin. The Supreme Court ruled that California is a preferred source of water supply rather than adjacent Colorado River watershed shared with other states and Indian tribes. It is very likely that California will keep control of the water wholesale operation as long as the political power of the south remains dominant and agriculture and urban development continues in spite of the lack of a natural water supply in the Southern California Basin.

Two forces are driving the fragmentation of public works. First, the rise of separate professional identity, particularly between transportation and water resources who serve different policy objectives, and the attention to environmental protection over the last 30 years have splintered traditional public works. The classic public works director no longer can hold an administrative umbrella above the myriad of functions at either the state or local level. Second, politically active interest groups are diverse, naturally demanding unique attention to their own public services. They see no advantage to battling for policy decisions and financial resources through a single public infrastructure agency or a comprehensive public works secretary. More direct competition across public works functions may result in less resources for any or all of the services.

C. The Case for Integration

In spite of the reality of disintegration in state government, we argue the case for the integration of public works at every level of public ownership. If infrastructure investment can be defended as necessary for a vibrant and growing economy, then the total amount of investment ought to be examined through a common policy lens. Such investment decisions can be more rational in terms of economic objectives as well as natural resource sustainability (Bernstein, 1998).

It is suggested that infrastructure will fare better if it is integrated, ensuring that investment dollars are available to meet service demands and renewal strategies for all functions. They will better coordinate functions, require fewer policy decisions, and present a stronger case in competition with other public programs. Such is not the case at this time, but here are suggested means to establish a higher degree of integration:

1. *Common legislative committees*, say, with the name "infrastructure and natural resources," requiring fewer committees and subcommittees, forcing interest groups to face the same policy makers who must integrate their choices into an infrastructure development policy.

2. *Single funding pools*, generated from earmarked fees and taxes, statewide bonds, and innovative debt and assessment mechanisms, can be created to serve the integrated policy choices. Infrastructure development banks, open to grants and/or loans, available to all public works functions, are increasingly popular in state government (Morris, 1996; Comptroller General, 1996).

3. *An infrastructure resource administrator*, with focused policy coordination by a single manager or the Governor's office, can be established. Infrastructure policy consolidation is the key, augmented by a state or national re-

search agenda it can be a powerful institutional voice for both economic and natural resource objectives.

Fewer administrative channels is critical, allowing aggregated decisions which are more professional and less politically divisive. The trade-offs between various public works functions should not be decided on the basis of segregated interest group politics, but on the basis of relative needs and cost-effectiveness to achieve macroeconomic and natural resource policy for the entire state. Political choices and legislative decisions must focus on service levels for each function and must determine the overall magnitude of public works investment to ensure the state's attractiveness as an industrial location. The economy demands high-performance public works systems, because economies can be hurt by weak-performing infrastructure and low-quality public works services (Lancaster and Genega, 1996; Poister, April 1997). The same argument applies to federal policy, yet the political and economic reasons for the demise of the national role overwhelm even the best arguments about investing in infrastructure to stimulate a sustainable national economy.

While such integration may change the influence of single-function interest groups, all stakeholders should participate in the strategy of each function, particularly at the regional level, where development decisions are increasingly made. If state policies focus on investment and economic impacts as well as sustainable natural resources, then an integrated public works policy better serves the broader infrastructure industry and all stakeholders.

No doubt public works integration is a reversal of the trend over the past 30 years, where the environmental movement created a more separate constituency, in and out of government. A return to a national and state infrastructure strategy is an idea needing debate since the combining of development and sustainability into one decision model will enhance consensus building for this often contentious issue. Rapid project deployment, with agreed environmental action known well in advance of project design, will serve the public interest for more efficient decision making, quicker project completion, and less litigation (Felbinger and Price, 1997).

V. ISSUES AND INNOVATIONS IN CALIFORNIA PUBLIC WORKS

As suggested by the research design presented earlier, a review of the California case highlights significant issues facing the State and presents important innovations accomplished by California over recent time. The following issues and innovations will likely be seen in other states. Research should be conducted to see how public works agencies elsewhere have responded to these and other initiatives.

A. Policy Issues

1. Devolution

Federal devolution would appear to give more power to the states by control of block grants and influence over infrastructure priorities. Yet the devolution stream flows downhill with states ultimately passing federal and state funding to the local level, possibly with minimal mandates.[2] California has sought to define the local level as the region, especially for public works where the rationality of regional systems is more persuasive than the demand for political control by municipal governments. Public works has resisted the devolution trend by recognizing the need for regional cooperation and coordinated planning, if not consolidation into larger institutions.

State government still has significant impact on regional or local public works given these roles:

Regulate Environmental, Health and Safety, and Quality-of-Work Life Standards

Public policy at the state level will continue to demand accountability by local/ regional agencies and independence for regulators in these areas, even though regulatory review can be enhanced by combining infrastructure development and environmental planning at the lowest level of government. Again, integrating these two objectives early in the planning cycle should reduce development time and cost and eliminate legal conflicts. Reducing the institutional and professional distance between developer and regulator is essential to improving the quality of regulatory services.

Determine Formulas for Distributing Resources to Local Regions

Distribution methods will have to be reasonable and fair, but most likely will be driven by population or tax base rather than by need or equity. In such cases, the needs of public works systems may be decided by population and political clout, to the detriment of equal service delivery across regions and systems often neglected in the past.

Require Regional Planning and Capital Decisions Across the Natural Boundaries of Infrastructure Systems

In many cases public works agencies are currently regionalized as seen above, with transit, water or, sewage districts. Airports or seaports are naturally regional, although in California, big cities like San Francisco, Oakland, Los Angeles, and

---

[2] For a current review of transportation policy and the role of states, see Truit (1997).

Long Beach protect their own enterprises. If no regional consolidation exists, regional collaboration is still desirable between cities and counties. It may be required or encouraged by state law. The San Francisco Bay Area, with several big and small seaports, has coordinated planning for seaport development under a process conducted by the Metropolitan Transportation Commission (MTC). But since little state or federal funding is involved with seaports, the actual regional plan is not rigid. The ports of Los Angeles and Long Beach, though quite separate institutions, actually conduct substantial joint planning and development. Most recently the ports are jointly creating the huge Alameda Corridor Project to improve rail and truck travel from the ports to a rail consolidation yard. Yet most regional cooperation occurs with the metropolitan planning organizations (MPOs) conducting regional transportation planning and priorities under a mandate by the State.

The MPO, often acting as an MTC, is a significant focus of infrastructure authority (Boschken, 1998). The MPO does effectively take power from local jurisdictions and the state, although Caltrans retains extensive engineering prowess and often provides design and construction services. Even when roadways are state-owned, the State conducts operations and maintenance, so they are more service provider than planner of facilities. The state has economies of scale and a huge memory, now doing less provision for and more production of roadway systems.

2. Investment Strategy

California has expressed support for renewed infrastructure investment, yet do capital resources follow the needs or deficits of infrastructure systems or do they follow growth and urban development? Maintenance resources tend to follow capital and not address deteriorating systems, weak service levels, or risks for public safety and health. A new debate on infrastructure condition has arisen with the recent Report Card on Infrastructure produced by the American Society of Civil Engineers, and the release of the Surface Transportation Policy Project study.[3] Both of these reports portray poor-performing infrastructure, costing citizens time and damages. Some public works officials argue such negative reports are exaggerated to support transportation investment; nonetheless, the debate should continue to add fodder to the difficult analysis of infrastructure resource

---

[3] Two recent reports add to the long standing debate as to the needs for public works investment. See the American Society of Civil Engineers news release (1998, March 5), "Civil engineers give nation's infrastructure bad grades, say it will cost $1 trillion to fix," Washington, DC, and Surface Transportation Policy Project's study of urban highway condition and vehicle damage, as reported in "Shabby highways called costly for California drivers" (1998, November 7), *San Francisco Chronicle*. This issue needs much more academic critique than it has received to date.

needs. The Rebuild America Coalition adds the views of public sector practitioners to the argument on deficits in infrastructure investment, yet there is no consensus in this policy debate as to the governmental role (Rendell, 1998; Levy and Cadette, 1998; Price, 1999).

The professional public works manager is inundated with opportunities to use information technology and decision support software to determine optimal maintenance and rehabilitation strategies, but sufficient budgets to reach these goals are rarely available (Berry et al., 1998; Shapard, 1997). The State does not invest in renewal with the same voracity they invest in capital for state assets or local systems. The argument, which State policy needs to demonstrate, is that capital funding by whatever creative means should ensure sufficient renewal expenditures. These are increasingly going to involve financial means that get revenues more directly from users and those who create demand for infrastructure systems, yet these funding innovations still need to include maintenance and rehabilitation (Price and Chapman, 1997).

Additionally, more study must be done to determine if the state's infrastructure investment policy relates to economic objectives or if the impact of investment decisions relate to the economic performance of the state economy. One surrogate measure of the economic health of the infrastructure is the propensity of industry and developers to locate or dislocate their private infrastructure in the state. Location decisions require data on the adequacy of public infrastructure and business locators demand public works investments, often as public sector contributions. The failure of public works policy to meet accepted standards of access, congestion, safety, and health will certainly cause business hesitance to locate in a community or region where the risk of poor public infrastructure performance is higher.

3. Privatizing Public Works

In California, as in many other states, there is a substantial social movement seeking the privatization of government activity. This discussion is not an extensive exploration into privatization behavior beyond the concepts and issues raised earlier, but it will demonstrate initiatives in the state. Public works in general, at all levels of government, has experimented with increased private activity to a greater extent than other public services. More is likely coming at the local level, where most public works is practiced.

The state has a very creative privatization initiative through its transportation agency. Caltrans has established a unit called Public-Private Partnerships, essentially leading the nation in highway privatization (Bloomfield et al., 1998; Chi, 1998). The state has won innovation awards for this achievement.

Caltrans' creative model seeks private development of tollways, with some meaningful state participation in what truly are partnerships, not full privatization.

They floated a request for proposals asking private ventures to propose development of new lanes, initially within existing corridors, with the private sector investing and reaping toll revenues. The State is certainly involved, from planning, financing, and operating perspectives. Caltrans' first winner was a proposal by a consortium, California Private Transportation Company (CPTC) to build HOT lanes within the Riverside Freeway (SR 91) for a reach of 10 miles, using congestion or value pricing and electronic toll collection. The distribution of efforts by both sectors in the SR 91 adventure is shown in the following table.

Development stage	Private co.	State of California
Land investment		Existing ownership
Plan/environmental objectives		Transportation plan
Engineering design and permits	CPTC	
Construction	CPTC	
Tollway operation	CPTC	
Roadway maintenance		Caltrans contract
Roadway policing		CHP contract

The advantage to the public was that they could avoid the capital investment needed, assuming these funds are more readily available in private financial markets. The project results in revenues for California since the State is delivering maintenance and patrol services to CPTC. More State highway privatization projects are being considered, but are not yet built. It is not clear what is causing the delay; maybe market hesitance. Future projects may be waiting until conclusions are drawn on the performance and success of the SR 91 venture. Here are some initial arguments about this award-winning innovation:

1.   The value pricing structure, as adapted by CPTC with usage, has improved congestion in the freeway and kept congestion from exceeding desirable limits in the tollway.

2.   All environmental interests seems satisfied that increased vehicle occupancy and shorter trip times result in meaningfully less pollution and construction within an existing median right of way did not result in significant environmental damage.

3.   Net operating revenues for CPTC appear reasonable in their annual reports, although their capital return period may still be unclear. Net operating revenues to the State are certainly positive, yet not intended to give them a financial payback on their contribution to the project.

4.   The risk to the private sector remains, especially if revenues decline or their need to raise fees creates demand sensitivity and diminishing revenue. This is a risk expected to be borne by a private investment, but should not create

any risk for the public sector. The State could realize a negative financial impact if CPTC is unable to keep its part of the bargain and fails in bankruptcy.

Yet the most striking aspect of this agreement is the partnership feature rather than the privatization move. It was possible for the State itself to have invested in the HOT lanes and collected the revenues. If it is good business for the private sector, could not the same argument be made for a public enterprise? In fact, another HOT project, San Joaquin Hills, was built in Orange County. This is a public tollway developed by a local authority instead of the State, but again with the State conducting services. A median HOT lane project, similar to SR 91, has been created in San Diego on Interstate 15. But it, too, is a local authority with State services.

Regarding water resources, California owns one major water diversion project, the California Water Project (CWP). There has been little talk about privatizing this system or even creating a major partnership with a private investor, mainly because the capital investment has been made. When the CWP deteriorates to the point where major capital renewal is necessary, the private sector could be asked to make this second investment and reap fees for transporting water. Maybe the private operator would take on the challenge to get additional supply and construct facilities elsewhere. The operation of the system could be conducted by private services, but likely with little advantage to the State. Private operation may cause less risk for the public if the private sector could collect revenues. A private CWP is not likely to reduce costs and may well raise water rates to ensure that the assets perform well for the contractor. In this case, what would serve the public interest (Council of State Government, 1998; Kraemer, 1998)?

At the same time, most of the privatization of the water resources system is emerging at the local level, where most of water retailers reside. Private water companies have existed in California for a long time, but now political pressure is strong to privatize many public water and sewer agencies through lease agreements rather than selling assets (Clark et al., 1997; Viscovich, 1998). Upfront cash payments are too inviting for many local governments to resist. They also minimize the revenue and cost risks and may take a fee or return for their ownership.

In solid waste public programs, competition is entering the equation as private operators are campaigning to get involved in waste collection and disposal, including hazardous materials.[4] Whether the local owners of existing disposal sites can compete against private entrepreneurs is an important question ahead for the solid waste industry (Wilt, 1997; O'Leary, 1997; Leavitt and Hadfield, 1998). But the State involvement has been limited to regulation, though

---

[4] For a comprehensive examination of implications of "Brownfields" sites for public works, see Meyer and Deitrick (1998).

encouraging private competition. The concept of "managed competition" has emerged as the basis for creating head-to-head battles between public and private waste operators. Waste collection competition has occurred for years, but now the battlefield is shifting to the disposal site. The privatization movement is alive and well.

Three questions remain for public works privatization, suggesting conditions and results to watch:

1. The share of *public investment and risk taking* is always a political concern. Caltrans has done well with SR 91, but other projects may require more risk by the State. The State may be forced to choose projects where the private sector will hesitate until the public takes a bigger share. Call it the S^3—sports stadium syndrome.

2. Is the public willing to play a more *entrepreneurial role with public works*, taking investment risks in order to reap returns that flow from revenue-based systems? Is it the role of government to realize positive net returns when funds can then be made available to other public functions? Public works such as large seaports have been recording large net revenues for years, so much that the State of California passed a law allowing local governments to reap a share of those "profits."

3. To capture both of the above two questions, a challenge is given to answer the comprehensive question as to whether the *public interest is truly being served by privatization* (Felbinger and Price, 1998). Does privatized public works provide higher quality services, reach all who have a right to receive service, at reasonable and equitable charges?

B. Innovations

1. Stakeholder Forums

As infrastructure decisions become more decentralized, they are also becoming more open to wider variety of stakeholders, particularly those directly benefited or affected in the local area. This model of decision making may or may not include political leadership, but does integrate professionals in and out of government agencies with business, environmental, and community interests (Mayo et al., 1998). These stakeholders get involved early in the development process and act as strategic planners, seeking agreements on plans and finances. They will need acceptance by local, state, or federal leadership, which are expected to approve plans and expenditures. The forum process should reach a consensus and agreement before significant design detail is selected, discovering contentious issues early, resolving them with the agreement, and leaving less grounds for dispute later in the development. Early agreements should eliminate later delays and reduce the overall time for permitting and approval. Three examples of such forums are briefly introduced:

1. The most substantial forum in California at this time is the CALFED Bay–Delta program, seeking to resolve longstanding disputes among those to have interests in the Delta over water quality and quantity. While the original mandate was protection of the Delta resource, CALFED is now discussing actions affecting statewide water strategy. As a result the local Delta and northern California interests see the process as serving southern California needs, and a consensus among all parties is less likely than earlier expected. This is a continuation of California's water wars between the "two states" and may not be resolvable at the forum.

2. A successful forum was recently completed with the process used in the Yolo Bypass Wildlife Reserve. In this case the forum was truly local, with the leading stakeholder as a nonprofit group—Ducks Unlimited. This nongovernmental entity led the forum to a development plan, where federal and state investment was assured even though governments did not directly influence the decision.

3. A very creative forum occurred with a new highway development project in Santa Clara County—SR 85. Instead of being a traditional state highway project within the state planning process, this development was driven by a local forum of interested citizens. They formed a local authority, received regional MPO support, got a consensus on design parameters, captured financing from federal and state sources without waiting in the State's overall priority list. As a result the freeway was built quicker, within estimates, and with less resistance from the community. One quote captures the payoff of this stakeholder forum: "The Traffic Authority virtually eliminated the possibility of litigation by spending literally hundreds of hours meeting with the people who would be impacted by Route 85's construction" (Innovation and cooperation, 1995).

2. Project Management

One principal framework for observing public works is the life cycle of infrastructure development, across the six stages introduced before. The development stages of the cycle, before operation and usage, address a unique structure over a fixed life and define a project. Projects are critical to public works organizations because they involve complex engineering systems, require large capital expenditure, and consume significant time. There is little argument that project outcomes expect technical functionality as designed, within the least cost and time. The following initiatives of the State address project performance:

a. Life Cycle Project Management

The project life cycle contains stages usually served by different specialists, necessitating a "hands-off" between professionals who serve different stages. Caltrans has chosen to assign a project manager to the development life, at least from the early concept, through design and construction. These managers take ownership of the project and can better coordinate "concurrent engineering" among designers and constructors. The expectation is that project life cycle managers will minimize the impacts of conflicts inside and outside the project, among all parties. Further, their presence should reduce the likelihood of cost and time overruns.

b. Accelerated Construction

Innovative project management includes a challenge to reduce completion time. Encouraged by the disasters of freeway collapse, Caltrans created an accelerated construction contract where design and bidding time were greatly reduced and contractors were required to begin immediately, working 24 hours seven days a week to meet target for a fast construction cycle (Roberts, 1997). Financial incentives were available to the contractor if time was reduced. The justification of this acceleration was the savings to the public by returning the freeway to full usage much earlier, and these dollar benefits are expected to exceed any payments by Caltrans to the contractor. A structural failure from an earthquake does demand some special concern for public delays, but why not consider this method to reduce cycle time for all projects?

c. Project Quality

Projects are more than an engineering task, more than project engineers and contractors. Customer and owner satisfaction must be measured, where users and those in proximity to the project site are important stakeholders to serve. Making projects "user friendly" is an objective the State is pursuing (Project quality management, 1996; Bowman and French, 1992; Poister, 1997; Poister and Larson, 1988). Consider these behaviors:

    1.   Conduct construction activities at times that minimize disruption to users and neighbors.

    2.   Create shorter traffic delay periods, avoiding high usage times and adjusting work to allow less waiting in traffic queues.

    3.   Interact with neighbors and businesses to plan construction around their needs; adapt to improve dust, noise, and congestion control.

    These innovations all focus on responsive, flexible performance in serving local demand, reducing the time and improving the quality of public works services. The next generation of innovations relies on technology, as seen in "intelligent transportation systems," should not only enhance quality but also increase the productivity of infrastructure systems (Newcombe, 1997).

VI. SUMMARY

The California case demonstrated a model for studying public works, and, while only one state, it plays a significant role in public works management and policy because of its size and unique infrastructure systems. Like most states, California owns and operates a major state highway network, even though the State's role is changing from a policy maker to a funder and regulator. California is still engaged in substantial highway design, construction, and maintenance, but increasingly under the influence of local/regional entities.

Across public works functions, there is a common fragmentation of functions between transportation, water resources, and environmental protection. While there are clear reasons for this disintegration, the case for integration has been made and should be tested to determine if benefits will accrue to infrastructure systems performance when policies and funding decisions are made together. Is it wise to separate infrastructure development from environmental planning? Is it wise to splinter water planning between quality and quantity decisions, to divide flood management from dam operation? The fragmenting of public works functions shown before creates hierarchical impediments to infrastructure management under the goal of political control and interest group preferences. Traditionally, dueling parties must come together early in development with one strategic focus, solving disputes earlier and easier.

California is unique with regard to statewide water projects because of the need to divert water supplies. The Federal Central Valley Project to send water upstream in the San Joaquin Valley to serve agriculture will likely devolve into a state, regional, or even privately operated system. Yet the majority of California's water purveyors are regional or local, with deliberate independence from the State. The State is not a good entrepreneur with its CVP because charges for water delivery are limited to provide a subsidy to water consumers. Consider this quote:

> The majority of DWR's funding, approximately 80%, comes from sale of water and power . . . if pricing was up structured, water revenues could not only support the department but create some desirable programs . . . we have asked General Obligation Bonds to do what increased user's fees might have done.[5]

In California, privatization initiatives do represent the "cutting edge" of privatization models for tollways. Yet it is unclear whether private sector involvement in development, operation, and even ownership will occur. More likely

---

[5] These comments by James Bailey represent his own views on DWR policies. But the idea of a self-sustaining department seems worth pursuing in these days of fiscal constraints and arguments that revenue sources should be tied to consumption and demand for public works services.

is the model of public-private partnerships seen here where the state (or local) governments remain active participants in infrastructure ownership and planning, with private sector capital and operation of more technically complex systems. Even public entrepreneurial efforts to develop and operate publicly owned toll-ways may be increasingly attractive. The bottom line for the privatization question is the public interest. In essence, will privatization serve to ensure fair and equitable access to infrastructure with continuing productivity improvements. The public interest is served when the private sector can realize a reasonable reward for private investment without denying the access and efficiency objectives and without creating any risk of lower service performance and unexpected costs/impacts for the public.

Solid waste in California is a local asset and operation, but the national battles between the public and private sectors to control waste collection and disposal will represent the management and policy debate for some time to come. This is a classic case of "managed competition," where some would argue the private sector should be fully engaged in ownership and operation but others make a case for public and private entities to freely compete for this business. Remember, the goal is to serve the public interest by service availability at reasonable costs with assurance that the public's environmental health will be sustained. Like tollways, waste management represents an opportunity for public entrepreneurs to conduct waste services and compete for this revenue stream. There is no justification for the position that only the private sector can be competitive while serving the public interest.

There should be no doubt that this exploration of public works at the state government level has set the stage for further investigation and inquiry of current practice and challenges facing new policies and methods. The following list briefly presents big questions, but serves as an agenda for continuing attention to infrastructure at all levels of this society.

1.   *Fragmentation.* Is functional disintegration occurring across the nation, are there any attempts to integrate public works? Is integration necessary to ensure needed funding?

2.   *Funding levels.* What is the level of investment in infrastructure to achieve system performance which minimizes risk; ensures access, safety, and health; and accomplishes the economic and environmental results?

3.   *State role.* Will the role of states in ownership, planning, and management of infrastructure development continue to wane? How will states justify continued investment?

4.   *Private role.* Will the private sector increase their role in public works? Will they be the only source of needed capital and risk taking? Will the public interest be served by privatizing?

5.   *Financial innovation.* Will tolls, user fees, benefit assessments, and revolving funds eliminate the use of general government funds for public works?

Will public works be weaned off general taxation, tying revenue sources to those who use and cause demand for these systems?

6. *Quality services.* Will the quality of public works services increase in the minds of infrastructure customers? Will public works agencies become learning, innovating, and improving organizations by reducing time and costs and delivering high-performance systems?

It is an exciting time for public works. The profession is innovating, heading in the right direction toward management strategies which serve the public interest. Yet public works managers may be derailed by an apathetic public and political leadership that fails to consider a rational long-term policy for infrastructure. New public and professional attention is on the horizon, and an academic base has been collected to create truly "pracademic" insights for these public assets.[6]

REFERENCES

Berry, B., and Foster. (1998). The determinants of services in implementing an expert system in state government, *Public Administration Review* 58:293–305.

Bernstein, H. M. (1997). A sustainable future: implementation a global research agenda, *Public Works Management and Policy* 1:271–287.

Bloomfield, P., Westerling, D., and Carey, R. (1998). Innovation and risk in a public private partnership, *Public Productivity and Management Review* 21:460–471.

Boschken, H. L. (1998). MPOs in charge: ISTEA mandates, bridge design and the struggle for power in the San Francisco Bay area, *Intermodal Fare*, Newsletter of the ASPA Section on Transportation Policy and Administration, summer.

Bowman, J. S., and French, B. J. (1992). Quality improvement in a state agency revisted, *Public Productivity and Management Review* 16:53–64.

Chi, K. S. (1998). Privatization in state government, *Public Administration Review* 58: 374–375.

Clark, C., Heilman, J. G., and Johnson, G. W. (1997). Privatization of wastewater treatment plants, *Public Works Management and Policy* 2:140–147.

Comptroller General. (1996). *State Infrastructure Banks: A Mechanism to Expand Federal Transportation Financing*, U.S. General Accounting Office, GAO/RCED-97-9, Washington.

Comptroller General. (1996). *Airport Privatization: Issues Related to the Sale or Lease of U.S. Commercial Airports*, U.S. General Accounting Office, GAO/RCED-97-3, Washington.

---

[6] The new academic contribution to public works is found in the first 2-1/2 years of the journal *Public Works Management and Policy*. An impressive list of authors from a wide set of disciplines has published in this scholarly journal, providing a central point for focusing attention to this field. PWMP's Web page can be seen at: www.uop.edu/~wprice/pwmpjournal

Council of State Government. (1998). *Private Practices: A Review of Privatization in State Government*, 5-044-9800, Author, Washington.

Fahey, J. (1998). How does TEA-21 impact you?, *APWA Reporter November*:7.

Felbinger, C. L. (1995). Conditions of confusion and conflict: rethinking the infrastructure–economic development linkage, *Building the Public City: The Politics, Governance and Finance of Public Infrastructure* (D. Perry, ed.), Sage Publications, Thousands Oaks, CA, pp. 103–137.

Felbinger, C. L. (1996). Road Construction and Finance in the United States. Report prepared for Transpacific Group, Tokyo, Japan.

Felbinger, C. L. (1997). Public works in the U.S.A., *The Challenge of Public Works Management: A Comparative Study of North America, Japan, and Europe* (B. Houlihan, ed.), International Institute of Administrative Sciences, Brussels.

Felbinger, C. L., and Price, W. T. (1997). Bringing innovation to public infrastructure, *Proceedings of Innovation in Urban Infrastructure* (T. H. W. Baker and M. A. Lacasse, eds.), American Public Works Association International Public Works Congress, pp. 2–12.

Felbinger, C. L., and Price, W. T. (1998). From the editors: Public works privatization, *Public Works Management and Policy* 2:283–285.

Giglio, J. (1998). Private toll roads: Is the glass 1/4 full or 3/4 empty, *Public Works Management and Policy* 2:286–293.

Glassman, J. K. (1998). Pay for your own roads, *US News and World Report*, Feb. 23: 55.

Gordon, C. (1997). Does America really need more infrastructure?, *Public Works Management and Policy* 2:129–139.

Haskins, S., Kelly, L., Brown, P., and Torres, R. (1998). The Seattle story: implementing the TOLT treatment facilities design-build-operate project, National Conference, American Society for Public Administration.

Innovation and cooperation . . . the spirit of California's Route 85. (1995). *Public Works 126*: 56+.

Kraemer, R. A. (1998). Privatization in the water industry, *Public Works Management and Review* 3:104–123.

Lancaster, H. M., and Genega, S. G. (1996). The paradox of federal infrastructure programs: aging infrastructure and constrained budgets, *Public Works Management and Policy 1*:107–119.

Leavitt, W. M., and Hadfield, J. S. (1998). Public/private competition in solid waste management: a case study of alternatives of flow control, *Public Works Management and Policy 3*:146–154.

Levy, S. J., and Cadette, W. M. (1998). Overcoming America's infrastructure deficit: a fiscally responsible plan for public capital investment, *Public Policy Brief*, Jerome Levy Economics Institute of Bard College, No. 40.

Lomax, A. (1998). TEA 21 ushers in a new era for surface transportation, *Intermodal Fare*, summer.

Luberoff, D. (1998). Can states be trusted?, *Governing*, March: 65; Luberoff, D. (1998). Old tea in new bottles, *Governing*, September: 72; Luberoff, D. (1998). The highway market, *Governing*, November: 82; Luberoff, D. (1997). A tale of two tables, *Governing*, May: 80.

Mayo, L. M., Lehman, D. A., and Harper, D. (1998). Step by step: involving engineers, county officials and residents in a decision, *Civil Engineering* 68:65–67.

Meyer, P., and Deitrick, S. (1998). Brownfields and public works: an introduction to the focus section. *Public Works Management and Policy* 2:202–209.

Morris, J. C. (1996). Institutional arrangements in an age of new federalism: public and private management in the state revolving fund program, *Public Works Management and Policy* 1:145–157.

Newcombe, T. (1997). Raising the highway IQ: making highways more efficient—an alternative to snarled traffic and new construction, and Intelligent transportation: international style'', *Government Technology* 10(5), 11(14).

O'Leary, R. (1997). Trash talk: the Supreme Court and the interstate transportation of waste, *Public Administration Review* 57:281–284.

Pagano, M. A. (1996). Local infrastructure intergovernmental grants and urban needs, *Public Works Management and Policy* 1:19–30.

Peters, R. A., and Hidalgo, J. (1997). An examination of the costs and benefits of state highway turnback programs, *Public Works Management and Policy* 1:350–359.

Poister, T. H., and Harris, R. H. (1997). The impacts of TQM in highway maintenance: benefit/cost implications, *Public Administration Review* 57:294–302.

Poister, T. H., and Larson, T. D. (1988). The revitalization of PennDot: a case study in effective public management, *Public Productivity and Management Review* 10:85–103.

Poister, T. H. (1997). A survey of performance measurement systems in state transportation departments, *Public Works Management and Policy* 1:323–341.

Poole, R. (1998). Private toll roads: changing the highway paradigm, *Public Works Management and Policy* 3:3–9.

Price, W. (1981). Seaports as public enterprise: some policy implications, *Making Ocean Policy* (F. W. Hoole, ed.), Westview Press, Boulder, CO, pp. 217–238.

Price, W., and Chapman, J. (1993). Getting public works maintenance off the general tax budget, National Tax Association, Annual Conference, St. Paul, MN.

Price, W. (1997). Public works management: in search of an academic field, *Public Works Administration: Current Public Policy Perspectives* (L. Brewer, ed.), Sage Publications, Thousands Oaks, CA, pp. 3–35.

Price, W. (1999). Reporting on the infrastructure report card: why grade the nation's public works? *Public Works Management and Policy* 4:58–87.

Project quality management. (1996). *A Guide to the Project Management Body of Knowledge*, Project Management Institute, pp. 83–92.

Rendell, E. G. (1998). A call to pay the U.S. infrastructure price tag, *Public Works Management and Policy* 3:99–103.

Roberts, J. (1997). Accelerated bridge reconstruction, *Proceedings of the 25th Annual Convention, Institute of Concrete Technology*.

Schachter, H. L. (1996). State departments of transportation research work programs, *Public Works Management and Policy* 1:174–184.

Shapard, R. (1997). From blacktop to desktop: five technologies changing public works, *American City and County*, September: 44+.

Truit, L. (1997). Transportation policy: deficits, devolution, and decentralization, *Public Works Management and Policy* 1:299–307.

Viskovich, B. (1998). The selling and leasing of city water utility, *Public Works Management and Policy 3*:169–172.

Wilt, C. (1997). The civil war of waste: Who will ultimately control the transport of solid waste, *Public Works Administration: Current Public Policy Perspectives* (L. Brewer, ed.), Sage Publications, Thousand Oaks, CA, pp. 201–220.

24
State Governing Challenges for the New Century

John J. Gargan
Kent State University, Kent, Ohio

The jobs of state government officials are difficult ones. In state capitals throughout the nation elected executives, appointed administrators, and career service managers juggle demands from voters and policy stakeholders to "do something" about everything from education of all types, to the justice system, to corrections, to developmental disabilities, to the ethical behavior of licensed professionals. And they deal with the issues, regardless of technical feasibility, resource availability, or divisions in public opinion. State officials daily confront Solomon-like choices regarding the ranking of equally valid priorities, the allocation of group benefits, or movement on strategic initiatives.

The issues dealt with frequently result from long-term factors such as those in the economy and demography. Hence the transformation of state and regional economies from steel, rubber, and manufacturing to those that are knowledge and technology based is due more to changing determinants of comparative advantage and the global mobility of capital than state efforts at economic development. Relatedly, population change reflects millions of decisions by individuals, families, and firms. Trends through the 1990s continued those of recent decades. Significant population increases in the South and West were from both interregional and international migration; slow growth in the Northeast and Midwest reflected interregional population losses offset by international population migration increases.

The reality of the changing conditions is that, in many instances, they are beyond state government control. Whether or not state officials can formulate administrative strategies and policies to effect change directly, they must be prepared to deal with the negative or positive consequences of change. For example, the 1990s were the worst and best of times for many states, including those of the Midwest. During the early years of the decade, the attention of officials throughout state governments was directed to the impacts of economies in recession—major budget deficits, high unemployment, revenue shortfalls, fiscal stress, and cutback management. The latter half of the decade saw balanced budgets, "rainy-day funds" of hundreds of millions of dollars, and income tax reductions. The changing conditions were the consequence of sustained state economic growth which, in turn, was generated by developments in the national and global economies. At the end of 1998 it was reported (Janofsky, 1998):

> Cautious spending and a robust national economy have left virtually all the states in solid financial condition for the fifth year in a row, according to a fiscal survey released today [by the National Governors' Association and the National Association of State Budget Officers].
>
> The healthy economy has allowed the states to give taxpayers the largest projected aggregate tax cuts in five years, $7 billion for the 1999 fiscal year. Twenty-nine states have reduced one tax or another.

I. STATE GOVERNING CAPACITY

The complexity of issues derived from structural changes—social conditions in older, central cites; destruction of a small-farm-based agriculture; loss of political clout in elections and representation in legislative bodies—is compounded by a heightened interconnectedness of their geographic, functional, and temporal aspects (Luke, 1992). Frequently the interconnections generate a multiplier effect so that decline leads to further decline in an exponential fashion. Dealing with the interconnections demands an unprecedented level of administrative and management finesse by public officials (Bailey, 1992) and tests the governing capacity of state governments.

Governing capacity is a measure of the ability to meet requirements and to satisfy expectations. A government's capacity is directly related to resources available and stakeholder expectations, and inversely related to the magnitude of problems confronting it, within an existing structural arrangement. Other things being equal, the more resources available and the higher the expectations about governmental performance, the greater the governing capacity; the more serious the problems with which the government must deal, the lower the governing capacity.

Over the past century, reformers have sought to build governing capacity by altering the arrangements for and the methods of conducting state government.

These alterations have taken several forms, ranging from conversion of the federal system, to adjustments in the structure of state government, to the promotion of innovative management practices. These reforms have not been easy. Since structure is never neutral and works to the advantage of particular values and interests, changes in arrangements change the values and interests benefited. People who are invested in arrangements and the career paths, service delivery systems, and the policy networks associated with them, can be expected to resist change.

II. FEDERALISM AND STATE GOVERNING CAPACITY

Federalism has constituted one of the most important, if not the most important, structural factors shaping state governing capacity. In the implementation of intergovernmental programs that capacity has been tested and the effects have been mixed. Depending on specific program details, federal funding has increased resources available. Conversely, the ability to meet requirements has on occasion been lowered by administrative regulations and grant form. The worst-case scenario, from a capacity perspective, has increased requirements and reduced resources, as reflected in state officials' criticisms of federally imposed unfunded mandates.

If the formal federal structure has remained intact, its operational form has been significantly altered over the past 40 years. National government involvement in more policy areas, higher levels of spending, and increased reliance on diverse arrangements—governmental, nongovernmental, nonprofit, for-profit, voluntary sectors—have produced an expansive and interdependent intergovernmental system (Milward, 1996).

Benefits of the expanded and interdependent system to the states are federal funds for such purposes as social and medical assistance to populations in need. State costs include some loss of discretion on spending matters and a diminution of executive branch autonomy. An obvious case of both has been Medicaid spending, which has consumed ever larger shares of state budgets. A fact regularly encountered by state decision makers is that Medicaid and other programs—welfare, special education—have significant fiscal and administrative impacts on state government but are guided by federal law, regulations, and funding, and are directly controlled only at the margins by state administrators.

The expanded and interdependent system involves more participants in the policy process and magnifies cooperation-coordination concerns of policy implementation. There is a dramatic change in administrative-management complexity in the shift from the lone agency delivering a program to new modes of service delivery involving (Kettl, 1996:7) multiagency, intergovernmental, and public-private-nonprofit partnerships. As O'Toole (1996:254) notes:

> The challenge of interagency implementation may be even more complicated . . . in that executing a program often requires building a *cluster* of networks for cooperation. The array needed for resource mobilization may be somewhat different from that needed for program operations, planning, or a host of other actions. Implementing public programs, then, often means developing and utilizing a whole series of functionally specific, partially overlapping network patterns.

Meeting the challenges of intergovernmental policy implementation has been a central concern of the public administration community. From the 1960s on, efforts have been directed to implementation improvement through changes at national points of policy adoption and at state-local points of policy delivery (Public Administration Review, 1975). A recurring theme in federal-state relations has been that of revamping programs to enhance state government flexibility by way of consolidating categorical grants, making greater use of block grants, and by tradeoffs that give states waivers to carry out federal policies on evidence of state ability to meet accountability criteria (National Performance Review, 1993).

Improvements in the performance of the intergovernmental system have entailed promotion of innovative management practices. A period of energetic state and local government capacity building activity began in the mid-1960s, peaked in the mid-1970s, and continued into the 1980s. Giving rise to renewed interest in capacity building were several factors. The dramatic increase in grant programs and grant money led to a heightened awareness by federal officials that solutions to national problems were contingent upon the implementation skills of state and local officials and the general competencies of state and local governments (Goggin et al., 1990). Difficulties encountered in coping with fiscal stress from the mid-1970s onward made state and local officials more sensitive to the priority of effective financial management and strategic planning practices.

III. REFORMING THE STRUCTURE OF STATE GOVERNMENT

Related to but analytically separate from changes in intergovernmental relations have been reforms geared to the modernization of state government for much of the past century. Drawing on public administration theory, looking to the recommendations of little Hoover commissions, and responding to pressures from business community and federal grant administrators, the reformers have directed the greater part of their attention to structural arrangements, powers of the governor, and the capabilities of the state work force (Conant, 1988).

A. Structural Arrangements

Considerable reform effort has been devoted to the reorganization of the executive branch. State constitutions were updated to remove detailed and outdated provisions which complicated administration and constrained innovation and were rewritten to reduce the number of state agencies and the number of agencies with plural executives. Organizational fragmentation was reduced by consolidating independent agencies into a limited number of departments. Changes were adopted to decrease the number of independently elected state executives. By transferring policy and regulatory authority from autonomous boards and commissions to executive agencies, decision making authority was made less dispersed.

The number of state departments, elective offices, boards, and commissions and the nature of their responsibilities vary from state to state, reflecting the variation in the form and success of reform movements and reorganization proposals. Though it is difficult to generalize about the movements and proposals, their thrust has been to rearrange structure to promote what have been identified as the "three standards of public bureaucratic performance: efficiency, effectiveness, and political or public accountability" (Elling, 1992:10).

In recent years, the specific targets of reform, and bases of theoretical support, have changed. But the reduction of organizational dispersion in state executive branches continues to be sought. Functions that have traditionally enjoyed a degree of autonomy, such as primary and secondary education, have been brought under greater gubernatorial control as they have become more election salient. Other structural reform matters, including the sunsetting of redundant boards and commissions, have been to a "cleaning up" of state government administration.

Changes in structural arrangements have been pronounced. Bowling and Wright (1998) write of a "revolution . . . in the administrative establishments of the states" which is manifested (p. 54) by improvements in such state agency factors as size (larger), scope (more extensive), structures (reorganized), quality (more professional), representativeness (more diverse), and responsiveness (more adaptive). They conclude (p. 55):

> The present administrative structures of state government are not necessarily models of efficiency, neatness, or symmetry. However, in their current reorganized form, they are a far cry from the rambling disorganization of a half century ago.

B. Powers of the Governor

Since an aim of many initiatives has been to centralize control and concentrate executive power, a major beneficiary of many state reform initiatives has been the governor. Executive leadership requires a governor to define policy direction and to set strategic goals. To empower public executives, "a principal focus of . . . reform initiatives" has been, in the words of the 1937 Brownlow Committee, "to make the chief executive the center of energy, direction, and administrative management" (Conant, 1988:893). It is assumed that the reforms make administrative sense by strengthening governors as chief executives and political sense by permitting governors to control agencies for which they are held politically accountable (Conant, 1988; Robinson, 1998).

Comparative studies of state government have devoted considerable attention to the powers of governors (Beyle, 1993). For example, a six-variable composite index of gubernatorial power was developed by the National Governors' Association. Three of the variables relate to "the governor's power within the executive branch"—tenure potential, appointments, budget authority." The other three—the legislature's role in the budget, veto power, political strength in legislature—relate to "the governor's power vis-à-vis the legislature" (Gray, Jacob, and Albriton, 1990:Appendix B).

For governors in some states the various powers are not always uniformly strong. Ohio governors, by way of illustration, are classified as "strong governors," scoring above the 50-state average on three (appointment power, budget-making power, and veto power) of the six measures, but below average on the other three (tenure potential, legislative budget-changing power, and political strength in the legislature).

Gubernatorial powers must be viewed in context. Other things being equal, governors with formal powers need not use up resources to overcome limits imposed by the lack of such powers. More fundamentally, the powers enhance heightened executive leadership and governing effectiveness resulting from expansion of the governor's several roles—chief policy strategist, chief administrator, chief legislator, and chief political leader. Further, better-educated and better-trained candidates have presented themselves to the electorate; the back-slapping "good-time Charlie" has been replaced by the politically astute and administratively competent chief executive officer (Sabato, 1983).

C. Capabilities of the State Work Force

Essential determinants of state governing capacity are the quality of state administrators and program managers (professionals *of* government) and the substantive knowledge and technical expertise of career service specialists (professionals *in* government). Elected officials and public personnel practitioners concern themselves with both types of professionals. As new issues emerge on public agendas, elected officials frequently turn to professionals *in* government for advice and technical solutions. To implement and coordinate the programs adopted to deal with the new issues they look to the knowledge and skill of professionals *of* government (Gargan, 1998).

Specifying the details of this state government professionals—governing capacity relationship is difficult. For one thing, the legal realities of American federalism mean that personnel practices are carried out in a variety of legal environments (Ban and Riccucci, 1993). In governing capacity terms, the key requirements to be met by the professionals vary from one state to another. The same is true for expectations of the professionals which form in different combinations and at different levels of fervor.

Interpretations of state personnel developments tend to follow either of two tracks. On the one hand, there is widespread recognition of improved conditions generally. Progress is also evident in specific fields, as with budgeting and financial management. Drawing on findings from five surveys of state officials between 1975 and 1995, Robert Lee (1997:137) found substantial advancement in the education and experience of budgeting professional staff (approximately half of whom have a master's degree by the 1990s), improvements in computer technology used, and growing sophistication in budgeting deliberations and practices. To the effects of personnel developments on state administration overall, Bowling and Wright (1998:58) conclude:

> In short, top-level management in state agencies has become more experienced, better educated, and notably professionalized, especially in administrative skill. From isolated and incidental instances of professionalism in the 1940s, state administration in the 1990s reflects both specialized professionalism and generalist management skills.

The second track of interpretation is much more critical, emphasizing how personnel systems limit governing capacity. Evidence abounds on this second track. In his survey of state administrators, Elling (1992:15) found that "of the six problems considered to be serious impediments by one-third or more of the managers, four concerned personnel matters. . . ." The rigidity of union contacts and tenure protection of the civil service system are frequently cited as a cause of inadequacies in the public sector and citizen discontent with governmental performance (Gargan, 1994).

Personnel problems have become severe enough to receive the attention of prestigious commissions established to study the national (National Commission on the Public Service, 1989) and state-local public services (National Commission on the State and Local Public Service, 1993; Thompson, 1993). Paul Volcker, the exemplary public servant and chair of the national commission, has referred in speeches and writings to emerging trends and a "quiet crisis" in the difficulties faced by the federal, state, and local governments in attracting highly qualified individuals to public sector careers. Unless the trends are altered, it is argued, "America will soon be left with a government of the mediocre, locked into careers of last resort or waiting for a chance to move on to other jobs" (National Commission on the Public Service, 1989:4).

Efforts have been made to overcome limitations of existing personnel systems. Statutes and administrative regulations have been adopted "to regulate the system of labor relations at the state and local levels of government" (Ban and Riccucci, 1993:75). Improved recruitment programs and new training opportunities have been undertaken. Adaptations have been made to permit greater flexibility in the assignment of career employees. In a number of states, full-scale senior executive services have been developed (Sherwood and Breyer, 1987), and in others, increasing use has been made of exempt managers "who serve at the will of and pleasure of their political superiors because of their role in policy-making and execution" (Roberts, 1988:21).

How successful state senior executive services and exempted managers will be, remains to be seen. Much depends on the political cultures of individual states and how governors reconcile the competing demands on them for political patronage and for policy and administrative expertise (Roberts, 1991). Even with improvements in state government organization, many governors continue to share executive power and to face extraordinarily difficult management problems. Hence the importance of politically astute professionals *of* government. Contemporary governors, like presidents, need help of a special kind. Each "can face performance expectations that outstrip his or her institutional resources and capacity to perform. Thus, both come to prize 'responsive competence' over 'neutral or organizational competence' " (Roberts, 1988:34).

IV. A NEW PARADIGM OF GOVERNANCE

The level of governing capacity achievable in state government is bounded and is influenced by a state's political culture and the qualities of its administrators and managers. Capacity also depends on the body of theory, definition of standards, and availability of empirically verified exemplar practices which constitute the state of the art in public administration.

The past quarter-century has seen changes in that state of the art and, perhaps, the emergence of a new paradigm of governance. From the 1970s onward, governments in the United States and abroad were altered in a transition from a paradigm derived from welfare economics to one derived from public-choice economics (Ostrom, 1998; Ingraham, Romzek, Associates, 1994; Kettl, 1996; Osborne and Gaebler, 1992).

The intellectual roots of the new paradigm are in market models emphasizing competition among service providers to overcome the inefficiencies of traditional monopolistic public bureaucracies. To increase competition, public organizations can be restructured and decisions about the provision of services can be separated from decisions on service production and delivery. At least in theory, by such tactical devices as agency decentralization, privatization, and contracting out, marketlike conditions will be simulated. Public managers are expected to behave like their private sector counterparts and maximize efficiency, engage in risk taking, and gain reputations as entrepreneurs. Those who perform effectively will be accordingly rewarded; those who fail will be fired or have their pay lowered.

Some governors who had been successful administrators with more traditional public administration practices have benefitted from changes in the state of the art. The practical importance of the emergent paradigm's emphasis on hard-headed management has been evident in political commentary. Following the 1998 elections, for example, David Rosenbaum observed in the *New York Times* (Nov. 5, 1998), ''Across the country in Tuesday's elections, governorships were won by pragmatic politicians who spurn the hard-edged ideology that dominates both parties in Congress.''

Paradigm tenets fit the political culture and acceptable approaches to governing of certain states. In his first inaugural address, Ohio's Republican Governor George Voinovich proclaimed:

> Gone are the days when public officials are measured by how much they spend on a problem. The new realities dictate that public officials are now judged on whether they can work harder and smarter, and do more with less. . . . We *must* distinguish between what we are able to do well, and what we cannot do at all. . . . In fact, the notion of not having government do *something* about *everything* is itself an extraordinary opportunity. . . . I'm well aware that talking about better management won't win any popularity contests, but I think some people miss the point. Better management of state resources— of state services—and of taxpayer dollars all add up to a better quality of life for the people of Ohio.

Popularity contests notwithstanding, forceful and creative management was a hallmark of the Voinovich executive branch. The governor's initiatives received national attention by way of sources like the National Governors' Association and *Governing: The Magazine of States and Localities*, which included him in a list of the ''best'' American governors of the 1990s (Ehrenhalt, 1998).

George Voinovich made real new approaches to administration in state government. As he claimed in his 1996 State of the State address, ''In Ohio, we are truly reinventing government!'' Even if lacking in mass appeal, quality management initiatives and programs based in market models, properly nurtured and sustained, may have permanent consequences for state governing capacity and, as in the case of Voinovich who was elected to the U.S. Senate on completion of his gubernatorial term, can have political appeal to key constituencies.

The extent to which a new paradigm and new approaches have resulted in a reinvention of state government remains an open question. Among the few efforts to examine reinvention activity was a mail survey by Brudney, Hebert, and Wright (1999) to 1229 agency heads in all 50 states. Those surveyed were asked if they had considered action on, planned action on, or partially or fully implemented a set of 11 reinvention items. Illustrative of the items are "Benchmarks for measuring program outcomes or results," "Privatization of major programs," and "Reduction in the number of levels in the agency hierarchy." Substantively, one item related to strategic planning, a second to the privatization of major programs, four to customer service, two to structural-organizational issues, and three to administrative rules.

Of the eleven reinvention items, just over half (six) were partially or fully implemented by at least half of the agencies (Brudney, Hebert, and Wright, 1999: 23). The three items ranking highest in partial or full implementation involved training to improve client service (81.5 percent), strategic planning (79.4 percent), and employee empowerment (76.6 percent). Ranking lowest were items concerned with simpler rules for personnel (28.9 percent), program privatization (23.0 percent), and discretion in fund carry over (21.3 percent). Variation among the items as to implementation is accompanied by variation in state implementation activity, with Florida, Oregon, and Texas most active and Alabama, Rhode Island, and New Hampshire least active. Nonetheless, conclude Brudney, Hebert, and Wright (1999:28–29), "Reinventing government has received wide publicity and prestigious political endorsements, but it appears to be more of a ripple than a reform wave at the state level."

V. CONCLUSION

State government administrators face multiple challenges in building the governing capacity to deal effectively with anticipated (and unanticipated) demands of the new century. As chapters in this handbook demonstrate, governing capacity demands effective strategic management. Strategic management builds upon competency in analytic and management skills, particularly in finances, human resources, and data and information collection, analysis, and use. State agencies with managers lacking in the basic skills will have difficulty building the internal management competency essential to survival in the turbulent environments of an increasingly interconnected external world.

Some of the most innovative public administration thinking in recent years has provided rationales for a so-called New Public Management and alternative approaches to administration and governing (Kaboolian, 1998). From this thinking, market models of administration have undoubtedly received the most attention from the professional public administration community. Real gains from the new approaches, such as the greater use of performance measures of policy outcomes, deregulation, and vouchers, are offset by some possible costs. Generations of public administration scholars and practitioners may be bemused by comments such as the following (Lynn, 1998:233):

> New Public Management reforms may also appear to emphasize the technical demands of administration, e.g., outcome measurement, more than the challenges of insuring democratic legitimacy, control, and accountability.

Though currently prominent, market-based models do not stand alone. Three approaches to governing, in addition to the market model based, are cited by B. Guy Peters (1996:25–37):

- **The "participatory" or "empowerment" approach.** In a state government or units in the state government adopting the approach, public employees and clients most knowledgeable about the actual conduct of programs, but given their low rankings in hierarchies most frequently excluded from discourse about the programs, would be given opportunities, empowered, to participate in decision making about program administration and management improvements.
- **The "flexible government" approach.** This approach centers on flexible and temporary organizations, recognizing that governmental problems increasingly "fall between the stools of the existing organizations" (Peters, 1996:31). By creatively using employees on temporary assignment or part-time employees, governmental organizations could be established to deal with crises or short-term interorganizational problems.
- **The "deregulating government" approach.** This approach has taken form in reinvention projects. A deregulating strategy aims to eliminate constraints on innovation in public organizations. Bureaucratic structures per se are viewed as less the problem than existing rules and "arcane procedures" which thwart imaginative and inventive public employees. Elimination of the inhibiting rules and procedures and involvement of all organizational levels will unleash public sector creativity and entrepreneurship.

There is not necessarily a single best approach for an entire state government or for individual agencies. Rather, the leadership task in organizational development is to determine the best possible fit between the alternative approaches to governing and combinations of context, problems, and resources. This forces recognition of the possibility that "we are experiencing ever-clearer *limits on the competence possible within our basic organization structure*" (Golembiewski, 1987:452).

At the outset, governing capacity was defined as the ability to meet requirements and to satisfy expectations. The definition accentuates the importance of *both* management and political factors in specific state contexts. The requirements to be met by a state's governing capacity, and the resources to be available to meet them, are determined by political processes at several levels of government, and the distribution of power within each. Even if the expectations to be satisfied have origins in such nonpolitical sources as the ethnic, religious, and social backgrounds of a population and historic or recent patterns of migration, the expectations are directed to political objects and are responded to by political officials.

The historical growth of the field and profession of public administration has involved an ongoing search for more effective tools of administration and management to meet requirements. Progress has been made in the search as a consequence of advancements in the critical triad of technology, doctrine, and organization. By adopting new technologies, reconceptualizing strategic and tactical doctrine, and creating new organizational structures, state governments have benefitted from the progress. The route from POSDCORB, to intergovernmental management, to New Public Management has been one followed by those seeking to raise state governing capacity to meet requirements.

In line with the purpose of this handbook, this concluding chapter and the chapters preceding it have emphasized administrative and management topics. Less emphasized have been aspects of the second governing capacity dimension—that of satisfying expectations. For the foreseeable future, satisfying expectations may well be as significant for state elected officials and the state career service as new approaches to administration and management.

Satisfying state government stakeholder expectations in an era of heightened sensitivity to cultural diversity, public cynicism, and distrust of government compounds the difficulty of achieving high governing capacity. Among the most significant challenges for the next generation of researchers and practitioners of state government is that of determining which governing approach and which accompanying organizational forms and management practices best correspond to various contexts in order to satisfy the expectations of policy stakeholders, citizens, and public employees. Meeting the challenge will increase the probability that the state's public interest is served.

REFERENCES

Bailey, M. T. (1992). Beyond rationality: Decisionmaking in an interconnected world, *Public Management in an Interconnected World: Essays in the Minnowbrook Tradition* (M. T. Bailey and R. T. Mayer, eds.), Greenwood, New York, pp. 33–52.
Ban, C., and Riccucci, N. (1993). Personnel systems and labor relations: Steps toward a

quiet revitalization, *Revitalizing State and Local Public Service* (F. J. Thompson, ed.), Jossey-Bass, San Francisco, pp. 71–103.

Beyle, T. L. (1993). Being governor, *The State of the States* (C. E. Van Horn, ed.), Congressional Quarterly Press, Washington, pp. 18–32.

Bowling, C. J., and Wright, D. S. (1998). Public administration in the fifty states: A half-century administrative revolution, *State and Local Govt. Rev.*, *30*: 1, 52–64.

Brudney, J. L., Hebert, F. T., and Wright, D. S. (1999). Reinventing government in the American states: Measuring and explaining administrative reform, *Publ. Adm. Rev.*, *59*: 19–30.

Conant, J. K. (1988). In the shadow of Wilson and Brownlow: Executive branch reorganization in the states, 1965–79, *Publ. Adm. Rev.*, *48*: 892–902.

Ehrenhalt, A. (1998). It pays to know where the bodies are buried, *Governing: The Magazine of States and Localities*, June.

Elling, R. C. (1992). *Public Management in the States: A Comparative Study of Administrative Performance and Politics*, Praeger, Westport, CT.

Gargan, J. J. (1994). Governing capacity and the personnel function, *Handbook of Public Sector Labor Relations* (J. Rabin, T. Vocino, W. B. Hildreth, and G. J. Miller, eds.), Marcel Dekker, New York, pp. 375–392.

Gargan, J. J. (1998). The public administration community and the search for professionalism, *Handbook of Public Administration* (2nd ed.) (J. Rabin, W. B. Hildreth, and G. J. Miller, eds.), Marcel Dekker, New York, pp. 1089–1161.

Goggin, M. L., Bowman, A. O'M., Lester, J. P., O'Toole, L. J. Jr. (1990). *Implementation Theory and Practice: Toward a Third Generation*, Scott/Foresman, Glenview, IL.

Golembiewski, R. T. (1987). Public sector organization: Why theory and practice should emphasize purpose, and how to do so, *A Centennial History of the American Administrative State* (R. C. Chandler, ed.), Free Press, New York, pp. 433–473.

Gray, V., Jacob, H., and Albriton R. B., eds. (1990). *Politics in the American States*, Scott, Foresman, Glenview, IL. Appendix B.

Ingraham, P. W., Romzek, B. S., and Associates. (1994). *New Paradigms for Government*, Jossey-Bass, San Francisco.

Janofsky, M. (1998). States continue in robust fiscal shape, *New York Times*, Dec. 31, 1998.

Kettl, D. F. (1996). Introduction, *The State of Public Management* (D. F. Kettl and H. B. Milward, eds.), Johns Hopkins University Press, Baltimore, pp. 1–12.

Kaboolian, L. (1998). The New Public Management: Challenging the boundaries of the management vs. administration debate, *Publ. Adm. Rev.*, *58*: 189–193.

Lee, R. D. (1997). A quarter century of state budgeting practices, *Publ. Adm. Rev.*, *57*: 133–140.

Luke, J. S. (1992). Managing interconnectedness: The new challenge for public administration, *Public Management in an Interconnected World: Essays in the Minnowbrook Tradition* (M. T. Bailey and R. T. Mayer, eds.), Greenwood, New York, pp. 13–32.

Lynn, L. E. Jr. (1998). The New Public Management: How to transform a theme into a legacy, *Publ. Adm. Rev.*, *58*: 231–236.

Milward, H. B. (1996). The changing character of the pubic sector, *Handbook of Public Administration* (2nd ed.) (J. L. Perry, ed.). Jossey-Bass, San Francisco, pp. 77–91.

National Commission on the Public Service. (1989). *Leadership for America: Rebuilding the Public Service*. Lexington Books, Lexington.

National Commission on the State and Local Public Service. (1993). *Hard Truths/Hard Choices*. Nelson A. Rockefeller Institute of Government.

National Performance Review. (1993). *From Red Tape to Results: Creating a Government That Works Better and Costs Less*, U.S. Government Printing Office, Washington.

Osborne, D., and Gaebler, T. (1992). *Reinventing Government*, Addison-Wesley, Reading, MA.

Ostrom, V. (1998). Some developments in the study of market choice, public choice, and institutional choice, *Handbook of Public Administration* (2nd ed.) (J. Rabin, W. B. Hildreth, and G. J. Miller, eds.), Marcel Dekker, New York, pp. 1065–1087.

O'Toole, L. J. Jr. (1996). Implementing public programs, *Handbook of Public Administration* (2nd. ed) (J. L. Perry, ed.), Jossey-Bass, San Francisco, pp. 250–262.

Peters, B. G. (1996). Models of governance for the 1990s, *The State of Public Management* (D. F. Kettl and H. B. Milward, eds.). Johns Hopkins University Press, Baltimore, pp. 15–44.

Public Administration Review (1975). Special Issue, *35*.

Roberts, D. D. (1988). A new breed of public executive: Top level exempt managers in state government, *Rev. Public Personnel Admin.*, *8*: 20–36.

Roberts, D. D. (1991). A personnel chameleon blending the political appointee and careerist traditions: Exempt managers in state government, *Public Personnel Management* (C. Ban and N. M. Riccucci, eds.), Longman, New York, pp. 190–204.

Rosenbaum, D. E. (1998). Middle of road led to victory in races for governors, *New York Times*, Nov. 5, 1998.

Robinson, J. E. (1998). The role of the independent political executive in state governance: Stability in the face of change, *Publ. Adm. Rev.*, *58*: 119–128.

Sabato, L. (1983). *Goodbye to Good-Time Charlie: The American Governorship Transformed*, Congressional Quarterly Press, Washington.

Sherwood, F. P., and Breyer, L. J. (1987). Executive personnel systems in the states, *Public Admin. Rev.*, *47*: 410–416.

Thompson, F. J. (1993). Introduction: Critical challenges to state and local public service, *Revitalizing State and Local Public Service* (F. J. Thompson, ed.), Jossey-Bass, San Francisco, pp. 1–38.

Index